THE NEW BOOK OF
KNOWLEDGE

Home and School
READING
AND
STUDY
GUIDES

SCHOLASTIC

Scholastic Library Publishing, Inc.

The editors of THE NEW BOOK OF KNOWLEDGE wish to acknowledge educational consultant Barbara Darga, whose experience as a teacher and whose research into current curriculum issues and trends guided the development and preparation of this edition of the HOME AND SCHOOL READING AND STUDY GUIDES.

The editors also wish to thank the teachers, librarians, and parents whose experiences, reviews, and suggestions help keep the information in these guides both useful and practical.

For the 2007 edition:
Editors: Donna M. Lusardi; Rosemarie Kent
Copy Editor: Sara A. Boak
Art Director: Wendy S. Allen
Composition: Linda Dillon
Production Manager: Teresa K. Ahearn
Production Supervisor: Patricia Raether

THE HOME AND SCHOOL READING GUIDE

THE HOME AND SCHOOL STUDY GUIDE

CONTENTS

PART I · THE READING GUIDE

PART II · THE STUDY GUIDE

PART III · ACTIVITIES

APPENDIX

PART I
THE READING GUIDE

INTRODUCTION

You have probably already discovered that THE NEW BOOK OF KNOWLEDGE is a valuable resource for finding information about a topic of special interest, beginning a school report or project, or answering a specific question.

In pursuing your search for information, you may also have had the experience of wanting to know even more about a topic than what you found in its many articles. No single reference work—even one as comprehensive as THE NEW BOOK OF KNOWLEDGE—can contain everything known about a topic. It simply isn't possible to hold within the covers of 21 volumes the vast storehouse of knowledge that has been accumulated during thousands of years of discovery, experience, and research.

The HOME AND SCHOOL READING GUIDE has been compiled to help you expand the information in THE NEW BOOK OF KNOWLEDGE. The READING GUIDE is a unique listing of more than 6,000 quality books dealing with hundreds of different topics. Almost every title in the list has been recommended by parent groups, teachers, librarians, literature specialists, or by young people themselves. Many of the books have also been cited by textbook publishers as recommended supplements to their science, social studies, or language arts series. Where can you find the books that may be of interest to you? The titles in the READING GUIDE should be readily available through your local bookstores or in your school or public library.

You will find the READING GUIDE a handy resource for building collections of books about many different subject areas for users at different ability levels. Because the READING GUIDE is updated each year, it will also help you keep such collections current and relevant to young people's school needs and extracurricular interests.

THE NEW BOOK OF KNOWLEDGE provides additional book listings in two of its articles: "Caldecott and Newbery Medals" and "Children's Literature," both in Volume C.

Nancy Larrick, the Children's Literature Adviser for THE NEW BOOK OF KNOWLEDGE, helped establish the guidelines for the development of the READING GUIDE. The original READING GUIDE was prepared by John T. Gillespie and Christine B. Gilbert, co-editors of *Best Books for Children*, published by the R. R. Bowker Company.

To make it easy for you to use the READING GUIDE with THE NEW BOOK OF KNOWLEDGE, book titles are listed under alphabetically arranged topic headings that correspond directly to the titles of THE NEW BOOK OF KNOWLEDGE articles. Wherever possible, books on a topic cover a range of ability levels from primary to advanced.

Key to abbreviations used in the READING GUIDE:

(P)	primary (through 4th grade)	ed.	editor; edited; edition
(I)	intermediate (5th through 8th grade)	illus.	illustrator; illustrated
		retel.	reteller; retelling
(A)	advanced (9th grade and up)	rev. ed.	revised edition
ad.	adapter; adapted	sel.	selector; selected
comp.	compiler; compiled	trans.	translator; translation

The following book lists are among the sources used in the preparation of the READING GUIDE:

Adventuring with Books: A Booklist for Pre-K—Grade 6. Kathryn M. Pierce, author, National Council of Teachers of English, March 2000.

Appraisal: Science Books for Young People. Published three times a year by the Children's Science Book Review Committee, sponsored by the Science and Mathematics Program of Boston University School of Education and the New England Roundtable of Children's Librarians.

Best Books for Children, by John T. Gillespie, Greenwood Publishing Group, 2001.

Best Books for Middle School and Junior High Readers, by John Gillespie and Catherine Barr, Greenwood Publishing Group, 2004.

Booklist. American Library Association.

Children's Books. New York Public Library. Published annually.

Children's Catalog, by Ann Price et al., H. W. Wilson, October 2001.

Children's Choices. October issues of *The Reading Teacher*, a project of the International Reading Association (IRA)–Children's Book Council Joint Committee.

The Elementary School Library Collection: A Guide to Books and Other Media, Phases 1-2-3, edited by Lauren K. Lee et al., 19th ed. Brodart, 1994.

The Horn Book Magazine. Horn Book, Inc.

Notable Children's Books, 1976–80. American Library Association, 1986.

Notable Social Studies Trade Books for Young People. May/June issues of *Social Education*, a professional journal of the National Council for the Social Studies.

Outstanding Science Trade Books for Children. March issues of *Science and Children*, *Science Scope*, and *The Science Teacher*, a joint project of the National Science Teachers Association and the Children's Book Council.

School Library Journal. R. R. Bowker.

A (LETTER)

Samoyault, Tiphaine. *Alphabetical Order: How the Alphabet Began.* Viking, 1998. *(P; I)*

ABOLITION MOVEMENT

Altman, Linda Jacobs. *Slavery and Abolition: In American History.* Enslow, 1999. *(I; A)*

Chang, Ina. *Separate Battle: Women and the Civil War.* Penguin Putnam, 1996 (reprint). *(I)*

Rockwell, Anne F. *Only Passing Through: The Story of Sojourner Truth.* Knopf, 2000. *(P; I)*

Zeinert, Karen. *The Amistad Slave Revolt and American Abolition.* Shoe String Press, 1997. *(I; A)*

ABORIGINES, AUSTRALIAN

Reynolds, Jan. *Down Under: Vanishing Cultures.* Harcourt, 1992. *(P; I)*

ABORTION

Herda, D. J. *Roe v. Wade: The Abortion Question.* Enslow, 1994. *(I; A)*

Lowenstein, Felicia. *The Abortion Battle: Looking at Both Sides.* Enslow, 1996. *(A)*

Roamine, Deborah S. *Roe vs. Wade: Abortion and the Supreme Court.* Lucent, 1998. *(I; A)*

ACID RAIN

Downs, Sandra. *Shaping the Earth: Erosion.* Lerner, 2000. *(I)*

Lucas, Eileen. *Acid Rain.* Children's Press, 1991. *(I)*

Morgan, Sally. *Acid Rain.* Scholastic, 1999. *(P; I)*

ADAMS, JOHN

Feinstein, Stephen. *John Adams.* Enslow, 2002. *(I; A)*

Gaines, Ann Graham. *John Adams: Our Second President.* Child's World, 2002. *(P; I)*

Harness, Cheryl. *The Revolutionary John Adams.* National Geographic Society, 2003. *(P; I)*

Kallen, Stuart A. *John Adams (Founding Fathers).* ABDO, 2002. *(P; I)*

Lukes, Bonnie L. *John Adams: Public Servant.* Reynolds, 2000. *(I)*

St. George, Judith. *John and Abigail Adams: An American Love Story.* Holiday House, 2001. *(I)*

Welsbacher, Anne. *John Adams.* ABDO, 1998. *(P)*

ADAMS, JOHN QUINCY

Feinstein, Stephen. *John Quincy Adams.* Enslow, 2002. *(I; A)*

McCollum, Sean. *John Quincy Adams (Encyclopedia of Presidents, Second Series).* Scholastic, 2003. *(I; A)*

Souter, Gerry, and Souter, Janet. *John Quincy Adams: Our Sixth President.* Child's World, 2002. *(P; I)*

ADHD

Beal, Eileen. *Everything You Need to Know About ADD/ADHD.* Rosen, 1998. *(I)*

Ingersoll, Barbara D. *Distant Drums, Different Drummers: A Guide for Young People with ADHD.* Cape, 1995. *(I; A)*

Morrison, Jaydene, and Simpson, Carolyn. *Coping with ADD/ADHD: Attention Deficit Disorder/Attention Deficit Hyperactivity Disorder.* Rosen, 1995. *(I; A)*

Quinn, Patricia O., and Stern, Judith M. *Putting on the Brakes: Young People's Guide to Understanding Attention Deficit Hyperactivity Disorder (ADHD).* Educational Publishing Foundation, 1991. *(P; I)*

ADOLESCENCE

Colman, Penny. *Girls: A History of Growing Up Female in America.* Scholastic, 2000. *(I)*

Harris, Robie H. *It's Perfectly Normal: Changing Bodies, Growing Up, Sex, and Sexual Health.* Candlewick Press, 2004 (10th ed.). *(I; A)*

ADOPTION

Banish, Roslyn, and Jordan-Wong, Jennifer. *A Forever Family.* HarperCollins, 1992. *(P)*

Girard, Linda Walvoord. *We Adopted You, Benjamin Koo.* Albert Whitman, 1992 (reprint). *(P; I)*

Gravelle, Karen, and Fischer, Susan. *Where Are My Birth Parents? A Guide for Teenage Adoptees.* Walker, 1993. *(A)*

Lindsay, Jeanne Warren. *Pregnant? Adoption Is an Option: Adoption from the Birthparent's Perspective.* Morning Glory Press, 1996. *(A)*

Liptak, Karen. *Adoption Controversies.* Watts, 1993. *(A)*

Rogers, Fred. *Let's Talk about It: Adoption.* Putnam, 1995. *(P)*

AERODYNAMICS

Berliner, Don. *Aviation: Reaching for the Sky.* Oliver Press, 1997. *(I)*

Schmidt, Norman. *Fabulous Paper Gliders.* Sterling, 1998. *(I; A)*

Schultz, Ron. *Looking inside Sports Aerodynamics.* Avalon Travel, 1992. *(I)*

AFGHANISTAN

Ali, Sharifah B. *Afghanistan.* Marshall Cavendish, 1995 (2nd ed.). *(I)*

Corona, Laurel. *Afghanistan.* Gale Group, 2002. *(I; A)*

Gritzner, Jeffrey A. *Afghanistan.* Chelsea House, 2002. *(I; A)*

Heinrichs, Ann. *Afghanistan.* Scholastic, 2003. *(P)*

Otfinoski, Steven. *Nations in Transition: Afghanistan.* Facts on File, 2003. *(I; A)*

AFRICA

Congo . . . in Pictures. Lerner, 1999. *(I; A)*

Morocco . . . in Pictures. Lerner, 1999. *(I; A)*

South Africa . . . in Pictures. Lerner, 1996 (rev. ed.). *(I; A)*

Tunisia . . . in Pictures. Lerner, 1998 rev. ed.). *(I; A)*

Altman, Susan, and Lechner, Susan. *Ancient Africa.* Scholastic, 2001. *(P)*

Abebe, Daniel. *Ethiopia . . . in Pictures.* Lerner, 1998 (rev. ed.). *(I; A)*

Baughan, Michael Gray. *Zimbabwe (Africa - Continent in the Balance Series).* ason Crest, 2004. *(I; A)*

Brennan, Kristine. *Burundi (Africa[<]EMBREAKContinent in the Balance Series).* Mason Crest, 2004. *(I; A)*

Corrigan, Jim. *Ethiopia (Africa - Continent in the Balance Series); Kenya (Africa - Continent in the Balance Series).* Mason Crest, 2004. *(I; A)*

Diagram Group. *Nations of Africa; Peoples of Central Africa; Peoples of East Africa; Peoples of North Africa; Peoples of Southern Africa; Peoples of West Africa.* Facts on File, 1997. *(I; A)*

Franklin, Sharon; Tull, Mary; and Shelton, Carol. *Africa: Understanding Geography and History through Art.* Raintree Steck-Vaughn, 2000. *(I; A)*

Harvey, Miles. *Look What Came from Africa.* Scholastic, 2001. *(P)*

Haskins, James S., and Benson, Kathleen. *African Beginnings.* Morrow, 1998. *(P; I)*

Koslow, Philip. *Asante: The Gold Coast; Benin: Lords of the River; Dahomey: The Warrior Kings; Yorubaland: The Flowering of Genius.* Chelsea House, 1996. *(I); Ancient Ghana: The Land of Gold.* Chelsea House, 1995. *(I)*

Mann, Kenny. *Egypt, Kush, Aksum: Northeast Africa; Kongo Ndongo: West Central Africa; Monomotapa, Great Zimbabwe, Zululand, Lesotho: Southern Africa; Zenj, Buganda: East Africa.* Silver Burdett Press, 1996. *(I)*

Montgomery, Bertha Vining, and Nabwire, Constance R. *Cooking the East African Way; Cooking the West African Way.* Lerner, 2001 (2nd ed.). *(I; A)*

Nelson, Julie. *Great African Kingdoms.* Raintree Steck-Vaughn, 2002. *(P)*

Osseo-Asare, Fran. *A Good Soup Attracts Chairs: A First African Cookbook for American Kids.* Pelican, 1993. *(I; A)*

Petersen, David. *Africa.* Scholastic, 1998. *(P; I)*

Zimmerman, Robert. *The Gambia.* Children's Press, 1994. *(A)*

AFRICA, LITERATURE OF

Aardema, Verna *Koi and the Kola Nuts: A Tale from Liberia.* Simon & Schuster, 1999 *Misoso: Once Upon a Time Tales from Africa.* Knopf, 1994. *(P)*

Feelings, Tom. *I Saw Your Face.* Penguin Group, 2005. *(P; I)*

Tadjo, Veronique. *Talking Drums: A Selection of Poems from Africa south of the Sahara.* Bloomsbury USA, 2004. *(I; A)*

Washington, Donna L. *A Pride of African Tales.* HarperCollins, 2003. *(P; I)*

AFRICAN AMERICANS

Altman, Susan. *The Encyclopedia of African-American Heritage.* Facts on File, 2001 (2nd ed.). *(I; A); Extraordinary Black Americans: From Colonial to Contem-*

porary Times. Scholastic, 2001 (2nd ed.). *(I)*

Ashabranner, Brent. *The New African Americans.* Linnet, 1999. *(I; A)*

Bolden, Tonya. *Maritcha: A Nineteenth-Century American Girl.* Abrams, 2004; *Wake Up Your Souls: A Celebration of African American Artists.* Abrams, 2003; *Tell All the Children Our Story: Memories and Mementos of Being Young and Black in America.* Abrams, 2002. *(I; A)*

Brodie, James Michael. *Created Equal: The Lives and Ideas of Black American Innovators.* Morrow, 1993. *(A)*

Buckley, Gail Lumet. *American Patriots: A Young People's Edition: The Story of Blacks in the Military from the Revolution to Desert Storm.* Crown, 2003. *(I; A)*

Byers, Ann. *African-American History from Emancipation to Today: Rising above the Ashes of Slavery.* Enslow, 2004. *(I; A)*

De Angelis, Gina. *Black Cowboys.* Chelsea House, 1997. *(I)*

Gaines, Ann Graham. *The Harlem Renaissance (In American History Series).* Enslow, 2002. *(I; A)*

Greene, Carol. *Thurgood Marshall: First African-American Supreme Court Justice.* Children's Press, 1991. *(P; I)*

Hacker, Carlotta. *Great African Americans in the Arts.* Crabtree, 1997. *(I)*

Harris, Jacqueline L. *The Tuskegee Airmen: Black Heroes of World War II.* Silver Burdett Press, 1995. *(I; A)*

Hayden, Robert C., and Loehle, Richard. *Nine African-American Inventors.* Twenty-First Century, 1992.

Hill, Laban Carrick. *Harlem Stomp!: A Cultural History of the Harlem Renaissance.* Little, 2004. *(I; A)*

Hoobler, Dorothy, and Hoobler, Thomas. *The African American Family Album.* Oxford University Press, 1995. *(I; A)*

Hoyt-Goldsmith, Diane, and Migdale, Lawrence. *Celebrating Kwanzaa.* Holiday House, 1994. *(P: I)*

Johnson, James Weldon. *Lift Every Voice and Sing.* Walker, 1993. *(P; I; A)*

Klots, Steve. *Richard Allen: Religious Leader and Social Activist.* Chelsea House, 1991. *(I)*

Lucas, Eileen. *Cracking the Wall: The Struggles of the Little Rock Nine.* Carolrhoda, 1998. *(P)*

Medearis, Angela Shelf. *Come This Far to Freedom: A History of African Americans.* Atheneum, 1993. *(I)*

Myers, Walter Dean. *Now Is Your Time: The African-American Struggle for Freedom.* HarperCollins, 1991. *(I; A)*

Parker, Janice. *Great African Americans in Film.* Crabtree, 1997. *(I)*

Parks, Rosa, with Haskins, Jim. *Rosa Parks: My Story.* Dial, 1992. *(I)*

Potter, Joan, and Clayton, Constance. *African-American Firsts.* Pinto Press, 1994 *(A); African Americans Who Were First.* Dutton/Cobblehill, 1997. *(I)*

Rediger, Pat. *Great African Americans in Business; Great African Americans in Civil Rights; Great African Americans in Literature.* Crabtree, 1996. *(P; I);*

Silverman, Jerry. *Just Listen to This Song I'm Singing: African-American History Through Song.* Millbrook, 1996. *(I; A)*

Sullivan, Otha Richard. *African American Inventors.* Wiley, 1997. *(I; A)*

Tate, Eleanora E., and Haskins, James. *African American Musicians.* Wiley, 2000. *(I; A)*

Trotter, Joe William. *From a Raw Deal to a New Deal?: African Americans, 1929-1945, Vol. 8.* Oxford University Press, 2006. *(A)*

Yannuzzi, Della A. *Madam C. J. Walker: Self-Made Businesswoman.* Enslow, 2000. *(I; A)*

AGRICULTURE

Gold, John C. *Environments of the Western Hemisphere.* Millbrook Press, 1997. *(I; A)*

Hughes, Meredith Sayles. *Spill the Beans and Pass the Peanuts: Legumes.* Lerner, 1999. *(P; I)*

Meltzer, Milton. *Food: How We Hunt and Gather It, How We Grow and Eat It.* Millbrook Press, 1998. *(P; I)*

Ventura, Piero. *Food: Its Evolution through the Ages.* Houghton Mifflin, 1994. *(P; I)*

Wilkes, Angela, and Thomas, Eric. *A Farm Through Time.* DK, 2001. *(P; I)*

Woods, Michael, and Woods, Mary B. *Ancient Agriculture: From Foraging to Farming.* Runestone, 2000. *(I)*

AGRICULTURE, UNITED STATES DEPARTMENT OF

Rosaler, Maxine. *The Department of Agriculture (This Is Your Government Series).* Rosen Central, 2005. *(A)*

AIDS

Cozic, Charles P., ed. *The AIDS Crisis.* Greenhaven, 1991. *(I; A)*

Ford, Michael Thomas. *The Voices of AIDS.* Morrow, 1995. *(I; A)*

Giblin, James Cross. *When Plague Strikes: The Black Death, Smallpox, AIDS.* HarperCollins, 1997. *(I; A)*

Gonzales, Doreen. *AIDS: Ten Stories of Courage.* Enslow, 1996. *(I)*

Manning, Karen. *AIDS: Can This Epidemic Be Stopped?* Millbrook Press, 1997. *(I; A)*

Nash, Carol Rust. *AIDS: Choices for Life.* Enslow, 1997. *(I; A)*

Silverstein, Alvin; Silverstein, Virginia; and Nunn, Laura Silverstein. *AIDS: An All-about Guide for Young Adults.* Enslow, 1999. *(A)*

White, Ryan, and Cunningham, Ann Marie. *Ryan White: My Own Story.* Dial, 1991. *(I; A)*

AIRPLANE MODELS

Schmidt, Norman. *Super Paper Airplanes.* Sterling, 2002; *Incredible Paper Flying Machines.* Sterling, 2001; *Great Paper Jets.* Sterling, 1999; *Fabulous Paper Gliders.* Sterling, 1998; *Paper Birds That Fly.* Sterling, 1997. *(I; A)*

AIR POLLUTION

Baines, John D. *Protecting Our Planet: Keeping the Air Clean, Vol. 3.* Raintree Steck-Vaughn, 1998. *(I)*

Branley, Franklyn. *It's Raining Cats and Dogs: All Kinds of Weather and Why We Have It.* Morrow/Avon, 1993. *(P; I)*

Chapman, Matthew, and Bowden, Rob. *Air Pollution: Our Impact on the Planet.* Raintree Steck-Vaughn, 2002. *(I; A)*

Kahl, Jonathan D.W. *Hazy Skies: Weather and the Environment.* Lerner, 1997. *(I)*

Miller, Christina G., and Berry, Louise A. *Air Alert: Rescuing the Earth's Atmosphere.* Simon & Schuster, 1996. *(I; A)*

Morgan, Sally. *Acid Rain; The Ozone Hole.* Scholastic, 1999. *(P; I)*

Yount, Lisa, and Rodgers, Mary M. *Our Endangered Planet.* Lerner, 1995. *(I)*

AIRPORTS

Davis, Meredith. *Up and Away!: Taking a Flight.* Mondo, 1997. *(P)*

Sullivan, George E. *How an Airport Really Works.* Dutton, 1993. *(I; A)*

ALABAMA

Brown, Dottie. *Alabama.* Lerner, 2001 (2nd ed.). *(P; I)*

Davis, Lucile. *Alabama.* Scholastic, 1999 (2nd ed.). *(I; A)*

Feeney, Kathy; Matusevich, Melissa N.; and Nichols, Lou Ellen. *Alabama.* Scholastic, 2002. *(P; I)*

Fradin, Dennis Brindell. *Alabama: From Sea to Shining Sea.* Scholastic, 1995. *(P; I)*

Greenfield, Eloise. *Rosa Parks.* HarperCollins, 1999. *(P)*

Martin, Michael A., and Craven, Jean. *Alabama: The Heart of Dixie.* Gareth Stevens, 2002. *(P; I)*

Parks, Rosa, and Haskins, James. *Rosa Parks: My Story.* Penguin Putnam, 1999. *(I)*

Shirley, David. *Alabama.* Marshall Cavendish, 2000. *(P; I)*

Summer, L. S. *Rosa Parks.* Child's World, 1999. *(P; I)*

Wills, Charles A. *A Historical Album of Alabama.* Millbrook Press, 1995. *(I)*

ALASKA

People of the Ice and Snow. Time-Life, 1994. *(I; A)*

Brown, Tricia. *Children of the Midnight Sun: Young Native Voices of Alaska.* Alaska Northwest Books, 1998. *(P; I)*

Cohen, Daniel. *The Alaska Purchase.* Millbrook Press, 1996. *(I)*

Dubois, Muriel L. *Alaska: Facts and Symbols.* Capstone/Hilltop, 2000. *(P)*

Flowers, Pam, and Dixon, Ann. *Alone across the Arctic: One Woman's Epic Journey by Dog Team.* Graphic Arts Center, 2001. *(I; A)*

Fradin, Dennis Brindell. *Alaska: From Sea to Shining Sea.* Scholastic, 1995. *(P; I)*

Fremon, David K. *The Alaska Purchase (In American History Series).* Enslow, 1999. *(I; A)*

Gold, Susan Dudley. *Land Pacts.* Millbrook Press, 1997. *(I; A)*

Johnston, Joyce. *Alaska.* Lerner, 2001 (2nd ed.). *(P; I)*

Kendall, Russell. *Eskimo Boy.* Scholastic, 1992. *(P)*

Petersen, David. *Denali National Park System.* Scholastic, 1997. *(P; I)*

Seder, Isaac. *Alaska: The Last Frontier.* Gareth Stevens, 2003. *(P; I)*

Somervill, Barbara A. *Alaska.* Scholastic, 2002. *(P; I)*

Whitcraft, Melissa. *Seward's Folly.* Scholastic, 2001. *(P; I)*

Younkin, Paula, and Hirschfelder, Arlene. *Indians of the Arctic and Subarctic.* Facts on File, 1991. *(I; A)*

ALBANIA

Dornberg, John. *Central and Eastern Europe.* Greenwood, 1995. *(A)*

Lear, Aaron E. *Albania.* Main Line Book Co., 1999. *(A)*

Wright, David K. *Albania (Enchantment of the World, Second Series).* Scholastic, 1997. *(I; A)*

ALBERTA

Yates, Sarah. *Alberta.* Lerner, 1998. *(P; I)*

ALCOHOLISM

Aaseng, Nathan. *Teens and Drunk Driving.* Gale Group, 2000. *(I; A)*

Barbour, Scott, ed. *Alcohol: Opposing Viewpoints.* Greenhaven, 1997. *(A)*

Clayton, Lawrence. *Alcohol Drug Dangers (Drug Dangers Series).* Enslow, 2001. *(I; A)*

Gerdes, Louise I. *Drunk Driving.* Gale Group, 2001. *(A)*

Holmes, Pamela. *Drugs, The Complete Story: Alcohol.* Raintree Steck-Vaughn, 1991. *(I)*

Hyde, Margaret O., and Setaro, John F. *Alcohol 101: An Overview for Teens.* Twenty-First Century, 1999. *(I; A)*

Monroe, Judy. *Alcohol.* Enslow, 1994. *(I; A)*

Ryan, Elizabeth A. *Straight Talk about Drugs and Alcohol.* Facts on File, 1996. *(I; A)*

Torr, James D., ed. *Alcoholism.* Greenhaven, 2000. *(I; A)*

Wijnberg, Ellen. *Alcohol.* Raintree Steck-Vaughn, 1993. *(I; A)*

ALCOTT, LOUISA MAY

Aller, Susan Bivin. *Beyond Little Women: A Story about Louisa May Alcott.* Lerner, 2004. *(P; I)*

Atkins, Jeannine. *Becoming Little Women: Louisa May at Fruitlands.* Penguin, 2001. *(P; I)*

Santrey, Laurence. *Louisa May Alcott: Young Writer.* Troll, 1997. *(P; I)*

Silverthorne, Elizabeth. *Louisa May Alcott.* Chelsea House, 2002. *(I; A)*

ALEXANDER

Van der Kiste, John. *The Romanovs 1818-1959: Alexander II of Russia and His Family.* Sutton, 1998. *(A)*

ALEXANDER THE GREAT

Greenblatt, Miriam. *Alexander the Great and Ancient Greece.* Marshall Cavendish, 2000. *(I; A)*

Meltzer, Milton. *Ten Kings: And the Worlds They Ruled.* Orchard Books, 2002. *(P; I)*

ALGAE

Lisowski, Marilyn, and Williams, Robert A. *Wetlands.* Scholastic, 1997. *(I; A)*

Rainis, Kenneth G., and Russell, Bruce J. *Guide to Microlife.* Scholastic, 1997. *(A)*

ALGERIA

Kaqda, Falaq. *Algeria.* Marshall Cavendish, 1997. *(I)*

Morrow, James. *Algeria.* Mason Crest, 2002. *(I; A)*

ALLEN, ETHAN

Stein, R. Conrad. *Ethan Allen and the Green Mountain Boys.* Children's Press, 2003. *(P; I)*

ALLERGIES

Brynie, Faith Hickman. *101 Questions About Your Immune System You Felt Defenseless to Answer: Until Now.* Twenty-First Century, 2000. *(I; A)*

Landau, Elaine. *Allergies.* Lerner, 1997. *(I; A)*

Lerner, Carol. *Plants That Make You Sniffle and Sneeze.* DIANE, 2004. *(P; I)*

Morgane, Wendy. *Allergies.* Twenty-First Century, 1999. *(I)*

Newman, Gerald, and Layfield, Eleanor N. *Allergies.* Watts, 1992. *(I; A)*

Parker, Steve. *Allergies.* Heinemann, 2004. *(I)*

Royston, Angela. *Why Do My Eyes Itch?: And Other Questions about Allergies.* Heinemann, 2002. *(P; I)*

Sexias, Judith S. *Allergies: What They Are, What They Do.* Greenwillow, 1991. *(P)*

Silverstein, Alvin, and Silverstein, Virginia B. *Allergies.* Scholastic, 2000. *(P; I)*

ALPHABET

Scrawl! Writing in Ancient Times. Runestone Press, 1994. *(I)*

Samoyault, Tiphaine. *Alphabetical Order: How the Alphabet Began.* Viking, 1998. *(P; I)*

ALUMINUM

Heiserman, David L. *Exploring Chemical Elements and Their Compounds.* McGraw-Hill, 1991. *(A)*

AMAZON RIVER

Castner, James L. *River Life: Deep in the Amazon; Surviving in the Rain Forest: Deep in the Amazon.* Marshall Cavendish, 2002; *Layers of Life: Deep in the Amazon; Native Peoples: Deep in the Amazon; Partners and Rivals: Deep in the Amazon; Rainforest Researchers: Deep in the Amazon.* Marshall Cavendish, 2001. *(I; A)*

Cousteau Society. *An Adventure in the Amazon.* Simon & Schuster, 1992. *(P; I)*

Pollard, Michael. *The Amazon.* Benchmark, 1997. *(P; I)*

Reynolds, Jan. *Amazon Basin: Vanishing Cultures.* Harcourt, 1993. *(P; I)*

Sandler, Michael, and Franck, Daniel H. *Rain Forests: Surviving in the Amazon.* Bearport, 2005. *(P; I)*

AMERICAN LITERATURE

Barbour, Scott. *American Modernism.* Gale Group, 1999. *(A)*

Berry, Skip L. *E. E. Cummings (Voices in Poetry); Emily Dickinson (Voices in Poetry); Langston Hughes (Voices in Poetry).* The Creative Company, 1994. *(A)*

Waxman, Laura Hamilton. *Uncommon Revolutionary: A Story about Thomas Paine.* Lerner, 2004. *(P; I)*

Weisbrod, Eva. *A Student's Guide to F. Scott Fitzgerald.* Enslow, 2004. *(I; A)*

Wright, Sarah Bird. *Edith Wharton A to Z: The Essential Guide to the Life and Work.* Facts on File, 1998. *(A)*

AMPHIBIANS

Gove, Doris. *Red-Spotted Newt.* Atheneum, 1994. *(I)*

Kalman, Bobbie, and Langille, Jacqueline. *What Is an Amphibian?* Crabtree/A Bobbie Kalman Bk., 1999. *(P)*

ANASAZI

Arnold, Caroline. *The Ancient Cliff Dwellers of Mesa Verde.* Houghton Mifflin, 2000. *(P; I)*

Lourie, Peter. *The Lost World of the Anasazi: Exploring the Mysteries of Chaco Canyon.* Boyds Mills Press, 2004. *(P; I)*

Petersen, David. *The Anasazi.* Scholastic, 1998. *(P)*

ANCIENT CIVILIZATIONS

Altman, Susan, and Lechner, Susan. *Ancient Africa; Ancient Egypt; Ancient Greece; Ancient Rome.* Scholastic, 2001. *(P)*

Barghusen, Joan D. *The Aztecs: End of a Civilization.* Gale Group, 2000. *(I; A)*

Burrell, Roy. *Oxford First Ancient History (Rebuilding the Past Series).* Oxford University Press, 1994. ; *The Greeks.* Oxford University Press, 1990. *(I)*

Caselli, Giovanni. *In Search of Knossos; In Search of Pompeii; In Search of Troy; In Search of Tutankhamun.* McGraw-Hill, 1999. *(P; I)*

Hoobler, Dorothy, and Hoobler, Thomas. *Lost Civilizations.* Walker, 1992. *(P; I)*

Hull, Robert. *Greece.* Raintree Steck-Vaughn, 1998. *(I; A)*

Landau, Elaine. *The Assyrians; The Sumerians.* Millbrook Press, 1997. *(I)*

Lourie, Peter. *Lost Treasure of the Inca; Tierra Del Fuego: A Journey to the End of the Earth.* Boyds Mills Press, 2002. *(I); The Mystery of the Maya: Uncovering the Lost City of Palenque.* Boyds Mills Press, 2001. *(P; I)*

Macdonald, Fiona. *A Greek Temple.* Peter Bedrick, 1992. *(P; I)*

Mann, Elizabeth. *The Great Pyramid: The Story of the Farmers, The God-King, and the Most Astounding Structure Ever Built.* Mikaya Press, 1996. *(P; I)*

Marston, Elsa. *The Ancient Egyptians.* Marshall Cavendish, 1996. *(I)*

Pearson, Anne. *Ancient Greece.* Knopf, 1992. *(P; I; A)*

Schomp, Virginia. *The Ancient Greeks.* Marshall Cavendish, 1996. *(I)*

Sheehan, Sean. *Ancient Rome.* Raintree Steck-Vaughn, 1999. *P; I); Great African Kingdoms.* Raintree Steck-Vaughn, 1998. *(I; A)*

Woods, Michael, and Woods, Mary B. *Ancient Communication; Ancient Computing; Ancient Construction; Ancient Warfare.* Lerner, 2000; *Ancient Agriculture; Ancient Machines; Ancient Medicine; Ancient Transportation.* Lerner, 1999. *(I; A)*

ANDERSEN, HANS CHRISTIAN

Hague, Michael. *Michael Hague's Favorite Hans Christian Andersen Fairy Tales.* Henry Holt, 2002. *(I)*

Hesse, Karen. *The Young Hans Christian Andersen.* Scholastic, 2005. *(P)*

ANDES

Falconer, Kieran. *Peru.* Marshall Cavendish, 1995 (2nd ed.). *(I; A)*

Lepthien, Emilie U. *Llamas.* Scholastic, 1997. *(P)*

Morrison, Marion. *Bolivia; Columbia; Ecuador; Peru; Venezuela.* Scholastic, 2001. *(I)*

ANGOLA

Fish, Bruce, and Fish, Becky Durost. *Angola, 1880 to the Present: Slavery, Exploitation and Revolt.* Chelsea House, 2001. *(A)*

Jordan, Manuel. *Chokwe (Angola, Zambia).* Rosen, 1997. *(I; A)*

Sheehan, Sean. *Angola.* Marshall Cavendish, 1999 (2nd ed.). *(I)*

ANIMAL RIGHTS

Bekoff, Marc A., and Meaney, Carron A., eds. *Encyclopedia of Animal Rights and Animal Welfare.* Greenwood Publishing Group, 1998. *(I; A)*

ANIMALS

Grolier Illustrated Encyclopedia of Animals. Scholastic, 1993. *(I; A)*

Arnold, Caroline. *Did You Hear That?: Animals with Super Hearing.* Charlesbridge, 2001. *(P; I); South American Animals.* Morrow, 1999. *(P)*

Brooks, Bruce. *Making Sense: Animal Perception and Communication.* Farrar, 1993. *(I)*

Cain, Nancy Woodard. *Animal Behavior Science Projects.* Wiley, 1995. *(I; A)*

Collard, Sneed B. *Making Animal Babies.* Houghton, 2000. *(P)*

Curtis, Patricia. *Animals You Never Even Heard Of.* Little, 1997. *(P); Aquatic Animals in the Wild and in Captivity.* Lodestar, 1992. *(I)*

Evans, Lisa Gollin. *An Elephant Never Forgets Its Snorkel: How Animals Survive without Tools and Gadgets.* Crown, 1992. *(I)*

Facklam, Marjorie. *Bees Dance and Whales Sing: The Mysteries of Animal Communication.* Gibbs Smith, 2001. *(I)*

Hickman, Pamela. *Animals in Motion: How Animals Swim, Jump, Slither and Glide.* Kids Can Press, 2000. *(P; I)*

Hodgkins, Fran. *Animals Among Us: Living with Suburban Wildlife.* Shoe String/Linnet, 2000. *(I)*

Jarrow, Gail, and Sherman, Paul. *Animal Baby Sitters.* Scholastic, 2001. *(P; I)*

Jordan, Tanis. *Jungle Days, Jungle Nights.* Houghton Mifflin, 1993. *(P)*

Kaner, Etta. *Animal Defenses: How Animals Protect Themselves.* Kids Can Press, 1999. *(P; I)*

Kitchen, Bert. *And So They Build.* Candlewick, 1993. *(P; I)*

Lauber, Patricia. *Fur, Feathers, and Flippers: How Animals Live Where They Do.* Scholastic, 1994. *(P; I)*

Martin, James, and Hamlin, Janet. *Living Fossils: Animals That Have Withstood the Test of Time.* Crown Books, 1997. *(P; I)*

McAlpine, Margaret. *Working with Animals.* Gareth Stevens, 2004. *(I; A)*

McClung, Robert M., and Hines, Bob. *Last of the Wild: Vanished and Vanishing Giants of the Animal World.* Shoe String Press, 1997. *(I; A)*

Perry, Phyllis J. *Animals That Hibernate; Animals Under the Ground.* Scholastic, 2001. *(P; I)*

Presnall, Judith. *Animals That Glow.* Watts, 1993. *(I)*

Riha, Suzanne. *Animal Journeys: Life Cycles and Migrations; Animals at Rest: Sleeping Patterns and Habitats.* Blackbirch, 1999. *(P; I)*

Robinson, W. Wright. *Animal Architects: How Mammals Build Their Amazing Homes.* Gale Group, 1999. *(I)*

Savage, Stephen. *Adaptation for Survival: Ears; Adaptation for Survival: Eyes; Adaptation for Survival: Hands and Feet; Adaptation for Survival: Mouths; Adaptation for Survival: Skin.* Raintree, 1995. *(P)*

Sayre, April Pulley. *Put on Some Antlers and Walk Like a Moose: How Scientists Find, Follow, and Study Wild Animals.* Millbrook Press, 1997. *(I)*

Settel, Joanne. *Exploding Ants: Amazing Facts About How Animals Adapt.* Simon & Schuster, 1999. *(P; I)*

Shedd, Warner. *The Kids' Wildlife Book: Exploring Animal Worlds through Indoor/Outdoor Experiences.* Williamson, 1994. *(P; I)*

Simon, Seymour. *They Walk the Earth: The Extraordinary Travels of Animals on Land.* Harcourt/Browndeer, 2000. *(P; I)*

Sowler, Sandie. *Amazing Animal Disguises; Amazing Armored Animals.* Knopf, 1992. *(P)*

Squire, Ann O. *African Animals.* Scholastic, 2001. *(P)*

Staub, Frank J. *The Signs Animals Leave.* Scholastic, 2001. *(P; I)*

Swan, Erin Pembrey. *Land Predators Around the World.* Scholastic, 2001; *Land Predators of North America.* Scholastic, 1999. *(P; I)*

Taylor, Barbara. *The Animals Atlas.* Knopf, 1992. *(I; A)*

Taylor, David. *Nature's Creatures of the Dark.* Dial, 1993. *(P; I)*

Thomas, Peggy. *Big Cat Conservation; Reptile Rescue.* Twenty-First Century, 2000. *(I)*

Whyman, Kate. *The Animal Kingdom.* Raintree Steck-Vaughn, 1999. *(I)*

Zoehfeld, Kathleen Weidner. *What Lives in a Shell?* HarperCollins, 1994. *(P)*

ANIMATION

Canemaker, John. *Winsor McCay: His Life and Art.* Abrams, 2005 (rev. ed.) ; *The Art and Flair of Mary Blair: An Appreciation.* Disney Press, 2003; *Walt Disney's Nine Old Men and the Art of Animation.* Disney Press, 2001. *(I; A)*

Scott, Elaine. *Look Alive: Behind the Scenes of an Animated Film.* Morrow, 1992. *(P; I; A)*

Thomas, Bob. *Disney's Art of Animation: From Mickey Mouse to Hercules.* Disney, 1997 (2nd ed.). *(P; I; A)*

ANTARCTICA

Armstrong, Jennifer. *Shipwreck at the Bottom of the World: The Extraordinary True Story of Shackelton and the Endurance.* Crown, 1998. *(I; A)*

Bocknek, Jonathan. *Antarctica: The Last Wilderness.* Smart Apple Media, 2004. *(I; A)*

Bramwell, Martyn; Crosby-Fairall, Marjorie; and Winterbotham, Ann. *DK Discoveries: Polar Exploration: Journeys to the Arctic & Antarctic.* DK, 1998. *(I; A)*

Burleigh, Robert. *Black Whiteness: Admiral Byrd Alone in the Antarctic.* Simon & Schuster, 1998. *(P; I)*

Chester, Jonathan. *A for Antarctica.* Tricycle, 1995. *(P; I)*

Currie, Stephen. *Polar Explorers.* Gale Group, 2002. *(I; A)*

Kimmel, Elizabeth Cody. *Ice Story: Shackelton's Lost Expedition.* Clarion, 1999. *(I)*

Kostyal, K. M. *Trial by Ice: A Photobiography of Sir Ernest Shackleton.* National Geographic Society, 1999. *(I)*

Matsen, Bradford. *An Extreme Dive Under the Antarctic Ice.* Enslow, 2003 *(I)*

Petersen, David. *Antarctica.* Scholastic, 1999. *(P; I)*

Theodorou, Rod. *From the Arctic to the Antarctic.* Heinemann, 2000. *(P)*

Webb, Sophie. *My Season with Penguins: An Antarctic Journal.* Houghton Mifflin, 2000. *(P; I)*

Wheeler, Sara. *Greetings from Antarctica.* Peter Bedrick, 1999. *(P; I)*

ANTHONY, SUSAN B.

Archer, Jules. *Breaking Barriers: The Feminist Revolution from Susan B. Anthony to Margaret Sanger to Betty Friedan.* Penguin Putnam, 1996. *(A)*

Kops, Deborah. *People at the Center of: Women's Suffrage.* Blackbirch Press, 2003. *(I)*

Monroe, Judy. *Susan B. Anthony Women's Voting Rights Trial: A Headline Court Case.* Enslow, 2002. *(I; A)*

ANTHROPOLOGY

Corbishley, Mike. *What Do We Know about Prehistoric People?* Peter Bedrick, 1995. *(I)*

Coville, Bruce. *Prehistoric People.* Doubleday, 1990. *(I)*

Gallant, Roy A. *Early Humans.* Marshall Cavendish/Benchmark, 1999. *(I; A)*

Jackson, Donna M. *The Bone Detectives: How Forensic Anthropologists Solve Crimes and Uncover Mysteries of the Dead.* Little, Brown, 1996. *(I; A)*

Martell, Hazel Mary. *Over 6,000 Years Ago: in the Stone Age.* Macmillan, 1992. *(I)*

Sattler, Helen Roney. *The Earliest Americans.* Clarion, 1993. (I; A)

ANTIBIOTICS

Day, Nancy. *Killer Superbugs: The Story of Drug-Resistant Diseases.* Enslow, 2001. *(I; A)*

Kaye, Judith. *The Life of Alexander Fleming.* Twenty-First Century, 1993. *(I)*

Smith, Linda Wasmer. *Louis Pasteur: Disease Fighter.* Enslow, 2001. *(I)*

APES

Gallardo, Evelyn. *Among the Orangutans: The Birute Galdikas Story.* Chronicle, 1993. *(P)*

Gogerly, Liz. *Dian Fossey.* Raintree, 2003. *(I)*

Pettit, Jayne. *Jane Goodall: Pioneer Researcher.* Scholastic, 1999. *(I)*

Pratt, Paula Bryant. *The Importance of Jane Goodall.* Gale Group, 1997. *(I; A)*

Roberts, Jack L. *The Importance of Dian Fossey.* Gale Group, 1995. *(I; A)*

Stonehouse, Bernard. *A Visual Introduction to Monkeys and Apes.* Facts on File, 1999. *(I; A)*

APPLE

Gibbons, Gail. *Apples.* Holiday, 2000. *(P)*

Schnieper, Claudia. *An Apple Tree through the Year.* Lerner, 1993. *(P; I)*

Wolfman, Judy, and Winston, David Lorenz. *Life on an Apple Orchard.* Lerner, 2003. *(P)*

AQUACULTURE

Bang, Molly. *Nobody Particular: One Woman's Fight to Save the Bays.* Chelsea Green, 2005. *(P; I)*

Koch, Frances King. *Mariculture: Farming the Fruits of the Sea.* Watts, 1992. *(P; I)*

ARABS

Corzine, Phyllis. *The Palestinian-Israeli Accord.* Gale Group, 1996. *(I; A)*

Ferber, Elizabeth. *Yasir Arafat: A Life of War and Peace.* Millbrook Press, 1995. *(I; A)*

Hall, Loretta, and Hall, Bridget K. *Arab American Biography; Arab American Voices.* Gale Group, 1999. *(I; A)*

Long, Cathryn J. *The Middle East in Search of Peace.* Millbrook Press, 1994. *(I)*

Williams, Mary E. *The Middle East.* Gale Group, 2000. *(A)*

ARACHNIDS

Berger, Melvin, and Berger, Gilda. *Do All Spiders Spin Webs?: Questions and Answers about Spiders; Do Tarantulas Have Teeth?: Questions and Answers about Poisonous Creatures.* Scholastic, 2000. *(P; I)*

Dykstra, Mary. *Amateur Zoologist: Explorations and Investigations.* Scholastic, 1995. *(I; A)*

ARCTIC

Currie, Stephen. *Polar Explorers.* Gale Group, 2002. *(I; A)*

Dudley, William, ed. *Endangered Oceans.* Thomson Gale, 1999. *(A)*

Flowers, Pam, and Dixon, Ann. *Alone across the Arctic: One Woman's Epic Journey by Dog Team.* Graphic Arts Center, 2001. *(I: A)*

Lynch, Wayne. *Arctic Alphabet: Exploring the North from A to Z.* Firefly, 1999. *(P; I)*

Osborn, Kevin. *The Peoples of the Arctic.* Chelsea House, 1990. *(I; A)*

Rozakis, Laurie E. *Matthew Henson and Robert Peary: The Race for the North Pole.* Gale Group, 1994. *(P; I)*

Sayre, April Pulley. *Ocean (Exploring Earth's Biomes Series).* Lerner, 1997. *(I)*

Steger, Will, and Bowermaster, Jon. *Over the Top of the World: Explorer Will Steger's Trek Across the Arctic.* Scholastic, 1996. *(P; I; A)*

Theodorou, Rod. *From the Arctic to the Antarctic.* Heinemann, 2000. *(P)*

Varilla, Mary, ed. *Scholastic Atlas of Oceans.* Scholastic, 2004. *(P; I)*

Vieira, Linda. *The Seven Seas: Exploring the World Ocean.* Walker, 2003. *(P; I)*

Younkin, Paula, and Hirschfelder, Arlene. *Indians of the Arctic and Subarctic.* Facts on File, 1991. *(I; A)*

ARGENTINA

Burgan, Michael. *Argentina.* Scholastic, 1999. *(P)*

Frank, Nicole, and Sita, Lisa. *Argentina.* Gareth Stevens, 2000. *(I)*

Gofen, Ethel Caro, and Jermyn, Leslie. *Argentina.* Marshall Cavendish, 2002 (2nd ed.). *(I; A)*

ARISTOTLE

Gay, Kathlyn. *Science in Ancient Greece.* Watts, 1998. *(I)*

Magee, Bryan. *The Story of Philosophy.* DK, 1999. *(A)*

Nardo, Don, ed. *Scientists of Ancient Greece.* Gale Group, 1998. *(I; A)*

Parker, Steve. *Aristotle and Scientific Thought.* Chelsea House, 1995. *(I)*

ARITHMETIC

Anno, Mitsumasa. *Anno's Math Games; nno's Math Games II; Anno's Math Games III.* Penguin Group, 1997 (reprint). *(P)*

Caron, Lucille. *Addition and Subtraction; Multiplication and Division.* Enslow, 2001; *Fractions and Decimals.* Enslow, 2000. *(P; I)*

Leedy, Loreen. *Subtraction Action.* Holiday House, 2000; *Mission: Addition.* Holiday House, 1999; *Fraction Action.* Holiday House, 1996. *(P)*

ARIZONA

Petersen, David. *Grand Canyon National Park.* Scholastic, 2001; *Saguaro National Park.* Scholastic, 2000; *Petrified Forest National Park.* Scholastic, 1997. *(P; I)*

Standard, Carole K. *Arizona.* Scholastic, 2002. *(P; I)*

Stanley, Jerry. *Frontier Merchants: Lionel and Barron Jacobs and the Jewish Pioneers Who Settled the West.* Crown, 1998. *(I; A)*

Thompson, Bill, and Thompson, Dorcas. *Geronimo.* Chelsea House, 2001. *(P; I)*

Weintraub, Aileen. *The Grand Canyon: The Widest Canyon.* Rosen, 2001. *(P; I)*

ARKANSAS

Altman, Linda Jacobs. *Arkansas.* Marshall Cavendish, 2000. *(P; I)*

Bailer, Darice, and Craven, Jean. *Arkansas: The Natural State.* Gareth Stevens, 2002. *(P; I)*

Dipiazza, Domenica. *Arkansas.* Lerner, 2001 (2nd ed.). *(P; I)*

Fradin, Dennis Brindell, and Fradin, Judith, Bloom. *Arkansas: From Sea to Shining Sea.* Scholastic, 1995. *(P; I)*

Macaulay, Ellen. *Arkansas.* Scholastic, 2001. *(P; I)*

ARMENIA

Batalden, Stephen K., and Batalden, Sandra L. *The Newly Independent States of Eurasia: Handbook of Former Soviet Republics. 2nd ed.* Greenwood, 1997. *(I; A)*

Greenberg, Keith Elliot. *Journey Between Two Worlds: An Armenian Family.* Lerner, 1997. *(P; I)*

Kherdian, David. *The Golden Bracelet.* Holiday House, 1998. *(P; I)*

Kort, Michael G. *The Handbook of the Former Soviet Union.* Millbrook Press, 1997. *(A)*

ARMSTRONG, NEIL A.

Bredeson, Carmen. *Neil Armstrong: A Space Biography.* Enslow, 1998. *(I)*

Brown, Don. *One Giant Leap: The Story of Neil Armstrong.* Houghton, 1998. *(P)*

Kramer, Barbara. *Neil Armstrong: The First Man on the Moon.* Enslow, 1997. *(I)*

ARNOLD, BENEDICT

Buranelli, Vincent. *American Spies and Traitors.* Enslow, 2004. *(I; A)*

Gaines, Ann Graham. *Benedict Arnold: Patriot or Traitor?* Enslow, 2000. *(I)*

King, David C. *Benedict Arnold and the American Revolution.* Blackbirch Press, 1998. *(I; A)*

Powell, Walter Louis. *Benedict Arnold: Revolutionary War Hero and Traitor.* PowerPlus Books, 2004. *(I)*

Sonneborn, Liz. *Benedict Arnold: Hero and Traitor (Leaders of the American Revolution Series).* Chelsea House, 2006. *(I)*

Wade, Mary Dodson. *Benedict Arnold.* Watts, 1994. *(P; I)*

ART

Aronson, Marc. *Art Attack: A Short Cultural History of the Avant-Garde.* Clarion, 1998. *(A)*

Bolden, Tonya. *Wake Up Your Souls: A Celebration of African American Artists.* Abrams, 2003. *(I; A)*

Connolly, Sean. *Henry Moore.* Heinemann, 1999. *(P; I)*

Cummings, Pat, ed. *Talking with Artists.* Bradbury, 1992. *(P; I); Talking with Artists, Volume Two.* Simon & Schuster, 1995. *(I; A)*

Greenberg, Jan, and Jordan, Sandra. *The American Eye: Eleven Artists of the Twentieth Century.* Delacorte, 1995; *The Painter's Eye: Learning to Look at Contemporary Art.* Delacorte, 1991. *(I; A)*

Micklethwait, Lucy. *A Child's Book of Art: Discover Great Paintings.* DK, 1999. *(P; I)*

Sills, Leslie. *Visions: Stories about Women Artists.* Albert Whitman, 1993. *(I)*

Welton, Jude. *Drawing: A Young Artist's Guide.* Dorling Kindersley, 1994. *(I; A)*

Wolfe, Gillian. *Oxford First Book of Art.* Oxford, 1999. *(P)*

Yenawine, Philip. *Colors; Lines; Shapes.* Delacorte, 1991. *(P)*

ARTHUR, CHESTER ALAN

Brunelli, Carol. *Chester A. Arthur: Our Twenty-First President.* Child's World, 2002. *(P; I)*

Elish, Dan. *Chester A. Arthur (Encyclopedia of Presidents, Second Series).* Scholastic, 2004. *(I; A)*

ARTHUR, KING

Bruce, Christopher W., ed. *Arthurian Name Dictionary.* Taylor & Francis, 1998. *(A)*

Crossley-Holland, Kevin. *The World of King Arthur and His Court: People, Places, Legend, and Lore.* Penguin Putnam, 1999 (First American Edition). *(I; A)*

Hodges, Margaret, retel. *Merlin and the Making of the King.* Holiday House, 2004. *(P; I); Of Swords and Sorcerers: The Adventures of King Arthur and His Knights.* Simon & Schuster, 1993. *(I); The Kitchen Knight: A Tale of King Arthur.* Holiday House, 1991. *(P; I)*

Williams, Marcia, illus. *King Arthur and the Knights of the Round Table.* Candlewick Press, 1996. *(P)*

Yolen, Jane. *Merlin (The Young Merlin Trilogy Series #3).* Harcourt, 1997; *Hobby (The Young Merlin Trilogy Series #2); Passager (The Young Merlin Trilogy Series #1).* Harcourt, 1996. *(P; I)*

ASIA

Clark, Cherese, and Clark, Charles. *The Central Asian States.* Gale Group, 2001. *(A)*

Merrill, Yvonne Y. *Hands-on Asia: Art Activities for All Ages.* K/ITS, 1999. *(I; A)*

Millett, Sandra. *Hmong of Southeast Asia.* Lerner, 2001. *(I)*

Pascoe, Elaine. *The Pacific Rim: East Asia at the Dawn of a New Century.* Millbrook Press, 1999. *(A)*

Petersen, David. *Asia.* Scholastic, 1998. *(P; I)*

Viesti, Joseph F., and Hall, Diane. *Celebrate! in South Asia; Celebrate! in Southeast Asia.* HarperCollins, 1996. *(P; I)*

ASTRONAUTS

Baird, Anne. *The U. S. Space Camp Book of Astronauts.* HarperCollins, 1996. *(I); Space Camp: The Great Adventure for NASA Hopefuls.* HarperCollins, 1995. *(P; I)*

Briggs, Carole S. *Women in Space.* Lerner, 1999. *(I)*

Burns, Khephra, and Miles, William. *Black Stars in Orbit: NASA's African American Astronauts.* Harcourt, 1995. *(I; A)*

Cassutt, Michael. *Who's Who in Space: The International Space Station Edition.* Thomson Gale, 1998 (3rd ed.). *(I; A)*

Cole, Michael D. *Astronauts: Training for Space.* Enslow, 1999. *(I)*

Mullane, R. Mike. *Liftoff! An Astronaut's Dream.* Silver Burdett Press, 1994. *(I)*

Richie, Jason. *Spectacular Space Travelers.* Oliver Press, 2002. *(I; A)*

ASTRONOMY

Berger, Melvin, and Berger, Gilda. *Do Stars Have Points?: Questions and Answers about Stars and Planets.* Scholastic, 1999. *(P; I)*

Boerst, William J. *Johannes Kepler: Discovering the Laws of Celestial Motion.* Reynolds, 2003. *(I; A)*

Branley, Franklyn M. *The Sun: Our Nearest Star.* HarperCollins, 2002 (rev. ed.). *(P)*

Camp, Carole Ann. *American Astronomers: Searchers and Wonderers.* Enslow, 1996. *(I; A)*

Cobb, Allan B. *How Do We Know how Stars Shine?* Rosen, 2001. *(I; A)*

Couper, Heather, and Henbest, Nigel. *Big Bang: The Story of the Universe.* DK, 1997. *(I; A); How the Universe Works.* Reader's Digest, 1994. *(I)*

Fradin, Dennis Brindell. *Searching for Alien Life.* Millbrook Press, 1997. *(I)*

Gallant, Roy A. *Earth's Place in Space.* Marshall Cavendish/ Benchmark, 1999. *(I; A)*

Goble, Todd. *Nicolas Copernicus: And the Founding of Modern Astronomy.* Reynolds, 2003. *(I; A)*

Gormley, Beatrice. *Maria Mitchell: The Soul of an Astronomer.* Eerdmans, William B., 1995. *(I; A)*

Jackson, Ellen. *Looking for Life in the Universe.* Houghton Mifflin, 2002. *(I)*

Lippincott, Kristen. *Astronomy.* Dorling Kindersley, 1994. *(I; A)*

Vbrova, Zuza. *Space and Astronomy.* Gloucester Press, 1990. *(I)*

Voekel, James R. *Johannes Kepler: And the New Astronomy.* Oxford University Press, 2001. *(I; A)*

Vogt, Gregory L. *Constellations; Milky Way; Stars.* Capstone Press, 2002. *(P); Milky Way and Other Galaxies.* Raintree, 2000. *(I; A); Deep Space Astronomy.* Millbrook Press, 1999. *(I; A); Asteroids, Comets, and Meteors; The Sun.* Millbrook Press, 1996. *(P; I); Solar System: Facts and Exploration.* Millbrook Press, 1995. *(I)*

ATLANTIC OCEAN

Dudley, William, ed. *Endangered Oceans.* Thomson Gale, 1999. *(A)*

Lambert, David. *The Kingfisher Young People's Book of Oceans.* Houghton Mifflin, 1997. *(P; I)*

Petersen, David, and Petersen, Christine. *The Atlantic Ocean.* Children's Press, 2001. *(P)*

Taylor, Leighton R. *The Atlantic Ocean.* Gale Group, 1999. *(P; I)*

ATMOSPHERE

Maslin, Mark. *Global Warming: Causes, Effects, and the Future.* Voyageur Press, 2002. *(A)*

Morgan, Sally. *The Ozone Hole.* Scholastic, 1999. *(P; I)*

Newton, David E. *The Ozone Dilemma: A Reference Handbook.* ABC-CLIO, 1994. *(A)*

Pringle, Laurence. *Global Warming: The Threat of Earth's Changing Climate.* Seastar Books, 2001; *Vanishing Ozone: Protecting Earth from Ultraviolet Radiation.* Morrow, 1995. *(I)*

Silverstein, Alvin; Silverstein, Virginia B.; and Nunn, Laura Silverstein. *Global Warming.* Lerner, 2003. *(I)*

ATOMS

Bortz, Alfred B. *Electron; Neutrino; Neutron; Photon; Proton; Quark.* Rosen, 2004. *(I; A)*

Brandolini, Anita J. *Fizz, Bubble and Flash!: Element Explorations and Atom Adventures for Hands-on Science Fun!* Ideals Publications, 2003. *(P; I)*

AUGUST

Updike, John. *A Child's Calendar.* Holiday House, 1999. *(P; I)*

Warner, Penny. *Kids' Holiday Fun: Great Family Activities Every Month of the Year.* Meadowbrook Press, 1997. *(P)*

AUGUSTUS

Baker, Rosalie F., and Baker, Charles F., III. *Ancient Romans: Expanding the Classical Tradition.* Oxford University Press, 1998 *(P; I)*

Greenblatt, Miriam. *Augustus Caesar and Ancient Rome.* Marshall Cavendish, 2000. *(P; I)*

AUSTEN, JANE

Bloom, Harold, ed. *Jane Austen's Pride and Prejudice (Bloom's Notes Series).* Chelsea House, 1995. *(A)*

LeFaye, Deirdre. *Jane Austen.* Oxford, 1999. *(A)*

AUSTRALIA

Collard, Sneed B. *Lizard Island: Science and Scientists on Australia's Great Barrier Reef.* Scholastic, 2000. *(I; A)*

Davis, Kevin A. *Look What Came from Australia.* Scholastic, 1999. *(P)*

Franklin, Sharon; Black, Cynthia A.; Langness, Teresa; and Krafchin, Rhonda. *Southwest Pacific.* Raintree Steck-Vaughn, 1999. *(I; A)*

Grupper, Jonathan. *Destination: Australia.* National Geographic, 2000. *(P; I)*

North, Peter, and McKay, Susan. *Welcome to Australia.* Gareth Stevens, 1999. *(P)*

Petersen, David. *Australia.* Scholastic, 1998. *(P; I)*

Reynolds, Jan. *Down Under: Vanishing Cultures.* Harcourt, 1992. *(P; I)*

AUTOMATION

Macaulay, David. *The New Way Things Work.* Houghton Mifflin, 1998. *(P; I; A)*

AVALANCHES AND LANDSLIDES

Downs, Sandra. *When the Earth Moves.* Twenty-First Century, 2000. *(P; I; A)*

Goodwin, Peter H. *Landslides, Slumps, and Creep.* Franklin Watts, 1998. *(P; I)*

AVIATION

Atkins, Jeannine. *Wings and Rockets: The Story of Women in Air and Space.* Farrar, 2003. *(I; A)*

Bellville, Cheryl Walsh. *The Airplane Book.* Carolrhoda, 1991. *(P; I)*

Berliner, Don. *Aviation: Reaching for the Sky.* Oliver Press, 1997 *(I)*

Burleigh, Robert. *Flight: The Journey of Charles Lindbergh.* Philomel, 1991. *(P; I)*

Busby, Peter. *First to Fly: How Wilbur and Orville Wright Invented the Airplane.* Crown, 2003. *(I)*

Canavan, Andrea. *Your Government: The Federal Aviation Administration.* Chelsea House, 2002. *(I; A)*

Lindblom, Steven. *Fly the Hot Ones.* Houghton, 1991. *(I; A)*

Maurer, Richard. *Airborne: The Search for the Secret of Flight.* Simon & Schuster, 1990. *(I)*

Nahum, Andrew. *Eyewitness: Flying Machine.* DK, 2004 (rev. ed.). *(I)*

Weiss, Harvey. *Strange and Wonderful Aircraft.* Houghton, 1995. *(I)*

AZTECS

Barghusen, Joan D. *The Aztecs: End of a Civilization.* Gale Group, 2000. *(I; A)*

Chrisp, Peter. *The Aztecs.* Raintree Steck-Vaughn, 1999. *(P; I)*

Dawson, Imogen. *Clothes and Crafts in Aztec Times.* Gareth Stevens, 2000. *(P; I)*

Flowers, Charles. *Cortes and the Conquest of the Aztec Empire in World History.* Enslow, 2001. *(I; A)*

Hull, Robert. *The Aztecs.* Raintree Steck-Vaughn, 1998. *(I; A)*

Stein, Richard Conrad. *The Aztec Empire.* Benchmark, 1996. *(I)*

B (LETTER)

Samoyault, Tiphaine. *Alphabetical Order: How the Alphabet Began.* Viking, 1998. *(P; I)*

BACTERIA

Berger, Melvin. *Germs Make Me Sick!* HarperCollins, 1995. *(P)*

Biddle, Wayne. *Field Guide to Germs.* Henry Holt, 1995. *(A)*

Facklam, Howard, and Facklam, Margery. *Bacteria; Parasites; Viruses.* Twenty-First Century, 1995. *(I)*

Nardo, Don. *Germs: Mysterious Microorganisms.* Gale Group, 1991. *(I; A)*

Rainis, Kenneth G., and Russell, Bruce J. *Guide to Microlife.* Scholastic, 1997. *(A)*

Ricciuti, Edward. *Microorganisms.* Blackbirch Press, 1994. *(I)*

BAHAMAS

Barlas, Robert. *Bahamas.* Marshall Cavendish, 2000. *(A)*

Hintz, Martin, and Hintz, Stephen V. *The Bahamas (Enchantment of the World, Second Series).* Scholastic, 1997. *(I; A)*

BAHRAIN

Cooper, Robert. *Bahrain.* Marshall Cavendish, 2000. *(I; A)*

Fox, Mary Virginia. *Bahrain.* Children's Press, 1995. *(I; A)*

McCoy, Lisa. *Bahrain.* Mason Crest, 2002. *(I; A)*

BALKANS

Black, Eric. *Bosnia.* Lerner, 1999. *(I; A)*

Kronenwetter, Michael. *The New Eastern Europe.* Watts, 1991. *(I; A)*

Milivojevic, Joann. *Serbia.* Children's Press, 1999. *(I; A)*

Otfinoski, Steven. *Bulgaria.* Facts on File, 1998. *(I; A)*

Reger, James P. *The Rebuilding of Bosnia.* Lucent, 1997. *(I)*

Sacco, Joe. *Safe Area Gorazde: The War in Eastern Bosnia, 1992-95.* Fantagraphics, 2001. *(A)*

BALLADS

Fox, Dan. *A Treasury of Children's Songs: Forty Favorites to Sing and Play.* Henry Holt, 2003; *Go In and Out the Window: An Illustrated Songbook for Young People.* Henry Holt, 1987. *(P)*

BALLET

Bussell, Darcey. *Ballet.* DK, 2000. *(P; I)*
Jessel, Camilla. *Ballet School.* Viking, 2000. *(P; I)*
Varriale, Jim. *Kids Dance: The Students of Ballet Tech.* Dutton, 1999. *(P; I)*

BALLOONS AND BALLOONING

Berliner, Don. *Aviation: Reaching for the Sky.* Oliver Press, 1997. *(I)*
Costanzo, Christie. *Hot Air Ballooning.* Capstone Press, 1991. *(P; I)*

BANDS AND BAND MUSIC

Venezia, Mike. *John Philip Sousa.* Children's Press, 1999. *(P)*
Zannos, Susan. *Masters of Music: The Life and Times of John Philip Sousa.* Mitchell Lane, 2003. *(I)*

BANGKOK (KRUNG THEP)

McNair, Sylvia. *Bangkok.* Children's Press, 2000. *(P)*

BANGLADESH

Laure, Jason. *Bangladesh.* Children's Press, 1992. *(I; A)*
Viesti, Joseph F., and Hall, Diane. *Celebrate! in South Asia.* HarperCollins, 1996. *(P;I)*
Whyte, Mariam. *Bangladesh.* Marshall Cavendish, 1999 (2nd ed.). *(I; A)*

BANKS AND BANKING

Godfrey, Neale S. *Neale S. Godfrey's Ultimate Kids' Money Book.* Simon & Schuster, 1998. *(P; I; A)*
Otfinoski, Steven. *The Kid's Guide to Money: Earning It, Saving It, Spending It, Growing It, Sharing It.* Scholastic, 1996. *(P; I)*

BARNUM, PHINEAS TAYLOR

Andronik, Catherine M. *Prince of Humbugs: A Life of P.T. Barnum.* Atheneum, 1994. *(I; A)*

BARRIE, SIR JAMES MATTHEW

Aller, Susan Bivin. *J. M. Barrie: The Magic behind Peter Pan.* Lerner, 1994. *(I)*

BARRYMORE FAMILY

Hoffman, Carol Stein. *Barrymores: Hollywood's First Family.* University of Kentucky Press, 2001. *(A)*

BARTON, CLARA

Chang, Ina. *Separate Battle: Women and the Civil War.* Penguin Putnam, 1996 (reprint). *(I)*
Tilton, Rafael. *Clara Barton.* Thomson Gale, 1995. *(I; A)*
Whitelaw, Nancy. *Clara Barton: Civil War Nurse.* Enslow, 1997. *(I)*

BASEBALL

Berler, Ron. *The Super Book of Baseball.* Sports Illustrated for Kids Books, 1991. *(I; A)*
Brundage, Buz. *Be a Better Hitter: Baseball Basics.* Sterling, 2000. *(I)*
Buckley, James. *Play Ball!* DK, 2002; *Baseball.* DK, 2000. *(P; I)*

BATS

Ackerman, Diane. *Bats: Shadows in the Night.* Crown Books, 1997. *(I)*
Earle, Ann. *Zipping, Zapping, Zooming Bats.* HarperCollins, 1995. *(P; I)*
Gibbons, Gail. *Bats.* Holiday, 1999. *(P)*
McNulty, Faith. *When I Lived with Bats.* Scholastic/Cartwheel, 1999. *(P)*
Pringle, Laurence. *Bats! Strange and Wonderful.* Boyds Mills, 2000. *(P; I)*; *Batman: Exploring the World of Bats.* Scribner's, 1991. *(P; I)*

BATTERIES

Bartholomew, Alan. *Electric Mischief: Battery-Powered Gadgets Kids Can Build (Kids Can Do It Series).* Kids Can Press, 2004. *(P; I)*
Challoner, Jack. *My First Batteries and Magnets.* DK, 1992. *(P)*

BATTLES

Crompton, Samuel Willard. *Hastings.* Chelsea House, 2002. *(I; A)*
Ferrie, Richard. *The World Turned Upside Down: George Washington and the Battle of Yorktown.* Holiday, 1999. *(I; A)*
Fraser, Mary Ann. *Vicksburg: The Battle That Won the Civil War.* Holt, 1999. *(I)*
Holmes, Richard. *Eyewitness Books: Battle.* DK, 2000. *(I; A)*
Nardo, Don. *Battle of Zama: Battles of the Ancient World.* Gale Group, 1996; *The Battle of Marathon: Battles of the Ancient World.* Gale Group, 1995. *(I; A)*
Pietrusza, David. *The Battle of Waterloo: Battles of the Nineteenth Century.* Gale Group, 1996; *The Invasion of Normandy: Battles of World War II.* Gale Group, 1995. *(I; A)*
Rice, Earl, Jr. *Strategic Battles in the Pacific.* Gale Group, 2000; *The Battle of Belleau Wood; The Battle of Britain; The Battle of Midway; The Inchon Invasion; The TET Offensive.* Gale Group, 1996. *(I; A)*
Sorrels, Roy. *The Alamo (In American History Series).* Enslow, 1996. *(I; A)*

BEARS

Berger, Melvin, and Berger, Gilda. *Do Bears Sleep All Winter?: Questions and Answers about Bears.* Scholastic, 2002. *(P; I)*

Hoshino, Michio. *The Grizzly Bear Family Book.* North-South Books, 1994. *(P; I)*

Larsen, Thor, illus. *The Polar Bear Family Book.* Sagebrush Education, 1996. *(P; I)*

Markle, Sandra. *Growing Up Wild: Bears.* Simon & Schuster/Atheneum, 2000. *(P)*

BEAVERS

Hodge, Deborah. *Beavers.* Kids Can Press, 1998. *(P; I)*

Rounds, Glen. *Beaver.* Holiday, 1999. *(P)*

BEETHOVEN, LUDWIG VAN

Callahan, John F. *Ludwig Van Beethoven: Composer.* Chelsea House, 1997. *(I)*

Thompson, Wendy. *Ludwig van Beethoven.* Viking, 1991. *(I)*

Venezia, Mike. *Ludwig Van Beethoven.* Children's Press, 1996. *(P)*

Zannos, Susan. *Masters of Music: The Life and Times of Ludwig Van Beethoven.* Mitchell Lane, 2003. *(I)*

BEETLES

Collard, Sneed B. *A Firefly Biologist at Work.* Scholastic, 2001. *(P; I)*

BEIJING

Barber, Nicola. *Great Cities of the World: Beijing.* Gareth Stevens, 2003. *(I)*

Kent, Deborah. *Beijing.* Children's Press, 1996. *(I)*

BELGIUM

Burgan, Michael. *Belgium (Enchantment of the World, Second Series).* Scholastic, 2000. *(I; A)*

Pateman, Robert. *Belgium.* Marshall Cavendish, 1995. *(I; A)*

BELIZE

Jermyn, Leslie. *Belize.* Marshall Cavendish, 2001. *(I; A)*

Maynard, Caitlin; Maynard, Thane; and Rullman, Stan. *Rain Forests and Reefs: A Kid's Eye-View of the Tropics.* Watts, 1996. *(I)*

Morrison, Marion. *Belize.* Children's Press, 1996. *(I; A)*

Staub, Frank J. *Children of Belize.* Lerner, 1997. *(P)*

BELL, ALEXANDER GRAHAM

Fisher, Leonard Everett. *Alexander Graham Bell.* Simon & Schuster/Atheneum, 1999. *(P; I)*

Matthews, Tom L. *Always Inventing: A Photobiography of Alexander Graham Bell.* National Geographic, 1999. *(P; I)*

BENEDICT XVI, POPE

Allen, John. *Pope Benedict XVI: Joseph Ratzinger.* Continuum International Publishing, 2005. *(A)*

Tobin, Greg. *Holy Father: Pope Benedict XVI: Pontiff for a New Era.* Sterling, 2005. *(A)*

BENIN

Franklin, Sharon; Tull, Mary; and Shelton, Carol. *Africa: Understanding Geography and History through Art.* Raintree Steck-Vaughn, 2000. *(I; A)*

Koslow, Philip. *Benin: Lords of the River; Dahomey: The Warrior Kings; Yorubaland: The Flowering of Genius.* Chelsea House, 1996. *(I)*

Mama, Raouf, trans. *Why Goats Smell Bad: And Other Stories from Benin.* Shoe String, 1997. *(I; A)*

BEOWULF

Bloom, Harold, ed. *Beowulf (Bloom's Notes Series).* Chelsea House, 1995. *(A)*

Crossley-Holland, Kevin, trans. *Beowulf.* Oxford University Press, 1999 (reprint). *(I; A)*

Thompson, Stephen P., ed. *Readings on Beowulf.* Greenhaven Press, 1998. *(A)*

BERLIN

Epler, Doris M. *The Berlin Wall: How It Rose and Why It Fell.* Millbrook, 1992. *(I; A)*

BETHUNE, MARY MCLEOD

Greenfield, Eloise. *Mary McLeod Bethune.* HarperCollins, 1994. *(P; I)*

Wolfe, Rinna Evelyn. *Mary McLeod Bethune.* Watts, 1992. *(P; I)*

BHUTAN

Cooper, Robert. *Bhutan.* Marshall Cavendish, 2001. *(I; A)*

Viesti, Joseph F., and Hall, Diane. *Celebrate! in South Asia.* HarperCollins, 1996. *(P; I)*

BHUTTO, BENAZIR

Englar, Mary. *Benazir Bhutto: Pakistani Prime Minister and Activist.* Capstone Press, 2003. *(I; A)*

BIBLE

Holy Bible. *King James Version Holy Bible Rev. Standard Version (Catholic Edition).* Many publishers.

Armstrong, Carole. *Women of the Bible: With Paintings from the Great Art Museums of the World.* Simon & Schuster, 1998. *(P; I)*

Manushkin, Fran. *Daughters of Fire: Heroines of the Bible.* Harcourt, 2001. *(P; I)*

Marcus, Amy Dockser. *The View from Nebo: How Archaeology is Rewriting the Bible and Reshaping the Middle East.* Little, 2000. *(A)*

Meltzer, Milton. *Ten Queens: Portraits of Women of Power.* Dutton, 1997. *(I; A)*

Rock, Lois, ed. *Words of Gold: A Treasury of Bible Poetry and Wisdom.* Eerdmans, 2000. *(P; I)*

BIBLE STORIES

Auld, Mary, retel. *Daniel in the Lions' Den; David and Goliath; Exodus from Egypt; Jacob and Esau; Joseph and His Brothers; Moses in the Bulrushes; Noah's Ark; The Story of Jonah.* Scholastic, 2000. *(P)*

Gerstein, Mordicai, reteller. *Noah and the Great Flood.* Simon, 1999. *(P)*

Wildsmith, Brian. *Mary.* Eerdmans, 2002; *Jesus; The Easter Story.* Eerdmans, 2000; *A Christmas Story; Exodus.* Eerdmans, 1998; *Joseph.* Eerdmans, 1997; *Saint Francis.* Eerdmans, 1996. *(P)*

BICYCLING

Bicycling Magazine's Editors et al. *Bicycling Magazine's Complete Guide to Bicycle Maintenance and Repair.* Rodale, 1996. *(A)*

Cycling. Boy Scouts of America, 1996. *(I; A)*

Otfinoski, Steven. *Pedaling Along: Bikes Then and Now.* Marshall Cavendish, 1996. *(P)*

Youngblut, Shelly. ed. *Way Inside ESPN's X Games.* Hyperion, 1998. *(I; A)*

BILL OF RIGHTS

Colman, Warren. *The Bill of Rights.* Scholastic, 1991. *(P)*

Krull, Kathleen. *A Kid's Guide to America's Bill of Rights: Curfews, Censorship, and the 100-Pound Giant.* Morrow, 1999. *(I)*

BIOCHEMISTRY

Boon, Kevin Alexander. *The Human Genome Project: What Does Decoding DNA Mean for Us?* Enslow, 2002. *(A)*

Gallant, Roy A. *Wonders of Biodiversity.* Benchmark, 2002. *(I)*

Hamilton, Janet. *James Watson: Solving the Mystery of DNA.* Enslow, 2004. *(I; A)*

Judson, Karen. *Genetic Engineering: Debating the Benefits and Concerns.* Enslow, 2001. *(I; A)*

Patent, Dorothy Hinshaw. *Biodiversity.* Houghton Mifflin, 1996. *(I; A)*

Silverstein, Alvin; Silverstein, Virginia; and Nunn, Laura Silverstein. *DNA.* Millbrook Press, 2002. *(A)*

Tagliaferro, Linda. *Genetic Engineering: Progress or Peril?* Lerner, 1997. *(I; A)*

Torr, James D. *Genetic Engineering.* Gale Group, 2000. *(A)*

Yount, Lisa. *Biotechnology and Genetic Engineering.* Facts on File, 2000; *Genetics and Genetic Engineering.* Facts on File, 1997. *(A)*

BIOGRAPHY, AUTOBIOGRAPHY, AND BIOGRAPHICAL NOVEL

Aller, Susan Bivin. *Beyond Little Women: A Story about Louisa May Alcott.* Lerner, 2004. *(P; I)*; *Mark Twain (A & E Biography Series).* Lerner, 2001. *(I; A)*

Dyer, Daniel. *Jack London: A Biography.* Scholastic, 2002. *(I; A)*

Englar, Mary. *I. M. Pei (Asian-American Biographies Series); Le Ly Hayslip (Asian-American Biographies Series).* Raintree, 2004. *(I)*

Escott, Colin. *Hank Williams: The Biography.* Back Bay Books, 2004. *(A)*

Fleischman, Sid. *The Abracadabra Kid: A Writer's Life.* Greenwillow, 1996. *(I; A)*

Hyland, William G. *George Gershwin: A New Biography.* Greenwood Press, 2003. *(A)*

Lester, Helen. *Author: A True Story.* Houghton/Lorraine, 1997. *(P)*

Meltzer, Milton. *Emily Dickinson: A Biography.* Lerner, 2006; *Herman Melville: A Biography.* Lerner, 2004; *Edgar Allan Poe: A Biography.* Lerner, 2003; *Walt Whitman: A Biography.* Lerner, 2002. *(I; A)*

Morgan, Judith, and Morgan, Neil. *Dr. Seuss and Mr. Geisel: A Biography.* Plenum, 2000. *(A)*

Peet, Bill. *Bill Peet: An Autobiography.* Houghton Mifflin, 1994. *(P; I)*

Robb, Graham. *Balzac: A Biography.* Norton, 2003. *(A)*

Zwonitzer, Mark, and Hirshberg, Charles. *Will You Miss Me When I'm Gone?: The Carter Family and Their Legacy in American Music.* Simon & Schuster, 2002. *(A)*

BIOLOGY

Baker, Beth. *Sylvia Earle: Guardian of the Sea.* Lerner, 2000. *(I)*

Bankston, John; Watson, James D.; and Crick, Francis. *Unlocking the Secrets of Science: Francis Crick and James Watson: Pioneers in DNA Research.* Mitchell Lane, 2002 *(I)*

Barrow, Lloyd H. *Science Fair Projects Investigating Earthworms.* Enslow, 2000. *(I)*

Brynie, Faith Hickman. *Genetics and Human Health: A Journey Within.* Millbrook Press, 1995. *(I; A)*

Gamlin, Linda. *Evolution.* DK, 1993. *(P; I)*

Jenkins, Steve. *Life on Earth: The Story of Evolution.* Houghton, 2002. *(P; I)*

Judson, Karen. *Genetic Engineering: Debating the Benefits and Concerns.* Enslow, 2001. *(I; A)*

Penny, Malcolm. *How Plants Grow.* Marshall Cavendish, 1996. *(P; I)*

Severs, Vesta-Nadine, and Whiting, Jim. *Oswald Avery and the Story of DNA.* Mitchell Lane, 2001. *(I; A)*

Silverstein, Alvin; Silverstein, Virginia; and Nunn, Laura Silverstein. *DNA.* Millbrook Press, 2002. *(A)*; *Evolution.* Millbrook Press, 1998. *(I; A)*

Snedden, Robert. *Cell Division and Genetics.* Heinemann, 2002. *(I; A)*

Stefoff, Rebecca. *Charles Darwin and the Evolution Revolution.* Oxford, 1996. *(I; A)*

Torr, James D. *Genetic Engineering.* Gale Group, 2000. *(A)*

Wallace, Holly, and Ganeri, Anita. *Cells and Systems.* Heinemann, 2000. *(P; I)*

Yount, Lisa. *Biotechnology and Genetic Engineering.* Facts on File, 2000; *Genetics and Genetic Engineering.* Facts on File, 1997. *(A)*

BIOTECHNOLOGY

DuPrau, Jeanne. *Cloning.* Gale Group, 2000. *(I; A)*

Edelson, Edward. *Genetics and Heredity.* Chelsea House, 1991. *(I; A)*

Hyde, Margaret O., and Setaro, John F. *Medicine's Brave New World: Bioengineering and the New Genetics.* Twenty-First Century, 2001. *(A)*

Jefferis, David. *Biotech: Frontiers of Medicine.* Crabtree, 2001. *(P; I)*

Marshall, Elizabeth L. *High-Tech Harvest: A Look at Genetically Engineered Foods.* Scholastic, 1999. *(I; A)*

Nardo, Don. *Cloning.* Gale Group, 2001. *(I; A)*

Rainis, Kenneth G., and Nassis, George. *Biotechnology Projects for Young Scientists.* Scholastic, 1998. *(A)*

Richardson, Hazel. *How to Clone a Sheep.* Scholastic, 2001. *(P; I)*

Snedden, Robert. *Medical Ethics: Changing Attitudes, 1900-2000 (20th Century Issues Series).* Raintree, 1999. *(I)*

Stanley, Debbie. *Genetic Engineering: The Cloning Debate (Focus on Science and Society Series).* Rosen, 2000. *(A)*

Torr, James D. *Genetic Engineering.* Gale Group, 2000. *(A)*

Yount, Lisa. *Biotechnology and Genetic Engineering.* Facts on File, 2000. *(A)*

BIRDS

Arnold, Caroline. *Birds: Natures Magnificent Flying Machines.* Charlesbridge, 2003. *(P; I)*

Arnosky, Jim. *Crinkleroot's 25 Birds Every Child Should Know.* Bradbury, 1993. *(P); Crinkleroot's Guide to Knowing the Birds.* Bradbury, 1992. *(P; I); Watching Water Birds.* National Geographic, 1997. *(P)*

Fleischman, Paul. *Townsend's Warbler.* Harper, 1992. *(I)*

Gans, Roma. *How Do Birds Find Their Way?* HarperCollins, 1996. *(P)*

Haus, Robyn. *Make Your Own Birdhouses and Feeders.* Ideals Publications, 2001. *(P; I)*

Hume, Rob. *Birdwatching.* Random House, 1993. *(I)*

Markle, Sandra. *Outside and Inside Birds.* Simon & Schuster, 1994. *(P; I)*

Martin, Patricia A. *California Condors; Northern Spotted Owls.* Scholastic, 2001. *(P)*

McDonald, Mary Ann. *Doves.* Child's World, 1999. *(P)*

Peters, Lisa Westberg. *This Way Home.* Holt, 1994. *(P; I)*

Sayre, April Pulley. *Secrets of Sound: Studying the Calls of Whales, Elephants, and Birds.* Houghton Mifflin, 2002. *(I; A); Endangered Birds of North America.* Millbrook Press, 1997. *(P; I)*

Sill, Cathryn. *About Birds: A Guide for Children.* Peachtree, 1991. *(P)*

Taylor, Barbara. *The Bird Atlas.* Dorling Kindersley, 1993. *(P; I)*

Thomas, Peggy. *Bird Alert.* Millbrook Press, 2000. *(I)*

Witmer, Lawrence M. *The Search for the Origin of Birds.* Watts, 1995. *(I; A)*

BIRDS AS PETS

Gutman, Bill. *Becoming Your Bird's Best Friend.* Millbrook Press, 1996. *(P; I)*

BLACK HOLES

Asimov, Isaac, and Hantula, Richard. *Black Holes, Pulsars, and Quasars.* Gareth Stevens, 2003 (updated edition). *(I)*

Couper, Heather, and Henbest, Nigel. *Black Holes.* Dorling Kindersley, 1996. *(I; A)*

BLACKWELL, ELIZABETH

Kline, Nancy. *Elizabeth Blackwell: A Doctor's Triumph.* Conari Press, 1997. *(A)*

Schleichert, Elizabeth. *The Life of Elizabeth Blackwell.* 21st Century Books, 1992. *(P; I)*

BLAIR, TONY

Hinman, Bonnie. *Tony Blair: Major World Leaders.* Chelsea House, 2002. *(I; A)*

Naden, Corinne J., and Blue, Rose J. *People in the News: Tony Blair.* Thomson Gale, 2002. *(I; A)*

BLOOD

Royston, Angela. *Why Do Bruises Change Color?: And Other Questions about Blood.* Heinemann, 2002. *(P; I)*

Sandeman, Anna. *Blood.* Millbrook, 1996. *(P)*

Schraff, Anne E. *Charles Drew: Pioneer in Medicine.* Enslow, 2003. *(P)*

Shackelford, Jole. *William Harvey and the Mechanics of the Heart.* Oxford, 2003. *(A)*

Viegas, Jennifer. *Heart: Learning How Our Blood Circulates.* Rosen, 2002. *(I; A)*

Yount, Lisa. *William Harvey: Discoverer of How Blood Circulates.* Enslow, 1994. *(I)*

BLY, NELLIE

Butcher, Nancy. *It Can't Be Done, Nellie Bly!: A Reporter's Race around the World.* Peachtree, 2003. *(P; I)*

Krensky, Stephen. *Nellie Bly: A Name to Be Reckoned With.* Simon & Schuster, 2003. *(I)*

BOATS AND BOATING

Motorboating. Boy Scouts of America, 1996; *Small-Boat Sailing.* Boy Scouts of America, 1995. *(I; A)*

Kentley, Eric. *Boat.* Knopf, 1992. *(I; A)*

Molzahn, Arlene Bourgeois. *Ships and Boats.* Enslow, 2003. *(P; I)*

Sandler, Martin W. *On the Waters of the USA: Ships and Boats in American Life.* Oxford University Press, 2003. *(I)*

BODY, HUMAN

Ballard, Carol. *The Heart and Circulatory System; The Stomach and Digestive System.* Raintree Steck-Vaughn, 1997. *(I)*

Berger, Melvin, and Berger, Gilda. *Why Don't Haircuts Hurt?: Questions and Answers about the Human Body.* Scholastic, 1999. *(P)*

Day, Trevor. *The Random House Book of 1001 Questions and Answers about the Human Body.* Random House, 1994. *(I)*

Ganeri, Anita. *Birth and Growth; Breathing; Eating; Moving.* Raintree Steck-Vaughn, 1994. *(P)*

Jukes, Mavis. *It's a Girl Thing: How to Stay Healthy, Safe, and in Charge.* Knopf, 1996. *(I; A)*

Lauersen, Niles H., and Stukane, Eileen. *You're in Charge: A Teenage Girl's Guide to Sex and Her Body.* Fawcett, 1993. *(I; A)*

Machotka, Hana. *Breathtaking Noses.* Morrow, 1992. *(P)*

Patterson, Claire. *It's OK to Be You: A Frank and Funny Guide to Growing Up.* Tricycle Press, 1994. *(I)*

Pringle, Laurence. *Hearing; Smell; Taste.* Marshall Cavendish/Benchmark, 1999. *(P; I)*

Rowan, Dr. Pete. *Some Body!* Knopf, 1995. *(P; I)*

Royston, Angela. *The Human Body and How It Works.* Random House, 1991. *(P; I)*

Stille, Darlene R. *The Digestive System; The Respiratory System.* Children's Press, 1998. *(P)*

Westheimer, Ruth. *Dr. Ruth Talks to Kids: Where You Came From, How Your Body Changes, and What Sex Is All About.* Macmillan, 1993. *(I; A)*

BODY CHEMISTRY

Brynie, Faith Hickman. *101 Questions About Food and Digestion That Have Been Eating at You Until Now.* Lerner, 2002. *(I; A)*

Gardner, Robert. *Health Science Projects about Nutrition.* Enslow, 2002. *(I; A)*

King, Hazel. *Body Needs: Carbohydrates for a Healthy Body.* Heinemann, 2003. *(P; I)*

Patent, Dorothy Hinshaw. *Biodiversity.* Houghton Mifflin, 1996. *(I; A)*; *Nutrition: What's in the Food We Eat.* Holiday House, 1992. *(P; I)*

Snedden, Robert. *Cell Division and Genetics.* Heinemann, 2002. *(I; A)*

Wallace, Holly, and Ganeri, Anita. *Cells and Systems.* Heinemann, 2000. *(P; I)*

Young, John K. *Hormones: Molecular Messengers.* Watts, 1994. *(I; A)*; *Cells: Amazing Forms and Functions.* Watts, 1990. *(I; A)*

Yount, Lisa. *Biotechnology and Genetic Engineering.* Facts on File, 2000. *(A)*

BODY SIGNALS

Berger, Melvin. *Why Don't Haircuts Hurt?: Questions and Answers about the Human Body.* Scholastic, 1999. *(P)*; *Why I Sneeze, Shiver, Hiccup, and Yawn.* HarperCollins, 1999. *(P)*

Conrad, David. *Burps, Boogers, and Bad Breath.* Compass Point Books, 2002. *(P)*

Lerner, Carol. *Plants That Make You Sniffle and Sneeze.* DIANE, 2004. *(P; I)*

Royston, Angela. *Why Do I Sneeze?: And Other Questions about Breathing.* Heinemann, 2002. *(P; I)*

Stangl, Jean. *What Makes You Cough, Sneeze, Burp, Hiccup, Yawn, Blink, Sweat, and Shiver?* Scholastic, 2000. *(P)*

Weber, Rebecca. *Body Language.* Compass Point Books, 2004. *(P)*

BOLIVIA

Hermes, Jules M. *The Children of Bolivia.* Carolrhoda, 1996. *(P; I)*

Morrison, Marion. *Bolivia.* Scholastic, 2001. *(I; A)*

BOONE, DANIEL

Armentrout, David, and Armentrout, Patricia. *Daniel Boone.* Rourke, 2002. *(P)*

Calvert, Patricia; Meltzer, Milton; and Faber, Harold. *Daniel Boone: Beyond the Mountains.* Marshall Cavendish, 2001. *(I)*

Sanford, William R., and Green, Carl R. *Daniel Boone: Wilderness Pioneer.* Enslow, 1997. *(I)*

BOSNIA AND HERZEGOVINA

Black, Eric. *Bosnia.* Lerner, 1999. *(I; A)*

Dornberg, John. *Central and Eastern Europe.* Greenwood, 1995. *(A)*

Fireside, Harvey, and Fireside, Bryna J. *Young People from Bosnia Talk about War.* Enslow, 1996. *(I; A)*

Reger, James P. *The Rebuilding of Bosnia.* Lucent, 1997. *(I)*

BOSTON

Gillis, Jennifer Blizin. *Life in Colonial Boston.* Heinemann, 2003. *(P)*

Kent, Deborah. *Boston.* Children's Press, 1998. *(P; I)*

BOTANY

Kalman, Bobbie, and Walker, Niki. *What Is a Plant?* Crabtree, 2000. *(P; I)*

Powledge, Fred. *Pharmacy in the Forest: How Medicines Are Found in the Natural World.* Simon & Schuster, 1998. *(I)*

BOY SCOUTS

Boys Scouts of America. *Bear: Cub Scout Book.* Boy Scouts of America, 1998 (rev. ed.). *(P)*

Boy Scouts of America. *The Boy Scout Handbook.* Boy Scouts of America, 1998 (11th ed.). *(I; A)*

Boy Scouts of America. *Fieldbook.* Boy Scouts of America, 2004 (4th ed.) *(I; A)*

Boy Scouts of America. *Wolf: Cub Scout Book.* Boy Scouts of America, 1998 (rev. ed.). *(P)*

Murphy, Claire Rudolf. *Friendship across Arctic Waters: Alasksan Cub Scouts Visit Their Soviet Neighbors.* Dutton, 1991. *(P; I)*

BRAHE, TYCHO

Boerst, William J. *Tycho Brahe: Mapping the Heavens.* Reynolds, 2003. *(I; A)*

BRAHMS, JOHANNES

Venezia, Mike. *Johannes Brahms.* Children's Press, 1999. *(P; I)*

Whiting, Jim. *Masters of Music: The Life and Times of Johannes Brahms.* Mitchell Lane, 2003. *(I)*

BRAZIL

Bender, Evelyn. *Brazil.* Chelsea House, 1998. *(I; A)*

Heinrichs, Ann. *Brazil.* Scholastic, 1997. *(P)*

Jermyn, Leslie. *Brazil.* Gareth Stevens, 1999. *(I)*

McGowan, Chris, and Pessanha, Ricardo. *The Brazilian Sound: Samba, Bossa Nova, and the Popular Music of Brazil.* Temple University Press, 1997. *(A)*

Richard, Christopher, and Jermyn, Leslie. *Brazil.* Marshall Cavendish, 2002 (2nd ed.). *(I)*

BREAD AND BAKING

Badt, Karin Luisa. *Pass the Bread!* Scholastic, 1997 (reprint). *(P; I)*

BRITISH COLUMBIA

Hancock, Lyn. *Destination Vancouver.* Lerner, 1997. *(I; A)*

LeVert, Suzanne, and Sheppard, George. *Let's Discover Canada: British Columbia.* Chelsea House, 1991. *(I; A)*

Taylor, Ronald J., and Douglas, George. *Mountain Plants of the Pacific Northwest: A Field Guide to Washington, Western British Columbia, and Southeastern Alaska.* Mountain Press, 1995. *(I; A)*

BRONTË SISTERS

Barnard, Robert. *The British Library Writers' Lives: Emily Brontë.* Oxford University Press, 2000. *(A)*

Bedard, Michael. *Glass Town: The Secret World of the Brontë Children.* Simon & Schuster, 1997. *(I)*

O'Neill, Jane. *The World of the Brontës.* Carlton, 1999. *(I; A)*

BRONZE AND BRASS

Beatty, Richard. *Copper.* Marshall Cavendish, 2000. *(P; I)*

Fodor, R. V. *Gold, Copper, Iron: How Metals Are Formed, Found, and Used.* Enslow, 1989. *(A)*

BRUNEI

Major, John S. *Land and People of Malaysia and Brunei.* HarperCollins, 1991. *(I; A)*

Wright, David K. *Brunei: Enchantment of the World.* Scholastic, 1991. *(I; A)*

BUCHANAN, JAMES

Lassieur, Allison. *James Buchanan (Encyclopedia of Presidents, Second Series).* Scholastic, 2004. *(I; A)*

Souter, Gerry, and Souter, Janet. *James Buchanan: Our Fifteenth President.* Child's World, 2002. *(P; I)*

BUDDHISM

Hewitt, Catherine. *Buddhism.* Steck-Vaughn, 1995. *(I; A)*

Netzley, Patricia D. *Buddhism.* Gale Group, 2002. *(I; A)*

BUFFALO BILL (WILLIAM FREDERICK CODY)

Robison, Nancy. *Buffalo Bill.* Watts, 1991. *(I)*

Sanford, William R., and Green, Carl R. *Buffalo Bill Cody: Showman of the Wild West.* Enslow, 1996. *(I)*

Shields, Charles J. *Buffalo Bill Cody.* Chelsea House, 2001. *(P; I)*

BULGARIA

Dornberg, John. *Central and Eastern Europe.* Greenwood, 1995. *(A)*

Otfinoski, Steven. *Bulgaria.* Facts on File, 1998. *(I; A)*

Resnick, Abraham. *Bulgaria.* Scholastic, 1995. *(I; A)*

BULLFIGHTING

Shubert, Adrian. *Death and Money in the Afternoon: A History of the Spanish Bullfight.* Oxford University Press, 2000. *(A)*

BURKINA FASO

McFarland, Daniel Miles, and Rupley, Lawrence. *Historical Dictionary of Burkina Faso.* Rowman & Littlefield, 1998 (2nd ed.). *(A)*

Nwanunobi, C. Onyeka. *Malinke (Burkina Faso, Côte d'Ivoire, Gambia, Guinea, Guinea Bissau, Liberia, Mali, Senegal, Sierra Leone).* Rosen, 1996. *(I; A)*; *Soninke (Burkina Faso, Côte d'Ivoirie, Ghana, Mali, Mauritania, Nigeria, Senegal).* Rosen, 1996. *(I; A)*

BURUNDI

Brennan, Kristine. *Burundi (Africa - Continent in the Balance Series).* Mason Crest, 2004. *(I; A)*

Eggers, Ellen K., and Weinstein, Warren. *Historical Dictionary of Burundi.* Rowman & Littlefield, 1997 (2nd ed.). *(A)*

BUSH, GEORGE

Bush, George Herbert Walker. *All the Best, George Bush: My Life in Letters and Other Writings.* Scribner, 1999. *(A)*

Francis, Sandra. *George Bush: Our Forty-First President.* Child's World, 2001. *(P; I)*

Ochester, Betsy. *George Bush (Encyclopedia of Presidents, Second Series).* Scholastic, 2005. *(I; A)*

BUSINESS

Mariotti, Steve. *The Young Entrepreneur's Guide to Starting and Running a Business.* (2nd ed.) Times, 2000. *(A)*

Otfinoski, Steven. *The Kid's Guide to Money: Earning It, Saving It, Spending It, Growing It, Sharing It.* Scholastic, 1996. *(P; I)*

BUTTERFLIES AND MOTHS

Boring, Mel. *Caterpillars, Bugs, and Butterflies.* Creative Publishing, 1997. *(P; I)*

Brimner, Larry Dane. *Butterflies and Moths.* Scholastic, 1999. *(P)*

Herberman, Ethan. *The Great Butterfly Hunt: The Mystery of the Migrating Monarchs.* Simon & Schuster, 1990. *(P; I; A)*

Lasky, Kathryn. *Monarchs.* Harcourt, 1993. *(P; I)*

Lavies, Bianca. *Monarch Butterflies: Mysterious Travelers.* Dutton, 1999. *(P; I)*

Pringle, Laurence P. *An Extraordinary Life: The Story of a Monarch Butterfly.* Orchard Books, 1996. *(P; I)*

C (LETTER)

Samoyault, Tiphaine. *Alphabetical Order: How the Alphabet Began.* Viking, 1998. *(P; I)*

CABOT, JOHN AND SEBASTIAN

Doak, Robin S. *Cabot (Exploring the World): John Cabot and the Journey to North America.* Compass Point Books, 2003. *(P; I)*

Maestro, Betsy C. *The Discovery of the Americas.* Lothrop, 1991. *(P)*

CACTUS

Bash, Barbara. *Desert Giant: The World of the Saguaro Cactus.* Gibbs Smith, 2002 (2nd ed.). *(P; I)*

Overbeck, Cynthia. *Cactus.* Lerner, 1994. *(P; I)*

CAESAR, GAIUS JULIUS

Shakespeare, William. *Julius Caesar.* Penguin, 2005. *(I; A)*

CAIRO

Rodenbeck, Max. *Cairo: The City Victorious.* Knopf, 1999. *(A)*

Stein, R. Conrad. *Cairo.* Children's Press, 1996. *(I)*

CALCUTTA (KOLKATA)

Rice, Tanya. *Mother Teresa.* Chelsea House, 1997. *(I)*

Tilton, Rafael. *Mother Teresa.* Thomson Gale, 1999. *(I; A)*

CALDECOTT, RANDOLPH

Bankston, John. *Randolph J. Caldecott and the Story of the Caldecott Medal.* Mitchell Lane, 2003. *(I)*

CALENDAR

Hughes, Paul. *The Days of the Week: Stories, Songs, Traditions, Festivals, and Surprising Facts About the Days of the Week from All Over the World; The Months of the Year: Stories, Songs, Traditions, Festivals, and Surprising Facts About the Months of the Year from All Over the World.* Garrett Educational, 1989. *(P; I)*

Maestro, Betsy. *The Story of Clocks and Calendars: Marking a Millenium.* Lothrop, 1999. *(P; I)*

Woods, Michael, and Woods, Mary B. *Ancient Computing: From Counting to Calendars.* Lerner, 2000. *(I)*

CALIFORNIA

Abbink, Emily. *Missions of the Monterey Bay Area.* Lerner, 1998. *(P; I)*

Altman, Linda Jacobs. *California.* Benchmark, 1996. *(I)*

Behrens, June. *Missions of the Central Coast.* Lerner, 1997. *(P; I)*

Brower, Pauline. *Missions of the Inland Valleys.* Lerner, 1998. *(P; I)*

Fradin, Dennis Brindell. *California: From Sea to Shining Sea.* Scholastic, 1994. *(P; I)*

Heinrichs, Ann. *California.* Children's Press, 1998. *(I)*

MacMillan, Diane. *Missions of the Los Angeles Area.* Lerner, 1999. *(P; I)*

Pelta, Kathy. *California.* Lerner, 2001 (2nd ed.). *(P; I)*

Petersen, David. *Death Valley National Park.* Scholastic, 1997. *(P; I)*

Wills, Charles A. *A Historical Album of California.* Millbrook Press, 1994. *(I)*

CAMBODIA

Cambodia . . . in Pictures. Lerner, 1996. *(I; A)*

De Silva, Dayaneetha, and Mesenas, Geraldine. *Cambodia.* Gareth Stevens, 2000. *(I)*

Kras, Sarah Louise. *Cambodia (Enchantment of the World, Second Series).* Scholastic, 2005. *(I; A)*

Pascoe, Elaine. *The Pacific Rim: East Asia at the Dawn of a New Century.* Millbrook Press, 1999. *(A)*

Sheehan, Sean. *Cambodia.* Marshall Cavendish, 1996. *(I)*

Viesti, Joseph F., and Hall, Diane. *Celebrate! in Southeast Asia.* HarperCollins, 1996. *(P; I)*

CAMELS

Ricciuti, Edward R. *What on Earth Is a Guanaco?* Gale Group, 1994. *(P; I)*

Squire, Ann O. *African Animals.* Scholastic, 2001. *(P)*

CAMEROON

Aniakor, Chike Cyril. *Heritage Library of African Peoples: Fang.* Rosen, 1997. *(I; A)*

Roschenthaler, Ute, and Chukwuezi, Barth. *Ejagham (Cameroon, Nigeria).* Rosen, 1996. *(I; A)*

CANADA

Christmas in Canada. World Book, 1997. *(I; A)*

Barlas, Bob; Tompsett, Norman; and McKay, Susan. *Welcome to Canada.* Gareth Stevens, 1999. *(P)*

Bowers, Vivien. *Only in Canada!: From the Colossal to the Kooky.* Maple Tree Press, 2002; *Wow Canada!:*

Exploring this Land from Coast to Coast to Coast. Firefly, 2000. *(P; I)*

Grabowski, John F. *Canada.* Gale Group, 1997. *(I; A)*

Landau, Elaine. *Canada.* Scholastic, 2000. *(P)*

Mercredi, Morningstar. *Fort Chipewyan Homecoming: A Journey to Native Canada.* Lerner, 1996. *(P; I)*

Sheppard, George. *Canada: Facts and Figures.* Chelsea House, 2001; *Alberta; Manitoba; Newfoundland; Northwest Territories; Nova Scotia; Ontario; Prince Edward Island; Saskatchewan.* Yukon, 2000. *(I; A)*

Younkin, Paula, and Hirschfelder, Arlene. *Indians of the Arctic and Subarctic.* Facts on File, 1991. *(I; A)*

CANADA, HISTORY OF

Barlas, Robert, and Tompsett, Norm. *Canada.* Gareth Stevens Audio, 1998. *(I)*

Bowers, Vivien. *Only in Canada!: From the Colossal to the Kooky.* Maple Tree Press, 2002. *(P; I)*

Xydes, Georgia. *Alexander MacKenzie and the Explorers of Canada.* Chelsea House, 1992. *(I)*

CANALS

Bial, Raymond. *The Canals.* Marshall Cavendish, 2001. *(I)*

Ditchfield, Christin. *Kayaking, Canoeing, Rowing, and Yachting.* Scholastic, 2000. *(P)*

Doherty, Craig A., and Doherty, Katherine M. *The Erie Canal.* Gale Group, 1996. *(I)*

Gaines, Ann Graham. *The Panama Canal in American History.* Enslow, 1999. *(I; A)*

Gold, Susan Dudley. *The Panama Canal Transfer: Controversy at the Crossroads.* Raintree Steck-Vaughn, 1999. *(I; A)*

Markun, Patricia Maloney. *It's Panama's Canal!* Shoe String/Linnet, 1999. *(I; A)*

CANCER

Bardhan, Sudipta. *Chemotherapy.* Thomson Gale, 2003. *(A)*

Krisher, Trudy. *Kathy's Hats: A Story of Hope.* Marianist Press, 1991. *(P)*

Lamb, Kirsten, and Lamb, Wendy. *Cancer.* Raintree, 2002. *(I)*

Landau, Elaine. *Cancer.* 21st Century Books, 1994. *(I; A)*

Thomas, Peggy. *Medicines from Nature.* Millbrook Press, 1997. *(I; A)*

CANDY AND CANDY MAKING

Burford, Betty M. *Chocolate by Hershey: A Story about Milton S. Hershey.* Lerner, 1994. *(P; I)*

Simon, Charnan. *Milton Hershey: Chocolate King, Town Builder.* Children's Press, 1998. *(P)*

CANOEING

Canoeing. Boy Scouts of America, 1996. *(I; A)*

Miller-Schroeder, Patricia. *Wings, Wheels and Keels: The Science of Transportation.* Raintree, 2000. *(P; I)*

CAPE VERDE

Lobban, Richard A., and Lopes, Marlene. *Historical Dictionary of the Republic of Cape Verde.* Rowman & Littlefield, 1995 (3rd ed.). *(A)*

CAPITOL, UNITED STATES

Hoig, Stan. *Capitol for the United States.* Dutton, 1990. *(P; I)*

CARBON

Sparrow, Giles. *Carbon.* Marshall Cavendish, 1999. *(P; I)*

CARIBBEAN SEA AND ISLANDS

McKenley, Yvonne. *A Taste of the Caribbean.* Raintree Steck-Vaughn, 1995. *(P; I)*

CAROLS

The First Noel: A Child's Book of Christmas Carols to Play and Sing. DK, 1998. *(P; I)*

Amery, Heather. *Christmas Carols.* Usborne Books, 1997 (rev. ed.). *(I; A)*

Fox, Dan. *A Treasury of Christmas Songs: Songs of the Season for Young People.* Henry Holt, 2004. *(P; I; A)*

CARROLL, LEWIS

Carpenter, Angelica Shirley. *Lewis Carroll: Through the Looking Glass.* Lerner, 2003. *(I; A)*

Carroll, Lewis. Mendelson, Edward, ed. *Poetry for Young People: Lewis Carroll.* Sterling, 2000. *(P; I)*

Halliwell, Sarah, ed. *19th Century: Artists, Writers, and Composers.* Raintree, 1998. *(I)*

CARSON, KIT

Faber, Harold. *John Charles Fremont: Pathfinder to the West.* Benchmark, 2002. *(I)*

Glass, Andrew. *A Right Fine Life: Kit Carson on the Santa Fe Trail.* Holiday House, 1997. *(P)*

Sanford, William R., and Green, Carl R. *Kit Carson: Frontier Scout.* Enslow, 1996. *(I)*

CARSON, RACHEL

Presnall, Judith Janda. *Rachel Carson.* Gale Group, 1994. *(I; A)*

Ransom, Candice F. *Listening to Crickets: A Story About Rachel Carson.* Lerner, 1993. *(P)*

Wadsworth, Ginger. *Rachel Carson: Voice for the Earth.* Lerner, 1992. *(I; A)*

CARTER, JAMES EARL, JR.

Carrigan, Mellonee. *Jimmy Carter: Beyond the Presidency.* Scholastic, 1995. *(P; I)*

Carter, Jimmy. *Talking Peace: A Vision for the Next Generation.* Penguin Putnam, 1996. *(I; A)*

Hobkirk, Lori. *James Earl Carter: Our Thirty-Ninth President.* Child's World, 2002. *(P; I)*

Kent, Deborah. *Jimmy Carter (Encyclopedia of Presidents, Second Series).* Scholastic, 2005. *(I; A)*

Lazo, Caroline Evensen. *Jimmy Carter: On the Road to Peace.* Silver Burdett Press, 1996. *(I; A)*

O'Shei, Tim. *Jimmy Carter.* Enslow, 2002. *(I; A)*

Richman, Daniel A. *James E. Carter.* Garrett Educational, 1989. *(I)*

CARTIER, JACQUES

West, Delno C., and West, Jean M. *Braving the North Atlantic: The Vikings, the Cabots, and Jacques Cartier Voyage to America.* Simon & Schuster, 1996. *(I)*

CARTOONS

Weiss, Harvey. *Cartoons and Cartooning.* Houghton, 1990. *(I; A)*

CARVER, GEORGE WASHINGTON

Carey, Charles W. *George Washington Carver.* Child's World, 1999. *(P; I)*

CASSATT, MARY

Muhlberger, Richard, and Metropolitan Museum of Art. *What Makes a Cassatt a Cassatt?* Viking, 1994. *(I)*

Turner, Robyn Montana. *Mary Cassatt.* Little, 1992. *(P; I)*

CASTLES

Day, Malcolm. *Castles and Forts.* McGraw-Hill, 1996. *(I)*

Gravett, Christopher. *Castle.* DK, 2000. *(P; I)*

Hicks, Peter. *How Castles Were Built.* Raintree Steck-Vaughn, 1998. *(I)*

Hinds, Kathryn. *Castle.* Marshall Cavendish, 2000. *(I)*

MacDonald, Fiona. *A Samurai Castle.* McGraw-Hill, 1995; *A Medieval Castle.* McGraw-Hill, 1993 *(I)*

McAleavy, Tony, and Chamberlain, Neville. *Life in a Medieval Castle.* Enchanted Lion Books, 2003. *(A)*

Nardo, Don. *The Medieval Castle.* Gale Group, 1997. *(I; A)*

Shuter, Jane. *Carisbrooke Castle.* Heinemann, 1999. *(I)*

Steele, Philip. *Castles.* Houghton Mifflin, 1995. *(P; I)*

CASTRO, FIDEL

Bentley, Judith. *Fidel Castro.* Silver Burdett Press, 1991. *(I; A)*

Beyer, Don E. *Castro: An Impact Biography.* Watts, 1993. *(I; A)*

Brown, Warren. *Fidel Castro: Cuban Revolutionary.* Millbrook Press, 1994. *(A)*

Madden, Paul. *Fidel Castro.* Rourke, 1993. *(I; A)*

Rice, Earle. *The Cuban Revolution.* Gale Group, 1994. *(I; A)*

CATS, WILD

Arnold, Caroline. *Bobcats.* Lerner, 1997. *(P)*; *Lion.* Morrow, 1995. *(P; I)*

Perry, Phyllis J. *The Snow Cats.* Scholastic, 1997. *(P; I)*

Silverstein, Alvin; Silverstein, Virgina B.; and Nunn, Laura Silverstein. *The Florida Panther.* Millbrook Press, 1997. *(I)*

Simon, Seymour. *Big Cats.* Harper, 1991. *(P; I)*

Thomas, Peggy. *Big Cat Conservation.* Millbrook Press, 2000. *(P; I)*

Thompson, Sharon Elaine. *Built for Speed: The Extraordinary, Enigmatic Cheetah.* Lerner, 1998. *(I; A)*

CATTLE

Marrin, Albert. *Cowboys, Indians, and Gunfighters: The Story of the Cattle Kingdom.* Simon & Schuster, 1993. *(I; A)*

Miller, Sara Swan. *Cows.* Scholastic, 2000. *(P)*

Older, Jules. *Cow.* Charlesbridge, 1997. *(P)*

Patent, Dorothy Hinshaw. *Cattle.* Carolrhoda, 1993. *(P; I)*

Pelta, Kathy. *Cattle Trails: "Get along Little Doggies."* Raintree Steck-Vaughn, 1997. *(I; A)*

Thomas, Heather Smith. *Your Calf: A Kid's Guide to Raising and Showing Beef and Dairy Calves.* Storey Books, 1997. *(I; A)*

Wolfman, Judy, and Winston, David Lorenz. *Life on a Dairy Farm.* Lerner, 2003; *Life on a Cattle Farm.* Lerner, 2001. *(P)*

CELLS

Young, John K. *Cells: Amazing Forms and Functions.* Watts, 1990. *(I; A)*

CELTS

Hinds, Kathryn. *The Celts of Northern Europe.* Marshall Cavendish, 1996. *(I; A)*

Martell, Hazel Mary. *The Celts.* Viking, 1995. *(I)*

Matthews, John. *Classic Celtic Fairy Tales.* Cassell, 1999. *(I)*

McGraw-Hill Staff. *Enchanted Kingdoms: Celtic Mythology.* NTC, 1998. *(I)*

CENSUS

Kassinger, Ruth. *U.S. Census: A Mirror of America.* Raintree Steck-Vaughn, 1999. *(I)*

CENTRAL AFRICAN REPUBLIC

Lyman, Francesca, and American Museum of Natural History. *Inside the Dzanga-Sangha Rain Forest.* Workman, 1998. *(P; I)*

O'Toole, Thomas E. *Central African Republic...in Pictures.* Lerner, 1996. *(I; A)*

CENTRAL AMERICA

Foley, Erin L. *Costa Rica.* Marshall Cavendish, 1997 (2nd ed); *El Salvador.* Marshall Cavendish, 1994. *(I; A)*

Frank, Nicole, and Vengadasalam, Leela. *Costa Rica.* Gareth Stevens, 2000. *(I)*

Franklin, Sharon; Tull, Mary; and Shelton, Carol. *Mexico and Central America.* Raintree Steck-Vaughn, 2000. *(I; A)*

Griffiths, John. *Nicaragua.* Chelsea House, 1998. *(I; A)*

Jermyn, Leslie. *Belize.* Marshall Cavendish, 2001. *(I; A)*

Kott, Jennifer. *Nicaragua.* Marshall Cavendish, 1994. *(I; A)*

Morrison, Marion. *Nicaragua.* Scholastic, 2003; *El Salvador.* Scholastic, 2001; *Belize.* Scholastic, 1996. *(I; A)*

Rau, Dana Meachen. *Panama.* Scholastic, 1999. *(P)*

CHAPLIN, CHARLIE

Schroeder, Alan. *Charlie Chaplin: The Beauty of Silence.* Watts, 1997. *(I; A)*

Turk, Ruth. *Charlie Chaplin: Genius of the Silent Screen.* Lerner, 2000. *(I; A)*

CHARLEMAGNE

Biel, Timothy L. *The Charlemagne.* Lucent, 1997. *(I; A)*

Greenblatt, Miriam. *Charlemagne and the Early Middle Ages.* Marshall Cavendish, 2002. *(I; A)*

MacDonald, Fiona. *The World in the Time of Charlemagne.* Silver Burdett Press, 1998. *(I)*

Meltzer, Milton. *Ten Kings: And the Worlds They Ruled.* Orchard Books, 2002. *(P; I)*

CHEKHOV, ANTON

Bloom, Harold, ed. *Anton Chekhov (Modern Critical Views Series).* Chelsea House, 1998. *(A)*

Halliwell, Sarah, ed. *19th Century: Artists, Writers, and Composers.* Raintree, 1998. *(I)*

CHEMISTRY

Bortz, Alfred B. *Electron; Neutrino; Neutron; Photon; Proton; Quark.* Rosen, 2004; *To the Young Scientist: Reflections on Doing and Living Science.* Scholastic, 1997. *(I; A)*

Corrick, James A. *Recent Revolutions in Chemistry.* Watts, 1986. *(I)*

Gallant, Roy A. *The Ever-Changing Atom.* Benchmark, 2000. *(P; I)*

Gardner, Robert. *Chemistry Science Fair Projects Using Acids, Bases, Metals, Salts, and Inorganic Stuff.* Enslow, 2004; *Science Projects Ideas about Kitchen Chemistry.* Enslow, 2002 (rev. ed.); *Science Projects about Chemistry.* Enslow, 1994. *(I; A)*

Heiserman, David L. *Exploring Chemical Elements and Their Compounds.* McGraw-Hill, 1991. *(A)*

CHESS

Albertini, Chicca. *The Great Book of Family Games.* Sterling, 2001. *(I; A)*

Berg, Barry. *Opening Moves: The Making of a Very Young Chess Champion.* Little, Brown, 2000. *(P; I)*

CHICAGO

Doherty, Craig A., and Doherty, Katherine M. *The Sears Tower.* Gale Group, 1995. *(I)*

Murphy, Jim. *The Great Fire.* Scholastic, 1995. *(P; I)*

Stein, Richard Conrad. *Chicago.* Grolier, 1997. *(I; A)*

CHILD ABUSE

DeKoster, Katie, and Swisher, Karin L., eds. *Child Abuse: Opposing Viewpoints.* Gale Group, 1994. *(A)*

Goldentyer, Debra. *Family Violence.* Steck-Vaughn, 1995. *(A)*

Grapes, Bryan J., ed. *Child Abuse.* Gale Group, 2001. *(I; A)*

Greenberg, Keith Elliot. *Family Abuse: Why Do People Hurt Each Other?* Millbrook Press, 1997. *(P; I)*

Havelin, Kate. *Child Abuse; Family Violence.* Capstone Press, 1999. *(I; A)*

Ito, Tom. *Child Abuse.* Gale Group, 1994. *(I; A)*

CHILD LABOR

Atkin, S. Beth. *Voices from the Fields: Children of Migrant Farmworkers Tell Their Stories.* Little, 1993. *(I; A)*

Freedman, Russell, and Hine, Lewis. *Kids at Work: Lewis Hine and the Crusade Against Child Labor.* Houghton Mifflin, 1998. *(I; A)*

Ennew, Judith. *Exploitation of Children.* Raintree Steck-Vaughn, 1996. *(I; A)*

Major, Kevin. *Free the Children: A Young Man Fights Against Child Labor and Proves that Children Can Change the World.* HarperCollins, 2000. *(I)*

Roberts-Davis, Tanya, comp. *We Need to Go to School: Voices of the Rugmark Children.* Douglas & McIntyre, 2001. *(I; A)*

Williams, Mary E., ed. *Child Labor and Sweatshops.* Gale Group, 1999. *(A)*

CHILDREN'S LITERATURE

Byars, Betsy. *The Moon and I.* Simon & Schuster, 1992. *(I)*

Carpenter, Angelica Shirley. *Lewis Carroll: Through the Looking Glass.* Lerner, 2003. *(I; A)*

Cleary, Beverly. *A Girl from Yamhill: A Memoir; My Own Two Feet: A Memoir.* HarperCollins, 1996 (reprint). *(I; A)*

Ehlert, Lois. *Under My Nose (Meet the Author Series).* Richard C. Owen, 1996. *(P)*

Engel, Dean, and Freedman, Florence B. *Ezra Jack Keats: A Biography with Illustrations.Fleming, Denise. Maker of Things (Meet the Author Series).* Richard C. Owen, 2003. *(P)* Silver Moon Press, 1995. *(P; I)*

German, Beverly. *E. B. White: Some Writer!* Atheneum, 1992. *(I)*

Kiefer, Barbara. *Wings of an Artist: Children's Book Illustrators Talk about Their Art.* Abrams, 1999. *(I; A)*

Lipson, Eden Ross. *The New York Times Parent's Guide to the Best Books for Children.* Crown, 2000 (3rd ed.). *(A)*

Locker, Thomas. *The Man Who Paints Nature (Meet the Author Series).* Richard C. Owen, 1999. *(P; I)*

Lowry, Lois. *Looking Back: A Book of Memories.* Walter Lorraine Books, 1998. *(P; I)*

Lyon, George Ella. *A Wordful Child (Meet the Author Series).* Richard C. Owen, 1996. *(P)*

Marcus, Leonard S. *Ways of Telling: Conversations on the Art of the Picture Book.* Dutton, 2002. *(I; A) Side by Side: Five Favorite Picture-Book Teams Go to Work.* Walker, 2001. *(P; I) Author Talk.* Simon & Schuster,

2000. *(I) Margaret Wise Brown: Awakened by the Moon.* HarperCollins, 1999. *(I) A Caldecott Celebration: Six Artists and Their Paths to the Caldecott Medal.* Walker, 1998. *(P; I)*

Wullschlager, Jackie. *Hans Christian Andersen: The Life of a Storyteller.* University of Chicago Press, 2002. *(A)*

CHILE

Dwyer, Christopher. *Chile.* Chelsea House, 1997. *(I; A)*

CHINA

Brown, Tricia. *Chinese New Year.* Henry Holt, 1997. *(P; I)*

Deedrick, Tami. *China.* Raintree Steck-Vaughn, 2001. *(P; I)*

Dolan, Sean. *Chiang Kai-Shek.* Chelsea House, 1989. *(I; A)*

Dramer, Kim. *People's Republic of China.* Children's Press, 1999. *(I; A)*

Green, Robert, ed. *China.* Gale Group, 1998. *(I; A)*

Hoyt-Goldsmith, Diane, and Migdale, Lawrence. *Celebrating Chinese New Year.* Holiday House, 1999. *(P; I)*

Kort, Michael G. *China Under Communism.* Millbrook Press, 1995. *(I; A)*

Marrin, Albert. *Mao Tse-Tung, and His China.* Penguin Putnam, 1993. *(I; A)*

Meltzer, Milton. *Ten Kings: And the Worlds They Ruled.* Orchard Books, 2002. *(P; I)*

Millar, Heather. *China's Tang Dynasty (Cultures of the Past Series).* Marshall Cavendish, 1996. *(I; A)*

Pascoe, Elaine. *The Pacific Rim: East Asia at the Dawn of a New Century.* Millbrook Press, 1999. *(A)*

Patent, Dorothy Hinshaw. *Incredible Story of China's Buried Warriors.* Marshall Cavendish, 2000. *(I)*

Stefoff, Rebecca. *Mao Zedong: Founder of the People's Republic of China.* Millbrook Press, 1996. *(I; A); Marco Polo and the Medieval Explorers.* Main Line, 1992. *(P; I)*

Stewart, Whitney. *Deng Xiaoping: Leader in a Changing China.* Lerner, 2001. *(I; A)*

Symynkywicz, Jeffrey B. *1989: The Year the World Changed.* Silver Burdett Press, 1995. *(I; A)*

Tull, Mary; Black, Cynthia A.; and Franklin, Tristan. *Northern Asia.* Raintree Steck-Vaughn, 1999. *(I; A)*

Twist, Clint. *Marco Polo: Overland to Medieval China.* Raintree Steck-Vaughn, 1994. *(P; I)*

Williams, Suzanne. *Made in China: Ideas and Inventions from Ancient China.* Pacific View Press, 1996. *(I; A)*

Yu, Ling. *Cooking the Chinese Way.* Lerner, 2001 (2nd ed.). *(I; A)*

Zhang, Song Nan. *The Children of China: An Artists Journey.* Tundra, 1998. *(P; I; A)*

CHINA, ART AND ARCHITECTURE OF

Lovett, Patricia. *Calligraphy and Illumination: A History and Practical Guide.* Abrams, 2000. *(A)*

Patent, Dorothy Hinshaw. *The Incredible Story of China's Buried Warriors.* Marshall Cavendish, 2000. *(I)*

Shuter, Jane. *Ancient Chinese Art.* Heinemann, 2001. *(P; I)*

Temko, Florence. *Traditional Crafts from China.* Lerner, 2000. *(P; I)*

Tull, Mary; Black, Cynthia A.; and Franklin, Tristan. *Northern Asia.* Raintree Steck-Vaughn, 1999. *(I; A)*

Zhensun, Zheng, and Low, Alice. *A Young Painter: The Life and Paintings of Wang Yani-China's Extraordinary Young Artist.* Scholastic, 1991. *(I; A)*

CHINA, LITERATURE OF

Bedard, Michael, adapt. *The Painted Wall and Other Strange Tales.* Tundra, 2003. *(I; A)*

Chang, Margaret Scrogin, and Chang, Raymond. *The Cricket Warrior: A Chinese Tale.* Simon & Schuster, 1994. *(P)*

Faurot, Jeannette L. *Asian-Pacific Folktales and Legends.* Simon & Schuster, 1995. *(A)*

Hong, Lily Toy, retel. *The Empress and the Silkworm.* Albert Whitman, 1995 ; *Two of Everything: A Chinese Folktale.* Albert Whitman, 1993. *(P)*

Krasno, Rena, and Chiang, Yeng-Fong. *Cloud Weavers: Ancient Chinese Legends.* Pacific View Press, 2003. *(P; I)*

Poole, Amy Lowry. *How the Rooster Got His Crown: A Chinese Folktale.* Holiday House, 1999. *(P)*

San Souci, Robert D. *Fa Mulan: The Story of a Woman Warrior.* Hyperion, 1998. *(P; I)*

Yacowitz, Caryn. *The Jade Stone: A Chinese Folktale.* Pelican Publishing, 2005. *(P)*

Yep, Lawrence. *The Rainbow People.* HarperCollins, 1992. *(I; A)*

Young, Ed. *The Lost Horse: A Chinese Folktale.* Harcourt, 2004. *(P); Lon Po Po: A Red-Riding Hood Story from China.* Putnam, 1996. *(I)*

Zhang, Song Nan, Zhang, Hao Yu. *A Time of Golden Dragons.* Tundra, 2000. *(P; I)*

CHOCOLATE

Burford, Betty M. *Chocolate by Hershey: A Story about Milton S. Hershey.* Lerner, 1994. *(P; I)*

Simon, Charnan. *Milton Hershey: Chocolate King, Town Builder.* Children's Press, 1998. *(P)*

CHOPIN, FREDERIC

Cavelletti, Carlo. *Chopin and Romantic Music.* Barron's Educational Series, 2000. *(I; A)*

Tames, Richard. *Frederic Chopin.* Watts, 1991. *(I)*

Venezia, Mike. *Frederic Chopin.* Children's Press, 2000. *(P)*

Whiting, Jim. *Masters of Music: The Life and Times of Frederic Chopin.* Mitchell Lane, 2004. *(I)*

CHRISTMAS

Christmas in Canada; Christmas in Switzerlalnd; Christmas in Ukraine. World Book, 1997. *(I; A)*

Bonnice, Sheery. *North American Christmas and Santa Claus Folklore.* Mason Crest, 2002. *(I)*

Hoyt-Goldsmith, Diane, and Migdale, Lawrence. *Las Posadas: An Hispanic Christmas Celebration.* Holiday House, 2000. *(P; I)*

Stevens, Kathryn J. *Christmas Trees.* Child's World, 1999. *(P)*

Thomas, Dylan. *A Child's Christmas in Wales.* Candlewick, 2004. *(P; I; A)*

Wildsmith, Brian. *A Christmas Story.* Eerdmans, 1996. *(P)*

CIRCULATORY SYSTEM

Arnold, Caroline. *Heart Disease.* Watts, 1990. *(I; A)*

Ballard, Carol. *The Heart and Circulatory System.* Raintree Steck-Vaughn, 1997. *(I)*

Brynie, Faith Hickman. *101 Questions About Blood and Circulation: with Answers Straight from the Heart.* Twenty-First Century, 2001. *(I; A)*

Parramon, Merce. *How Our Blood Circulates.* Chelsea House, 1993. *(I)*

Sandeman, Anna. *Blood.* Millbrook Press, 1996. *(P)*

Silverstein, Alvin; Silverstein, Virginia; and Silverstein, Robert. *The Circulatory System.* 21st Century Books, 1994. *(I)*

Simon, Seymour. *The Heart: Our Circulatory System.* Morrow, 1996. *(I)*

Yount, Lisa. *William Harvey: Discoverer of How Blood Circulates.* Enslow, 1994. *(I)*

CIRCUS

Granfield, Linda. *Circus: An Album.* Dorling Kindersley, 1998. *(I)*

Perkins, Catherine. *Most Excellent Book of How to Be a Clown.* Millbrook Press, 1996. *(P; I)*

CIVIL RIGHTS

Bridges, Ruby. *Through My Eyes.* Scholastic, 1999. *(P; I)*

Collier, Christopher, and Collier, James L. *Reconstruction and the Rise of Jim Crow: 1864-1896.* Marshall Cavendish/Benchmark, 1999. *(I)*

Fradin, Dennis Brindell, and Fradin, Judith Bloom. *Ida B. Wells: Mother of the Civil Rights Movement.* Clarion, 2000. *(I; A)*

Levy, Debbie. *Civil Liberties.* Lucent, 1999. *(I; A)*

Meltzer, Milton. *The Bill of Rights: How We Got It and What It Means.* Crowell, 1990. *(A)*

Ramen, Fred. *Rights of the Accused (Individual Rights and Civil Responsibilities Series).* Rosen, 2001. *(A)*

Rochelle, Belinda. *Witnesses to Freedom: Young People Who Fought for Civil Rights.* Lodestar, 1993. *(I; A)*

Vernell, Marjorie. *Leaders of Black Civil Rights.* Lucent, 1999. *(I; A)*

Wormser, Richard. *The Rise and Fall of Jim Crow: The African-American Struggle against Discrimination, 1865-1954.* Watts, 1999. *(I; A)*

CIVIL RIGHTS MOVEMENT

Booker, Christopher B. *African-Americans and the Presidency: A History of Broken Promises.* Scholastic, 2000. *(A)*

Dudley, Mark E. *Brown v. Board of Education (1954): School Desegregation.* Lerner, 1995. *(I; A)*

Dudley, William, ed. *The Civil Rights Movement.* Greenhaven, 1996. *(A)*

Dunn, John M. *The Civil Rights Movement.* Gale Group, 1997. *(I; A)*

Winters, Paul A., ed. *The Civil Rights Movement.* Greenhaven, 2000. *(A)*

CIVIL WAR, UNITED STATES

Adler, David A. *A Picture Book of Robert E. Lee.* Holiday House, 1998. *(P)*

Archer, Jules. *A House Divided: The Lives of Ulysses S. Grant and Robert E. Lee.* Scholastic, 1996. *(I)*

Armstrong, Jennifer. *Photo by Brady: A Picture of the Civil War.* Simon & Schuster, 2005. *(I; A)*

Arnold, James R., and Wiener, Roberta. *Divided in Two: The Road to Civil War, 1861.* Lerner, 2001. *(I)*

Barney, William L. *The Civil War and Reconstruction: A Student Companion.* Oxford, 2001. *(I; A)*

Beller, Susan Provost. *Billy Yank and Johnny Reb: Soldiering in the Civil War.* Millbrook Press, 2000; *Confederate Ladies of Richmond.* Millbrook Press, 1999; *Never Were Men So Brave: The Irish Brigade During the Civil War.* Simon & Schuster, 1998; *To Hold this Ground: A Desperate Battle at Gettysburg.* Simon & Schuster, 1995; *Cadets at War: The True Story of Teenage Heroism at the Battle of New Market.* F & W Publications, 1991. *(I; A)*

Brooks, Victor. *African Americans in the Civil War; Civil War Forts; Secret Weapons in the Civil War.* Chelsea House, 2000. *(P; I)*

Carter, Alden R. *Battle of the Ironclads: The Monitor and the Merrimack.* Watts, 1993. *(I)*

Chang, Ina. *A Separate Battle: Women and the Civil War.* Lodestar, 1991. *(I)*

Colbert, Nancy. *The Firing on Fort Sumter: A Splintered Nation Goes to War.* Morgan Reynolds, 2000. *(I; A)*

Corrick, James A. *Life among the Soldiers and Cavalry.* Lucent, 2000; *The Battle of Gettysburg: Battles of the Civil War.* Gale Group, 1996. *(I; A)*

Damon, Duane. *When This Cruel War Is Over: The Civil War Home Front.* Lerner, 1996. *(I; A)*

Day, Nancy. *Your Travel Guide to Civil War America.* Lerner, 2000. *(I)*

Dodd, Craig. *Going to War in the 19th Century.* Scholastic, 2001. *(I)*

Haskins, Jim. *Black, Blue and Gray: African Americans in the Civil War.* Simon & Schuster, 1998. *(I)*

Kennett, Lee B. *Marching through Georgia: The Story of Soldiers and Civilians during Sherman's Campaign.* HarperCollins, 1995. *(A)*

Kerby, Mona. *Robert E. Lee: Southern Hero of the Civil War.* Enslow, 1997. *(I; A)*

Mettger, Zak. *Till Victory Is Won: Black Soldiers in the Civil War.* Penguin, 1994. *(I)*

Marrin, Albert. *Commander in Chief: Abraham Lincoln and the Civil War.* Penguin Putnam, 1997; *Virginia's*

General: Robert E. Lee and the Civil War; Unconditional Surrender: U. S. Grant and the Civil War. Simon & Schuster, 1994. *(I; A)*

Meltzer, Milton, ed. *Voices from the Civil War: A Documentary History of the Great American Conflict.* Crowell, 1989. *(I; A)*

Ray, Delia. *Behind the Blue and the Gray: The Soldier's Life in the Civil War.* Lodestar, 1991. *(I; A)*

Reef, Catherine. *Gettysburg.* Silver Burdett Press, 1992. *(P; I)*

Reger, James P. *Civil War Generals of the Confederacy.* Gale Group, 1998. *(I; A)*; *Battle of Antietam; Life in the South During the Civil War.* Gale Group, 1997. *(I; A)*

Robertson, James I., Jr. *Civil War! America Becomes One Nation.* Knopf, 1992. *(I; A)*

Sateren, Shelley Swanson. *A Civil War Drummer Boy: The Diary of William Bircher.* Capstone Press, 1999. *(P; I)*

Seidman, Rachel Filene. *The Civil War: A History in Documents.* Oxford, 2000. *(A)*

Steele, Christy. *A Confederate Girl: The Diary of Carrie Berry, 1864.* Capstone Press, 1999. *(P; I)*

Werner, Emmy E. *Reluctant Witnesses: Children's Voices from the Civil War.* Westview, 1998. *(A)*

Wert, Jeffry D. *A Brotherhood of Valor: The Common Soldiers of the Stonewall Brigade, C.S.A., and the Iron Brigade, U.S.A.* Simon & Schuster, 1999. *(A)*

Zeinert, Karen. *Tragic Prelude: Bleeding Kansas.* Shoe String Press, 2000; *Those Courageous Women of the Civil War.* Millbrook Press, 1998. *(I; A)*

CLAY, HENRY

Burgan, Michael. *Henry Clay.* Child's World, 2004. *(P; I)*

CLEVELAND, STEPHEN GROVER

Gaines, Ann Graham. *Grover Cleveland: Our Twenty-Second and Twenty-Fourth President.* Child's World, 2002. *(P; I)*

Ochester, Betsy. *Grover Cleveland (Encyclopedia of Presidents, Second Series).* Scholastic, 2004. *(I; A)*

CLIMATE

Friedman, Katherine. *What If the Polar Ice Caps Melted?* Scholastic, 2002. *(I; A)*

Maslin, Mark. *Global Warming: Causes, Effects, and the Future.* Voyageur Press, 2002. *(A)*

Pringle, Laurence P. *Global Warming: The Threat of Earth's Changing Climate.* Seastar Books, 2001. *(I)*

Scoones, Simon. *Climate Change: Our Impact on the Planet.* Raintree Steck-Vaughn, 2002. *(I)*

Smith, Trevor. *Earth's Changing Climate.* Smart Apple Media, 2004. *(I; A)*

CLINTON, HILLARY

Boyd, Aaron. *First Lady: The Story of Hillary Rodham Clinton.* Reynolds, 1994. *(I)*

Greenberg, Keith Elliot. *Bill and Hillary, the Clintons: Working Together in the White House.* Gale Group, 1994. *(P; I)*

Kozar, Richard. *Hillary Rodham Clinton.* Chelsea House, 1998. *(I; A)*

Stacey, T. J. *Hillary Rodham Clinton: Activist 1st Lady.* Enslow, 1994. *(I; A)*

CLINTON, WILLIAM

Cohen, Daniel. *The Impeachment of William Jefferson Clinton.* Twenty-First Century, 1999. *(I; A)*

Cwiklik, Robert. *Bill Clinton: President of the 90's.* Millbrook, 1997. *(I)*

Gaines, Ann Graham. *William J. Clinton: Our Forty-Second President.* Child's World, 2001. *(P; I)*

Gallen, David. *Bill Clinton as They Know Him.* Gallen, 1994. *(A)*

Howard, Todd, ed. *William J. Clinton.* Gale Group, 2001. *(A)*

Kelly, Michael. *Bill Clinton.* Chelsea House, 1998. *(I; A)*

CLOCKS

Dash, Joan. *The Longitude Prize.* Farrar, 2000. *(I; A)*

Duffy, Trent. *The Turning Point Inventions: The Clock.* Simon & Schuster, 2000. *(I; A)*

Koscielniak, Bruce. *About Time: A First Look at Time and Clocks.* Houghton Mifflin, 2004. *(P; I)*

Maestro, Betsy C. *The Story of Clocks and Calendars: Marking a Millennium.* Morrow, 1999. *(P; I)*

Older, Jules. *Telling Time: How to Tell Time on Digital and Analog Clocks!* Charlesbridge, 2000. *(P)*

Williams, John. *Water Projects.* Steck-Vaughn, 1997. *(I)*

CLOUDS

Branley, Franklyn Mansfield. *Down Comes the Rain: Stage 2.* HarperCollins, 1999. *(P)*

CLOWNS

Burgess, Ron. *Be a Clown!: Techniques from a Real Clown.* Ideals Publications, 2001. *(P; I)*

Perkins, Catherine. *Most Excellent Book of How to Be a Clown.* Millbrook Press, 1996. *(P; I)*

COAL AND COAL MINING

Bartoletti, Susan Campbell. *Growing Up in Coal Country.* Houghton Mifflin, 1999. *(I)*

Ditchfield, Christin; Jenner, Jan; and Cornwell, Linda. *Coal.* Scholastic, 2001. *(P)*

Kittinger, Jo S. *A Look at Rocks: From Coal to Kimberlite.* Scholastic, 1998. *(I)*

COLD WAR

Anderson, Dale. *The Cold War Years.* Raintree Steck-Vaughn, 2001. *(I; A)*

Burgan, Michael. *The Collapse; The Hot Conflicts; The Separation; The Threats.* Raintree Steck-Vaughn, 2001. *(I; A)*

Dudley, William, ed. *The Cold War.* Greenhaven Press, 1992. *(A)*

Grant, R. G. *The Berlin Wall.* Raintree Steck-Vaughn, 1998. *(I; A)*

Kort, Michael G. *The Cold War.* Millbrook Press, 1994. *(A)*

Sherrow, Victoria. *Joseph McCarthy and the Cold War.* Blackbirch, 1998. *(I; A)*

Taylor, David. *The Cold War.* Heinemann, 2001. *(I)*

Warren, James A. *Cold War: The American Crusade against World Communism, 1945-1991, Vol. 1.* HarperCollins, 1996. *(A)*

Winkler, Allan M. *The Cold War: A History in Documents.* Oxford University Press, 2000. *(A)*

COLOMBIA

Boraas, Tracey. *Colombia.* Capstone Press, 2002. *(P)*

DuBois, Jill, and Jermyn, Leslie. *Colombia.* Marshall Cavendish, 2002 (2nd ed.). *(I; A)*

Haynes, Tricia. *Colombia.* Chelsea House, 1998. *(I; A)*

Jermyn, Leslie, and Vengadasalam, Leela. *Colombia.* Gareth Stevens, 1999. *(I)*

Morrison, Marion. *Colombia.* Scholastic, 2001. *(I)*

COLONIAL LIFE IN AMERICA

Aronson, Marc. *Witch-Hunt: Mysteries of the Salem Witch Trials.* Simon & Schuster, 2003. *(A)*

Brenner, Barbara. *If You Were There in 1776.* Simon & Schuster, 1994. *(P; I)*

Carlson, Laurie M. *Colonial Kids: An Acivity Guide to Life in the New World.* Chicago Press Review, 1997. *(P; I)*

Day, Nancy. *Your Travel Guide to Colonial America.* Lerner, 2000. *(I)*

Enslow, Anne, and Enslow, Ridley. *Music of the American Colonies.* Enslow, 2000. *(I; A)*

Howarth, Sarah. *Colonial People; Colonial Places.* Millbrook Press, 1994. *(I)*

Ichord, Loretta Frances. *Hasty Pudding, Johnnycakes, and Other Good Stuff: Cooking in Colonial America.* Millbrook Press, 1999. *(P; I)*

Maestro, Betsy, and Maestro, Giulio. *The New Americans: Colonial Times, 1620-1689.* HarperCollins, 1998. *(P)*

Sateren, Shelley Swanson. *Going to School in Colonial America.* Capstone Press, 2001. *(P; I)*

Stefoff, Rebecca. *The Colonies.* Marshall Cavendish, 2000. *(I)*

Steins, Richard. *Colonial America, Vol. 2.* Raintree Steck-Vaughn, 2000. *(I)*

Wilbur, C. Keith. *Homebuilding and Woodworking in Colonial America.* Chelsea House, 1997. *(A)*

COLOR

Boerst, William J. *Isaac Newton: Organizing the Universe.* Morgan Reynolds, 2003. *(I; A)*

Levine, Shar, and Johnstone, Leslie. *The Optics Book: Fun Experiments with Light, Vision, and Color.* Sterling, 1999. *(I)*

Nassau, Kurt. *Experimenting with Color.* Scholastic, 1997. *(I; A)*

COLORADO

Ayer, Eleanor H. *Colorado.* Benchmark, 1997. *(P; I)*

Aylesworth, Thomas G., and Aylesworth, Virgina L. *The Southwest: Colorado, New Mexico, Texas.* Chelsea House, 1995. *(I)*

Blashfield, Jean F. *Colorado.* Scholastic, 1999 (2nd ed.). *(I; A)*

Elias, Megan. *Colorado: The Centennial State.* Gareth Stevens, 2002. *(P; I)*

Fradin, Dennis Brindell. *Colorado: From Sea to Shining Sea.* Scholastic, 1994. *(P; I)*

Miller, Amy; Matusevich, Melissa N.; and Meyer, Kim R. *Colorado.* Scholastic, 2002. *(P; I)*

Petersen, David. *Great Sand Dunes National Monument.* Scholastic, 2000; *Dinosaur National Monument.* Scholastic, 1995; *Rocky Mountain National Park.* Scholastic, 1993. *(P; I)*

Wills, Charles A. *A Historical Album of Colorado.* Millbrook Press, 1996. *(I)*

COLUMBUS, CHRISTOPHER

Aaseng, Nathan. *You Are the Explorer.* Oliver Press, 2000. *(I; A)*

Brenner, Barbara. *If You Were There in 1492: Everyday Life in the Time of Columbus.* Simon & Schuster, 1998. *(I)*

Columbus, Christopher. *The Log of Christopher Columbus' First Voyage to America in the Year 1492: As Copied out in Brief by Bartholomew Las Casas.* Linnet Books, 1989. *(P; I)*

Gallagher, Carole S. *Christopher Columbus and the Discovery of the New World.* Chelsea House, 1999. *(I)*

Landau, Elaine. *Columbus Day: Celebrating a Famous Explorer.* Enslow, 2001. *(P)*

Meltzer, Milton. *Columbus and the World around Him.* Watts, 1990. *(I; A)*

Pelta, Kathy. *Discovering Christopher Columbus.* Lerner, 1991. *(I; A)*

COMIC BOOKS

McCloud, Scott. *Understanding Comics.* Kitchen Sink Press, 1997 (2nd ed.). *(I)*

Pellowski, Michael Morgan. *The Art of Making Comic Books.* Lerner, 1995. *(I; A)*

COMMERCE, UNITED STATES DEPARTMENT OF

Goldberg, Jan. *The Department of Commerce (This Is Your Government Series).* Rosen, 2005. *(P)*

COMMONWEALTH OF INDEPENDENT STATES

Batalden, Stephen K., and Batalden, Sandra L. *The Newly Independent States of Eurasia: Handbook of Former Soviet Republics.* Greenwood, 1997 (2nd ed.). *(A)*

Clark, Mary Jane Behrends. *The Commonwealth of Independent States.* Millbrook Press, 1992. *(I)*

Kort, Michael G. *The Handbook of the Former Soviet Union.* Millbrook Press, 1997. *(I; A)*

Otfinoski, Steven. *Boris Yeltsin and the Rebirth of Russia.* Millbrook Press, 1995. *(I; A)*

Resnick, Abraham. *The Commonwealth of Independent States.* Scholastic, 1993. *(I; A)*

COMMONWEALTH OF NATIONS

Lace, William W. *The British Empire: The End of Colonialism.* Lucent, 2000. *(I; A)*

COMMUNICATION

Wilson, Anthony. *Communications.* Kingfisher, 1999. *(I; A)*

Woods, Michael, and Woods, Mary B. *Ancient Communication: From Grunts to Graffiti.* Lerner, 2000. *(I)*

COMPUTERS

Aaseng, Nathan. *Business Builders in Computers.* Oliver Press, 2000. *(I; A)*

Bortz, Alfred B. *Mind Tools: The Science of Artificial Intelligence.* Watts, 1992. *(I; A)*

Brimner, Larry Dane. *E-Mail.* Scholastic, 1997. *(P; I)*

Dunn, John M. *World History: Computer Revolution.* Lucent Books, 2001. *(I; A)*

Eberts, Marjorie; Gisler, Margaret; and Olsen, Maria. *Careers for Computer Buffs and Other Technological Types.* NTC, 1998 (2nd ed.). *(A)*

Ehrenhaft, Daniel. *Marc Andreessen: Web Warrior.* Millbrook Press, 2001. *(I)*

Gaines, Ann G. *Unlocking the Secrets of Science: Tim Berners-Lee and the Development of the World Wide Web.* Mitchell Lane, 2001. *(I)*

Henderson, Harry. *The Internet.* Lucent, 1998. *(I)*

Jefferis, David. *Internet: The Electronic Global Village.* Crabtree, 2001. *(P; I)*

Koehler, Lora. *Internet.* Children's Press, 1995. *(P; I)*

Marshall, Elizabeth L., and Heweston, Nicholas. *A Student's Guide to the Internet.* Millbrook Press, 2000 (rev. ed.). *(I; A)*

Owen, Trevor, and Owston, Ron. *The Learning Highway: Smart Students and the Net.* Key Porter, 1998. *(A)*

Pascoe, Elaine. *Virtual Reality: Beyond the Looking Glass.* Gale Group, 1997. *(P; I)*

Williams, Brian K. *Computers.* Heinemann, 2001. *(I)*

Wolinsky, Art. *Communicating on the Internet; Creating and Publishing Web Pages on the Internet.* Enslow, 1999. *(I)*; *The History of the Internet and the World Wide Web; Locating and Evaluating Information on the Internet.* Enslow, 1999. *(I; A)*

CONGO, DEMOCRATIC REPUBLIC OF

Congo...in Pictures. Lerner, 1999. *(I; A)*

Barter, James. *The Congo.* Lucent, 2003. *(I; A)*

Franklin, Sharon; Tull, Mary; and Shelton, Carol. *Africa: Understanding Geography and History through Art.* Raintree Steck-Vaughn, 2000. *(I; A)*

Kushner, Nina. *Democratic Republic of the Congo.* Gareth Stevens, 2001. *(I; A)*

CONGO, REPUBLIC OF

Franklin, Sharon; Tull, Mary; and Shelton, Carol. *Africa: Understanding Geography and History through Art.* Raintree Steck-Vaughn, 2000. *(I; A)*

Okeke, Chika, and Okeke, M. F. *Kongo.* Rosen, 1997. *(I; A)*

CONGO RIVER

Congo...in Pictures. Lerner, 1999. *(I; A)*

Barter, James. *The Congo.* Lucent, 2003. *(I; A)*

CONNECTICUT

Bailer, Darice, and Craven, Jean. *Connecticut: The Constitution State.* Gareth Stevens, 2002. *(P; I)*

Fradin, Dennis Brindell, and Fradin, Judith Bloom. *Connecticut: From Sea to Shining Sea.* Scholastic, 1995. *(P; I)*

Furstinger, Nancy. *Connecticut.* Scholastic, 2001. *(P; I)*

Gelman, Amy. *Connecticut.* Lerner, 2002 (2nd ed.). *(P; I)*

Girod, Christina M. *The Thirteen Colonies: Connecticut.* Gale Group, 2001. *(I)*

McNair, Sylvia, and Kent, Deborah. *Connecticut.* Scholastic, 1999 (2nd ed.). *(I; A)*

Wills, Charles A. *A Historical Album of Connecticut.* Millbrook Press, 1995. *(I)*

CONRAD, JOSEPH

Bloom, Harold, ed. *Joseph Conrad's Heart of Darkness and The Secret Sharer (Bloom's Notes Series).* Chelsea House, 1995. *(A)*

Fletcher, Chris. *Joseph Conrad.* Oxford University Press, 1999. *(A)*

Swisher, Clarice, ed. *Joseph Conrad (Literary Companion to American Literature).* Thomson Gale, 1997. *(A)*

CONSERVATION

DeStefano, Susan. *Theodore Roosevelt: Conservation President.* Millbrook Press, 1993. *(P; I)*

Dolan, Edward F. *American Wilderness and Its Future: Conservation Versus Use.* Watts, 1992. *(I; A)*

Gardner, Robert. *Experimenting with Energy Conservation.* Watts, 1992. *(I; A)*

Kessler, Christina, and Mswati III. *All the King's Animals: The Return of Endangered Wildlife to Swaziland.* Boyds Mills Press, 1995. *(P; I)*

Koebner, Linda. *Zoo Book: The Evolution of Wildlife Conservation Centers.* Tor Books, 1994. *(I; A)*

Lewis, Barbara A., and Espeland, Pamela. *Kid's Guide to Service Projects: Over 500 Service Ideas for Young People Who Want to Make a Difference.* Free Spirit, 1995. *(I; A)*

Tagliaferro, Linda. *Galapagos Islands: Nature's Delicate Balance at Risk.* Lerner, 2000. *(I)*

Thomas, Peggy. *Big Cat Conservation; Bird Alert; Marine Mammal Preservation; Reptile Rescue.* Millbrook Press, 2000. *(I)*

Whitman, Sylvia. *This Land is Your Land: The American Conservation Movement.* Lerner, 1994. *(I)*

CONSTANTINE THE GREAT

Baker, Rosalie F., and Baker, Charles F., III. *Ancient Romans: Expanding the Classical Tradition.* Oxford University Press, 1998. *(A)*

Bator, Robert. *Daily Life in Ancient and Modern Istanbul.* Lerner, 2000. *(P; I)*

Corrick, James A. *The Byzantine Empire.* Lucent, 1997. *(I)*

Nardo, Don, ed. *Rulers of Ancient Rome.* Gale Group, 1998. *(I; A)*

CONSUMER PROTECTION

Bowen, Nancy. *Ralph Nader: Man with a Mission.* Millbrook Press, 2002. *(I; A)*

Celsi, Teresa Noel. *Ralph Nader: The Consumer Revolution.* Millbrook Press, 1994. *(I; A)*

Menhard, Francha Roffe. *Teen Consumer Smarts: Shop, Save and Steer Clear of Scams.* Enslow, 2002. *(I; A)*

CONTINENTAL CONGRESS

Feinberg, Barbara Silberdick. *Articles of Confederation: The First Constitution of the United States.* Millbrook Press, 2002. *(I; A)*

Fradin, Dennis Brindell. *The Signers: The 56 Stories Behind the Declaration of Independence.* Walker, 2002. *(I)*

Freedman, Russell. *Give Me Liberty!: The Story of the Declaration of Independence.* Holiday House, 2000. *(I)*

Weber, Michael. *Young Republic.* Raintree Steck-Vaughn, 2000. *(I)*

CONTINENTS

Gallant, Roy A. *Dance of the Continents.* Marshall Cavendish, 2000. *(I)*

Petersen, David. *Africa; Antarctica; Asia; Australia; Europe; North America; South America.* Children's Press, 1998; *Continents.* Children's Press, 1996. *(P)*

Taylor, Barbara. *Earth Explained: A Beginner's Guide to Our Planet.* Twenty-First Century, 1997. *(I)*

COOKING

Betty Crocker's Cookbook for Boys and Girls. John Wiley & Sons, 2003. *(P; I)*

Albyn, Carole Lisa, and Webb, Lois Sinaiko. *The Multicultural Cookbook for Students.* Greenwood, 1993. *(I; A)*

Bisignano, Alphonse. *Cooking the Italian Way.* Lerner, 2001 (2nd ed.). *(I; A)*

Christian, Rebecca. *Cooking the Spanish Way.* Lerner, 2001 (2nd ed.). *(I; A)*

Coronado, Rosa. *Cooking the Mexican Way.* Lerner, 2001 (2nd ed.). *(I; A)*

D'Amico, Joan, and Drummond, Karen Eich. *The United States Cookbook: Fabulous Foods and Fascinating Facts from All 50 States.* Wiley, 2000. *(I)*

Hargittai, Magdolna. *Cooking the Hungarian Way.* Lerner, 2003 (2nd ed.). *(I; A)*

Johnson, Sylvia A. *Tomatoes, Potatoes, Corn, and Beans: How the Foods of the Americas Changed Cooking Around the World.* Atheneum, 1997. *(I; A)*

Montgomery, Bertha Vining, and Nabwire, Constance R. *Cooking the East African Way; Cooking the West African Way.* Lerner, 2001 (2nd ed.). *(I; A)*

Munsen, Sylvia. *Cooking the Norwegian Way.* Lerner, 2002 (2nd ed.). *(I; A)*

Osseo-Asare, Fran. *A Good Soup Attracts Chairs: A First African Cookbook for American Kids.* Pelican, 1993. *(I; A)*

Parnell, Helga. *Cooking the German Way.* Lerner, 2003 (2nd ed.). *(I; A)*

Plotkin, Gregory, and Plotkin, Rita. *Cooking the Russian Way.* Lerner, 2003 (2nd ed.). *(I; A)*

Ralph, Judy. *The Peanut Butter Cookbook for Kids.* Hyperion, 1995. *(I)*

Villios, Lynne W. *Cooking the Greek Way.* Lerner, 2002 (2nd ed.). *(I; A)*

Webb, Lois Sinaiko. *Holidays of the World Cookbook for Students.* Greenwood, 1995. *(I; A)*

Yu, Ling. *Cooking the Chinese Way.* Lerner, 2001 (2nd ed.). *(I; A)*

Zalben, Jane Breskin. *To Every Season: A Family Holiday Cookbook.* Simon & Schuster, 1999. *(P; I)*

Zamojska-Hutchins, Danuta. *Cooking the Polish Way.* Lerner, 2002 (2nd ed.). *(I; A)*

COOLIDGE, CALVIN

Maupin, Melissa. *Calvin Coolidge: Our Thirtieth President.* Child's World, 2002. *(P; I)*

Stein, R. Conrad. *Calvin Coolidge (Encyclopedia of Presidents, Second Series).* Scholastic, 2004. *(I; A)*

COPPER

Beatty, Richard. *Copper.* Marshall Cavendish, 2000. *(P; I)*

CORALS

Cerullo, Mary M. *Coral Reef: A City That Never Sleeps.* Dutton, 1996. *(P; I)*

Collard, Sneed B. *One Night in the Coral Sea.* Charlesbridge, 2005. *(P; I)*

Cousteau Society. *Corals: The Sea's Great Builders.* Simon & Schuster, 1992. *(P; I)*

Maynard, Caitlin; Maynard, Thane; and Rullman, Stan. *Rain Forests and Reefs: A Kid's-Eye View of the Tropics.* Watts, 1996. *(I)*

Sargent, William. *Night Reef: Dusk to Dawn on a Coral Reef.* Watts, 1991. *(P; I)*

Segaloff, Nat, and Erickson, Paul. *A Reef Comes to Life: Creating an Undersea Exhibit.* Watts, 1991. *(I)*

CORK

Plomer, Anna Llimos. *Let's Create!: Wood and Cork*. Gareth Stevens, 2003. *(P; I)*

CORTÉS, HERNANDO

Aaseng, Nathan. *You Are the Explorer*. Oliver Press, 2000. *(I; A)*

Calvert, Patricia. *Hernando Cortés: Fortune Favored the Bold*. Benchmark, 2002. *(I)*

De Angelis, Gina. *Hernando Cortés and the Conquest of Mexico*. Chelsea House, 1999. *(I)*

COSMIC RAYS

Branley, Franklyn Mansfield. *Superstar: The Supernova of 1987*. HarperCollins, 1990. *(P; I)*

COSTA RICA

Costa Rica . . . in Pictures. Lerner, 1997. *(I)*

Collard, Sneed B. *Monteverde: Science and Scientists in a Costa Rican Cloud Forest*. Scholastic, 1998. *(I; A)*

Foley, Erin L. *Costa Rica*. Marshall Cavendish, 1997 (2nd ed.). *(I; A)*

Frank, Nicole, and Vengadasalam, Leela. *Costa Rica*. Gareth Stevens, 2000. *(I)*

Haynes, Tricia. *Costa Rica*. Chelsea House, 1998. *(I; A)*

Morrison, Marion. *Costa Rica (Enchantment of the World, Second Series)*. Scholastic, 1998. *(I; A)*

COUNTRY MUSIC

Kallen, Stuart A. *History of Country Music*. Gale Group, 2002. *(I; A)*

Orgill, Roxanne. *Shout, Sister, Shout! Ten Girl Singers Who Shaped a Century*. Simon & Schuster, 2001. *(I; A)*

COURTS

DeVillers, David. *The John Brown Slavery Revolt Trial: A Headline Court Case*. Enslow, 2000; *Marbury v. Madison: Powers of the Supreme Court*. Enslow, 1998. *(I; A)*

Fireside, Harvey. *Mississippi Burning Civil Rights Murder Conspiracy Trial*. Enslow, 2002. *(I; A)*; *Plessy v. Ferguson: Separate But Equal?* Enslow, 1997. *(A)*

Ogawa, Brian K. *To Tell the Truth*. Volcano Press, 1997. *(I)*

Telgen, Diane. *Brown v. Board of Education*. Omnigraphics, 2005. *(A)*

Wormser, Richard L. *Defending the Accused: Stories from the Courtroom*. Scholastic, 2001. *(I; A)*

CRABS

Blaxland, Beth. *Crustaceans: Crabs, Crayfishes, and Their Relatives*. Chelsea House, 2002. *(P; I)*

CRANE, STEPHEN

Sufrin, Mark. *Stephen Crane*. Atheneum, 1992. *(I; A)*

Szumski, Bonnie, ed. *Stephen Crane*. Thomson Gale, 1997. *(A)*

CREDIT CARDS

Godfrey, Neale S. *Neale S. Godfrey's Ultimate Kids' Money Book*. Simon & Schuster, 1998. *(P; I; A)*

CRICKET

Eastaway, Robert. *Cricket Explained*. St. Martin's Press, 1993. *(A)*

CRIMEAN WAR

Bachrach, Deborah. *The Crimean War*. Lucent, 1997. *(A)*

CROCHETING

Kinsler-Blakley, Gwen. *Crocheting*. Kids Can Press, 2003. *(P; I)*

Messent, Jan. *Wool'n Magic: Creative Uses of Yarn...Knitting, Crochet, Embroidery*. Search Press, 1997. *(A)*

O'Reilly, Susan. *Knitting and Crocheting*. Raintree Steck-Vaughn, 1994. *(P; I)*

CROCODILES AND ALLIGATORS

Arnosky, Jim. *All about Alligators*. Scholastic, 1994. *(P)*

Jango-Cohen, Judith. *Crocodiles*. Benchmark, 2000. *(P; I)*

Landau, Elaine. *Fearsome Alligators*. Enslow, 2003. *(P; I)*

Simon, Seymour. *Crocodiles and Alligators*. HarperCollins, 1999. *(I)*

Sloan, Christopher. *Super Croc and Other Prehistoric Crocodiles*. National Geographic, 2002. *(I)*

Souza, Dorothy M. *Roaring Reptiles*. Lerner, 1992. *(P; I)*

Thomas, Peggy. *Reptile Rescue*. Millbrook Press, 2000. *(P; I)*

CUBA

Ancona, George. *Cuban Kids*. Marshall Cavendish, 2000. *(P; I)*

Bentley, Judith. *Fidel Castro*. Silver Burdett Press, 1991. *(I; A)*

Crouch, Clifford W. *Cuba*. Chelsea House, 1997. *(I)*

Gay, Kathlyn. *Leaving Cuba: From Operation Pedro Pan to Elian*. Twenty-First Century, 2001. *(I; A)*

Hughes, Susan, and Fast, April. *Cuba the Culture*. Crabtree, 2004. *(P; I)*

Madden, Paul. *Fidel Castro*. Rourke, 1993. *(I; A)*

Petersen, Christine, and Petersen, David. *Cuba*. Scholastic, 2002. *(P; I)*

Regler, Margaret, and Hoff, Rhoda. *Uneasy Neighbors: Cuba and the United States*. Watts, 1997. *(A)*

Sheehan, Sean. *Cuba*. Marshall Cavendish, 1995. *(I; A)*

Sherrow, Victoria, and Heweston, Nicholas. *Cuba*. Twenty-First Century, 2001. *(I; A)*

Staub, Frank J. *Children of Cuba*. Lerner, 1996. *(P; I)*

CURIE, MARIE AND PIERRE

Fox, Karen. *The Chain Reaction: Pioneers of Nuclear Science*. Watts, 1998. *(I; A)*

Hazell, Rebecca. *Heroines: Great Women Through the Ages*. Abbeville Press, 1996. *(I)*

Tracy, Kathleen. *Pierre and Marie Curie and the Discovery of Radium.* Mitchell Lane, 2004. *(I)*

CURLING

Hansen, Warren, and Martin, Kevin. *Curling: The History, The Players, The Game.* Key Porter Books, 2000. *(A)*

CYPRUS

Cyprus . . . in Pictures. Lerner, 1992. *(I)*

CZECH REPUBLIC

Dornberg, John. *Central and Eastern Europe.* Greenwood, 1995. *(A)*

Kronenwetter, Michael. *New Eastern Europe.* Watts, 1991. *(I; A)*

Sioras, Efstathia. *Czech Republic.* Marshall Cavendish, 1998 (2nd ed.). *(I; A)*

D (LETTER)

Samoyault, Tiphaine. *Alphabetical Order: How the Alphabet Began.* Viking, 1998. *(P; I)*

DAIRYING AND DAIRY PRODUCTS

Bial, Raymond. *Portrait of a Farm Family.* Houghton Mifflin, 1995. *(P; I)*

Doyle, Malachy. *Cow.* McElderry, 2002. *(P)*

King, Hazel. *Milk and Yogurt.* Heinemann, 1998. *(P; I)*

Older, Jules. *Ice Cream.* Charlesbridge, 2002; *Cow.* Charlesbridge, 1997. *(P; I)*

Patent, Dorothy Hinshaw. *Cattle.* Carolrhoda, 1993. *(P; I)*

Peterson, Cris. *Century Farm: One Hundred Years on a Family Farm.* Boyds Mills Press, 1999. *(P)*

Powell, Jillian. *Milk.* Steck-Vaughn, 1997. *(P; I)*

Wolfman, Judy, and Winston, David Lorenz. *Life on a Dairy Farm.* Lerner, 2003; *Life on a Goat Farm.* Lerner, 2001. *(P)*

DALI, SALVADOR

Carter, David. *Salvador Dali.* Chelsea, 1994. *(I; A)*

Halliwell, Sarah, ed. *20th Century: Post-1945 Artists, Writers, and Composers.* Raintree, 1998. *(I)*

DALTON, JOHN

Kjelle, Marylou Morano, and Whiting, Jim. *John Dalton and the Atomic Theory.* Mitchell Lane, 2004. *(I)*

DAMS

Doherty, Craig A., and Doherty, Katherine M. *Hoover Dam.* Blackbirch Press, 1995. *(I)*

Mann, Elizabeth. *The Hoover Dam: The Story of Hard Times, Tough People and the Taming of a Wild River.* Firefly, 2001. *(P; I; A)*

DANCE

Augustyn, Frank, and Tanaka, Shelley. *Footnotes: Dancing the World's Best-Loved Ballets.* Millbrook Press, 2002. *(I; A)*

Barboza, Steven. *I Feel Like Dancing: A Year with Jacques D'Amboise and the National Dance Institute.* Crown, 1992. *(P; I)*

Ford, Carin T. *Legends of American Dance and Choreography.* Enslow, 2000. *(I; A)*

Glover, Savion, and Weber, Bruce. *Savion!: My Life in Tap.* Morrow, 2000. *(I; A)*

Gottlieb, Robert. *George Balanchine: The Ballet Maker (Eminent Lives Series).* HarperCollins, 2004. *(A)*

Grau, Andree. *Eyewitness: Dance.* DK, 2000. *(P; I)*

Hebach, Susan. *Tap Dancing.* Scholastic, 2001. *(I: A)*

Tomblin, Gill. *Illustrated Book of Ballet Stories.* DK, 2000. *(P; I)*

DARWIN, CHARLES ROBERT

Altman, Linda Jacobs. *Mr. Darwin's Voyage: People in Focus.* Silver Burdett Press, 1995. *(I; A)*

Evans, Nathan Edward. *Charles Darwin: Revolutionary Biologist.* Lerner, 1993. *(I; A)*

Hyndley, Kate. *Voyage of the Beagle.* Watts, 1989. *(I)*

Nardo, Don, ed. *Charles Darwin.* Greenhaven, 1999. *(A)*

Parker, Steve. *Charles Darwin and Evolution.* Harper, 1992. *(I)*

Patent, Dorothy Hinshaw. *Charles Darwin: The Life of a Revolutionary Thinker.* Holiday House, 2001. *(I; A)*

Stefoff, Rebecca. *Charles Darwin and the Evolution Revolution.* Oxford, 1996. *(I; A)*

DAYS OF THE WEEK

Hughes, Paul, and Burn, Jeffrey. *The Days of the Week: Stories, Songs, Traditions, Festivals, and Surprising Facts about the Days of the Week All over the World.* Garrett Educational, 1989. *(P; I)*

Nelson, Robin. *Day; Months; Week.* Lerner, 2001. *(P)*

DEATH

Altman, Linda Jacobs. *Death: An Introduction to Medical-Ethical Dilemmas.* Enslow, 2000. *(I; A)*

Grimes, Nikki. *What is Goodbye?* Hyperion, 2004. *(P; I)*

Hyde, Margaret O., and Setaro, John F. *When the Brain Dies First.* Watts, 2000. *(A)*

Perl, Lila, and Heweston, Nicholas. *Dying to Know: About Death, Funeral Customs, and Final Resting Places.* Millbrook Press, 2001. *(I)*

Sloan, Christopher. *Bury the Dead: Tombs, Corpses, Mummies, Skeletons, and Rituals.* National Geographic, 2002. *(I; A)*

Walker, Richard. *A Right to Die?* Scholastic, 1997. *(I)*

DEBATES AND DISCUSSIONS

Dunbar, Robert E. *How to Debate.* Watts, 1994. *(A)*

Simpson, Carolyn. *High Performance through Negotiation.* Rosen, 1996. *(I; A)*

DECEMBER

Updike, John. *A Child's Calendar.* Holiday House, 1999. *(P; I)*

Warner, Penny. *Kids' Holiday Fun: Great Family Activities Every Month of the Year.* Meadowbrook Press, 1997. *(P)*

DECLARATION OF INDEPENDENCE

Brenner, Barbara. *If You Were There in 1776.* Simon & Schuster, 1994. *(P; I)*

Dalgliesh, Alice. *The Fourth of July Story.* Simon & Schuster, 1995 (2nd ed.). *(P; I)*

Fradin, Dennis Brindell. *The Signers: The 56 Stories Behind the Declaration of Independence.* Walker, 2002. *(I)*

Freedman, Russell. *Give Me Liberty: The Story of the Declaration of Independence.* Holiday House, 2000. *(I)*

DECORATIVE ARTS

Avi-Yonah, Michael. *Piece by Piece!: Mosaics of the Ancient World.* Lerner, 1993. *(I; A)*

Dawson, Imogen. *Clothes and Crafts in the Middle Ages.* Silver Burdett Press, 1998. *(P; I)*

Giblin, James Cross. *Be Seated: A Book about Chairs.* HarperCollins, 1993 *(P; I); Let There Be Light: A Book about Windows.* HarperCollins, 1988. *(I; A)*

Lerner Geography Department. *Dazzling!: Jewelry of the Ancient World.* Lerner, 1995. *(I; A)*

Steele, Philip. *Clothes and Crafts in Ancient Greece.* Gareth Stevens, 2000. *(P; I)*

DEER

Arnosky, Jim. *All about Deer.* Scholastic, 1996. *(P)*

Hodge, Deborah. *Deer, Moose, Elk & Caribou.* Kids Can Press, 1998. *(P; I)*

Patent, Dorothy Hinshaw. *Deer and Elk.* Houghton Mifflin, 1994. *(I)*

DEFENSE, UNITED STATES DEPARTMENT OF

Heinsohn, Beth, and Cohen, Andrew. *The Department of Defense.* Chelsea House, 1990. *(P; I)*

DEGAS, EDGAR

Janson, H. W., and Janson, Anthony F. *History of Art for Young People.* Abrams, 1997 (rev. ed.). *(I; A)*

Muhlberger, Richard, and Metropolitan Museum of Art. *What Makes a Degas a Degas?* Viking, 1993. *(I)*

Venezia, Mike. *Edgar Degas.* Children's Press, 2000. *(P; I)*

Welton, Jude. *Eyewitness: Impressionism.* DK, 2000. *(P; I; A)*

DELAWARE

Blashfield, Jean F. *Delaware.* Scholastic, 2000 (2nd ed.). *(I; A)*

Brown, Dottie. *Delaware.* Lerner, 2002 (2nd ed.). *(P; I)*

Fontes, Justine, and Fontes, Ron. *Delaware: The First State.* Gareth Stevens, 2003. *(P; I)*

Melchiore, Susan McCarthy, and Schlesinger, Arthur Meier. *Caesar Rodney: American Patriot (Colonial Leaders Series).* Chelsea House, 2000. *(P; I)*

Miller, Amy. *Delaware.* Scholastic, 2001. *(P; I)*

Schuman, Michael A. *Delaware.* Marshall Cavendish, 2000. *(P; I)*

DEPRESSION, GREAT

Cooper, Michael L. *Dust to Eat: Drought and Depression in the 1930s.* Houghton Mifflin, 2004. *(P; I)*

Farrell, Jacqueline. *The Great Depression.* Lucent, 1996. *(I; A)*

McElvaine, Robert S. *The Depression and the New Deal: A History in Documents.* Oxford, 2000. *(A)*

Meltzer, Milton. *Brother, Can You Spare a Dime?: The Great Depression of 1929-1933.* Facts on File, 1990. *(I; A)*

Nardo, Don, ed. *The Great Depression.* Greenhaven, 1999. *(A)*

Schraff, Anne E., and Feinberg, Barbara Silberdick. *Great Depression and the New Deal: America's Economic Collapse and Recovery.* Watts, 1990. *(I; A)*

DESERTS

Claybourne, Anna. *Deserts (Geography Fact Files Series).* Smart Apple Media, 2004. *(I; A)*

Fridell, Ron. *Life in the Desert.* Scholastic, 2005. *(P; I)*

Jenkins, Martin. *Deserts (Endangered People and Places Series).* Lerner, 1996. *(I)*

Patent, Dorothy Hinshaw. *Life in a Desert (Ecosystems in Action Series).* Lerner, 2003. *(I; A)*

Radley, Gail. *Grasslands and Deserts.* Lerner, 2003. *(P; I)*

Ricciuti, Edward R. *Biomes of the World: Desert.* Marshall Cavendish, 1996.

Weintraub, Aileen. *The Sahara Desert: The Biggest Desert (Great Record Breakers in Nature Series).* PowerKids Press, 2003. *(P; I)*

Wright-Frierson, Virginia. *A Desert Scrapbook: Dawn to Dusk in the Sonoran Desert.* Simon & Schuster, 1996. *(P; I)*

Yolen, Jane. *Welcome to the Sea of Sand.* Putnam, 1996. *(P)*

DIANA, PRINCESS OF WALES

Brennan, Kristine. *Diana, Princess of Wales.* Chelsea House, 1998. *(I; A)*

Wood, Richard. *Diana: The People's Princess.* Raintree Steck-Vaughn, 1998. *(P; I)*

DICKENS, CHARLES

Caravantes, Peggy. *The Best of Times: The Story of Charles Dickens.* Morgan Reynolds, 2005. *(I; A)*

Halliwell, Sarah, ed. *19th Century: Artists, Writers, and Composers.* Raintree, 1998. *(I)*

DICKINSON, EMILY

Berry, Skip L. *Emily Dickinson (Voices in Poetry).* The Creative Company, 1994. *(A)*

Steffens, Bradley. *Emily Dickinson.* Lucent, 1997. *(I; A)*

Vecchione, Patrice, ed. *Revenge and Forgiveness: An Anthology of Poems.* Henry Holt, 2004. *(I; A)*

DICTIONARIES

The American Heritage Children's Science Dictionary. Houghton Mifflin, 2003. *(P; I)*; *The American Heritage Student Dictionary.* Houghton Mifflin, 2003. *(I; A)*; *The American Heritage High School Dictionary.* Houghton Mifflin, 2002 (4th ed.). *(A)*; *The American Heritage Student Science Dictionary.* Houghton Mifflin, 2002. *(I; A)*

Scholastic Children's Dictionary. Scholastic, 2002 (new & updated ed.). *(P; I)*

DIES AND MOLDS

Good, Keith. *Shape It!: Magnificent Projects for Molding Materials.* Lerner, 1999. *(P; I)*

DIGESTIVE SYSTEM

Avraham, Regina. *The Digestive System.* Chelsea House, 2000. *(A)*

Ballard, Carol. *The Stomach and Digestive System.* Raintree Steck-Vaughn, 1997. *(I)*

Brynie, Faith Hickman. *101 Questions About Food and Digestion That Have Been Eating at You Until Now.* Lerner, 2002. *(I; A)*

Ganeri, Anita. *Eating.* Raintree Steck-Vaughn, 1996. *(P)*

Gold, Susan Dudley. *The Digestive and Excretory Systems.* Enslow, 2003. *(P; I)*

Maurer, Tracy. *Digestion.* Rourke, 1999. *(P)*

Stille, Darlene R. *The Digestive System.* Children's Press, 1998. *(P)*

Swanson, Diane. *Burp! The Most Interesting Book You'll Ever Read about Eating.* Kids Can Press, 2001. *(P; I)*

Toriello, James. *Stomach: Learning How We Digest.* Rosen, 2002. *(I; A)*

Walker, Pam, and Wood, Elaine. *Digestive System.* Lucent, 2003. *(I; A)*

DINOSAURS

Aliki. *Digging Up Dinosaurs.* HarperCollins, 1988. *(P)*

Berger, Melvin, and Berger, Gilda. *Did Dinosaurs Live in Your Backyard?: Questions and Answers about Dinosaurs.* Scholastic, 1999. *(P)*

Bishop, Nic. *Digging for Bird-Dinosaurs: An Expedition to Madagascar.* Houghton, 2000. *(I)*

Cohen, Daniel, and Cohen, Susan. *Where to Find Dinosaurs Today.* Dutton/Cobblehill, 1992. *(I)*

Currie, Philip J., and Mastin, Colleayn O. *The Newest and Coolest Dinosaurs.* Grasshopper, 1998. *(I)*

Dingus, Lowell, and Chiappe, Luis. *The Tiniest Giants: Discovering Dinosaur Eggs.* Doubleday, 1999. *(I)*

Facklam, Marjorie. *Tracking Dinosaurs in the Gobi.* Millbrook Press, 1997. *(I)*

Funston, Sylvia. *The Dinosaur Question and Answer Book: Everything Kids Want to Know about Dinosaurs, Fossils and Paleontology.* Joy Street/Little, 1992. *(P; I)*

Gay, Tanner Ottley. *Dinosaurs and Their Relatives in Action.* Aladdin, 1990. *(P)*

Gillette, J. Lynette. *Search for Seismosaurus.* Dial, 1994. *(P; I)*

Lessem, Don. *Bigger than T-Rex.* Crown, 1997; *Seismosaurus: The Longest Dinosaur; Utahraptor: The Deadliest Dinosaur.* Lerner, 1996; *Ornithomimids: The Fastest Dinosaur; Troodon: The Smartest Dinosaur.* Lerner, 1995. *(P; I)*

Lindsay, William. *DK Great Dinosaur Atlas.* DK, 1999. *(P; I)*

Markle, Sandra. *Outside and Inside Dinosaurs.* Aladdin, 2003. *(P; I)*

Marrin, Albert, and Andrews, Roy Chapman. *Secrets from the Rocks: Dinosaur Hunting with Roy Chapman Andrews.* Penguin Putnam, 2002. *(P; I)*

Nardo, Don. *The Extinction of the Dinosaurs.* Gale Group, 2001. *(I; A)*

Norell, Mark A., and Dingus, Lowell. *A Nest of Dinosaurs: The Story of Oviraptor.* Doubleday, 1999. *(I; A)*

Patent, Dorothy Hinshaw. *In Search of the Maiasaurs.* Marshall Cavendish, 1999. *(I)*

Relf, Patricia. *A Dinosaur Named Sue: The Story of the Colossal Fossil.* Scholastic, 2000. *(I)*

Willis, Paul, ed. *Dinosaurs.* Reader's Digest, 1999. *(P; I)*

Zimmerman, Howard. *Beyond the Dinosaurs!: Sky Dragons, Sea Monsters, Mega Mammals and Other Prehistoric Beasts.* Simon & Schuster, 2001; *Dinosaurs!: The Biggest, Baddest, Strangest, Fastest.* Simon & Schuster, 2000. *(P; I)*

Zoehfeld, Kathleen Weidner. *Did Dinosaurs Have Feathers?* HarperCollins, 2003. *(P)*; *Dinosaurs Big and Small.* HarperCollins, 2002. *(P)*; *Dinosaur Parents, Dinosaur Young: Uncovering the Mystery of Dinosaur Families.* Houghton Mifflin, 2001. *(P; I)*; *Terrible Tyrannosaurs.* HarperCollins, 2000. *(P)*; *Dinosaur Babies.* HarperCollins, 1999. *(P)*

DISABILITIES, PEOPLE WITH

Aaseng, Nathan. *Cerebral Palsy.* Watts, 1991. *(I; A)*

Aldape, Virginia Totorica. *Nicole's Story: A Book about a Girl with Juvenile Rheumatoid Arthritis (Meeting the Challenge Series).* Lerner, 1996. *(P; I)*

Bergman, Thomas. *Going Places: Children Living with Cerebral Palsy.* Gareth Stevens, 1991. *(P; I)*

Levinson, Harold N., and Sanders, Addie. *The Upside-Down Kids: Helping Dyslexic Children Understand Themselves and Their Disorder.* Evans, 1991. *(P; I)*

Porterfield, Kay Marie. *Straight Talk about Learning Disabilities.* Facts on File, 1999. *(I; A)*

DISARMAMENT

Gold, Susan Dudley. *Arms Control.* 21st Century, 1997. *(A)*

DISEASES

Aaseng, Nathan. *Multiple Sclerosis.* Watts, 2000. *(I; A)*

Aldape, Virginia Totrica. *Nicole's Story: A Book about a Girl with Juvenile Rheumatoid Arthritis.* Lerner, 1996. *(P; I)*

Altman, Linda Jacobs. *Plague and Pestilence: A History of Infectious Disease.* Enslow, 1998. *(I; A)*

Friedlander, Mark P. *Outbreak: Disease Detectives at Work.* Lerner, 2000. *(I; A)*

Giblin, James Cross. *When Plague Strikes: The Black Death, Smallpox, and AIDS.* HarperCollins, 1995. *(I; A)*

Hoff, Brent H., and Smith, Carter. *Mapping Epidemics: A Historical Atlas of Disease.* Watts, 2000. *(A)*

Latta, Sara L. *Food Poisoning and Foodborne Diseases.* Enslow, 1999. *(I; A)*

Zonderman, Jon, and Shader, Laurel. *Environmental Diseases; Nutritional Diseases.* Millbrook Press, 1995. *(I; A)*

DISINFECTANTS AND ANTISEPTICS

Watt, Susan. *Chlorine.* Marshall Cavendish, 2001. *(P; I)*

DISNEY, WALT

Canemaker, John. *Walt Disney's Nine Old Men and the Art of Animation.* Disney Press, 2001. *(I; A)*

Cole, Michael D. *Walt Disney: Creator of Mickey Mouse.* Enslow, 1996. *(I)*

Ford, Barbara. *Walt Disney: A Biography.* Walker, 2000. *(P; I)*

Hahn, Don. *Disney's Animation Magic: A Behind-the-Scenes Look at How an Animated Film Is Made.* Disney Press, 1996. *(P; I)*

Schroeder, Russell, ed. *Walt Disney: His Life in Pictures.* Disney, 1996. *(P; I)*

Selden, Bernice. *The Story of Walt Disney: Maker of Magical Worlds.* Gareth Stevens, 1996. *(P; I)*

Thomas, Bob. *Building a Company: Roy O. Disney and the Creation of an Entertainment Empire.* Disney Press, 1998. *(A)*; *Disney's Art of Animation: From Mickey Mouse to Hercules.* Disney, 1997 (2nd ed.). *(P; I; A)*

Watts, Steven. *Magic Kingdom: Walt Disney and the American Way of Life.* University of Missouri Press, 2001 (reprint). *(A)*

DIVING

Carson, Charles. *Make the Team: Swimming and Diving.* Little, 1991. *(P; I)*

Ditchfield, Christin. *Swimming and Diving.* Scholastic, 2000. *(P)*

Page, Jason. *Swimming: Sprints, Medleys, Diving, Water Polo, and Lots, Lots More.* Lerner, 2000. *(P; I; A)*

DIX, DOROTHEA LYNDE

Schleichert, Elizabeth. *The Life of Dorothea Dix.* 21st Century Books, 1992. *(P; I)*

DOCTORS

Storring, Rod. *A Doctor's Life: A Visual History of Doctors and Nurses Through the Ages.* Dutton, 1998. *(P; I)*

DOGS

George, Jean Craighead. *How to Talk to Your Dog.* HarperCollins, 2000. *(P)*

Ring, Elizabeth. *Performing Dogs: Stars of Stage, Screen, and Television; Ranch and Farm Dogs: Herders and Guards; Search and Rescue Dogs: Expert Trackers and Trailers.* Millbrook, 1994. *(P; I)*

DOLLHOUSES

Boulton, Vivienne. *The Dollhouse Decorator.* Dorling Kindersley, 1992. *(I; A)*

Harrop, Jane. *Dolls House Do-It-Yourself: Finishing Touches.* F & W Publications, 2004; *Dolls House Do-It-Yourself: Toys and Games.* F & W Publications, 2003. *(A)*

Hawkins, Sue. *Dolls House Do-It-Yourself: Embroidered Accessories.* F & W Publications, 2004; *Dolls House Do-It-Yourself: Carpets and Rugs.* F & W Publications, 2003. *(A)*

Theiss, Nola. *The Complete Guide to Remodeling and Expanding Your Dollhouse.* Sterling, 1993. *(I; A)*

DOLLS

Goodfellow, Caroline G.; Coleman, Dorothy; and Coleman, Evelyn Jane. *The Ultimate Doll Book.* Barnes & Noble, 2001. *(I; A)*

McGraw, Sheila. *Dolls Kids Can Make.* Firefly, 1995. *(I; A)*

Young, Robert S. *Dolls.* Silver Burdett Press, 1992. *(I)*

DOLPHINS AND PORPOISES

Dolphins and Porpoises. Facts on File, 1990. *(I)*

Berger, Melvin, and Berger, Gilda. *Is a Dolphin a Fish?: Questions and Answers about Dolphins.* Scholastic, 2002; *Do Whales Have Belly Buttons?: Questions and Answers about Whales and Dolphins.* Scholastic, 1999. *(P; I)*

Bright, Michael. *Dolphins.* DK, 2002. *(A)*

Cerullo, Mary M. *Dolphins: What They Can Teach Us.* Dutton, 1999. *(P; I)*

Dudzinski, Kathleen. *Meeting Dolphins: My Adventures in the Sea.* National Geographic, 2000. *(P; I)*

Grover, Wayne. *Dolphin Adventure: A True Story.* Greenwillow, 1990. *(P)*

Read, Andrew. *Porpoises.* Voyageur, 1999. *(I)*

Samuels, Amy. *Follow That Fin! Studying Dolphin Behavior.* Raintree Steck-Vaughn, 1999. *(P; I)*

Stoops, Erik Daniel; Martin, Jeffrey L.; and Stone, Debbie L. *Dolphins.* Sterling, 1996. *(P; I)*

Thomas, Peggy. *Marine Mammal Preservation.* Millbrook Press, 2000. *(I)*

Walker, Sally M. *Dolphins.* Carolrhoda, 1999. *(P; I)*

Wilson, Ben. *Dolphins of the World.* Voyageur Press, 2001. *(I; A)*

DOMINICAN REPUBLIC

Creed, Alexander. *Dominican Republic.* Chelsea House, 1999. *(I; A)*

Foley, Erin L. *Dominican Republic.* Marshall Cavendish, 1995 (2nd ed.). *(I; A)*

DONATELLO

Barter, James E., ed. *Artists of the Renaissance.* Thomson Gale, 1998. *(I; A)*

Janson, H. W., and Janson, Anthony F. *History of Art for Young People.* Abrams, 1997 (rev. ed.). *(I; A)*

DOVES AND PIGEONS

McDonald, Mary Ann. *Doves.* Child's World, 1999. *(P)*

Nofsinger, Ray, and Hargrove, Jim. *Pigeons and Doves.* Scholastic, 1993. *(P)*

Patent, Dorothy Hinshaw. *Pigeons.* Clarion Books, 1997. *(P; I)*

DOWN SYNDROME

Bowman-Kruhm, Mary. *Everything You Need to Know about Down Syndrome.* Rosen, 2000. *(P; I)*

Tocci, Salvatore. *Down Syndrome.* Watts, 2000. *(I; A)*

DOYLE, SIR ARTHUR CONAN

Doyle, Arthur Conan. Meyers, Jeffrey, and Meyers, Valerie, eds. *The Sir Arthur Conan Doyle Reader: From Sherlock Holmes to Spiritualism.* Rowman & Littlefield, 2002. *(A)*

Pascal, Janet B. *Arthur Conan Doyle: Beyond Baker Street.* Oxford, 2000. *(I; A)*

DRAMA

Bany-Winters, Lisa. *Show Time!: Music, Dance, and Drama Activities for Kids.* Chicago Review Press, 2000. *(P; I)*

Bloom, Harold, ed. *Arthur Miller's Death of a Salesman (Bloom's Notes Series); Arthur Miller's The Crucible (Bloom's Notes Series); Sophocles: The Oedipus Plays (Bloom's Notes Series).* Chelsea House, 1995. *(A)*

Boland, Robert, and Argentini, Paul. *Musicals!: Directing School and Community Theatre.* Rowman & Littlefield, 1997. *(A)*

Burton, Marilee Robin. *Artists at Work.* Chelsea Clubhouse, 2003. *(P)*

Egendorf, Laura K. *Elizabethan Drama.* Thomson Gale, 2000. *(A)*

Halliwell, Sarah, ed. *20th Century: Post-1945 Artists, Writers, and Composers; 20th Century: Pre-1945 Artists, Writers, and Composers; 19th Century: Artists, Writers, and Composers; The Romantics: Artists, Writers, and Composers.* Raintree, 1998; *18th Century: Artists, Writers, and Composers; 17th Century: Artists, Writers, and Composers; Impressionism and Postimpressionism: Artists, Writers, and Composers.;* Raintree, 1997; *Renaissance: Artists and Writers.* Marshall Cavendish, 1997. *(I)*

Holden, Amanda, ed. *The New Penguin Opera Guide.* Penguin Group, 2002 (rev. ed.). *(A)*

Nardo, Don, ed. *Greek Drama.* Greenhaven, 1999. *(A)*

Novak, Elaine A., and Novak, Deborah. *Staging Musical Theatre: A Complete Guide for Directors, Choreographers, and Producers.* F & W Publications, 1996. *(A)*

Whiting, Jim. *Masters of Music: The Life and Times of George Gershwin; Masters of Music: The Life and Times of Gilbert and Sullivan.* Mitchell Lane, 2004. *(I)*

Zinsser, William Knowlton. *Easy to Remember: The Great American Songwriters and Their Songs for Broadway Shows and Hollywood Musicals.* Godine, David R., 2001. *(A)*

DREISER, THEODORE

Loving, Jerome. *The Last Titan: A Life of Theodore Dreiser.* University of California Press, 2005. *(A)*

DRED SCOTT DECISION

Herda, D. J. *The Dred Scott Case: Slavery and Citizenship.* Enslow, 1994. *(I; A)*

DREYFUS, ALFRED

Finkelstein, Norman H. *Captain of Innocence.* Penguin, 1991. *(I; A)*

DRIVER EDUCATION

Greenberger, Robert. *Careers without College for People Who Love to Drive.* Rosen, 2003. *(I; A)*

Skurzynski, Gloria. *Almost the Real Thing: Simulation in Your High-Tech World.* Simon & Schuster, 1991. *(I)*

Winters, Adam. *Everything You Need to Know about Being a Teen Driver.* Rosen, 2000. *(I; A)*

DRUM

Dearling, Robert, ed. *The Illustrated Encyclopedia of Musical Instruments.* Gale Research, 1996. *(I; A)*

DU BOIS, W. E. B.

Cryan-Hicks, Kathryn T. *W. E. B. Du Bois: Crusader for Peace.* Discovery, 1991. *(I)*

Hinman, Bonnie. *A Stranger in My Own House: The Story of W. E. B. Du Bois.* Morgan Reynolds, 2005. *(I; A)*

McKissack, Patricia C., and McKissack, Fredrick L. *W. E. B. Du Bois.* Scholastic, 1990. *(I; A)*

Troy, Don. *W. E. B. Du Bois.* Child's World, 1999. *(P; I)*

DUNBAR, PAUL LAURENCE

Reef, Catherine. *Paul Laurence Dunbar: Portrait of a Poet.* Enslow, 2000. *(I; A)*

E (LETTER)

Samoyault, Tiphaine. *Alphabetical Order: How the Alphabet Began.* Viking, 1998. *(P; I)*

EAGLES

Grambo, Rebecca L. *Eagles.* Voyageur, 1999. *(I)*

Horton, Casey. *Eagles.* Benchmark, 1996. *(I)*

Penny, Malcolm. *Golden Eagle: Habitats, Life Cycles, Food Chains, Threats.* Raintree, 2002. *(P; I)*

EAR

Silverstein, Alvin, and Nunn, Laura Silverstein. *Senses and Sensors: Hearing.* Lerner, 2001. *(I)*

EARHART, AMELIA

Adler, David A. *A Picture Book of Amelia Earhart.* Holiday House, 1998. *(P)*

Par, Jan. *Amelia Earhart: First Lady of Flight.* Watts, 1997. *(I)*

Randolph, Blythe. *Amelia Earhart.* Marshall Cavendish, 1991. *(I; A)*

Szabo, Corrine. *Sky Pioneer: A Photobiography of Amelia Earhart.* National Geographic, 1997. *(P; I)*

EARP, WYATT

Staeger, Rob. *Wyatt Earp.* Chelsea House, 2001. *(P; I)*

Thrasher, Thomas E. *Gunfighters.* Gale Group, 2000. *(I)*

EARTH

Alessandrello, Anna. *The Earth: Origins and Evolution.* Steck-Vaughn, 1994. *(I; A)*

Asimov, Isaac, and Hantula, Richard. *Earth.* Gareth Stevens, 2002 (rev. ed.). *(P; I)*

Bortz, Alfred B. *Collision Course!: Cosmic Impacts and Life on Earth.* Lerner, 2001. *(I; A)*

Brimner, Larry Dane. *Earth.* Scholastic, 1999. *(P)*

Clifford, Nick J. *Incredible Earth.* Firefly, 1996. *(I)*

Curtis, Neil; Muirden, James; and Allaby, Michael. *Planet Earth: Visual Factfinder.* Houghton Mifflin, 1993. *(I)*

Durell, Ann; Paterson, Katherine; and George, Jean Craighead, eds. *The Big Book for Our Planet.* Dutton, 1993. *(P; I)*

Gibbons, Gail. *Planet Earth/Inside Out.* Morrow, 1995. *(P; I)*

Knapp, Brian. *Earth Science: Discovering the Secrets of the Earth.* Grolier, 2000 (8 vols.). *(I; A)*

Miller, Ron. *Worlds Beyond: Earth and the Moon.* Lerner, 2003. *(I)*

Nicolson, Cynthia Pratt. *The Earth.* Kids Can Press, 1997. *(P; I)*

Patent, Dorothy Hinshaw. *Shaping the Earth.* Clarion, 2000. *(P; I)*

Sattler, Helen Roney. *Our Patchwork Planet.* Lothrop, 1995. *(I; A)*

Taylor, Barbara. *Earth Explained: A Beginner's Guide to Our Planet.* Twenty-First Century, 1997. *(I)*

Van Rose, Susanna. *Earth.* Dorling Kindersley, 1994. *(I; A)*

Vogt, Gregory L. *Earth.* Millbrook Press, 1996. *(P; I)*

Zoehfeld, Kathleen Weidner. *How Are Mountains Made?* HarperCollins, 1995. *(P)*

EARTH, HISTORY OF

Clifford, Nick. *Inside Guides: Incredible Earth.* DK, 1996. *(I)*

Doyle, Peter; Bennett, Matthew R.; and Baxter, Alistair N. *Key to Earth History: An Introduction to Stratigraphy.* Wiley, 2001. *(I; A)*

Nicolson, Cynthia Pratt. *The Earth.* Kids Can Press, 1997. *(P; I)*

Patent, Dorothy Hinshaw. *Shaping the Earth.* Houghton Mifflin, 2000. *(P; I)*

Redfern, Ron. *Origins: The Evolution of Continents, Oceans and Life.* University of Oklahoma Press, 2001. *(A)*

Taylor, Barbara. *Earth Explained: A Beginner's Guide to Our Planet.* Twenty-First Century, 1997. *(I)*

EARTH-MOVING MACHINERY

Jennings, Terry J. *Cranes, Dumptrucks, Bulldozers, and Other Building Machines.* Kingfisher, 1993. *(I)*

Royston, Angela. *Diggers and Dump Trucks.* Aladdin, 1991. *(P)*

EARTHQUAKES

Barnard, Bryn. *Dangerous Planet: Natural Disasters That Changed History.* Crown Books, 2003. *(I; A)*

Berger, Melvin, and Berger, Gilda. *Why Do Volcanoes Blow Their Tops?: Questions and Answers about Volcanoes and Earthquakes.* Scholastic, 2000. *(P)*

Meister, Cari. *Earthquakes.* ABDO, 1999. *(P; I)*

Nicolson, Cynthia Pratt. *Disaster: Earthquake.* Kids Can Press, 2002. *(P; I)*

Sherrow, Victoria. *San Francisco Earthquake, 1989: Death and Destruction.* Enslow, 1998. *(P; I)*

Vogel, Carole G. *Shock Waves through Los Angeles: The Northridge Earthquake.* Little, 1996. *(P; I)*

Walker, Sally M. *Earthquakes.* Lerner, 1996. *(P; I)*

Worth, Richard. *The San Francisco Earthquake (Environmental Disasters Series).* Facts on File, 2005. *(I)*

EASTER

Gulevich, Tanya. *Encyclopedia of Easter, Carnival and Lent: Over 150 Alphabetically Arranged Entries Covering All Aspects of Easter, Carnival and Lent.* Omnigraphics, 2001. *(I; A)*

Kimmel, Eric A., reteller. *The Birds' Gift: A Ukrainian Easter Story.* Holiday House, 1999. *(P)*

Merrick, Patrick. *Easter Bunnies.* Child's World, 1999. *(P)*

Sanders, Nancy I. *Easter.* Scholastic, 2003. *(P)*

Thompson, Lauren. *Love One Another: The Story of Easter.* Scholastic, 2000. *(P)*

EASTMAN, GEORGE

Ford, Carin T. *George Eastman: The Kodak Camera Man.* Enslow, 2004. *(P)*

ECLIPSES

Aronson, Billy. *Eclipses: Nature's Blackouts.* Watts, 1997. *(I)*

ECOLOGY

Preparing for a Career in the Environment. Ferguson, 1998. *(A)*

Behler, Deborah A. *The Rain Forests of the Pacific Northwest.* Marshall Cavendish, 2000. *(I; A)*

Bial, Raymond. *A Handful of Dirt.* Walker, 2000. *(P; I)*

Black, Wallace B., and Willis, Terri. *Cars: An Environmental Challenge.* Scholastic, 1992. *(I; A)*

Blaustein, Daniel. *Everglades and the Gulf Coast.* Marshall Cavendish, 2000. *(I)*

Bograd, Larry. *The Rocky Mountains.* Marshall Cavendish, 2000. *(I)*

Carr, Terry. *Spill!: The Story of the Exxon Valdez.* Watts, 1991. *(I; A)*

Castner, James L. *River Life: Deep in the Amazon; Surviving in the Rain Forest: Deep in the Amazon.* Marshall Cavendish, 2002; *Layers of Life: Deep in the Amazon; Native Peoples: Deep in the Amazon; Partners and Rivals: Deep in the Amazon; Rainforest Researchers: Deep in the Amazon.* Marshall Cavendish, 2001. *(I; A)*

Fanning, Odom. *Opportunities in Environmental Careers.* VGM, 1995. *(A)*

Lavies, Bianca. *Compost Critters.* Dutton, 1993. *(P; I)*

Leuzzi, Linda. *Life Connections: Pioneers in Ecology.* Watts, 2000; *To the Young Environmentalist: Lives Dedicated to Preserving the Natural World.* Scholastic, 1998. *(I; A)*

Markley, Oliver W., and McCuan, Walter R., eds. *21st Century Earth: Opposing Viewpoints.* Greenhaven Press, 1996. *(I; A)*

Mudd-Ruth, Maria. *The Mississippi River; The Pacific Coast.* Marshall Cavendish, 2000. *(I; A)*; *The Deserts of the Southwest.* Marshall Cavendish, 1998. *(I)*

Sayre, April Pulley. *Tundra.* Henry Holt, 1997. *(I)*

Skelton, Olivia, and Skelton, Renee. *The Atlantic Coast.* Marshall Cavendish, 2000. *(I; A)*

Tagliaferro, Linda. *Galapagos Islands: Nature's Delicate Balance at Risk.* Lerner, 2000. *(I)*

ECUADOR

Beirne, Barbara. *The Children of the Ecuadorean Highlands.* Lerner, 1996. *(P; I)*

Daniels, Amy S. *Ecuador.* Gareth Stevens, 2002. *(I)*

Morrison, Marion. *Ecuador.* Scholastic, 2000. *(I)*

Tagliaferro, Linda. *Galapagos Islands: Nature's Delicate Balance at Risk.* Lerner, 2000. *(I)*

EDISON, THOMAS ALVA

Adair, Gene. *Thomas Alva Edison: Inventing the Electric Age.* Oxford, 1996. *(I; A)*

Adler, David A. *A Picture Book of Thomas Alva Edison.* Holiday House, 1996. *(P)*

Buranelli, Vincent. *Thomas Alva Edison.* Silver Burdett, 1989. *(I)*

Ford, Carin T. *Thomas Edison: Inventor.* Enslow, 2002. *(P)*

Murcia, Rebecca Thatcher. *Thomas Edison: Great Inventor.* Mitchell Lane, 2004. *(I)*

Sproule, Anna. *Thomas A. Edison: The World's Greatest Inventor.* Gale Group, 2000. *(I; A)*

EELS

Halton, Cheryl Mays. *Those Amazing Eels.* Dillon, 1990. *(I)*

Hirschmann, Kris. *Moray Eels.* Gale Group, 2002. *(P; I)*

Wu, Norbert. *Beneath the Waves: Exploring the Hidden World of the Kelp Forest.* Chronicle, 1997. *(P; I)*

EGGS AND EMBRYOS

Griffin, Margaret, and Seed, Deborah. *The Amazing Egg Book.* Addison Wesley Longman, 1990. *(P; I)*

EGYPT

Aykroyd, Clarissa. *Egypt.* Mason Crest, 2002. *(I; A)*

Heinrichs, Ann. *Egypt (Enchantment of the World, Second Series).* Scholastic, 2006. *(I; A)*

Shuter, Jane. *Egypt.* Raintree Steck-Vaughn, 1998. *(I; A)*

Solecki, John. *Hosni Mubarak.* Chelsea House, 1991. *(I)*

EGYPT, ANCIENT

Altman, Susan, and Lechner, Susan. *Ancient Egypt.* Scholastic, 2001. *(P)*

Baker, Rosalie F., and Baker, Charles F. *Ancient Egyptians: Building for Eternal Glory.* Oxford, 2001. *(I; A)*

Bianchi, Robert S. *The Nubians: People of the Ancient Nile.* Millbrook Press, 1994. *(A)*

Broida, Marian. *Ancient Egyptians and Their Neighbors: An Activity Guide.* Chicago Review, 1999. *(I)*

David, Rosalie. *Discovering Ancient Egypt.* Facts on File, 1994. *(A)*

Fletcher, Joann, and Malam, John. *Mummies: And the Secrets of Ancient Egypt.* DK, 2001. *(P; I)*

Greenblatt, Miriam. *Hatshepsut and Ancient Egypt.* Marshall Cavendish, 2000. *(I; A)*

Greene, Jacqueline Dembar. *Slavery in Ancient Egypt and Mesopotamia.* Watts, 2000. *(P; I)*

Marston, Elsa. *The Ancient Egyptians.* Marshall Cavendish, 1996. *(I)*

Millard, Anne. *Going to War in Ancient Egypt.* Scholastic, 2001. *(I)*

Perl, Lila, and Weihs, Erika. *Mummies, Tombs, and Treasure: Secrets of Ancient Egypt.* Houghton Mifflin, 1991. *(P; I)*

EGYPTIAN ART AND ARCHITECTURE

Hodge, Susie. *Ancient Egyptian Art.* Heinemann, 1997. *(P; I)*

Mann, Elizabeth. *The Great Pyramid: The Story of the Farmers, The God-King, and the Most Astounding Structure Ever Built.* Mikaya Press, 1996. *(P; I)*

Tyldesley, Joyce. *The Mummy: Unwrap the Ancient Secrets of the Mummies' Tombs.* Carlton, 2000. *(A)*

EINSTEIN, ALBERT

Bernstein, Jeremy. *Albert Einstein and the Frontiers of Physics.* Oxford, 1996. *(I; A)*

Goldberg, Jake. *Albert Einstein: The Rebel behind Relativity.* Watts, 1996. *(I; A)*

Goldenstern, Joyce. *Albert Einstein: Physicist and Genius.* Enslow, 2001. *(I; A)*

McPherson, Stephanie Sammartino. *Ordinary Genius: The Story of Albert Einstein.* Carolrhoda, 1995. *(I)*

Parker, Steve. *Albert Einstein and Relativity.* Chelsea House, 1995. *(P)*

Severance, John B. *Einstein: Visionary Scientist.* Clarion, 1999. *(I; A)*

ELECTRIC GENERATORS

Berger, Melvin. *Switch On, Switch Off.* HarperCollins, 1990. *(P)*

ELECTRICITY

Ardley, Neil. *Electricity.* New Discovery, 1992. *(I)*

Billings, Charlene W. *Superconductivity: From Discovery to Breakthrough.* Dutton, 1991. *(P; I)*

Dispezio, Michael. *Awesome Experiments in Electricity and Magnetism.* Sterling, 1999. *(I; A)*

Fleisher, Paul. *Waves: Principles of Light, Electricity, and Magnetism.* Lerner, 2001. *(I; A)*

Gardner, Robert. *Science Projects about Elecricity and Magnets.* Enslow, 1994. *(P; I)*

Good, Keith. *Zap It!: Exciting Electricity Activities.* Lerner, 1999. *(P; I)*

Math, Irwin. *Tomorrow's Technology: Experimenting with the Science of the Future.* Simon & Schuster, 1992. *(A)*

Wood, Robert W., and Wright, Bill. *Electricity and Magnetism Fundamentals.* Chelsea House, 1998. *(I; A)*

Zubrowski, Bernie. *Blinkers and Buzzers.* Morrow, 1991. *(I)*

ELECTRON MICROSCOPE

Tomb, Howard. *Microaliens: Dazzling Journeys with an Electron Microscope.* Farrar, 1993. *(I)*

ELEMENTS, CHEMICAL

Angliss, Sarah. *Gold.* Marshall Cavendish, 2000. *(I)*

Beatty, Richard. *Manganese.* Marshall Cavendish, 2004; *Copper; Phosphorus; Sulfur.* Marshall Cavendish, 2000. *(I)*

Farndon, John. *Aluminum; Calcium; Hydrogen.* Marshall Cavendish, 2000; *Nitrogen; Oxygen.* Marshall Cavendish, 1998. *(I)*

ELEPHANTS

Darling, Kathy. *The Elephant Hospital.* Lerner, 2000. *(P; I)*

Grace, Eric S. *Elephants.* Sierra Club, 1996. *(P)*

Johnston, Marianne. *Mastodons, Mammoths, and Modern-Day Elephants.* Rosen, 2003. *(P; I)*

MacMillan, Dianne M. *Elephants: Our Last Land Giants.* Lerner, 1993. *(P; I)*

Moss, Cynthia. *Little Big Ears: The Story of Ely.* Simon & Schuster, 1996. *(P)*

Patent, Dorothy Hinshaw. *African Elephants: Giants of the Land.* Holiday, 1991. *(P; I)*

Poole, Joyce. *Elephants.* Voyageur Press, 1997. *(A)*

Pringle, Laurence P. *Elephant Woman: Cynthia Moss Explores the World of Elephants.* Simon & Schuster, 1997. *(I)*

Sayre, April Pulley. *Secrets of Sound: Studying the Calls of Whales, Elephants, and Birds.* Houghton Mifflin, 2002. *(I; A)*

Schwabacher, Martin. *Elephants.* Marshall Cavendish, 2000. *(P; I)*

Smith, Roland, and Schmidt, Michael J. *In the Forest with the Elephants.* Harcourt, 1998. *(P; I)*

ELIJAH

Goldin, Barbara Diamond. *Journeys with Elijah: Eight Tales of the Prophet.* Harcourt/Gulliver, 1999. *(P; I)*

ELIZABETH I

Hazell, Rebecca. *Heroines: Great Women through the Ages.* Abbeville Press, 1996. *(I)*

Lace, William W. *Elizabeth I and Her Court.* Thomson Gale, 2002. *(I; A)*

Meltzer, Milton. *Ten Queens: Portraits of Women of Power.* Dutton, 1997. *(I; A)*

Thomas, Jane Resh. *Behind the Mask: The Life of Queen Elizabeth I.* Clarion, 1998. *(I; A)*

Weir, Alison. *The Life of Elizabeth I.* Ballantine, 1998; *The Children of Henry VIII.* Ballantine, 1997. *(A)*

ELIZABETH II

Barton-Wood, Sara. *Queen Elizabeth II: Monarch of Our Times (Famous Lives Series).* Harcourt, 2002. *(P; I)*

EMERSON, RALPH WALDO

Bloom, Harold, ed. *Ralph Waldo Emerson.* Chelsea House, 1992. *(A)*

EMOTIONS

Sherrow, Victoria. *Dropping Out.* Marshall Cavendish, 1995. *(I; A)*

Vecchione, Patrice, ed. *Revenge and Forgiveness: An Anthology of Poems.* Henry Holt, 2004. *(I; A)*

ENDANGERED SPECIES

Becker, John E. *Florida Panther.* Gale Group, 2003; *Bald Eagle; Bats; Manatees; North American Beaver; North American River Otters.* Gale Group, 2002. *(P; I)*

Cohen, Daniel. *The Modern Ark: Saving Endangered Species.* Penguin, 1995. *(I; A)*

Denton, Peter. *World Wildlife Fund.* Silver Burdett Press, 1994. *(I; A)*

Dobson, David. *Can We Save Them?* Charlesbridge, 1997. *(P)*

Dudley, William, ed. *Endangered Oceans*. Gale Group, 1999. *(A)*

Jackson, Donna M. *The Wildlife Detectives*. Houghton Mifflin, 2002. *(P; I)*

McMillan, Bruce. *A Beach for the Birds*. Houghton Mifflin, 1993. *(P; I)*

Penny, Malcolm. *Endangered Species: Our Impact on the Planet*. Raintree Steck-Vaughn, 2002. *(I)*

Powell, Jillian. *World Organizations: World Wildlife Fund*. Scholastic, 2001. *(I; A)*

Pringle, Laurence. *Saving Our Wildlife*. Enslow, 1990. *(I; A)*

Ricciuti, Edward. *Wildlife Special Agent: Protecting Endangered Species*. Blackbirch, 1996. *(P; I)*

Sayre, April Pulley. *Endangered Birds of North America*. Millbrook Press, 1997. *(P; I)*

Thomas, Peggy. *Big Cat Conservation; Bird Alert; Marine Mammal Preservation; Reptile Rescue*. Millbrook Press, 2000. *(I)*

Vergoth, Karin, and Lampton, Christopher. *Endangered Species*. Watts, 1999. *(I)*

ENGINEERING

Bortz, Alfred B. *Techno-Matter: The Materials Behind the Marvels*. Lerner, 2001. *(A)*; *To the Young Scientist: Reflections on Doing and Living Science*. Scholastic, 1997. *(I; A)*

Gies, Frances, and Gies, Joseph. *Cathedral, Forge, and Waterwheel: Technology and Invention in the Middle Ages*. HarperCollins, 1994. *(A)*

Johmann, Carol A., and Rieth, Elizabeth J. *Bridges! Amazing Structures to Design, Build and Test*. Williamson, 1999. *(P; I)*

Mann, Elizabeth. *The Great Pyramid: The Story of the Farmers, The God-King, and the Most Astounding Structure Ever Built*. Mikaya Press, 1996. *(P; I)*

Maze, Stephanie. *I Want to Be an Engineer*. Harcourt, 1999. *(P; I)*

McAlpine, Margaret. *Working in Engineering*. Gareth Stevens, 2005. *(I; A)*

Pasternak, Ceel, and Thornburg, Linda. *Cool Careers for Girls in Engineering*. Impact, 1999. *(I)*

ENGLAND

Blashfield, Jean F. *England*. Scholastic, 1997. *(I)*

Burgan, Michael. *England*. Scholastic, 1999. *(P)*

Davis, Kevin A. *Look What Came from England*. Scholastic, 1999. *(P)*

Lyle, Garry. *England*. Chelsea House, 1999. *(I; A)*

ENGLAND, HISTORY OF

Ashby, Ruth. *Elizabethan England*. Marshall Cavendish, 1999. *(I)*

Brooks, Polly Schoyer. *Queen Eleanor: Independent Spirit of the Medieval World: A Biography of Eleanor of Aquitaine*. Houghton Mifflin, 1999 (reprint). *(I; A)*

Crompton, Samuel Willard. *Hastings*. Chelsea House, 2002. *(I; A)*

Hinds, Kathryn. *Medieval England*. Marshall Cavendish, 2001. *(I; A)*

Konstam, Angus, and Kean, Roger. *Atlas of Medieval Europe*. Facts on File, 2000. *(A)*

Thomas, Jane Resh. *Behind the Mask: The Life of Queen Elizabeth I*. Clarion, 1998. *(I; A)*

Weatherly, Myra S. *William Marshal: Medieval England's Greatest Knight*. Reynolds, 2001. *(I)*

Weir, Alison. *Eleanor of Aquitaine: A Life; Henry VIII: The King and His Court*. Ballantine, 2001; *The Life of Elizabeth I*. Ballantine, 1998; *The Children of Henry VIII*. Ballantine, 1997; *The Princes in the Tower; The Wars of the Roses*. Ballantine, 1995; *The Six Wives of Henry VIII*. Ballantine, 1993. *(A)*

ENGLISH ART AND ARCHITECTURE

Ashby, Ruth. *Elizabethan England*. Marshall Cavendish, 1999. *(I)*

Kenner, Robert. *J. M. W. Turner: Introductions to Art*. Abrams, 1995. *(I; A)*

Lace, William W. *Elizabethan England*. Lucent, 1994. *(I; A)*

McLanathan, Richard. *Peter Paul Rubens*. Abrams, 1995. *(I; A)*

Shuter, Jane. *Carisbrooke Castle*. Heinemann, 1999. *(I)*

Smith, Nigel. *The Houses of Parliament: Their History and Purpose*. Raintree Steck-Vaughn, 1997. *(I; A)*

ENGLISH LITERATURE

Aller, Susan Bivin. *J. M. Barrie: The Magic behind Peter Pan*. Lerner, 1994. *(I)*

Aronson, Marc. *Sir Walter Raleigh and the Quest for El Dorado*. Clarion, 2000. *(I; A)*

Ashby, Ruth. *Elizabethan England*. Marshall Cavendish, 1999. *(I)*

Dominic, Catherine C., ed. *Epics for Students*. Gale Group, 1997. *(A)*

Thompson, Stephen P., ed. *Readings on Beowulf*. Greenhaven Press, 1998. *(A)*

ENGLISH MUSIC

Anderson, Matthew T. *Handel, Who Knew What He Liked*. Candlewick Press, 2001. *(P)*

Getzinger, Donna, and Felsenfeld, Daniel. *George Frideric Handel and Music for Voices*. Morgan Reynolds, 2004. *(I; A)*

Halliwell, Sarah, ed. *19th Century: Artists, Writers, and Composers*. Raintree, 1998; *18th Century: Artists, Writers, and Composers*. Raintree, 1997; *17th Century: Artists, Writers, and Composers*. Raintree, 1997. *(I)*

Krull, Kathleen. *Lives of the Musicians: Good Times, Bad Times (And What the Neighbors Thought)*. Raintree Steck-Vaughn, 1998. *(I; A)*

ENLIGHTENMENT, AGE OF

Giblin, James Cross. *The Amazing Life of Benjamin Franklin*. Scholastic, 2000. *(P; I)*

Halliwell, Sarah. *The 18th Century: Artists, Writers, and Composers.* Raintree Steck-Vaughn, 1997. *(I)*

Jaffe, Steven H. *Who Were the Founding Fathers?: Two Hundered Years of Reinventing American History.* Holt, 1996. *(I; A)*

ENVIRONMENT

Preparing for a Career in the Environment. Ferguson, 1998. *(A)*

Bowden, Rob. *Sustainable World: Environments.* Thomson Gale, 2004; *Food Supply: Our Impact on the Planet; Overcrowded World?: Our Impact on the Planet; Waste, Recycling and Reuse: Our Impact on the Planet.* Raintree Steck-Vaughn, 2002. *(I; A)*

Chapman, Matthew, and Bowden, Rob. *Air Pollution: Our Impact on the Planet.* Raintree Steck-Vaughn, 2002. *(I; A)*

Fanning, Odom. *Opportunities in Environmental Careers.* VGM, 1995. *(A)*

Gold, John C. *Environments of the Western Hemisphere.* Twenty-First Century, 1997. *(I; A)*

Kouhoupt, Rudy, and Marti, Donald B. *How on Earth Do We Recycle Metal?* Millbrook, 1992. *(I)*

Lauber, Patricia. *She's Wearing a Dead Bird on Her Head!* Hyperion, 1995. *(P); You're aboard Spaceship Earth.* HarperCollins, 1996. *(P)*

Lowery, Linda. *Earth Day.* Lerner, 2003 (rev. ed.). *(P)*

McLeish, Ewan. *Energy Resources: Our Impact on the Planet; Rain Forests: Our Impact on the Planet.* Raintree Steck-Vaughn, 2002. *(I; A)*

Nelson, Corinna. *Working in the Environment.* Lerner, 1999. *(I)*

Netzley, Patricia D. *Environmental Groups.* Gale Group, 1997. *(I; A)*

Penny, Malcolm. *Endangered Species: Our Impact on the Planet.* Raintree Steck-Vaughn, 2002. *(I)*

Pringle, Laurence. *The Environmental Movement: From Its Roots to the Challenges of a New Century.* HarperCollins, 2000. *(I)*

Scoones, Simon. *Climate Change: Our Impact on the Planet.* Raintree Steck-Vaughn, 2002. *(I)*

Stanley, Phyllis M. *American Environmental Heroes.* Enslow, 1996. *(I; A)*

Walker, Jane. *The Ozone Hole.* Gloucester, 1993. *(I; A)*

Zeaman, John. *Overpopulation.* Scholastic, 2002. *(I; A)*

Zonderman, Jon, and Shader, Laurel. *Environmental Diseases.* Millbrook Press, 1995. *(I; A)*

ENZYMES

Ballard, Carol. *The Stomach and Digestive System.* Raintree Steck-Vaughn, 1997. *(I)*

Ganeri, Anita. *Eating.* Raintree Steck-Vaughn, 1996. *(P)*

Maurer, Tracy. *Digestion.* Rourke, 1999. *(P)*

Showers, Paul. *What Happens to a Hamburger?* HarperCollins, 2001. *(P)*

Stille, Darlene R. *The Digestive System.* Children's Press, 1998. *(P)*

ERICSON, LEIF

Klingel, Cynthia Fitterer, and Noyed, Robert B. *Leif Eriksson: Norwegian Explorer.* Child's World, 2002. *(P; I)*

Simon, Charnan. *Leif Eriksson and the Vikings.* Children's Press, 1991. *(I)*

ERIC THE RED

Gallagher, Jim. *Viking Explorers.* Chelsea House, 2000. *(P; I)*

Klingel, Cynthia Fitterer, and Noyed, Robert B. *Leif Eriksson: Norwegian Explorer.* Child's World, 2002. *(P; I)*

Simon, Charnan. *Leif Eriksson and the Vikings.* Children's Press, 1991. *(I)*

West, Delno C., and West, Jean M. *Braving the North Atlantic: The Vikings, the Cabots, and Jacques Cartier Voyage to America.* Simon & Schuster, 1996. *(I)*

ERIE CANAL

Doherty, Craig A., and Doherty, Katherine M. *The Erie Canal.* Blackbirch Press, 1996. *(P; I)*

Harness, Cheryl. *The Amazing Impossible Erie Canal.* Simon & Schuster, 1995. *(P; I)*

Lourie, Peter. *Erie Canal: Canoeing America's Great Waterway.* Boyds Mills Press, 1999. *(P; I)*

Santella, Andrew. *The Erie Canal (We the People Series).* Compass Point Books, 2004. *(P; I)*

ERITREA

Berg, Lois Anne. *An Eritrean Family.* Lerner, 1996. *(I)*

ESTONIA

Estonia: Then and Now. Lerner, 1992. *(I; A)*

Flint, David C. *The Baltic States: Estonia, Latvia, Lithuania.* Millbrook Press, 1992. *(P; I)*

ETHICS

Jussim, Daniel. *Medical Ethics.* Silver Burdett, 1990. *(I; A)*

ETHNIC GROUPS

Levinson, David H. *Ethnic Groups Worldwide: A Ready Reference Handbook.* Greenwood, 1998. *(I; A)*

ETIQUETTE

Barmier, James. *Life in America 100 Years Ago: Manners and Customs.* Chelsea House, 1995. *(I)*

Dougherty, Karla. *The Rules to Be Cool: Etiquette and Netiquette.* Enslow, 2001. *(I; A)*

Dunnewind, Stephanie. *Come to Tea: Fun Tea Party Themes, Recipes, Crafts, Games, Etiquette and More.* Sterling, 2002. *(P; I)*

Lauber, Patricia. *What You Never Knew about Fingers, Forks, and Chopsticks.* Simon & Schuster, 1999. *(P; I)*

Lewis, Barbara A. *Being Your Best: Character Building for Kides 7-10.* Free Spirit, 1999; *What Do You Stand*

For? A Kid's Guide to Building Character. Free Spirit, 1997. *(I; A)*

Packer, Alex J. *How Rude! Handbook of Family Manners for Teens: Avoiding Strife in Family Life; How Rude! Handbook of Friendship and Dating Manners for Teens: Surviving the Social Scene; How Rude! Handbook of School Manners for Teens: Civility in the Hallowed Halls.* Free Spirit Publishing, 2004; *How Rude!: The Teenagers' Guide to Good Manners, Proper Behavior, and Not Grossing People Out.* Free Spirit Publishing, 1997. *(I; A)*

Polisar, Barry Louis. *Don't Do That!: A Child's Guide to Bad Manners, Ridiculous Rules, and Inadequate Etiquette.* Rainbow Morning Music, 1995. *(P)*

Post, Peggy, and Senning, Cindy Post. *Emily Post's The Guide to Good Manners for Kids.* HarperCollins, 2004. *(P; I)*

EUROPE

National Geographic World Atlas for Young Explorers. National Geographic Society, 2003 (rev. ed.). *(P; I)*

Caselli, Giovanni. *The Roman Empire and the Dark Ages.* McGraw-Hill, 1998. *(I)*

Konstam, Angus, and Kean, Roger. *Atlas of Medieval Europe.* Facts on File, 2000. *(A)*

McGowen, Tom. *Frederick the Great, Bismarck, and the Building of the German Empire in World History.* Enslow, 2002. *(I; A)*

Petersen, David. *Europe.* Scholastic, 1998. *(P; I)*

EUROPEAN UNION

Powell, Jillian. *World Organizations: European Union.* Scholastic, 2001. *(I; A)*

Press, Petra. *European Union.* Gareth Stevens, 2003. *(I)*

EVEREST, MOUNT

Brennan, Kristine. *Sir Edmund Hillary: Modern-Day Explorer.* Chelsea House, 2000. *(I)*

Jenkins, Steve. *The Top of the World: Climbing Mount Everest.* Houghton, 1999. *(P; I)*

EVOLUTION

Alessandrello, Anna. Serini, Rocco, trans. *The Earth: Origins and Evolution.* Steck-Vaughn, 1994. *(I; A)*

Altman, Linda Jacobs. *Mr. Darwin's Voyage: People in Focus.* Silver Burdett Press, 1995. *(I; A)*

Bailey, Marilyn. *Evolution: Opposing Viewpoints.* Gale Group, 1990. *(I; A)*

Evans, Nathan Edward. *Charles Darwin: Revolutionary Biologist.* Lerner, 1993. *(I; A)*

Gamlin, Linda. *Evolution.* DK, 1993. *(P; I)*

Garassino, Alessandro. Serini, Rocco, trans. *Life: Origins and Evolution.* Steck-Vaughn, 1994. *(I; A)*

Jenkins, Steve. *Life on Earth: The Story of Evolution.* Houghton, 2002. *(P; I)*

Patent, Dorothy Hinshaw. *Charles Darwin: The Life of a Revolutionary Thinker.* Holiday House, 2001; *Biodiversity.* Houghton Mifflin, 1996. *(I; A)*

Ruiz, Andres Llamas. *Evolution.* Sterling, 1996. *(P; I)*

Silverstein, Alvin; Silverstein, Virginia; and Nunn, Laura Silverstein. *Evolution.* Millbrook Press, 1998. *(I; A)*

Stefoff, Rebecca. *Charles Darwin and the Evolution Revolution.* Oxford, 1996. *(I; A)*

EXPERIMENTS AND OTHER SCIENCE ACTIVITIES

Food and the Kitchen: Step-by-Step Science Activity Projects from the Smithsonian Institution. Gareth Stevens, 1993. *(I)*

Adams, Richard, and Gardner, Robert. *Ideas for Science Projects.* Watts, 1997; *More Ideas for Science Projects.* Watts, 1998. *(I; A)*

Barrow, Lloyd H. *Science Fair Projects Investigating Earthworms.* Enslow, 2000. *(P; I)*

Gardner, Robert. *Bicycle Science Projects: Physics on Wheels.* Enslow, 2004; *Science Projects about Methods of Measuring; Science Projects about Solids, Liquids, and Gases; Science Projects about Sound; Science Projects about the Physics of Sports; Science Projects about the Physics of Toys and Games.* Enslow, 2000; *Science Projects about Kitchen Chemistry; Science Projects about Physics in the Home; Science Projects about Plants; Science Projects about the Environment and Ecology.* Enslow, 1999. *(I; A)*

Goodstein, Madeline. *Sports Science Projects: The Physics of Balls in Motion.* Enslow, 1999. *(I; A)*

Krieger, Melanie Jacobs. *How to Excel in Science Competitions.* Enslow, 1999. (rev. ed.) *(I; A)*

Levine, Shar, and Johnstone, Leslie. *Shocking Science: Fun and Fascinating Electrical Experiments.* Sterling, 2000. *(P; I)* ; *The Optics Book: Fun Experiments with Light, Vision, and Color.* Sterling, 1999. *(I)*

Marks, Diana F. *Glues, Brews, and Goos: Recipes and Formulas for Almost Any Classroom Project.* Teacher Ideas, 1996. *(I)*

McLoughlin, Andrea. *Simple Science Experiments.* Scholastic/Cartwheel, 1996. *(P)*

Richards, Jon. *Chemicals and Reactions.* Millbrook/Cooper, 2000. *(P; I)*

Richards, Roy. *101 Science Surprises: Exciting Experiments with Everyday Materials.* Sterling, 1993. *(P; I)*

VanCleave, Janice. *Janice VanCleave's Guide to More of the Best Science Fair Projects; Janice VanCleave's Solar System: Mind Boggling Experiments You Can Turn into Science Fair Projects.* Wiley, 2000; *Janice VanCleave's 203 Icy, Freezing, Frosty, Cool and Wild Experiments.* Wiley, 1999. *(I)*; *Janice VanCleave's Earth Science for Every Kid: 101 Easy Experiments That Really Work.* Wiley, 1991. *(P; I)*; *Janice VanCleave's The Human Body for Every Kid: Easy Activities That Make Learning Science Fun.* Wiley, 1995. *(I)*; *Janice VanCleave's Physics for Every Kid.* Wiley 1991. *(I)*; *Janice VanCleave's Play and Find Out about the Human Body: Easy Experiments for Young Children.* Wiley, 1998. *(P)*; *Janice VanCleave's Play and Find Out about Nature: Easy Experiments for Young Children.* Wiley, 1997. *(P)*; *Janice VanCleave's*

Play and Find Out about Science: Easy Experiments for Young Children. Wiley, 1996. *(P)*

EXPLORATION AND DISCOVERY

Aaseng, Nathan. *You Are the Explorer.* Oliver Press, 2000. *(I; A)*

Alter, Judy. *Exploring and Mapping the American West.* Scholastic, 2001. *(P; I); Extraordinary Explorers and Adventurers.* Scholastic, 2001. *(I; A)*

Armstrong, Jennifer. *Shipwreck at the Bottom of the World: The Extraordinary True Story of Shackelton and the Endurance.* Crown, 1998. *(I; A)*

Atkins, Jeannine. *How High Can We Climb?: The Story of Women Explorers.* Farrar, 2005. *(I)*

Beattie, Owen, and Geiger, John. *Buried in Ice: The Mystery of a Lost Arctic Expedition.* Scholastic, 1992. *(I; A)*

Burleigh, Robert. *Black Whiteness: Admiral Byrd Alone in the Antarctic.* Simon & Schuster, 1998. *(P; I)*

Currie, Stephen. *Polar Explorers.* Gale Group, 2002. *(I; A)*

Fisher, Leonard Everett. *Prince Henry the Navigator.* Macmillan, 1990. *(P; I)*

Gallagher, Jim. *Viking Explorers.* Chelsea House, 2000. *(P; I)*

Kimmel, Elizabeth Cody. *Ice Story: Shackelton's Lost Expedition.* Clarion, 1999. *(I)*

Krensky, Stephen. *Who Really Discovered America?* Hastings House, 1991. *(I)*

Maestro, Betsy. *The Discovery of the Americas.* Lothrop, 1991. *(P)*

Matthews, Rupert. *Explorer.* Knopf, 1991. *(I; A)*

Maurer, Richard. *The Wild Colorado: The True Adventures of Fred Dellenbaugh, Age 17, on the Second Powell Expedition into the Grand Canyon.* Crown, 1999. *(I; A)*

McCurdy, Michael. *Trapped by the Ice!: Shackelton's Amazing Antarctic Adventure.* Walker, 1997. *(P; I)*

Polk, Milbry, and Tiegreen, Mary. *Women of Discovery: A Celebration of Intrepid Women Who Explored the World.* Crown, 2001. *(A)*

Schraff, Anne E. *American Heroes of Exploration and Flight.* Enslow, 1996. *(I; A)*

Slung, Michele B. *Living with Cannibals and Other Women's Adventures.* National Geographic Society, 2001. *(A)*

Steger, Will, and Bowermaster, Jon. *Over the Top of the World: Explorer Will Steger's Trek Across the Arctic.* Scholastic, 1996. *(P; I; A)*

Turk, Jon. *Cold Oceans: Adventures in Kayak, Rowboat, and Dogsled.* HarperCollins, 1999. *(A)*

EXTINCTION

Arnold, Caroline. *On the Brink of Extinction: The California Condor.* Harcourt, 1993. *(P; I)*

Facklam, Howard, and Facklam, Marjorie. *Plants: Extinction or Survival?* Enslow, 1990. *(I; A)*

Facklam, Marjorie. *And Then There Was One: The Mysteries of Extinction, Vol. 1.* Little, Brown, 1993. *(P; I)*

Hecht, Jeff. *Vanishing Life: The Mystery of Mass Extinctions.* Simon & Schuster, 1993. *(I; A)*

Hoff, Mary King, and Rodgers, Mary M. *Our Endangered Planet: Groundwater.* Lerner, 1991. *(I)*

Hoyt, Erich. *Extinction A-Z.* Enslow, 1991. *(A)*

Lessem, Don. *Dinosaurs to Dodos: An Encyclopedia of Extinct Animals.* Scholastic, 1999. *(P; I; A)*

Stefoff, Rebecca. *Extinction.* Chelsea House, 1992. *(I; A)*

EXTRASENSORY PERCEPTION (ESP)

Deem, James M. *How to Read Your Mother's Mind.* Houghton, 1994. *(P; I)*

Landau, Elaine. *ESP.* Lerner, 1996. *(P; I)*

Netzley, Patricia D. *ESP.* Lucent, 2000. *(I; A)*

EYE

Goldstein, Margaret J., and Beirne, Barbara. *Household History: Eyeglasses.* Lerner, 1997. *(P; I)*

Silverstein, Alvin; Silverstein, Virginia B.; and Nunn, Laura Silverstein. *Can You See the Chalkboard?* Scholastic, 2001. *(P; I); Senses and Sensors: Seeing.* Lerner, 2001. *(I)*

Viegas, Jennifer. *Eye: Learning How We See.* Rosen, 2002. *(I; A)*

F (LETTER)

Samoyault, Tiphaine. *Alphabetical Order: How the Alphabet Began.* Viking, 1998. *(P; I)*

FABLES

Climo, Shirley. *The Little Red Ant and the Great Big Crumb: A Mexican Fable.* Houghton Mifflin, 2004. *(P)*

Jacobs, Joseph, ed. *Fables of Aesop.* Dover, 2002. *(P; I)*

FAIRS AND EXPOSITIONS

Alter, Judy. *Meet Me at the Fair: County, State, and World's Fair Expositions.* Scholastic, 1997. *(P; I)*

Bial, Raymond. *County Fair.* Houghton, 1992. *(P; I)*

Lewin, Ted. *Fair!* Lothrop, 1997. *(P)*

FAIRY TALES

Blackaby, Susan, retel. *The Emperor's New Clothes; The Little Mermaid; The Princess and the Pea; The Steadfast Tin Soldier; The Ugly Duckling; Thumbelina.* Picture Window Books, 2003. *(P)*

Climo, Shirley. *The Persian Cinderella.* HarperCollins, 1999; *The Korean Cinderella.* HarperCollins, 1996. *(P)*

Kessler, Brad, and Harris, Joel Chandler. *Brer Rabbit and Boss Lion.* Simon & Schuster, 2005. *(P)*

Lang, Andrew. *The Blue Fairy Book.* NuVision, 2004 (and other Lang Fairy Books). *(P; I)*

Philip, Neil, ed. *Fairy Tales of Eastern Europe.* Clarion, 1991. *(I)*

FAMILY

Erlbach, Arlene. *The Families Book: True Stories about Real Kids and the People They Live with and Love.* Free Spirit, 1996. *(P; I)*

Kerley, Barbara. *You and Me Together: Moms, Dads, and Kids Around the World.* National Geographic Society, 2005. *(P)*

FAMINE

Lampton, Christopher F. *Famine.* Millbrook, 1994. *(P; I)*

FARMS AND FARMING

Artley, Bob. *Once Upon a Farm.* Pelican, 2000. *(P; I; A)*

Bowden, Rob. *Sustainable World: Food and Farming.* Thomson Gale, 2004. *(I; A)*

Goldberg, Jacob. *The Disappearing American Farm.* Watts, 1996. *(A)*

Paladino, Catherine. *One Good Apple: Growing Our Food for the Sake of the Earth.* Houghton, 1999. *(I)*

Peterson, Cris. *Century Farm: One Hundred Years on a Family Farm.* Boyds Mills Press, 1999. *(P)*

Wilkes, Anglea, and Thomas, Eric. *A Farm Through Time.* DK, 2001. *(P; I)*

Wolfman, Judy, and Winston, David Lorenz. *Life on an Apple Orchard; Life on a Dairy Farm.* Lerner, 2003; *Life on a Cattle Farm; Life on a Crop Farm; Life on a Goat Farm; Life on a Horse Farm; Life on a Pig Farm.* Lerner, 2001. *(P)*

Woods, Michael, and Woods, Mary B. *Ancient Agriculture: From Foraging to Farming.* Lerner, 2000. *(I)*

FARRAGUT, DAVID

Stein, R. Conrad. *David Farragut: First Admiral of the U. S. Navy.* Child's World, 2005. *(P; I)*

FASCISM

Downing, David. *Fascism.* Heinemann, 2002; *Benito Mussolini (Leading Lives Series).* Heinemann, 2001. *(I; A)*

Giesecke, Ernestine. *Governments around the World.* Heinemann, 2000. *(P; I)*

Tames, Richard L. *Fascism.* Raintree, 2001. *(I)*

FATHER'S DAY

Robinson, Fay. *Father's Day Crafts.* Enslow, 2005. *(P; I)*

FEET AND HANDS

Badt, Karin Luisa. *On Your Feet!* Scholastic, 1995. *(P)*

Savage, Stephen. *Adaptation for Survival: Hands and Feet.* Raintree, 1995. *(P)*

Sherman, Josepha. *Upper Limbs: Learning How We Use Our Arms, Elbows, Forearms, and Hands.* Rosen, 2002. *(I; A)*

FERDINAND AND ISABELLA

Meltzer, Milton. *Ten Queens: Portraits of Women of Power.* Dutton, 1997. *(I; A)*

FIBER OPTICS

Hecht, Jeff. *City of Light: The Story of Fiber Optics.* Oxford University Press, 2004 (2nd ed.). *(A)*

Kassinger, Ruth G. *Glass: From Cinderella's Slippers to Fiber Optics.* Lerner, 2003. *(I)*

Lloyd, Gill, and Jefferis, David. *The History of Optics.* Raintree Steck-Vaughn, 1995. *(I)*

Math, Irwin. *Tomorrow's Technology: Experimenting with the Science of the Future.* Simon & Schuster, 1992. *(A)*

FIBERS

Keeler, Patricia, and McCall, Francis X., Jr. *Unraveling Fibers.* Atheneum, 1995. *(P; I)*

FICTION

Bloom, Harold. *Jewish Women Fiction Writers.* Chelsea House, 1998. *(A)*

Bredeson, Carmen. *American Writers of the 20th Century.* Enslow, 1996. *(I; A)*

Datnow, Claire L. *American Science Fiction and Fantasy Writers.* Enslow, 1999. *(I)*

Dommermuth-Costa, Carol. *Agatha Christie: Writer of Mystery.* Lerner, 1997. *(I; A)*

Reid, Suzanne Elizabeth. *Presenting Young Adult Science Fiction.* Twayne, 1998. *(I; A)*

FIELD HOCKEY

Adelson, Bruce. *The Composite Guide to Field Hockey.* Chelsea House, 2000. *(I; A)*

Lee, Veronica; Small, Eric; and Saliba, Susan. *Field Hockey.* Mason Crest, 2003. *(P; I)*

Swissler, Becky. *Winning Field Hockey for Girls.* Facts on File, 2003. *(I; A)*

FIJI

Ngcheong-Lum, Roseline. *Fiji.* Marshall Cavendish, 2000. *(I; A)*

FILLMORE, MILLARD

Santella, Andrew. *Millard Fillmore.* Compass Point Books, 2003. *(P; I)*

Santow, Dan. *Millard Fillmore (Encyclopedia of Presidents, Second Series).* Scholastic, 2004. *(I; A)*

Souter, Gerry, and Souter, Janet. *Millard Fillmore: Our Thirteenth President.* Child's World, 2002. *(P; I)*

FINGER PAINTING

Carreiro, Carolyn. *Hand-Print Animal Art.* Williamson, 1997. *(P; I)*

FINGERPRINTING

Jones, Charlotte Foltz. *Fingerprints and Talking Bones: How Real-Life Crimes Are Solved.* Bantam Doubleday Dell, 1999. *(I)*

Tocci, Salvatore. *High-Tech IDs: From Finger Scans to Voice Patterns.* Sagebrush Education Resources, 2000. *(I; A)*

FINLAND

McNair, Sylvai. *Finland (Enchantment of the World, Second Series).* Scholastic, 1997. *(I; A)*

Zhong, Meichun. *Finland.* Gareth Steens, 2001. *(I)*

FIRE FIGHTING AND PREVENTION

Beil, Karen Magnuson. *Fire in Their Eyes: Wildfires and the People Who Fight Them.* Harcourt, 1999. *(I; A)*

Bingham, Caroline. *Fire Truck.* Dorling Kindersley, 1995. *(P)*

Bourgeois, Paulette. *Fire Fighters.* Kids Can Press, 1998. *(P)*

Greenberg, Keith Elliot. *Smokejumper: Firefighter from the Sky.* Blackbirch Press, 1995. *(P; I)*

Kalman, Maira. *Fireboat: The Heroic Adventures of the John J. Harvey.* Putnam, 2002. *(P)*

Lee, Mary Price, and Lee, Richard S. *Careers in Firefighting.* Rosen, 1993. *(I; A)*

Winkleman, Katherine K. *Firehouse.* Walker, 1994. *(P)*

FIRST AID

Boelts, Maribeth, and Boelts, Darwin. *Kids to the Rescue! First Aid Techniques for Kids.* Parenting Press, 1992. *(P; I)*

Boy Scouts of America Staff. *First Aid.* Boy Scouts, 1995 (updated edition). *(I; A)*

Masoff, Joy. *Emergency!* Scholastic Reference, 1999. *(I)*

FIRST AMENDMENT FREEDOMS

Barbour, Scott, ed. *Free Speech.* Greenhaven, 1999. *(A)*

Evans, J. Edward. *Freedom of Religion.* Lerner, 1990. *(I; A)*; *Freedom of Speech.* Lerner, 1990. *(I; A)*

Herda, D. J. *New York Times v. United States: National Security and Censorship.* Enslow, 1994. *(I; A)*

Pascoe, Elaine. *Freedom of Expression: The Right to Speak out in America.* Millbrook Press, 1992. *(I; A)*

Zeinert, Karen. *Free Speech: From Newspapers to Music Lyrics.* Enslow, 1995. *(I; A)*

FIRST LADIES

Beller, Susan Provost. *Woman of Independence: The Life of Abigail Adams.* F & W Publications, 1992. *(I; A)*

St. George, Judith. *John and Abigail Adams: An American Love Story.* Holiday House, 2001. *(I)*

Stacey, T. J. *Hillary Rodham Clinton: Activist First Lady.* Enslow, 1994. *(I; A)*

FISH

Bailey, Jill. *How Fish Swim.* Marshall Cavendish, 1996. *(P; I)*

Buttfield, Helen. *Secret Life of Fishes: From Angels to Zebras on the Coral Reef.* Abrams, 2000. *(I)*

Castner, James L. *River Life: Deep in the Amazon.* Marshall Cavendish, 2002. *(P; I)*

Cerullo, Mary M. *The Truth about Great White Sharks.* Chronicle, 2000. *(P; I)*; *Dolphins: What They Can Teach Us.* Dutton, 1999. *(P; I)*; *The Octopus: Phantom of the Sea.* Cobblehill, 1997. *(I; A)*; *Coral Reef: A City That Never Sleeps.* Dutton, 1996. *(P; I)*

Clapham, Phil. *Whales of the World.* Voyageur Press, 2001. *(I; A)*

Hirschmann, Kris. *Moray Eels; Sea Stars.* Gale Group, 2002. *(P; I)*

Johnson, Rebecca L. *The Great Barrier Reef: A Living Laboratory.* Lerner, 1991. *(I)*

Kovacs, Deborah, and Madin, Kate. *Beneath Blue Waters: Meetings with Remarkable Deep-Sea Creatures.* Viking Penguin, 1996. *(I)*

Landau, Elaine. *Angelfish; Piranhas; Sea Horses; Siamese Fighting Fish.* Scholastic, 1999. *(P; I)*

Morgan, Sally, and Lalor, Pauline. *Ocean Life.* Sterling, 2001. *(I; A)*

Pascoe, Elaine. *Freshwater Fish (Nature Close-up Series).* Thomson Gale, 2004; *Tadpoles (Nature Close-up Series).* Thomson Gale, 1996. *(P; I)*

Perrine, Doug. *Sharks and Rays of the World.* Voyageur Press, 1999. *(I; A)*

Spilsbury, Louise A., and Spilsbury, Richard. *Classifying Fish.* Heinemann, 2003. *(P; I)*

Van Blaricom, Glenn R. *Sea Otters.* Voyageur Press, 2001. *(I; A)*

Walker, Sally M. *Fossil Fish Found Alive: The Amazing Quest for the Coelacanth.* Carolrhoda, 2002. *(I)*

FISHING

Arnosky, Jim. *Hook, Line, and Seeker: A Beginner's Guide to Fishing, Boating, and Watching Water Wildlife.* Scholastic, 2005. *(I)*; *Flies in the Water, Fish in the Air: A Personal Introduction to Fly Fishing.* The Countryman Press, 1992. *(I; A)*

Bailey, John. *The Young Fishing Enthusiast: A Practical Guide for Kids.* DK, 1999. *(I; A)*

Kurlansky, Mark, and Schindler, S. D. *The Cod's Tale.* Penguin, 2001. *(P; I)*

Patchett, Fiona, ed. *Starting Fishing.* Usborne Books, 1999. *(P; I)*

FISSION

Barron, Rachel Stiffler. *Lise Meitner: Discoverer of Nuclear Fission.* Morgan Reynolds, 2000. *(I; A)*

FITZGERALD, F. SCOTT

Bloom, Harold, ed. *F. Scott Fitzgerald's The Great Gatsby (Bloom's Notes Series).* Chelsea House, 1995. *(A)*

Bredeson, Carmen. *American Writers of the 20th Century.* Enslow, 1996. *(I; A)*

DeKoster, Katie, ed. *Readings on F. Scott Fitzgerald.* Greenhaven Press, 1997. *(A)*

Halliwell, Sarah, ed. *20th Century: Pre-1945 Artists, Writers, and Composers.* Raintree, 1998. *(I)*

Lazo, Caroline Evensen. *F. Scott Fitzgerald: Voice of the Jazz Age.* Lerner, 2003. *(I; A)*

Pelzer, Linda Claycomb. *Student Companion to F. Scott Fitzgerald.* Greenwood Press, 2000. *(A)*

Tate, Mary Jo. *F. Scott Fitzgerald A to Z: The Essential Reference to His Life and Work.* Facts on File, 1999. *(A)*

Tessitore, John. *F. Scott Fitzgerald: The American Dreamer.* Watts, 2001. *(I; A)*

Weisbrod, Eva. *A Student's Guide to F. Scott Fitzgerald.* Enslow, 2004. *(I; A)*

FLAGS

Brandt, Sue R. *State Flags: Including the Commonwealth of Puerto Rico.* Scholastic, 1992. *(I; A)*

Ferry, Joseph. *The American Flag (American Symbols and Their Meanings Series).* Mason Crest, 2002. *(I)*

Johnson, Linda Carlson. *Our National Symbols.* Millbrook Press, 1994. *(P)*

Sonneborn, Liz. *The Pledge of Allegiance: The Story Behind Our Patriotic Promise; The Star-Spangled Banner: The Story Behind Our National Anthem.* Chelsea Clubhouse, 2004. *(P; I)*

FLEMING, SIR ALEXANDER

Bankston, John. *Unlocking the Secrets of Science: Alexander Fleming and the Story of Penicillin.* Mitchell Lane, 2001. *(I)*

Kaye, Judith. *The Life of Alexander Fleming.* Twenty-First Century, 1993. *(I)*

FLOATING AND BUOYANCY

Challoner, Jack. *Floating and Sinking.* Raintree Steck-Vaughn, 1997. *(P)*

FLOODS

Gow, Mary. *Johnstown Flood: The Day the Dam Burst (American Disasters Series).* Enslow, 2003. *(I)*

Hiscock, Bruce. *The Big Rivers: The Missouri, the Mississippi, and the Ohio.* Atheneum, 1997. *(P; I)*

Thompson, Luke. *Natural Disasters: Floods.* Scholastic, 2000. *(I)*

FLORIDA

Blaustein, Daniel. *Everglades and the Gulf Coast.* Marshall Cavendish, 2000. *(I)*

Bryant, Philip S. *Zora Neale Hurston.* Raintree, 2003. *(P)*

Chang, Perry. *Florida.* Marshall Cavendish, 1998. *(P; I)*

Chui, Patricia, and Craven, Jean. *Florida: The Sunshine State.* Gareth Stevens, 2002. *(P; I)*

Fradin, Dennis Brindell. *Florida: From Sea to Shining Sea.* Scholastic, 1994. *(P; I)*

Heinrichs, Ann. *Florida.* Children's Press, 1998. *(I)*

FLOUR AND FLOUR MILLING

Harbison, E. M. *Loaves of Fun: A History of Bread with Activities and Recipes from around the World.* Chicago Review Press, 1997. *(P; I)*

Hughes, Meredith Sayles, and Hughes, E. Thomas. *Glorious Grasses: The Grains.* Lerner, 1998. *(P; I)*

FLOWERS

Burns, Diane L. *Wildflowers, Blooms, and Blossoms.* Sagebrush Education Resources, 1998. *(P; I)*

Hewitt, Sally. *It's Science: Plants and Flowers.* Scholastic, 1998. *(P)*

Penny, Malcolm. *How Plants Grow.* Marshall Cavendish, 1996. *(P; I)*

Ryden, Hope. *Wildflowers Around the Year.* Houghton Mifflin, 2001. *(P; I)*

FOG AND SMOG

Donald, Rhonda Lucas. *Air Pollution.* Scholastic, 2001. *(P)*

Kahl, Jonathan D. W. *Hazy Skies: Weather and the Environment.* Lerner, 1997. *(I)*

Llewellyn, Claire. *Wild, Wet and Windy: The Weather-From Hurricanes to Monsoons (SuperSmarts Series).* Candlewick Press, 1997. *(P)*

Miller, Christina G., and Berry, Louise A. *Air Alert: Rescuing the Earth's Atmosphere.* Simon & Schuster, 1996. *(I; A)*

FOLK ART

Franklin, Sharon; Black, Cynthia A.; and Krafchin, Rhonda. *Southwest Pacific.* Raintree Steck-Vaughn, 1999. *(I; A)*

Franklin, Sharon; Tull, Mary; and Black, Cynthia A. *Scandinavia.* Raintree Steck-Vaughn, 2000. *(I; A)*

Franklin, Sharon; Tull, Mary; and Shelton, Carol. *Mexico and Central America.* Raintree Steck-Vaughn, 2000. *(I; A)*

Lovett, Patricia. *Calligraphy and Illumination: A History and Practical Guide.* Abrams, 2000. *(A)*

Tull, Mary, and Franklin, Sharon. *North America.* Raintree Steck-Vaughn, 1999. *(I; A)*

Tull, Mary; Franklin, Tristan; and Black, Cynthia A. *Northern Asia.* Raintree Steck-Vaughn, 1999. *(I; A)*

Wilson, Sule Greg C. *African American Quilting: The Warmth of Tradition.* Rosen, 1999. *(P; I)*

FOLK MUSIC

Cohn, Amy L., comp. *From Sea to Shining Sea: A Treasury of American Folklore and Folk Songs.* Scholastic, 1993. *(P; I; A)*

Krull, Kathleen. *I Hear America Singing!: Folk Songs for American Families.* Alfred A. Knopf, 2003; *Gonna Sing My Head Off!: American Folk Songs for Children.* Alfred A. Knopf, 1995. *(P; I)*

Partridge, Elizabeth. *This Land Was Made for You and Me: The Life and Songs of Woody Guthrie.* Viking, 2002. *(I; A)*

Sieling, Peter. *North American Folk Music; North American Folk Songs.* Mason Crest, 2002. *(I; A)*

FOOD SUPPLY

Bowden, Rob. *Food Supply: Our Impact on the Planet.* Raintree Steck-Vaughn, 2002. *(I)*

McCoy, J. J. *How Safe Is Our Food Supply?* Watts, 1990. *(A)*

Patent, Dorothy Hinshaw. *Where Food Comes From.* Holiday, 1991. *(P)*

FOOTBALL

Donnelly, Karen J. *Football Hall of Famers: Deacon Jones.* Rosen, 2003. *(I)*

Gallagher, Aileen. *Football Hall of Famers: Walter Payton.* Rosen, 2003. *(I)*

Helmer, Diana Star, and Owens, Thomas S. *The History of Football.* Rosen, 2003. *(P)*

Holden, Steve. *Football: Passing; Football: Rushing and Tackling.* Scholastic, 2000. *(I; A)*

Hulm, David. *Football Hall of Famers: Fran Tarkenton.* Rosen, 2003. *(I)*

Jaques, Trevor D. *Australian Football: Steps to Success.* Human Kinetics Publishers, 1994. *(A)*

Kennedy, Mike. *Football.* Scholastic, 2001. *(P)*

Miller, J. David. *The Super Book of Football.* Sports Illustrated for Kids Books, 1990. *(I)*

Ramen, Fred. *Football Hall of Famers: Joe Montana.* Rosen, 2003. *(I)*

Roensch, Greg. *Football Hall of Famers: Vince Lombardi.* Rosen, 2003. *(I)*

FORCES

Dispezio, Michael. *Awesome Experiments in Force and Motion.* Sterling, 1999. *(I; A)*

Hewitt, Sally. *It's Science: Forces Around Us.* Scholastic, 1998. *(P)*

Lafferty, Peter. *Force and Motion.* Dorling Kindersley, 1992. *(I)*

FORD, GERALD R.

Francis, Sandra. *Gerald R. Ford: Our Thirty-Eighth President.* Child's World, 2002. *(P; I)*

Stein, R. Conrad. *Gerald R. Ford (Encyclopedia of Presidents, Second Series).* Scholastic, 2005. *(I; A)*

FOREIGN AID

Egendorf, Laura, ed. *The Third World.* Greenhaven, 2000. *(A)*

FORENSIC SCIENCE

Campbell, Andrea. *Forensic Science: Evidence, Clues, and Investigation.* Chelsea House, 1999. *(I; A)*

Fridell, Ron. *Solving Crimes: Pioneers of Forensic Science.* Watts, 2000. *(I; A)*

Innes, Brian. *Crime and Detection: Forensic Science.* Mason Crest, 2002. *(I; A)*

Jackson, Donna M. *The Wildlife Detectives: How Forensic Scientists Fight Crimes Against Nature.* Houghton Mifflin, 2000. *(P; I)*; *The Bone Detectives: How Forensic Anthropologists Solve Crimes and Uncover Mysteries of the Dead.* Little, Brown, 1996. *(I; A)*

Jones, Charlotte Foltz. *Fingerprints and Talking Bones: How Real-Life Crimes Are Solved.* Bantam Doubleday Dell, 1999. *(I)*

Oxlade, Chris. *Crime Detection.* Heinemann, 1997. *(P; I)*

FORTS AND FORTIFICATION

Bial, Raymond. *Forts: Building America.* Marshall Cavendish, 2001. *(I)*

Gravett, Christopher. *Castle.* DK, 2000. *(P; I)*

Hicks, Peter. *How Castles Were Built.* Raintree Steck-Vaughn, 1998. *(I)*

Hinds, Kathryn. *Castle.* Marshall Cavendish, 2000. *(I)*

MacDonald, Fiona. *A Samurai Castle.* McGraw-Hill, 1995; *A Medieval Castle; A Roman Fort.* McGraw-Hill, 1993. *(I)*

Mann, Elizabeth. *The Great Wall: The Story of 4,000 Miles of Earth and Stone That Turned a Nation into a Fortress.* Firefly, 1997. *(P; I; A)*

Steedman, Scott. *A Frontier Fort on the Oregon Trail.* McGraw-Hill, 1994. *(P; I)*

FOSSEY, DIAN

Gogerly, Liz. *Dian Fossey.* Raintree, 2003. *(I)*

Jerome, Leah. *Dian Fossey.* Bantam, 1991. *(I)*

FOSSILS

Aaseng, Nathan. *American Dinosaur Hunters.* Enslow, 1996. *(I)*

Bishop, Nic. *Digging for Bird-Dinosaurs: An Expedition to Madagascar.* Houghton Mifflin, 2000. *(I)*

Heiligman, Deborah. *Mary Leakey: In Search of Human Beginnings.* Freeman, 1995. *(I)*

Pascoe, Elaine. *New Dinosaurs: Skeletons in the Sand.* Gale Group, 1997. *(P; I)*

Patent, Dorothy Hinshaw. *In Search of the Maiasaurs.* Marshall Cavendish, 1999. *(I)*

Tyldesley, Joyce. *The Mummy: Unwrap the Ancient Secrets of the Mummies' Tombs.* Carlton, 2000. *(A)*

Walker, Sally M. *Fossil Fish Found Alive: The Amazing Quest for the Coelacanth.* Carolrhoda, 2002. *(I)*

FOSTER CARE

Blomquist, Geraldine M., and Blomquist, Paul. *Coping as a Foster Child.* Rosen, 1991. *(A)*

Davies, Nancy Millichap. *Foster Care.* Watts, 1994. *(I; A)*

Warren, Andrea. *We Rode the Orphan Trains.* Houghton Mifflin, 2001; *Orphan Train Rider: One Boy's True Story.* Houghton Mifflin, 1998. *(I)*

FOUNDERS OF THE UNITED STATES

Collier, James Lincoln. *The Benjamin Franklin You Never Knew; The Alexander Hamilton You Never Knew; The George Washington You Never Knew.* Scholastic, 2004. *(P; I)*

FRACTIONS AND DECIMALS

Adler, David A. *Fraction Fun.* Holiday House, 1997. *(P)*

King, Andrew. *Making Fractions.* Millbrook Press, 1998. *(P)*

Leedy, Loreen. *Fraction Action.* Holiday House, 1996. *(P)*

Stienecker, David L., and Maccabe, Richard. *Fractions.* Marshall Cavendish, 1995. *(P; I)*

FRANCE

Brooks, Polly Schoyer. *Queen Eleanor: Independent Spirit of the Medieval World.* Houghton Mifflin, 1999 (reprint). *(I; A)*

Bullen, Susan. *The Alps and Their People.* Raintree Steck-Vaughn, 1994. *(P; I)*

Byers, Helen. *Colors of France.* Lerner, 2001. *(P)*

Carroll, Bob. *Napoleon Bonaparte.* Gale Group, 1994. *(I; A)*

Costain, Meredith, and Collins, Paul. *Welcome to France.* Chelsea House, 2001. *(P; I)*

Gofen, Ethel C. *France.* Marshall Cavendish, 1995 (2nd ed.). *(I; A)*

Harvey, Miles. *Look What Comes from France.* Watts, 1999. *(P; I)*

Landau, Elaine. *France.* Scholastic, 2000. *(I; A)*

McGowen, Tom. *Frederick the Great, Bismarck, and the Building of the German Empire in World History.* Enslow, 2002. *(I; A)*

Pietrusza, David. *The Battle of Waterloo: Battles of the Nineteenth Century.* Gale Group, 1996; *The Invasion of Normandy: Battles of World War II.* Gale Group, 1995. *(I; A)*

FRANCE, LANGUAGE OF

Wright, Nicola. *Getting to Know: France and French.* Barron's, 1993. *(P; I)*

FRANCE, MUSIC OF

Cavelletti, Carlo. *Chopin and Romantic Music.* Barron's Educational Series, 2000. *(I; A)*

FRANCIS OF ASSISI, SAINT

Mayo, Margaret. *Brother Sun, Sister Moon: The Life and Stories of St. Francis.* Little, Brown, 2000. *(P)*

FRANK, ANNE

Gold, Alison Leslie. *Memories of Anne Frank: Reflections of a Childhood Friend.* Scholastic, 1997. *(P; I)*

Koestler-Grack, Rachel A. *The Story of Anne Frank.* Chelsea House, 2004. *(P)*

Muller, Melissa. *Anne Frank: The Biography.* Metropolitan, 1998. *(A)*

Poole, Josephine. *Anne Frank.* Random House, 2005. *(P; I)*

Pressler, Mirjam. *Anne Frank: A Hidden Life.* Dutton, 2000. *(A)*

Wukovits, John F. *Anne Frank.* Lucent, 1998. *(I; A)*

FRANKLIN, BENJAMIN

Franklin, Benjamin. *The Autobiography of Benjamin Franklin.* Airmont, n.d. *(A)*; *Poor Richard.* Peter Pauper, n.d. *(I; A)*

Gaustad, Edwin S. *Benjamin Franklin: Inventing America.* Oxford University Press, 2004. *(I; A)*

Giblin, James Cross. *The Amazing Life of Benjamin Franklin.* Scholastic, 2006. *(P; I)*

Heiligman, Deborah. *The Mysterious Ocean Highway: Benjamin Franklin and the Gulf Stream.* Raintree Steck-Vaughn, 1999. *(P; I)*

Kallen, Stuart A. *Benjamin Franklin (Founding Fathers).* ABDO, 2001. *(P; I)*

FREMONT, JOHN CHARLES

Faber, Harold. *John Charles Fremont: Pathfinder to the West.* Benchmark, 2002. *(I)*

FRENCH AND INDIAN WAR

Collier, Christopher, and Collier, James L. *The French and Indian War, 1660-1763.* Marshall Cavendish, 1997. *(I)*

Maestro, Betsy C. *Struggle for a Continent: The French and Indian Wars 1689-1763.* Morrow, 2000. *(P; I)*

Minks, Benton, and Minks, Louise. *The French and Indian War.* Lucent, 1994. *(I; A)*

FRENCH GUIANA

Morrison, Marion. *French Guiana.* Children's Press, 1995. *(I; A)*

FRENCH REVOLUTION

Otfinoski, Steven. *Triumph and Terror: The French Revolution.* Facts on File, 1993. *(A)*

Stewart, Gail B. *Life during the French Revolution.* Lucent, 1995. *(I; A)*

FREUD, SIGMUND

Reef, Catherine. *Sigmund Freud: Pioneer of the Mind.* Houghton Mifflin, 2001. *(I)*

FROGS AND TOADS

Badger, David P. *Frogs.* Voyageur Press, 2000. *(A)*

Pascoe, Elaine. *Tadpoles (Nature Close-up Series).* Thomson Gale, 1996. *(P; I)*

Tagholm, Sally. *The Frog.* Kingfisher, 2000. *(P)*

FROST, ROBERT

Bober, Natalie S. *A Restless Spirit: The Story of Robert Frost.* Henry Holt, 1998 (rev. ed.). *(I; A)*

Parini, Jay. *Robert Frost: A Life.* Henry Holt, 2000. *(A)*

Vecchione, Patrice, ed. *Revenge and Forgiveness: An Anthology of Poems.* Henry Holt, 2004. *(I; A)*

FRUITGROWING

Hughes, Meredith Sayles. *Tall and Tasty: Fruit Trees.* Lerner, 2000; *Yes, We Have Bananas!: Fruits from*

Shrubs and Vines. Lerner, 1999. *(P; I)*

Jaspersohn, William. *Cranberries.* Houghton, 1991. *(P; I)*

FULTON, ROBERT

Bowen, Andy Russell. *A Head Full of Notions: A Story about Robert Fulton.* Lerner, 1997. *(P; I)*

Ford, Carin T. *Robert Fulton: The Steamboat Man.* Enslow, 2004. *(P)*

Pierce, Morris A. *Robert Fulton and the Development of the Steamboat.* PowerKids Press, 2003. *(I)*

FUNERAL CUSTOMS

Colman, Penny. *Corpses, Coffins, and Crypts: A History of Burial.* Holt, 1997. *(I; A)*

Johnston, Marianne. *Let's Talk about Going to a Funeral.* Rosen/Power Kids Press, 1998. *(P)*

Perl, Lila, and Heweston, Nicholas. *Dying to Know: About Death, Funeral Customs, and Final Resting Places.* Millbrook Press, 2001. *(I)*

FUNGI

Pascoe, Elaine. *Slime, Molds, and Fungi (Nature Close-up Series).* Thomson Gale, 1998. *(P; I)*

Rainis, Kenneth G., and Russell, Bruce J. *Guide to Microlife.* Scholastic, 1997. *(A)*

Silverstein, Alvin; Silverstein, Virginia B.; and Silverstein, Robert A. *Fungi (Kingdoms of Life Series).* Lerner, 1997. *(I; A)*

FUR TRADE IN NORTH AMERICA

Riendeau, Roger E. *A Brief History of Canada.* Facts on File, 1999. *(A)*

Sundling, Charles W. *Mountain Men of the Frontier.* ABDO, 2000. *(P; I)*

G (LETTER)

Samoyault, Tiphaine. *Alphabetical Order: How the Alphabet Began.* Viking, 1998. *(P; I)*

GABON

Aniakor, Chike Cyril. *Heritage Library of African Peoples: Fang.* Rosen, 1997. *(I; A)*

GALILEO

Goldsmith, Mike. *Galileo Galilei.* Raintree Steck-Vaughn, 2002. *(P; I)*

Hightower, Paul W. *Galileo: Astronomer and Physicist.* Enslow, 2001. *(A)*

Mason, Paul. *Galileo.* Heinemann, 2002. *(I)*

Sis, Peter. *Starry Messenger: Galileo Galilei.* Farrar/Foster, 1996. *(P; I)*

White, Michael. *Galileo Galilei: Inventor, Astronomer and Rebel.* Blackbirch Press, 1999. *(I)*

GAMA, VASCO DA

Aaseng, Nathan. *You Are the Explorer.* Oliver Press, 2000. *(I; A)*

Calvert, Patricia. *Vasco Da Gama: So Strong a Spirit.* Marshall Cavendish, 2004. *(I)*

GAMBIA, THE

Hughes, Arnold, and Gailey, Harry A. *Historical Dictionary of the Gambia.* Rowman & Littlefield, 1999 (3rd ed.). *(A)*

Nwanunobi, C. Onyeka. *Malinke (Burkina Faso, Côte d'Ivoire, Gambia, Guinea, Guinea Bissau, Liberia, Mali, Senegal, Sierra Leone).* Rosen, 1996. *(I; A)*

Zimmerman, Robert. *The Gambia.* Children's Press, 1994. *(A)*

GANDHI, MOHANDAS KARAMCHAND

Fisher, Leonard Everett. *Gandhi.* Simon & Schuster, 1995. *(P; I)*

Martin, Christopher. *Mohandas Gandhi.* Lerner, 2000. *(I; A)*

Severance, John B. *Gandhi, Great Soul.* Houghton Mifflin, 1997. *(I; A)*

Sherrow, Victoria. *Mohandas Gandhi: The Power of the Spirit.* Millbrook Press, 1994. *(I; A)*

GANGES RIVER

Cumming, David. *The Ganges.* Raintree Steck-Vaughn, 1993. *(I)*

GARDENS AND GARDENING

Chasek, Ruth. *Essential Gardening for Teens.* Scholastic, 2000. *(I; A)*

Congdon, Vicky. *Garden Fun!: Indoors and Out, in Pots and Small Spots.* Ideals Publications, 2002. *(P; I)*

Creasy, Rosalind. *Blue Potatoes, Orange Tomatoes: How to Grow a Rainbow Garden.* Sierra, 1994. *(P; I)*

Krementz, Jill. *A Very Young Gardener.* Dial, 1991. *(P)*

GARFIELD, JAMES ABRAM

Ackerman, Kenneth D. *Dark Horse: The Surprise Election and Political Murder of President James A. Garfield.* Avalon, 2004. *(A)*

Brunelli, Carol. *James A. Garfield: Our Twentieth President.* Child's World, 2002. *(P; I)*

Jones, Rebecca C. *The President Has Been Shot: True Stories of the Attacks on Ten U.S. Presidents.* Penguin Putnam, 1996. *(I; A)*

Kent, Deborah. *James A. Garfield (Encyclopedia of Presidents, Second Series).* Scholastic, 2004. *(I; A)*

GARIBALDI, GIUSEPPE

Viola, Herman J., and Viola, Susan. *Giuseppe Garibaldi.* Chelsea House, 1987. *(I; A)*

GASES

Darling, David. *From Glasses to Gases: The Science of Matter.* Silver Burdett Press, 1992. *(P; I)*

Gardner, Robert. *Science Projects about Solids, Liquids, and Gases.* Enslow, 2000. *(I; A)*

Mebane, Robert C., and Rybolt, Thomas R. *Air and Other Gases.* Twenty-First Century, 1995. *(I)*

Zoehfeld, Kathleen Weidner, and Meisel, Paul. *What Is The World Made Of?: All about Solids, Liquids, and Gases.* Turtleback Books, 1998. *(P)*

GEMS

Symes, R. F., and Harding, Roger. *Crystal & Gem.* Knopf, 1991. *(I)*

GENETICS

Aaseng, Nathan. *Genetics: Unlocking The Secrets of Life.* Oliver Press, 1996. *(I; A)*

Boon, Kevin Alexander. *The Human Genome Project: What Does Decoding DNA Mean for Us?* Enslow, 2002. *(A)*

Dowswell, Paul. *Genetics: The Impact on Our Lives.* Raintree Steck-Vaughn, 2001. *(I; A)*

DuPrau, Jeanne. *Cloning.* Gale Group, 2000. *(I; A)*

Edelson, Edward. *Gregor Mendel and the Roots of Genetics.* Oxford, 2001; *Genetics and Heredity.* Chelsea House, 1990. *(I; A)*

Levy, Debbie. *Medical Ethics (Overview Series).* Thomson Gale, 2000. *(I; A)*

Marshall, Elizabeth L. *High-Tech Harvest: A Look at Genetically Engineered Foods.* Scholastic, 1999. *(I; A)*; *The Human Genome Project: Cracking the Code within Us.* Watts, 1996. *(A)*

Miller-Schroeder, Patricia, ed. *The Revolution in Genetics.* Smart Apple Media, 2003. *(I; A)*

Nardo, Don. *Cloning.* Gale Group, 2001. *(I; A)*

Patent, Dorothy Hinshaw. *Biodiversity.* Houghton Mifflin, 1996. *(I; A)*; *Grandfather's Nose: Why We Look Alike or Different.* Watts, 1989. *(P)*

Rainis, Kenneth G., and Nassis, George. *Biotechnology Projects for Young Scientists.* Scholastic, 1998. *(A)*

Richardson, Hazel. *How to Clone a Sheep.* Scholastic, 2001. *(P; I)*

Snedden, Robert. *Cell Division and Genetics; DNA and Genetic Engineering.* Heinemann, 2002. *(I; A)*; *Medical Ethics: Changing Attitudes, 1900-2000 (20th Century Issues Series).* Raintree, 1999. *(I)*

Stanley, Debbie. *Genetic Engineering: The Cloning Debate (Focus on Science and Society Series).* Rosen, 2000. *(A)*

Torr, James D. *Genetic Engineering.* Gale Group, 2000. *(A)*

GENEVA CONVENTIONS

Gold, Susan Dudley. *Human Rights.* Lerner, 1997. *(I; A)*

GENOCIDE

Altman, Linda Jacobs. *Genocide: The Systematic Killing of a People.* Enslow, 1995. *(I; A)*

Grant, R.G. *Genocide.* Raintree Steck-Vaughn, 1999. *(I; A)*

Warren, Andrea. *Surviving Hitler: A Boy in the Nazi Death Camps.* HarperCollins, 2001. *(I)*

GEOGRAPHY

Dorling Kindersley Children's Atlas. DK, 2000. *(P; I)*

Grolier Incorporated. *Lands and Peoples* (6 volumes). Grolier, 2005. *(I)*

National Geographic World Atlas for Young Explorers: A Complete World Reference for Adventurous Minds. National Geographic Society, 1998. *(P; I)*

Arnold, Caroline. *The Geography Book: Activities for Exploring, Mapping, and Enjoying Your World.* Wiley, 2001. *(P; I)*

Grabham, Sue, ed. *Circling the Globe: A Young People's Guide to Countries and Cultures of the World.* Houghton Mifflin, 1995. *(I)*

Lafleur, Claude. *Our Planet Today.* Gareth Stevens, 2001. *(I; A)*

Levinson, David. *Human Environments: A Cross-Cultural Encyclopedia.* ABC-CLIO, 1995. *(A)*

Lye, Keith. *The Complete Atlas of the World.* Raintree Steck-Vaughn, 1997. *(I)*

Maurer, Richard. *Wild Colorado.* Crown, 1999. *(I; A)*

GEOLOGY

Brimner, Larry Dane. *Glaciers.* Scholastic, 2000. *(P)*

Carless, Jennifer. *Renewable Energy: A Concise Guide to Green Alternatives.* Walker, 1993. *(A)*

Erickson, Jon. *An Introduction to Fossils and Minerals; Plate Tectonics; Rock Formations and Unusual Geologic Structures.* Facts on File, 2001; *Making of the Earth: Geological Forces That Shape Our Planet.* Facts on File, 2000. *(A)*

Gallant, Roy A. *Dance of the Continents.* Marshall Cavendish, 1999. *(I; A)*; *Limestone Caves.* Watts, 1998. *(P; I)*; *Story of Dunes: Sand on the Move.* Scholastic, 1998. *(P; I)*

Goodwin, Peter H. *Landslides, Slumps, and Creep.* Scholastic, 1998. *(P; I)*

Kittinger, Jo S. *A Look at Rocks: From Coal to Kimberlite.* Scholastic, 1998. *(I)*

Lewis, J. Patrick. *Earth and You - a Closer View: Nature's Features.* Dawn, 2001. *(P)*

Oldershaw, Cally. *Atlas of Geology and Landforms: An A-Z Guide.* Scholastic, 2001. *(I)*

Patent, Dorothy Hinshaw. *Shaping the Earth.* Houghton Mifflin, 2000. *(I; A)*

Silverstein, Alvin; Silverstein, Virginia; and Nunn, Laura Silverstein. *Plate Tectonics.* Millbrook Press, 1998. *(I; A)*

Stein, Paul. *Ice Ages of the Future.* Rosen, 2001. *(I)*

VanCleave, Janice, and Ettlinger, Doris. *Janice VanCleave's Rocks and Minerals: Mind-Boggling Experiments You Can Turn into Science Fair Projects.* Econo-Clad, 1996. *(I)*

GEOMETRY

VanCleave, Janice. *Janice VanCleave's Geometry for Every Kid.* Wiley, 1994. *(I)*

GEORGIA

Britton, Tamara L. *Georgia Colony.* ABDO, 2002. *(P)*

Fradin, Dennis Brindell. *Georgia: From Sea to Shining Sea.* Scholastic, 1995. *(P; I)*

Gentry, Tony. *Alice Walker.* Chelsea House, 1992. *(I; A)*

Girod, Christina M. *The Thirteen Colonies: Georgia.* Gale Group, 2001. *(I)*

Holtz, Eric Siegfried. *Georgia: Empire State of the South.* Gareth Stevens, 2002. *(P; I)*

Ladoux, Rita C. *Georgia.* Lerner, 2002 (2nd ed.). *(P; I)*

Masters, Nancy Robinson. *Georgia.* Scholastic, 1999 (2nd ed.). *(I; A)*

Otfinoski, Steven. *Georgia.* Marshall Cavendish, 2000. *(P; I)*

Stechschulte, Pattie; Matusevich, Melissa N.; and Children's Services Quadrant Council. *Georgia.* Scholastic, 2001. *(P; I)*

Wills, Charles A. *A Historical Album of Georgia.* Millbrook Press, 1996. *(I)*

GERMANY

Ayer, Eleanor H. *Germany: In the Heartland of Europe.* Benchmark, 1996. *(I)*

Blashfield, Jean F. *Germany.* Scholastic, 2003. *(I)*

Bradley, Catherine, and Bradley, John. *Germany: The Reunification of a Nation.* Gloucester Press, dist. by Watts, 1991. *(I)*

Davis, Kevin A. *Look What Came from Germany.* Scholastic, 1999. *(P)*

Flint, David. *Germany.* Steck-Vaughn, 1994. *(I)*

Lace, William W. *Hitler and the Nazis.* Gale Group, 2000; *The Nazis.* Gale Group, 1998. *(I; A)*

Marrin, Albert. *Hitler.* Penguin Putnam, 1993. *(I; A)*

McGowen, Tom. *Frederick the Great, Bismarck, and the Building of the German Empire in World History.* Enslow, 2002. *(I; A)*

Parnell, Helga. *Cooking the German Way.* Lerner, 2003 (2nd ed.). *(I; A)*

Pfeiffer, Christine. *Germany: A Nation Reunited.* Silver Burdett Press, 1998 (2nd ed.). *(I; A)*

Pollard, Michael. *The Rhine.* Marshall Cavendish, 1997. *(I)*

Symynkywicz, Jeffrey B. *Germany: United Again.* Simon & Schuster, 1995. *(I; A)*

GERSHWIN, GEORGE

Krull, Kathleen. *Lives of the Musicians: Good Times, Bad Times (And What the Neighbors Thought).* Raintree Steck-Vaughn, 1998. *(I; A)*

Rosenberg, Deena. *Fascinating Rhythm: The Collaboration of George and Ira Gershwin.* University of Michigan Press, 1998 (reprint). *(A)*

GETTYSBURG ADDRESS

Armstrong, Jennifer. *A Three-Minute Speech: Lincoln's Remarks at Gettysburg.* Simon & Schuster, 2003. *(P; I)*

Feinberg, Barbara Silberdick. *Abraham Lincoln's Gettysburg Address: Four Score and More.* Twenty-First Century, 2000. *(I)*

Lincoln, Abraham. *The Gettysburg Address.* Houghton Mifflin, 1998. *(I)*

GHANA

Blauer, Ettagle, and Laure, Jason. *Ghana.* Scholastic, 1999. *(I; A)*

Jacobsen, Karen. *Ghana.* Scholastic, 1992. *(P)*

Koslow, Philip. *Ancient Ghana: The Land of Gold.* Chelsea House, 1995. *(I)*

McKissack, Frederick L., and McKissack, Patricia C. *Royal Kingdoms of Ghana, Mali, and Songhay: Life in Medieval Africa.* Holt, 1995. *(I)*

Nelson, Julie. *Great African Kingdoms.* Raintree Steck-Vaughn, 2002. *(P)*

Nwanunobi, C. Onyeka. *Soninke (Burkina Faso, Côte d'Ivoire, Ghana, Mali, Mauritania, Nigeria, Senegal).* Rosen, 1996. *(I; A)*

GHOSTS

Matthews, John. *The Barefoot Book of Giants, Ghosts and Goblins: Traditional Tales from around the World.* Barefoot, 1999. *(P; I)*

Walker, Paul Robert. *Giants!: Stories from around the World.* Harcourt, 1995. *(P; I)*

GIOTTO DI BONDONE

Corrain, Lucia. *Giotto and Medieval Art: The Lives and Works of the Medieval Artists.* NTC, 1995. *(I)*

Janson, H. W., and Janson, Anthony F. *History of Art for Young People.* Abrams, 1997 (rev. ed.). *(I; A)*

GIRAFFES

Markert, Jenny. *Giraffes.* Child's World, 2001 (2nd ed.). *(P)*

Sattler, Helen Roney. *Giraffes, the Sentinels of the Savannahs.* Lothrop, 1990. *(I)*

GIRL SCOUTS

Junior Girl Scout Activity Book. Girl Scouts of the United States of America, 1992. *(I; A)*

Trefoil Round the World. World Association of Girl Guides and Girl Scouts, 1997. *(I; A)*

Bergerson, Chris; Unger, Karen; and Caban, Maria. *Junior Girl Scout Handbook.* Girl Scouts of the United States of America, 2001 (2nd ed.). *(I)*

Boas, Elisabeth K., ed. *Interest Projects for Cadette and Senior Girl Scouts.* Girl Scouts of the United States of America, 1997. *(I; A)*

Sparks, Karen Unger. *Brownie Girl Scout Handbook.* Girl Scouts of the United States of America, 1993 (rev. ed.). *(P; I)*

GLACIERS

Bramwell, Martyn. *Glaciers and Ice Caps.* Watts, 1994. *(I)*

Brimner, Larry Dane. *Glaciers.* Scholastic, 2000. *(P)*

Gordon, John E. *Glaciers.* Voyageur Press, 2001. *(I; A)*

GLANDS

Young, John K. *Hormones: Molecular Messengers.* Watts, 1994. *(I; A)*

GLASS

Avi-Yonah, Michael. *Piece by Piece!: Mosaics of the Ancient World.* Lerner, 1993. *(I; A)*

Kassinger, Ruth G. *Glass: From Cinderella's Slippers to Fiber Optics.* Lerner, 2003. *(I)*

Llewellyn, Claire. *Material World: Glass.* Scholastic, 2001. *(P; I)*

Tocci, Salvatore. *Experiments with a Hand Lens.* Scholastic, 2002. *(P)*

GLENN, JOHN H., JR.

Kramer, Barbara. *John Glenn: A Space Biography.* Enslow, 1998. *(I)*

GLIDERS

Berliner, Don. *Aviation: Reaching for the Sky.* Oliver Press, 1997. *(I)*

Schmidt, Norman. *Fabulous Paper Gliders.* Sterling, 1998. *(I; A)*

GODDARD, ROBERT HUTCHINGS

Bankston, John. *Unlocking the Secrets of Science: Robert Goddard and the Liquid Rocket Engine.* Mitchell Lane, 2001. *(I; A)*

GOLD, DISCOVERIES OF

Dolan, Edward F. *The Gold Rush.* Marshall Cavendish, 2002. *(P)*

Jones, Charlotte Foltz. *Yukon Gold: The Story of the Klondike Gold Rush.* Holiday, 1999. *(I)*

Meltzer, Milton. *Gold: The True Story of Why People Search for It, Mine It, Trade It, Steal It, Mint It, Hoard It, Shape It, Wear It, Fight and Kill for It.* HarperCollins, 1993. *(P; I)*

Murphy, Claire Rudolph, and Haigh, Jane G. *Children of the Gold Rush.* Roberts Rinehart, 1999. *(I)*

Schnazer, Rosalyn. *Gold Fever: Tales of the California Gold Rush.* National Geographic Society, 1999. *(P; I)*

Shepherd, Donna Walsh. *The Klondike Gold Rush.* Watts, 1998. *(P; I)*

Van Steenwyk, Elizabeth. *The California Gold Rush: West with the Forty-Niners.* Scholastic, 1991. *(I)*

GOLF

Adams, Mike, and Tomasi, T. J. *Play Golf for Juniors: The Academy of Golf at PGA National.* Firefly Books, 2000. *(I; A)*

Anderson, Dave. *The Story of Golf.* William Morrow, 1998. *(I; A)*

Collins, David R. *Tiger Woods, Golfing Champion.* Pelican, 1999. *(I)*

Curtis, Bruce, and Morelli, Jay. *Beginning Golf.* Sterling, 2001. *(I)*

Ditchfield, Christin. *Golf.* Scholastic, 2003. *(P)*

Gordon, John. *The Kids Book of Golf.* Kids Can Press, 2001. *(P; I)*

Owens, Dede, and Bunker, Linda K. *Golf: Steps to Success.* Human Kinetics Publishers, 1995 (2nd ed.). *(A)*

Soul, Robert, and Faldo, Nick. *The Young Golfer: A Young Enthusiast's Guide to Golf.* DK, 1999. *(I; A)*

Uschan, Michael V. *Golf.* Thomson Gale, 2000. *(P; I)*

Wakeman, Nancy. *Babe Didrikson Zaharias: Driven to Win.* Lerner, 2000. *(P; I)*

Wilner, Barry. *Superstars of Women's Golf.* Chelsea House, 1997. *(I)*

GOODALL, JANE

Lucas, Eileen. *Jane Goodall, Friend of the Chimps.* Millbrook, 1992. *(I)*

GORBACHEV, MIKHAIL

Butson, Thomas G. *Mikhail Gorbachev.* Chelsea House, 1991 (reprint). *(A)*

Langley, Andrew. *Mikhail Gorbachev.* Heinemann, 2003. *(P; I)*

Streissguth, Thomas, and Haig, Alexander Meigs. *Soviet Leaders from Lenin to Gorbachev.* Oliver Press, 1992. *(I; A)*

Sullivan, George E. *Mikhail Gorbachev.* Silver Burdett Press, 1990 (rev. ed.). *(I)*

GOYA, FRANCISCO

Janson, H. W., and Janson, Anthony F. *History of Art for Young People.* Abrams, 1997 (rev. ed.). *(I; A)*

Muhlberger, Richard, and Metropolitan Museum of Art. *What Makes a Goya a Goya?* Viking, 1994. *(I)*

Riboldi, Silvia; Schiaffino, Mariarosa; and Trojer, Thomas. *Goya.* NTC, 1999. *(I)*

Waldron, Ann. *Francisco Goya.* Abrams, 1992. *(I)*

GRAINS AND GRAIN PRODUCTS

Gelman, Rita Golden. *Rice Is Life.* Holt, 2000. *(P)*

Kalz, Jill. *Grains.* Smart Apple Media, 2004. *(P)*

GRANT, ULYSSES SIMPSON

Alter, Judy. *Ulysses S. Grant.* Enslow, 2002. *(I; A)*

Archer, Jules. *A House Divided: The Lives of Ulysses S. Grant and Robert E. Lee.* Scholastic, 1996. *(I)*

Gaines, Ann Graham. *Ulysses S. Grant: Our Eighteenth President.* Child's World, 2001. *(P; I)*

King, David C. *Ulysses S. Grant: Leader of the Union Army.* Gale Group, 2001. *(I; A)*

Marrin, Albert. *Unconditional Surrender: U. S. Grant and the Civil War.* Simon & Schuster, 1994. *(I; A)*

O'Brien, Steven. *Ulysses S. Grant.* Chelsea House, 1990. *(I; A)*

GRAPES AND BERRIES

Hughes, Meredith Sayles. *Yes, We Have Bananas: Fruits from Shrubs and Vines.* Lerner, 1999. *(P; I)*

GREAT LAKES

Armbruster, Ann. *Lake Erie; Lake Huron; Lake Michigan; Lake Ontario; Lake Superior.* Scholastic, 1996. *(P)*

Katz, Sharon. *The Great Lakes.* Marshall Cavendish, 1998. *(I; A)*

Prevost, John F. *Lake Superior.* ABDO, 2002. *(P)*

Ylvisaker, Anne, and Fortner, Rosanne W. *Lake Erie; Lake Huron; Lake Michigan; Lake Ontario; Lake Superior.* Capstone Press, 2003. *(P)*

GREECE

Davis, Kevin A. *Look What Came from Greece.* Scholastic, 1999. *(P)*

Heinrichs, Ann. *Greece.* Scholastic, 2001. *(P; I)*

Lyle, Garry. *Greece.* Chelsea House, 1999. *(I; A)*

Petersen, Christine, and Petersen, David. *Greece.* Scholastic, 2002. *(P; I)*

Sioras, Efstathia. *Greece.* Gareth Stevens, 1998. *(P)*

Villios, Lynne W. *Cooking the Greek Way.* Lerner, 2002 (2nd ed.). *(I; A)*

GREEK MYTHOLOGY

Colum, Padraic, retel. *The Children's Homer: The Adventures of Odysseus and the Tale of Troy.* Simon & Schuster, 2004. *(I; A)*

Lombardo, Stanley, retel. *The Iliad.* Houghton Mifflin, 2004. *(I)*

GREENAWAY, KATE

Kate Greenaway's Apple Pie Book. Merrimack, 1990. *(P)*

Greenaway, Kate. *Kate Greenaway Nursery Rhyme Classics.* Smithmark, 1990. *(P; I: A)*

Taylor, Ina. *The Art of Kate Greenaway: A Nostalgic Portrait of Childhood.* Pelican, 1991. *(A)*

GREENLAND

Blashfield, Jean F. *Greenland (Enchantment of the World, Second Series).* Scholastic, 2005. *(I; A)*

GREENPEACE

Brown, Paul. *Greenpeace.* Silver Burdett, 1995. *(I; A)*

GRENADA

Cheng, Pang Guek. *Grenada.* Marshall Cavendish, 2000. *(I)*

GRIMM, JACOB AND WILHELM

Grimm, Wilhelm Carl, and Grimm, Jacob Ludwig Carl. *Grimm's Complete Fairy Tales.* Barnes & Noble, 1996 (13th ed.). *(I; A)*; *The Brothers Grimm Fairy Tales.* Alfred A. Knopf, 1992. *(I)*

Hettinga, Donald R. *The Brothers Grimm: Two Lives, One Legacy.* Houghton Mifflin, 2001. *(I; A)*

Koralek, Jenny, retel. *A Treasury of Stories from the Brothers Grimm.* Houghton Mifflin, 1996. *(P)*

GUATEMALA

Guatemala . . . in Pictures. Lerner, 1997. *(I)*

Franklin, Sharon; Tull, Mary; and Shelton, Carol. *Mexico and Central America: Understanding Geography and History through Art.* Raintree Steck-Vaughn, 2000. *(I; A)*

Haynes, Tricia. *Guatemala.* Chelsea House, 1998. *(I; A)*

Hermes, Jules M. *The Children of Guatemala.* Carolrhoda, 1997. *(P; I)*

Mann, Elizabeth. *Tikal: The Center of the Maya World.* Firefly, 2002. *(I)*

GUITAR

Dearling, Robert, ed. *The Illustrated Encyclopedia of Musical Instruments.* Gale Research, 1996. *(I; A)*

Gourse, Leslie. *Fancy Fretwork: The Great Jazz Guitarists.* Scholastic, 2000. *(I; A)*

Laufer, Peter, and Roth, Susan. *Made in Mexico.* National Geographic Society, 2000. *(P; I)*

Woods, Samuel G. *Guitars: From Start to Finish.* Blackbirch, 1999. *(P; I)*

GUNS AND AMMUNITION

Rifle Shooting. Boy Scouts of America, 1990. *(I; A)*

Cox, Vic. *Guns, Violence, and Teens.* Enslow, 1997. *(I; A)*

Dolan, Edward F., and Scariano, Margaret M. *Guns in the United States.* Watts, 1994. *(A)*

O'Neill, Terry. *Gun Control.* Gale Group, 2000. *(A)*

Richie, Jason. *Weapons: Designing the Tools of War.* Oliver Press, 2000. *(I; A)*

Streissguth, Thomas. *Gun Control: The Pros and Cons.* Enslow, 2001. *(I; A)*

GUYANA

Jermyn, Leslie. *Guyana.* Marshall Cavendish, 2000. *(I; A)*

Morrison, Marion. *Guyana.* Scholastic, 2003. *(I; A)*

GYMNASTICS

Bragg, Linda Wallenberg. *Play-by-Play Gymnastics.* Lerner, 2000. *(P; I; A)*

Green, Septima. *Shannon Miller: American Gymnast—from Girlhood Dreams to Olympic Glory.* Avon, 1996. *(P; I)*

Kuklin, Susan. *Going to My Gymnastics Class.* Bradbury, 1991. *(P)*

Miller, Shannon, and Richardson, Nancy Ann. *Winning Every Day: Gold Medal Advice for a Happy, Healthy Life!* Bantam, 1998. *(I; A)*

Schlegel, Elfi, and Dunn, Claire Ross. *The Gymnastics Book: The Young Performer's Guide to Gymnastics.* Firefly Books, 2000. *(P; I)*

Whitlock, Steve. *Gymnastics for Girls.* Sports Illustrated for Kids, 1991. *(I; A)*

H (LETTER)

Samoyault, Tiphaine. *Alphabetical Order: How the Alphabet Began.* Viking, 1998. *(P; I)*

HAITI

Cheong-Lum, Roseline Ng. *Haiti.* Marshall Cavendish, 1994. *(I; A)*

Goldish, Meish. *Crisis in Haiti.* Millbrook, 1995. *(I)*

HALLOWEEN

Barth, Edna. *Witches, Pumpkins, and Grinning Ghosts: The Story of the Halloween Symbols.* Houghton Mifflin, 2000. *(P; I)*

Greene, Carol. *The Story of Halloween.* HarperCollins, 2004. *(P)*

Hintz, Martin, and Hintz, Kate. *Halloween: Why We Celebrate the Way We Do.* Scholastic, 1998. *(P; I)*

Rau, Dana Meachen. *Halloween.* Scholastic, 2001. *(P)*

Ross, Kathy. *All New Crafts for Halloween.* Lerner, 2003. *(P; I)*

Stevens, Kathryn J. *Halloween Jack-O'-Lanterns.* Child's World, 1999. *(P)*

HALS, FRANS

Janson, H. W., and Janson, Anthony F. *History of Art for Young People.* Abrams, 1997 (rev. ed.). *(I; A)*

HAMILTON, ALEXANDER

Whitelaw, Nancy. *More Perfect Union: The Story of Alexander Hamilton.* Morgan Reynolds, 1997. *(I)*

HANCOCK, JOHN

Fritz, Jean. *Will You Sign Here, John Hancock?* Putnam, 1997. (rev. ed.) *(I)*

Kallen, Stuart A. *John Hancock (Founding Fathers).* ABDO, 2002. *(P; I)*

HANDBALL

Clanton, Reita E., and Dwight, Mary Phyl. *Team Handball: Steps to Success.* Human Kinetics Publishers, 1996. *(A)*

HANNIBAL

Green, Robert. *Hannibal.* Watts, 1996. *(I)*

Nardo, Don. *The Battle of Zama; The Punic Wars.* Lucent, 1996. *(I; A)*

HANUKKAH

Behrens, June. *Hanukkah.* Scholastic, 1991. *(P)*

Drucker, Malka. *The Family Treasury of Jewish Holidays.* Little, 1994. *(P; I)*

Hoyt-Goldsmith, Diane, and Migdale, Lawrence. *Celebrating Hanukkah.* Holiday House, 1998. *(P: I)*

Rau, Dana Meachen. *Chanukah.* Scholastic, 2000. *(P; I)*

Zakarin, Debra Mostow. *Happening Hanukkah: Creative Ways to Celebrate.* Penguin Putnam, 2002. *(P; I)*

HARDING, WARREN G.

Kent, Deborah. *Warren G. Harding (Encyclopedia of Presidents, Second Series).* Scholastic, 2004. *(I; A)*

Souter, Gerry, and Souter, Janet. *Warren G. Harding: Our Twenty-Ninth President.* Child's World, 2002. *(P; I)*

HARDY, THOMAS

Halliwell, Sarah, ed. *19th Century: Artists, Writers, and Composers.* Raintree, 1998. *(I)*

Lefebure, Molly. *Thomas Hardy's World: The Life, Work and Times of the Great Novelist Poet.* Carlton, 1999. *(A)*

Wright, Sarah Bird. *Thomas Hardy A to Z: The Essential Reference to His Life and Work.* Facts on File, 2002. *(A)*

HARMONICA

Dearling, Robert, ed. *The Illustrated Encyclopedia of Musical Instruments.* Gale Research, 1996. *(I; A)*

HARP

Dearling, Robert, ed. *The Illustrated Encyclopedia of Musical Instruments.* Gale Research, 1996. *(I; A)*

HARRISON, BENJAMIN

Barber, James G. *Eyewitness: Presidents.* DK, 2000. *(P; I)*

Francis, Sandra. *Benjamin Harrison: Our Twenty-Third President.* Child's World, 2002. *(P; I)*

Krull, Kathleen. *Lives of the Presidents: Fame, Shame and What the Neighbors Thought.* Raintree Steck-Vaughn, 1998. *(I)*

Pascoe, Elaine. *First Facts about the Presidents.* Blackbirch, 1996. *(I)*

HARVEY, WILLIAM

Yount, Lisa. *William Harvey: Discoverer of How Blood Circulates.* Enslow, 1994. *(I)*

HAWAII

Doak, Robin S. *Hawaii: The Aloha State.* Gareth Stevens, 2003. *(P; I)*

Fradin, Dennis Brindell. *Hawaii: From Sea to Shining Sea.* Scholastic, 1996. *(P; I)*

Goldberg, Jake. *Hawaii.* Marshall Cavendish, 1998. *(I; A)*

Hintz, Martin. *Hawaii.* Scholastic, 1999 (2nd ed.). *(I; A)*

Johnston, Joyce. *Hawaii.* Lerner, 2001. *(P; I)*

Krensky, Stephen. *Pearl Harbor.* Simon & Schuster, 2001. *(P)*

Nelson, Sharlene P., and Nelson, Ted. *Hawaii Volcanoes National Park.* Scholastic, 1998. *(P)*

Neri, P. J.; Matusevich, Melissa N.; and Davis, Maile. *Hawaii.* Scholastic, 2002. *(P; I)*

Petersen, David. *Haleakala National Park.* Scholastic, 2001. *(P; I)*

Stanley, Fay. *The Last Princess: The Story of Princess Ka'iulani of Hawaii.* Four Winds, 1991. *(P; I)*

Staub, Frank J. *Children of Hawaii.* Lerner, 1998. *(P; I)*

Takaki, Rebecca T., and Takaki, Ronald. *Raising Cane: The World of Plantation Hawaii.* Chelsea House, 1994. *(I; A)*

HAWTHORNE, NATHANIEL

Diorio, Mary Ann. *A Student's Guide to Nathaniel Hawthorne.* Enslow, 2004. *(I; A)*

San Souci, Daniel D. *Feathertop: Based on the Tale by Nathaniel Hawthorne.* Doubleday, 1992. *(P)*

HAYES, RUTHERFORD B.

Francis, Sandra. *Rutherford B. Hayes: Our Nineteenth President.* Child's World, 2002. *(P; I)*

Kent, Zachary. *Rutherford B. Hayes: Nineteenth President of the United States.* Scholastic, 1995. *(I)*

Otfinoski, Steven. *Rutherford B. Hayes (Encyclopedia of Presidents, Second Series).* Scholastic, 2004. *(I; A)*

HEALTH

Brynie, Faith Hickman. *Genetics and Human Health: A Journey Within.* Millbrook Press, 1995. *(I; A)*

Kinch, Michael P. *Warts.* Scholastic, 2000. *(P)*

Lassieur, Allison; Silverstein, Virginia B.; and Nunn, Laura Silverstein. *Head Lice.* Scholastic, 2000. *(P)*

McGinty, Alice B. *Staying Healthy: Dental Care; Staying Healthy: Eating Right; Staying Healthy: Good Hygiene; Staying Healthy: Let's Exercise; Staying Healthy: Personal Safety; Staying Healthy: Sleep and Rest.* Rosen, 2003. *(P)*

Parsons, Alexandra. *Fit for Life.* Scholastic, 1996. *(P; I)*

Peters, Celeste A. *Allergies, Asthma and Exercise: The Science of Health.* Raintree, 1999. *(P; I)*

Salter, Charles A. *The Nutrition-Fitness Link: How Diet Can Help Your Body and Mind.* Lerner, 1993. *(I; A)*

Schwager, Tina, and Schuerger, Michele. *The Right Moves: A Girl's Guide to Getting Fit and Feeling Good.* Free Spirit, 1998. *(I; A)*

HEALTH AND HUMAN SERVICES, UNITED STATES DEPARTMENT OF

Broberg, Merle. *The Department of Health and Human Services.* Chelsea House, 1989. *(P; I)*

HEALTH FOODS

Chandler, Gary, and Graham, Kevin. *Making a Better World: Natural Foods and Products.* Lerner, 1996. *(I)*

Krizmanic, Judy. *The Teen's Vegetarian Cookbook.* Penguin, 1999; *A Teen's Guide to Going Vegetarian.* Penguin, 1994. *(I; A)*

HEART

Beckelman, Laurie. *Transplants.* Silver Burdett Press, 1990. *(P; I)*

Brynie, Faith Hickman. *101 Questions About Blood and Circulation: with Answers Straight from the Heart.* Twenty-First Century, 2001. *(I; A)*

Parramon, Merce. *How Our Blood Circulates.* Chelsea House, 1993. *(I)*

Silverstein, Alvin; Silverstein, Robert; and Silverstein, Virginia B. *The Circulatory System.* Lerner, 1995. *(I)*

Simon, Seymour. *The Heart: Our Circulatory System.* Morrow, 1996. *(I)*

Viegas, Jennifer. *Heart: Learning How Our Blood Circulates.* Rosen, 2002. *(I; A)*

HELICOPTERS

Berliner, Don. *Aviation: Reaching for the Sky.* Oliver Press, 1997. *(I)*

Nahum, Andrew. *Eyewitness: Flying Machine.* DK, 2004 (rev. ed.). *(I)*

Otfinoski, Steven, and Otfinoski, Paul. *Whirling Around: Helicopters Then and Now.* Marshall Cavendish, 1999. *(P)*

Parker, Steve. *High in the Sky: Flying Machines.* Candlewick Press, 1997. *(P)*

Rinard, Judith E. *The Story of Flight: From the Smithsonian National Air and Space Museum.* Firefly Books, 2002. *(P; I)*

HELIUM

Heiserman, David L. *Exploring Chemical Elements and Their Compounds.* McGraw-Hill, 1991. *(A)*

Stwertka, Albert. *SuperConductors: The Irresistible Future.* Watts, 1991. *(I; A)*

HEMINGWAY, ERNEST

Bloom, Harold, ed. *Ernest Hemingway's A Farewell to Arms (Bloom's Notes Series); Ernest Hemingway's The Old Man and the Sea (Bloom's Notes Series); Ernest Hemingway's The Sun Also Rises (Bloom's Notes Series).* Chelsea House, 1995. *(A)*

Meehan, Elizabeth. *Twentieth-Century American Writers.* Gale Group, 2000. *(I; A)*

HENRY, O.

Bloom, Harold, ed. *Bloom's Major Short Story Writers: O. Henry.* Chelsea House, 1999. *(A)*

HENRY, PATRICK

Adler, David A., and Wallner, John C. *A Picture Book of Patrick Henry.* Holiday House, 1995. *(P)*

Kallen, Stuart A. *Patrick Henry (Founding Fathers).* ABDO, 2001. *(P; I)*

Kukla, Amy, and Kukla, Jon. *Patrick Henry: The Voice of the Revolution.* Rosen, 2002. *(P; I)*

HENSON, MATTHEW

Currie, Stephen. *Polar Explorers.* Gale Group, 2002. *(I; A)*

Gilman, Michael. *Matthew Henson: Arctic Explorer.* Holloway House, 1991. *(I; A)*

Litwin, Laura Baskes. *Matthew Henson: Co-Discoverer of the North Pole.* Enslow, 2001. *(I; A)*

Schraff, Anne E. *American Heroes of Exploration and Flight.* Enslow, 1996. *(I; A)*

Weidt, Maryann N. *Matthew Henson.* Lerner, 2002. *(P)*

HERALDRY

Fradon, Dana. *Harold the Herald: A Book about Heraldry.* Dutton, 1990. *(P; I)*

HERBS AND SPICES

Hughes, Meredith Sayles. *Flavor Foods: Spices and Herbs.* Lerner, 2000. *(P; I)*

Lilly, Melinda. *Spices.* Chelsea House, 1993. *(I; A)*

HIBERNATION

Bastian, Lois Brunner, and Carlstead, Kathy. *Chipmunk Family.* Scholastic, 2000. *(P; I)*

Brimner, Larry Dane. *Animals That Hibernate.* Watts, 1991. *(P; I)*

Perry, Phyllis J. *Animals That Hibernate.* Scholastic, 2001. *(P; I)*

Souza, Dorothy M. *It's a Mouse!* Lerner, 1997. *(P)*

HICKOK, JAMES BUTLER ("WILD BILL")

Thrasher, Thomas E. *Gunfighters.* Gale Group, 2000. *(I)*

HIEROGLYPHIC WRITING SYSTEMS

Coulter, Laurie. *Secrets in Stone: All about Maya Hieroglyphs.* Little, 2001. *(P; I)*

Giblin, James Cross. *The Riddle of the Rosetta Stone: Key to Ancient Egypt.* HarperCollins, 1993. *(I)*

Roehrig, Catharine. *Fun with Hieroglyphs.* Viking, 1990. *(I)*

HIJACKING

Beyer, Mark. *Sky Marshals.* Children's Press, 2003. *(P; I)*

Buell, Tonya. *The Crash of United Flight 93 on September 11, 2001.* Rosen, 2003. *(I)*

HIKING AND BACKPACKING

Andryszewski, Tricia. *Step by Step along the Appalachian Trail; Step by Step along the Pacific Crest Trail.* Lerner, 1998. *(P; I)*

Arnosky, Jim. *Crinkleroot's Guide to Walking in Wild Places.* Simon & Schuster, 1990. *(P)*

Dewey, Jennifer Owens. *Finding Your Way: The Art of Natural Navigation.* Lerner, 2001. *(I)*

Hooks, Kristine. *Essential Hiking for Teens.* Scholastic, 2000. *(I; A)*

HILLARY, SIR EDMUND

Brennan, Kristine. *Sir Edmund Hillary: Modern-Day Explorer.* Chelsea House, 2000. *(I)*

Coburn, Broughton. *Triumph on Everest: A Photobiography of Sir Edmund Hillary.* National Geographic, 2000. *(I)*

Hacking, Sue Muller. *Mount Everest and Beyond: Sir Edmund Hillary.* Marshall Cavendish, 1996. *(P; I)*

Stewart, Whitney, and Keiser, Anne B. *Sir Edmund Hillary: To Everest and Beyond.* Lerner, 1996. *(I)*

HIMALAYAS

Reynolds, Jan. *Himalaya: Vanishing Cultures.* Harcourt, 1991. *(P; I)*

HISPANIC AMERICANS

Gonzales, Doreen. *Cesar Chavez: Leader for Migrant Farm Workers.* Enslow, 1996. *(I; A)*

Goodnough, David. *José Martí: Cuban Patriot and Poet.* Enslow, 1996. *(I; A)*

Hoyt-Goldsmith, Diane, and Migdale, Lawrence. *Las Posadas: A Hispanic Christmas Celebration.* Holiday House, 2000; *Migrant Workers: A Boy from the Rio Grande Valley.* Holiday House, 1996; *Day of the Dead: A Mexican-American Celebration.* Holiday House, 1994. *(P; I)*

Perl, Lila; Haskins, James; Meltzer, Milton; and Benson, Kathleen. *North across the Border: The Story of the Mexican Americans.* Marshall Cavendish, 2002. *(I; A)*

Raintree Hispanic Stories. (Written in both English and Spanish) *Simón Bolívar; Hernando De Soto; David Farragut; Miguel Hildago Y Costilla; Jose Marti; Luis Muñoz Marín; Diego Rivera; Junípero Serra; Luis W. Alvarez; Juana Ines De La Cruz; Carlos Finlay; Bernardo de Gálvez; Queen Isabella I; Benito Juárez; Vilma Martínez; Pedro Menéndez De Avilés.* Raintree, 1989-90. *(P; I)*

HITLER, ADOLF

Altman, Linda Jacobs. *The Holocaust, Hitler, and Nazi Germany.* Enslow, 1999. *(I)*

Cartlidge, Cherese, and Clark, Charles. *Life of a Nazi Soldier.* Gale Group, 2001. *(I; A)*

Giblin, James Cross. *The Life and Death of Adolf Hitler.* Houghton Mifflin, 2002. *(I; A)*

Rice, Earle. *The Fall of the Third Reich: Demise of the Nazi Dream.* Gale Group, 2000. *(I; A)*

Stalcup, Brenda, ed. *Adolf Hitler.* Greenhaven, 2000. *(I; A)*

HOBBIES

The Muppet Workshop, and St. Pierre, Stephanie. *The Muppets Big Book of Crafts: 100 Great Projects to Snip, Sculpt, Stitch, and Stuff.* Workman, 2000. *(P; I)*

Baker, Diane. *Make Your Own Hairwear: Beaded Barrettes, Clips, Dangles and Headbands.* Ideals Publications, 2001. *(P; I)*

Blanchette, Peg, and Thibault, Terri. *Really Cool Felt Crafts.* Ideals Publications, 2002; *Kids' Easy Knitting Projects.* Ideals Publications, 2000. *(P; I)*

Churchill, E. Richard. *Building with Paper.* Sterling, 1990. *(I)*

Congdon, Vicky. *Garden Fun!: Indoors and Out, in Pots and Small Spots.* Ideals Publications, 2002. *(P; I)*

Davis, Jodie, and Jaskiel, Stan, illus. *Make Your Own Teddy Bears and Bear Clothes.* Ideals Publications, 2000. *(P; I)*

Friedman, Debra, and Kurisu, Jane. *Picture This: Fun Photography and Crafts.* Kids Can Press, 2003. *(P; I)*

Haus, Robyn. *Make Your Own Birdhouses and Feeders.* Ideals Publications, 2001. *(P; I)*

Hendry, Linda, and Rebnord, Lisa. *Making Picture Frames.* Sagebrush Education Resources, 1999. *(P; I)*

Jackson, Paul. *Festive Folding: Decorative Origami for Parties and Celebrations.* North Light Books, 1991. *(P; I)*

Johnson, Ginger. *Make Your Own Christmas Ornaments.* Ideals Publications, 2002. *(P; I)*

Lohf, Sabine. *Nature Crafts.* Children's Press, 1990. *(P; I)*

Mayne, Don. *Draw Your Own Cartoons!* Ideals Publications, 2000. *(P; I)*

Mayne, Don, and Stetson, Emily. *Drawing Horses (That Look Real).* Ideals Publications, 2002. *(P; I)*

McGill, Ormond. *Paper Magic: Creating Fantasies and Performing Tricks with Paper.* Millbrook, 1992. *(P; I)*

Phillips, Matt. *Make Your Own Fun Frames!* Ideals Publications, 2001. *(P; I)*

Plomer, Anna Llimos. *Let's Create!: Clay; Let's Create!: Metal; Let's Create!: Paper; Let's Create!: Plants and Seeds; Let's Create!: Recyclables; Let's Create!: Stones and "Stuff"; Let's Create!: Wood and Cork.* Gareth Stevens, 2003. *(P; I)*

Schwarz, Renee. *Funky Junk: Cool Stuff to Make with Hardware.* Kids Can Press, 2003. *(P; I)*

Stetson, Emily. *40 Knots to Know: Hitches, Loops, Bends and Bindings.* Ideals Publications, 2002. *(P; I)*

Thibault, Terri, and Hoffman, Beth. *Kids' Easy Quilting Projects.* Ideals Publications, 2000. *(P; I)*

HOISTING AND LOADING MACHINERY

Lampton, Christopher. *Sailboats, Flag Poles, Cranes: Using Pulleys as Simple Machines.* Millbrook Press, 1991. *(P)*

HOLBEIN, HANS, THE YOUNGER

Janson, H. W., and Janson, Anthony F. *History of Art for Young People.* Abrams, 1997 (rev. ed.). *(I; A)*

HOLIDAYS

Bledsoe, Karen E. *Chinese New Year Crafts.* Enslow, 2005. *(P; I)*

Coil, Suzanne M., and Osborne, Mitchel L. *Mardi Gras!* Simon & Schuster, 1993. *(I)*

Gnojewski, Carol. *Martin Luther King, Jr. Day: Honoring a Man of Peace.* Enslow, 2002. *(P)*

Gulevich, Tanya. *Encyclopedia of Christmas and New Year's: Over 240 Alphabetically Arranged Entries Covering Christmas, New Year's, and Related Days of Observance.* Omnigraphics, 2003 (2nd ed.); *Encyclopedia of Easter, Carnival and Lent: Over 150 Alphabetically Arranged Entries Covering All Aspects of Easter, Carnival and Lent.* Omnigraphics, 2001. *(I; A)*

Harris, Zoe, and Williams, Suzanne. *Pinatas and Smiling Skeletons: Celebrating Mexican Festivals.* Pacific View Press, 1998. *(P; I)*

Lewis, Earl B., illus. *Magid Fasts for Ramadan.* Houghton Mifflin, 2000 (reprint). *(P)* (fiction)

MacMillan, Dianne M. *Ramadan and Id al-Fitr (Best Holiday Books Series).* Enslow, 1994. *(P)*

Markham, Lois. *Harvest (World Celebrations and Ceremonies Series).* Thomson Gale, 1998. *(P; I)*

Pinkney, Andrea Davis. *Seven Candles for Kwanzaa.* Dial, 1993. *(P)*

Viesti, Joe, and Hall, Diane. *Celebrate! In Central America.* Lothrop, 1997. *(P; I)*; *Celebrate! In South Asia; Celebrate! In Southeast Asia.* Lothrop, 1996. *(P; I)*

Webb, Lois Sinaiko. *Holidays of the World Cookbook for Students.* Greenwood, 1995. *(I; A)*

HOLISTIC MEDICINE

Ferguson's Careers in Focus: Alternative Health Care. Facts on File, 2003. *(A)*

Billitteri, Thomas J. *Alternative Medicine.* Lerner, 2001. *(I; A)*

Rattenbury, Jeanne. *Understanding Alternative Medicine.* Scholastic, 1999. *(I)*

HOLOCAUST

Adler, David A. *We Remember the Holocaust.* Henry Holt, 1995. *(P; I)*

Altman, Linda Jacobs. *The Holocaust, Hitler, and Nazi Germany.* Enslow, 1999; *The Holocaust Ghettos.* Enslow, 1998. *(I; A)*

Ayer, Eleanor H. *In the Ghettos: Teens Who Survived the Ghettos of the Holocaust.* Rosen, 1999. *(I)*; *The Survivors.* Lucent, 1997. *(I; A)*

Cefrey, Holly. *Dr. Josef Mengele: The Angel of Death.* Rosen, 2001. *(I; A)*

Chaikin, Miriam. *A Nightmare in History: The Holocaust 1933-1945.* Houghton Mifflin, 1992. *(I; A)*

Frank, Anne. *Anne Frank: Diary of a Young Girl.* Doubleday, 1967. *(I; A)*

Friedman, Ina R. *The Other Victims: First Person Stories of Non-Jews Persecuted by the Nazis.* Houghton, 1990. *(I)*

Greenfield, Howard. *The Hidden Children.* Ticknor & Fields, 1993. *(I)*

Handler, Andrew, and Meschel, Susan V., comp. and ed. *Young People Speak: Surviving the Holocaust in Hungary.* Watts, 1993. *(A)*

Nieuwsma, Milton J., ed. *Kinderlager: An Oral History of Young Holocaust Survivors.* Holiday, 1998. *(I; A)*

Novac, Ana. *The Beautiful Days of My Youth: My Six Months in Auschwitz.* Henry Holt, 1997. *(I; A)*

Oertelt, Henry A., and Samuels, Stephanie Oertelt. *An Unbroken Chain: My Journey through the Nazi Holocaust.* Lerner, 2000. *(A)*

Opdyke, Irene Gut, and Armstrong, Jennifer. *In My Hands: Memories of a Holocaust Rescuer.* Knopf/Borzoi, 1999. *(I; A)*

Sherrow, Victoria. *The Righteous Gentiles.* Lucent, 1997. *(I; A)*

Spielberg, Steven, and Survivors of the Shoah Visual History Foundation. *The Last Days.* St. Martin's, 1999. *(A)*

Toll, Nelly S. *Behind the Secret Window: A Memoir of a Hidden Childhood During World War Two.* Dial, 1993. *(I; A)*

Warren, Andrea. *Surviving Hitler: A Boy in the Nazi Death Camps.* HarperCollins, 2001. *(I)*

Weinberg, Jeshajahu, and Elieli, Rina. *The Holocaust Museum in Washington: The Story of Its Creation.* Rizzoli International, 1995. *(A)*

HOMELESSNESS

Stearman, Kaye. *Homelessness.* Raintree Steck-Vaughn, 1999. *(I)*

Wolf, Bernard. *Homeless.* Orchard Books, 1995. *(P; I)*

HOMER, WINSLOW

Venezia, Mike. *Winslow Homer.* Scholastic, 2004. *(P)*

HOMES AND HOUSING

Bial, Raymond. *Tenement: Immigrant Life on the Lower East Side.* Houghton Mifflin, 2002. *(I)*

Morris, Ann. *Houses and Homes.* Lothrop, 1992. *(P)*

White, Sylvia. *Welcome Home!* Scholastic, 1997 (reprint). *(P; I)*

Wilkinson, Philip. *The Master Builders.* Chelsea House, 1993. *(I; A)*

Yue, Charlotte, and Yue, David. *The Wigwam and the Longhouse.* Houghton Mifflin, 2000; *The Igloo.* Houghton Mifflin, 1992; *The Pueblo.* Houghton Mifflin, 1991. *(P; I)*

HOMING AND MIGRATION

Arnold, Caroline. *Birds: Nature's Magnificent Flying Machines.* Charlesbridge, 2003. *(P; I)*; *Did You Hear That?: Animals with Super Hearing.* Charlesbridge, 2001. *(P; I)*; *Hawk Highway in the Sky: Watching Raptor Migration.* Harcourt, 1997. *(I)*

Johnston, Marianne. *Sea Turtles: Past and Present.* Rosen, 2003. *(P; I)*

Lasky, Kathryn. *Monarchs.* Harcourt, 1993. *(I)*

Simon, Seymour. *They Walk the Earth: The Extraordinary Travels of Animals on Land.* Harcourt, 2000; *They Swim the Seas: The Mystery of Animal Migration.* Harcourt, 1998; *Ride the Wind: Airborne Journeys of Animals and Plants.* Harcourt, 1997. *(P; I)*

HONDURAS

Haynes, Tricia. *Honduras.* Chelsea House, 1998. *(I; A)*

McGaffey, Leta. *Honduras.* Marshall Cavendish, 1999. *(I; A)*

HONEY

Johnson, Sylvia A. *A Beekeeper's Year.* Little, 1994. *(P; I)*

Micucci, Charles. *The Life and Times of the Honey Bee.* Houghton Mifflin, 1995. *(P)*

HONG KONG

Barber, Nicola. *Great Cities of the World: Hong Kong.* Gareth Stevens, 2004. *(I)*

Kaqda, Falaq. *Hong Kong.* Marshall Cavendish, 1998. *(I)*

Lyle, Garry. *Hong Kong.* Chelsea House, 1998. *(I; A)*

HOOFED MAMMALS

Bailey, Jill. *Mission Rhino: Earth's Endangered Creatures.* Raintree Steck-Vaughn, 1992. *(P; I)*

Bredeson, Carmen. *Animals That Migrate.* Scholastic, 2001. *(P; I)*

Clutton-Brock, Juliet. *Eyewitness: Horse.* DK, 2000. *(P; I)*

Swan, Erin Pembrey. *Camels and Pigs: What They Have in Common.* Watts, 2000. *(P; I)*

Walker, Sally M. *Hippos.* Lerner, 1997. *(P; I)*

HOOVER, HERBERT CLARK

Holford, David M. *Herbert Hoover.* Enslow, 1999. *(I)*

Kendall, Martha E. *Herbert Hoover (Encyclopedia of Presidents, Second Series).* Scholastic, 2004. *(I; A)*

Souter, Gerry, and Souter, Janet. *Herbert Hoover: Our Thirty-First President.* Child's World, 2001. *(P; I)*

HORSEBACK RIDING

Binder, Sibylle Luise, and Wolf, Gefion. *Riding for Beginners.* Sterling, 1999. *(I; A)*

Bolte, Betty. *Dressage; Jumping.* Chelsea House, 2001. *(I)*

Cole, Joanna. *Riding Silver Star.* Morrow, 1996. *(P; I)*

Pritchard, Louise. *My Pony Book.* Dorling Kindersley, 1998. *(P; I)*

HORSE RACING

Baker, Kent. *Thoroughbred Racing.* Chelsea House, 2001. *(I)*

Duvowski, Mark, and Duvowski, Cathy East. *A Horse Named Seabiscuit.* Penguin Putnam, 2003. *(P)*

Gutman, Bill. *Overcoming the Odds: Julie Krone.* Raintree Steck-Vaughn, 1996. *(P; I)*

Wolfman, Judy, and Winston, David Lorenz. *Life on a Horse Farm.* Lerner, 2001. *(P)*

HORSES

Budd, Jackie. *The Complete Guide to Horses and Ponies: Horse and Pony Jumping; The Complete Guide to Horses and Ponies: Horse and Pony Tack; The Complete Guide to Horses and Ponies: Understanding Horses and Ponies.* Gareth Stevens, 1999; *The Complete Guide to Horses and Ponies: Horse and Pony Breeds; The Complete Guide to Horses and Ponies: Horse and Pony Care; The Complete Guide to Horses and Ponies: Learning to Ride Horses and Ponies.* Gareth Stevens, 1998. *(I; A)*

Budiansky, Stephen. *The World according to Horses: How They Run, See, and Think.* Holt, 2000. *(P; I)*

Clutton-Brock, Juliet. *Horse.* Knopf, 1992. *(I; A)*

Edwards, Elwyn Hartley, and Lemon, Sharon Ralls. *The Ultimate Horse Book.* DK, 1991. *(A)*

Felber, Bill. *The Horse in War.* Chelsea House, 2001. *(I)*

Holub, Joan. *Why Do Horses Neigh?* Penguin Putnam, 2003. *(P)*

Lauber, Patricia. *The True-or-False Book of Horses.* HarperCollins, 2000. *(P)*

Patent, Dorothy Hinshaw. *Horses.* Lerner, 2001; *Where the Wild Horses Roam.* Houghton Mifflin, 1993; *Miniature Horses.* Dutton, 1991. *(P; I)*

HORSESHOE CRAB

Crenson, Victoria. *Horseshoe Crabs and Shorebirds: Story of a Food Web.* Marshall Cavendish, 2003. *(P; I)*

Day, Nancy. *The Horseshoe Crab.* Silver Burdett Press, 1992. *(P)*

Martin, James, and Hamlin, Janet. *Living Fossils: Animals That Have Withstood the Test of Time.* Crown Books, 1997. *(P; I)*

HORSESHOE PITCHING

Boga, Steven. *Horseshoes (A handbook of all the rules, strategies, tips, and techniques you need to be a better player).* Stackpole Books, 1996. *(A)*

HOSPITALS

Crofford, Emily. *Frontier Surgeons: A Story about the Mayo Brothers.* Lerner, 1989. *(P; I)*

Darling, David. *The Health Revolution: Surgery and Medicine in the Twenty-First Century.* Silver Burdett Press, 1995. *(I; A)*

Dooley, Virginia. *Tubes in My Ears: My Trip to the Hospital.* Mondo, 1996. *(P)*

Grinney, Ellen Heath. *Encyclopedia of Health: Hospital.* Chelsea House, 1991. *(I; A)*

Howe, James. *The Hospital Book.* Crown, 1995 (rev. ed.). *(P)*

Johnston, Marianne. *Let's Talk About Going to the Hospital; Let's Talk About When Someone You Love is in the Hospital.* Rosen, 2003. *(P)*

Miller, G. Wayne. *Work of Human Hands: Surgical Wonder at Children's Hospital.* Random House, 1993. *(A)*

Mulcahy, Robert. *Medical Technology: Inventing the Instruments.* Oliver Press, 1997. *(I)*

Murphy, Patricia J. *Everything You Need to Know about Staying in the Hospital.* Rosen, 2000. *(I)*

Rogers, Fred. *Going to the Hospital.* Penguin Putnam, 1997. *(P)*

Winkler, Kathy. *Inventors and Inventions: Radiology.* Marshall Cavendish, 1996. *(P; I)*

HOUSING AND URBAN DEVELOPMENT, UNITED STATES DEPARTMENT OF

Bernotas, Bob. *The Department of Housing and Urban Development.* Chelsea House, 1990. *(P; I)*

HOUSTON

McComb, David G. *Texas: An Illustrated History.* Oxford, 1995. *(I; A)*

HOUSTON, SAMUEL

Collier, Christopher, and Collier, James L. *Hispanic America, Texas, and the Mexican War 1835-1850.* Benchmark, 1998. *(I)*

Fritz, Jean, and Primavera, Elise. *Make Way for Sam Houston.* Putnam, 1998. *(I)*

McComb, David G. *Texas: An Illustrated History.* Oxford, 1995. *(I; A)*

Sorrels, Roy. *The Alamo in American History.* Enslow, 1996. *(I)*

HUDSON, HENRY

Doak, Robin S. *Hudson (Exploring the World): Henry Hudson Searches for a Passage to Asia.* Compass Point Books, 2003. *(P; I)*

Edwards, Judith. *Henry Hudson and His Voyages of Exploration in World History.* Enslow, 2002. *(I; A)*

Goodman, Joan Elizabeth, and Duke, Bette. *Beyond the Sea of Ice: The Voyages of Henry Hudson.* Firefly, 1999. *(P; I)*

Sherman, Josepha. *Henry Hudson: English Explorer of the Northwest Passage.* Rosen, 2003. *(I)*

HUGHES, LANGSTON

Berry, Skip L. *Langston Hughes (Voices in Poetry).* The Creative Company, 1994. *(A)*

Bryant, Philip S. *Langston Hughes.* Raintree, 2003. *(P; I)*

Medina, Tony. *Love to Langston.* Lee & Low, 2002. *(P; I)*

Meltzer, Milton. *Langston Hughes: An Illustrated Edition.* Millbrook Press, 1997. *(I; A)*

HULL, CORDELL

Butler, Michael A. *Cautious Visionary: Cordell Hull and Trade Reform, 1933-1937.* Kent State University Press, 1998. *(A)*

HUMAN RIGHTS

Gold, Susan Dudley. *Human Rights.* 21st Century, 1997. *(I; A)*

Lucas, Eileen. *Contemporary Human Rights Activists.* Facts on File, 1997. *(I; A)*

HUMMINGBIRDS

Rauzon, Mark J. *Hummingbirds.* Watts, 1997. *(P; I)*

Tyrrell, Esther Quesada, and Tyrrell, Robert A. *Hummingbirds: Jewels in the Sky.* Random House, 1992. *(P; I)*

HUMOR

Cox, Clinton. *Mark Twain: America's Humorist, Dreamer, Prophet: A Biography.* Scholastic, 1999. *(I; A)*

Prelutsky, Jack. *Scranimals.* HarperCollins, 2002. *(P; I)*; *The Frogs Wore Red Suspenders.* HarperCollins, 2002. *(P)*; *Awful Ogre's Awful Day.* Greenwillow Books, 2001. *(P)*; *It's Raining Pigs and Noodles.* HarperCollins, 2000. *(P)*; *The Gargoyle on the Roof.* Greenwillow Books, 1999. *(P)*; *A Pizza the Size of the Sun.* Greenwillow Books, 1996. *(P; I)*

HUNDRED YEARS' WAR

Lace, William W. *Hundred Years' War.* Lucent, 1994. *(I; A)*

HUNGARY

Dornberg, John. *Central and Eastern Europe.* Greenwood, 1995. *(A)*

Esbenshade, Richard S. *Hungary.* Marshall Cavendish, 1994. *(I; A)*

Hargittai, Magdolna. *Cooking the Hungarian Way.* Lerner, 2003 (2nd ed.). *(I; A)*

Lundrigan, Nicole. *Hungary.* Gareth Stevens, 2002. *(P; I)*

Steins, Richard. *Hungary: Crossroads of Europe.* Benchmark, 1997. *(P; I)*

Whiting, Jim. *Masters of Music: The Life and Times of Franz Liszt.* Mitchell Lane, 2004. *(I)*

HUNTING

Newton, David E. *Hunting.* Watts, 1992. *(I; A)*

HURRICANES

Allaby, Michael. *Hurricanes (Dangerous Weather Series).* Facts on File, 2003 (2nd ed.). *(I; A)*

Berger, Melvin, and Berger, Gilda. *Do Tornadoes Really Twist?: Questions and Answers about Tornadoes and Hurricanes.* Scholastic, 2000. *(P)*

Gaffney, Timothy R. *Aircraft: Hurricane Hunters.* Enslow, 2001. *(I)*

Greenberg, Keith Elliot. *Storm Chaser: Into the Eye of a Hurricane.* Blackbirch Press, 1997. *(P; I)*

Kahl, Jonathan D. *Weather Watch: Forecasting the Weather.* Lerner, 1999; *Storm Warning: Tornadoes and Hurricanes.* Lerner, 1993. *(I)*

Kramer, Stephen P. *Eye of the Storm: Chasing Storms with Warren Faidley.* Penguin Putnam, 1997. *(P; I)*

Larson, Erik. *Isaac's Storm: A Man, a Time, and the Deadliest Hurricane in History.* Crown, 2000. *(A)*

Lauber, Patricia. *Hurricanes: Earth's Mightiest Storms.* Scholastic, 1996. *(I; A)*

Llewellyn, Claire. *Wild, Wet and Windy: The Weather-From Hurricanes to Monsoons (SuperSmarts Series).* Candlewick Press, 1997. *(P)*

Meister, Cari. *Hurricanes.* ABDO, 1999. *(P; I)*

Sherrow, Victoria. *Hurricane Andrew: Nature's Rage.* Enslow, 1998. *(P; I)*

Simon, Seymour. *Hurricanes.* HarperCollins, 2003. *(P; I)*

Torres, John Albert. *Hurricane Katrina and the Destruction of New Orleans, 2005 (Monumental Milestones Series).* Mitchell Lane, 2006. *(I)*

HUSSEIN, SADDAM

Anderson, Dale. *Saddam Hussein.* Lerner, 2003. *(I; A)*

Shields, Charles J. *Saddam Hussein: Major World Leaders.* Chelsea House, 2002. *(I; A)*

Stefoff, Rebecca. *Saddam Hussein: Absolute Ruler of Iraq.* Millbrook Press, 1995. *(I; A)*

Wakin, Edward. *Contemporary Political Leaders of the Middle East.* Facts on File, 1995. *(I; A)*

HUSSEIN I

Wakin, Edward. *Contemporary Political Leaders of the Middle East.* Facts on File, 1995. *(I; A)*

HYDROGEN

Farndon, John. *Hydrogen.* Marshall Cavendish/Benchmark, 1999. *(I)*

Heiserman, David L. *Exploring Chemical Elements and Their Compounds.* McGraw-Hill, 1991. *(A)*

HYENAS AND THE AARDWOLF

Morgan, Sally. *Predators: Hyenas.* Raintree, 2003. *(P; I)*

Moser, Barry, illus., and Moser, Madeline, comp. *Ever Heard of an Aardwolf?: A Miscellany of Uncommon Animals.* Harcourt, 1996. *(P; I)*

I (LETTER)

Samoyault, Tiphaine. *Alphabetical Order: How the Alphabet Began.* Viking, 1998. *(P; I)*

IBSEN, HENRIK

Bloom, Harold, ed. *Henrik Ibsen.* Chelsea House, 1998. *(A)*

Halliwell, Sarah, ed. *19th Century: Artists, Writers, and Composers.* Raintree, 1998. (I)

ICEBERGS

Simon, Seymour. *Icebergs and Glaciers.* Morrow, 1999. (rev. ed.) *(P; I)*

ICE CREAM

Keller, Kristin Thoennes. *From Milk to Ice Cream.* Capstone Press, 2005. *(P)*

Older, Jules. *Ice Cream.* Charlesbridge, 2002. *(P; I)*

ICE HOCKEY

Kennedy, Mike. *Ice Hockey.* Watts, 2003. *(I)*

Leonetti, Mike. *Hockey Now!* Firefly, 1999. *(I; A)*

Raber, Thomas R. *Wayne Gretzky: Hockey Great.* Lerner, 1999. *(I; A)*

Stewart, Mark. *Hockey: A History of the Fastest Game on Ice.* Scholastic, 1998. *(I; A)*

Sullivan, George. *All about Hockey.* Putnam, 1998. *(P; I)*

ICELAND

Bratvold, Gretchen, ed. *Iceland...in Pictures.* Lerner, 1996. *(I; A)*

Pitkanen, Matti A., and Harkonen, Reijo. *The Grandchildren of the Vikings.* Lerner, 1996. *(P; I)*

Russell, William. *Iceland.* Rourke, 1994. *(P)*

Somervill, Barbara A. *Iceland.* Scholastic, 2003. *(I; A)*

Wilcox, Jonathan. *Iceland.* Marshall Cavendish, 1996. *(I; A)*

ICE-SKATING

Boitano, Brian; Harper, Suzanne; and Fleming, Peggy. *Boitano's Edge: Inside the Real World of Figure Skating.* Simon & Schuster, 1997. *(I; A)*

Edelson, Paula. *Nancy Kerrigan.* Chelsea House, 1998. *(I)*

Feldman, Jane. *I Am a Skater.* Random House, 2002. *(P; I)*

Kunzle-Watson, Karin, and De Armond, Steve. *Ice Skating: Steps to Success.* Human Kinetics Publishers, 1995. *(A)*

IDAHO

Edwards, Karen. *Idaho: The Gem State.* Gareth Stevens, 2003. *(P; I)*

Fradin, Dennis Brindell. *Idaho: From Sea to Shining Sea.* Scholastic, 1996. *(P; I)*

George, Charles, and George, Linda. *Idaho.* Scholastic, 2000 (2nd ed.). *(I; A)*

Pelta, Kathy. *Idaho.* Lerner, 2002 (2nd ed.). *(P; I)*

Stefoff, Rebecca. *Idaho.* Marshall Cavendish, 2000. *(P; I)*

ILIAD

Bloom, Harold, ed. *Homer's Iliad (Bloom's Notes Series).* Chelsea House, 1995. *(A)*

Colum, Padraic, retel. *The Children's Homer: The Adventures of Odysseus and the Tale of Troy.* Simon & Schuster, 2004. *(I; A)*

Lombardo, Stanley, retel. *The Iliad.* Houghton Mifflin, 2004. *(I)*

McCarty, Nick, retel. *The Iliad.* Houghton Mifflin, 2000. *(I)*

Nardo, Don. *Greek and Roman Mythology.* Thomson Gale, 1997. *(I)*; *Readings on Homer (Literary Companion Series).* Thomson Gale, 1997. *(A)*

Sutcliff, Rosemary, adapted. *Black Ships before Troy.* Lincoln, Frances Limited, 2005. *(P; I)*

ILLINOIS

Anderson, Kathy P. *Illinois.* Lerner, 2001 (2nd ed.). *(P; I)*

Boekhoff, P. M., and Kallen, Stuart A. *Illinois.* Gale Group, 2001. *(P; I)*

Brill, Marlene Targ. *Illinois.* Benchmark, 1996. *(I)*

Doherty, Craig A., and Doherty, Katherine M. *The Sears Tower.* Gale Group, 1995. *(I)*

Feeley, Kathleen, and Craven, Jean. *Illinois: The Prairie State.* Gareth Stevens, 2002. *(P; I)*

Murphy, Jim. *The Great Fire.* Scholastic, 1995. *(P; I)*

Santella, Andrew. *Illinois.* Children's Press, 1998. *(I)*

Somervill, Barbara A. *Illinois: From Sea to Shining Sea.* Scholastic, 2001. *(P; I)*

Wills, Charles A. *A Historical Album of Illinois.* Millbrook Press, 1994. *(I)*

ILLUMINATED MANUSCRIPTS

Wilson, Elizabeth B. *Bibles and Bestiaries: A Guide to Illuminated Manuscripts.* Farrar, 1994. *(I; A)*

IMAGING, DIAGNOSTIC

Winkler, Kathy. *Radiology.* Benchmark, 1996. *(I; A)*

IMMIGRATION

Archibald, Erika F. *Journey Between Two Worlds: A Sudanese Family.* Lerner, 1997. *(P; I)*

Ashabranner, Brent. *To Seek a Better World: The Haitian Minority in America.* Cobblehill, 1997; *Beckoning Borders: Illegal Immigration to America.* Cobblehill, 1996; *Still a Nation of Immigrants.* Cobblehill, 1993. *(I; A)*

Catalano, Julie. *The Mexican Americans.* Chelsea House, 1995. *(I; A)*

Chicoine, Stephen. *Journey Between Two Worlds: A Liberian Family.* Lerner, 1997. *(P; I)*

Coleman, Lori. *Vietnamese in America (In America Series).* Lerner, 2004. *(P; I)*

Collier, Christopher, and Collier, James L. *A Century of Immigration: 1820-1924.* Marshall Cavendish/Benchmark, 1999. *(I)*

Freedman, Russell. *Immigrant Kids.* Sagebrush Education Resources, 1995. *(I)*

Gogol, Sara. *Journey Between Two Worlds: A Mien Family.* Lerner, 1996. *(P; I)*

Goldstein, Margaret J. *Irish in America (In America Series).* Lerner, 2004. *(P; I)*

Greenberg, Keith Elliot. *Journey Between Two Worlds: A Haitain Family; Journey Between Two Worlds: An Armenian Family.* Lerner, 1997. *(P; I)*

Hoobler, Dorothy, and Hoobler, Thomas. *The Chinese American Family Album.* Oxford University Press, 1994. *(I; A)*

Meltzer, Milton; Benson, Kathleen; Perl, Lila; and Haskins, James. *Bound for America: The Story of the European Immigrants.* Marshall Cavendish, 2001. *(I; A)*

Perl, Lila; Haskins, James; Meltzer, Milton; and Benson, Kathleen. *North across the Border: The Story of the Mexican Americans.* Marshall Cavendish, 2002. *(I; A)*

Rebman, Renee C. *Life on Ellis Island.* Gale Group, 2000. *(I)*

Reimers, David M., and Stotsky, Sandra. *A Land of Immigrants.* Chelsea House, 1995. *(I; A)*

IMMUNE SYSTEM

Aaseng, Nathan. *Autoimmune Diseases.* Watts, 1995. *(I; A)*

IMPERIALISM

Flowers, Charles. *Cortes and the Conquest of the Aztec Empire in World History.* Enslow, 2001. *(I; A)*

Gallagher, Jim. *Sir Francis Drake and the Foundation of a World Empire.* Chelsea House, 2000. *(P; I)*

Lace, William W. *The British Empire: The End of Colonialism.* Gale Group, 2000. *(I; A)*

Worth, Richard. *Pizarro and the Conquest of the Incan Empire in World History.* Enslow, 2000. *(I; A)*

INCOME TAX

Grote, Joann A. *Your Government: The Internal Revenue Service.* Chelsea House, 2000. *(I; A)*

INDEPENDENCE HALL

Steen, Sandra, and Steen, Susan. *Independence Hall.* Silver Burdett Press, 1994. *(P; I)*

INDIA

Cumming, David. *India.* Raintree, 1995. *(P)*

Dhanjal, Beryl. *Amritsar.* Silver Burdett Press, 1994. *(I)*

Harvey, Miles. *Look What Came from India.* Scholastic, 1999. *(P)*

Hermes, Jules M. *The Children of India.* Carolrhoda, 1993. *(P; I)*

Hinds, Kathryn. *India's GUPTA Dynasty (Cultures of the Past Series).* Marshall Cavendish, 1996. *(I; A)*

Howard, Dale E. *India: Games People Play!* Scholastic, 1996. *(P; I)*

Shalant, Phyllis. *Look What We've Brought You from India: Crafts, Games, Recipes, Stories, and Other Cultural Activities from Indian Americans.* Silver Burdett Press, 1997. *(I)*

Wolpert, Stanley A. *A New History of India.* Oxford University Press, 2003 (7th ed.). *(A)*

INDIANA

Brunelle, Lynn, and Craven, Jean. *Indiana: The Hoosier State.* Gareth Stevens, 2002. *(P; I)*

Fradin, Dennis Brindell, and Fradin, Judith Bloom. *Indiana: From Sea to Shining Sea.* Scholastic, 1995. *(P; I)*

Ling, Bettina; Cornwell, Linda; and McGriff, Nancy. *Indiana.* Scholastic, 2003. *(P; I)*

Swain, Gwenyth. *Indiana.* Lerner, 2001 (2nd ed.). *(P; I)*

INDIAN OCEAN

Dudley, William, ed. *Endangered Oceans.* Thomson Gale, 1999. *(A)*

Taylor, Leighton R. *The Indian Ocean.* Blackbirch Press, 1998. *(P; I)*

INDIANS, AMERICAN

The Indians of California. Time-Life, 1994. *(A)*

Aller, Susan Bivin. *Sitting Bull; Tecumseh.* Lerner, 2004. *(P; I)*

Ancona, George. *Powwow.* Harcourt, 1993. *(P; I)*

Ashabranner, Brent. *A Strange and Distant Shore: Indians of the Great Plains in Exile.* Cobblehill, 1996. *(I; A)*

Ayer, Eleanor H. *The Anasazi.* Walker, 1993. *(I)*

Bial, Raymond. *The Arapaho; The Chumash; The Shawnee; The Wampanoag.* Marshall Cavendish, 2003; *The Blackfeet; The Choctaw; The Long Walk: The Story of Navajo Captivity; The Mandan; The Nez Perce; The Tlingit.* Marshall Cavendish, 2002; *The Inuit; The Shoshone.* Marshall Cavendish, 2001; *The Apache; The Cheyenne; The Haida; The Huron; The Powhatan.*

Marshall Cavendish, 2000; *The Comanche; The Ojibwe; The Pueblo; The Seminole.* Marshall Cavendish, 1999; *The Cherokee; The Iroquois; The Navajo; The Sioux.* Marshall Cavendish, 1998. *(I; A)*

Brennan, Kristine. *Crazy Horse.* Chelsea House, 2001. *(P; I)*

Brill, Marlene Targ. *The Trail of Tears: The Cherokee Journey from Home.* Millbrook Press, 1995. *(I)*

Brown, Tricia. *Children of the Midnight Sun: Young Native Voices of Alaska.* Alaska Northwest Books, 1998. *(I)*

Elish, Dan; Haskins, James; Meltzer, Milton; Perl, Lila, and Benson, Kathleen. *Trail of Tears: The Story of the Cherokee Removal.* Marshall Cavendish, 2001. *(I; A)*

Freedman, Russell. *The Life and Death of Crazy Horse.* Holiday House, 1997. *(P; I)*

Glassman, Bruce. *Wilma Mankiller: Chief of the Cherokee Nation.* Blackbirch Press: Rosen, 1992. *(I)*

Green, Rayna. *Women in American Indian Society.* Chelsea House, 1992. *(I; A)*

Griffin, Lana T. *The Navajo.* Raintree Steck-Vaughn, 1999. *(P; I)*

Harvey, Karen, ed. *American Indian Voices.* Millbrook, 1995. *(I)*

Hirschfelder, Arlene B. *Squanto, 1585?-1622 (American Indian Biographies).* Capstone Press, 2004. *(P; I)*

Hirschfelder, Arlene B., and Singer, Beverly R., eds. *Rising Voices: Writings of Young Native Americans.* Scribner's, 1992. *(I; A)*

Hoyt-Goldsmith, Diane, and Migdale, Lawrence. *Lacrosse: The National Game of the Iroquois.* Holiday House, 1998; *Buffalo Days.* Holiday House, 1997; *Apache Rodeo.* Holiday House, 1995; *Totem Pole.* Holiday House, 1994; *Pueblo Storyteller.* Holiday House, 1991. *(P; I)*

Kallen, Stuart A. *Native Americans of the Northeast.* Lucent, 2000. *(A)*; *Native American Chiefs and Warriors; Native Americans of the Great Lakes.* Lucent, 1999. *(I; A)*

Kavasch, E. Barrie. *The Seminoles.* Raintree Steck-Vaughn, 1999. *(P; I)*

Koslow, Philip. *The Seminole Indians.* Chelsea, 1994. *(I)*

Monroe, Jean Guard, and Williamson, Ray A. *First Houses: Native American Homes and Sacred Structures.* Houghton, 1993. *(I; A)*

Monroe, Judy, and Gaiashkibos, Judi M. *Chief Red Cloud, 1822-1909 (American Indian Biographies).* Capstone Press, 2004. *(P; I)*

Pasqua, Sandra M. *The Navajo Nation.* Bridgestone, 2000. *(P)*

Remington, Gwen. *The Sioux.* Lucent, 1999. *(I)*

Rodanas, Kristina, adapt. *Dance of the Sacred Circle: A Native American Tale.* Little, 1994. *(P)*

Rumford, James. *Sequoyah: The Cherokee Man Who Gave His People Writing.* Houghton Mifflin, 2004. *(P)*

St. George, Judith. *Crazy Horse.* Putnam, 1994. *(I)*

Sayer, Chloe. *The Incas.* Raintree Steck-Vaughn, 1998. *(I; A)*

Sherrow, Victoria. *Political Leaders and Peacemakers.* Facts on File, 1994. *(I; A)*

Sita, Lisa. *Indians of the Great Plains: Traditions, History, Legends, and Life; Indians of the Southwest: Traditions, History, Legends, and Life.* Gareth Stevens, 2000. *(P; I)*

Taylor, C. J. *Bones in the Basket: Native Stories of the Origin of People.* Tundra Books, 1994. *(P; I)*

Terry, Michael Bad Hand. *Daily Life in a Plains Indian Village: 1868.* Clarion, 1999. *(P; I)*

Trottier, Maxine. *Native Crafts: Inspired by North America's First Peoples.* Kids Can Press, 2000. *(P; I)*

Wilkinson, Philip. *The Master Builders.* Chelsea House, 1993. *(I; A)*

Yue, Charlotte, and Yue, David. *The Wigwam and the Longhouse.* Houghton Mifflin, 2000. *(I)*

Zemlicka, Shannon. *Quanah Parker (History Maker Bios Series).* Lerner, 2004. *(P; I)*; *Pocahontas (On My Own Biographies Series).* Lerner, 2002. *(P)*

INDIAN WARS OF NORTH AMERICA

Aller, Susan Bivin. *Tecumseh.* Lerner, 2004. *(P; I)*

Anderson, Paul Christopher. *George Armstrong Custer: The Indian Wars and the Battle at the Little Bighorn.* PowerKids Press, 2004. *(I)*

Ferrell, Nancy Warren. *The Battle of Little Bighorn in American History.* Enslow, 1996. *(I; A)*

Marker, Sherry, and Bowman, John Stewart. *Plains Indian Wars.* Facts on File, 2003 (2nd ed.). *(A)*

Wilson, Claire. *Joseph Brant: Mohawk Chief.* Chelsea House, 1992. *(I; A)*

INDONESIA

Fisher, Frederick. *Indonesia.* Gareth Stevens, 1999. *(P; I)*

Franklin, Sharon; Black, Cynthia A.; Langness, Teresa; and Krafchin, Rhonda. *Southwest Pacific.* Raintree Steck-Vaughn, 1999. *(I; A)*

Lim, Robin. *Indonesia.* Lerner, 2000. *(P)*

Lyle, Garry. *Indonesia.* Chelsea House, 1998. *(I; A)*

Mirpuri, Gouri, and Cooper, Robert. *Indonesia.* Marshall Cavendish, 2001 (2nd ed.). *(I; A)*

Pascoe, Elaine. *The Pacific Rim: East Asia at the Dawn of a New Century.* Millbrook Press, 1999. *(A)*

Viesti, Joseph F., and Hall, Diane. *Celebrate! in Southeast Asia.* HarperCollins, 1996. *(P; I)*

INDUSTRIAL REVOLUTION

Bartoletti, Susan Campbell. *Growing Up in Coal Country.* Houghton Mifflin, 1999. *(I)*

Bland, Ceclia. *The Mechanical Age: The Industrial Revolution in England.* Facts on File, 1995. *(I; A)*

Collier, Christopher, and Collier, James L. *The Rise of Industry: 1860-1900.* Marshall Cavendish/Benchmark, 1999. *(I)*

Ross, Stewart. *The Industrial Revolution.* Scholastic, 2001. *(I; A)*

Sproule, Anna, and Pollard, Michael. *James Watt: Master of the Steam Engine.* Gale Group, 2001. *(I)*

Stanley, Jerry. *Big Annie of Calumet: A True Story of the Industrial Revolution.* Crown, 1996. *(I)*

INFLUENZA

Aronson, Virginia. *Influenza Pandemic of 1918-1919.* Chelsea House, 2000. *(I)*

Getz, David. *Purple Death: The Mysterious Flu of 1918.* Henry Holt, 2000. *(P; I)*

Monroe, Judy. *Influenza and Other Viruses.* Capstone Press, 2001. *(I)*

Peters, Stephanie True. *Epidemic!: The 1918 Influenza Pandemic.* Marshall Cavendish, 2004. *(I; A)*

INSECTS

Berger, Melvin, and Berger, Gilda. *How Do Flies Walk Upside Down?: Questions and Answers about Insects.* Scholastic, 1999. *(P)*

Camper, Cathy. *Bugs Before Time: Prehistoric Insects and Their Relatives.* Simon & Schuster, 2002. *(P; I)*

Collard, Sneed B. *A Firefly Biologist at Work.* Scholastic, 2001. *(P; I)*

Facklam, Howard, and Facklam, Margery. *Insects.* Twenty-First Century, 1995. *(I)*

Jackson, Donna M. *The Bug Scientists.* Houghton Mifflin, 2004. *(P; I)*

Johnson, Jinny. *Simon & Schuster Children's Guide to Insects and Spiders.* Simon & Schuster, 1997. *(P; I)*

Jordan, Tanis. *Jungle Days, Jungle Nights.* Houghton Mifflin, 1993. *(P)*

Pascoe, Elaine. *Dragonflies and Damselflies (Nature Close-up Series).* Thomson Gale, 2005; *Mantids (Nature Close-up Series).* Thomson Gale, 2004; *Beetles (Nature Close-up Series); Flies (Nature Close-up Series).* Thomson Gale, 2001; *Ants (Nature Close-up Series); Crickets and Grasshoppers (Nature Close-up Series).* Thomson Gale, 1998; *Butterflies and Moths (Natures Close-up Series).* Thomson Gale, 1996. *(P; I)*

Perry, Phyllis J. *Fiddlehoppers: Crickets, Katydids and Locusts.* Scholastic, 1995. *(P; I)*

INTERIOR, UNITED STATES DEPARTMENT OF THE

Clement, Fred. *The Department of the Interior.* Chelsea House, 1989. *(P; I)*

INUIT

Alexander, Bryan, and Alexander, Cherry. *What Do We Know about the Inuit.* McGraw-Hill, 1995. *(P; I)*

Bierhorst, John, ed. *Dancing Fox: Arctic Folktales.* Morrow, 1997. *(I)*

Foa, Maryclare. *Songs Are Thought: Poems of the Inuit.* Orchard, 1995. *(I)*

Kendall, Russ. *Eskimo Boy: Life in an Inupiaq Eskimo Village.* Scholastic, 1992. *(I; A)*

Kusugak, Michael Arvaarluk. *Arctic Stories.* Firefly, 1998. *(P; I)*; *My Arctic 1, 2, 3.* Firefly, 1996. *(P)*

Lassieur, Allison. *The Inuit.* Bridgestone, 2000. *(P)*

Newman, Shirlee Petkin. *The Inuits.* Scholastic, 1994. *(P; I)*

Reynolds, Jan. *Frozen Land: Vanishing Cultures* Harcourt, 1993. *(P; I)*

Stewart, Gail B. *Life in an Eskimo Village.* Lucent, 1995. *(I; A)*

INVENTIONS

Baker, Christopher W. *Scientific Visualization: The New Eyes of Science.* Millbrook, 2000. *(I)*

Bankston, John. *Unlocking the Secrets of Science: Robert Jarvik and the First Artificial Heart.* Mitchell Lane, 2002. *(I; A)*

Dash, Joan. *The Longitude Prize.* Farrar, 2000. *(I; A)*

Dommermuth-Costa, Carol. *Nikola Tesla: A Spark of Genius.* Lerner, 1994. *(I)*

Evans, Sarah S. *World of Invention: History's Most Significant Inventions and the People Behind Them.* Gale Group, 1993. *(A)*

Gates, Phil. *Nature Got There First: Inventions Inspired by Nature.* Kingfisher, 1995. *(I; A)*

Jeffrey, Laura S. *American Inventors of the 20th Century.* Enslow, 1996. *(P; I)*

Jones, Charlotte Foltz. *Accidents May Happen: Fifty Inventions Discovered by Mistake.* Delacorte, 1996. *(P; I)*

Karenes, Frances A., and Bean, Suzanne M. *Girls and Young Women Inventing.* Free Spirit, 1995. *(I)*

McKissack, Patricia C., and McKissack, Fredrick L. *African-American Inventors.* Millbrook Press, 1994. *(I; A)*

Richie, Jason. *Weapons: Designing the Tools of War.* Oliver Press, 2000. *(I; A)*

St. George, Judith. *So You Want to Be an Inventor?* Penguin Putnam, 2002. *(I)*

Sobey, Edwin J. *How to Enter and Win an Invention Contest.* Enslow, 1999. *(I; A)*

Streissguth, Thomas. *Communications: Sending the Message.* Oliver Press, 1997. *(I; A)*

Sullivan, Otha Richard. *African American Inventors.* Wiley, 1997. *(I; A)*

IODINE

Gray, Leon. *Iodine.* Marshall Cavendish, 2004. *(I)*

Heiserman, David L. *Exploring Chemical Elements and Their Compounds.* McGraw-Hill, 1991. *(A)*

IONS AND IONIZATION

Shepherd, Donna Walsh. *Auroras.* Watts, 1995. *(I)*

IOWA

Balcavage, Dynise. *Iowa: From Sea to Shining Sea.* Scholastic, 2001. *(P; I)*

Hintz, Martin. *Iowa.* Scholastic, 2000 (2nd ed.). *(I; A)*

Ladoux, Rita. *Iowa.* Lerner, 2002 (2nd ed.). *(P; I)*

Martin, Michael A., and Craven, Jean. *Iowa: The Hawkeye State.* Gareth Stevens, 2002. *(P; I)*

Morrice, Polly. *Iowa.* Marshall Cavendish, 1998. *(P; I)*

IRAN

Bodnarchuk, Kari J. *Kurdistan: Region under Siege.* Lerner, 2000. *(A)*

Cartlidge, Cherese, and Clark, Charles. *Iran.* Gale Group, 2002. *(I; A)*

Fox, Mary Virginia. *Iran.* Scholastic, 1993 (rev. ed.). *(I)*

Gritzner, Jeffrey A. *Iran.* Chelsea House, 2003. *(I; A)*

Habeeb, William Mark. *Iran.* Mason Crest, 2002. *(I; A)*

Lyle, Garry. *Iran.* Chelsea House, 1997. *(I; A)*

Shepard, Aaron. *Forty Fortunes: A Tale of Iran.* Houghton Mifflin, 1999. *(P)*

Spencer, William. *The United States and Iran.* Twenty-First Century, 2000. *(I; A)*

IRAN-CONTRA AFFAIR

Lawson, Don, and Feinberg, Barbara Silberdick. *America Held Hostage: The Iran Hostage Crisis and the Iran-Contra Affair.* Watts, 1991. *(I)*

IRAQ

Bodnarchuk, Kari J. *Kurdistan: Region under Siege.* Lerner, 2000. *(A)*

Kent, Zachary. *The Persian Gulf War: The Mother of All Battles.* Enslow, 1994. *(I; A)*

King, John. *The Gulf War.* Silver Burdett Press, 1991. *(I; A)*

Pimlott, John. *Middle East: A Background to the Conflicts.* Watts, 1991. *(I)*

IRAQ WAR

Al-Windawi, Thura. *Thura's Diary: My Life in Wartime Iraq.* Penguin Group, 2004. *(A)*

Carlisle, Rodney P. *America at War: Iraq War.* Facts on File, 2004. *(A)*

Shostak, Arthur B., ed. *Beyond 9/11 and the Iraq War (Defeating Terrorism/Developing Dreams); In the Shadow of War (Defeating Terrorism/Defeloping Dreams); The Turning Point: The Rocky Road to Peace and Reconstruction (Defeating Terrorism/ Developing Dreams).* Chelsea House, 2004; *Culture Clash/Media Demons (Defeating Terrorism/Developing Dreams); Trade Towers/War Clouds (Defeating Terrorism/Developing Dreams).* Chelsea House, 2003. *(A)*

Yancey, Diane. *Iraq War.* Thomson Gale, 2004. *(I; A)*

IRELAND

Bartoletti, Susan Campbell. *Black Potatoes: The Story of the Great Irish Famine, 1845 to 1850.* Houghton Mifflin, 2001. *(I; A)*

Blashfield, Jean F. *Ireland.* Scholastic, 2002. *(I)*

Daly, Ita. *Irish Myths and Legends.* Oxford, 2001. *(P; I)*

Gottfried, Ted. *Northern Ireland: Peace in Our Time?* Millbrook Press, 2002. *(I; A)*

Harvey, Miles. *Look What Came from Ireland.* Scholastic, 2001. *(P)*

Innes, Brian. *United Kingdom.* Raintree Steck-Vaughn, 2002. *(P; I)*

January, Brendan. *Ireland.* Scholastic, 1999. *(P)*

Kent, Deborah. *Cities of the World: Dublin.* Scholastic, 1997. *(P; I)*

Levy, Patricia M. *Ireland.* Marshall Cavendish, 1996 (2nd ed.). *(I; A)*

Lyons, Mary E., ed. *Feed the Children First: Irish Memories of the Great Hunger.* Simon & Schuster, 2002. *(P; I)*

IRVING, WASHINGTON

Collins, David R. *Washington Irving: Storyteller for a New Nation.* Morgan Reynolds, 2000. *(I)*

Irving, Washington. *Rip Van Winkle.* Simon & Schuster, 2004. *(P)*

ISLAM

Clark, Charles. *Islam.* Gale Group, 2001. *(I; A)*

Stanley, Diane. *Saladin: Noble Prince of Islam.* Morrow, 2002. *(P; I)*

ISLAMIC ART AND ARCHITECTURE

Macaulay, David. *Mosque.* Houghton Mifflin, 2003. *(I; A)*

Wilson, Elizabeth B. *Bibles and Bestiaries: A Guide to Illuminated Manuscripts.* Farrar, 1994. *(I; A)*

ISLANDS

Pelta, Kathy. *Rediscovering Easter Island.* Lerner, 2001. *(I; A)*

Pitkanen, Matti A., and Harkonen, Reijo. *The Grandchildren of the Vikings.* Lerner, 1996. *(P; I)*

Steele, Philip. *Geography Detective: Islands.* Carolrhoda, 1996. *(I)*

ISRAEL

Burstein, Chaya M. *A Kid's Catalog of Israel.* Jewish Publication Society, 1998 (rev. ed.); *Our Land of Israel.* UAHC Press, 1997. *(P; I)*

Corzine, Phyllis. *Palestinian-Israeli Accord.* Gale Group, 1996. *(I; A)*

Finkelstein, Norman H. *Theodor Herzl: Architect of a Nation.* Lerner, 1991; *Friends Indeed: The Special Relationship of Israel and the United States.* Millbrook Press, 1998. *(I; A)*

Fisher, Frederick; Spencer, Shannon; and Chang, Ken. *Israel.* Gareth Stevens, 2000. *(I)*

Garfinkle, Adam M. *Israel.* Mason Crest, 2002. *(I; A)*

Grossman, Laurie M. *Children of Israel.* Lerner, 2000. *(P; I)*

Kort, Michael G. *Yitzhak Rabin: Israel's Soldier Statesman.* Millbrook Press, 1996. *(I; A)*

Landau, Elaine. *Israel.* Scholastic, 2000. *(P)*

Long, Cathryn J. *The Middle East in Search of Peace.* Millbrook Press, 1996. *(P; I)*

McCullough, L. E. *Israel Reborn: Legends of the Diaspora and Israel's Modern Rebirth.* Smith & Kraus, 2000. *(P; I)*

Schroeter, Daniel J. *Israel: An Illustrated History.* Oxford, 1998. *(A)*

Silverman, Maida. *Israel: The Founding of a Modern Nation.* Dial, 1998. *(I; A)*

Williams, Mary E. *The Middle East.* Gale Group, 2000. *(A)*

ITALY

Bisignano, Alphonse. *Cooking the Italian Way.* Lerner, 2001 (2nd ed.). *(I; A)*

Blashfield, Jean F. *Italy.* Scholastic, 1999. *(I)*

Bullen, Susan. *The Alps and Their People.* Raintree Steck-Vaughn, 1994. *(P; I)*

Foster, Leila Merrell. *Italy.* Lucent, 1998. *(I)*

Harvey, Miles. *Look What Came from Italy.* Scholastic, 1999. *(P)*

Hausam, Josephine Sander. *Italy.* Gareth Stevens, 1999. *(P; I)*

Petersen, Christine, and Petersen, David. *Italy.* Scholastic, 2002. *(P; I)*

Winter, Jane Kohen, and Jermyn, Leslie. *Italy.* Marshall Cavendish, 2003 (2nd ed.). *(I; A)*

ITALY, ART AND ARCHITECTURE OF

Blashfield, Jean F. *Italy.* Scholastic, 1999. *(I)*

Corrain, Lucia. *Giotto and Medieval Art: The Lives and Works of the Medieval Artists.* NTC, 1995; *The Art of the Renaissance.* NTC, 1997. *(I)*

Faerna, Jose Maria. *Modigliani.* Abrams, 1997. *(A)*

Harvey, Miles. *Look What Came from Italy.* Scholastic, 1999. *(P)*

Hausam, Josephine Sander. *Italy.* Gareth Stevens, 1999. *(P; I)*

Janson, H. W., and Janson, Anthony F. *History of Art for Young People.* Abrams, 1997 (rev. ed.). *(I; A)*

Muhlberger, Richard, and Metropolitan Museum of Art. *What Makes a Leonardo a Leonardo?* Viking, 1994; *What Makes a Raphael a Raphael?* Viking, 1993. *(I)*

Petersen, Christine, and Petersen, David. *Italy.* Scholastic, 2002. *(P; I)*

Stanley, Diane. *Michelangelo.* HarperCollins, 2000. *(I)*

Winter, Jane Kohen, and Jermyn, Leslie. *Italy.* Marshall Cavendish, 2003 (2nd ed.). *(I; A)*

Zaunders, Bo. *Gargoyles, Girders, and Glass Houses: Magnificent Master Builders.* Penguin Putnam, 2004. *(P; I)*

ITALY, LANGUAGE AND LITERATURE OF

Bloom, Harold, ed. *Dante's Inferno (Bloom's Notes Series).* Chelsea House, 1995. *(A)*

Greenblatt, Miriam. *Lorenzo de Medici and Renaissance Italy.* Marshall Cavendish, 2002. *(I; A)*

Wright, Nicola. *Getting to Know: Italy and Italian.* Barron's, 1993. *(P; I)*

ITALY, MUSIC OF

Berger, William. *Puccini without Excuses: A Refreshing Reassessment of the World's Most Popular Composer.*

Knopf, 2005; *The NPR Curious Listener's Guide to Opera.* Penguin Group, 2002; *Verdi with a Vengeance: An Energetic Guide to the Life and Complete Works of the King of Opera.* Knopf, 2000; *Wagner without Fear: Learning to Love-and Even Enjoy-Opera's Most Demanding Genius.* Random House, 1998. *(A)*

Geras, Adele, and Beck, Ian. *The Random House Book of Opera Stories.* Random House, 1998. *(P; I)*

Getzinger, Donna, and Felsenfeld, Daniel. *Antonio Vivaldi and the Baroque Tradition.* Morgan Reynolds, 2004. *(I; A)*

IVES, CHARLES

Block, Geoffrey Holden, and Burkholder, J. Peter, eds. *Charles Ives and the Classical Tradition.* Yale University Press, 2004. *(A)*

IVORY

Havill, Juanita. *Sato and the Elephants.* Lothrop, 1993. *(P; I; A)*

IVORY COAST (CÔTE D'IVOIRE)

Habeeb, William Mark. *Ivory Coast (Africa - Continent in the Balance Series).* Mason Crest, 2004. *(I; A)*

Nwanunobi, C. Onyeka. *Malinke (Burkina Faso, Côte d'Ivoire, Gambia, Guinea, Guinea Bissau, Liberia, Mali, Senegal, Sierra Leone).* Rosen, 1996. *(I; A)*; *Soninke (Burkina Faso, Côte d'Ivoirie, Ghana, Mali, Mauritania, Nigeria, Senegal).* Rosen, 1996. *(I; A)*

Sheehan, Patricia. *Ivory Coast.* Marshall Cavendish, 2000. *(P; I)*

J (LETTER)

Samoyault, Tiphaine. *Alphabetical Order: How the Alphabet Began.* Viking, 1998. *(P; I)*

JACKSON, ANDREW

Collier, Christopher, and Collier, James Lincoln. *Andrew Jackson's America: 1824-1850.* Marshall Cavendish, 1998. *(I; A)*

Doherty, Kieran. *Andrew Jackson (Encyclopedia of Presidents, Second Series).* Scholastic, 2003. *(I; A)*

Feinstein, Stephen. *Andrew Jackson.* Enslow, 2002. *(I; A)*

Gaines, Ann Graham. *Andrew Jackson: Our Seventh President.* Child's World, 2002. *(P; I)*

Meltzer, Milton. *Andrew Jackson: And His America.* Scholastic, 1993. *(I; A)*

Whitelaw, Nancy. *Andrew Jackson: Frontier President.* Reynolds, 2000. *(I; A)*

JACKSON, JESSE

Haskins, James. *Jesse Jackson: Civil Rights Activist.* Enslow, 2000. *(I; A)*

JACKSON, THOMAS JONATHAN ("STONEWALL")

Fritz, Jean. *Stonewall.* Putnam, 1997. *(P)*

Hughes, Christopher. *Thomas Stonewall Jackson.* Gale Group, 2001. *(I)*

JAMAICA

Brownlie, Alison. *We Come From Jamaica.* Raintree Steck-Vaughn, 2000. *(P)*

Gunning, Monica. *Under the Breadfruit Tree: Island Poems.* Boyds Mills Press, 1998. *(P; I)*

Sheehan, Sean. *Jamaica.* Benchmark, 1996. *(I)*

Wilson, Amber. *Jamaica the Culture.* Crabtree, 2003. *(P; I)*

JAMES, JESSE

Bruns, Roger A. *Jesse James: Legendary Outlaw.* Enslow, 1998. *(P; I)*

Wukovits, John F. *Jesse James.* Chelsea House, 1996. *(I)*

JAMESTOWN

Collier, Christopher, and Collier, James L. *The Paradox of Jamestown, 1585-1700.* Marshall Cavendish, 1997. *(I; A)*

Edwards, Judith. *Jamestown, John Smith, and Pocahontas (In American History Series).* Enslow, 2002. *(I; A)*

JANUARY

Updike, John. *A Child's Calendar.* Holiday House, 1999. *(P; I)*

Warner, Penny. *Kids' Holiday Fun: Great Family Activities Every Month of the Year.* Meadowbrook Press, 1997. *(P)*

JAPAN

Brown, Tricia. *Konnichiwa: I Am a Japanese-American Girl.* St. Martin's Press, 1999. *(P; I)*

Cobb, Vicki. *This Place is Crowded: Japan.* Walker, 1992. *(P)*

Harvey, Miles. *Look What Comes from Japan.* Watts, 1999. *(P; I)*

Pascoe, Elaine. *The Pacific Rim: East Asia at the Dawn of a New Century.* Millbrook Press, 1999. *(A)*

Roberson, John R. *Japan Meets the World: The Birth of a Super Power.* Millbrook, 1998. *(I; A)*

JAPANESE ART AND ARCHITECTURE

Finley, Carol. *Art of Japan: Wood-Block Color Prints.* Lerner, 1998. *(I; A)*

Lovett, Patricia. *Calligraphy and Illumination: A History and Practical Guide.* Abrams, 2000. *(A)*

MacDonald, Fiona. *A Samurai Castle.* NTC, 1995. *(I)*

Ray, Deborah Kogan. *Hokusai: The Man Who Painted a Mountain.* Farrar, Straus & Giroux, 2001. *(I)*

JAPANESE LITERATURE

Haviland, Virginia, retel. *Favorite Fairy Tales Told in Japan.* Morrow, 1996. *(P; I)*

JEFFERSON, THOMAS

Ferris, Jeri Chase. *Thomas Jefferson: Father of Liberty.* Carolrhoda, 1998. *(I)*

Fisher, Leonard Everett. *Monticello.* Holiday House, 1998. *(I)*

Harness, Cheryl. *Thomas Jefferson.* National Geographic Society, 2004. *(P; I)*

Old, Wendie C. *Thomas Jefferson.* Enslow, 1997. *(I)*

Whitelaw, Nancy. *Thomas Jefferson: Philosopher and President.* Reynolds, 2001. *(I; A)*

JELLYFISH AND OTHER COELENTERATES

Gowell, Elizabeth Tayntor. *Sea Jellies: Rainbows in the Sea.* Watts, 1993. *(I)*

Taylor, Leighton. *Jellyfish.* Lerner, 1998. *(P)*

JERUSALEM

Pirotta, Saviour. *Jerusalem.* Silver Burdett Press, 1993. *(I)*

Waldman, Neil. *The Golden City: Jerusalem's 3,000 Years.* Boyds Mills Press, 2000. *(P)*

JESUS CHRIST

Mayer, Marianna. *Young Jesus of Nazareth.* Morrow, 1999. *(P; I)*

JEWS

Chaikin, Miriam. *Menorahs, Mezuzas, and Other Jewish Symbols.* Houghton Mifflin, 2003. *(I)*

Corona, Laurel. *Immigrants in America: Jewish Americans.* Lucent, 2004. *(P; I)*

Mann, Kenny. *The Ancient Hebrews.* Marshall Cavendish, 1998. *(I; A)*

Solomon, Norman. *Historical Dictionary of Judaism.* Rowman & Littlefield, 1998. *(I; A)*

JOAN OF ARC, SAINT

Armstrong, Carole. *Lives and Legends of the Saints: With Paintings from the Great Art Museums of the World.* Simon & Schuster, 1995. *(I; A)*

Hazell, Rebecca. *Heroines: Great Women Through the Ages.* Abbeville Press, 1996. *(I)*

Poole, Josephine. *Joan of Arc.* Random House, 2005. *(P; I)*

JOGGING AND RUNNING

Batten, Jack. *The Man Who Ran Faster Than Everyone: The Story of Tom Longboat.* Tundra, 2002. *(I; A)*

Savage, Jeff. *Running.* Silver Burdett Press, 1995. *(P; I)*

JOHN PAUL II, POPE

Pope John Paul II. *For the Children: Words of Love and Inspiration from His Holiness Pope John Paul II.* Scholastic, 2000. *(P; I)*

Wilson, Jay. *Pope John Paul II: Religious Leader.* Chelsea House, 1992. *(P; I)*

JOHNSON, ANDREW

Alter, Judy. *Andrew Johnson.* Enslow, 2002. *(I; A)*

Harper, Judith E. *Andrew Johnson: Our Seventeenth President.* Child's World, 2002. *(P; I)*

JOHNSON, JAMES WELDON

Haskell, Robert E. *Harlem Renaissance.* Thomson Gale, 2003. *(A)*

Johnson, James Weldon. *Lift Every Voice and Sing: The Negro National Anthem.* Hyperion, 2001. *(P; I)*

JOHNSON, LYNDON BAINES

Schuman, Michael A. *Lyndon B. Johnson.* Enslow, 1998. *(I; A)*

Williams, Jean Kinney. *Lyndon B. Johnson (Encyclopedia of Presidents, Second Series).* Scholastic, 2005. *(I; A)*

JOKES AND RIDDLES

Jansen, John. *Playing Possum: Riddles about Kangaroos, Koalas, and Other Marsupials.* Lerner, 1995. *(P; I)*

JOLLIET, LOUIS AND MARQUETTE, JACQUES

Binns, Tristan Boyer. *Louis Jolliet.* Heinemann, 2002. *(I)*

JONES, JOHN PAUL

Lutz, Norma Jean. *John Paul Jones: Father of the U. S. Navy.* Chelsea House, 2000. *(P; I)*

JORDAN

Jordan . . . in Pictures. Lerner, 1992. *(I)*

Foster, Leila Merrell. *Jordan.* Children's Press, 1994. *(I)*

JUDAISM

Brown, Tricia. *Chaim: The Story of a Russian Émigré Boy.* Henry Holt, 1994. *(P; I)*

Chaikin, Miriam. *Menorahs, Mezuzas, and Other Jewish Symbols.* Houghton Mifflin, 2003. *(I)*

Drucker, Malka. *The Family Treasury of Jewish Holidays.* Little, 1994. *(P; I)*

Kimmel, Eric. *Bar Mitzvah: A Jewish Boy's Coming of Age.* Viking, 1995. *(I; A)*

Kolatch, Alfred J. *Let's Celebrate Our Jewish Holidays.* Jonathan David, 1997. *(P)*

Silverman, Maida, retel. *Festival of Freedom: The Story of Passover.* Simon & Schuster, 1991; *Festival of Esther: The Story of Purim.* Simon & Schuster, 1989. *(P)*

Weitzman, Elizabeth. *I Am Jewish American.* Rosen/Power Kids Press, 1998. *(P)*

Wood, Angela. *Judaism.* Steck-Vaughn, 1995. *(I; A)*

Yolen, Jane. *Milk and Honey: A Year of Jewish Holidays.* Penguin Putnam, 1996. *(P; I)*

JUDO

Casey, Kevin K. *Martial Arts: Judo.* Rourke, 1994. *(I)*

Chesterman, BarSnaby. *Judo.* Mason Crest, 2002. *(I)*

JULY

Updike, John. *A Child's Calendar.* Holiday House, 1999. *(P; I)*

Warner, Penny. *Kids' Holiday Fun: Great Family Activities Every Month of the Year.* Meadowbrook Press, 1997. *(P)*

JUNGLES

Berger, Melvin, and Berger, Gilda. *Does It Always Rain in the Rain Forest?: Questions and Answers about Rain Forests.* Scholastic, 2002. *(P)*

Johnson, Rebecca L. *A Walk in the Rain Forest (Biomes of North America Series).* Lerner, 2000. *(P; I)*

Tocci, Salvatore. *Life in the Tropical Forests.* Scholastic, 2005. *(P; I)*

JUPITER

Brimner, Larry Dane; Goodwin, Peter; and Cornwell, Linda. *Jupiter.* Scholastic, 1999. *(P)*

Cole, Michael D. *Galileo Spacecraft: Mission to Jupiter.* Enslow, 1999. *(I)*

Miller, Ron. *Worlds Beyond: Jupiter.* Lerner, 2002. *(I)*

JURY

Ehrenfreund, Norbert. *You're the Jury: Solve Twelve Real-Life Court Cases Along with the Juries Who Decided Them.* Holt, 1992. *(A)*

JUSTICE, UNITED STATES DEPARTMENT OF

Greene, Meg. *Your Government: The Drug Enforcement Administration.* Chelsea House, 2000. *(I; A)*

Harmon, Daniel E. *Your Government: The Attorney General's Office.* Chelsea House, 2000. *(I; A)*

JUVENILE CRIME

Atkin, S. Beth. *Voices from the Streets: Young Former Gang Members Tell Their Stories.* Little, 1996. *(I; A)*

Bosch, Carl. *Schools Under Siege: Guns, Gangs, and Hidden Dangers.* Enslow, 1997. *(I; A)*

Gedatus, Gus Mark. *Gangs and Violence.* Capstone Press, 2000. *(I; A)*

Goldentyer, Debra. *Preteen Pressures: Street Violence.* Raintree, 1998. *(P; I)*; *Teen Hot Line: Dropping Out of School; Teen Hot Line: Gangs.* Steck-Vaughn, 1993. *(I)*

Hempelman, Kathleen A. *Teen Legal Rights.* Greenwood, 2000 (rev. ed.). *(A)*

Hyde, Margaret O. *Kids in and out of Trouble: Juveniles and the Law.* Dutton, 1995. *(I; A)*

Johnson, Julie. *Why Do People Join Gangs?* Raintree, 2001. *(I)*

Margolis, Jeffrey A. *Teen Crime Wave: A Growing Problem.* Enslow, 1997. *(I; A)*

K (LETTER)

Samoyault, Tiphaine. *Alphabetical Order: How the Alphabet Began.* Viking, 1998. *(P; I)*

KALEIDOSCOPE

Newlin, Gary. *Simple Kaleidoscopes: 24 Spectacular Scopes to Make.* Sterling, 1996. *(I; A)*

KANGAROOS

Jansen, John. *Playing Possum: Riddles about Kangaroos, Koalas, and Other Marsupials.* Lerner, 1995. *(P; I)*

Lepthien, Emilie U. *Kangaroos.* Scholastic, 1995. *(P)*

KANSAS

Bjorklund, Ruth. *Kansas.* Marshall Cavendish, 2000. *(P; I)*

Fredeen, Charles. *Kansas.* Lerner, 2001 (2nd ed.). *(P; I)*

Ingram, W. Scott, and Craven, Jean. *Kansas: The Sunflower State.* Gareth Stevens, 2002. *(P; I)*

Zeinert, Karen. *Tragic Prelude: Bleeding Kansas.* Shoe String Press, 2000. *(I; A)*

KENNEDY, JOHN FITZGERALD

Anderson, Catherine Corley. *John F. Kennedy: Young People's President.* Lerner, 1991. *(I; A)*

Cooper, Ilene. *Jack: The Early Years of John F. Kennedy.* Penguin Putnam, 2003. *(I)*

Goldman, Martin S. *John F. Kennedy: Portrait of a President.* Facts on File, 1995. *(A)*

Harper, Judith E. *John F. Kennedy: Our Thirty-Fifth President.* Child's World, 2001. *(P; I)*

Harrison, Barbara, and Terris, Daniel. *Twilight Struggle: The Life of John Fitzgerald Kennedy.* HarperCollins, 1992. *(I; A)*

Swisher, Clarice, ed. *John F. Kennedy.* Greenhaven, 1999. *(A)*

KENNEDY, ROBERT F. AND EDWARD M.

Harrison, Barbara, and Terris, Daniel. *A Ripple of Hope: The Life of Robert F. Kennedy.* Dutton, 1997. *(I; A)*

Mills, Judie. *Robert Kennedy.* Millbrook, 1998. *(A)*

KEYBOARD INSTRUMENTS

Blackwood, Alan. *Playing the Piano and Keyboards.* Stargazer Books, 2004. *(P; I)*

KING, MARTIN LUTHER, JR.

Aaseng, Nathan. *The Peace Seekers: The Nobel Peace Prize.* Lerner, 1991. *(I; A)*

Adler, David A. *Dr. Martin Luther King, Jr.* Holiday House, 2003. *(P)*

Andryszewski, Tricia. *The March on Washington, 1963: Gathering to Be Heard.* Millbrook Press, 1996. *(I)*

Gnojewski, Carol. *Martin Luther King, Jr. Day: Honoring a Man of Peace.* Enslow, 2002. *(P)*

King, Martin Luther, Jr. *Why We Can't Wait.* Harper, 1964. *(A)*

Marzollo, Jean. *Happy Birthday, Martin Luther King.* Scholastic, 1993. *(P)*

McKissack, Patricia C., and McKissack, Fredrick. *Martin Luther King, Jr.: Man of Peace*. Enslow, 2001 (rev. ed.). *(P)*

Murray, Peter. *Dreams: The Story of Martin Luther King, Jr.* Child's World, 1998. *(P)*

KINGDOMS OF LIVING THINGS

Kelsey, Elin. *Strange New Species: Astonishing Discoveries of Life on Earth*. Maple Tree Press, 2005. *(I)*

Silverstein, Alvin; Silverstein, Virginia B.; and Silverstein, Robert A. *Fungi (Kingdoms of Life Series); Invertebrates (Kingdoms of Life Series); Monerans and Protists (Kingdoms of Life Series); Plants (Kingdoms of Life Series); Vertebrates (Kingdoms of Life Series)*. Lerner, 1997. *(I; A)*

KISSINGER, HENRY

Israel, Fred L. *Henry Kissinger*. Chelsea House, 1986. *(I; A)*

KITES

Kingfisher Books, and Grisewood, Sara. *Step-by-Step Crafts for Children*. Larousse Kingfisher Chambers, 2000. *(P; I)*

Schmidt, Norman. *Best Ever Paper Kites*. Sterling, 2002; *The Great Kite Book*. Sterling, 1997. *(I; A)*

KLEE, PAUL

Janson, H. W., and Janson, Anthony F. *History of Art for Young People*. Abrams, 1997(rev. ed.). *(I; A)*

KNIGHTS, KNIGHTHOOD, AND CHIVALRY

Gravett, Christopher. *The World of the Medieval Knight*. Peter Bedrick, 1996. *(I)*

Weatherly, Myra S. *William Marshal: Medieval England's Greatest Knight*. Reynolds, 2001. *(I)*

KNITTING

Blanchette, Peg. *Kid's Easy Knitting Projects*. Williamson, 2000. *(P; I)*

Clewer, Caroline. *Kids Can Knit: Fun and Easy Projects for Small Knitters*. Barron's Educational, 2003. *(P; I)*

Falick, Melanie D. *Kids Knitting: Projects for Kids of All Ages*. Workman, 1998. *(I)*

O'Reilly, Susan. *Arts and Crafts: Knitting and Crocheting*. Raintree Steck-Vaughn, 1994. *(P; I)*

Sadler, Judy Ann. *Knitting*. Kids Can Press, 2002. *(P; I)*

KNOTS

Adkins, Jan. *String: Tying It Up, Tying It Down*. Simon & Schuster, 1992. *(I; A)*

KOALAS

Burt, Denise. *Koalas*. Carolrhoda, 1999. *(P; I)*

Jansen, John. *Playing Possum: Riddles about Kangaroos, Koalas, and Other Marsupials*. Lerner, 1995. *(P; I)*

Lepthien, Emilie U. *Koalas*. Scholastic, 1991. *(P)*

KOREA, NORTH

Landau, Elaine. *Korea*. Children's Press, 1999. *(P)*

Nash, Amy K. *North Korea*. Chelsea House, 1997. *(I)*

Pascoe, Elaine. *The Pacific Rim: East Asia at the Dawn of a New Century*. Millbrook Press, 1999. *(A)*

KOREA, SOUTH

Landau, Elaine. *Korea*. Children's Press, 1999. *(P)*

Pascoe, Elaine. *The Pacific Rim: East Asia at the Dawn of a New Century*. Millbrook Press, 1999. *(A)*

Solberg, S. E. *The Land and People of Korea*. HarperCollins, 1991. *(I)*

KOREAN WAR

Ashabranner, Brent K. *Great American Memorials: Remembering Korea*. Lerner, 2001. *(I; A)*

Granfield, Linda. *I Remember Korea: Veterans Tell Their Stories of the Korean War, 1950-1953*. Houghton Mifflin, 2003. *(I; A)*

Rice, Earl, Jr. *The Inchon Invasion; The TET Offensive*. Gale Group, 1996. *(I; A)*

KURDS

Bodnarchuk, Kari J. *Kurdistan: Region under Siege*. Lerner, 2000. *(A)*

KUWAIT

O'Shea, Maria. *Kuwait*. Marshall Cavendish, 1999. *(I)*

Pimlott, John. *Middle East: A Background to the Conflicts*. Watts, 1991. *(I)*

L (LETTER)

Samoyault, Tiphaine. *Alphabetical Order: How the Alphabet Began*. Viking, 1998. *(P; I)*

LABOR, UNITED STATES DEPARTMENT OF

Young Person's Occupational Outlook Handbook: Descriptions for America's Top 250 Jobs. JIST Works, 2001 (3rd ed.). *(I; A)*

Casil, Amy Sterling. *The Department of Labor (This Is Your Government Series)*. Rosen Central, 2005. *(A)*

Morem, Susan. U. S. Department of Labor Staff, ed. *How to Get a Job and Keep It.: Career and Life Skills You Need to Succeed*. Facts on File, 2002. *(A)*

Mulford, Carolyn. *Elizabeth Dole: Public Servant*. Enslow, 1992. *(I; A)*

LACE

Meech, Sue. *1900-20: Linen and Lace*. Gareth Stevens, 1999. *(P; I)*

LAFAYETTE, MARQUIS DE

Fritz, Jean. *Why Not, Lafayette?* Putnam, 1999. *(I)*

LAKES

Beatty, Richard. *Rivers, Lakes, Streams, and Ponds (Biomes Atlases Series)*. Raintree, 2003. *(I)*

Donovan, Sandra. *Animals of Rivers, Lakes and Ponds.* Raintree Steck-Vaughn, 2002. *(P)*

Hoff, Mary, and Rodgers, Mary M. *Rivers and Lakes.* Lerner, 1991. *(I)*

Levete, Sarah. *Closer Look at Rivers and Lakes.* Millbrook Press, 1999. *(I)*

Sayre, April Pulley. *Lake and Pond.* Millbrook Press, 1997. *(I)*

LANGUAGES

Charles, Arthur H., and Rowh, Mark. *How to Learn a Foreign Language.* Scholastic, 1994. *(A)*

LAOS

Laos . . . in Pictures. Lerner, 1996. *(I; A)*

Coburn, Jewell Reinhart. *Jouanah: A Hmong Cinderella.* Shen's Books, 1997. *(P; I)*

Mansfield, Stephen. *Laos.* Marshall Cavendish, 1998. *(I)*

Viesti, Joseph F., and Hall, Diane. *Celebrate! in Southeast Asia.* HarperCollins, 1996. *(P; I)*

Zickgraf, Ralph, and Buckmaster, Margie. *Laos.* Chelsea House, 1997. *(I; A)*

LAPLAND

Bullen, Susan. *The Alps and Their People.* Raintree Steck-Vaughn, 1994. *(P; I)*

Hodge, Deborah. *Deer, Moose, Elk & Caribou.* Kids Can Press, 1999. *(P)*

Reynolds, Jan. *Far North: Vanishing Cultures.* Harcourt, 1992. *(P; I)*

LASERS

Asimov, Isaac. *How Did We Find Out about Lasers?* Walker, 1990. *(I)*

Billings, Charlene W. *Lasers: The New Technology of Light.* Facts on File, 1992. *(I; A)*

Boekhoff, P. M., and Kallen, Stuart A. *Lasers.* Thomson Gale, 2001. *(P; I)*

Morgan, Nina. *20th Century Inventions: Lasers, Vol. 6.* Raintree, 1997. *(I; A)*

Nardo, Don. *Lasers.* Lucent, 2003. *(I; A)*

LATIN AMERICA

Franklin, Sharon; Tull, Mary; and Shelton, Carol. *Mexico and Central America.* Raintree Steck-Vaughn, 2000. *(I; A)*

Hoyt-Goldsmith, Diane, and Migdale, Lawrence. *Celebrating a Quinceanera: A Latina's Fifteenth Birthday Celebration.* Holiday House, 2002. *(P; I)*

Main, Mary. *Isabel Allende: Award-Winning Latin American Author.* Enslow, 2005. *(I; A)*

Petersen, David. *South America.* Children's Press, 1998. *(P)*

Tenenbaum, Barbara A. *Latin America: History and Culture.* Gale Group, 1999. *(I; A)*

LATIN AMERICA, ART AND ARCHITECTURE OF

Mann, Elizabeth. *Machu Picchu: The Story of the Amazing Incas and Their City in the Clouds.* Firefly, 2000. *(P; I; A)*

Merrill, Yvonne Y. *Hands-On Latin America: Art Activities For All Ages.* KITS, 1998. *(I)*

LATITUDE AND LONGITUDE

Dash, Joan. *The Longitude Prize.* Farrar, 2000. *(I; A)*

LATVIA

Latvia: Then and Now. Lerner, 1992. *(I; A)*

Barlas, Robert. *Latvia.* Marshall Cavendish, 2000. *(I; A)*

Flint, David C. *The Baltic States: Estonia, Latvia, Lithuania.* Millbrook Press, 1992. *(P; I)*

LAW AND LAW ENFORCEMENT

Billitteri, Thomas J. *The Gault Case: Legal Rights for Young People.* Enslow, 2000. *(I; A)*

Camenson, Blythe. *Real People Working in Law (On the Job Series).* NTC, 1997. *(A)*

Davis, Mary L. *Working in Law and Justice.* Lerner, 1999. *(I)*

Ehrenfreund, Norbert, and Treat, Lawrence. *You're the Jury.* Holt, 1992. *(A)*

Hempelman, Kathleen A. *Teen Legal Rights.* Greenwood, 2000 (rev. ed.). *(A)*

Hyde, Margaret O. *Kids in and out of Trouble: Juveniles and the Law.* Dutton, 1995. *(I; A)*

Italia, Bob. *Courageous Crimefighters.* Oliver Press, 1995. *(I; A)*

Landau, Elaine. *Your Legal Rights: From Custody Battles to School Searches, the Headline-Making Cases That Affect Your Life.* Walker, 1995. *(I; A)*

Nuñez, Sandra, and Marx, Trish. *And Justice For All: The Legal Rights of Young People.* Millbrook Press, 1997. *(I; A)*

Stinchcomb, James A. *Opportunities in Law Enforcement and Criminal Justice Careers.* McGraw-Hill, 2002 (2nd ed.). *(A)*

Thomas, William David, and McAlpine, Margaret. *Working in Law Enforcement.* Gareth Stevens, 2005. *(I; A)*

Wormser, Richard L. *Defending the Accused: Stories from the Courtroom.* Scholastic, 2001. *(I; A)*

LEAD

Heiserman, David L. *Exploring Chemical Elements and Their Compounds.* McGraw-Hill, 1991. *(A)*

Watt, Susan. *Lead.* Marshall Cavendish, 2001. *(I)*

LEAGUE OF NATIONS

Gold, Susan Dudley. *Human Rights.* Lerner, 1997. *(I; A)*

Grant, Reg G. *World War I: Armistice 1918.* Raintree, 2001. *(I)*

Schraff, Anne E. *Woodrow Wilson.* Enslow, 1997. *(I)*

LEAKEY FAMILY

Heiligman, Deborah. *Mary Leakey: In Search of Human Beginnings.* Freeman, 1995. *(I)*

Lambert, Lisa Ann. *The Leakeys.* Rourke, 1993. *(I; A)*

Willis, Delta. *The Leakey Family: Leaders in the Search for Human Origins.* Facts on File, 1992. *(A)*

LEBANON

Marston, Elsa. *Lebanon: New Light in an Ancient Land.* Silver Burdett Press, 1994. *(I)*

Willis, Terri. *Lebanon (Enchantment of the World, Second Series).* Scholastic, 2005. *(I; A)*

LEE FAMILY

Furgang, Kathy. *Declaration of Independence and Richard Henry Lee of Virginia.* Rosen, 2003. *(P)*

LENIN, VLADIMIR ILICH

Edwards, Judith. *Lenin and the Russian Revolution in World History.* Enslow, 2001. *(I; A)*

LEONARDO DA VINCI

Byrd, Robert. *Leonardo, Beautiful Dreamer.* Dutton, 2003. *(P; I)*

Halliwell, Sarah, ed. *Renaissance: Artists and Writers.* Marshall Cavendish, 1997. *(I)*

Herbert, Janis. *Leonardo da Vinci for Kids: His Life and Ideas: 21 Activities.* Chicago Review, 1998. *(I)*

Janson, H. W., and Janson, Anthony F. *History of Art for Young People.* Abrams, 1997 (rev. ed.). *(I; A)*

Muhlberger, Richard, and Metropolitan Museum of Art. *What Makes a Leonardo a Leonardo?* Viking, 1994. *(I)*

LESOTHO

Van Wyk, Gary N. *Basotho (Lesotho, South Africa).* Rosen, 1996. *(I; A)*

LETTER WRITING

Leedy, Loreen. *Messages in the Mailbox: How to Write a Letter.* Holiday, 1991. *(P)*

Otfinoski, Steven. *Scholastic Guide to Putting It in Writing.* Scholastic, 1993. *(I)*

LEWIS, SINCLAIR

Bloom, Harold, ed. *Sinclair Lewis.* Chelsea House, 1992. *(A)*

LEWIS AND CLARK EXPEDITION

Alter, Judy. *Exploring and Mapping the American West.* Scholastic, 2001. *(I)*

Ambrose, Stephen. *Lewis & Clark: Voyage of Discovery.* National Geographic, 1998. *(A)*

Edwards, Judith. *Lewis and Clark's Journey of Discovery (In American History Series).* Enslow, 1999. *(I; A)*

Faber, Harold; Meltzer, Milton; and Calvert, Patricia. *Lewis and Clark: From Ocean to Ocean.* Marshall Cavendish, 2001. *(I)*

Kozar, Richard. *Lewis and Clark: Explorers of the Louisiana Purchase.* Chelsea House, 1999. *(I)*

Marcovitz, Hal. *Sacagawea: Guide for the Lewis and Clark Expedition.* Chelsea House, 2000. *(I)*

Morley, Jacqueline, and Salariya, David. *Across America: The Story of Lewis and Clark.* Scholastic, 1999. *(P; I)*

Patent, Dorothy Hinshaw. *Plants on the Trail with Lewis and Clark.* Houghton Mifflin, 2003. *(I)*

Schanzer, Rosalyn. *How We Crossed the West: The Adventures of Lewis and Clark.* National Geographic Society, 1997. *(P)*

LIBERIA

Aardema, Verna. *Koi and the Kola Nuts: A Tale from Liberia.* Simon & Schuster, 1999. *(P)*

Levy, Patricia M. *Liberia.* Marshall Cavendish, 1998. (2nd ed.). *(I; A)*

Mirepoix, Camille, and Sullivan, Mary Jo. *Liberia... in Pictures.* Lerner, 1996 (rev. ed.). *(I; A)*

Nwanunobi, C. Onyeka. *Malinke (Burkina Faso, Côte d'Ivoire, Gambia, Guinea, Guinea Bissau, Liberia, Mali, Senegal, Sierra Leone).* Rosen, 1996. *(I; A)*

Reef, Catherine. *This Our Dark Country: The American Settlers of Liberia.* Houghton Mifflin, 2002. *(I; A)*

LIBERTY, STATUE OF

Ashley, Susan, and Nations, Susan. *The Statue of Liberty.* Weekly Reader Early Learning Library, 2003. *(P)*

LIBERTY BELL

Hess, Debra. *The Liberty Bell.* Marshall Cavendish, 2003. *(P; I)*

Johnson, Linda Carlson. *Our National Symbols.* Millbrook Press, 1994. *(P)*

Sakurai, Gail. *The Liberty Bell.* Children's Press, 1996. *(P; I)*

LIBRARIES

Cummins, Julie. *The Inside-Outside Book of Libraries.* Dutton, 1996. *(P)*

Fowler, Allan. *The Library of Congress.* Scholastic, 1997. *(P; I)*

Wu, Dana Ying-Hui. *Our Libraries.* Lerner, 2001. *(P)*

LIE DETECTION

Segrave, Kerry. *Lie Detectors: A Social History.* McFarland & Co., 2003. *(A)*

LIES

Hayes, Joe. *Juan Verdades: The Man Who Couldn't Tell a Lie.* Scholastic, 2001. *(P; I)* (fiction)

Moncure, Jane Belk. *Honesty.* Child's World, 1996 (rev. ed.). *(P; I)*

Shannon, George, and O'Brien, John. *True Lies: 10 Tales for You to Judge.* Morrow, 1998. *(P)*

LIFE

Berger, Melvin. *How Life Began.* Doubleday, 1991. *(P; I)*

Burnie, David. *Life.* Dorling Kindersley, 1994. *(I; A)*

Facklam, Margery. *Partners for Life: The Mysteries of Animal Symbiosis, Vol. 1.* Little, 1991. *(P; I)*

Kelsey, Elin. *Strange New Species: Astonishing Discoveries of Life on Earth.* Maple Tree Press, 2005. *(I)*

Silverstein, Alvin; Silverstein, Virginia; and Nunn, Laura Silverstein. *Symbiosis.* Millbrook Press, 1998. *(I; A)*

LIGHT

Burnie, David. *Light.* Dorling Kindersley, 1992. *(I; A)*

Doherty, Paul, and Rathjen, Don. *The Magic Wand and Other Bright Experiments on Light and Color.* Wiley, 1995. *(I)*

Lafferty, Peter. *Light and Sound.* Marshall Cavendish, 1996. *(I)*

Lauber, Patricia. *What Do You See and How Do You See It?* Crown, 1994. *(P; I)*

Levine, Shar, and Johnstone, Leslie. *The Optics Book: Fun Experiments with Light, Vision and Color.* Sterling, 1999. *(I)*

Skurzynski, Gloria. *Waves: The Electromagnetic Universe.* National Geographic, 1996. *(I)*

Tomecek, Steve. *Bouncing and Bending Light: Phantastic Physical Phenomena.* Freeman, 1995. *(P; I)*

LIGHTING

Aust, Siegfried. *Light!: A Bright Idea.* Lerner, 1992. *(P; I)*

Gardner, Robert. *Science Projects about Light.* Enslow, 1994. *(I)*; *Experimenting with Light.* Watts, 1991. *(I; A)*; *Investigate and Discover Light.* Silver Burdett Press, 1991. *(P; I)*

Levine, Shar, and Johnstone, Leslie. *The Optics Book: Fun Experiments With Light, Vision and Color.* Sterling, 1999. *(I)*

LINCOLN, ABRAHAM

Alter, Judy. *Abraham Lincoln.* Enslow, 2002. *(I; A)*

Armstrong, Jennifer. *A Three-Minute Speech: Lincoln's Remarks at Gettysburg.* Simon & Schuster, 2003. *(P; I)*

Bowler, Sarah. *Abraham Lincoln: Our Sixteenth President.* Child's World, 2002. *(P; I)*

Burchard, Peter. *Lincoln and Slavery.* Simon, 1999. *(I; A)*

Cohn, Amy L., and Schmidt, Suzy. *Abraham Lincoln.* Scholastic, 2001. *(P)*

Feinberg, Barbara Silberdick. *Abraham Lincoln's Gettysburg Address: Four Score and More.* Twenty-First Century, 2000. *(I)*

Gross, Ruth Belov. *True Stories about Abraham Lincoln.* Lothrop, 1990. *(P)*

Holford, David M. *Lincoln and the Emancipation Proclamation (In American History Series).* Enslow, 2002. *(I; A)*

Holzer, Harold, comp. and ed. *Abraham Lincoln the Writer: A Treasury of His Greatest Speeches and Letters.* Boyds Mills, 2000. *(I; A)*

Kops, Deborah. *Abraham Lincoln: Holding the Union Together.* Gale Group, 2001. *(I; A)*

Marrin, Albert. *Commander in Chief: Abraham Lincoln and the Civil War.* Penguin Putnam, 1997. *(I; A)*

Morris, Jan. *Lincoln: A Foreigner's Quest.* Simon & Schuster, 2000. *(A)*

LINNAEUS, CAROLUS

Anderson, Margaret Jean. *Carl Linnaeus: Father of Classification.* Enslow, 1997. *(I; A)*

LIONS

Schafer, Susan. *Lions.* Marshall Cavendish, 2000. *(P; I)*

Stonehouse, Bernard. *A Visual Introduction to Wild Cats.* Facts on File, 1999. *(P; I; A)*

LIQUID OXYGEN AND OTHER LIQUID GASES

Billings, Charlene W. *Superconductivity: From Discovery to Breakthrough.* Dutton, 1991. *(P; I)*

Farndon, John. *Hydrogen.* Marshall Cavendish, 2000 *(I)*; *Nitrogen; Oxygen.* Marshall Cavendish, 1999. *(P; I)*

Fleisher, Paul. *Liquids and Gases: Principles of Fluid Mechanics.* Lerner, 2001. *(I; A)*

Stwertka, Albert. *SuperConductors: The Irresistible Future.* Watts, 1991. *(I; A)*

LIQUIDS

Gardner, Robert. *Science Projects about Solids, Liquids, and Gases.* Enslow, 2000. *(I; A)*

Mebane, Robert C., and Rybolt, Thomas R. *Water and Other Liquids.* Twenty-First Century, 1995. *(I)*

Zoehfeld, Kathleen Weidner, and Meisel, Paul. *What Is The World Made Of?: All about Solids, Liquids, and Gases.* Turtleback Books, 1998. *(P)*

LISTER, JOSEPH

McTavish, Douglas. *Joseph Lister: Pioneers of Science.* Watts, 1992. *(I; A)*

LISZT, FRANZ

Halliwell, Sarah, ed. *The Romantics: Artists, Writers, and Composers.* Raintree, 1998. *(I)*

Rosen, Charles. *The Romantic Generation.* Harvard University Press, 1998. *(A)*

Walker, Alice. *Franz Liszt: The Final Years, 1861-1886, Vol. 3.* Cornell University Press, 1997 (reprint); *Franz Liszt: The Weimar Years, 1848-1861, Vol. 2.* Cornell University Press, 1993 (reprint); *Franz Liszt: The Virtuoso Years, 1811-1847, Vol. 1.* Cornell University Press, 1988 (revised). *(A)*

Whiting, Jim. *Masters of Music: The Life and Times of Franz Liszt.* Mitchell Lane, 2004. *(I)*

LITERATURE

Bloom, Harold. *Jewish Women Fiction Writers.* Chelsea House, 1998. *(A)*

Datnow, Claire L. *American Science Fiction and Fantasy Writers.* Enslow, 1999. *(I)*

Reid, Suzanne Elizabeth. *Presenting Young Adult Science Fiction.* Twayne, 1998. *(I; A)*

Vecchione, Patrice, ed. *Truth & Lies: An Anthology of Poems.* Holt, 2001. *(I; A)*

LITHUANIA

Lithuania: Then and Now. Lerner, 1992. *(I)*

Chicoine, Stephen, and Ashabranner, Brent. *Lithuania: The Nation That Would Be Free.* Cobblehill, 1995. *(I)*

Flint, David C. *The Baltic States: Estonia, Latvia, Lithuania.* Millbrook Press, 1992. *(P; I)*

Kaqda, Sakina. *Lithuania.* Marshall Cavendish, 1997. *(I; A)*

LITTLE LEAGUE BASEBALL

Kreutzer, Peter A., and Kerley, Ted. *Little League's Official How-to-Play Baseball Book: Based On the Best-selling Video by Mastervision.* Broadway Books, 2003 (revised and updated). *(P; I)*

Sullivan, George. *Baseball Kids.* Dutton, 1990. *(P; I)*

LIZARDS

Cherry, James. *Loco for Lizards.* Northland Publishing, 2000. *(I; A)*

Souza, Dorothy M. *Catch Me If You Can; Roaring Reptiles.* Lerner, 1992. *(P; I)*

LLAMAS

Arnold, Caroline. *Llama.* Morrow, 1992. *(P)*

Lepthien, Emilie U. *Llamas.* Children's Press, 1997. *(P)*

LOCOMOTIVES

Weitzman, David L. *Locomotive: Building an Eight-Wheeler.* Houghton Mifflin, 1999. *(I)*

Zimmermann, Karl. *Steam Locomotives: Whistling, Chugging, Smoking Iron Horses of the Past.* Boyds Mills Press, 2004. *(P; I)*

LONDON, JACK

Bankston, John. *Classic Storytellers: Jack London.* Mitchell Lane, 2004. *(I)*

Dyer, Daniel. *Jack London: A Biography.* Scholastic, 2002. *(I; A)*

Halliwell, Sarah, ed. *19th Century: Artists, Writers, and Composers.* Raintree, 1998. *(I)*

Lisandrelli, Elaine Slivinski. *Jack London: A Writer's Adventurous Life.* Enslow, 1998. *(I; A)*

Schroeder, Alan. *Jack London.* Chelsea House, 1991. *(I; A)*

Streissguth, Thomas. *Jack London.* Lerner, 2000. *(I)*

LONG FAMILY

LeVert, Suzanne. *Huey Long: The Kingfish of Louisiana.* Facts on File, 1995. *(I; A)*

LOS ANGELES

Jaskol, Julie, and Lewis, Brian. *City of Angels: In and around Los Angeles.* Dutton, 1999. *(P; I)*

MacMillan, Diane. *Missions of the Los Angeles Area.* Lerner, 1999. *(P; I)*

LOUISIANA

Gildart, Leslie S. *Louisiana: The Pelican State.* Gareth Stevens, 2003. *(P; I)*

Hintz, Martin. *Louisiana.* Children's Press, 1998. *(I)*; *Destination New Orleans.* Lerner, 1997. *(I; A)*

Ladoux, Rita. *Louisiana.* Lerner, 2001 (2nd ed.). *(P; I)*

LeVert, Suzanne. *Louisiana.* Marshall Cavendish, 1997. *(P; I)*

LULLABIES

McKellar, Shona, comp. *A Child's Book of Lullabies.* DK, 1997. *(P)*

LUMBER AND LUMBERING

Cowan, Mary Morton. *Timberrr!: A History of Logging in New England.* Lerner, 2003. *(I; A)*

Nelson, Sharlene P., and Nelson, Ted. *Bull Whackers to Whistle Punks: Logging in the Old West.* Scholastic, 1996. *(P; I)*

LUNGS

Ganeri, Anita. *Breathing.* Raintree Streck-Vaughn, 1994. *(P)*

LUTHER, MARTIN

Flowers, Sarah. *The Reformation.* Gale Group, 1995. *(I; A)*

LUXEMBOURG

Heinrichs, Ann. *Luxembourg (Enchantment of the World, Second Series).* Scholastic, 2005. *(I; A)*

Sheehan, Patricia. *Luxembourg.* Marshall Cavendish, 1997 (2nd ed.). *(I; A)*

LYMPHATIC SYSTEM

Ballard, Carol. *The Heart and Circulatory System.* Raintree Steck-Vaughn, 1997. *(I)*

Brynie, Faith Hickman. *101 Questions About Blood and Circulation: with Answers Straight from the Heart.* Twenty-First Century, 2001; *101 Questions About Your Immune System You Felt Defenseless to Answer...Until Now.* Twenty-First Century, 2000. *(I; A)*

Parramon, Merce. *How Our Blood Circulates.* Chelsea House, 1993. *(I)*

M (LETTER)

Samoyault, Tiphaine. *Alphabetical Order: How the Alphabet Began.* Viking, 1998. *(P; I)*

MACARTHUR, DOUGLAS

Fox, Mary Virginia. *Douglas MacArthur.* Lucent, 1999. *(I; A)*

MACKENZIE, SIR ALEXANDER

Xydes, Georgia. *Alexander MacKenzie and the Explorers of Canada.* Chelsea House, 1992. *(I)*

MACRAMÉ

Bress, Helene. *The Macramé Book.* Flower Valley Press, 1999. *(A)*

Gryski, Camilla. *Friendship Bracelets.* William Morrow & Co., 1993. *(P; I; A)*

South, Lianne, and Robins, Deri. *Creative Bracelets.* Scholastic, 2000. *(I)*

MADAGASCAR

Blauer, Ettagle, and Laure, Jason. *Madagascar.* Scholastic, 2000. *(I; A)*

MADISON, JAMES

Gaines, Ann Graham. *James Madison: Our Fourth President.* Child's World, 2002. *(P; I)*

Kallen, Stuart A. *James Madison (Founding Fathers).* ABDO, 2002. *(P; I)*

Welsbacher, Anne. *James Madison.* ABDO, 1998 (rev. ed.). *(P; I)*

MAGELLAN, FERDINAND

Burgan, Michael. *Magellan: Ferdinand Magellan and the First Trip around the World.* Compass Point Books, 2001. *(P; I)*

Gallagher, Jim. *Ferdinand Magellan and the First Voyage around the World.* Chelsea House, 1999. *(I)*

Levinson, Nancy Smiler. *Magellan: And the First Voyage Around the World.* Houghton Mifflin, 2001. *(I; A)*

MacDonald, Fiona. *Magellan: A Voyage around the World.* Scholastic, 1998. *(P; I)*

MAGIC

Bulloch, Ivan, and James, Diane. *I Want to Be a Magician.* World Book, 1997. *(P)*

Cox, Clinton. *Houdini: Master of Illusion.* Scholastic, 2001. *(I; A)*

Eldin, Peter. *The Most Excellent Book of How to Do Card Tricks.* Millbrook Press, 1996. *(P; I)*

Haskins, Jim, and Benson, Kathleen. *Conjure Times: The History of Black Magicians in America.* Walker, 2001. *(I)*

Woog, Adam. *Harry Houdini.* Gale Group, 1994. *(I; A)*

MAGNESIUM

Heiserman, David L. *Exploring Chemical Elements and Their Compounds.* McGraw-Hill, 1991. *(A)*

Uttley, Colin. *Magnesium.* Marshall Cavendish/Benchmark, 1999. *(I)*

MAGNETS AND MAGNETISM

Billings, Charlene W. *Superconductivity: From Discovery to Breakthrough.* Dutton, 1991. *(P; I)*

Dispezio, Michael. *Awesome Experiments in Electricity and Magnetism.* Sterling, 1999. *(I; A)*

Fleisher, Paul. *Waves: Principles of Light, Electricity, and Magnetism.* Lerner, 2001. *(I; A)*

Gardner, Robert, and Ettlinger, Doris. *Electricity and Magnetism.* Twenty-First Century, 1995. *(I; A)*

Math, Irwin. *Tomorrow's Technology: Experimenting with the Science of the Future.* Simon & Schuster, 1992. *(A)*

Tomecek, Steve. *Simple Attraction.* Scientific American, 1995. *(P; I)*

MAINE

Blanchard, Paula. *Sarah Orne Jewett: Her World Her Work.* Addison-Wesley, 1995. *(A)*

DeFord, Deborah H. *Maine: The Pine Tree State.* Gareth Stevens, 2003. *(P; I)*

Dornfeld, Margaret. *Maine.* Marshall Cavendish, 2001. *(P; I)*

Engfer, LeeAnne. *Maine.* Lerner, 1991. *(I)*

Fazio, Wende. *Acadia National Park.* Scholastic, 1999. *(P; I)*

Kent, Deborah. *Maine.* Scholastic, 1999 (2nd ed.). *(I; A)*

Webster, Christine. *Maine.* Scholastic, 2003. *(P; I)*

MALAYSIA

Major, John S. *Land and People of Malaysia and Brunei.* HarperCollins, 1991. *(I; A)*

Munan, Heidi, and Foo, Yuk Yee. *Malaysia.* Marshall Cavendish, 2001 (2nd ed.). *(I; A)*

Pascoe, Elaine. *The Pacific Rim: East Asia at the Dawn of a New Century.* Millbrook Press, 1999. *(A)*

Viesti, Joseph F., and Hall, Diane. *Celebrate! in Southeast Asia.* HarperCollins, 1996. *(P; I)*

MALCOLM X

Brown, Kevin. *Malcolm X: His Life and Legacy.* Millbrook, 1995. *(I; A)*

Myers, Walter Dean. *Malcolm X: A Fire Burning Brightly.* HarperCollins, 2000. *(I; A)*; *Malcolm X: By Any Means Necessary.* Scholastic, 1993. *(A)*

Stine, Megan. *The Story of Malcolm X, Civil Rights Leader.* Dell, 1994. *(I)*

MALI

Brooks, Larry. *Daily Life in Ancient and Modern Timbuktu.* Lerner, 1999. *(I)*

MALTA

Sheehan, Sean. *Malta.* Marshall Cavendish, 2000. *(I; A)*

MAMMALS

Grolier Illustrated Encyclopedia of Animals. Scholastic, 1993. *(I; A)*

Patent, Dorothy Hinshaw. *Why Mammals Have Fur.* Cobblehill, 1995. *(P; I)*

Sherrow, Victoria, and Cohen, Sandee. *Endangered Mammals of North America.* Millbrook Press, 1995. *(I)*

Simon, Seymour. *They Walk the Earth: The Extraordinary Travels of Animals on Land.* Harcourt, 2000; *They Swim the Seas: The Mystery of Animal Migration.* Harcourt, 1998. *(P; I)*

MANATEES

Johnson, Rebecca L. *The Great Barrier Reef: A Living Laboratory.* Lerner, 1991. *(I)*

Ripple, Jeff. *Manatees and Dugongs of the World.* Voyageur Press, 1999. *(I; A)*

Staub, Frank. *Manatees.* Lerner, 1998. *(P)*

Walker, Sally M. *Manatees.* Carolrhoda, 1999. *(P; I)*

MANDELA, NELSON

Cooper, Floyd. *Mandela: From the Life of the South African Statesman.* Philomel, 1996. *(P)*

Denenberg, Barry. *Nelson Mandela: No Easy Walk to Freedom.* Scholastic, 1991. *(I)*

MANET, ÉDOUARD

Janson, H. W., and Janson, Anthony F. *History of Art for Young People.* Abrams, 1997 (rev. ed.). *(I; A)*

Welton, Jude. *Eyewitness: Impressionism.* DK, 2000. *(P; I; A)*

Wright, Patricia. *Eyewitness Art: Manet.* DK, 1993. *(P; I)*

MAO ZEDONG

Marrin, Albert. *Mao Tse-Tung, and His China.* Penguin Putnam, 1993. *(I; A)*

Stefoff, Rebecca. *Mao Zedong: Founder of the People's Republic of China.* Millbrook, 1996. *(I; A)*

MAPLE SYRUP AND MAPLE SUGAR

Carney, Margaret. *At Grandpa's Sugar Bush.* Kids Can Press, 1998. *(P)*

Chall, Marsha Wilson. *Sugarbush Spring.* HarperCollins, 2000. *(P)*

MAPS AND GLOBES

Dorling Kindersley Children's Atlas. DK, 2000. *(P; I)*

National Geographic World Atlas for Young Explorers: A Complete World Reference for Adventurous Minds. National Geographic Society, 1998. *(P; I)*

Alter, Judy. *Exploring and Mapping the American West.* Scholastic, 2001. *(P; I)*

Arnold, Caroline. *The Geography Book: Activities for Exploring, Mapping, and Enjoying Your World.* Wiley, 2001. *(P; I)*

Bramwell, Martyn. *How Maps Are Made; Mapping Our World; Mapping the Seas and Airways; Maps in Everyday Life.* Lerner, 1998. *(I)*

Grabham, Sue, ed. *Circling the Globe: A Young People's Guide to Countries and Cultures of the World.* Houghton Mifflin, 1995. *(I)*

Johnson, Sylvia A. *Mapping the World.* Simon & Schuster/Atheneum, 1999. *(P; I)*

Lye, Keith. *The Complete Atlas of the World.* Raintree Steck-Vaughn, 1997. *(I)*

MARBLES

Levine, Shar, and Scudamore, Vicki. *Marbles: A Player's Guide.* Sterling, 1999. *(P; I)*

MARCH

Updike, John. *A Child's Calendar.* Holiday House, 1999. *(P; I)*

Warner, Penny. *Kids' Holiday Fun: Great Family Activities Every Month of the Year.* Meadowbrook Press, 1997. *(P)*

MARS

Fradin, Dennis Brindell. *Is There Life on Mars?* Simon & Schuster/Margaret K. McElderry Bks., 1999. *(I; A)*

Kelch, Joseph W. *Millions of Miles to Mars.* Messner, 1995. *(I)*

Ride, Sally, and O'Shaughnessy, Tam. *The Mystery of Mars.* Crown, 1999. *(P; I)*

Simon, Seymour. *Destination: Mars.* HarperCollins, 2000. *(P; I)*

Spangenburg, Ray; Moser, Diane; and Moser, Kit. *A Look at Mars: Out of This World.* Scholastic, 2000. *(I; A)*

Stille, Darlene R. *Mars.* Child's World, 2003. *(P)*

Vogt, Gregory L. *Mars.* Millbrook Press, 1996; *Viking and the Mars Landing.* Millbrook Press, 1991. *(I)*

Wunsch, Susi Trautmann. *The Adventures of Sojourner: The Mission to Mars That Thrilled the World.* Mikaya Press, 1998. *(I; A)*

MARSHALL, GEORGE C.

Lubetkin, Wendy. *George Marshall.* Chelsea House, 1990. *(I)*

Saunders, Alan. *George C. Marshall: A General for Peace.* Facts on File, 1995. *(A)*

MARSHALL, JOHN

Kallen, Stuart A. *John Marshall (Founding Fathers).* ABDO, 2002. *(P; I)*

Silberdick-Feinberg, Barbara. *John Marshall: The Great Chief Justice.* Enslow, 1995. *(I; A)*

MARSUPIALS

Jansen, John. *Playing Possum: Riddles about Kangaroos, Koalas, and Other Marsupials.* Lerner, 1995. *(P; I)*

Lepthien, Emilie U. *Kangaroos.* Scholastic, 1995; *Opossums.* Scholastic, 1994; *Koalas.* Scholastic, 1991. *(P)*

MARX, KARL

Bussing-Burks, Marie. *Influential Economists.* Oliver Press, 2002. *(A)*

MARYLAND

Dubois, Muriel L. *Maryland: Facts and Symbols.* Capstone/Hilltop, 2000. *(P)*

Fradin, Dennis Brindell; Callcott, George H.; and Hillerich, Robert L. *Maryland: From Sea to Shining Sea.* Scholastic, 1997. *(P; I)*

Johnston, Joyce. *Maryland.* Lerner, 2002 (2nd ed.). *(P; I)*

Martin, Michael A., and Craven, Jean. *Maryland: The Old Line State.* Gareth Stevens, 2002. *(P; I)*

Rauth, Leslie. *Maryland.* Marshall Cavendish, 2000. *(P; I)*

Somervill, Barbara A. *Maryland.* Scholastic, 2003. *(P; I)*

Streissguth, Thomas. *The Thirteen Colonies: Maryland.* Gale Group, 2001. *(I)*

MASON-DIXON LINE

St. George, Judith. *Mason and Dixon's Line of Fire.* Putnam, 1991. *(I; A)*

MASSACHUSETTS

Barenblat, Rachel, and Craven, Jean. *Massachusetts: The Bay State.* Gareth Stevens, 2002. *(P; I)*

Bjornlund, Lydia. *The Thirteen Colonies: Massachusetts.* Gale Group, 2001. *(I)*

Fradin, Dennis Brindell. *Massachusetts: From Sea to Shining Sea.* Scholastic, 1994. *(P; I)*

LeVert, Suzanne. *Massachusetts.* Marshall Cavendish, 2000. *(P; I)*

Lewis, Taylor Biggs, and Heard, Virginia Scott. *Nantucket: Gardens and Houses.* Little, Brown & Co., 1990. *(A)*

McNair, Sylvia. *Massachusetts.* Children's Press, 1998. *(I)*

Warner, J. F. *Massachusetts.* Lerner, 2001 (2nd ed.). *(P; I)*

MATERIALS SCIENCE

Billings, Charlene W. *Superconductivity: From Discovery to Breakthrough.* Dutton, 1991. *(P; I)*

Bortz, Alfred B. *Techno-Matter: The Materials Behind the Marvels.* Lerner, 2001. *(A)*

Fodor, R. V. *Gold, Copper, Iron: How Metals Are Formed, Found, and Used.* Enslow, 1989. *(A)*

Gallant, Roy A. *The Ever-Changing Atom.* Benchmark, 2000. *(P; I)*

Goldstein, Natalie. *How Do We Know the Nature of the Atom.* Rosen, 2001. *(I; A)*

Lampton, Christopher. *SuperConductors.* Enslow, 1989. *(I)*

Stwertka, Albert. *SuperConductors: The Irresistible Future.* Watts, 1991. *(I; A)*

Tomb, Howard, and Kunkel, Dennis. *Microaliens: Dazzling Journeys with an Electron Microscope.* Farrar, 1993. *(I)*

MATHEMATICS

Anno, Mitsumasa. *Anno's Math Games; Anno's Math Games II; Anno's Math Games III.* Penguin Group, 1997 (reprint). *(P)*

Caron, Lucille, and St. Jacques, Philip M. *Addition and Subtraction; Geometry; Multiplication and Division.* Enslow, 2001; *Fractions and Decimals; Math Success; Percents and Ratios; Pre-Algebra and Algebra.* Enslow, 2000. *(P; I)*

Cushman, Jean. *Do You Wanna Bet? Your Chance to Find Out About Probability.* Clarion, 1991. *(I)*

Leedy, Loreen. *Subtraction Action.* Holiday House, 2000; *Mission: Addition.* Holiday House, 1999; *Fraction Action.* Holiday House, 1996. *(P)*

McMillan, Bruce. *Jellybeans for Sale.* Scholastic, 1996. *(P)*

Murphy, Stuart J. *Mall Mania (Mathstart Series); Rodeo Time (Mathstart Series).* HarperCollins, 2006; *Leaping Lizards (Mathstart Series); Same Old Horse (Mathstart Series).* HarperCollins, 2005; *Coyotes All Around (Mathstart Series).* HarperCollins, 2003; *Dinosaur Deals (Mathstart Series).* HarperCollins, 2001; *Betcha! (Mathstart Series); Divide and Ride (Mathstart Series); Elevator Magic (Mathstart Series); Every Buddy Counts (Mathstart Series); Game Time! (Mathstart Series).* HarperCollins, 1997. *(P)*

Reeves, Diane Lindsey. *Career Ideas for Kids Who Like Math.* Facts on File, 2000. *(I)*

Roy, Jennifer Rozines, and Roy, Gregory. *Addition in the Forest (Math All around Us Series); Holiday Fractions (Math All around Us Series); Numbers on the Street (Math All around Us Series); Patterns in Nature (Math All around Us); Sorting at the Ocean (Math All around Us Series); Subtraction at School (Math All around Us Series).* Benchmark Books, 2005. *(P)*

Schwartz, David M. *Millions to Measure.* HarperCollins, 2003; *On Beyond a Million: An Amazing Math Journey.* Random House, 2001; *How Much Is a Million?* HarperCollins, 1997; *If You Made a Million.* HarperCollins, 1994. *(P)*

Scieszka, Jon. *Math Curse.* Viking, 1995. *(P; I)*

Tang, Greg. *Math for All Seasons (Mind-Stretching Math Riddles Series); Math Potatoes: Mind-Stretching Brain Food.* Scholastic, 2005; *The Grapes of Math (Mind-Stretching Math Riddles Series).* Scholastic, 2004; *Math Appeal (Mind-Stretching Math Riddles Series); Math-terpieces: The Art of Problem-Solving.* Scholastic, 2003; *The Best of Times: Math Strategies that Multiply.* Scholastic, 2002. *(P; I)*

VanCleave, Janice. *Math for Every Kid: Activities That Make Learning Math Fun.* John Wiley, 1991. *(P; I)*

Wingard-Nelson, Rebecca. *Algebra I and Algebra II; Data, Graphing, and Statistics; Problem Solving and Word Problems; Trigonometry.* Enslow, 2004. *(I)*

Zaslavsky, Claudia. *Math Games and Activities from around the World.* Chicago Review Press, 1998. *(I; A)*

MATTER

Clark, John. *Matter and Energy: Physics in Action.* Oxford University Press, 1995. *(I; A)*

Cobb, Vicki. *Why Can't You Unscramble an Egg?: and Other Not Such Dumb Questions about Matter.* Lodestar, 1990. *(P; I)*

Gardner, Robert. *Science Projects about Solids, Liquids, and Gases.* Enslow, 2000. *(I; A)*

Mebane, Robert C., and Rybolt, Thomas R. *Air and Other Gases; Salts and Solids; Water and Other Liquids.* Twenty-First Century, 1995. *(I)*

MAURITANIA

Goodsmith, Lauren. *The Children of Mauritania: Days in the Desert and by the River Shore.* Lerner, 1994. *(I)*

MAYA

Day, Nancy. *Your Travel Guide to the Ancient Mayan Civilization.* Lerner, 2000. *(I)*

Fisher, Leonard Everett. *Gods and Goddesses of the Ancient Maya.* Holiday, 1999. *(P; I)*

Galvin, Irene Flum, and Stein, R.C. *The Ancient Maya.* Marshall Cavendish, 1997. *(I)*

Gerson, Mary-Joan, retel. *People of Corn: A Mayan Story.* Little, Brown & Co., 1995. *(P)*

MAYFLOWER

Leeuwen, Jean Van. *Across the Wide Dark Sea: The Mayflower Journey.* Dial Books for Young Readers, 1995. *(P)*

McCLINTOCK, BARBARA

Fine, Edith Hope. *Barbara McClintock: Nobel Prize Geneticist.* Enslow, 1998. *(I)*

Hacker, Carlotta. *Nobel Prize Winners.* Crabtree, 1999. *(P; I)*

McKINLEY, WILLIAM

Feinstein, Stephen. *William McKinley.* Enslow, 2002. *(I; A)*

Klingel, Cynthia Fitterer, and Noyed, Robert B. *William McKinley: Our Twenty-Fifth President.* Child's World, 2002. *(P; I)*

MEAD, MARGARET

Castiglia, Julie. *Margaret Mead.* Silver Burdett, 1989. *(I; A)*

Pollard, Michael. *Margaret Mead: Bringing World Cultures Together.* Gale Group, 1999. *(A)*

Tilton, Rafael. *Margaret Mead.* Gale Group, 1994. *(I; A)*

MEAT AND MEAT PACKING

Cooper, Jason. *Dairy Products; Poultry.* Rourke, 2002; *Beef.* Rourke, 1997. *(P)*

MEDICINE

Boon, Kevin Alexander. *The Human Genome Project: What Does Decoding DNA Mean for Us?* Enslow, 2002. *(A)*

Darling, David. *The Health Revolution: Surgery and Medicine in the Twenty-First Century; Micromachines and Nanotechnology: The Amazing New World of the Ultrasmall.* Silver Burdett Press, 1995. *(I; A)*

Dowswell, Paul. *Medicine.* Heinemann, 2001. *(I)*

Mabie, Margot C. J. *Bioethics and the New Medical Technology.* Simon & Schuster, 1993. *(A)*

Marshall, Elizabeth L. *Conquering Infertility: Medical Challenges and Moral Dilemmas.* Watts, 1997; *The Human Genome Project: Cracking the Code within Us.* Watts, 1996. *(A)*

Miller, Brandon Marie. *Just What the Doctor Ordered: The History of American Medicine.* Lerner, 1997. *(I)*

Mulcahy, Robert. *Medical Technology: Inventing the Instruments.* Oliver Press, 1997; *Diseases: Finding the Cure.* Oliver Press, 1996. *(I)*

Thomas, Peggy. *Medicines from Nature.* Millbrook Press, 1997. *(I; A)*

Townsend, John. *A Painful History of Medicine: Bedpans, Blood, and Bandages: A History of Hospitals; A Painful History of Medicine: Pills, Powders, and Potions: A History of Medication; A Painful History of Medicine: Pox, Pus, and Plagues: A History of Disease and Infection; A Painful History of Medicine: Scalpels, Stitches, and Scars: A History of Surgery.* Raintree, 2005. *(I; A)*

MEIR, GOLDA

Hitzeroth, Deborah. *Golda Meir.* Lucent, 1998. *(I)*

MELONS

Hughes, Meredith Sayles. *Yes, We Have Bananas: Fruits from Shrubs and Vines.* Lerner, 1999. *(P; I)*

MELVILLE, HERMAN

Bloom, Harold, ed. *Herman Melville's Billy Budd, Benito Cereno, and Bartleby the Scrivener (Bloom's Notes Series); Herman Melville's Moby Dick (Bloom's Notes Series).* Chelsea House, 1995. *(A)*

Rollyson, Carl E., and Paddock, Lisa Olson. *Herman Melville A to Z: The Essential Reference to His Life and Work.* Facts on File, 2001. *(A)*

MENDEL, GREGOR JOHANN

Brynie, Faith Hickman. *Genetics and Human Health: A Journey Within.* Millbrook Press, 1995. *(I; A)*

Edelson, Edward. *Gregor Mendel and the Roots of Genetics.* Oxford, 2001. *(I; A)*

Klare, Roger. *Gregor Mendel: Father of Genetics.* Enslow, 1997. *(I)*

Yount, Lisa. *Genetics and Genetic Engineering.* Facts on File, 1997. *(A)*

MENSTRUATION

Berger, Gilda. *PMS: Premenstrual Syndrome: A Guide for Young Women.* Hunter House, 1993. *(I; A)*

Gravelle, Karen, and Gravelle, Jennifer. *The Period Book: Everything You Don't Want to Ask (but Need to Know).* Walker, 1996. *(P; I)*

MENTAL ILLNESS

Campbell, Nancy M. *Panic Disorder (Perspectives on Mental Health Series).* Capstone Press, 2001. *(I)*

Cobain, Bev. *When Nothing Matters Anymore: A Survival Guide for Depressed Teens.* Free Spirit, 1998. *(I; A)*

Hurley, Jennifer A., ed. *Mental Health.* Greenhaven, 1999. *(I; A)*

Hyde, Margaret O., and Forsyth, Elizabeth H. *Know about Mental Illness.* Walker, 1996. *(I)*

Kelly, Evelyn B. *Coping with Schizophrenia.* Rosen, 1999. *(I; A)*

Leigh, Vanora. *Mental Illness.* Raintree Steck-Vaughn, 1999. *(I)*

Moe, Barbara A. *Coping with Mental Illness.* Rosen, 2001. *(I; A)*

Silverstein, Alvin; Silverstein, Virginia B.; and Nunn, Laura Silverstein. *Depression.* Enslow, 1997. *(I; A)*

Wolff, Lisa, ed. *Teen Depression.* Gale Group, 1998. *(I; A)*

MERCURY

Brimner, Larry Dane. *Mercury.* Scholastic, 1999. *(P)*

Simon, Seymour. *Mercury.* Morrow, 1992. *(P)*

MESOPOTAMIA

Crisp, Peter. *Mesopotamia: Iraq in Ancient Times.* Enchanted Lion Books, 2004. *(P; I)*

Greene, Jacqueline Dembar. *Slavery in Ancient Egypt and Mesopotamia.* Watts, 2000. *(P; I)*

Meltzer, Milton. *Ten Kings: And the Worlds They Ruled.* Orchard Books, 2002. *(P; I)*

Moss, Carol. *Science in Ancient Mesopotamia.* Watts, 1999. *(P; I)*

Service, Pamela F. *Mesopotamia.* Marshall Cavendish, 1998. *(I; A)*

Swisher, Clarice. *The Ancient Near East.* Gale Group, 1995. *(I; A)*

METALS AND METALLURGY

Beatty, Richard. *Manganese.* Marshall Cavendish, 2004; *Copper.* Marshall Cavendish, 2000. *(I)*

Farndon, John. *Aluminum.* Marshall Cavendish, 2000. *(I)*

Fodor, R. V. *Gold, Copper, Iron: How Metals Are Formed, Found, and Used.* Enslow, 1989. *(A)*

Gray, Leon. *Tin.* Marshall Cavendish, 2003. *(I)*

Plomer, Anna Llimos. *Let's Create!: Metal.* Gareth Stevens, 2003. *(P; I)*

Sparrow, Giles. *Nickel.* Marshall Cavendish, 2004 ; *Iron.* Marshall Cavendish, 1999. *(I)*

Tocci, Salvatore. *Aluminum; Copper; Gold; Iron; Silver; Tin.* Scholastic, 2005. *(P)*

Watt, Susan. *Mercury.* Marshall Cavendish, 2004; *Silver; Titanium.* Marshall Cavendish, 2002; *Lead.* Marshall Cavendish, 2001. *(I)*

METAMORPHOSIS

Bailey, Jill. *How Caterpillars Turn into Butterflies.* Marshall Cavendish, 1998. *(P; I)*

Goor, Nancy, and Goor, Ron. *Insect Metamorphosis: From Egg to Adult.* Simon & Schuster, 1998. *(P)*

Ruiz, Andres Llamas, and Arredondo, Francisco. *Metamorphosis.* Sterling, 1996. *(P; I)*

MEXICAN WAR

The Mexican War of Independence. Lucent, 1997. *(A)*

Carey, Charles W. *Mexican War: Mr. Polk's War.* Enslow, 2002. *(I; A)*

Gold, Susan Dudley. *Land Pacts.* Millbrook Press, 1997. *(I; A)*

Nardo, Don. *The Mexican-American War.* Lucent, 1991. *(I; A)*

Sorrels, Roy. *The Alamo in American History.* Enslow, 1996. *(I)*

MEXICO

Ancona, George. *Fiestas: Viva Mexico!; Folk Arts: Viva Mexico!; Foods: Viva Mexico; Past: Viva Mexico!; People: Viva Mexico!* Marshall Cavendish, 2001. *(P; I)*

Aykroyd, Clarissa. *Government of Mexico.* Mason Crest, 2002. *(I)*

Burt, Janet. *Provinces of the Pacific North of Mexico.* Mason Crest, 2002. *(I)*

Carey, Charles W. *Mexican War: Mr. Polk's War.* Enslow, 2002. *(I; A)*

Coronado, Rosa. *Cooking the Mexican Way.* Lerner, 2001 (2nd ed.). *(I; A)*

Day-MacLeod, Deirdre. *Central States of Mexico.* Mason Crest, 2002. *(I)*

Day-MacLeod, Deirdre, and Burt, Janet. *States of the Pacific North of Mexico.* Mason Crest, 2002. *(I)*

Field, Randi. *Gulf States of Mexico.* Mason Crest, 2002. *(I)*

Flowers, Charles. *Cortés and the Conquest of the Aztec Empire in World History.* Enslow, 2001. *(I; A)*

Franklin, Sharon; Tull, Mary; and Shelton, Carol. *Mexico and Central America: Understanding Geography and History through Art.* Raintree Steck-Vaughn, 2000. *(I; A)*

Harvey, Miles. *Look What Came from Mexico.* Scholastic, 1999. *(P)*

Heinrichs, Ann. *Mexico.* Scholastic, 1997. *(P)*

Hernandez, Roger E., ed. *Art and Architecture of Mexico; Famous People of Mexico; Festivals of Mexico; Food of Mexico; Geography of Mexico; History of Mexico.* Mason Crest, 2002. *(I)*

Hoyt-Goldsmith, Diane, and Migdale, Lawrence. *Celebrating a Quinceanera: A Latina's Fifteenth Birthday Celebration.* Holiday House, 2002. *(P; I)*

Kalman, Bobbie. *Mexico the Culture; Mexico the Land; Mexico the People.* Crabtree, 2001. *(P; I)*

Nantus, Sheryl. *States of the Pacific South of Mexico.* Mason Crest, 2002. *(I)*

Palacios, Argentina. *Viva Mexico! The Story of Benito Juárez and Cinco de Mayo.* Steck-Vaughn Publishers, 1993. *(I)*

Sanna, Ellyn. *Mexico: Facts and Figures.* Mason Crest, 2002. *(I)*

Stokes, Erica M. *Economy of Mexico; Sports of Mexico.* Mason Crest, 2002. *(I)*

Williams, Colleen Madonna. *People of Mexico.* Mason Crest, 2002. *(I)*

MICHELANGELO

Barter, James E., ed. *Artists of the Renaissance.* Thomson Gale, 1998. *(I; A)*

Giudici, Vittorio, and Galante, L. R. *The Sistine Chapel: Its History and Masterpieces.* NTC, 2000. *(I)*

Halliwell, Sarah, ed. *Renaissance: Artists and Writers.* Marshall Cavendish, 1997. *(I)*

Janson, H. W., and Janson, Anthony F. *History of Art for Young People.* Abrams, 1997 (rev. ed.). *(I; A)*

McLanathan, Richard B. *Michelangelo.* Abrams, 1993. *(I; A)*

Stanley, Diane. *Michelangelo.* HarperCollins, 2000. *(I)*

Ventura, Piero. *Michelangelo's World.* Putnam, 1990. *(P; I)*

MICHIGAN

Barenblat, Rachel, and Craven, Jean. *Michigan: The Wolverine State.* Gareth Stevens, 2002. *(P; I)*

Brill, Marlene Targ. *Michigan.* Marshall Cavendish, 1998. *(P; I)*

Fradin, Dennis Brindell. *Michigan: From Sea to Shining Sea.* Scholastic, 1994. *(P; I)*

Hintz, Martin, and Stein, R. Conrad. *Michigan.* Scholastic, 1998 (2nd ed.). *(I; A)*

Johnson, Elizabeth M.; Matusevich, Melissa N.; Streit, M. Jill. *Michigan.* Scholastic, 2002. *(P; I)*

Sirvaitis, Karen. *Michigan.* Lerner, 2002 (2nd ed.). *(P; I)*

Wills, Charles A. *A Historical Album of Michigan.* Millbrook Press, 1996. *(I)*

MICROBIOLOGY

Berger, Melvin. *Germs Make Me Sick!* HarperCollins, 1995. *(P)*

Biddle, Wayne. *Field Guide to Germs.* Henry Holt, 1995. *(A)*

Dashefsky, H. Steven. *Microbiology: High-School Science Fair Experiments.* McGraw-Hill, 1995. *(A)*

Facklam, Howard, and Facklam, Margery. *Bacteria; Parasites; Viruses.* Twenty-First Century, 1995. *(I)*

Snedden, Robert. *Scientists and Discoveries.* Heinemann, 2000. *(I; A)*

MICRONESIA, FEDERATED STATES OF

Hermes, Jules M. *The Children of Micronesia.* Carolrhoda, 1995. *(I)*

MICROSCOPES

Kassinger, Ruth G. *Glass: From Cinderella's Slippers to Fiber Optics.* Lerner, 2003. *(I)*

Kramer, Stephen P. *Hidden Worlds: Looking Through a Scientist's Microscope.* Houghton Mifflin, 2003. *(P; I)*

Levine, Shar, and Johnstone, Leslie. *The Microscope Book.* Sterling, 1997. *(I)*

Nachtigall, Werner. *Exploring with the Microscope: A Book of Discovery and Learning.* Sterling, 1995. *(A)*

Rainis, Kenneth G., and Russell, Bruce J. *Guide to Microlife.* Scholastic, 1997. *(A)*

Tomb, Howard, and Kunkel, Dennis. *Microaliens: Dazzling Journeys with an Electron Microscope.* Farrar, Straus & Giroux, 1993. *(I; A)*

Yount, Lisa. *Antoni Van Leeuwenhoek: First to See Microscopic Life.* Enslow, 1996. *(I)*

MICROWAVES

Asimov, Isaac. *How Did We Find Out about Microwaves?* Walker, 1989. *(P; I)*

MIDDLE AGES

Anderson, Dale. *Churches and Religion in the Middle Ages.* Gareth Stevens, 2006; *Monks and Monasteries in the Middle Ages.* Gareth Stevens, 2005. *(I)*

Greenblatt, Miriam. *Charlemagne and the Early Middle Ages.* Marshall Cavendish, 2002. *(I; A)*

Hanawalt, Barbara A. *The European World, 400-1450.* Oxford University Press, 2005. *(A)*; *The Middle Ages: An Illustrated History.* Oxford University Press, 1998. *(I; A)*

Hinds, Kathryn. *Life in the Renaissance: The Church.* Benchmark, 2003; *Medieval England.* Marshall Cavendish, 2001; *Life in the Middle Ages: The Castle; Life in the Middle Ages: The Church; Life in the Middle Ages: The City; Life in the Middle Ages: The Countryside.* Benchmark, 2000. *(I; A)*

Kallen, Stuart A. *A Medieval Merchant.* Thomson Gale, 2005. *(I; A)*

Sherrow, Victoria. *Life in a Medieval Monastery.* Thomson Gale, 2000. *(I; A)*

MIDDLE EAST

Climo, Shirley. *The Persian Cinderella.* HarperCollins, 1999. *(P)*

Collinson, Alan. *Mountains.* Dillon, 1992. *(I; A)*

Harik, Ramsay M., and Marston, Elsa. *Women in the Middle East: Tradition and Change.* Scholastic, 1996. *(I; A)*

Hickox, Rebecca. *The Golden Sandal: A Middle Eastern Cinderella Story.* Holiday House, 1998. *(P)*

King, John. *The Gulf War.* Silver Burdett Press, 1991. *(I; A)*

Long, Cathryn J. *The Middle East in Search of Peace.* Millbrook, 1994. *(I)*

MILK

Bourgeois, Paulette; Ross, Catherine; and Wallace, Susan. *The Amazing Milk Book.* General Distribution Services, 1997. *(P; I)*

Cooper, Jason. *Dairy Products.* Rourke, 2002. *(P)*

Doyle, Malachy. *Cow.* McElderry, 2002. *(P)*

King, Hazel. *Milk and Yogurt.* Heinemann, 1998. *(P; I)*

Powell, Jillian. *Milk.* Raintree Publishers, 1997. *(P; I)*

Wolfman, Judy, and Winston, David Lorenz. *Life on a Dairy Farm.* Lerner, 2003. *(P)*

MILKY WAY

Gustafson, John R. *Stars, Clusters and Galaxies.* Silver Burdett Press, 1993. *(I; A)*

Simon, Seymour. *Galaxies.* Morrow, 1991. *(P; I)*

MILTON, JOHN

Bloom, Harold, ed. *John Milton's Paradise Lost (Bloom's Notes Series).* Chelsea House, 1995. *(A)*

MINERALS

Bates, Robert L. *The Challenge of Mineral Resources.* Enslow, 1991. *(A)*

MINES AND MINING

Kalman, Bobbie, and Calder, Kate. *The Life of a Miner.* Crabtree/A Bobbie Kalman Bk., 1999. *(P; I)*

MINNESOTA

Carlson, Jeffrey D. *A Historical Album of Minnesota.* Millbrook Press, 1993. *(I)*

Fradin, Dennis Brindell. *Minnesota: From Sea to Shining Sea.* Scholastic, 1995. *(P; I)*

Hasday, Judy L.; Matusevich, Melissa N.; and Pettinger, Joyce. *Minnesota.* Scholastic, 2003. *(P; I)*

Hintz, Martin. *Minnesota.* Scholastic, 2000 (2nd ed.); *Destination Duluth.* Lerner, 1997. *(I; A)*

Pollock, Miriam Heddy; Jaffe, Peter; and Craven, Jean. *Minnesota: Land of 10,000 Lakes.* Gareth Stevens, 2002. *(P; I)*

Porter, A. P. *Minnesota.* Lerner, 2001 (2nd ed.). *(P; I)*

Schwabacher, Martin, and Stefoff, Rebecca. *Minnesota.* Marshall Cavendish, 1999. *(P; I)*

MINT

Abeyta, Jennifer. *Coins.* Scholastic, 2000. *(I; A)*

Attebury, Nancy Garhan. *Out and about at the United States Mint (Field Trips Series).* Capstone Press, 2005. *(P; I)*

Maestro, Betsy, and Maestro, Giulio. *The Story of Money.* Houghton Mifflin, 1995. *(P)*

Otfinoski, Steven. *Coin Collecting for Kids.* Innovative Kids, 2000. *(P)*

Reiter, Ed, and Travers, Scott A. *The New York Times Guide to Coin Collecting: Do's, Don'ts, Facts, Myths, and a Wealth of History.* St. Martin's Press, 2002. *(A)*

MISSISSIPPI

Figueroa, Acton. *Mississippi: The Magnolia State.* Gareth Stevens, 2003. *(P; I)*

Fradin, Dennis Brindell. *Mississippi: From Sea to Shining Sea.* Scholastic, 1996. *(P; I)*

George, Charles, and George, Linda. *Mississippi.* Scholastic, 1999 (2nd ed.). *(I; A)*

Shirley, David. *Mississippi.* Marshall Cavendish, 1999. *(P; I)*

Twain, Mark. *Life on the Mississippi.* Oxford University Press, 1996. *(I; A)*

Van Steenwyk, Elizabeth. *Ida B. Wells-Barnett: Woman of Courage.* Watts, 1992. *(I; A)*

MISSISSIPPI RIVER

Hiscock, Bruce. *The Big Rivers: The Missouri, the Mississippi, and the Ohio.* Atheneum, 1997. *(P; I)*

Lauber, Patricia. *Flood: Wrestling with the Mississippi.* National Geographic, 1996. *(P; I)*

Mudd-Ruth, Maria. *The Mississippi River.* Marshall Cavendish, 2000. *(I; A)*

Prevost, John F. *Mississippi River.* ABDO, 2002. *(P)*

Walsh, Kieran J. *Great Rivers of the World: The Mississippi.* Gareth Stevens, 2003. *(P; I)*

MISSOURI

Bennett, Michelle. *Missouri.* Marshall Cavendish, 2001. *(P; I)*

Doherty, Craig A., and Doherty, Katherine M. *The Gateway Arch.* Gale Group, 1995. *(I)*

Fradin, Dennis Brindell. *Missouri: From Sea to Shining Sea.* Scholastic, 1995. *(P; I)*

Hintz, Martin. *Missouri.* Scholastic, 1999 (2nd ed.); *St. Louis.* Lerner, 1998. *(I; A)*

Ingram, W. Scott, and Craven, Jean. *Missouri: The Show Me State.* Gareth Stevens, 2002. *(P; I)*

Ladoux, Rita. *Missouri.* Lerner, 2002 (2nd ed.). *(P; I)*

Lago, Mary Ellen. *Missouri.* Scholastic, 2003. *(P; I)*

MODELING, FASHION

Giacobello, John. *Careers in the Fashion Industry.* Rosen, 2003 (rev. ed.). *(A)*

O'Donnell, Kerri. *Careers in Modeling.* Rosen, 2001. *(I; A)*

MOLDOVA

Moldova: Then and Now. Lerner, 1992. *(I; A)*

Sheehan, Patricia. *Moldova.* Marshall Cavendish, 2000. *(I; A)*

MOLIÈRE

Bloom, Harold, ed. *Moliere (Modern Critical Views Series).* Chelsea House, 2001. *(A)*

MOLLUSKS

Blaxland, Beth. *Cephalopods: Octopuses, Squids, and Their Relatives; Mollusks: Snails, Clams, and Their Relatives.* Chelsea House, 2002. *(P; I)*

Pascoe, Elaine. *Snails and Slugs.* Blackbirch Press, 1998. *(I)*

MONET, CLAUDE

Janson, H. W., and Janson, Anthony F. *History of Art for Young People.* Abrams, 1997 (rev. ed.). *(I; A)*

Muhlberger, Richard, and Metropolitan Museum of Art. *What Makes a Monet a Monet?* Viking, 1993. *(I)*

Venezia, Mike. *Monet.* Children's Press, 1990. *(P)*

Waldron, Ann. *Claude Monet.* Abrams, 1991. *(I; A)*

Welton, Jude. *Eyewitness: Impressionism.* DK, 2000. *(P; I; A)*

MONGOLIA

Cheng, Pang Guek. *Mongolia.* Marshall Cavendish, 1999. *(I)*

Meltzer, Milton. *Ten Kings: And the Worlds They Ruled.* Orchard Books, 2002. *(P; I)*

Reynolds, Jan. *Mongolia: Vanishing Cultures.* Harcourt, 1994. *(P; I)*

MONKEYS

Jordan, Tanis. *Jungle Days, Jungle Nights.* Houghton Mifflin, 1993. *(P)*

Maynard, Thane. *Primates: Apes, Monkeys, Prosimians.* Watts, 1995. *(I)*

Stonehouse, Bernard. *A Visual Introduction to Monkeys and Apes.* Facts on File, 1999. *(I; A)*

MONROE, JAMES

Gaines, Ann Graham. *James Monroe: Our Fifth President.* Child's World, 2002. *(P; I)*

Kallen, Stuart A. *James Monroe (Founding Fathers).* ABDO, 2002. *(P; I)*

Old, Wendie C. *James Monroe.* Enslow, 1998. *(I; A)*

Santella, Andrew. *James Monroe (Encyclopedia of Presidents, Second Series).* Scholastic, 2003. *(I; A)*

MONTANA

Bennett, Clayton. *Montana.* Marshall Cavendish, 2001. *(I)*

Fradin, Dennis Brindell. *Montana: From Sea to Shining Sea.* Scholastic, 1995. *(P; I)*

George, Charles, and George, Linda. *Montana.* Scholastic, 2000 (2nd ed.). *(I; A)*

Hirschmann, Kris. *Montana: The Treasure State.* Gareth Stevens, 2003. *(P; I)*

Hoyt-Goldsmith, Diane, and Migdale, Lawrence. *Buffalo Days.* Holiday House, 1997. *(P; I)*

Ladoux, Rita. *Montana.* Lerner, 2002 (2nd ed.). *(P; I)*

Williams, Judith M. *Montana.* Scholastic, 2002. *(P; I)*

MONTREAL

Rogers, Stillman D. *Cities of the World: Montreal.* Scholastic, 2000. *(P; I)*

MOON

Branley, Franklyn M. *What the Moon Is Like.* HarperCollins, 2000. *(P)*

Carruthers, Margaret W. *The Moon.* Scholastic, 2003. *(I)*

Graham, Ian. *The Best Book of the Moon.* Kingfisher, 1999. *(P; I)*

Hughes, David. *The Moon.* Facts on File, 1990. *(P; I)*

Miller, Ron. *Worlds Beyond: Earth and the Moon.* Lerner, 2003. *(I)*

Nicolson, Cynthia Pratt. *The Moon.* Kids Can Press, 1997. *(P; I)*

MORMONS

Nash, Carol Rust. *The Mormon Trail and the Latter-Day Saints (In American History Series).* Enslow, 1999. *(I; A)*

MOROCCO

Morocco in Pictures. Lerner, 1996 (rev. ed.). *(I; A)*

Blauer, Ettagle, and Laure, Jason. *Morocco.* Scholastic, 1999. *(I; A)*

Cassanos, Lynda Cohen. *Morocco.* Mason Crest, 2002. *(I; A)*

Hermes, Jules M. *The Children of Morocco.* Carolrhoda, 1995. *(P; I)*

Seward, Pat. *Morocco.* Benchmark, 1995. *(I)*

MORSE, SAMUEL F. B.

Kerby, Mona. *Samuel Morse.* Watts, 1991. *(P; I)*

MOSCOW

Adelman, Deborah. *The "Children of Perestroika" Come of Age: Young People of Moscow Talk about Life in the New Russia.* Sharpe, 1994. *(A)*

Kent, Deborah. *Moscow.* Children's Press, 2000. *(I)*

Steele, Philip. *Great Cities of the World: Moscow.* Gareth Stevens, 2003. *(I)*

MOSES

Auld, Mary, retel. *Exodus from Egypt; Moses in the Bulrushes.* Scholastic, 2000. *(P)*

Wildsmith, Brian. *Exodus.* Eerdmans, 1999. *(P)*

MOSES, GRANDMA

Nikola-Lisa, W., and Moses, Grandma. *Year with Grandma Moses.* Henry Holt, 2000. *(P; I)*

Venezia, Mike. *Grandma Moses.* Scholastic, 2004. *(P)*

MOSSES

Greenway, Theresa. *Mosses and Liverworts.* Raintree Steck-Vaughn, 1992. *(I)*

MOTION

Doherty, Paul, and Rathjen, Don. *The Spinning Blackboard and Other Dynamic Experiments on Force and Motion.* Wiley, 1996. *(I; A)*

Farndon, John. *Motion.* Benchmark, 2002. *(I)*

Taylor, Kim. *Action.* John Wiley, 1992. *(I)*

MOTION PICTURES

Adair, Gene. *Alfred Hitchcock: Filming Our Fears.* Oxford University Press, 2002. *(I; A)*

Apel, Melanie Ann. *Cool Careers without College for Film and Television Buffs.* Rosen, 2002. *(I; A)*

Blakely, Gloria. *Danny Glover (Black Americans of Achievement Series).* Chelsea House, 2001. *(I; A)*

Camenson, Blythe. *Real People Working in Entertainment (On the Job Series).* NTC, 1999. *(A)*

De Angelis, Gina. *Gregory Hines (Black Americans of Achievement Series); Morgan Freeman (Black Americans of Achievement Series).* Chelsea House, 1999. *(I; A)*

Fitzgerald, Dawn, and Tuttle, Dennis. *Angela Bassett (Black Americans of Achievement Series).* Chelsea House, 2001. *(I; A)*

Hoffman, Carol Stein. *Barrymores: Hollywood's First Family.* University of Kentucky Press, 2001. *(A)*

Kramer, Barbara. *Ron Howard: Child Star and Hollywood Director (People to Know Series).* Enslow, 1998. *(I; A)*

Lommel, Cookie. *African Americans in Film and Television (American Mosaic: African-American Contribution Series).* Chelsea House, 2003. *(I)*; *Cuba Gooding Jr. (Black Americans of Achievement Series).* Chelsea House, 2000. *(I; A)*

McAlpine, Margaret. *Working in Film and Television.* Gareth Stevens, 2004. *(I; A)*

Meachum, Virginia. *Steven Spielberg: Hollywood Filmmaker.* Enslow, 1996. *(P; I)*

Naden, Corinne J., and Blue, Rose J. *Halle Berry (Black Americans of Achievement Series).* Chelsea House, 2001. *(I; A)*

Netzley, Patricia D. *Encyclopedia of Movie Special Effects.* Facts on File, 2001. *(A)*

Parkinson, David. *The Young Oxford Book of the Movies.* Oxford, 1997. *(I; A)*

Rowland-Warne, L. *Eyewitness: Costume.* DK, 2000. *(P; I)*

Rubin, Susan Goldman. *Steven Spielberg: Crazy for Movies.* Abrams, 2001. *(I; A)*

Wessling, Katherine. *Backstage at a Movie Set (Backstage Pass Series).* Children's Press, 2003. *(I)*

Wormser, Richard. *To the Young Filmmaker: Conversations with Working Filmmakers.* Scholastic, 2001. *(I; A)*

Wren, Laura Lee. *Christopher Reeve: Hollywood's Man of Courage (People to Know Series).* Enslow, 1999. *(I; A)*

Zannos, Susan. *Drew Barrymore (Real Life Reader Biography Series).* Mitchell Lane, 2000. *(P; I)*

MOUNTAINS

Bullen, Susan. *The Alps and Their People.* Raintree Steck-Vaughn, 1994. *(P; I)*

Harris, Tim. *Mountains and Highlands (Biomes Atlases Series).* Raintree, 2003. *(I)*

Price, Martin F. *Mountains: Geology, Natural History, and Ecosystems.* Voyageur Press, 2002. *(A)*

Stronach, Neil. *Mountains.* Lerner, 1996. *(I)*

Zoehfeld, Kathleen Weidner. *How Mountains Are Made.* HarperCollins, 1999. *(P)*

MOZAMBIQUE

Blauer, Ettagle, and Laure, Jason. *Mozambique.* Scholastic, 1995. *(I; A)*

James, R. S. *Mozambique.* Chelsea House, 1997. *(P; I)*

MOZART, WOLFGANG AMADEUS

Allman, Barbara. *Musical Genius: A Story about Wolfgang Amadeus Mozart.* Lerner, 2004. *(P; I)*

Bankston, John. *Masters of Music: The Life and Times of Wolfgang Amadeus Mozart.* Mitchell Lane, 2003. *(I)*

Gay, Peter. *Mozart.* Viking, 1999. *(A)*

Geras, Adele, and Beck, Ian. *The Random House Book of Opera Stories.* Random House, 1998. *(P; I)*

Krull, Kathleen. *Lives of the Musicians: Good Times, Bad Times (And What the Neighbors Thought).* Raintree Steck-Vaughn, 1998. *(I; A)*

Pancella, Peggy. *Wolfgang Amadeus Mozart.* Heinemann, 2005. *(P)*

MUIR, JOHN

Anderson, Peter. *John Muir: Wilderness Prophet.* Scholastic, 1995. *(P)*

Warrick, Karen Clemens. *John Muir: Crusader for the Wilderness.* Enslow, 2002. *(I; A)*

MUMMIES

Buell, Janet. *Ancient Horsemen of Siberia; Greenland Mummies.* Millbrook Press, 1998. *(I; A)*; *Bog Bodies; Ice Maiden of the Andes.* Twenty-First Century, 1997. *(I)*

Deem, James M. *Bodies from the Bog.* Houghton Mifflin, 1998. *(I)*

Fletcher, Joann, and Malam, John. *Mummies: And the Secrets of Ancient Egypt.* DK, 2001. *(P; I)*

Jackson, Donna M. *The Bone Detectives: How Forensic Anthropologists Solve Crimes and Uncover Mysteries of the Dead.* Little, 1996. *(I; A)*

McCall, Henrietta. *Egyptian Mummies.* Watts, 2000. *(P; I)*

Patent, Dorothy Hinshaw. *Secrets of the Ice Man.* Marshall Cavendish, 1998. *(I; A)*

Pemberton, Delia. *Egyptian Mummies: People from the Past.* Harcourt, 2001. *(P; I)*

Perl, Lila, and Weihs, Erika. *Mummies, Tombs, and Treasure: Secrets of Ancient Egypt.* Houghton Mifflin, 1991. *(P; I)*

Reinhard, Johan. *Discovering the Inca Ice Maiden.* National Geographic, 1998. *(I; A)*

Wilcox, Charlotte. *Mummies, Bones and Body Parts.* Lerner, 2000. *(I; A)*

MUSCULAR SYSTEM

Silverstein, Alvin; Silverstein, Virginia; and Silverstein, Robert. *The Muscular System.* 21st Century Books, 1994. *(I)*

MUSEUMS

Ayer, Eleanor H. *U. S. Holocaust Memorial Museum: America Keeps the Memory Alive.* Silver Burdett Press, 1995. *(I; A)*

Cutchins, Judy, and Johnston, Ginny. *Are Those Animals Real?: How Museums Prepare Wildlife Exhibits.* Morrow, 1995 (rev. ed.). *(I)*

D'Archinbaud, Nicholas; Forgeau, Annie; and Saint-Hilaire, Yves. *Louvre: Portrait of a Museum.* Abrams, 2001. *(A)*

de Farcy, Elizabeth, ed. *The Louvre.* Knopf, 1995. *(A)*

L'Hommedieu, Arthur John. *Working at a Museum.* Scholastic, 1999. *(P)*

Paolucci, Antonio. *Great Museums of Europe.* Skira, 2003. *(A)*

Richardson, Joy. *Inside the Museum: A Children's Guide to the Metropolitan Museum of Art.* Abrams, 1993. *(P; I)*

Thompson, Peggy; Moore, Barbara; and Eron, Carol. *The Nine-Ton Cat: Behind the Scenes at an Art Museum.* Houghton Mifflin, 1997. *(I; A)*

MUSHROOMS

Laessoe, Thomas. *Smithsonian Handbook: Mushrooms.* Sagebrush, 2002. *(I; A)*

Pascoe, Elaine. *Slime, Molds, and Fungi.* Blackbirch, 1998. *(P; I)*

MUSICAL INSTRUMENTS

Dearling, Robert, ed. *The Illustrated Encyclopedia of Musical Instruments.* Gale Research, 1996. *(I; A)*

Koscielniak, Bruce. *The Story of the Incredible Orchestra: An Introduction to Musical Instruments and the Symphony Orchestra.* Houghton Mifflin, 2000. *(P; I)*

Montagu, Jeremy. *Timpani and Percussion.* Yale University Press, 2002. *(A)*

Temple, Bob. *Trombones (Music Makers Series); Tubas (Music Makers Series).* Child's World, 2002. *(P)*

Walton, Simon. *Playing the Flute, Recorder, and Other Woodwinds.* Stargazer Books, 2004. *(P; I)*

Woods, Samuel G. *Guitars: From Start to Finish.* Blackbirch, 1999. *(P; I)*

MUSICAL THEATER

Bany-Winters, Lisa. *Show Time!: Music, Dance, and Drama Activities for Kids.* Chicago Review, 2000. *(P; I)*

Malam, John. *Song and Dance.* Grolier, 2000. *(I)*

MUSSOLINI, BENITO

Downing, David. *Fascism.* Heinemann, 2002; *Benito Mussolini (Leading Lives Series).* Heinemann, 2001. *(I; A)*

MYANMAR

Ledgard, Edna, retel. *Snake Prince and Other Stories: Burmese Folk Tales.* Interlink, 1999. *(I)*

Viesti, Joseph F., and Hall, Diane. *Celebrate! in South Asia.* HarperCollins, 1996. *(P; I)*

Wright, David K. *Burma; Malaysia.* Children's Press, 1996. *(I)*

Yin, Saw Myat. *Myanmar.* Marshall Cavendish, 2001 (2nd ed.). *(I; A)*

MYCENAEAN CULTURE

Connolly, Peter. *Ancient Greece.* Oxford, 2001. *(I)*

Pearson, Anne. *Eyewitness: Ancient Greece.* DK, 2000. *(I)*

Schomp, Virginia. *The Ancient Greeks.* Marshall Cavendish, 1996. *(I)*

N (LETTER)

Samoyault, Tiphaine. *Alphabetical Order: How the Alphabet Began.* Viking, 1998. *(P; I)*

NAILS, SCREWS, AND RIVETS

Welsbacher, Anne. *Screws.* Capstone Press, 2001. *(P; I)*

NAMIBIA

Anozie, F. N. *Khoekhoe (Namibia, South Africa).* Rosen, 1997. *(I; A)*

Biesele, Megan, and Loloo, Kxao. *San (Botswana, Namibia, South Africa).* Rosen, 1997. *(I; A)*

Blauer, Ettagle, and Laure, Jason. *Namibia.* Scholastic, 1993. *(I; A)*

Udechukwu, Ada Obi. *Herero (Botswana, Namibia).* Rosen, 1996. *(I; A)*

NAPOLEON I

Foreman, Laura, and Phillips, Ellen Blue. *Napoleon's Lost Fleet: Bonaparte, Nelson, and the Battle of the Nile.* Discovery Channel, 1999. *(A)*

Marrin, Albert. *Napoleon and the Napoleonic Wars.* Viking, 1991. *(A)*

McGowen, Tom. *Frederick the Great, Bismarck, and the Building of the German Empire in World History.* Enslow, 2002. *(I; A)*

NARCOTICS

Hanan, Jessica. *When Someone You Love Is Addicted.* Rosen, 1999. *(I)*

McLaughlin, Miriam Smith, and Hazouri, Sandra Peyser. *Addiction: The High That Brings You Down.* Enslow, 1997. *(I; A)*

Oliver, Marilyn Tower. *Drugs: Should They Be Legalized?* Enslow, 1996. *(I; A)*

NAST, THOMAS

Pflueger, Lynda. *Thomas Nast: Political Cartoonist.* Enslow, 2000. *(I)*

Shirley, David. *Thomas Nast: Cartoonist and Illustrator.* Watts, 1998. *(I; A)*

NATIONAL ANTHEMS AND PATRIOTIC SONGS

Quiri, Patricia Ryon. *The National Anthem.* Children's Press, 1998. *(P)*

Sonneborn, Liz. *America the Beautiful: The Story Behind Our National Hymn; The Star-Spangled Banner: The Story Behind Our National Anthem.* Chelsea Clubhouse, 2004. *(P; I)*

St. Pierre, Stephanie. *Our National Anthem.* Millbrook Press, 1994. *(P)*

NATIONAL ASSOCIATION FOR THE ADVANCEMENT OF COLORED PEOPLE (NAACP)

Fradin, Dennis Brindell, and Fradin, Judith Bloom. *Ida B. Wells: Mother of the Civil Rights Movement.* Clarion, 2000. *(I; A)*

Harris, Jacqueline L. *History and Achievement of the NAACP.* Watts, 1992. *(A)*

Hauser, Pierre. *Great Ambitions: From the 'Separate but Equal' Doctrine to the Birth of the NAACP.* Chelsea House, 1995. *(A)*

Jordan, Denise M. *Julian Bond: Civil Rights Activist and Chairman of the NAACP.* Enslow, 2001. *(I; A)*

Ovington, Mary White, and Luker, Ralph E., ed. *Black and White Sat Down Together: The Reminiscences of an NAACP Founder.* Feminist Press at The City University of New York, 1996. *(A)*

Paterra, M. Elizabeth. *Kweisi Mfume: Congressman and NAACP Leader.* Enslow, 2001. *(I; A)*

Wilson, Sondra Kathryn. *In Search of Democracy: The NAACP Writings of James Weldon Johnson, Walter White, and Roy Wilkins (1920-1977).* Oxford University Press, 1999. *(A)*

NATIONAL FOREST SYSTEM

Dolan, Edward F. *American Wilderness and Its Future: Conservation Versus Use.* Watts, 1992. *(I; A)*

Lasky, Kathryn. *John Muir: America's First Environmentalist.* Candlewick Press, 2006. *(P)*

Parker, Edward. *Protecting Our Planet: Forests for the Future, Vol. 1.* Raintree Steck-Vaughn, 1998. *(I)*

Patent, Dorothy Hinshaw. *Yellowstone Fires: Flames and Rebirth.* Holiday House, 1990. *(P; I)*

Vogt, Gregory. *Forests on Fire: The Fight to Save Our Trees.* Watts, 1990. *(A)*

NATIONAL INSTITUTES OF HEALTH

Jussim, Daniel. *Medical Ethics.* Silver Burdett Press, 1990. *(I; A)*

Yount, Lisa. *Issues in Biomedical Ethics.* Gale Group, 1997. *(I; A)*

NATIONAL PARK SYSTEM

Doherty, Craig A., and Doherty, Katherine M. *The Empire State Building.* Gale Group, 1997; *The Erie Canal.* Gale Group, 1996; *Hoover Dam; Mount Rushmore; The Gateway Arch; The Golden Gate Bridge; The Sears Tower; The Washington Monument.* Gale Group, 1995. *(I)*

Dolan, Edward F. *American Wilderness and Its Future: Conservation Versus Use.* Watts, 1992. *(I; A)*

Fazio, Wende. *Acadia National Park.* Scholastic, 1999. *(P; I)*

Gartner, Robert. *Exploring Careers in the National Parks.* Rosen, 1999 (rev. ed.). *(A)*

Nelson, Sharlene P., and Nelson, Ted. *Hawaii Volcanoes National Park.* Scholastic, 1998. *(P)*

Patent, Dorothy Hinshaw. *Yellowstone Fires: Flames and Rebirth.* Holiday House, 1990. *(P; I)*

Petersen, David. *Grand Canyon National Park; Haleakala National Park; National Parks; Yellowstone National Park.* Scholastic, 2001; *Arches National Park; Chaco Culture National Historical Park; Great Sand Dunes National Monument; Saguaro National Park.* Scholastic, 2000; *Death Valley National Park; Denali National Park System; Petrified Forest National Park.* Scholastic, 1997; *Bryce Canyon National Park.* Scholastic, 1996; *Dinosaur National Monument.* Scholastic, 1995; *Rocky Mountain National Park; Great Smoky Mountains National Park; Zion National Park.* Scholastic, 1993; *Grand Teton National Park; Waterton-Glacier International Peace Park.* Scholastic, 1992. *(P; I)*

NATURAL RESOURCES

Camp, William G. C., and Daugherty, Thomas B. *Managing Our Natural Resources.* 4th ed. Delmar Thomson Learning, 2000. *(I; A)*

Cossi, Olga. *Water Wars: The Fight to Control and Conserve Nature's Most Precious Resource.* Silver Burdett Press, 1993. *(I)*

Parker, Steve. *The Earth's Resources.* Raintree Steck-Vaughn, 2000. *(I)*

Pringle, Laurence P. *The Environmental Movement: From Its Roots to the Challenge of a New Century.* Morrow, 2000. *(I; A)*

NATURE, STUDY OF

Burnie, David. *How Nature Works: 100 Ways Parents and Kids Can Share the Secrets of Nature.* Reader's Digest, 1991. *(I)*

Keene, Ann T. *Earthkeepers: Observers and Protectors of Nature.* Oxford, 1993. *(I; A)*

Parker, Steve. *The Random House Book of How Nature Works.* Random House, 1993. *(I)*

Potter, Jean. *Nature in a Nutshell for Kids: Over 100 Activities You Can Do in Ten Minutes or Less.* John Wiley, 1995. *(P)*

Sayre, April Pulley. *Put on Some Antlers and Walk Like a Moose: How Scientists Find, Follow, and Study Wild Animals.* Millbrook Press, 1997. *(I)*

NAVIGATION

Dash, Joan. *The Longitude Prize.* Farrar, 2000. *(I; A)*

Wilkinson, Philip. *Ships: History, Battles, Discovery, Navigation.* Larousse, 2000. *(P; I)*

NAZISM

Altman, Linda Jacobs. *The Holocaust, Hitler, and Nazi Germany.* Enslow, 1999. *(I)*

Cartlidge, Cherese, and Clark, Charles. *Life of a Nazi Soldier.* Gale Group, 2001. *(I; A)*

Freeman, Charles. *The Rise of the Nazis, Vol. 7.* Raintree Steck-Vaughn, 1998. *(I; A)*

Rice, Earle. *The Fall of the Third Reich: Demise of the Nazi Dream.* Gale Group, 2000. *(I; A)*

Stewart, Gail B. *Hitler's Reich.* Gale Group, 1994. *(I; A)*

NEBRASKA

Bjorklund, Ruth. *Nebraska.* Marshall Cavendish, 2002. *(P; I)*

Flocker, Michael E., and Craven, Jean. *Nebraska: The Cornhusker State.* Stevens, 2002. *(P; I)*

Fradin, Dennis Brindell. *Nebraska: From Sea to Shining Sea.* Scholastic, 1996. *(P; I)*

McNair, Sylvia. *Nebraska.* Scholastic, 1999 (2nd ed.). *(I; A)*

Porter, A. P. *Nebraska.* Lerner, 2002 (2nd ed.). *(P; I)*

Wills, Charles A. *A Historical Album of Nebraska.* Millbrook Press, 1995. *(I)*

NEBULAS

Branley, Franklyn M. *Superstar: The Supernova of 1987.* HarperCollins, 1990. *(P; I)*

NEON AND OTHER NOBLE GASES

Heiserman, David L. *Exploring Chemical Elements and Their Compounds.* McGraw-Hill, 1991. *(A)*

Thomas, Jens. *Noble Gases.* Marshall Cavendish, 2002. *(I)*

Tocci, Salvatore. *Hydrogen and the Noble Gases.* Scholastic, 2005. *(P)*

NEPAL

Burbank, Jon. *Nepal.* Marshall Cavendish, 2002 (2nd ed.). *(I; A)*

Heinrichs, Ann. *Nepal.* Scholastic, 1996. *(I; A)*

Margolies, Barbara A. *Kanu of Kathmandu: A Journey in Nepal.* Four Winds, 1992. *(P; I)*

Pitkanen, Matti A. *Children of Nepal.* Lerner, 1990. *(P)*

Viesti, Joseph F., and Hall, Diane. *Celebrate! in South Asia.* HarperCollins, 1996. *(P; I)*

NEPTUNE

Asimov, Isaac. *How Did We Find Out about Neptune?* Walker, 1990. *(I; A)*

Branley, Franklyn M. *Neptune: Voyager's Final Target.* HarperCollins, 1992. *(P; I)*

Simon, Seymour. *Neptune.* Morrow, 1991. *(P; I)*

NERVOUS SYSTEM

Gold, Martha V. *The Nervous System.* Enslow, 2004. *(I)*

Silverstein, Alvin; Silverstein, Virginia; and Silverstein, Robert. *The Nervous System.* 21st Century Books, 1994. *(I)*

NETHERLANDS

Davis, Kevin A. *Look What Came from the Netherlands.* Scholastic, 2001. *(P)*

Heinrichs, Ann. *The Netherlands.* Scholastic, 2003. *(P)*

Hintz, Martin. *The Netherlands (Enchantment of the World, Second Series).* Scholastic, 1999.

Ngcheong-Lum, Roseline. *Netherlands.* Gareth Stevens, 2002. *(P; I)*

Seward, Pat. *Netherlands.* Marshall Cavendish, 1995 (2nd ed.). *(I; A)*

NEW BRUNSWICK

Levert, Suzanne. *New Brunswick.* Chelsea House, 2000. *(I)*

NEWFOUNDLAND AND LABRADOR

Jackson, Lawrence. *Newfoundland and Labrador.* Lerner, 1995. *(P)*

NEW HAMPSHIRE

Blohm, Craig E. *The Thirteen Colonies: New Hampshire.* Gale Group, 2001. *(I)*

Brown, Dottie. *New Hampshire.* Lerner, 2002 (2nd ed.). *(P; I)*

Dubois, Muriel L. *New Hampshire: Facts and Symbols.* Capstone/Hilltop, 2000. *(P)*

Fradin, Dennis Brindell. *New Hampshire: From Sea to Shining Sea.* Scholastic, 1994. *(P; I)*

Mattern, Joanne. *New Hampshire: The Granite State.* Gareth Stevens, 2003. *(P; I)*

Otfinoski, Steven. *New Hampshire.* Marshall Cavendish, 1999. *(P; I)*

Shannon, Terry Miller. *New Hampshire.* Scholastic, 2002. *(P; I)*

Stein, R. Conrad. *New Hampshire.* Scholastic, 2000 (2nd ed.). *(I; A)*

NEW JERSEY

Fradin, Dennis Brindell. *New Jersey: From Sea to Shining Sea.* Scholastic, 1994. *(P; I)*

Fredeen, Charles. *New Jersey.* Lerner, 2001 (2nd ed.). *(P; I)*

Holtz, Eric Siegfried. *New Jersey: The Garden State.* Gareth Stevens, 2002. *(P; I)*

Moragne, Wendy. *New Jersey.* Marshall Cavendish, 2000. *(P; I)*

Scholl, Elisabeth J. *New Jersey.* Scholastic, 2001. *(P; I)*

Stein, R. Conrad. *New Jersey.* Children's Press, 1998. *(I)*

Streissguth, Thomas. *The Thirteen Colonies: New Jersey.* Gale Group, 2001. *(I)*

Wills, Charles A., and Topper, Frank. *A Historical Album of New Jersey.* Millbrook Press, 1995. *(I)*

NEW MEXICO

Burgan, Michael. *New Mexico: Land of Enchantment.* Gareth Stevens, 2003. *(P; I)*

De Angelis, Therese. *New Mexico.* Scholastic, 2002. *(P; I)*

Fradin, Judith Bloom, and Fradin, Dennis Brindell. *New Mexico: From Sea to Shining Sea.* Scholastic, 1994. *(P; I)*

Kent, Deborah. *New Mexico.* Children's Press, 1999. *(I; A)*

McDaniel, Melissa, and Hoffman, Nancy. *New Mexico.* Marshall Cavendish, 1999. *(P; I)*

Petersen, David. *Chaco Culture National Historical Park.* Scholastic, 2000. *(P; I)*

Swentzell, Rina. *Children of Clay: A Family of Pueblo Potters.* Lerner, 1993. *(P; I)*

NEW ORLEANS

Hintz, Martin. *Destination New Orleans.* Lerner, 1997. *(P; I)*

Prentzas, G. S. *Cities of the World: New Orleans.* Scholastic, 1998. *(P; I)*

Torres, John Albert. *Hurricane Katrina and the Destruction of New Orleans, 2005 (Monumental Milestones Series).* Mitchell Lane, 2006. *(I)*

NEWSPAPERS

Cohen, Daniel. *Yellow Journalism: Scandal, Sensationalism, and Gossip in the Media.* Twenty-First Century, 2000. *(I; A)*

Crisman, Ruth. *Hot off the Press: Getting the News into Print.* Lerner, 1991. *(I; A)*

Hamill, Pete. *News Is a Verb: Journalism at the End of the Twentieth Century.* Ballantine Books, 1998. *(I; A)*

Leedy, Loreen. *The Furry News: How to Make a Newspaper.* Holiday House, 1996. *(P)*

Waters, Sarah A. *How Newspapers Are Made.* Facts on File, 1995. *(I)*

NEWTON, ISAAC

Allan, Tony. *Isaac Newton.* Heinemann, 2002. *(I)*

Hizeroth, Deborah, and Leon, Sharon. *The Importance of Sir Isaac Newton.* Lucent, 1994. *(I; A)*

White, Michael. *Sir Isaac Newton: Discovering Laws That Govern the Universe.* Blackbirch Press, 1999. *(I)*

NEW YEAR CELEBRATIONS AROUND THE WORLD

Bledsoe, Karen E. *Chinese New Year Crafts.* Enslow, 2005. *(P; I)*

Robinson, Fay. *Chinese New Year: A Time for Parades, Family, and Friends.* Enslow, 2001. *(P)*

NEW YORK

Avakian, Monique, and Smith, Carter. *A Historical Album of New York.* Millbrook Press, 1994. *(I)*

Ball, Jacqueline A.; Behrens, Kristen; and Craven, Jean. *New York: The Empire State.* Gareth Stevens, 2002. *(P; I)*

Cotter, Kristin. *New York.* Scholastic, 2001. *(P; I)*

Doherty, Craig A., and Doherty, Katherine M. *The Empire State Building.* Gale Group, 1997. *(I)*

Fischer, Laura. *Life in New Amsterdam, New York.* Heinemann, 2003. *(P)*

Fradin, Dennis Brindell. *New York: From Sea to Shining Sea.* Scholastic, 1994. *(P; I)*

Gelman, Amy. *New York.* Lerner, 2001 (2nd ed.). *(P; I)*

Kent, Deborah, and Stein, R. Conrad. *New York.* Scholastic, 1999 (2nd ed.). *(I; A)*

Schomp, Virginia. *New York.* Benchmark, 1996. *(I)*

Woog, Adam. *The Thirteen Colonies: New York.* Gale Group, 2001. *(I)*

NEW YORK CITY

Doherty, Craig A., and Doherty, Katherine M. *The Empire State Building.* Gale Group, 1997. *(I)*

Gillis, Jennifer Blizin. *Life on the Lower East Side.* Heinemann, 2003. *(P)*

Homberger, Eric. *Mrs. Astor's New York: Money and Power in a Gilded Age.* Yale University Press, 2002; *The Historical Atlas of New York City.* Henry Holt, 1994. *(A)*

Jakobsen, Kathy. *My New York.* Little, 1993. *(P)*

Walsh, Frank. *Great Cities of the World: New York City.* Gareth Stevens, 2003. *(I)*

Zaunders, Bo. *Gargoyles, Girders, and Glass Houses: Magnificent Master Builders.* Penguin Putnam, 2004. *(P; I)*

NEW ZEALAND

Keyworth, Valerie. *New Zealand: Land of the Long White Cloud.* Silver Burdett Press, 1998 (2nd ed.). *(P; I)*

Landau, Elaine. *Australia and New Zealand.* Scholastic, 1999. *(P)*

Robson, Michael. *New Zealand...in Pictures.* Lerner, 1995. *(I; A)*

Shepherd, Donna Walsh. *New Zealand.* Scholastic, 2002. *(I)*

Theunissen, Steve. *The Maori of New Zealand.* Lerner, 2003. *(I)*

NICARAGUA

Franklin, Sharon; Tull, Mary; and Shelton, Carol. *Mexico and Central America: Understanding Geography and History through Art.* Raintree Steck-Vaughn, 2000. *(I; A)*

Griffiths, John. *Nicaragua.* Chelsea House, 1998. *(I; A)*

Kott, Jennifer. *Nicaragua.* Marshall Cavendish, 1994. *(I; A)*

Morrison, Marion. *Nicaragua.* Scholastic, 2003. *(I; A)*

NICHOLAS

Duffy, James P., and Ricci, Vincent L. *Czars: Russia's Rulers for Over One Thousand Years.* Facts on File, 1995. *(A)*

NICKEL

Heiserman, David L. *Exploring Chemical Elements and Their Compounds.* McGraw-Hill, 1991. *(A)*

NIGERIA

Adeeb, Hassan, and Adeeb, Bonnetta. *Nigeria: One Nation, Many Cultures.* Benchmark, 1995. *(I)*

Anda, Michael O. *Yoruba (Nigeria).* Rosen, 1996. *(I; A)*

Blauer, Ettagle, and Laure, Jason. *Nigeria.* Scholastic, 2001. *(I; A)*

Brownlie, Alison. *We Come From Nigeria.* Raintree Steck-Vaughn, 2000. *(P)*

Gerson, Mary-Joan, retel. *Why the Sky is Far Away: A Nigerian Folktale.* Little, Brown & Co., 1995. *(P)*

Hamilton, Janice. *Nigeria... in Pictures.* Lerner, 2003 (rev. ed.). *(I; A)*

Harmon, Daniel E., and Leakey, Richard E. *Nigeria.* Chelsea House, 2000. *(I; A)*

Levy, Patricia M. *Nigeria.* Marshall Cavendish, 1996 (2nd ed.). *(I; A)*

Millar, Heather. *The Kingdom of Benin in West Africa.* Marshall Cavendish, 1996. *(I)*

Roschenthaler, Ute, and Chukwuezi, Barth. *Ejagham (Cameroon, Nigeria).* Rosen, 1996. *(I; A)*

Walker, Ida. *Nigeria (Africa - Continent in the Balance Series).* Mason Crest, 2004. *(I; A)*

NIGHTINGALE, FLORENCE

Gorrell, Gena K. *Heart and Soul: The Story of Florence Nightingale.* Tundra Books, 2000. *(I)*

NITROGEN

Farndon, John. *Nitrogen.* Marshall Cavendish, 1998. *(P; I)*

Heiserman, David L. *Exploring Chemical Elements and Their Compounds.* McGraw-Hill, 1991. *(A)*

NIXON, RICHARD M.

Barron, Rachel. *Richard Nixon: American Politician.* Morgan Reynolds, 1998. *(I; A)*

Fremon, David K. *The Watergate Scandal (In American History Series).* Enslow, 1997. *(I; A)*

Gaines, Ann Graham. *Richard M. Nixon: Our Thirty-Seventh President.* Child's World, 2001. *(P; I)*

Genovese, Michael A. *The Watergate Crisis.* Greenwood, 1999. *(A)*

Hay, Jeff. *Richard M. Nixon.* Gale Group, 2001. *(A)*

Herda, D. J. *United States v. Nixon: Watergate and the President.* Enslow, 1996. *(I; A)*

NOBEL PRIZES

Aaseng, Nathan. *The Disease Fighters: The Nobel Prize in Medicine.* Lerner, 1995; *The Peace Seekers: The Nobel Peace Prize.* Lerner, 1991. *(I; A)*

Goodnough, David. *Pablo Neruda: Nobel Prize-Winning Poet.* Enslow, 1998. *(I; A)*

Keene, Ann T. *Peacemakers: Winners of the Nobel Peace Prize.* Oxford University Press, 1998. *(I; A)*

Santella, Andrew. *Martin Luther King, Jr.: Civil Rights Leader and Nobel Prize Winner.* Child's World, 2003. *(P; I)*

NOISE

Wright, Lynne. *The Science of Noise.* Raintree Steck-Vaughn, 2000. *(I)*

NOMADS

Halliburton, Warren J. *Nomads of the Sahara.* Burdett Press, 1992. *(I)*

Jenkins, Martin. *Deserts (Endangered People and Places Series).* Lerner, 1996. *(I)*

NORSE MYTHOLOGY

Climo, Shirley, retel. *Stolen Thunder: A Norse Myth.* Houghton Mifflin, 1994. *(P; I)*

Fisher, Leonard Everett. *Gods and Goddesses of the Ancient Norse.* Holiday House, 2001. *(P)*

Philip, Neil, retel. *The Illustrated Book of Myths: Tales and Legends of the World.* DK, 1995. *(I)*

Zeitlin, Steve J. *The Four Corners of the Sky: Creation Stories and Cosmologies from around the World.* Henry Holt, 2000. *(I; A)*

NORTH AMERICA

Petersen, David. *North America.* Children's Press, 1998. *(P)*

Simon, Seymour. *Winter across America.* Hyperion, 1994. *(P; I)*

NORTH CAROLINA

Alex, Nan; Matusevich, Melissa N.; and Burton, Mel. *North Carolina.* Scholastic, 2001. *(P; I)*

Hintz, Martin, and Hintz, Stephen. *North Carolina.* Children's Press, 1998. *(I)*

Rafle, Sarah, and Craven, Jean. *North Carolina: The Tar Heel State.* Gareth Stevens, 2002. *(P; I)*

Schulz, Andrea. *North Carolina.* Lerner, 2001 (2nd ed.). *(P; I)*

Shirley, David. *North Carolina.* Marshall Cavendish, 2001. *(P; I)*

Uschan, Michael V. *The Thirteen Colonies: North Carolina.* Gale Group, 2001. *(I)*

NORTH DAKOTA

Fontes, Justine, and Fontes, Ron. *North Dakota: The Peace Garden State.* Gareth Stevens, 2003. *(P; I)*

Hintz, Martin. *North Dakota.* Scholastic, 2000 (2nd ed.). *(I; A)*

McDaniel, Melissa. *North Dakota.* Marshall Cavendish, 2001. *(P; I)*

Silverman, Robin Landew; Matusevich, Melissa N.; and Reinertson-Sand, Mary. *North Dakota.* Scholastic, 2003. *(P; I)*

NORTHERN IRELAND

Northern Ireland...in Pictures. Lerner, 1997. *(I)*

Gottfried, Ted. *Northern Ireland: Peace in Our Time?* Millbrook Press, 2002. *(I; A)*

Innes, Brian. *United Kingdom.* Raintree Steck-Vaughn, 2002. *(P; I)*

Killeen, Richard. *The Easter Rising.* Raintree Steck-Vaughn, 1995. *(I)*

O'Connor, Alan, and McMahon, Patricia. *One Belfast Boy.* Houghton Mifflin, 1999. *(P; I)*

Ross, Michael Elsohn. *Children of Northern Ireland.* Lerner, 2000. *(P)*

NORTHWEST PASSAGE

Beattie, Owen, and Geiger, John. *Buried in Ice: The Mystery of a Lost Arctic Expedition.* Scholastic, 1993. *(I; A)*

Chrisp, Peter. *The Search for a Northern Route.* Thomson Learning, 1993. *(P; I)*

Currie, Stephen. *Polar Explorers.* Gale Group, 2002. *(I; A)*

Delgado, James P. *Across the Top of the World: The Quest for the Northwest Passage.* Facts on File, 1999. *(A)*

Sundling, Charles W. *Explorers of the Frontier.* ABDO, 2000. *(P; I)*

NORWAY

Norway...in Pictures. Lerner, 1995. *(I)*

Blashfield, Jean F. *Norway.* Scholastic, 2000. *(I)*

Charbonneau, Claudette, and Lander, Patricia S. *The Land and People of Norway.* HarperCollins, 1992. *(I)*

Kagda, Sakina. *Norway.* Marshall Cavendish, 1995. *(I; A)*

Klingel, Cynthia Fitterer, and Noyed, Robert B. *Leif Eriksson: Norwegian Explorer.* Child's World, 2002. *(P; I)*

Landau, Elaine. *Norway.* Scholastic, 2000. *(P)*

NOVA SCOTIA

Sheppard, George, and LeVert, Suzanne. *Nova Scotia.* Chelsea House, 2000. *(I)*

NUCLEAR ENERGY

Andryszewski, Tricia. *What to Do about Nuclear Waste.* Millbrook, 1995. *(I; A)*

Barron, Rachel Stiffler. *Lise Meitner: Discoverer of Nuclear Fission.* Morgan Reynolds, 2000. *(I; A)*

Bryan, Nichol. *Chernobyl: Nuclear Disaster (Environmental Disasters Series).* Gareth Stevens, 2003. *(I; A)*

Cheney, Glenn Alan. *Nuclear Proliferation: The Problems and Possibilities.* Watts, 1999. *(I; A)*

Cohen, Daniel. *The Manhattan Project.* Millbrook, 1999. *(I; A)*

Cole, Michael D. *Three Mile Island: Nuclear Disaster (American Disasters Series).* Enslow, 2002. *(I)*

Daley, Michael J. *Nuclear Power: Promise or Peril?* Lerner, 1996. *(I; A)*

Fox, Karen. *The Chain Reaction: Pioneers of Nuclear Science.* Watts, 1998. *(I; A)*

Hampton, Wilborn. *Meltdown: A Race against Nuclear Disaster at Three Mile Island: A Reporter's Story.* Candlewick Press, 2001. *(I; A)*

Holland, Gini. *Nuclear Energy.* Benchmark, 1996. *(I; A)*

Ingram, W. Scott. *The Chernobyl Nuclear Disaster (Environmental Disasters Series).* Facts on File, 2005. *(I)*

Kidd, J. S., and Kidd, Renee A. *Quarks and Sparks: The Story of Nuclear Power.* Facts on File, 1999. *(I; A)*

Lampton, Christopher. *Nuclear Accident.* Millbrook, 1992. *(I)*

Wilcox, Charlotte. *Powerhouse: Inside a Nuclear Power Plant.* Carolrhoda, 1996. *(I; A)*

NUMBER PATTERNS

Ball, Johnny. *Go Figure!: A Totally Cool Book about Numbers; Think of a Number: A Fascinating Look at the World of Numbers.* DK, 2005. *(I)*

Zaslavsky, Claudia. *Number Sense and Nonsense.* Chicago Review Press, 2001. *(P; I)*

NUMBER PUZZLES AND GAMES

Allen, Robert. *Mensa: Mind Mazes for Kids; Mensa: Number Puzzles for Kids; Mensa: Secret Codes for Kids; Mensa: Word Puzzles for Kids.* Scholastic, 2000. *(P; I)*

Niederman, Derrick. *Hard-to-Solve Math Puzzles.* Sterling, 2001. *(I; A)*

NUMBERS AND NUMBER SYSTEMS

Hartmann, Wendy. *One Sun Rises: An African Wildlife Counting Book.* Dutton, 1994. *(P)*

Heinst, Marie. *My First Number Book.* Dorling Kindersley, 1992. *(P)*

Schmandt-Besserat, Denise. *The History of Counting.* Morrow, 1999. *(P; I)*

NUNAVUT

Finley, Carol. *Art of the Far North: Inuit Sculpture, Drawing, and Printmaking.* Lerner, 1998. *(P; I)*

Oberman, Sheldon. *The Shaman's Nephew: A Life in the Far North.* Stoddart, 2000. *(P; I)*

Wallace, Mary. *The Inuksuk Book.* Firefly, 1999. *(P; I)*

NURSERY RHYMES

Craig, Helen. *The Random House Book of Nursery Stories.* Random House, 2000. *(P)*

Crews, Nina. *The Neighborhood Mother Goose.* HarperCollins, 2003. *(P)*

De Paola, Tomie. *Tomie de Paola's Mother Goose Favorites.* Penguin Putnam, 2000. *(P)*

Greenberg, David T. *Whatever Happened to Humpty Dumpty?: And Other Surprising Sequels to Mother Goose Rhymes.* Little, 1999. *(P; I)*

Lobel, Arnold. *The Arnold Lobel Book of Mother Goose.* Random House, 2003 (reissue). *(P)*

Opie, Iona Archibald. *Here Comes Mother Goose.* Candlewick Press, 1999; *My Very First Mother Goose.* Candlewick Press, 1996. *(P)*

Wyndham, Robert, sel. *Chinese Mother Goose Rhymes.* Penguin, 1997. *(P)*

Yaccarino, Dan, illus. *Dan Yaccarino's Mother Goose.* Random House, 2004. *(P)*

NURSES AND NURSING

What Can I Do Now/Nursing. Ferguson, 1998. *(A)*

Frederickson, Keville. *Opportunities in Nursing Careers.* VGM, 1995. *(A)*

Storring, Rod. *A Doctor's Life: A Visual History of Doctors and Nurses Through the Ages.* Dutton, 1998. *(P; I)*

Waugh, Ingela. *Home Health Aide.* Scholastic, 2004. *(I)*

Witty, Margot. *A Day in the Life of an Emergency Room Nurse.* Troll, 1996. *(I)*

NUTRITION

Brynie, Faith Hickman. *101 Questions about Food and Digestion That Have Been Eating at You until Now.* Lerner, 2002. *(I; A)*

Hughes, Meredith Sayles. *Spill the Beans and Pass the Peanuts: Legumes.* Lerner, 1999. *(P; I)*

Parsons, Alexandra. *Fit for Life.* Scholastic, 1996. *(P; I)*

Patent, Dorothy Hinshaw. *Nutrition: What's in the Food We Eat.* Holiday, 1992. *(P; I)*

Petrie, Kristin. *Conquering Carbs; Fit and Fats; The Food Pyramid; Nutrition; Vitamins are Vital.* ABDO, 2003. *(P)*

Rockwell, Lizzy. *Good Enough to Eat: A Kid's Guide to Food and Nutrition.* HarperCollins, 1999. *(P)*

Silverstein, Dr. Alvin. *Carbohydrates; Fats; Proteins; Vitamins and Minerals.* Millbrook, 1992. *(I)*

VanCleave, Janice. *Janice VanCleave's Food and Nutrition for Every Kid: Easy Activities That Make Learning Science Fun.* Wiley, 1999. *(I)*

Zonderman, Jon, and Shader, Laurel. *Nutritional Diseases.* Millbrook Press, 1995. *(I; A)*

NYLON AND OTHER SYNTHETIC FIBERS

Keeler, Patricia A., and McCall, Francis X., Jr. *Unraveling Fibers.* Macmillan, 1995. *(P; I)*

O (LETTER)

Samoyault, Tiphaine. *Alphabetical Order: How the Alphabet Began.* Viking, 1998. *(P; I)*

OATS

Hughes, Meredith Sayles, and Hughes, E. Thomas. *Glorious Grasses: The Grains.* Lerner, 1998. *(I)*

OCCUPATIONAL HEALTH AND SAFETY

Wax, Nina. *Occupational Health.* Chelsea House, 1994. *(A)*

OCEANS AND SEAS OF THE WORLD

Lambert, David. *The Kingfisher Young People's Book of Oceans.* Houghton Mifflin, 1997. *(P; I)*

Landau, Elaine. *Ocean Mammals.* Scholastic, 1997. *(P)*

Petersen, Christine, and Petersen, David. *The Atlantic Ocean; The Gulf of Mexico; The Pacific Ocean.* Scholastic, 2001. *(P; I)*

Sauvain, Philip Arthur. *Geography Detective: Oceans.* Lerner, 1997. *(P; I)*

OCTOBER

Updike, John. *A Child's Calendar.* Holiday House, 1999. *(P; I)*

Warner, Penny. *Kids' Holiday Fun: Great Family Activities Every Month of the Year.* Meadowbrook Press, 1997. *(P)*

OCTOPUSES, SQUIDS, AND OTHER CEPHALOPODS

Lauber, Patricia. *An Octopus is Amazing.* HarperCollins, 1996. *(P)*

Markert, Jenny. *Octopuses.* Child's World, 2001 (2nd ed.). *(P)*

Markle, Sandra. *Outside and Inside the Giant Squid.* Walker, 2003. *(I)*

Martin, James. *Tentacles: The Amazing World of Octopus, Squid, and Their Relatives.* Crown, 1993. *(I)*

OHIO

Brown, Dottie. *Ohio.* Lerner, 2001 (2nd ed.). *(P; I)*

Kline, Nancy. *Ohio.* Scholastic, 2001. *(P; I)*

Martin, Michael A., and Craven, Jean. *Ohio: The Buckeye State.* Gareth Stevens, 2002. *(P; I)*

Sherrow, Victoria. *Ohio.* Marshall Cavendish, 1998. *(P; I)*

Wills, Charles A. *A Historical Album of Ohio.* Millbrook Press, 1996. *(I)*

OILS AND FATS

Nottridge, Rhoda. *Fats.* Lerner, 1993. *(P)*

O'KEEFFE, GEORGIA

Lowery, Linda. *Georgia O'Keefe.* Carolrhoda, 1996. *(P)*

Nicholson, Lois. P. *Georgia O'Keeffe.* Lucent, 1995. *(I; A)*

OLYMPIC GAMES

Aaseng, Nathan. *Women Olympic Champions.* Lucent, 2000; *Great Summer Olympic Moments; Great Winter Olympic Moments.* Lerner, 1990. *(I; A)*

Anderson, Dave. *The Story of the Olympics.* HarperCollins, 2000. *(I; A)*

Blacklock, Dyan. *Olympia: Warrior Athletes of Ancient Greece.* Walker, 2001. *(I)*

Uschan, Michael V. *Male Olympic Champions.* Lucent, 1999. *(I; A)*

Woff, Richard. *The Ancient Greek Olympics.* Oxford, 2000. *(I)*

Wukovits, John F. *The Encyclopedia of the Winter Olympics.* Scholastic, 2002. *(I)*

OPTICAL ILLUSIONS

Kid's Bathroom Book: Optical Illusions. Sterling, 2003. *(P; I)*

Doherty, Paul, and Rathjen, Don. *The Cheshire Cat and Other Eye-Popping Experiments on How We See the World.* Wiley, 1995. *(I)*

Jennings, Terry J. *101 Amazing Optical Illusions: Fantastic Visual Tricks.* Sterling, 1997. *(I)*

OPTICAL INSTRUMENTS

Levine, Shar, and Johnstone, Leslie. *The Optics Book: Fun Experiments with Light, Vision and Color.* Sterling, 1999; *The Microscope Book.* Sterling, 1997. *(I)*

ORATORY

Boyko, Carrie. *Hold Fast Your Dreams: Twenty Commencement Speeches.* Scholastic, 1996. *(A)*

Gilbert, Sara. *You Can Speak Up in Class.* Morrow, 1991. *(I; A)*

ORCHESTRA

Blackwood, Alan. *Playing the Piano and Keyboards.* Stargazer Books, 2004; *The Orchestra: An Introduction to the World of Classical Music.* Millbrook Press, 1993. *(P; I)*

Montagu, Jeremy. *Timpani and Percussion.* Yale University Press, 2002. *(A)*

OREGON

Ingram, W. Scott, and Craven, Jean. *Oregon: The Beaver State.* Gareth Stevens, 2002. *(P; I)*

Stefoff, Rebecca. *Oregon.* Marshall Cavendish, 1997. *(P; I)*

Wills, Charles A. *A Historical Album of Oregon.* Millbrook Press, 1995. *(I)*

ORIGAMI

Biddle, Steve, and Biddle, Megumi. *Beginner's Origami: Birds, Beasts, Bugs, and Butterflies.* Viking, 2003; *Paper Capers: A First Book of Paper-Folding Fun.* Barron's, 2002; *Planet Origami: Cosmic Paper Folding for Kids.* Barron's, 1998; *Horrorgami: Spooky Paper Folding for Children.* Barron's, 1996. *(I)*

Smith, Soonboke. *Origami for the First Time.* Sterling, 2004. *(I; A)*

Ungert, Ruth. *Easy Origami Animals.* Sterling, 2003. *(P)*

ORTHODONTICS

Kendall, Bonnie L.; Camenson, Blythe; and Sidney, Elizabeth C. *Dental Care Careers.* McGraw-Hill, 2000. *(A)*

ORWELL, GEORGE

Agathocleous, Tanya. *George Orwell: Battling Big Brother.* Oxford, 2000. *(I; A)*

OSCEOLA

Koestler-Grack, Rachel A. *Osceola, 1804-1838 (American Indian Biographies).* Capstone Press, 2002. *(P; I)*

Sanford, William Reynolds. *Osceola: Seminole Warrior.* Enslow, 1994. *(I)*

OSTRICHES AND OTHER FLIGHTLESS BIRDS

Barrett, Norman S. *Flightless Birds.* Scholastic, 1991. *(P)*

OTTERS AND OTHER MUSTELIDS

Aronsky, Jim. *Otters Under Water.* Putnam, 1992. *(P)*

Van Blaricom, Glenn R. *Sea Otters.* Voyageur Press, 2001. *(I; A)*

Wexo, John Bonnett. *Skunks and Their Relatives.* Creative, 1999. *(I)*

Wu, Norbert. *Beneath the Waves: Exploring the Hidden World of the Kelp Forest.* Chronicle, 1997. *(P; I)*

OVERLAND TRAILS

Blackwood, Gary L. *Life on the Oregon Trail.* Lucent, 1999. *(I)*

Calabro, Marian. *The Perilous Journey of the Donner Party.* Clarion, 1999. *(I)*

Faber, Harold. *John Charles Fremont: Pathfinder to the West.* Benchmark, 2002. *(I)*

Kozar, Richard. *Daniel Boone and the Exploration of the Frontier; Lewis and Clark: Explorers of the Louisiana Purchase.* Chelsea House, 1999. *(I)*

Lavender, David Sievert. *The Santa Fe Trail.* Holiday House, 1995. *(P; I)*

Pelta, Kathy. *Cattle Trails: "Get along Little Doggies"; Eastern Trails: From Footpaths to Turnpikes; The Royal Roads: Spanish Trails in North America; Trails to the West: Beyond the Mississippi.* Raintree Steck-Vaughn, 1997. *(I; A)*

OWLS

Arnosky, Jim. *All about Owls.* Scholastic, 1995. *(P)*

George, Jean Craighead. *The Moon of the Owls.* HarperCollins, 1993. *(I)*

Miller, Sara Swan, and Savage, Stephen. *Owls: The Silent Hunters.* Scholastic, 2000. *(P)*

Silverstein, Alvin; Silverstein, Robert; and Silverstein, Virginia B. *The Spotted Owl.* Millbrook Press, 1994. *(I)*

OXYGEN

Farndon, John. *Oxygen.* Marshall Cavendish, 1998. *(P; I)*

Fitzgerald, Karen. *The Story of Oxygen.* Watts, 1996. *(I; A)*

OYSTERS, CLAMS, AND OTHER BIVALVES

Guiberson, Brenda Z. *Exotic Species: Invaders in Paradise.* Millbrook Press, 1999. *(P; I)*

OZONE

Cefrey, Holly. *What If the Hole in the Ozone Layer Grows Larger?* Scholastic, 2002. *(I; A)*

Nardo, Don. *Ozone (Our Environment Series)*. Thomson Gale, 2005. *(I)*

Newton, David E. *Ozone Dilemma: A Reference Handbook*. ABC-CLIO, 1994. *(A)*

Pringle, Laurence. *Vanishing Ozone: Protecting Earth from Ultraviolet Radiation*. Morrow, 1995. *(I)*

P (LETTER)

Samoyault, Tiphaine. *Alphabetical Order: How the Alphabet Began*. Viking, 1998. *(P; I)*

PACIFIC OCEAN AND ISLANDS

Franklin, Sharon; Black, Cynthia A.; Langness, Teresa; and Krafchin, Rhonda. *Southwest Pacific*. Raintree Steck-Vaughn, 1999. *(I; A)*

Petersen, David, and Petersen, Christine. *The Pacific Ocean*. Children's Press, 2001. *(P)*

Sayre, April Pulley. *Ocean (Exploring Earth's Biomes Series)*. Lerner, 1997. *(I)*

Simon, Seymour. *Oceans*. HarperCollins, 2006. *(P; I)*

Taylor, Leighton R. *The Pacific Ocean*. Gale Group, 1998. *(P; I)*

PAINE, THOMAS

Crompton, Samuel Willard. *Thomas Paine and the Fight for Liberty (Leaders of the American Revolution Series)*. Chelsea House, 2005. *(I)*

PAINTING

Capek, Michael. *Murals: Cave, Cathedral, to Street*. Lerner, 1996. *(A)*

Solga, Kim. *Paint!* F & W Publications, 1991. *(P; I)*

PAKISTAN

Haque, Jameel. *Pakistan*. Gareth Stevens, 2002. *(I)*

Rumalshah, Mano. *Pakistan*. Hamish Hamilton, 1992. *(P; I)*

Viesti, Joseph F., and Hall, Diane. *Celebrate! in South Asia*. HarperCollins, 1996. *(P; I)*

Wagner, Heather Lehr. *India and Pakistan*. Chelsea House, 2002. *(I; A)*

Weston, Mark. *The Land and People of Pakistan*. HarperCollins, 1992. *(A)*

PALESTINE

Carew-Miller, Anna. *Palestinians*. Mason Crest, 2002. *(I; A)*

PANAMA

Augustin, Byron. *Panama (Enchantment of the World, Second Series)*. Scholastic, 2005. *(I; A)*

Haynes, Tricia. *Panama*. Chelsea House, 1998. *(I; A)*

Rau, Dana Meachen. *Panama*. Children's Press, 1999. *(I)*

PANAMA CANAL

Gaines, Ann Graham. *The Panama Canal in American History*. Enslow, 1999. *(I; A)*

Gold, Susan Dudley. *The Panama Canal Transfer: Controversy at the Crossroads*. Raintree Steck-Vaughn, 1999. *(I; A)*

Mann, Elizabeth. *Panama Canal: The Story of How a Jungle Was Conquered and the World Made Smaller*. Firefly, 1998. *(P; I; A)*

Markun, Patricia Maloney. *It's Panama's Canal!* Linnet, 1999. *(I)*

Winkelman, Barbara Gaines. *The Panama Canal*. Children's Press, 1999. *(I)*

PANDAS

Bailey, Jill. *Project Panda*. Steck-Vaughn, 1990. *(P; I)*

Berger, Melvin, and Berger, Gilda. *Where Have All the Pandas Gone?* Scholastic, 1999. *(P; I)*

Dudley, Karen. *Giant Pandas*. Raintree Steck-Vaughn, 1997. *(P; I)*

PAPER

Doney, Meryl. *World Crafts: Papercraft*. Scholastic, 1998. *(I; A)*

Draper, Allison Stark. *Choosing a Career in the Pulp and Paper Industry*. Rosen, 2001. *(A)*

Fiarotta, Phyllis, and Fiarotta, Noel. *Cups and Cans and Paper Plate Fans: Craft Projects from Recycled Materials*. Sterling, 1992. *(P)*

Jaspersohn, William. *Timber: From Trees to Wood Products, Vol. 1*. Little, Brown & Co., 1996. *(P)*

Llewellyn, Claire. *Material World: Paper*. Scholastic, 2001. *(P; I)*

Plomer, Anna Llimos. *Let's Create!: Paper*. Gareth Stevens, 2003. *(P; I)*

PAPIER-MÂCHÉ

McGraw, Sheila. *Papier-Mâché for Kids*. Firefly, 1991. *(P; I)*

Schwartz, Renee F. *Papier-Mâché*. Kids Can Press, 2000. *(I)*

PAPUA NEW GUINEA

Fox, Mary Virginia. *Papua New Guinea*. Children's Press, 1996. *(P; I)*

PARAGUAY

Augustin, Byron. *Paraguay (Enchantment of the World, Second Series)*. Scholastic, 2005. *(I; A)*

Wilkinson, Philip. *The Master Builders*. Chelsea House, 1993. *(I; A)*

PARENT-TEACHER ASSOCIATIONS

Lewis, Barbara A., and Espeland, Pamela. *Kid's Guide to Service Projects: Over 500 Service Ideas for Young People Who Want to Make a Difference*. Free Spirit, 1995. *(I; A)*

PARKS AND PLAYGROUNDS

Alter, Judy. *Amusement Parks: Roller Coasters, Ferris Wheels and Cotton Candy.* Scholastic, 1997. *(P; I)*

Simon, Charnan. *Milton Hershey: Chocolate King, Town Builder.* Children's Press, 1998. *(P)*

PARLIAMENTARY PROCEDURE

Jones, O. Garfield. *Parliamentary Procedure at a Glance.* Viking, 1991. (rev. ed.) *(A)*

PARROTS

Horton, Casey. *Parrots.* Benchmark Books, 1996. *(I)*

PARTIES

Barnes, Emilie. *Let's Have a Tea Party.* Harvest House, 1997. *(P; I)*

Bastyra, Judy. *Parties for Kids.* Larousse Kingfisher, 1998. *(I; A)*

Levine, Shar, and Grafton, Allison. *Einstein's Science Parties: Easy Parties for Curious Kids.* Wiley, 1994. *(P; I)*

Ross, Kathy. *The Best Birthday Parties Ever!: A Kid's Do-It-Yourself Guide.* Millbrook Press, 1999. *(P; I)*

Warner, Penny, and Sanford, Jason. *Kids' Outdoor Parties.* Simon & Schuster, 1999. *(P; I)*

PARTS OF SPEECH

Heller, Ruth. *Fantastic! Wow! And Unreal!: A Book About Interjections and Conjunctions.* Putnam, 2000; *Mine, All Mine: A Book about Pronouns.* Putnam, 1999; *Behind the Mask: A Book about Prepositions; Kites Sail High: A Book about Verbs; Many Luscious Lollipops: A Book about Adjectives; Merry-Go-Round: A Book about Nouns; Up, Up and Away: A Book about Adverbs.* Putnam, 1998. *(P; I)*

PASSOVER

De Paola, Tomie. *My First Passover.* Putnam, 1991. *(P)*

Drucker, Malka. *The Family Treasury of Jewish Holidays.* Little, 1994. *(P; I)*

Fluek, Toby Knobel. *Passover As I Remember It.* Knopf, 1994. *(P; I; A)*

Manushkin, Fran. *Miriam's Cup: A Passover Story.* Scholastic, 1998; *The Matzah That Papa Brought Home.* Scholastic, 1995. *(P)*

Musleah, Rahel. *Why on This Night?: A Passover Haggadah for Family Celebration.* Simon & Schuster, 2000. *(I)*

PASTEUR, LOUIS

Armentrout, David, and Armentrout, Patricia. *Louis Pasteur.* Rourke, 2002. *(P)*

Parker, Steve. *Louis Pasteur and Germs.* Chelsea House, 1995. *(P)*

Robbins, Louise E. *Louis Pasteur and the Hidden World of Microbes.* Oxford, 2001. *(I; A)*

Smith, Linda Wasmer. *Louis Pasteur: Disease Fighter.* Enslow, 1997. *(I)*

PAULING, LINUS

Newton, David E. *Linus Pauling: Scientist and Advocate.* Facts on File, 1994. *(A)*

Pasachoff, Naomi E. *Linus Pauling: Advancing Science, Advocating Peace.* Enslow, 2004. *(I; A)*

PEACE CORPS

Peace Corps, ed. *To Touch the World: The Peace Corps Experience.* Peace Corps, 1995. *(A)*

Peters, Celeste A. *Peace Corps.* Weigl Publishers, 2002. *(I)*

PEACE MOVEMENTS

Aaseng, Nathan. *The Peace Seekers: The Nobel Peace Prize.* Lerner, 1991. *(I; A)*

Abrams, Irwin. *Nobel Peace Prize and the Laureates: An Illustrated Biographical History, 1901-2001.* Watson Publishing International, 2001 (Centennial Edition). *(A)*

Caravantes, Peggy. *Waging Peace: The Story of Jane Addams.* Reynolds, 2004. *(I)*

Carter, Jimmy. *Talking Peace: A Vision for the Next Generation.* Penguin Putnam, 1996 (2nd ed.). *(I; A)*

Harvey, Bonnie Carman. *Jane Addams: Nobel Prize Winner and Founder of Hull House.* Enslow, 1999. *(I)*

Keene, Ann T. *Peacemakers: Winners of the Nobel Peace Prize.* Oxford University Press, 1998. *(I; A)*

Peace Corps, ed. *To Touch the World: The Peace Corps Experience.* Peace Corps, 1995. *(A)*

Peters, Celeste A. *Peace Corps.* Weigl Publishers, 2002. *(I)*

Ross, Stewart. *World Watch: United Nations.* Raintree, 2004; *The United Nations.* Heinemann, 2002. *(I; A)*

Santella, Andrew. *Martin Luther King, Jr.: Civil Rights Leader and Nobel Prize Winner.* Child's World, 2003. *(P; I)*

Schraff, Anne E. *Ralph Bunche: Winner of the Nobel Peace Prize.* Enslow, 1999; *Women of Peace: Nobel Prize Winners.* Enslow, 1994. *(I; A)*

Tarsitano, Frank. *United Nations.* Gareth Stevens, 2003. *(I)*

PELÉ

Krull, Kathleen. *Lives of the Athletes: Thrills, Spills (And What the Neighbors Thought).* Raintree Steck-Vaughn, 1999. *(I; A)*

PENGUINS

Paladino, Catherine. *Pomona: The Birth of a Penguin.* Watts, 1991. *(P)*

Rauzon, Mark J. *Seabirds.* Watts, 1996. *(P; I)*

Vernon, Adele. *The Hoiho: New Zealand's Yellow-Eyed Penguin.* Putnam, 1991. *(I)*

Webb, Sophie. *My Season with Penguins: An Antarctic Journal.* Houghton Mifflin, 2000. *(P; I)*

PENN, WILLIAM

Kroll-Smith, Steve. *William Penn: Founder of Pennsylvania.* Holiday House, 2000. *(I)*

Lutz, Norma Jean, and Schlesinger, Arthur Meier. *William Penn: Founder of Democracy (Colonial Leaders Series).* Chelsea House, 2000. *(P; I)*

PENNSYLVANIA

Fradin, Dennis Brindell. *Pennsylvania: From Sea to Shining Sea.* Scholastic, 1995. *(P; I)*

Ingram, Scott, and Craven, Jean. *Pennsylvania: The Keystone State.* Gareth Stevens, 2002. *(P; I)*

Kroll-Smith, Steve. *William Penn: Founder of Pennsylvania.* Holiday House, 2000. *(I)*

Lutz, Norma Jean, and Schlesinger, Arthur Meier. *William Penn: Founder of Democracy (Colonial Leaders Series).* Chelsea House, 2000. *(P; I)*

Peters, Stephen. *Pennsylvania.* Marshall Cavendish, 2000. *(P; I)*

Pickles, Dewayne E., and Israel, Fred. *The Amish (Immigrant Experience Series).* Chelsea House, 1996. *(I)*

Sherrow, Victoria. *The Thirteen Colonies: Pennsylvania.* Gale Group, 2001. *(I)*

Somervill, Barbara A.; Scanlon, Donna L.; Matusevich, Melissa N. *Pennsylvania.* Scholastic, 2003. *(P; I)*

Swain, Gwenyth. *Pennsylvania.* Lerner, 2001 (2nd ed.). *(P; I)*

PERCUSSION INSTRUMENTS

Dearling, Robert, ed. *The Illustrated Encyclopedia of Musical Instruments.* Gale Research, 1996. *(I; A)*

PERICLES

Poulton, Michael. *Pericles and the Ancient Greeks.* Raintree Steck-Vaughn, 1992. *(I)*

PERSIAN GULF WAR

Gay, Kathlyn, and Gay, Martin. *Persian Gulf War.* 21st Century Books, 1996. *(I)*

Kent, Zachary. *The Persian Gulf War: The Mother of All Battles.* Enslow, 1994. *(I; A)*

King, John. *The Gulf War.* Silver Burdett Press, 1991. *(I; A)*

PERU

Heisey, Janet. *Peru.* Gareth Stevens, 2001. *(I)*

Landau, Elaine. *Peru.* Scholastic, 2000. *(P)*

Mann, Elizabeth. *Machu Picchu: The Story of the Amazing Incas and Their City in the Clouds.* Firefly, 2000. *(P; I; A)*

Morrison, Marion. *Peru.* Scholastic, 2000. *(I)*

Worth, Richard. *Pizarro and the Conquest of the Incan Empire in World History.* Enslow, 2000. *(I; A)*

PETER THE GREAT

Meltzer, Milton. *Ten Kings: And the Worlds They Ruled.* Orchard Books, 2002. *(P; I)*

Roberson, John R. *Transforming Russia, 1682-1991.* Simon & Schuster, 1992. *(I; A)*

Stanley, Diane. *Peter the Great.* William Morrow & Co., 1999. *(P; I)*

PETROLEUM AND PETROLEUM REFINING

Aaseng, Nathan. *Business Builders in Oil.* Oliver Press, 2000. *(I; A)*

Ditchfield, Christin; Jenner, Jan; and Cornwell, Linda. *Oil.* Scholastic, 2001. *(P)*

Gunderson, Cory Gideon. *The Need for Oil.* ABDO, 2003. *(P; I)*

Lampton, Christopher. *Oil Spill.* Lerner, 1992. *(P; I)*

Pringle, Laurence. *Oil Spills: Damage, Recovery, and Prevention.* Morrow, 1993. *(P; I)*

PETS

Benjamin, Carol Lea. *Surviving Your Dog's Adolescence: A Positive Training Program.* John Wiley, 1993. *(A)*;

Gutman, Bill. *Becoming Your Bird's Best Friend.* Millbrook Press, 1996. *(P; I)*

Peterson-Fleming, Judy, and Fleming, Bill. *Kitten Training and Critters, Too!; Puppy Training and Critters, Too!* Morrow/Tamborine, 1996. *(P)*

PHILADELPHIA

Clay, Rebecca. *Kidding around Philadelphia: A Young Person's Guide to the City.* John Muir, 1990. *(P; I)*

Murphy, Jim. *An American Plague: The True and Terrifying Story of the Yellow Fever Epidemic of 1793.* Houghton Mifflin, 2003. *(I; A)*

PHILIPPINES

Kinkade, Sheila. *Children of the Philippines.* Lerner, 1996. *(P; I)*

Lepthien, Emilie U. *The Philippines.* Scholastic, 1994. *(P)*

Olesky, Walter. *The Philippines (Enchantment of the World, Second Series).* Scholastic, 2000. *(I; A)*

Pascoe, Elaine. *The Pacific Rim: East Asia at the Dawn of a New Century.* Millbrook Press, 1999. *(A)*

Schraff, Anne E. *Philippines.* Lerner, 2000. *(P; I)*

Viesti, Joseph F., and Hall, Diane. *Celebrate! in Southeast Asia.* HarperCollins, 1996. *(P; I)*

PHILOSOPHY

Cobb, Vicki. *Why Can't I Live Forever?: And Other Not Such Dumb Questions about Life.* NAL, 1997. *(P; I)*

Law, Stephen. *Philosophy Rocks!: Find out What It Means.* Disney Press, 2002. *(I; A)*

Magee, Bryan. *The Story of Philosophy.* DK, 1998. *(A)*

PHOTOGRAPHY

Ford, Carin T. *George Eastman: The Kodak Camera Man.* Enslow, 2004. *(P)*

Friedman, Debra, and Kurisu, Jane. *Picture This: Fun Photography and Crafts.* Kids Can Press, 2003. *(P; I)*

Gaines, Ann Graham. *American Photographers: Capturing the Image.* Enslow, 2002. *(I)*

King, Dave. *My First Photography Book: A Life-Size Guide to Taking Creative Photographs and Making Exciting Projects with Your Prints.* DK, 1994. *(P; I)*

Lawlor, Laurie. *Window on the West: The Frontier Photography of William Henry Jackson.* Holiday, 1999. *(I)*

Moss, Miriam. *Fashion Photographer.* Crestwood, 1991. *(I)*

Partridge, Elizabeth. *Restless Spirit: The Life and Work of Dorothea Lange.* Viking, 1998. *(I; A)*

Rubin, Susan Goldman. *Margaret Bourke-White: Her Pictures Were Her Life.* Abrams, 1999. *(I; A)*

Sullivan, George. *Black Artists in Photography.* Cobblehill, 1996. *(I; A)*

Varriale, Jim. *Take a Look Around: Photography Activities for Young People.* Millbrook, 1999. *(I)*

Wallace, Joseph. *The Camera.* Simon & Schuster, 2000. *(I; A)*

PHOTOSYNTHESIS

Ross, Bill. *Straight from the Bear's Mouth: The Story of Photosynthesis.* Atheneum, 1995. *(I)*

Silverstein, Alvin; Silverstein, Virginia; and Nunn, Laura Silverstein. *Photosynthesis.* Millbrook Press, 1998. *(I; A)*

PHYSICAL EDUCATION

Morris, Ann. *That's Our Gym Teacher! (That's Our School Series).* Lerner, 2003. *(P)*

PHYSICAL FITNESS

Bull, Deborah C., and Eike, Torje. *Totally Fit.* DK, 1998. *(I)*

Garell, Dale C., and Nardo, Don. *Exercise.* Chelsea House, 1992. *(I)*

Reef, Catherine. *Eat the Right Stuff: Food Facts; Stay Fit: Build a Strong Body; Think Positive: Cope with Stress.* Twenty-First Century, 1995. *(I)*

PHYSICS

Adams, Richard C., and Goodwin, Peter H. *Physics Projects for Young Scientists: Rev. ed. 2000.* Watts, 2000. *(I; A)*

Bortz, Fred. *Catastrophe! Great Engineering Failure—& Success.* Freeman, 1995. *(I; A)*; *Mind Tools: The Science of Artificial Intelligence.* Watts, 1992. *(I; A)*

Cobb, Vicki. *Why Can't You Unscramble an Egg?: and Other Not Such Dumb Questions about Matter.* Lodestar, 1990. *(P; I)*

Couper, Heather, and Henbest, Nigel. *Big Bang: The Story of the Universe.* DK, 1997. *(I; A)*

Gallant, Roy A. *The Ever-Changing Atom.* Marshall Cavendish/Benchmark, 1999. *(I; A)*

Gardner, Robert. *Science Projects about the Physics of Sports; Science Projects about the Physics of Toys and Games.* Enslow, 2000; *Science Projects about Physics in the Home.* Enslow, 1999. *(I; A)*

Gribbin, John, and Gribbin, Mary. *Time & Space: Explore the Changing Ideas about Our Universe—From the Flat Earth to the Latest Research into Black Holes.* Dorling Kindersley, 1994. *(I; A)*

Supplee, Curt. *Physics in the 20th Century.* Abrams, 1999. *(A)*

PIANO

Blackwood, Alan. *Playing the Piano and Keyboards.* Stargazer Books, 2004. *(P; I)*

Dearling, Robert, ed. *The Illustrated Encyclopedia of Musical Instruments.* Gale Research, 1996. *(I; A)*

Krull, Kathleen. *Lives of the Musicians: Good Times, Bad Times (And What the Neighbors Thought).* Raintree Steck-Vaughn, 1998. *(I; A)*

PICASSO, PABLO

Beardsley, John. *Pablo Picasso.* Abrams, 1991. *(I; A)*

Janson, H. W., and Janson, Anthony F. *History of Art for Young People.* Abrams, 1997 (rev. ed.). *(I; A)*

Lowery, Linda. *Pablo Picasso.* Lerner, 1999. *(P)*

Muhlberger, Richard, and Metropolitan Museum of Art. *What Makes a Picasso a Picasso?* Viking, 1994. *(I)*

PIERCE, FRANKLIN

DiConsiglio, John. *Franklin Pierce (Encyclopedia of Presidents, Second Series).*

Ferry, Steven. *Franklin Pierce: Our Fourteenth President.* Child's World, 2002. *(P; I)*

PIGS

Ling, Mary. *Pig.* Dorling Kindersley, 1993. *(P)*

Miller, Sara Swan. *Pigs.* Scholastic, 2000. *(P)*

Wolfman, Judy, and Winston, David Lorenz. *Life on a Pig Farm.* Lerner, 2001. *(P)*

PINEAPPLE

Hughes, Meredith Sayles. *Yes, We Have Bananas: Fruits from Shrubs and Vines.* Lerner, 1999. *(P; I)*

PIONEER LIFE

Bentley, Judith. *Settling the West: Explorers, Trappers, and Guides; Settling the West: Brides, Midwives, and Widows.* Lerner, 1997. *(I; A)*

Graves, Kerry A. *Going to School in Pioneer Times.* Capstone Press, 2001. *(P; I)*

Ichord, Loretta Frances. *Skillet Bread, Sourdough, and Vinegar Pie.* Lerner, 2003. *(P; I)*

Katz, William Loren. *Black Pioneers: An Untold Story.* Atheneum, 1999. *(I)*

Stanley, Jerry. *Frontier Merchants: Lionel and Barron Jacobs and the Jewish Pioneers Who Settled the West.* Crown, 1998. *(I; A)*

PIZARRO, FRANCISCO

Bernhard, Brendan. *Pizarro, Orellana, and the Exploration of the Amazon.* Chelsea House, 1991. *(A)*

De Angelis, Gina. *Francisco Pizarro and the Conquest of the Inca.* Chelsea House, 2000. *(I)*

Marrin, Albert. *Inca and Spaniard: Pizarro and the Conquest of Peru.* Simon & Schuster, 1991. *(I; A)*

Worth, Richard. *Pizarro and the Conquest of the Incan Empire in World History.* Enslow, 2000. *(I; A)*

PLANETS

Asimov, Isaac. *Colonizing the Planets and Stars.* Gareth Stevens, 1990. *(P; I)*

Berger, Melvin, and Berger, Gilda. *Do Stars Have Points?: Questions and Answers about Stars and Planets.* Scholastic, 1999. *(P; I)*

Branley, Franklyn M. *The Planets in Our Solar System.* Crowell, 1998 (rev. ed.). *(P)*

Lauber, Patricia. *Journey to the Planets.* Crown, 1993 (rev. ed.). *(I; A)*

Levy, David H. *Stars and Planets: Discovery.* Barnes & Noble, 2003 (3rd ed.). *(P; I)*

PLANKTON

Cerullo, Mary M. *Sea Soup: Zooplankton.* Tilbury House, 2001; *Sea Soup: Phytoplankton.* Tilbury House, 1999. *(I)*

Dykstra, Mary. *Amateur Zoologist: Explorations and Investigations.* Scholastic, 1995. *(I; A)*

Wu, Norbert. *Beneath the Waves: Exploring the Hidden World of the Kelp Forest.* Chronicle, 1997. *(P; I)*

PLANTS

Batten, Mary. *Hungry Plants.* Golden, 2000. *(P)*

Bocknek, Jonathan. *The Science of Plants.* Gareth Stevens, 1999. *(P; I)*

Coil, Suzanne M. *Poisonous Plants.* Watts, 1991. *(P; I)*

Dowden, Anne O. *From Flower to Fruit.* Harper, 1995 (rev. ed.). *(I; A)*

Gardner, Robert. *Science Projects about Plants.* Enslow, 1999. *(I; A)*

Kerrod, Robin. *Plant Life.* Marshall Cavendish, 1994. *(P; I)*

Kidd, J. S., and Kidd, Renee A. *Mother Nature's Pharmacy: Potent Natural Medicines (Science and Society Series).* Facts on File, 2005; *Mother Nature's Pharmacy: Potent Medicines from Plants (Science and Society Series).* Facts on File, 1998. *(I; A)*

Kite, L. Patricia. *Insect-Eating Plants.* Millbrook, 1995. *(P; I)*

Patent, Dorothy Hinshaw. *Plants on the Trail with Lewis and Clark.* Houghton Mifflin, 2003. *(I)*

Penny, Malcolm. *How Plants Grow.* Marshall Cavendish, 1996. *(P; I)*

Powledge, Fred. *Pharmacy in the Forest: How Medicines Are Found in the Natural World.* Simon & Schuster, 1998. *(I)*

Rhoades, Diane. *Garden Crafts for Kids: 50 Great Reasons to Get Your Hands Dirty.* Sterling, 1998. *(P; I)*

Waters, Marjorie. *The Victory Garden Kids' Book.* Globe Pequot Press, 1994. *(P; I; A)*

PLATYPUS AND SPINY ANTEATERS

Short, Joan; Bird, Bettina; and Green, Jack. *Platypus.* Mondo, 1996. *(P; I)*

Squire, Ann O. *Anteaters, Sloths, and Armadillos.* Watts, 1999. *(I)*

PLAYS

Bruchac, Joseph. *Pushing Up the Sky: Seven Native American Plays for Children.* Dial, 2000. *(P; I)*

McCullough, L. E. *Anyone Can Produce Plays with Kids: The Absolute Basics of Staging Your Own At-Home, In-School, Round-the-Neighborhood Plays.* Smith & Kraus, 1998. *(A)*

Surface, Mary Hall. *Most Valuable Player and Four Other All-Star Plays for Middle and High School Audiences (Young Actors Series).* Smith & Kraus, 1999. *(A)*; *Short Scenes and Monologues for Middle School Actors (Young Actors Series).* Smith & Kraus, 1999. *(I)*

Winther, Barbara. *Plays from Hispanic Tales.* Plays, 1998. *(I)*

PLUTO

Asimov, Isaac. *How Did We Find Out about Pluto?* Walker, 1991. *(I; A)*; *Pluto: A Double Planet?* Gareth Stevens, 1990. *(P; I)*

PLYMOUTH COLONY

Doherty, Kieran. *William Bradford: Rock of Plymouth.* Twenty-First Century, 1999. *(I; A)*

Penner, Lucille Recht. *The Pilgrims at Plymouth.* Random, 1996. *(P)*

POISONS

Dowden, Anne Ophelia. *Poisons in Our Path: Plants That Harm and Heal.* HarperCollins, 1994. *(P; I)*

Latta, Sara L. *Food Poisoning and Foodborne Diseases.* Enslow, 1999. *(I; A)*

Pascoe, Elaine. *Spreading Menace: Salmonella Attack and the Hunger Craving.* Thomson Gale, 2003. *(I)*

Rosaler, Maxine. *Botulism (Epidemics Series).* Rosen, 2003. *(I)*

POLAND

Poland...in Pictures. Lerner, 1994. *(I)*

Dornberg, John. *Central and Eastern Europe.* Greenwood, 1995. *(A)*

Grajnert, Paul. *Poland.* Gareth Stevens, 2002. *(P; I)*

Heale, Jay. *Poland.* Marshall Cavendish, 1994. *(I; A)*

Hintz, Martin. *Poland (Enchantment of the World, Second Series).* Scholastic, 1998. *(I; A)*

Zamojska-Hutchins, Danuta. *Cooking the Polish Way.* Lerner, 2002 (2nd ed.). *(I; A)*

POLICE

Almonte, Paul, and Desmond, Theresa. *Police, People and Power.* Silver Burdett Press, 1992. *(I)*

Stinchcomb, James A. *Opportunities in Law Enforcement and Criminal Justice Careers.* McGraw-Hill, 2002 (2nd ed.). *(A)*

POLITICAL PARTIES

The New World Order. Greenhaven, 1991. *(A)*

Fish, Bruce, and Fish, Becky Durost. *The History of the Democratic Party.* Chelsea House, 2000. *(I; A)*

Morin, Isobel V. *Politics, American Style: Political Parties in American History.* Twenty-First Century, 1999. *(I)*

Sullivan, George E. *Choosing the Candidates.* Silver Burdett Press, 1991. *(I)*

POLK, JAMES KNOX

Carey, Charles W. *Mexican War: Mr. Polk's War.* Enslow, 2002. *(I; A)*

Gaines, Ann Graham. *James Polk: Our Eleventh President.* Child's World, 2002. *(P; I)*

McCollum, Sean. *James K. Polk (Encyclopedia of Presidents, Second Series).* Scholastic, 2004. *(I; A)*

POLLOCK, JACKSON

Greenberg, Jan, and Jordan, Sandra. *Action Jackson.* Millbrook/Roaring Brook, 2002. *(P; I)*

Halliwell, Sarah, ed. *20th Century: Post-1945 Artists, Writers, and Composers.* Raintree, 1998. *(I)*

Janson, H. W., and Janson, Anthony F. *History of Art for Young People.* Abrams, 1997 (rev. ed.). *(I; A)*

POLO, MARCO

Stefoff, Rebecca. *Marco Polo and the Medieval Explorers.* Main Line, 1992. *(P; I)*

Twist, Clint. *Marco Polo: Overland to Medieval China.* Raintree Steck-Vaughn, 1994. *(P; I)*

POMPEII

Deem, James M. *Bodies from the Ash: Life and Death in Ancient Pompeii.* Houghton Mifflin, 2005. *(P; I)*

Patent, Dorothy Hinshaw. *Lost City of Pompeii.* Marshall Cavendish, 2000. *(I)*

PONCE DE LÉON, JUAN

Dolan, Sean. *Juan Ponce De Léon.* Chelsea House, 1995. *(I)*

Harmon, Daniel E. *Juan Ponce de Léon and the Search for the Fountain of Youth.* Chelsea House, 1999. *(I)*

PONTIAC

Bland, Celia. *Pontiac: Ottawa Rebel.* Chelsea House, 1994. *(I)*

PONY EXPRESS

Dolan, Edward F. *The Pony Express.* Marshall Cavendish, 2002. *(P)*

Geis, Jacqueline. *The First Ride: Blazing the Trail for the Pony Express.* Hambleton-Hill, 1994. *(P)*

Harness, Cheryl. *They're Off!: The Story of the Pony Express.* Aladdin, 2002. *(P)*

Kroll, Steven. *Pony Express!* Scholastic, 1996. *(P)*

McCormick, Anita Louise. *The Pony Express in American History.* Enslow, 2001. *(I)*

Savage, Jeff. *Pony Express Riders of the Wild West.* Enslow, 1995. *(P; I)*

Van der Linde, Laurel. *The Pony Express.* Simon & Schuster, 1993. *(I)*

Yancey, Diane. *Life on the Pony Express.* Gale Group, 2001. *(A)*

POPULATION

Bowden, Rob. *Overcrowded World?: Our Impact on the Planet.* Raintree Steck-Vaughn, 2002. *(I)*

Cooper, Michael L. *Bound for the Promised Land: The Great Black Migration.* Penguin, 1995. *(I; A)*

Markley, Oliver W., and McCuan, Walter R., eds. *21st Century Earth.* Gale Group, 1996. *(I; A)*

Nardo, Don. *Population.* Gale Group, 2000. *(A)*

Winckler, Suzanne, and Rodgers, Mary M. *Population Growth.* Lerner, 1991. *(I)*

Zeaman, John. *Overpopulation.* Scholastic, 2002. *(I; A)*

PORTUGAL

Portugal...in Pictures. Lerner, 1996. *(I)*

Blauer, Ettagle, and Laure, Jason. *Portugal.* Scholastic, 2001. *(I; A)*

Ngcheong-Lum, Roseline. *Portugal.* Gareth Stevens, 2000. *(I)*

POSTAL SERVICE

Bolick, Nancy O'Keefe. *Mail Call: The History of the U.S. Postal Service.* Watts, 1995. *(I)*

Burns, Peggy. *Stepping Through History: The Mail.* Steck-Vaughn, 1994. *(P; I)*

Kule, Elaine A. *The U. S. Mail (Transportation and Communication Series).* Enslow, 2002. *(P)*

Skurzynski, Gloria. *Here Comes the Mail.* Simon & Schuster, 1993. *(P)*

POTATOES

Meltzer, Milton. *The Amazing Potato: A Story in Which the Incas, Conquistadors, Marie Antoinette, Thomas Jefferson, Wars, Famines, Immigrants, and French Fries All Play a Part.* HarperCollins, 1992. *(I)*

POTTER, HELEN BEATRIX

Johnson, Jane. *My Dear Noel: The Story of a Letter from Beatrix Potter.* Dial Books, 1999. *(P)*

Malam, John. *Beatrix Potter.* Lerner, 1998. *(P)*

Wallner, Alexandra. *Beatrix Potter.* Holiday, 1995. *(P)*

POTTERY

Schwartz, Deborah; Sullivan, Missy; and the Brooklyn Museum. *The Native American Look Book: Art and Activities for Kids.* New Press, 2000. *(I)*

POULTRY

Miller, Sara Swan. *Chickens.* Scholastic, 2000. *(P)*

Patent, Dorothy Hinshaw. *Wild Turkeys.* Lerner, 1999. *(P)*

POVERTY

Berek, Judith. *No Place to Be: Voices of Homeless Children.* Houghton, 1992. *(I; A)*

Bial, Raymond. *Tenement: Immigrant Life on the Lower East Side.* Houghton Mifflin, 2002. *(I)*

Criswell, Sara Dixon. *Homelessness.* Lucent, 1998. *(I; A)*

Greenberg, Keith Elliot. *Erik is Homeless.* Lerner, 1992. *(P; I)*

Kowalski, Kathiann M. *Poverty in America: Causes and Issues.* Enslow, 2003. *(I; A)*

Nichelason, Margery G. *Homeless or Hopeless?: A Pro/ Con Issue.* Lerner, 1993. *(I; A)*

Rozakis, Laurie E. *Homelessness: Can We Solve the Problem?* Twenty-First Century, 1995. *(I)*

Stearman, Kaye. *Homelessness.* Raintree Steck-Vaughn, 1999. *(I; A)*

Worth, Richard. *Poverty.* Lucent, 1997. *(A)*

POWELL, COLIN

Banta, Melissa. *Colin Powell: A Complete Soldier.* Chelsea, 1994. *(I)*

Hughes, Libby. *Colin Powell: A Man of Quality.* Silver Burdett Press, 1996. *(I; A)*

Landau, Elaine. *Colin Powell: Four Star General.* Watts, 1991. *(I)*

Shichtman, Sandra H. *Colin Powell: Have a Vision. Be Demanding.* Enslow, 2005. *(I; A)*

POWER PLANTS

Wilcox, Charlotte. *Powerhouse: Inside a Nuclear Power Plant.* Carolrhoda, 1996. *(I; A)*

PRAYER

Thanks Be to God: Prayers from around the World. Macmillan, 1990. *(P; I)*

Brown, Susan Taylor. *Can I Pray with My Eyes Open?* Hyperion, 1999. *(P)*

Godwin, Laura. *Barnyard Prayers.* Hyperion, 2000. *(P)*

PREHISTORIC ANIMALS

Bonner, Hannah. *When Bugs Were Big, Plants Were Strange, and Tetrapods Stalked the Earth: A Cartoon Prehistory of Life Before Dinosaurs.* National Geographic, 2004. *(P; I)*

Giblin, James Cross. *The Mystery of the Mammoth Bones: And How It Was Solved.* HarperCollins, 1999. *(I)*

Thompson, Sharon Elaine. *Death Trap: The Story of the La Brea Tar Pits.* Lerner, 1994. *(I)*

Walker, Sally M. *Fossil Fish Found Alive: The Amazing Quest for the Coelacanth.* Carolrhoda, 2002. *(I)*

Zimmerman, Howard. *Beyond the Dinosaurs!: Sky Dragons, Sea Monsters, Mega Mammals and Other Prehistoric Beasts.* Simon & Schuster, 2001; *Dinosaurs!: The Biggest, Baddest, Strangest, Fastest.* Simon & Schuster, 2000. *(P; I)*

PREHISTORIC ART

Hodge, Susie. *Prehistoric Art.* Heinemann, 1997. *(P; I)*

Lambert, David, and Diagram Group Staff. *Encyclopedia of Prehistory.* Facts on File, 2002. *(I; A)*

PREHISTORIC PEOPLE

Arnold, Caroline. *Stone Age Farmers Beside the Sea: Scotland's Prehistoric Village of Skara Brae.* Houghton Mifflin, 1997. *(I)*

Buell, Janet. *Ancient Horsemen of Siberia; Greenland Mummies.* Millbrook Press, 1998. *(I; A); Bog Bodies; Ice Maiden of the Andes.* Twenty-First Century, 1997. *(I)*

Facchini, Fiorenzo. *Humans: Origins and Evolution.* Steck-Vaughn, 1994. *(I; A)*

Patent, Dorothy Hinshaw. *Mystery of the Lascaux Cave; Secrets of the Ice Man.* Marshall Cavendish, 1998. *(I)*

Reinhard, Johan. *Discovering the Inca Ice Maiden.* National Geographic, 1998. *(I; A)*

Sattler, Helen Roney. *The Earliest Americans.* Houghton Mifflin, 2001. *(I; A)*

PRESIDENCY OF THE UNITED STATES

Aaseng, Nathan. *You Are the President; You Are the President II, 1800-1899.* Oliver Press, 1994. *(I; A)*

Blassingame, Wyatt. *The Look-It-Up Book of Presidents.* Random House, 2004 (rev. ed.). *(P; I)*

Davis, Kenneth C. *Don't Know Much About the Presidents.* HarperCollins, 2001. *(P; I)*

Gorman, Jacqueline Laks. *President.* Gareth Stevens, 2005. *(P)*

Krull, Kathleen. *Lives of the Presidents: Fame, Shame (And What the Neighbors Thought).* Raintree Steck-Vaughn, 1998. *(I)*

Morris, Juddi. *At Home with the Presidents.* Wiley, 1999. *(I)*

Parker, Nancy Winslow. *The President's Cabinet and How it Grew.* HarperCollins, 1991. *(P; I)*

Pascoe, Elaine. *First Facts about the Presidents.* Blackbirch, 1996. *(I)*

Roberts, Russell. *Presidents and Scandals.* Gale Group, 2001. *(A)*

St. George, Judith. *So You Want to Be President? (P; I); In the Line of Fire: Presidents' Lives at Stake.* Holiday House, 1999. *(A)*

Santella, Andrew. *U.S. Presidential Inaugurations.* Scholastic, 2001. *(P; I)*

Woronoff, Kristen. *American Inaugurals: The Speeches, the Presidents and Their Times.* Gale Group, 2002. *(A)*

PRIMATES

Maynard, Thane. *Primates: Apes, Monkeys, Prosimians.* Watts, 1995. *(I)*

Powzyk, Joyce Ann. *In Search of Lemurs: My Days and Nights in a Madagascar Rain Forest.* National Geographic, 1998. *(P; I)*

PRINTING

The History of Making Books: From Clay Tablets, Papyrus Rolls, and Illuminated Manuscripts to the Printing Press. Scholastic, 1996. *(P; I)*

Koscielniak, Bruce. *Johann Gutenberg and the Amazing Printing Press.* Houghton Mifflin, 2003. *(P; I)*

PRISONS

Oliver, Marilyn Tower. *Alcatraz Prison (In American History Series).* Enslow, 1998. *(I; A)*

Owens, Lois Smith, and Gordon, Vivian Verdell. *Think about Prisons and the Criminal Justice System.* Walker, 1991. *(I; A)*

Warburton, Lois. *Prisons.* Lucent, 1993. *(I; A)*

Williams, Stanley "Tookie," and Becnel, Barbara Cottman. *Life in Prison.* Morrow, 1998. *(I; A)*

PROPAGANDA

Simon, Charnan. *Hollywood at War: The Motion Picture Industry and World War II.* Watts, 1993. *(I)*

Steffens, Bradley, and Buggey, Joanne. *Free Speech: Identifying Propaganda Techniques.* Greenhaven Press, 1992. *(I)*

PROTESTANTISM

Kroll-Smith, Steve. *William Penn: Founder of Pennsylvania.* Holiday House, 2000. *(I)*

Williams, Jean Kinney. *The Shakers.* Watts, 1997. *(I; A)*; *The Amish.* Scholastic, 1996. *(I; A)*

PUBLIC HEALTH

Aronson, Virginia. *Influenza Pandemic of 1918-1919.* Chelsea House, 2000. *(I)*

Bianchi, Anne. *C. Everett Koop: The Health of a Nation.* Millbrook Press, 1992. *(I; A)*

Colman, Penny. *Toilets, Bathtubs, Sinks, and Sewers: A History of the Bathroom.* Simon & Schuster, 1994. *(I)*

Giblin, James Cross. *When Plague Strikes: The Black Death, Smallpox, AIDS.* HarperCollins, 1997. *(I; A)*

Hawxhurst, Joan C. *Antonia Novello: U.S. Surgeon General.* Millbrook Press, 1995. *(P; I)*

Holmes, Pamela. *Drugs, The Complete Story: Alcohol.* Raintree Steck-Vaughn, 1991. *(I)*

Powell, Jillian. *World Organizations: World Health Organization.* Scholastic, 2001. *(I; A)*

Yount, Lisa. *Epidemics.* Lucent, 1999. *(I; A)*

PUBLIC LANDS

Dolan, Edward F. *American Wilderness and Its Future: Conservation Versus Use.* Watts, 1992. *(I; A)*

PUBLIC SPEAKING

Gilbert, Sara. *You Can Speak Up in Class.* Morrow, 1991. *(I; A)*

Holzer, Harold, ed. *Abraham Lincoln, the Writer: A Treasury of His Greatest Speeches and Letters.* Boyds Mills Press, 2000. *(I; A)*

PUBLISHING

The History of Making Books: From Clay Tablets, Papyrus Rolls, and Illuminated Manuscripts to the Printing Press. Scholastic, 1996. *(P; I)*

Carter, Robert A.; Pattis, S. William; and Camenson, Blythe. *Opportunities in Publishing Careers.* McGraw-Hill, 2000 (rev. ed.). *(I; A)*

Garcia, John. *The Success of Hispanic Magazine: A Publishing Success Story.* Walker, 1995. *(I; A)*

Kiefer, Barbara. *Wings of an Artist: Children's Book Illustrators Talk about Their Art.* Abrams, 1999. *(I; A)*

Locker, Thomas. *The Man Who Paints Nature (Meet the Author Series).* Richard C. Owen, 1999. *(P; I)*

Markham, Lois. *Avi (Meet the Author Series).* Creative Teaching Press, 1996; *Lois Lowry (Meet the Author Series).* Creative Teaching Press, 1995. *(I)*

Pringle, Laurence P. *Nature! Wild and Wonderful (Meet the Author Series).* Richard C. Owen, 1997. *(P)*

Raatma, Lucia. *How Books Are Made.* Scholastic, 1998. *(P)*

Rhatigan, Joe. *In Print!: 40 Cool Publishing Projects for Kids.* Sterling, 2004. *(P; I)*

Simon, Seymour. *From Paper Airplanes to Outer Space (Meet the Author Series).* Richard C. Owen, 2000. *(P; I)*

PUCCINI, GIACOMO

Berger, William. *Puccini without Excuses: A Refreshing Reassessment of the World's Most Popular Composer.* Knopf, 2005. *(A)*

Geras, Adele, and Beck, Ian. *The Random House Book of Opera Stories.* Random House, 1998. *(P; I)*

Holden, Amanda, ed. *The New Penguin Opera Guide.* Penguin Group, 2002 (rev. ed.). *(A)*

PUERTO RICO

Banting, Erinn. *Puerto Rico the People and Culture.* Crabtree, 2003. *(P; I)*

Fradin, Dennis Brindell, and Fradin, Judith Bloom. *Puerto Rico: From Sea to Shining Sea.* Scholastic, 1996. *(P; I)*

Harlan, Judith. *Puerto Rico: Deciding Its Future.* 21st Century Books, 1996. *(I; A)*

Johnston, Joyce. *Puerto Rico.* Lerner, 2001 (2nd ed.). *(P; I)*

Levy, Patricia M. *Puerto Rico.* Marshall Cavendish, 1995 (2nd ed.). *(I; A)*

McKenley, Yvonne. *A Taste of the Caribbean.* Raintree Steck-Vaughn, 1995. *(P; I)*

Schwebacher, Martin. *Puerto Rico.* Marshall Cavendish, 2001. *(P; I)*

PULITZER PRIZES

Whitelaw, Nancy. *Joseph Pulitzer and the New York World.* Morgan Reynolds, 1999. *(I; A)*

PULSARS

Asimov, Isaac, and Hantula, Richard. *Black Holes, Pulsars, and Quasars.* Gareth Stevens, 2003 (updated edition). *(I)*

PUNCTUATION

Terban, Marvin. *Punctuation Power: Punctuation and How to Use It.* Scholastic, 2000. *(P; I; A)*

PUNIC WARS

Green, Robert. *Hannibal.* Watts, 1996. *(I)*

Nardo, Don. *The Battle of Zama; The Punic Wars.* Lucent, 1996. *(I; A)*

PUPPETS AND MARIONETTES

Buetter, Barbara MacDonald. *Simple Puppets from Everyday Materials.* Sterling, 1996. *(P)*

Lade, Roger. *The Most Excellent Book of How to Be a Puppeteer.* Copper Beech, 1996. *(P; I)*

PURIM

Drucker, Malka. *The Family Treasury of Jewish Holidays.* Little, 1994. *(P; I)*

PURITANS

Collier, Christopher, and Collier, James L. *Pilgrims and Puritans, 1620-1676.* Marshall Cavendish, 1997. *(I; A)*

PYRAMIDS

Kent, Peter. *Great Building Stories of the Past.* Oxford, 2001. *(P; I)*

Mann, Elizabeth. *The Great Pyramid: The Story of the Farmers, The God-King, and the Most Astounding Structure Ever Built.* Mikaya Press, 1996. *(P; I)*

Mellett, Peter. *Pyramids.* Southwater, 2000. *(P; I)*

Morley, Jacqueline, and Bergin, Mark. *An Egyptian Pyramid.* NTC, 1993. *(P; I)*

Putnam, James. *Eyewitness: Pyramid.* DK, 2000. *(P; I)*

Q (LETTER)

Samoyault, Tiphaine. *Alphabetical Order: How the Alphabet Began.* Viking, 1998. *(P; I)*

QUAKERS

Kroll-Smith, Steve. *William Penn: Founder of Pennsylvania.* Holiday House, 2000. *(I)*

Lutz, Norma Jean, and Schlesinger, Arthur Meier. *William Penn: Founder of Democracy (Colonial Leaders Series).* Chelsea House, 2000. *(P; I)*

Williams, Jean Kinney. *The Quakers (American Religious Experience Series).* Scholastic, 1998. *(I; A)*

QUEBEC

Gillis, Jennifer Blizin. *Life in New France, Quebec.* Heinemann, 2003. *(P)*

Kizilos, Peter. *Quebec: Province Divided.* Lerner, 1999. *(I; A)*

LeVert, Suzanne. *Quebec.* Chelsea House, 1990. *(I)*

R (LETTER)

Samoyault, Tiphaine. *Alphabetical Order: How the Alphabet Began.* Viking, 1998. *(P; I)*

RABBITS AND HARES

Boring, Mel. *Rabbits, Squirrels, and Chipmunks.* Creative Publishing, 1997. *(P; I)*

Evans, Mark. *Rabbit: A Practical Guide to Caring for Your Rabbit.* DK, 2001. *(P; I)*

Holub, Joan. *Why Do Rabbits Hop?: And Other Questions about Rabbits, Guinea Pigs, Hamsters, and Gerbils.* Penguin Putnam, 2003. *(P)*

Jeffrey, Laura S. *Hamsters, Gerbils, Guinea Pigs, Rabbits, Ferrets, Mice, and Rats: How to Choose and Care for a Small Mammal.* Enslow, 2004. *(P; I)*

Lepthien, Emilie U. *Rabbits and Hares.* Scholastic, 1994. *(P)*

Miller, Sara Swan. *Rabbits, Pikas, and Hares.* Scholastic, 2002. *(P; I)*

Tagholm, Sally. *The Rabbit.* Kingfisher, 2000. *(P)*

RACCOONS AND THEIR RELATIVES

Jacobs, Lee. *Raccoon.* Gale Group, 2002. *(P)*

Merrick, Patrick. *Raccoons.* Child's World, 1998. *(P)*

RACES, HUMAN

Gallant, Roy A. *Early Humans.* Benchmark, 2000. *(I)*

Glover, David M. *The Young Oxford Book of the Human Being: The Body, The Mind, and The Way We Live.* Oxford University Press, 1997. *(I; A)*

RACING

Page, Jason. *On the Water: Rowing, Yachting, Canoeing, and Lots, Lots, More.* Lerner, 2000. *(P; I; A)*

Sherman, Josepha. *Barrel Racing.* Heinemann, 2001. *(P; I)*

Stewart, Mark. *The Pettys: Triumphs and Tragedies of Auto Racing's First Family.* Millbrook Press, 2001. *(P; I)*; *Auto Racing: A History of Fast Cars and Fearless Drivers.* Watts, 1998. *(I; A)*

Youngblood, Ed. *Dirt Track Racing; Superbike Racing.* Capstone Press, 2000. *(P; I)*

RACISM

Cooper, Michael L. *Remembering Manzanar: Life in a Japanese Relocation Camp.* Houghton Mifflin, 2002. *(A)*; *Fighting For Honor: Japanese Americans and World War II.* Houghton Mifflin, 2000. *(I; A)*; *Double V Campaign: African-Americans in World War II.* Penguin Group, 1997. *(I)*

Gay, Kathlyn. *Neo-Nazis: A Growing Threat.* Enslow, 1997. *(A)*

Green, Jen. *Dealing with Racism.* Copper Beech, 1998. *(P)*

Pascoe, Elaine. *Racial Prejudice: Why Can't We Overcome?* Watts, 1997. *(I; A)*

Williams, Mary E, ed. *Discrimination.* Gale Group, 2002. *(A); Issues in Racism.* Lucent, 2000. *(I; A)*

RADIATION

Andryszewski, Tricia. *What to Do about Nuclear Waste.* Lerner, 1995. *(I; A)*

Cheney, Glenn Alan. *They Never Knew: The Victims of Nuclear Testing.* Scholastic, 1996. *(I; A)*

Skurzynski, Gloria. *Waves: The Electro-Magnetic Universe.* National Geographic, 1996. *(P; I)*

RADIO

Finkelstein, Norman H. *Sounds in the Air: The Golden Age of Radio.* Simon & Schuster, 1993. *(I; A)*

RADIO ASTRONOMY

Fradin, Dennis Brindell. *Is There Life on Mars?* Simon & Schuster, 1999. *(I; A); Searching for Alien Life: Is Anyone Out There?* Twenty-First Century, 1997. *(I)*

RADIOMETRIC DATING

Liptak, Karen. *Dating Dinosaurs and Other Old Things.* Millbrook Press, 1992. *(I; A)*

RAILROADS

Blumberg, Rhoda. *Full Steam Ahead: The Race to Build a Transcontinental Railroad.* National Geographic, 1996. *(P; I)*

Levinson, Nancy Smiler. *She's Been Working on the Railroad.* Lodestar, 1997. *(I; A)*

Perl, Lila. *To the Golden Mountain: The Chinese Who Built the Transcontinental Railroad.* Marshall Cavendish, 2002. *(I; A)*

Streissguth, Thomas. *The Transcontinental Railroad.* Lucent, 1999. *(I)*

Winslow, Mimi; Bentley, Judith; and Culleton, Pat. *Loggers and Railroad Workers.* Lerner, 1997. *(I)*

Wormser, Richard L. *The Iron Horse: How Railroads Changed America.* Walker, 1993. *(I; A)*

RAIN, SNOW, SLEET, AND HAIL

Branley, Franklyn M. *Snow Is Falling.* HarperCollins, 2000. *Down Comes the Rain;* 1997. *(P)*

Gardner, Robert. *Science Project Ideas about Rain.* Enslow, 1997. *(I)*

Llewellyn, Claire. *Wild, Wet and Windy: The Weather-From Hurricanes to Monsoons (SuperSmarts Series).* Candlewick Press, 1997. *(P)*

Rodgers, Alan, and Streluk, Angella. *Precipitation.* Heinemann, 2002. *(P; I)*

RAINBOW

Kramer, Stephen. *Theodoric's Rainbow.* Scientific American, 1995. *(I)*

Krupp, E. C. *The Rainbow and You.* HarperCollins, 2000. *(P)*

RAIN FORESTS

Castner, James L. *Layers of Life: Deep in the Amazon; Native Peoples: Deep in the Amazon; Partners and Rivals: Deep in the Amazon; Rainforest Researchers: Deep in the Amazon; River Life: Deep in the Amazon; Surviving in the Rain Forest: Deep in the Amazon.* Marshall Cavendish, 2001. *(I; A)*

Collard, Sneed B. *Monteverde: Science and Scientists in a Costa Rican Cloud Forest.* Scholastic, 1998. *(I; A)*

Johnson, Linda Carlson. *Rain Forests: A Pro/Con Issue.* Enslow, 1999. *(I)*

Johnson, Rebecca L. *A Walk in the Rain Forest (Biomes of North America Series).* Lerner, 2000. *(P; I)*

Lewington, Anna, and Parker, Edward. *People of the Rain Forests.* Raintree Steck-Vaughn, 1998. *(P; I)*

Lyman, Francesca, and American Museum of Natural History. *Inside the Dzanga-Sangha Rain Forest.* Workman, 1998. *(P; I)*

McLeish, Ewan. *Rain Forests: Our Impact on the Planet.* Raintree Steck-Vaughn, 2002. *(I)*

Pirotta, Saviour. *People in the Rain Forest; Predators in the Rain Forest; Rivers in the Rain Forest; Trees and Plants in the Rain Forest.* Raintree Steck-Vaughn, 1998. *(P)*

Radley, Gail. *Forests and Jungles.* Lerner, 2001. *(P; I)*

Ricciuti, Edward R. *Biomes of the World: Rainforest.* Marshall Cavendish, 1995. *(P; I)*

Wright-Frierson, Virginia. *A North American Rain Forest Scrapbook.* Walker, 2003. *(P)*

RALEIGH, SIR WALTER

Aronson, Marc. *Sir Walter Raleigh and the Quest for El Dorado.* Clarion, 2000. *(I; A)*

Chippendale, Neil. *Sir Walter Raleigh and the Search for El Dorado.* Chelsea House, 2001. *(I)*

Korman, Susan, and Schlesinger, Arthur Meier. *Sir Walter Raleigh: English Explorer and Author.* Chelsea House, 2000. *(P; I)*

RANCH LIFE

De Angelis, Gina. *Black Cowboys.* Chelsea House, 1997. *(I)*

Klausmeier, Robert. *Cowboy.* Lerner, 1995. *(P; I)*

Sandler, Martin W. *Cowboys: A Library of Congress Book.* HarperCollins, 2000. *(P; I)*

REAGAN, RONALD WILSON

Doherty, Kieran. *Ronald Reagan (Encyclopedia of Presidents, Second Series).* Scholastic, 2005. *(I; A)*

Johnson, Darv. *The Reagan Years.* Thomson Gale, 1999. *(I)*

Morris, Jeffrey Brandon. *The Reagan Way.* Lerner, 1995. *(I; A)*

REAL ESTATE

Aaseng, Nathan. *Business Builders in Real Estate.* Oliver Press, 2001. *(I; A)*

RECONSTRUCTION PERIOD

Barney, William L. *The Civil War and Reconstruction: A Student Companion.* Oxford, 2001. *(I; A)*

Collier, Christopher, and Collier, James L. *Reconstruction and the Rise of Jim Crow, 1864-1896.* Marshall Cavendish, 2000. *(I; A)*

Hansen, Joyce. *"Bury Me Not in a Land of Slaves": African-Americans in the Time of Reconstruction.* Watts, 2000. *(I; A)*

McPherson, James M. *Fields of Fury: The American Civil War.* Simon & Schuster, 2002. *(A)*

Seidman, Rachel Filene. *The Civil War: A History in Documents.* Oxford, 2000. *(A)*

Smith, John David. *Black Voices from Reconstruction, 1865-1877.* Millbrook Press, 1996. *(A)*

Weber, Michael. *Civil War and Reconstruction.* Raintree Steck-Vaughn, 2000. *(I)*

Ziff, Marsha. *Reconstruction Following the Civil War in American History.* Enslow, 1999. *(I; A)*

RECYCLING

Boekhoff, P. M. *Recycling (Our Environment Series).* Thomson Gale, 2004. *(I)*

Bowden, Rob. *Sustainable World: Waste.* Thomson Gale, 2004; *Waste, Recycling and Reuse: Our Impact on the Planet.* Raintree Steck-Vaughn, 2002. *(I; A)*

Burton, Jane, and Taylor, Kim. *Nature and Science of Waste.* Gareth Stevens, 1999. *(P; I)*

Chandler, Gary, and Graham, Kevin. *Making a Better World: Recycling.* Lerner, 1997. *(I)*

Cozic, Charles P., ed. *Garbage and Waste.* Thomson Gale, 1997. *(A)*

Diehn, Gwen; Smith, Heather; Krautwurst, Terry; and Anderson, Alan. *Nature Smart.* Sterling, 2003. *(P; I)*

Fiarotta, Phyllis, and Fiarotta, Noel. *Cups and Cans and Paper Plate Fans: Craft Projects from Recycled Materials.* Sterling, 1992. *(P)*

Foster, Joanna. *Cartons, Cans, and Orange Peels: Where Does Our Garbage Go?* Houghton Mifflin, 1991. *(I)*

Gay, Kathlyn. *Garbage and Recycling.* Enslow, 1991. *(I; A)*

Gutnik, Martin J. *Recycling: Learning the Four R's: Reduce, Reuse, Recycle, Recover.* Enslow, 1993; *Experiments That Explore Recycling.* Millbrook Press, 1992. *(I; A)*

Silverstein, Alvin; Silverstein, Robert; and Silverstein, Virginia B. *Recycling: Meeting the Challenge of the Trash Crisis.* Putnam, 1992. *(I)*

REFERENCE MATERIALS

Grolier Illustrated Encyclopedia of Animals. Scholastic, 1993. *(I; A)*

National Geographic World Atlas for Young Explorers. National Geographic Society, 2003 (rev. ed.). *(P; I)*

Burrell, Roy. *Oxford First Ancient History.* Oxford University Press, 1994. *(I; A)*

REFORMATION

Flowers, Sarah. *The Reformation.* Lucent, 1995. *(I; A)*

REFRIGERATION

Ford, Barbara. *Keeping Things Cool: The Story of Refrigeration and Air Conditioning.* Walker, 1986. *(I; A)*

REINDEER AND CARIBOU

Hodge, Deborah. *Deer, Moose, Elk & Caribou.* Kids Can Press, 1999. *(P)*

RELATIVITY

Swisher, Clarice. *Relativity.* Greenhaven Press, 1990. *(I)*

RELIGIONS OF THE WORLD

Bial, Raymond. *Amish Home.* Houghton Mifflin, 1995. *(I)*

Butler, Jon. *Religion in Colonial America.* Oxford, 2000. *(I)*

Ellwood, Robert, and Alles, Gregory D., eds. *The Encyclopedia of World Religions.* Facts on File, 1998. *(I; A)*

Fisher, James T. *Catholics in America.* Oxford, 2000. *(I)*

Gellman, Rabbi Marc, and Hartman, Monsignor Thomas. *How Do You Spell God?: Answers to the Big Questions from around the World.* Morrow, 1997. *(I; A)*

Ghazi, Suhaib Hamid. *Ramadan.* Holiday, 1996. *(P)*

Langley, Myrtle. *Religion.* Knopf, 1996. *(P; I; A)*

Lugira, Aloysius. *African Religion.* Facts on File, 1999. *(I; A)*

Maestro, Betsy. *The Story of Religion.* Clarion, 1996. *(P; I)*

Nardo, Don, ed. *The Rise of Christianity.* Greenhaven, 1998. *(A)*

Osborne, Mary Pope. *One World, Many Religions: The Ways We Worship.* Knopf, 1996. *(I)*

Peare, Catherine O. *John Woolman: Child of Light.* Vanguard, n.d. *(I; A)*

Pickles, Dewayne E., and Israel, Fred. *The Amish (Immigrant Experience Series).* Chelsea House, 1996. *(I)*

Raboteau, Albert J. *African-American Religion.* Oxford University, 1999. *(A)*

Wacker, Grant. *Religion in Nineteenth Century America.* Oxford, 2000. *(I)*

Wagner, Katherine. *Life in an Amish Community (Way People Live Series).* Thomson Gale, 2001. *(I; A)*

Williams, Jean Kinney. *The Quakers (American Religious Experience Series).* Scholastic, 1998; *The Christian Scientists (American Religious Experience Series); The Shakers (American Religious Experience Series).* Scholastic, 1997; *The Amish (American Religious Experience Series); The Mormons (American Religious Experience Series).* Scholastic, 1996. *(I; A)*

RENAISSANCE

Barter, James E. *Renaissance Florence.* Thomson Gale, 2002. *(I; A)*

Caselli, Giovanni. *The Renaissance and the New World.* NTC, 1998. *(I; A)*

Greenblatt, Miriam. *Lorenzo de Medici and Renaissance Italy.* Marshall Cavendish, 2002. *(I; A)*

Howarth, Sarah. *Renaissance People; Renaissance Places.* Millbrook, 1992. *(I; A)*

RENOIR, PIERRE AUGUSTE

Janson, H. W., and Janson, Anthony F. *History of Art for Young People.* Abrams, 1997 (rev. ed.). *(I; A)*

Parsons, Tom. *Pierre Auguste Renoir: Art for Young People.* Sterling, 1996. *(P; I)*

Rayfield, Susan. *Pierre-Auguste Renoir.* Abrams, 1998. *(I; A)*

Welton, Jude. *Eyewitness: Impressionism.* DK, 2000. *(P; I; A)*

REPRODUCTION

Burton, Robert. *Egg: A Photographic Story of Hatching.* DK, 1994. *(P)*

Harris, Robie H., and Emberley, Michael. *It's So Amazing!: A Book about Eggs, Sperm, Birth, Babies, and Families.* Candlewick, 2002. *(P)*

Wallace, Holly, and Ganeri, Anita. *Cells and Systems.* Heinemann, 2000. *(P; I)*

REPRODUCTION, HUMAN

Harris, Robie H. *It's So Amazing!: A Book about Eggs, Sperm, Birth, Babies, and Families.* Candlewick, 1999. *(P; I)*

Parker, Steve. *Our Bodies: Reproduction.* Raintree, 2004. *(I); Look at Your Body: Reproduction & Growth.* Millbrook Press, 1998. *(P; I); Human Body: The Reproductive System.* Raintree Steck-Vaughn, 1997. *(I)*

Silverstein, Alvin; Silverstein, Virginia; and Silverstein, Robert. *The Reproductive System.* 21st Century Books, 1994. *(I)*

Walker, Pam, and Clark, Chris. *Reproductive System.* Lucent, 2002. *(I; A)*

REPTILES

Mattison, Christopher. *The Care of Reptiles and Amphibians in Captivity.* Blandford Press, 1992 (3rd ed.). *(I; A)*

McCarthy, Colin, and Arnold, Nick. *Reptile.* Knopf, 1991. *(I)*

Miller, Sara Swan. *Radical Reptiles.* Scholastic, 2001. *(P; I)*

Miller-Schroeder, Patricia. *Scales, Slime and Salamanders: The Science of Reptiles and Amphibians.* Raintree, 2000. *(P; I)*

Perry, Phyllis J. *Crocodilians: Reminders of the Age of Dinosaurs.* Watts, 1997. *(P; I)*

Snedden, Robert. *What Is a Reptile?* Sierra Club, 1995. *(I)*

Souza, Dorothy M. *Roaring Reptiles.* Lerner, 1992. *(P; I)*

Spilsbury, Louise A., and Spilsbury, Richard. *Classifying Reptiles.* Heinemann, 2003. *(P; I)*

RESEARCH

Heiligman, Deborah. *The Kid's Guide to Research.* Scholastic, 1999. *(I)*

McInerney, Claire Fleischman. *Tracking the Facts: How to Develop Research Skills.* Lerner, 1990. *(I)*

Sullivan, Helen, and Sernoff, Linda. *Research Reports: A Guide for Middle and High School Students.* Millbrook Press, 1996. *(I; A)*

RETARDATION, MENTAL

McNey, Martha. *Leslie's Story: A Book about a Girl with Mental Retardation.* Lerner, 1996. *(P; I)*

REVERE, PAUL

Adler, David A.; Wallner, John; and Wallner, Alexandra. *A Picture Book of Paul Revere.* Holiday House, 1995. *(P)*

Brandt, Keith, and Livingston, Francis. *Paul Revere: Son of Liberty.* Troll, 1997 (reissue). *(P; I)*

Ford, Carin T. *Paul Revere: Patriot.* Enslow, 2003. *(P)*

Wagner, Heather Lehr. *Paul Revere: Messenger for Freedom (Leaders of the American Revolution Series).* Chelsea House, 2005. *(I)*

REVOLUTIONARY WAR

Aronson, Marc. *The Real Revolution: The Global Story of American Independence.* Houghton Mifflin, 2005. *(I; A)*

Beller, Susan Provost. *Yankee Doodle and the Redcoats: Soldiering in the Revolutionary War.* Lerner, 2003. *(I)*

Bliven, Bruce, Jr. *The American Revolution.* Random, 1996 (reissue). *(I; A)*

Egger-Bovet, Howard, and Smith-Baranzini, Marlene. *Book of the American Revolution.* Little, 1994. *(I)*

Murphy, Jim. *A Young Patriot: The American Revolution As Experienced by One Boy.* Clarion, 1996. *(I; A)*

Wagner, Heather Lehr. *Paul Revere: Messenger for Freedom (Leaders of the American Revolution Series).* Chelsea House, 2005. *(I)*

Zeinert, Karen. *Those Remarkable Women of the American Revolution.* Millbrook Press, 1996. *(I; A)*

RHINOCEROSES

Arnold, Caroline. *Rhino.* Morrow, 1995. *(P; I)*

Miller, Sara Swan. *Horses and Rhinos: What They Have in Common.* Scholastic, 1999. *(P; I)*

Walker, Sally M. *Rhinos.* Lerner, 1996. *(P; I)*

RHODE ISLAND

Fradin, Dennis Brindell. *Rhode Island: From Sea to Shining Sea.* Scholastic, 1997. *(P; I)*

Klein, Ted. *Rhode Island.* Scholastic, 1997. *(P; I)*

Kling, Andrew A. *The Thirteen Colonies: Rhode Island.* Gale Group, 2001. *(I)*

Mattern, Joanne. *Rhode Island: The Ocean State.* Gareth Stevens, 2003. *(P; I)*

Warner, J. F. *Rhode Island.* Lerner, 2002 (2nd ed.). *(P; I)*

RICE

Gelman, Rita Golden. *Rice Is Life.* Henry Holt, 2000. *(P)*

Hughes, Meredith Sayles, and Hughes, E. Thomas. *Glorious Grasses: The Grains.* Lerner, 1998. *(I)*

RIO DE JANEIRO

Kent, Deborah. *Rio de Janeiro.* Children's Press, 1996. *(P; I)*

Morrison, Marion. *Great Cities of the World: Rio de Janeiro.* Gareth Stevens, 2004. *(I)*

RIVERS

Beatty, Richard. *Rivers, Lakes, Streams, and Ponds (Biomes Atlases Series).* Raintree, 2003. *(I)*

Bryan, Nichol. *Danube: Cyanide Spill (Environmental Disasters Series.* Gareth Stevens, 2003. *(I; A)*

Castner, James L. *River Life: Deep in the Amazon.* Marshall Cavendish, 2002. *(P; I)*

Donovan, Sandra. *Animals of Rivers, Lakes and Ponds.* Raintree Steck-Vaughn, 2002. *(P)*

Fink, Patricia *Rivers and Streams.* Watts, 1999. *(I; A)*

Lourie, Peter. *Mississippi River: A Journey Down the Father of Waters.* Boyds Mills Press, 2000. *(P; I)*; *Rio Grande: From the Rocky Mountains to the Gulf of Mexico.* Boyds Mills Press, 1999. *(P; I)*; *Amazon: A Young Reader's Look at the Last Frontier.* Boyds Mills Press, 1998. *(P; I)*; *In the Path of Lewis and Clark: Traveling the Missouri.* Silver Burdett Press, 1996. *(I; A)*; *Hudson River: An Adventure from the Mountains to the Sea.* Boyds Mills Press, 1992. *(P; I)*

Mudd-Ruth, Maria. *The Mississippi River.* Marshall Cavendish, 2000. *(I; A)*

Pollard, Michael. *The Rhine.* Marshall Cavendish, 1997. *(I)*

Powledge, Fred. *Working River.* Farrar, 1995. *(P; I)*

Rawlins, Carol B. *The Orinoco River.* Watts, 1999. *(P; I)*

Sayre, April Pulley. *River and Stream.* Millbrook Press, 1997. *(I)*

Whitcraft, Melissa. *The Niagara River.* Watts, 2001; *The Hudson River; The Tigris and Euphrates Rivers.* Watts, 1999. *(P; I)*

ROBINSON, JACK ROOSEVELT (JACKIE)

Ford, Carin T. *Jackie Robinson: All I Ask Is That You Respect Me as a Human Being.* Enslow, 2005. *(I; A)*

Jacobs, William Jay. *They Shaped the Game.* Simon & Schuster, 1994. *(P; I)*

Krull, Kathleen. *Lives of the Athletes: Thrills, Spills (And What the Neighbors Thought).* Raintree Steck-Vaughn, 1999. *(I; A)*

Robinson, Sharon. *Promises to Keep: How Jackie Robinson Changed America.* Scholastic, 2004. *(P; I)*; *Stealing Home: An Intimate Family Portrait by the Daughter of Jackie Robinson.* HarperCollins, 1996. *(A)*

ROBOTS

Berger, Fredericka. *Robots: What They Are, What They Do.* Greenwillow, 1992. *(P)*

Gifford, Clive. *How to Build a Robot.* Scholastic, 2001. *(P; I)*

Hellman, Hal. *Beyond Your Senses: The World of Sensors.* Dutton, 1997. *(I)*

Skurzynski, Gloria. *Robots: Your High-Tech World.* Bradbury, 1990. *(I)*

Sonenklar, Carol. *Robots Rising.* Holt, 1999. *(P; I)*

ROCKETS

Bankston, John. *Unlocking the Secrets of Science: Robert Goddard and the Liquid Rocket Engine.* Mitchell Lane, 2001. *(I; A)*

Maurer, Richard. *Rocket! How a Toy Launched the Space Age.* Crown, 1995. *(I)*

ROCK MUSIC

Bergamini, Andrea. *History of Rock Music.* Barron's 2000. *(I; A)*

Bustard, Anne. *Buddy: The Story of Buddy Holly.* Simon & Schuster, 2005. *(P; I)*

Gentry, Tony. *Elvis Presley.* Chelsea House, 1994. *(I; A)*

Powell, Stephanie. *Hit Me with Music: How to Start, Manage, Record, and Perform with Your Own Rock Band.* Millbrook Press, 1995. *(I; A)*

ROCKS

Christian, Peggy. *If You Find a Rock.* Harcourt, 2000. *(P)*

Kittinger, Jo S. *A Look at Minerals: From Galena to Gold.* Scholastic, 1999 *(I)*; *A Look at Rocks: From Coal to Kimberlite.* Scholastic, 1998. *(I)*

Parker, Steve. *Eyewitness Explorers: Rocks and Minerals.* DK, 1997. *(P; I)*

Ricciuti, Edward R. *National Audubon Society First Field Guide: Rocks and Minerals.* Scholastic, 1998. *(I; A)*

ROCKWELL, NORMAN

Gherman, Beverly. *Norman Rockwell: Storyteller with a Brush.* Atheneum, 2000. *(I)*

RODENTS

Bastian, Lois Brunner. *Chipmunk Family.* Scholastic, 2000. *(P; I)*

Evans, Mark. *Guinea Pig: A Practical Guide to Caring for Your Guinea Pig.* DK, 2001. *(P; I)*

Hansen, Elvig. *Guinea Pigs.* Lerner, 1993. *(P; I)*

Holub, Joan. *Why Do Rabbits Hop?: And Other Questions about Rabbits, Guinea Pigs, Hamsters, and Gerbils.* Penguin Putnam, 2003. *(P)*

Kalman, Bobbie, and Langille, Jacqueline. *What Is a Rodent?* Crabtree/A Bobbie Kalman Bk., 1999. *(P)*

Markle, Sandra. *Outside and Inside Rats and Mice.* Simon & Schuster, 2001. *(P; I)*

Miller, Sara Swan. *Rodents: From Mice to Muskrats.* Scholastic, 1999. *(P; I)*

Perry, Phyllis J. *Animals That Hibernate; Animals Under the Ground.* Scholastic, 2001. *(P; I)*

ROMAN CATHOLIC CHURCH

Fisher, James T. *Catholics in America.* Oxford, 2000. *(I; A)*

ROMANIA

Romania...in Pictures. Lerner, 1993. *(I)*

Dornberg, John. *Central and Eastern Europe.* Greenwood, 1995. *(A)*

Sheehan, Sean. *Romania.* Marshall Cavendish, 1994. *(I; A)*

Willis, Terri, and Carran, Betty B. *Romania (Enchantment of the World, Second Series).* Scholastic, 2001. *(I; A)*

ROMAN NUMERALS

Giesert, Arthur. *Roman Numerals I to MM.* Houghton, 1995. *(P; I)*

ROME

Barghusen, Joan D. *Daily Life in Ancient and Modern Rome.* Lerner, 1999. *(P; I)*

ROME, ANCIENT

Altman, Susan, and Lechner, Susan. *Ancient Rome.* Scholastic, 2001. *(P)*

Baker, Rosalie F., and Baker, Charles F., III. *Ancient Romans: Expanding the Classical Tradition.* Oxford University Press, 1998. *(A)*

Barghusen, Joan D. *Daily Life in Ancient and Modern Rome.* Lerner, 1999. *(P; I)*

Connolly, Peter. *Ancient Rome.* Oxford, 2001. *(I)*

Connolly, Peter, and Dodge, Hazel. *The Ancient City: Life in Classical Athens and Rome.* Oxford, 2000. *(A)*

Corbishley, Michael. *Ancient Rome (Cultural Atlas for Young People).* Facts on File, 2003 (2nd ed.). *(I)*

Greenblatt, Miriam. *Augustus Caesar and Imperial Rome.* Marshall Cavendish, 2001. *(I; A); Augustus Caesar and Ancient Rome.* Marshall Cavendish, 2000. *(P; I)*

Harris, Jacqueline L. *Science in Ancient Rome.* Grolier, 1998. *(I)*

Mulvihill, Margaret. *Roman Forts.* Watts, 1990. *(I)*

Nardo, Don. *Ancient Rome; The Roman Empire.* Gale Group, 2001; *Cleopatra; The Ancient Romans; The End of Ancient Rome.* Gale Group, 2000; *Rulers of Ancient Rome; The Decline and Fall of the Roman Empire.* Gale Group, 1998; *Greek and Roman Mythology; Life in Ancient Rome; The Age of Augustus.* Gale Group, 1997; *Caesar's Conquest of Gaul; The Importance of Julius Caesar.* Gale Group, 1996; *Greek and Roman Theater.* Gale Group, 1994. *(I; A)*

ROOSEVELT, ELEANOR

Cooney, Barbara. *Eleanor.* Viking, 1996. *(P)*

Fleming, Candace. *Our Eleanor: A Scrapbook Look at Eleanor Roosevelt's Remarkable Life.* Simon & Schuster, 2005. *(P; I)*

Freedman, Russell. *Eleanor Roosevelt: A Life of Discovery.* Clarion, 1993. *(I; A)*

Kulling, Monica. *Eleanor Everywhere: The Life of Eleanor Roosevelt.* Random, 1999. *(P)*

Morey, Eileen. *Eleanor Roosevelt.* Thomson Gale, 1994. *(I; A)*

Roosevelt, Eleanor. *The Autobiography of Eleanor Roosevelt.* Da Capo Press, 1992. *(A)*

Westervelt, Virginia Veeder. *Here Comes Eleanor: A New Biography of Eleanor Roosevelt for Young People.* Avisson, 1999. *(I)*

ROOSEVELT, FRANKLIN D.

Feinberg, Barbara Silverdick. *Franklin D. Roosevelt (Encyclopedia of Presidents, Second Series).* Scholastic, 2005. *(I; A)*

Knapp, Ron. *Franklin D. Roosevelt.* Enslow, 2002. *(I)*

Maupin, Melissa. *Franklin D. Roosevelt: Our Thirty-Second President.* Child's World, 2001. *(P; I)*

Nardo, Don. *Franklin D. Roosevelt: U.S. President.* Chelsea House, 1995. *(I; A)*

Phillips, Anne. *The Franklin Delano Roosevelt Memorial.* Scholastic, 2000. *(P; I)*

Schuman, Michael A. *Franklin D. Roosevelt: The Four-Term President.* Enslow, 1996. *(I)*

ROOSEVELT, THEODORE

DeStefano, Susan. *Theodore Roosevelt: Conservation President.* Twenty-First Century, 1993. *(I)*

Fritz, Jean. *Bully for You, Teddy Roosevelt!* Putnam, 1991. *(I)*

Gaines, Ann Graham. *Theodore Roosevelt: Our Twenty-Sixth President.* Child's World, 2001. *(P; I)*

Meltzer, Milton. *Theodore Roosevelt and His America.* Grolier, 1994. *(A)*

Schuman, Michael A. *Theodore Roosevelt.* Enslow, 1997. *(I; A)*

Whitelaw, Nancy. *Theodore Roosevelt Takes Charge.* Albert Whitman, 1991. *(I; A)*

ROSS, BETSY

Cox, Vicki. *Betsy Ross: A Flag for a New Nation (Leaders of the American Revolution Series).* Chelsea House, 2006. *(I)*

Miller, Susan Martins. *Betsy Ross: American Patriot.* Chelsea House, 2000. *(P; I)*

Roop, Peter. *Betsy Ross (In Their Own Words Series).* Scholastic, 2002. *(P; I)*

ROWING

Ditchfield, Christin. *Kayaking, Canoeing, Rowing, and Yachting.* Scholastic, 2000. *(P)*

Page, Jason. *On the Water: Rowing, Yachting, Canoeing, and Lots, Lots, More.* Lerner, 2000. *(P; I; A)*

ROWLING, J. K.

Rowling, J. K., and Fraser, Lindsey. *Conversations with J. K. Rowling.* Scholastic, 2001. *(P; I)*

Steffens, Bradley. *J. K. Rowling*. Lucent, 2002. *(I)*

RUSSIA

Corona, Laurel. *The Russian Federation*. Gale Group, 2001. *(A)*

Gottfried, Ted. *Road to Communism; Stalinist Empire*. Twenty-First Century, 2002. *(A)*

Gray, Bettyanne, and Levin, Nora. *Manya's Story: Faith and Survival in Revolutionary Russia*. Lerner, 1995. *(A)*

Greenblatt, Miriam. *Peter the Great and Tsarist Russia*. Marshall Cavendish, 2000. *(I; A)*

Harvey, Miles. *Look What Comes from Russia*. Watts, 1999. *(P; I)*

Kendall, Russell. *Russian Girl: Life in an Old Russian Town*. Scholastic, 1995. *(P)*

Kort, Michael. *Russia*. Facts on File, 1998. *(I; A)*

Murrell, Kathleen Berton. *Russia*. Knopf/Borzoi, 1998. *(I; A)*

Plotkin, Gregory, and Plotkin, Rita. *Cooking the Russian Way*. Lerner, 2003 (2nd ed.). *(I; A)*

Resnick, Abraham. *Union of Soviet Socialist Republics: A Survey from 1917 to 1991*. Scholastic, 1992 (rev. ed.). *(I; A)*

Rice, Terence M. *Russia*. Gareth Stevens, 1999. *(I)*

Wade, Rex A. *The Bolshevik Revolution and Russian Civil War*. Greenwood, 2000. *(A)*

RUTH, GEORGE HERMAN (BABE)

Burleigh, Robert. *Home Run: The Story of Babe Ruth*. Harcourt, 1998. *(P)*

Jacobs, William Jay. *They Shaped the Game*. Simon & Schuster, 1994. *(P; I)*

Krull, Kathleen. *Lives of the Athletes: Thrills, Spills (And What the Neighbors Thought)*. Raintree Steck-Vaughn, 1999. *(I; A)*

RWANDA

Aardema, Verna. *Sebgugugu the Glutton: A Bantu Tale from Rwanda*. Eerdmans, William B., 1993. *(P)*

Bodnarchuk, Kari. *Rwanda: Country Torn Apart*. Lerner, 1999. *(I; A)*

Chikwende, Vincent Emenike, and Twagilimana, Aimable. *Hutu and Tutsi*. Rosen, 1997. *(I; A)*

Greenberg, Keith. *Rwanda: Fierce Clashes in Central America*. Blackbirch, 1996. *(P;I)*

Koopmans, Andy. *Rwanda (Africa - Continent in the Balance Series)*. Mason Crest, 2004. *(I; A)*

S (LETTER)

Samoyault, Tiphaine. *Alphabetical Order: How the Alphabet Began*. Viking, 1998. *(P; I)*

SAFETY

Gutman, Bill. *Be Aware of Danger*. Henry Holt, 1997; *Hazards at Home*. Millbrook Press, 1997; *Recreation Can Be Risky*. Millbrook Press, 1996. *(I)*

Latta, Sara L. *Food Poisoning and Foodborne Diseases*. Enslow, 1999. *(I; A)*

Roberts, Robin. *Sports Injuries: How to Stay Safe and Keep on Playing*. Millbrook Press, 2001. *(P; I)*

Silverstein, Alvin; Silverstein, Virginia B.; and Nunn, Laura Silverstein. *Pains and Sprains*. Scholastic, 2003; *Burns and Blisters*. Scholastic, 2002; *Broken Bones*. Scholastic, 2001. *(P; I)*

Zonderman, Jon, and Shader, Laurel. *Environmental Diseases*. Millbrook Press, 1995. *(I; A)*

SAILING

Into the Wind: Sailboats Then and Now. Marshall Cavendish, 1996. *(P; I)*

Small-Boat Sailing. Boy Scouts of America, 1995. *(I; A)*

SAINT KITTS AND NEVIS

McKenley, Yvonne. *A Taste of the Caribbean*. Raintree Steck-Vaughn, 1995. *(P; I)*

SAINT LOUIS

Doherty, Craig A., and Doherty, Katherine M. *The Gateway Arch*. Gale Group, 1995. *(I)*

Hintz, Martin. *Destination St. Louis*. Lerner, 1998. *(P; I)*

SAINT LUCIA

McKenley, Yvonne. *A Taste of the Caribbean*. Raintree Steck-Vaughn, 1995. *(P; I)*

SAINTS

Kennedy, Robert F., Jr. *Saint Francis of Assisi: A Life of Joy*. Hyperion, 2005. *(P)*

Kimmel, Eric A. *Brother Wolf, Sister Sparrow: Stories about Saints and Animals*. Holiday House, 2003. *(P; I)*

Mayo, Margaret. *Brother Sun, Sister Moon: The Life and Stories of St. Francis*. Little, Brown, 2000. *(P; I)*

Morgan, Nina, and Wood, Richard. *Mother Teresa: Saint of the Poor*. Raintree Steck-Vaughn, 1998. *(P; I)*

Mulvihill, Margaret, and Farmer, David Hugh. *The Treasury of Saints and Martyrs*. Penguin, 1999. *(P; I)*

Schmidt, Gary D. *Saint Ciaran: The Tale of a Saint of Ireland*. Eerdmans, William B., 2000. *(P; I)*

Visconti, Guido. *Clare and Francis*. Eerdmans, 2004. *(P; I)*

Wildsmith, Brian. *Saint Francis*. Eerdmans, 1996. *(P)*

SAINT VINCENT AND THE GRENADINES

McKenley, Yvonne. *A Taste of the Caribbean*. Raintree Steck-Vaughn, 1995. *(P; I)*

SALT

Mebane, Robert C., and Rybolt, Thomas. *Salts and Solids*. Twenty-First Century, 1995. *(I)*

SALT LAKE CITY

Doubleday, Veronica. *Salt Lake City*. Silver Burdett Press, 1994. *(I)*

SALVATION ARMY

Green, Roger J. *Catherine Booth: A Biography of the Cofounder of the Salvation Army.* Baker Books, 1996. *(I; A)*

SAN ANTONIO

McComb, David G. *Texas: An Illustrated History.* Oxford, 1995. *(I; A)*

Sorrels, Roy. *The Alamo in American History.* Enslow, 1996. *(I)*

SANDBURG, CARL

Krull, Kathleen. *Lives of the Writers: Comedies, Tragedies (And What the Neighbors Thought).* Raintree Steck-Vaughn, 1998. *(I; A)*

Meltzer, Milton. *Carl Sandburg: A Biography.* Twenty-First Century, 1999. *(I; A)*

Niven, Penelope. *Carl Sandburg: A Biography.* University of Illinois Press, 1994. *(A)*

Sandburg, Carl. *The Complete Poems of Carl Sandburg.* Harcourt, 2003 (revised and expanded edition). *(A)*

Sandburg, Carl, and Niven, Penelope. *Carl Sandburg: Adventures of a Poet.* Harcourt, 2003. *(I)*

Yannella, Philip R. *The Other Carl Sandburg.* University Press of Mississippi, 1996. *(A)*

SANITATION

Bowden, Rob. *Waste, Recycling and Reuse: Our Impact on the Planet.* Raintree Steck-Vaughn, 2002. *(I; A)*

Burton, Jane, and Taylor, Kim. *Nature and Science of Waste.* Gareth Stevens, 1999. *(P; I)*

Chandler, Gary, and Graham, Kevin. *Making a Better World: Recycling.* Lerner, 1997. *(I)*

Colman, Penny. *Toilets, Bathtubs, Sinks, and Sewers: A History of the Bathroom.* Simon & Schuster, 1994. *(I)*

Coombs, Karen Mueller. *Flush!: Treating Wastewater.* Lerner, 1995. *(P; I)*

Cozic, Charles P.; Leone, Bruno; Stalcup, Brenda; and Barbour, Scott, eds. *Garbage and Waste.* Gale Group, 1997. *(A)*

Diehn, Gwen; Smith, Heather; Krautwurst, Terry; and Anderson, Alan. *Nature Smart.* Sterling, 2003. *(P; I)*

Foster, Joanna. *Cartons, Cans, and Orange Peels: Where Does Our Garbage Go?* Houghton Mifflin, 1991. *(I)*

Gay, Kathlyn. *Global Garbage: Exporting Trash and Toxic Waste.* Watts, 1992; *Garbage and Recycling.* Enslow, 1991. *(I; A)*

Gutnik, Martin J. *Recycling: Learning the Four R's: Reduce, Reuse, Recycle, Recover.* Enslow, 1993; *Experiments That Explore Recycling.* Millbrook Press, 1992. *(I; A)*

Ross, Allison J. *Choosing a Career in Waste Management.* Rosen, 2001. *(I; A)*

Wilcox, Charlotte. *Trash!* Lerner, 1993. *(P; I)*

Zonderman, Jon, and Shader, Laurel. *Environmental Diseases.* Millbrook Press, 1995. *(I; A)*

SASKATCHEWAN

Richardson, Gillian. *Saskatchewan.* Lerner, 1998. *(P; I)*

SATELLITES, ARTIFICIAL

Branley, Franklyn M. *The International Space Station.* HarperCollins, 2000. *(P)*; *From Sputnik to Space Shuttles: Into the New Space Age.* HarperCollins, 1989. *(P; I)*

Kupperberg, Paul. *Spy Satellites.* Rosen, 2003. *(I)*

SATURN

Asimov, Isaac, and Hantula, Richard. *Saturn.* Gareth Stevens, 2002 (revised and updated edition). *(P; I)*

Bortolotti, Dan. *Exploring Saturn.* Firefly Books, 2003. *(I; A)*

SAUDI ARABIA

Heinrichs, Ann. *Saudi Arabia.* Scholastic, 2001. *(I; A)*

Keating, Susan Katz. *Saudi Arabia.* Mason Crest, 2002. *(I; A)*

Reed, Jennifer Bond. *The Saudi Royal Family: Major World Leaders.* Chelsea House, 2002. *(I; A)*

SCANDINAVIA

Ferris, Julie. *Viking World: A Guide to 11th Century Scandinavia.* Houghton Mifflin, 2000. *(P; I)*

Franklin, Sharon; Tull, Mary; and Shelton, Carol. *Scandinavia: Understanding Geography and History through Art.* Raintree Steck-Vaughn, 2000. *(I; A)*

SCHLIEMANN, HEINRICH

Caselli, Giovanni. *In Search of Troy: One Man's Quest for Homer's Fabled City.* NTC, 1999. *(P; I)*

Wilkinson, Philip. *The Mediterranean.* Chelsea House, 1993. *(I; A)*

SCHWEITZER, ALBERT

Crawford, Gail, and Renna, Giani. *Albert Schweitzer.* Silver Burdett Press, 1990. *(I; A)*

Robles, Harold. *Albert Schweitzer: An Adventurer for Humanity.* Millbrook Press, 1994. *(I)*

SCIENCE

The American Heritage Children's Science Dictionary. Houghton Mifflin, 2003. *(P; I)*; *The American Heritage Student Science Dictionary.* Houghton Mifflin, 2002. *(I; A)*

Berger, Joseph R., and Lederman, Leon M. *The Young Scientists: America's Future and the Winning of the Westinghouse.* Addison-Wesley, 1993. *(A)*

Boon, Kevin Alexander. *The Human Genome Project: What Does Decoding DNA Mean for Us?* Enslow, 2002. *(A)*

January, Brendan. *Science in the Renaissance.* Watts, 1999. *(P; I)*

Judson, Karen. *Genetic Engineering: Debating the Benefits and Concerns.* Enslow, 2001. *(I; A)*

Nardo, Don. *Cloning; Vaccines.* Gale Group, 2001. *(I; A)*

Peters, Celeste A. *Circuits, Shocks and Lightning: The Science of Electricity; Peppers, Popcorn and Pizza: The Science of Food.* Raintree, 2000; *Allergies, Asthma and Exercise: The Science of Health.* Raintree, 1999. *(P; I)*

Silverstein, Alvin; Silverstein, Virginia; and Nunn, Laura Silverstein. *DNA.* Millbrook Press, 2002. *(A)*; *Photosynthesis; Symbiosis.* Millbrook Press, 1998. *(I; A)*

Spangenburg, Ray, and Moser, Diane. *The History of Science from 1895 to 1945; The History of Science from 1946 to the 1990s.* Facts on File, 1994. *(I; A)*

Torr, James D. *Genetic Engineering.* Gale Group, 2000. *(A)*

VanCleave, Janice. *Janice VanCleave's A + Projects in Earth Science: Winning Experiments for Science Fairs and Extra Credit.* Wiley, 1999. *(I; A)*

Woods, Geraldine. *Science of the Early Americas.* Watts, 1999. *(P; I)*

Yount, Lisa. *Biotechnology and Genetic Engineering.* Facts on File, 2000 ; *A to Z of Women in Science and Math (Encyclopedia of Women Series).* Facts on File, 1999. *(A)*

SCIENCE FAIRS

Barrow, Lloyd H. *Science Fair Projects Investigating Earthworms.* Enslow, 2000. *(I)*

Cain, Nancy Woodard. *Animal Behavior Science Projects.* Wiley, 1995. *(I; A)*

Dashefsky, H. Steven. *Zoology: 49 Science Fair Projects.* McGraw-Hill, 1994. *(I)*

Gardner, Robert. *Health Science Projects about Nutrition.* Enslow, 2002; *Health Science Projects about Anatomy and Physiology; Health Science Projects about Heredity; Health Science Projects about Your Senses.* Enslow, 2001; *Science Projects about Methods of Measuring; Science Projects about Solids, Liquids, and Gases; Science Projects about Sound; Science Projects about the Physics of Sport; Science Projects about the Physics of Toys and Games.* Enslow, 2000; *Science Projects about Kitchen Chemistry; Science Projects about Physics in the Home; Science Projects about Plants; Science Projects about the Environment and Ecology.* Enslow, 1999; *Science Project Ideas about Trees.* Enslow, 1997; *Science Projects about Light.* Enslow, 1994. *(I; A)*

Gardner, Robert, and Conklin, Barbara Gardner. *Health Science Projects about Psychology; Health Science Projects about Sports Performance.* Enslow, 2002. *(I; A)*

Krieger, Melanie Jacobs. *How to Excel in Science Competitions.* Enslow, 1999 (rev. ed.). *(I; A)*

Simon, Seymour. *How to Be an Ocean Scientist in Your Own Home.* HarperCollins, 1999. *(P; I)*

Sobey, Ed. *How to Enter and Win an Invention Contest.* Enslow, 1999. *(I; A)*

VanCleave, Janice. *Janice VanCleave's Guide to More of the Best Science Fair Projects; Janice VanCleave's Solar System: Mind Boggling Experiments You Can Turn into Science Fair Projects.* Wiley, 2000. *(I)*

SCIENCE FICTION

Datnow, Claire L. *American Science Fiction and Fantasy Writers.* Enslow, 1999. *(I)*

LeGuin, Ursula. *The Last Book of Earthsea.* Atheneum, 1990. *(I)*

Streissguth, Thomas. *Science Fiction Pioneer: A Story about Jules Verne.* Lerner, 2000. *(P; I)*

SCOPES TRIAL

Blake, Arthur. *The Scopes Trial: Defending the Right to Teach.* Millbrook, 1994. *(P; I)*

SCORPIONS

Hillyard, Paul. *Spiders and Scorpions: A Unique First Visual Reference.* Reader's Digest, 1995. *(P; I)*

Pringle, Laurence. *Scorpion Man: Exploring the World of Scorpions.* Simon & Schuster, 1994. *(I)*

SCOTLAND

Meek, James. *The Land and People of Scotland.* Lippincott, 1990. *(I; A)*

Stein, R. Conrad. *Scotland.* Scholastic, 2001. *(I; A)*

SCULPTURE

Faerna, Jose Maria. *Botero; Brancusi; Modigliani.* Abrams, 1997; *Duchamp.* Abrams, 1996. *(A)*

Janson, H. W., and Janson, Anthony F. *History of Art for Young People.* Abrams, 1997 (rev. ed.). *(I; A)*

SEA LIONS

DuTemple, Lesley A. *Seals and Sea Lions.* Lerner, 1998. *(P)*

Grace, Eric S. *Seals.* Little, 1991. *(I; A)*

Johnson, Sylvia A. *Elephant Seals.* Lerner, 1989. *(P; I)*

Patent, Dorothy Hinshaw. *Seals, Sea Lions and Walruses.* Holiday, 1990. *(P; I)*

Sherrow, Victoria. *Seals, Sea Lions & Walruses.* Watts, 1991. *(P)*

SEALS

Matthews, Downs. *Harp Seal Pups.* Simon & Schuster, 1996. *(P)*

Patent, Dorothy Hinshaw. *Seals, Sea Lions and Walruses.* Holiday, 1990. *(P; I)*

Rotter, Charles. *Seals.* Child's World, 2001. *(P)*

Sherrow, Victoria. *Seals, Sea Lions & Walruses.* Watts, 1991. *(P)*

Wu, Norbert. *Beneath the Waves: Exploring the Hidden World of the Kelp Forest.* Chronicle, 1997. *(P; I)*

SEASONS

Branley, Franklyn M. *Sunshine Makes the Seasons.* HarperCollins, 2005. *(P)*

Gibbons, Gail. *The Reasons for Seasons.* Holiday, 1995. *(P)*

SEATTLE

Snelson, Karen. *Seattle: Downtown America.* Silver Burdett Press, 1992. *(P)*

Stein, R. Conrad. *Seattle.* Children's Press, 1999. *(P; I)*

SEGREGATION

Fireside, Harvey. *Plessy v. Ferguson: Separate But Equal?* Enslow, 1997. *(A)*

Fremon, David K. *The Jim Crow Laws and Racism in American History.* Enslow, 2000. *(I; A)*

Somerlott, Robert. *The Little Rock School Desegregation Crisis (In American History Series).* Enslow, 2001. *(I; A)*

SEMANTICS

Scholastic Dictionary of Synonyms, Antonyms, and Homonyms. Scholastic, 2001. *(I; A)*

SENEGAL

Beaton, Margaret. *Senegal.* Scholastic, 1997. *(I; A)*

Berg, Elizabeth L. *Senegal.* Marshall Cavendish, 1999 (2nd ed.). *(I; A)*

Brownlie, Alison. *Senegal.* Heinemann, 1996. *(P; I)*

Nwanunobi, C. Onyeka. *Malinke (Burkina Faso, Côte d'Ivoire, Gambia, Guinea, Guinea Bissau, Liberia, Mali, Senegal, Sierra Leone).* Rosen, 1996. *(I; A)*; *Soninke (Burkina Faso, Côte d'Ivoirie, Ghana, Mali, Mauritania, Nigeria, Senegal).* Rosen, 1996. *(I; A)*

SEPTEMBER

Updike, John. *A Child's Calendar.* Holiday House, 1999. *(P; I)*

Warner, Penny. *Kids' Holiday Fun: Great Family Activities Every Month of the Year.* Meadowbrook Press, 1997. *(P)*

SERBIA

Milivojevic, Joann. *Serbia.* Children's Press, 1999. *(I; A)*

SEUSS, DR.

Krull, Kathleen. *The Boy on Fairfield Street.* Random House, 2004. *(P)*

Weidt, Maryann N. *Oh, the Places He Went: A Story About Dr. Seuss.* Carolrhoda, 1994. *(P; I)*

SEWING

Eaton, Jan. *The Encyclopedia of Sewing Techniques.* Barron, 1987. *(A)*

McAllister, Buff. *Sewing with Felt: Learn Basic Stitches to Create More than 60 Colorful Projects.* Boyds Mills Press, 2003. *(P; I)*

SHAKESPEARE, WILLIAM

Aliki. *William Shakespeare and the Globe.* HarperCollins, 1999. *(P; I)*

Ferris, Julie. *Shakespeare's London: A Guide to Elizabethan London.* Kingfisher, 2000. *(P; I)*

Halliwell, Sarah, ed. *17th Century: Artists, Writers, and Composers.* Raintree, 1997. *(I)*

Vecchione, Patrice, ed. *Revenge and Forgiveness: An Anthology of Poems.* Henry Holt, 2004. *(I; A)*

SHARKS, RAYS, AND CHIMAERAS

Arnold, Caroline. *Giant Shark: Megalodon, the Super Prehistoric Predator.* Houghton Mifflin, 2000. *(P; I)*

Batten, Mary. *Shark Attack Almanac.* Random, 1997. *(I)*

Berman, Ruth. *Sharks.* Lerner, 1995. *(P; I)*

Cerullo, Mary M. *The Truth About Great White Sharks.* Chronicle, 2000. *(P; I)*

Gibbons, Gail. *Sharks.* Holiday, 1992. *(P)*

Harman, Amanda, and Horton, Casey. *Endangered!: Sharks.* Marshall Cavendish, 1996. *(P; I)*

Mallory, Kenneth. *Swimming with Hammerhead Sharks.* Houghton Mifflin, 2001. *(P; I)*

Markle, Sandra. *Outside and Inside Sharks.* Atheneum, 1996. *(I)*

Perrine, Doug. *Sharks and Rays of the World.* Voyageur, 2000. *(A)*

Zoehfeld, Kathleen Weidner. *Great White Shark: Ruler of the Sea.* Soundprints, 1995. *(P)*

SHEEP

Mattern, Joanne. *The Bighorn Sheep.* Capstone Press, 1999. *(P)*

Miller, Sara Swan. *Sheep.* Scholastic, 2000. *(P)*

Paladino, Catherine. *Springfleece: A Day of Sheepshearing.* Little, 1990. *(P; I)*

Simmons, Paula; and Salsbury, Darrell L. *Your Sheep: A Kid's Guide to Raising and Showing.* Storey Books, 1992. *(I; A)*

SHELLS

Arthur, Alex. *Eyewitness: Shell.* DK, 2000. *(I)*

Tibbitts, Christiane Kump. *Seashells, Crabs, and Sea Stars.* Creative Publishing, 1997. *(P; I)*

SHERMAN, WILLIAM TECUMSEH

Kent, Zachary. *William Tecumseh Sherman: Union General.* Enslow, 2002. *(I)*

King, David C. *William Tecumseh Sherman.* Gale Group, 2002. *(I)*

Whitelaw, Nancy. *William Tecumseh Sherman: Defender and Destroyer.* Morgan Reynolds, 1996. *(I; A)*

SHIPS AND SHIPPING

Ballard, Robert D. *The Lost Wreck of the Isis.* Scholastic, 1994; *Exploring the Titanic.* Scholastic, 1993; *Exploring the Bismarck.* Scholastic, 1991. *(P; I)*

Houghton, Gillian. *Wreck of the Andrea Gail: Three Days of a Perfect Storm.* Rosen, 2003. *(I)*

Wilkinson, Philip. *Ships: History, Battles, Discovery, Navigation.* Larousse Kingfisher Chambers, 2000. *(P; I)*

SHORT STORIES

Aller, Susan Bivin. *Mark Twain (A & E Biography Series)*. Lerner, 2001. *(I; A)*

Anderson, William. *River Boy: The Story of Mark Twain*. HarperCollins, 2003. *(P; I)*

Camfield, Gregg, ed. *Stories for Young People: Mark Twain*. Sterling, 2005. *(I; A)*

Diorio, Mary Ann. *A Student's Guide to Herman Melville*. Enslow, 2006. *(I; A)*

Fargnoli, A. Nicholas, and Gillespie, Michael P. *James Joyce A to Z: The Essential Reference to His Life and Writings*. Facts on File, 1995. *(A)*

Fargnoli, A. Nicholas, and Golay, Michael. *William Faulkner A to Z: The Essential Reference to His Life and Work*. Facts on File, 2001. *(A)*

Fletcher, Chris. *Joseph Conrad*. Oxford University Press, 1999. *(A)*

Halliwell, Sarah, ed. *20th Century: Pre-1945 Artists, Writers, and Composers; 19th Century: Artists, Writers, and Composers*. Raintree, 1998. *(I)*

Lazo, Caroline Evensen. *F. Scott Fitzgerald: Voice of the Jazz Age*. Lerner, 2003. *(I; A)*

Lyttle, Richard B. *Mark Twain-The Man and His Adventure*. Simon & Schuster, 1994. *(I; A)*

Mee, Susie. *Downhome: An Anthology of Southern Women Writers*. Harcourt, 1995. *(A)*

Meehan, Elizabeth. *Twentieth-Century American Writers*. Gale Group, 2000. *(I; A)*

Meltzer, Milton. *Herman Melville: A Biography*. Lerner, 2004. *(I; A)*

Oliver, Charles M. *Ernest Hemingway A to Z: The Essential Reference to His Life and Work*. Facts on File, 1999. *(A)*

Otfinoski, Steven. *Extraordinary Short Story Writing*. Scholastic, 2006. *(I)*

Peltak, Jennifer. *Edgar Allan Poe*. Chelsea House, 2003. *(I; A)*

Pingelton, Timothy J. *A Student's Guide to Ernest Hemingway*. Enslow, 2005. *(I; A)*

Rollyson, Carl E., and Paddock, Lisa Olson. *Herman Melville A to Z: The Essential Reference to His Life and Work*. Facts on File, 2001. *(A)*

Sova, Dawn B. *Edgar Allan Poe A to Z: The Essential Reference to His Life and Work*. Facts on File, 2001. *(A)*

Szumski, Bonnie, ed. *Stephen Crane*. Thomson Gale, 1997. *(A)*

Tate, Mary Jo. *F. Scott Fitzgerald A to Z: The Essential Reference to His Life and Work*. Facts on File, 1999. *(A)*

Yannuzzi, Della A. *Ernest Hemingway: Writer and Adventurer*. Enslow, 1998. *(I; A)*

Salem Press Staff, and May, Charles E., eds. *Short Story Writers*. Salem Press, 1997. *(A)*

Weisbrod, Eva. *A Student's Guide to F. Scott Fitzgerald*. Enslow, 2004. *(I; A)*

Whiting, Jim. *Classic Storytellers: Ernest Hemingway*. Mitchell Lane, 2005. *(I)*

SIBERIA

Buell, Janet. *Ancient Horsemen of Siberia*. Millbrook Press, 1998. *(I; A)*

Hautzig, Esther. *The Endless Steppe: Growing up in Siberia*. HarperCollins, 1995. *(P; I; A)*

SILVER

Tocci, Salvatore. *Silver*. Scholastic, 2005. *(P)*

SINGAPORE

Baker, James Michael, and Baker, Junia Marion. *Singapore*. Gareth Stevens, 2002. *(I)*

Barber, Nicola. *Great Cities of the World: Singapore*. Gareth Stevens, 2005. *(I)*

Layton, Lesley. *Singapore*. Marshall Cavendish, 1990. *(I)*

Pascoe, Elaine. *The Pacific Rim: East Asia at the Dawn of a New Century*. Millbrook Press, 1999. *(A)*

Viesti, Joseph F., and Hall, Diane. *Celebrate! in Southeast Asia*. HarperCollins, 1996. *(P; I)*

SKATEBOARDING

Andrejtschitsch, Jan; Schmidt, Petra; and Kallee, Raimund. *Action Skateboarding*. Sterling, 1992. *(A)*

Burke, L. M. *Skateboarding!: Surf the Pavement*. Rosen, 2000. *(P; I)*

Kennedy, Mike. *Skateboarding*. Scholastic, 2001. *(P; I)*

SKELETAL SYSTEM

Llewellyn, Claire. *The Big Book of Bones: An Introduction to Skeletons*. Peter Bedrick, 1998. *(I)*

Parker, Steve. *Our Bodies: The Skeleton and Muscles*. Raintree, 2004. *(I)*; *The Skeleton and Muscular System*. Raintree-Steck Vaughn, 1997. *(I)*; *Look at Your Body: Skeleton*. Millbrook Press, 1996. *(P; I)*

Royston, Angela. *Why Do Bones Break?: And Other Questions about Bones and Muscles*. Heinemann, 2002. *(P; I)*

Sandeman, Anna. *Bones*. Millbrook, 1995. *(P)*

Silverstein, Alvin; Silverstein, Virginia; and Silverstein, Robert. *The Skeletal System*. 21st Century Books, 1994. *(I)*

Walker, Pam, and Wood, Elaine. *Skeletal and Muscular System*. Lucent, 2003. *(I; A)*

Walker, Richard. *The Visual Dictionary of the Skeleton*. Dorling Kindersley, 1995. *(I; A)*

SKIN DIVING

Earle, Sylvia A. *Dive: My Adventures in the Deep Frontier*. National Geographic Society, 1999. *(P; I)*

SLAVERY

Altman, Linda Jacobs. *Politics of Slavery: Fiery National Debates Fueled by the Slave Economy*. Enslow, 2004; *Slavery and Abolition (In American History Series)*. Enslow, 1999. *(I; A)*

Bailey, John. *The Lost German Slave Girl: The Extraordinary True Story of the Slave Sally Miller and Her*

Fight for Freedom. Grove/Atlantic, 2004. *(A)*

Bial, Raymond. *The Strength of These Arms: Life in the Slave Quarters.* Houghton, 1997. *(I)*

Byers, Ann. *African-American History from Emancipation to Today: Rising above the Ashes of Slavery.* Enslow, 2004. *(I; A)*

Collier, Christopher, and Collier, James L. *Slavery and the Coming of the Civil War: 1831-1861.* Marshall Cavendish/Benchmark, 1999. *(I)*

Eskridge, Ann E. *Slave Uprisings and Runaways: Fighting for Freedom and the Underground Railroad.* Enslow, 2004. *(I; A)*

Everett, Gwen. *John Brown: One Man against Slavery.* Rizzoli, 1994. *(I; A)*

Haskins, Jim. *Get on Board: The Story of the Underground Railroad.* Scholastic, 1993. *(I; A)*

Johnson, Dolores. *Seminole Diary: Remembrances of a Slave.* Macmillan, 1994. *(P; I)*

Lilley, Stephen R. *Fighters against American Slavery.* Lucent, 1998. *(I; A)*

McNeese, Tim. *The Rise and Fall of American Slavery: Freedom Denied, Freedom Gained.* Enslow, 2004. *(I; A)*

Stearman, Kaye. *Slavery Today.* Raintree Steck-Vaughn, 1999. *(I)*

Tapper, Suzanne Cloud. *Voices from Slavery's Past: Yearning to Be Heard.* Enslow, 2004. *(I; A)*

SLOVAKIA

Dornberg, John. *Central and Eastern Europe.* Greenwood, 1995. *(A)*

Kinkade, Sheila. *Children of Slovakia.* Lerner, 2000. *(P; I)*

SMITH, JOHN

Bruchac, Joseph. *Pocahontas.* Harcourt, 2005. *(I; A)*

Doherty, Kieran. *To Conquer is to Live: The Life of Captain John Smith.* Lerner, 2001. *(I)*

Edwards, Judith. *Jamestown, John Smith, and Pocahontas (In American History Series).* Enslow, 2002. *(I; A)*

SMITHSONIAN INSTITUTION

Collins, Mary. *The Smithsonian Institution.* Children's Press, 2000. *(P; I)*

SMOKING

Cohen, Philip. *Drugs, The Complete Story: Tobacco.* Raintree Steck-Vaughn, 1991. *(I)*

Haughton, Emma. *A Right to Smoke?* Scholastic, 1997. *(I)*

Hirschfelder, Arlene. *Kick Butts! A Kid's Action Guide to a Tobacco-Free America.* Simon & Schuster/Messner, 1998. *(I; A)*

Hyde, Margaret O., and Setaro, John F. *Smoking 101: An Overview for Teens.* Twenty-First Century, 2005. *(I; A)*

Kranz, Rachel. *Straight Talk about Smoking.* Facts on File, 1999. *(I; A)*

Lang, Susan, and Marks, Beth H. *Teens & Tobacco: A Fatal Attraction.* 21st Century Books, 1996. *(A)*

MacDonald, Joan Vos. *Tobacco and Nicotine Drug Dangers (Drug Dangers Series).* Enslow, 2001. *(I; A)*

Pietrusza, David. *Smoking.* Lucent, 1997. *(I)*

SNAKES

Arnold, Caroline. *Snake.* Morrow, 1991. *(P; I)*

Berger, Melvin, and Berger, Gilda. *Can Snakes Crawl Backward?: Questions and Answers about Reptiles.* Scholastic, 2002. *(P; I)*

Maestro, Betsy. *Take a Look at Snakes.* Scholastic, 1992. *(P)*

Markle, Sandra. *Outside and inside Snakes.* Macmillan, 1995. *(I)*

Montgomery, Sy. *The Snake Scientist.* Houghton, 1999. *(I)*

Patent, Dorothy Hinshaw. *Slinky, Scaly, Slithery Snakes.* Walker, 2000. *(P; I)*

Rubio, Manny. *Rattlesnake: Portrait of a Predator.* Smithsonian, 1998. *(A)*

SNOWBOARDING

Brimner, Larry Dane. *Snowboarding.* Watts, 1998. *(P; I)*

Hayhurst, Chris. *Snowboarding!: Shred the Powder.* Rosen, 1999. *(P; I)*

Iguchi, Bryan. *Snowboarding.* DK, 2000. *(P; I; A)*

Jensen, Julie. *Beginning Snowboarding.* Lerner, 1995. *(P)*

Lurie, Jon. *Play-by-Play Snowboarding.; Fundamental Snowboarding.* Lerner, 1995. *(P; I)*

Sullivan, George E. *Snowboarding: A Complete Guide for Beginners.* Penguin Group, 1996. *(P; I)*

SOCCER

Arnold, Caroline. *Soccer: From Neighborhood Play to the World Cup.* Watts, 1991. *(P; I)*

Buxton, Ted; Leith, Alex; Drewitt, Jim; and Jago, Gordon. *Soccer Skills: For Young Players.* Firefly Books, 2000. *(I; A)*

Cope, Suzanne. *Great Soccer: Team Defense.* Scholastic, 2001. *(I; A)*

Helmer, Diana Star, and Owens, Thomas S. *The History of Soccer.* Rosen, 2003. *(P)*

Jensen, Julie. *Beginning Soccer.* Lerner, 1995. *(P; I)*

Kennedy, Mike. *Soccer.* Scholastic, 2001. *(P; I)*

Lineker, Gary. *Soccer.* DK, 2000. *(P; I)*

Longman, Jere. *The Girls of Summer: The U.S. Women's Soccer Team and How It Changed the World.* HarperCollins, 2000. *(A)*

Luxbacher, Joseph A. *Soccer: Steps to Success.* Human Kinetics Publishers, 1996 (2nd ed.). *(A)*

Page, Jason. *Ball Games: Soccer, Table Tennis, Handball, Hockey, Badminton, and Lots, Lots More.* Lerner, 2000. *(P; I)*

Rutledge, Rachel. *The Best of the Best in Soccer.* Millbrook Press, 1998. *(I)*

Sherman, Josepha. *Competitive Soccer for Girls.* Rosen, 2002. *(P; I)*

SOCIAL STUDIES

Jackson, Ellen B. *Turn of the Century.* Charlesbridge, 1998. *(P; I)*

SOCIAL WORK

Isler, Claudia. *Volunteering to Help in Your Neighborhood.* Children's Press, 2000. *(I; A)*

Lewis, Barbara A., and Espeland, Pamela. *Kid's Guide to Social Action: How to Solve the Problems You Choose - and Turn Creative Thinking into Positive Action.* Free Spirit, 1998; *Kid's Guide to Service Projects: Over 500 Service Ideas for Young People Who Want to Make a Difference.* Free Spirit, 1995. *(I; A)*

SOCIOLOGY

Bowden, Rob. *Overcrowded World?: Our Impact on the Planet.* Raintree Steck-Vaughn, 2002. *(I)*

Lewis, Barbara A.; Espeland, Pamela; and Pernu, Caryn. *Kid's Guide to Social Action: How to Solve the Problems You Choose - and Turn Creative Thinking into Positive Action.* Free Spirit, 1998 (rev. ed.) *(I; A)*

Nardo, Don. *Population.* Gale Group, 2000. *(A)*

Zeaman, John. *Overpopulation.* Scholastic, 2002. *(I; A)*

SOFTBALL

Nitz, Kristin W. *Play-by-Play: Softball.* Lerner, 2000. *(I)*

U.S. Olympic Committee. *A Basic Guide to Softball.* Gareth Stevens, 2001. *(P; I; A)*

SOILS

Bial, Raymond. *A Handful of Dirt.* Walker, 2000. *(P; I)*

Bocknek, Jonathan. *The Science of Soil.* Gareth Stevens, 1999. *(P; I)*

Bryant-Mole, Karen. *Soil.* Raintree Steck-Vaughn, 1996. *(P)*

Gallant, Roy A. *Story of Dunes: Sand on the Move.* Scholastic, 1998. *(P; I)*

Lavies, Bianca. *Compost Critters.* Dutton, 1993. *(P; I)*

Prager, Ellen J. *Sand.* National Geographic, 2000. *(P)*

Rybolt, Thomas R., and Mebane, Robert C. *Environmental Experiments about Land.* Enslow, 1993. *(P; I)*

SOLAR ENERGY

Carless, Jennifer. *Renewable Energy: A Concise Guide to Green Alternatives.* Walker, 1993. *(A)*

Gardner, Robert. *Experimenting with Energy Conservation.* Watts, 1992. *(I; A)*

Hirschmann, Kris. *Solar Energy (Our Environment Series).* Thomson Gale, 2005. *(I)*

McLeish, Ewan. *Energy Resources: Our Impact on the Planet.* Raintree Steck-Vaughn, 2002. *(I)*

Smith, Trevor. *Renewable Energy Resources.* Smart Apple Media, 2004. *(I; A)*

SOLAR SYSTEM

Aronson, Billy. *Eclipses: Nature's Blackouts; Meteors: The Truth behind Shooting Stars.* Scholastic, 1996. *(I)*

Boerst, William J. *Isaac Newton: Organizing the Universe; Johannes Kepler: Discovering the Laws of Celestial Motion; Tycho Brahe: Mapping the Heavens.* Reynolds, 2003. *(I; A)*

Branley, Franklyn Mansfield. *The Planets in Our Solar System.* HarperCollins, 1998. *(P)*

Fradin, Dennis Brindell, and Sipiera, Paul P. *Comets and Meteor Showers.* Scholastic, 1997. *(P; I)*

Graun, Ken. *Our Earth and the Solar System.* Ken Press, 2001. *(P; I)*

Simon, Seymour. *Our Solar System.* Morrow, 1992. *(P; I)*

Sipiera, Paul B. *The Solar System.* Scholastic, 1997. *(P)*

Wilsdon, Christina, and Summers, Frank. *Solar System: An A-Z Guide.* Scholastic, 2000. *(P; I)*

SOLIDS

Berger, Melvin *Solids, Liquids, and Gases.* Putnam, 1989. *(I; A)*

Gardner, Robert. *Science Projects about Solids, Liquids, and Gases.* Enslow, 2000. *(I; A)*

Mebane, Robert C., and Rybolt, Thomas R. *Salts and Solids.* Twenty-First Century, 1995. *(I)*

Zoehfeld, Kathleen Weidner, and Meisel, Paul. *What Is The World Made Of?: All about Solids, Liquids, and Gases.* Turtleback Books, 1998. *(P)*

SOMALIA

Ferry, Joseph. *Somalia.* Mason Crest, 2002. *(I; A)*

Matthews, Jo, and Ganeri, Anita. *I Remember Somalia.* Raintree Steck-Vaughn, 1994. *(I)*

SOUND AND ULTRASONICS

Gardner, Robert. *Science Projects about Sound.* Enslow, 2000. *(I; A)*

Lampton, Christopher. *Sound: More Than What You Hear.* Enslow, 1992. *(I; A)*

SOUTH AFRICA

Anozie, F. N. *Khoekhoe (Namibia, South Africa).* Rosen, 1997. *(I; A)*

Biesele, Megan, and Loloo, Kxao. *San (Botswana, Namibia, South Africa).* Rosen, 1997. *(I; A)*

Blauer, Ettagle, and Laure, Jason. *South Africa.* Scholastic, 1998. *(I; A)*

Brownlie, Alison. *We Come from South Africa.* Raintree Steck-Vaughn, 2000 *(P)*

Canesso, Claudia. *South Africa.* Chelsea House, 1999. *(I; A)*

Franklin, Sharon; Tull, Mary; and Shelton, Carol. *Africa: Understanding Geography and History through Art.* Raintree Steck-Vaughn, 2000. *(I; A)*

Van Wyk, Gary N. *Basotho (Lesotho, South Africa).* Rosen, 1996. *(I; A)*

SOUTH AMERICA

Boraas, Tracey. *Colombia.* Capstone Press, 2002. *(P)*

Burgan, Michael. *Argentina.* Scholastic, 1999. *(P)*

Daniels, Amy S. *Ecuador.* Gareth Stevens, 2002. *(I)*

DeSpain, Pleasant. *Emerald Lizard: Fifteen Latin American Tales to Tell in English and Spanish.* August House, 1999. *(I)*

DuBois, Jill, and Jermyn, Leslie. *Colombia.* Marshall Cavendish, 2002 (2nd ed.). *(I; A)*

Gerson, Mary-Joan, retel. *Fiesta Femenina: Celebrating Women in Mexican Folktale.* Barefoot Books, 2005. *(P; I; People of Corn: A Mayan Story.* Little, Brown & Co., 1995. *(P); How Night Came from the Sea: A Story from Brazil.* Little, Brown & Co., 1994. *(P; I)*

Gofen, Ethel Caro, and Jermyn, Leslie. *Argentina.* Marshall Cavendish, 2002 (2nd ed.). *(I; A)*

Haynes, Tricia. *Colombia.* Chelsea House, 1998. *(I; A)*

Heisey, Janet. *Peru.* Gareth Stevens, 2001. *(I)*

Jaffe, Nina. *The Golden Flower: A Taino Myth from Puerto Rico.* Simon & Schuster, 1996. *(P; I)*

Jermyn, Leslie. *Guyana; Paraguay.* Marshall Cavendish, 2000 (2nd ed.) *(I; A); Brazil.* Gareth Stevens, 1999. *(I); Peru.* Gareth Stevens, 1998. *(P; I); Uruguay.* Marshall Cavendish, 1998 (2nd ed.). *(I; A)*

Jermyn, Leslie, and Vengadasalam, Leela. *Colombia.* Gareth Stevens, 1999. *(I)*

Landau, Elaine. *Peru.* Scholastic, 2000. *(P)*

Lourie, Peter. *Lost Treasure of the Inca; Tierra Del Fuego: A Journey to the End of the Earth.* Boyds Mills Press, 2002. *(I); The Mystery of the Maya: Uncovering the Lost City of Palenque.* Boyds Mills Press, 2001. *(P; I)*

Lyle, Garry. *Peru.* Chelsea House, 1998 *(I; A)*

Morrison, Marion. *Guyana.* Scholastic, 2003 *(I); Bolivia; Columbia; Ecuador; Peru; Venezuela.* Scholastic, 2001. *(I); Paraguay; Venezuela.* Chelsea House, 1999. *(P; I); French Guiana.* Children's Press, 1995. *(I; A); Uruguay.* Children's Press, 1992. *(I; A)*

Nishi, Dennis. *Inca Empire.* Gale Group, 2000. *(I; A)*

Petersen, David. *South America.* Children's Press, 1998. *(P)*

Richard, Christopher, and Jermyn, Leslie. *Brazil.* Marshall Cavendish, 2002 (2nd ed.). *(I)*

Winter, Jane Kohen, and Baguley, Kitt. *Venezuela.* Marshall Cavendish, 2002 (2nd ed.). *(I; A)*

SOUTH CAROLINA

Fradin, Dennis Brindell. *South Carolina: From Sea to Shining Sea.* Scholastic, 1994. *(P; I)*

Fredeen, Charles. *South Carolina.* Lerner, 2002 (2nd ed.). *(P; I)*

Girod, Christina M. *The Thirteen Colonies: South Carolina.* Gale Group, 2001. *(I)*

Hoffman, Nancy. *South Carolina.* Marshall Cavendish, 2000. *(P; I)*

Stein, R. Conrad. *South Carolina.* Scholastic, 1999 (2nd ed.). *(I; A)*

Volkwein, Ann M. *South Carolina: The Palmetto State.* Gareth Stevens, 2002. *(P; I)*

Weatherly, Myra S. *South Carolina.* Scholastic, 2001. *(P; I)*

SOUTH DAKOTA

Brennan, Kristine. *Crazy Horse.* Chelsea House, 2001. *(P; I)*

Doherty, Craig A., and Doherty, Katherine M. *Mount Rushmore.* Gale Group, 1995. *(I)*

Feeney, Kathy. *South Dakota Facts and Symbols.* Capstone Press, 2001. *(P)*

Fradin, Dennis Brindell, and Fradin, Judith Bloom. *South Dakota: From Sea to Shining Sea.* Scholastic, 1995. *(P; I)*

Hirschmann, Kris. *South Dakota: The Mount Rushmore State.* Gareth Stevens, 2003. *(P; I)*

Marcovitz, Hal. *Sitting Bull.* Chelsea House, 2001. *(P; I)*

Santella, Andrew. *Mount Rushmore.* Children's Press, 1999. *(P; I)*

Shepher, Donna Walsh. *South Dakota.* Scholastic, 2001. *(I; A)*

Sirvaitis, Karen. *South Dakota.* Lerner, 2001 (2nd ed.). *(P; I)*

SOUTHEAST ASIA

Vietnam...in Pictures. Lerner, 1998. *(I; A)*

Baker, James Michael, and Baker, Junia Marion. *Singapore.* Gareth Stevens, 2002. *(I)*

Fisher, Frederick. *Indonesia.* Gareth Stevens, 1999. *(P; I)*

Khng, Pauline. *Myanmar.* Gareth Stevens, 2000. *(P; I)*

Mansfield, Stephen. *Laos.* Marshall Cavendish, 1998 (2nd ed.). *(I)*

McNair, Sylvia. *Thailand.* Children's Press, 1998. *(P; I)*

Millett, Sandra. *Hmong of Southeast Asia.* Lerner, 2001. *(P; I)*

Munan, Heidi, and Foo, Yuk Yee. *Malaysia.* Marshall Cavendish, 2001 (2nd ed.). *(I; A)*

Pascoe, Elaine. *The Pacific Rim: East Asia at the Dawn of a New Century.* Millbrook Press, 1999. *(A)*

Schraff, Anne E. *Philippines.* Lerner, 2000. *(P; I)*

Sheehan, Sean. *Cambodia.* Marshall Cavendish, 1996 (2nd ed.). *(I)*

Viesti, Joseph F., and Hall, Diane. *Celebrate! in Southeast Asia.* HarperCollins, 1996. *(P; I)*

Vuong, Lynette Dyer. *The Golden Carp and Other Tales of Vietnam.* HarperCollins, 1993; *The Brocaded Slipper and Other Vietnamese Tales.* HarperCollins, 1992. *(P)*

Yin, Saw Myat. *Myanmar.* Marshall Cavendish, 2001 (2nd ed.). *(I; A)*

Zickgraf, Ralph, and Buckmaster, Margie. *Laos.* Chelsea House, 1997. *(I; A)*

SPACE EXPLORATION AND TRAVEL

Becklake, Sue. *Space: Stars, Planets, and Spacecraft.* Dorling Kindersley, 1991. *(I; A)*

Bond, Peter. *DK Guide to Space: A Photographic Journey through the Universe.* DK, 1999. *(P; I)*

Cassutt, Michael. *Who's Who in Space: The International Space Station Edition.* Thomson Gale, 1998 (3rd ed.). *(I; A)*

Fradin, Dennis Brindell. *Searching for Alien Life.* Millbrook Press, 1997. *(I)*

Harris, Alan, and Weissman, Paul. *The Great Voyager Adventure: A Guided Tour through the Solar System.* Messner, 1990. *(I)*

Jackson, Ellen. *Looking for Life in the Universe.* Houghton Mifflin, 2002. *(I)*

Lauber, Patricia. *Journey to the Planets.* Crown, 1993 (4th ed.). *(I; A)*

Vogt, Gregory L. *Disasters in Space Exploration; Space Mission Patches.* Millbrook Press, 2001. *(I)*; *John Glenn's Return to Space.* Millbrook Press, 2000. *(I)*; *Deep Space Astronomy.* Millbrook Press, 1999. *(I; A)*; *Solar System: Facts and Exploration.* Millbrook Press, 1995. *(I)*; *Space Exploration Projects for Young Scientists.* Scholastic, 1995. *(I; A)*; *Magellan and the Radar Mapping of Venus.* Millbrook Press, 1992; *Apollo and the Moon Landing: Missions in Space; Viking and the Mars Landing: Missions in Space; Voyager: Missions in Space.* Millbrook Press, 1991. *(P; I)*

SPACE PROBES

Ride, Sally, and O'Shaughnessy, Tam. *Voyager: An Adventure to the Edge of the Solar System.* Crown, 1992. *(P; I)*

Sherman, Josepha. *Deep Space Observation Satellites.* Rosen, 2003. *(I)*

Wunsch, Susi Trautmann. *The Adventures of Sojourner: The Mission to Mars That Thrilled the World.* Mikaya Press, 1998. *(I; A)*

SPACE SHUTTLES

Cole, Michael D. *Challenger: America's Space Tragedy; Columbia: First Flight of the Space Shuttle.* Enslow, 1995. *(I)*

Lassieur, Allison. *The Space Shuttle.* Children's Press, 2000. *(P; I)*

Spangenburg, Ray; Moser, Diane; and Moser, Kit. *Onboard the Space Shuttle: Out of This World.* Scholastic, 2002. *(I; A)*

SPACE STATIONS

Dyson, Marianne J. *Space Station Science: Life in Free Fall.* Scholastic, 1999. *(I)*

Nicolson, Cynthia Pratt. *Exploring Space.* Kids Can Press, 2000. *(P; I)*

Sipiera, Diane M., and Sipiera, Paul P. *Space Stations.* Grolier, 1998. *(P; I)*

SPACE TELESCOPES

Cole, Michael D. *Hubble Space Telescope: Exploring the Universe.* Enslow, 1999. *(I)*

Simon, Seymour. *Destination: Space.* HarperCollins, 2002; *Out of Sight: Pictures of Hidden Worlds.* Chronicle, 2000. *(I)*

SPAIN

Christian, Rebecca. *Cooking the Spanish Way.* Lerner, 2001 (2nd ed.). *(I; A)*

Davis, Kevin A. *Look What Came from Spain.* Scholastic, 2001. *(P)*

Hodges, Margaret. *Don Quixote and Sancho Panza.* Scribner's, 1992. *(I; A)*

Rogers, Lura. *Spain.* Scholastic, 2001. *(I)*

Selby, Anna. *Spain.* Raintree Publishers, 1994. *(I)*

SPAIN, ART AND ARCHITECTURE OF

Carter, David. *Salvador Dali: Spanish Painter.* Chelsea House, 1994. *(I; A)*

Janson, H. W., and Janson, Anthony F. *History of Art for Young People.* Abrams, 1997 (rev. ed.). *(I; A)*

Muhlberger, Richard, and Metropolitan Museum of Art. *What Makes a Goya a Goya?* Viking, 1994. *(I)*

Riboldi, Silvia; Schiaffino, Mariarosa; and Trojer, Thomas. *Goya.* NTC, 1999. *(I)*

Venezia, Mike. *El Greco.* Children's Press, 1998. *(P)*

Waldron, Ann. *Francisco Goya.* Abrams, 1992. *(I)*

SPAIN, LANGUAGE AND LITERATURE OF

De Saulles, Janet, and Wright, Nicola. *Getting to Know: Spain and Spanish.* Barron's, 1993. *(P; I)*

Halliwell, Sarah, ed. *20th Century: Post-1945 Artists, Writers, and Composers; 20th Century: Pre-1945 Artists, Writers, and Composers; 19th Century: Artists, Writers, and Composers; The Romantics: Artists, Writers, and Composers.* Raintree, 1998; *18th Century: Artists, Writers, and Composers; 17th Century: Artists, Writers, and Composers; Impressionism and Postimpressionism: Artists, Writers, and Composers.* Raintree, 1997; *Renaissance: Artists and Writers.* Marshall Cavendish, 1997. *(I)*

Moss, Joyce. *Spanish and Portuguese Literatures and Their Times (The Iberian Peninsula), Vol. 5 (World Literature and Its Times Series).* Thomson Gale, 2001. *(A)*

SPANISH-AMERICAN WAR

Dolan, Edward F., and Quinn, Stephen. *Spanish-American War.* Millbrook Press, 2001. *(I; A)*

Marrin, Albert. *The Spanish-American War.* Atheneum, 1991. *(I; A)*

McNeese, Tim. *Remember the Maine!: The Spanish-American War Begins.* Reynolds, 2001. *(I; A)*

Wukovits, John F. *Spanish-American War.* Gale Group, 2001. *(I; A)*

SPANISH ARMADA

Kelsey, Harry. *Sir Francis Drake: The Queen's Pirate.* Yale University Press, 2000. *(A)*

Lace, William W. *Defeat of the Spanish Armada.* Gale Group, 2001. *(I; A)*

Marrin, Albert. *The Sea King: Sir Francis Drake and His Times.* Simon & Schuster, 1995. *(I; A)*

Whitfield, Peter. *Sir Francis Drake.* New York University Press, 2004. *(A)*

SPECIAL OLYMPICS

Brown, Fern G., and Rich, Mary P., ed. *Special Olympics.* Watts, 1992. *(P; I)*

Dinn, Sheila. *Hearts of Gold: A Celebration of Special Olympics and Its Heroes.* Thomson Gale, 1995. *(P; I)*

SPELUNKING

Gibbons, Gail, and Gibbons, Dave. *Caves and Caverns.* Harcourt, 1996. *(P; I)*

SPIDERS

Fowler, Allan. *Spiders Are Not Insects.* Children's Press, 1996. *(P)*

Greenberg, Daniel A. *Spiders.* Marshall Cavendish, 2001. *(P; I)*

Hillyard, Paul. *Spiders and Scorpions: A Unique First Visual Reference.* Reader's Digest, 1995. *(P; I)*

Markle, Sandra. *Outside and Inside Spiders.* Simon & Schuster, 1994. *(P; I)*

SPIES

Alonso, Karen. *Alger Hiss Communist Spy Trial: A Headline Court Case.* Enslow, 2001. *(I; A)*

Ziff, John. *Espionage and Treason.* Chelsea House, 1999. *(I; A)*

SRI LANKA

Sri Lanka...in Pictures. Lerner, 1997. *(I; A)*

Viesti, Joseph F., and Hall, Diane. *Celebrate! in South Asia.* HarperCollins, 1996. *(P; I)*

Wanasundera, Nanda Pethiyagoda. *Sri Lanka.* Marshall Cavendish, 2002 (2nd ed.). *(I; A)*

Zimmermann, Robert. *Sri Lanka.* Scholastic, 1992. *(I; A)*

STALIN, JOSEPH

Cunningham, Kevin. *Joseph Stalin and the Soviet Union (World Leaders Series).* Morgan Reynolds, 2006. *(I; A)*

Gottfried, Ted. *Stalinist Empire.* Twenty-First Century, 2002. *(A)*

Ross, Stewart. *U. S. S. R. under Stalin.* Watts, 1991. *(I; A)*

STAMPS AND STAMP COLLECTING

Abeyta, Jennifer. *Stamps (High Interest Book Series).* Scholastic, 2000. *(I; A)*

STANTON, ELIZABETH CADY

Fritz, Jean. *You Want Women to Vote, Lizzie Stanton?* Putnam, 1995. *(I)*

STARFISH

Hurd, Edith Thacher. *Starfish.* HarperCollins, 2000. *(P)*

Stefoff, Rebecca. *Starfish.* Marshall Cavendish, 1996. *(P)*

STARS

Gibbons, Gail. *Stargazers.* Holiday, 1992. *(P)*

Gustafson, John R. *Stars, Clusters and Galaxies.* Silver Burdett Press, 1993. *(I)*

Nicolson, Cynthia Pratt. *The Stars.* Kids Can Press, 1998. *(P; I)*

STATE, UNITED STATES DEPARTMENT OF

Burgan, Michael. *Madeleine Albright.* Millbrook Press, 1998. *(I; A)*

Byman, Jeremy. *Madame Secretary: The Story of Madeleine Albright.* Reynolds, 1997. *(I; A)*

Dolan, Edward F., and Scariano, Margaret M. *Shaping U. S. Foreign Policy: Profiles of Twelve Secretaries of State.* Watts, 1996. *(I; A)*

Hasday, Judy L. *Madeleine Albright.* Chelsea House, 1996. *(I; A)*

Howard, Megan. *Madeleine Albright.* Lerner, 1998. *(I; A)*

Kent, Zachary. *William Seward: The Mastermind of the Alaska Purchase.* Enslow, 2001. *(I; A)*

Wellman, Sam. *Your Government: The Secretary of State.* Chelsea House, 2000. *(I; A)*

STEINBECK, JOHN

Halliwell, Sarah, ed. *20th Century: Pre-1945 Artists, Writers, and Composers.* Raintree, 1998. *(I)*

Ito, Tom. *The Importance of John Steinbeck.* Gale Group, 1994. *(I; A)*

Tessitore, John. *John Steinbeck: A Writer's Life.* Scholastic, 2001. *(I; A)*

STOMACH

Avraham, Regina. *The Digestive System.* Chelsea House, 2000. *(A)*

Ballard, Carol. *The Stomach and Digestive System.* Raintree Steck-Vaughn, 1997. *(I)*

Brynie, Faith Hickman. *101 Questions About Food and Digestion That Have Been Eating at You Until Now.* Lerner, 2002. *(I; A)*

Monroe, Judy. *Coping with Ulcers, Heartburn, and Stress-Related Stomach Disorders.* Rosen, 2000. *(A)*

Parker, Steve. *Our Bodies: Digestion.* Raintree, 2004. *(I); Food and Digestion.* Scholastic, 1998 (rev. ed.). *(P; I); Look at Your Body: Digestion.* Millbrook Press, 1997. *(P; I); Eating a Meal: How You Eat, Drink and Digest.* Watts, 1991. *(P; I)*

Silverstein, Alvin; Silverstein, Robert; and Silverstein, Virginia B. *The Digestive System.* Lerner, 1997. *(I)*

Toriello, James. *Stomach: Learning How We Digest.* Rosen, 2002. *(I; A)*

Walker, Pam, and Wood, Elaine. *Digestive System.* Lucent, 2003. *(I; A)*

STORYTELLING

Hamilton, Martha, and Weiss, Mitch. *How and Why Stories: World Tales Kids Can Read and Tell.* August House, 1999. *(P; I)*

Hettinga, Donald R. *The Brothers Grimm: Two Lives, One Legacy.* Houghton Mifflin, 2001. *(I; A)*

Lang, Andrew. *The Blue Fairy Book.* NuVision, 2004. *(P; I)*

Trelease, Jim, ed. *Hey! Listen to This: Stories to Read Aloud.* Viking Penguin, 1992. *(A)*

STOWE, HARRIET BEECHER

Griskey, Michele. *Classic Storytellers: Harriet Beecher Stowe.* Mitchell Lane, 2005. *(I)*

Johnston, Norma. *Harriet: The Life and World of Harriet Beecher Stowe.* William Morrow, 1996. *(I)*

STRAVINSKY, IGOR

Venezia, Mike. *Igor Stravinsky.* Children's Press, 1997. *(P)*

STRINGED INSTRUMENTS

Blackwood, Alan. *Playing the Piano and Keyboards.* Stargazer Books, 2004. *(P; I)*

Dearling, Robert, ed. *The Illustrated Encyclopedia of Musical Instruments.* Gale Research, 1996. *(I; A)*

STUDY, HOW TO

Fry, Ron. *"Ace" Any Test; How to Study.* Career, 1996. *(I; A)*

SUDAN

Archibald, Erika F. *Journey Between Two Worlds: A Sudanese Family.* Lerner, 1997. *(P; I)*

Lobban, Jr., Richard A.; Kramer, Robert S.; and Fluehr-Lobban, Carolyn. *Historical Dictionary of the Sudan.* Rowman & Littlefield, 2002 (3rd ed.). *(A)*

Snyder, Gail. *Sudan.* Mason Crest, 2002. *(I; A)*

Zwier, Lawrence J. *Sudan: North against South.* Lerner, 1999. *(I; A)*

SUGAR

Carney, Margaret. *At Grandpa's Sugar Bush.* Kids Can Press, 1998. *(P)*

Chall, Marsha Wilson. *Sugarbush Spring.* HarperCollins, 2000. *(P)*

Haas, Jessie. *Sugaring.* Greenwillow, 1996. *(P)*

Keller, Kristin Thoennes. *Maple Trees to Maple Syrup.* Capstone Press, 2004. *(P)*

Landau, Elaine. *Sugar.* Scholastic, 2000. *(P)*

Nottridge, Rhoda. *Sugars.* Lerner, 1993. *(P; I)*

Wittstock, Laura Waterman. *Ininatig's Gift of Sugar: Traditional Native Sugarmaking.* Lerner, 1993. *(P; I)*

SUN

Branley, Franklyn M. *The Sun: Our Nearest Star.* HarperCollins, 2002 (rev. ed.). *(P)*

Gardner, Robert. *Science Project Ideas about the Sun.* Enslow, 1997. *(I)*

Petersen, Christine. *Solar Power.* Scholastic, 2004. *(P)*

Tocci, Salvatore. *Experiments with the Sun and the Moon.* Scholastic, 2003. *(P)*

Vogt, Gregory L. *The Sun.* Millbrook Press, 1996. *(P; I)*

SUPREME COURT OF THE UNITED STATES

Aaseng, Nathan. *Great Justices of the Supreme Court.* Oliver Press, 1992. *(I; A)*

Alonso, Karen. *Loving v. Virginia: Interracial Marriage.* Enslow, 2000; *Schenck v. United States: Restrictions on Free Speech.* Enslow, 1999. *(I; A)*

Banfield, Susan. *The Bakke Case: Quotas in College Admissions.* Enslow, 1998. *(I; A)*

Baum, Lawrence. *The Supreme Court.* Congressional Quarterly, 1998 (6th ed.). *(A)*

Billitteri, Thomas J. *The Gault Case: Legal Rights for Young People.* Enslow, 2000. *(I; A)*

Compston, Christine L. *Earl Warren: Justice for All.* Oxford, 2002. *(A)*

Gold, Susan Dudley. *Veronia School District v. Acton: Drug Testing in the Schools.* Benchmark Books, 2005; *Roberts v. U. S. Jaycees (1984): Women's Rights.* Millbrook Press, 1997. *(I; A)*

Good, Diane L. *Brown v. Board of Education.* Children's Press, 2004. *(I)*

Herda, D. J. *Furman v. Georgia: The Death Penalty Case; New York Times v. United States: National Security and Censorship; Roe v. Wade: The Abortion Question; The Dred Scott Case: Slavery and Citizenship.* Enslow, 1994. *(I; A)*

McElroy, Lisa Tucker. *Meet My Grandmother: She's a Supreme Court Justice.* Millbrook, 1999. *(P)*

McPherson, Stephanie Sammartino. *Lau v. Nichols: Bilingual Education in Public Schools.* Enslow, 2000. *(I; A)*

Prentzas, G. S. *Thurgood Marshall: Supreme Court Justice.* Chelsea House, 1994. *(I)*

Quiri, Patricia Ryon. *The Supreme Court.* Scholastic, 1999. *(P)*

Riley, Gail Blasser. *Miranda v. Arizona: Rights of the Accused.* Enslow, 1994. *(I; A)*

Romaine, Deborah S. *Roe v. Wade: Abortion and the Supreme Court.* Gale Group, 1998. *(I; A)*

Rowh, Mark. *Thurgood Marshall: Civil Rights Attorney and Supreme Court Justice.* Enslow, 2002. *(I)*

SURFING

Brimner, Larry Dane. *Surfing.* Scholastic, 1998. *(I)*

Voeller, Edward A. *Extreme Surfing.* Capstone Press, 2000. *(I)*

SURGERY

Brink, Benjamin. *David's Story: A Book about Surgery.* Lerner, 1996. *(P; I)*

Parker, Steve, and West, David. *Brain Surgery for Beginners and Other Major Operations for Minors.* Millbrook Press, 1995. *(I)*

Woods, Michael, and Woods, Mary B. *Ancient Medicine: From Sorcery to Surgery.* Lerner, 1999. *(I)*

SURINAME

Beatty, Noelle Blackmer. *Suriname.* Chelsea House, 1997. *(I; A)*

Lieberg, Carolyn S. *Suriname.* Scholastic, 1995. *(I; A)*

SURREALISM

Carter, David. *Salvador Dali: Spanish Painter.* Chelsea House, 1994. *(I; A)*

Gaff, Jackie, and Oliver, Clare. *1920-40: Realism and Surrealism.* Gareth Stevens, 2001. *(P; I)*

SWAZILAND

Blauer, Ettagle, and Laure, Jason. *Swaziland.* Scholastic, 1996. *(I; A)*

Booth, Alan R., and Grotpeter, John J. *Historical Dictionary of Swaziland.* Rowman & Littlefield, 2000 (2nd ed.). *(A)*

Kessler, Christina, and Mswati III. *All the King's Animals: The Return of Endangered Wildlife to Swaziland.* Boyds Mills Press, 1995. *(P; I)*

SWEDEN

Sweden...in Pictures. Lerner, 1998 (rev. ed.). *(P; I)*

Pitkanen, Matti A., and Harkonen, Reijo. *The Grandchildren of the Vikings.* Lerner, 1996. *(P; I)*

SWIMMING

Boelts, Maribeth. *A Kid's Guide to Staying Safe Around Water.* Rosen, 2003. *(P)*

Carson, Charles. *Make the Team: Swimming and Diving.* Little, 1991. *(P; I)*

Ditchfield, Christin. *Swimming and Diving.* Scholastic, 2000. *(P)*

Thomas, David G. *Swimming: Steps to Success.* Human Kinetics Publishers, 1996 (2nd ed.); *Advanced Swimming: Steps to Success.* Human Kinetics Publishers, 1990. *(A)*

SWITZERLAND

Christmas in Switzerland. World Book, 1997. *(I; A)*

Bullen, Susan. *The Alps and Their People.* Raintree Steck-Vaughn, 1994. *(P; I)*

Harvey, Miles. *Look What Came from Switzerland.* Scholastic, 2001. *(P)*

Levy, Patricia. *Switzerland.* Marshall Cavendish, 1994. *(P; I)*

SYRIA

Syria...in Pictures. Lerner, 1992. *(I; A)*

Bodnarchuk, Kari J. *Kurdistan: Region under Siege.* Lerner, 2000. *(A)*

Kummer, Patricia K. *Syria (Enchantment of the World, Second Series).* Scholastic, 2005. *(I; A)*

South, Coleman. *Syria.* Marshall Cavendish, 1995 (2nd ed.). *(I; A)*

Sullivan, Anne Marie. *Syria.* Mason Crest, 2002. *(I; A)*

T (LETTER)

Samoyault, Tiphaine. *Alphabetical Order: How the Alphabet Began.* Viking, 1998. *(P; I)*

TAFT, WILLIAM HOWARD

Doherty, Kieran. *William Howard Taft (Encyclopedia of Presidents, Second Series).* Scholastic, 2004. *(I; A)*

Maupin, Melissa. *William Howard Taft: Our Twenty-Seventh President.* Child's World, 2002. *(P; I)*

TAIWAN

Moiz, Azra. *Taiwan.* Marshall Cavendish, 1995. *(I; A)*

Pascoe, Elaine. *The Pacific Rim: East Asia at the Dawn of a New Century.* Millbrook Press, 1999. *(A)*

Russell, William. *Taiwan.* Rourke, 1994. *(P)*

TAJIKISTAN

Tajikistan. Lerner, 1993. *(I)*

TAJ MAHAL

Moorcroft, Christine. *The Taj Mahal.* Raintree Steck-Vaughn, 1997. *(P; I)*

TAXATION

Giesecke, Ernestine. *State Government.* Heinemann, 2000. *(P; I)*

TAXIDERMY

Cutchins, Judy, and Johnston, Ginny. *Are Those Animals Real? How Museums Prepare Wildlife Exhibits.* Morrow, 1995 (rev. ed.). *(P; I)*

TCHAIKOVSKY, PETER ILYICH

Halliwell, Sarah, ed. *The Romantics: Artists, Writers, and Composers.* Raintree, 1998. *(I)*

Krull, Kathleen. *Lives of the Musicians: Good Times, Bad Times (And What the Neighbors Thought).* Raintree Steck-Vaughn, 1998. *(I; A)*

Thompson, Wendy. *Pyotr Ilyich Tchaikovsky.* Viking, 1993. *(I; A)*

Venezia, Mike. *Peter Tchaikovsky.* Children's Press, 1995. *(P)*

Whiting, Jim. *Masters of Music: The Life and Times of Peter Ilych Tchaikovsky.* Mitchell Lane, 2003. *(I)*

TEACHERS AND TEACHING

Calhoun, Florence J. *(I)World of Work: Choosing a Career in Teaching.* Rosen, 2000. *(I; A)*

Camenson, Blythe. *Real People Working in Education (On the Job Series).* NTC, 1997. *(A)*

TECHNOLOGY

Science, Technology, and Society: The Impact of Science in the 20th Century. Thomson Gale, 2002. *(I; A)*

Baker, Christopher W. *Virtual Reality: Experiencing Illusion.* Millbrook, 2000. *(I)*

Burnie, David. *Machines and How They Work.* Dorling Kindersley, 1991. *(I; A)*

Diagram Group. *Weapons: An International Encyclopedia from 5000 B.C. to 2000 A.D.* St. Martin's, 1990. *(I; A)*

Eberts, Marjorie; Gisler, Margaret; and Olsen, Maria. *Careers for Computer Buffs and Other Technological Types.* NTC, 1998 (2nd ed.). *(A)*

Gies, Frances, and Gies, Joseph. *Cathedral, Forge, and Waterwheel: Technology and Invention in the Middle Ages.* HarperCollins, 1994. *(A)*

Math, Irwin. *Tomorrow's Technology: Experimenting with the Science of the Future.* Scribner's, 1992. *(I; A)*

Morgan, Kate. *The Story of Things.* Walker, 1991. *(P; I)*

Parker, Steve. *Everyday Things & How They Work; The Random House Book of How Things Work.* Random House, 1991. *(I)*

Skurzynski, Gloria. *Almost the Real Thing: Simulation in Your High-Tech World.* Bradbury, 1991. *(I)*

Stacy, Tom. *Wings, Wheels & Sails.* Random House, 1991. *(P; I)*

Wilson, Anthony. *Communications: How the Future Began.* Larousse Kingfisher Chambers, 1999. *(P; I)*

TEETH

Kendall, Bonnie L.; Camenson, Blythe; and Sidney, Elizabeth C. *Dental Care Careers.* McGraw-Hill, 2000. *(A)*

McGinty, Alice B. *Staying Healthy: Dental Care.* Scholastic, 1999. *(P)*

TELEPHONE

Alphin, Elaine Marie. *Household History: Telephones.* Lerner, 2001. *(P; I)*

Berger, Melvin, and Berger, Gilda. *Telephones, Televisions, and Toilets: How They Work and What Can Go Wrong.* Chelsea House, 1998. *(P; I)*

Webb, Marcus. *Telephones: Words Over Wires.* Lucent Books, 1992. *(I)*

TELEVISION

Apel, Melanie Ann. *Cool Careers without College for Film and Television Buffs.* Rosen, 2002. *(I; A)*

Berger, Melvin, and Berger, Gilda. *Telephones, Televisions, and Toilets: How They Work and What Can Go Wrong.* Chelsea House, 1998. *(P; I)*

Borgenicht, David. *Sesame Street Unpaved: Scripts, Stories, Secrets, and Songs.* Hyperion, 1998. *(A)*

Riehecky, Janet. *Television.* Benchmark, 1996. *(P; I)*

TENNESSEE

Feeney, Kathy. *Tennessee: Facts and Symbols.* Capstone/Hilltop, 2000. *(P)*

Fradin, Dennis Brindell. *Tennessee: From Sea to Shining Sea.* Scholastic, 1996. *(P; I)*

Kent, Deborah. *Tennessee.* Scholastic, 2001 (2nd ed.). *(I; A)*

Peck, Barbara. *Tennessee: The Volunteer State.* Gareth Stevens, 2002. *(P; I)*

Petersen, David. *Great Smoky Mountains National Park.* Scholastic, 1993. *(P; I)*

Sirvaitis, Karen. *Tennessee.* Lerner, 2002 (2nd ed.). *(P; I)*

Weatherly, Myra S. *Tennessee.* Scholastic, 2001. *(P; I)*

TENNIS

Brown, Jim M. *Tennis: Steps to Success.* Human Kinetics Publishers, 1995 (2nd ed.). *(A)*

Ditchfield, Christin. *Tennis.* Scholastic, 2003. *(P)*

Macy, Sue. *Winning Ways: A Photohistory of American Women in Sports.* Henry Holt, 1996. *(I; A)*

Rutledge, Rachel. *The Best of the Best in Tennis.* Millbrook Press, 1998. *(I)*

Vicario, Arantxa Sanchez. *Tennis.* DK, 2000. *(P; I)*

Wright, David K. *Arthur Ashe: Breaking the Color Barrier in Tennis.* Enslow, 1996. *(I)*

TERRORISM

Andryszewski, Tricia. *Terrorism in America (Headliners Series).* Millbrook Press, 2003. *(I; A)*

Buell, Tonya. *Terrorist Attacks: Crash of United Flight 93 on September 11, 2001.* Rosen, 2003. *(I)*

Cart, Michael; Aronson, Marc; and Carus, Marianne, eds. *911: The Book of Help.* Cricket Books, 2002. *(I; A)*

Currie, Stephen. *Terrorists and Terrorist Groups.* Gale Group, 2002. *(A)*

Fridell, Ron. *Terrorism: Political Violence at Home and Abroad.* Enslow, 2001. *(I; A)*

Gaines, Anne, and Sarat, Austin. *Terrorism.* Chelsea House, 1998. *(I; A)*

Gay, Kathlyn. *Silent Death: The Threat of Chemical and Biological Terrorism.* Twenty-First Century, 2001. *(I; A)*

Greenberg, Keith Elliot. *Bomb Squad Officer: Expert with Explosives.* Blackbirch Press, 1995. *(P)*

Sherrow, Victoria. *The Oklahoma City Bombing: Terror in the Heartland; The World Trade Center Bombing: Terror in the Towers.* Enslow, 1998. *(P; I)*

TERRORISM, WAR ON

Donovan, Sandra. *Protecting America: A Look at the People Who Keep Our Country Safe.* Lerner, 2004. *(P; I)*

TESTS AND TEST TAKING

How to Get Better Test Scores: Grades 3-4; How to Get Better Test Scores: Grades 5-6; How to Get Better Test Scores: Grades 7-8. Random House, 1991. *(P; I)*

TEXAS

Aylesworth, Thomas G., and Aylesworth, Virgina L. *The Southwest: Colorado, New Mexico, Texas.* Chelsea House, 1995. *(I)*

Barenblat, Rachel, and Craven, Jean. *Texas: The Lone Star State.* Gareth Stevens, 2002. *(P; I)*

Bredeson, Carmen. *Texas.* Marshall Cavendish, 1997. *(P; I); The Battle of the Alamo: The Fight for Texas Territory; The Spindletop Gusher: The Story of the Texas Oil Boom.* Millbrook Press, 1996. *(I)*

Haley, James L., and Edmondson, J. R. *Jim Bowie: Frontier Legend, Alamo Hero.* Rosen, 2003. *(I; A)*

Hanson-Harding, Alexandra; Larson, Jeanette; and Matusevich, Melissa N. *Texas*. Scholastic, 2001. *(P; I)*

Hoyt-Goldsmith, Diane, and Migdale, Lawrence. *Migrant Workers: A Boy from the Rio Grande Valley*. Holiday House, 1996. *(P; I)*

McComb, David G. *Texas: An Illustrated History*. Oxford, 1995. *(I; A)*

Pelta, Kathy. *Texas*. Lerner, 2001 (2nd ed.). *(P; I)*

Sorrels, Roy. *The Alamo in American History*. Enslow, 1996. *(I)*

Wills, Charles A. *A Historical Album of Texas*. Millbrook Press, 1995. *(I)*

THANKSGIVING DAY

Barth, Edna. *Turkey, Pilgrims, and Indian Corn: The Story of the Thanksgiving Symbols*. Houghton, 2000. *(P; I)*

Kessel, Joyce K. *Squanto and the First Thanksgiving*. Lerner, 2003. *(P)*

Landau, Elaine. *Thanksgiving Day: A Time to Be Thankful*. Enslow, 2001. *(P)*

THATCHER, MARGARET

Moskin, Marietta D. *Margaret Thatcher of Great Britain*. Silver Burdett, 1990. *(I; A)*

THEATER

Boland, Robert, and Argentini, Paul. *Musicals!: Directing School and Community Theatre*. Rowman & Littlefield, 1997. *(A)*

Burton, Marilee Robin. *Artists at Work*. Chelsea Clubhouse, 2003. *(P)*

Egendorf, Laura K. *Elizabethan Drama*. Thomson Gale, 2000. *(A)*

Miller, Kimberly M. *Backstage at a Play (Backstage Pass Series)*. Children's Press, 2003. *(I)*

Nardo, Don. *Greek Drama*. Thomson Gale, 1999. *(A)*

Novak, Elaine A., and Novak, Deborah. *Staging Musical Theatre: A Complete Guide for Directors, Choreographers, and Producers*. F & W Publications, 1996. *(A)*

Zinsser, William Knowlton. *Easy to Remember: The Great American Songwriters and Their Songs for Broadway Shows and Hollywood Musicals*. Godine, David R., 2001. *(A)*

THIRTEEN AMERICAN COLONIES

Aronson, Marc. *John Winthrop, Oliver Cromwell, and the Land of Promise*. Houghton Mifflin, 2004. *(I; A)*

Beller, Susan Provost. *Woman of Independence: The Life of Abigail Adams*. F & W Publications, 1992. *(I; A)*

Bjornlund, Lydia. *The Thirteen Colonies: Massachusetts*. Gale Group, 2001. *(I)*

Blohm, Craig E. *The Thirteen Colonies: New Hampshire*. Gale Group, 2001. *(I)*

Bremer, Francis J. *John Winthrop: America's Forgotten Founding Father*. Oxford University Press, 2005. *(A)*

Daugherty, James. *The Landing of the Pilgrims*. Random, 1996. *(I)*

Dean, Ruth, and Thompson, Melissa. *Life in the American Colonies*. Gale Group, 1998. *(I)*

Fradin, Dennis Brindell. *Connecticut Colony; Delaware Colony; Georgia Colony; Maryland Colony; Massachusetts Colony; New Hampshire Colony; New Jersey Colony; New York Colony; North Carolina Colony; Pennsylvania Colony; Rhode Island Colony; South Carolina Colony; Virginia Colony*. Scholastic, 1986-1992. *(I)*

Hakim, Joy. *Making Thirteen Colonies*. Oxford, 1993. *(I; A)*

Hossell, Karen Price. *The Thirteen Colonies: Virginia*. Gale Group, 2001. *(I)*

Kallen, Stuart A. *The Thirteen Colonies: Delaware*. Gale Group, 2001. *(I)*

Kent, Deborah. *African-Americans in the Thirteen Colonies*. Scholastic, 1996. *(P; I)*

Kling, Andrew A. *The Thirteen Colonies: Rhode Island*. Gale Group, 2001. *(I)*

Lukes, Bonnie L. *Colonial America*. Lucent, 1999. *(I; A)*

Sherrow, Victoria. *The Thirteen Colonies: Pennsylvania*. Gale Group, 2001. *(I)*

Stefoff, Rebecca. *The Colonies*. Marshall Cavendish, 2000. *(I)*

Streissguth, Thomas. *The Thirteen Colonies: Maryland; The Thirteen Colonies: New Jersey*. Gale Group, 2001. *(I)*

Uschan, Michael V. *The Thirteen Colonies: North Carolina*. Gale Group, 2001. *(I)*

Woog, Adam. *The Thirteen Colonies: New York*. Gale Group, 2001. *(I)*

THOREAU, HENRY DAVID

Locker, Thomas. *Walking with Henry: Based on the Life and Works of Henry David Thoreau*. Fulcrum, 2002. *(P; I)*

Miller, Douglas T. *Henry David Thoreau: A Man for All Seasons*. Replica Books, 1999. *(I; A)*

Reef, Catherine. *Henry David Thoreau: A Neighbor to Nature*. 21st Century Books, 1991. *(P; I)*

THORPE, JAMES FRANCIS (JIM)

Krull, Kathleen. *Lives of the Athletes: Thrills, Spills (And What the Neighbors Thought)*. Raintree Steck-Vaughn, 1999. *(I; A)*

THUNDER AND LIGHTNING

Branley, Franklyn M. *Flash, Crash, Rumble, and Roll*. HarperCollins, 1999. *(P)*

Hopping, Lorraine Jean. *Wild Weather: Lightning!* Scholastic, 1999. *(P)*

Simon, Seymour. *Lightning*. Morrow, 1997. *(P; I)*

Staub, Frank. *The Kids' Book of Clouds & Sky*. Sterling, 2004. *(I)*

TIDES

Berger, Melvin. *What Makes an Ocean Wave?: Questions and Answers about Oceans and Ocean Life*. Scholastic, 2001. *(P; I)*

TIGERS

Dutemple, Lesley A. *Tigers.* Lerner, 1996. *(P)*

Harman, Amanda. *Tigers.* Marshall Cavendish, 1995. *(P; I)*

Stonehouse, Bernard. *A Visual Introduction to Wild Cats.* Facts on File, 1999. *(P; I; A)*

TIME

Branley, Franklyn. *Keeping Time.* Houghton, 1993. *(I)*

Chapman, Gillian. *Exploring Time.* Lerner, 1995. *(P; I)*

Gribbin, John, and Gribbin, Mary. *Time and Space.* DK, 1994. *(I; A)*

Koscielniak, Bruce. *About Time: A First Look at Time and Clocks.* Houghton Mifflin, 2004. *(P; I)*

Llewellyn, Claire. *My First Book of Time.* DK, 1992. *(P)*

Matthews, Rupert. *Everyday History: Telling the Time.* Scholastic, 2000. *(P)*

Murphy, Stuart J. *Rodeo Time (Mathstart Series).* Harper-Collins, 2006; *Game Time! (Mathstart Series).* HarperCollins, 1997. *(P)*

Older, Jules. *Telling Time.* Charlesbridge, 2000. *(P)*

Skurzynski, Gloria. *On Time: From Seasons to Split Seconds.* National Geographic, 2000. *(P; I)*

TIN

Gray, Leon. *Tin.* Marshall Cavendish, 2003. *(I)*

TINTORETTO

Janson, H. W., and Janson, Anthony F. *History of Art for Young People.* Abrams, 1997 (rev. ed.). *(I; A)*

TITIAN

Halliwell, Sarah, ed. *Renaissance: Artists and Writers.* Marshall Cavendish, 1997. *(I)*

Janson, H. W., and Janson, Anthony F. *History of Art for Young People.* Abrams, 1997 (rev. ed.). *(I; A)*

TOBACCO

Cohen, Philip. *Drugs, The Complete Story: Tobacco.* Raintree Steck-Vaughn, 1991. *(I)*

Heyes, Eileen. *Tobacco, USA: The Industry behind the Smoke Curtain.* Twenty-First Century, 1999. *(I; A)*

TOLKIEN, J. R. R.

Levine, Stuart P. *The Importance of J. R. R. Tolkien.* Thomson Gale, 2003. *(I; A)*

TOMATOES

Watts, Barrie. *Tomato.* Silver Burdett Press, 1995. *(P)*

TOOLS

Good, Keith. *Gear Up!: Marvelous Machine Projects.* Lerner, 2003. *(P; I)*

Schwarz, Renee. *Funky Junk: Cool Stuff to Make with Hardware.* Kids Can Press, 2003. *(P; I)*

TORNADOES

Allaby, Michael. *Tornadoes (Dangerous Weather Series).* Facts on File, 2004 (2nd ed.). *(I; A)*

Mogil, H. Michael. *Tornadoes.* Voyageur Press, 2001. *(I; A)*

Sherrow, Victoria. *Plains Outbreak Tornadoes: Killer Twisters.* Enslow, 1998. *(P; I)*

TOULOUSE-LAUTREC, HENRI DE

Bryant, Jennifer Fisher. *Henri de Toulouse-Lautrec: Artist.* Chelsea House, 1995. *(P; I)*

Janson, H. W., and Janson, Anthony F. *History of Art for Young People.* Abrams, 1997 (rev. ed.). *(I; A)*

Venezia, Mike. *Henri de Toulouse-Lautrec.* Children's Press, 1995. *(P)*

TOYS

Aaseng, Nathan. *Business Builders in Toys.* Oliver Press, 2002. *(I; A)*

Wulffson, Don. *Toys! Amazing Stories behind Some Great Inventions.* Holt, 2000. *(P; I)*

TRACK AND FIELD

Jackson, Colin. *The Young Track and Field Athlete: A Young Enthusiast's Guide to Track and Field Athletics.* Dorling Kindersley, 1996. *(P; I)*

Knotts, Bob. *Track and Field.* Scholastic, 2000. *(P)*

McKissack, Patricia C., and McKissack, Frederick. *Jesse Owens: Olympic Star.* Enslow, 2001 (rev. ed.). *(P; I)*

TRANSPORTATION

Barter, James E. *Building the Transcontinental Railroad.* Gale Group, 2001. *(I)*

Berliner, Don. *Aviation: Reaching for the Sky.* Oliver Press, 1997. *(I)*

Grant, R. G. *Flight: 100 Years of Aviation.* DK, 2002. *(A)*

Whitman, Sylvia. *Get Up and Go!: The History of American Road Travel.* Lerner, 1996. *(I)*

Woods, Michael, and Woods, Mary B. *Ancient Transportation: From Camels to Canals.* Lerner, 1999. *(I)*

TREATIES

Corzine, Phyllis. *The Palestinian-Israeli Accord.* Lucent, 1996. *(I; A)*

Dunn, John M. *The Relocation of the North American Indian.* Lucent, 1994. *(I; A)*

Gold, Susan Dudley. *Land Pacts.* Twenty-First Century, 1997. *(I; A)*

TREES

Arnosky, Jim. *Crinkleroot's Guide to Knowing the Trees.* Bradbury, 1992. *(P)*

Hughes, Meredith Sayles. *Hard to Crack: Nut Trees; Tall and Tasty: Fruit Trees.* Lerner, 2000. *(P; I)*

Pine, Jonathan. *Trees.* HarperCollins, 1995. *(I)*

TRINIDAD AND TOBAGO

McKenley, Yvonne. *A Taste of the Caribbean.* Raintree Steck-Vaughn, 1995. *(P; I)*

TROJAN WAR

Caselli, Giovanni. *In Search of Troy: One Man's Quest for Homer's Fabled City.* NTC, 1999. *(P; I)*

TRUCKS AND TRUCKING

Mitchell, Joyce Slayton. *Tractor-Trailer Trucker: A Powerful Truck Book.* Tricycle, 2000. *(P; I)*

TRUMAN, HARRY S.

Alter, Judy. *Harry S. Truman.* Enslow, 2002. *(I; A)*

Feinberg, Barbara Silberdick. *Harry S. Truman.* Watts, 1994. *(A)*

Gaines, Ann Graham. *Harry S. Truman: Our Thirty-Third President.* Child's World, 2001. *(P; I)*

Otfinoski, Steven. *Harry S. Truman (Encyclopedia of Presidents, Second Series).* Scholastic, 2005. *(I; A)*

TUBMAN, HARRIET

Bentley, Judith. *Harriet Tubman.* Watts, 1990. *(A)*

Chang, Ina. *Separate Battle: Women and the Civil War.* Penguin Putnam, 1996 (reprint). *(I)*

Hazell, Rebecca. *Heroines: Great Women Through the Ages.* Abbeville Press, 1996. *(I)*

Pinkney, Andrea Davis. *Let It Shine: Stories of Black Women Freedom Fighters.* Harcourt, 2000. *(I)*

Sullivan, George E. *Harriet Tubman (In Their Own Words Series).* Scholastic, 2002. *(P; I)*

Taylor, M. W. *Harriet Tubman.* Chelsea House, 1990. *(I)*

TUNISIA

Tunisia... in Pictures. Lerner, 1998 (rev. ed.). *(I; A)*

Carew-Miller, Anna. *Tunisia.* Mason Crest, 2002. *(I; A)*

Fox, Mary Virginia. *Tunisia.* Scholastic, 1994 (rev. ed.). *(I)*

Nardo, Don. *Battle of Zama: Battles of the Ancient World.* Gale Group, 1996. *(I; A)*

TUNNELS

Borchelt, Kelly L. *The Longest Tunnel.* Thomson Gale, 2004. *(I; A)*

Landau, Elaine. *Tunnels.* Scholastic, 2001. *(P)*

Vanderwarker, Peter. *The Big Dig: Reshaping an American City.* Little, 2001. *(I)*

TURTLES

Arnosky, Jim. *All about Turtles.* Scholastic, 2000. *(P)*

Gibbons, Gail. *Turtles.* Holiday, 1995. *(P)*

Guiberson, Brenda Z. *Into the Sea.* Holt, 1996. *(P)*

Lepthien, Emilie U. *Sea Turtles.* Scholastic, 1997. *(P)*

Staub, Frank. *Sea Turtles.* Lerner, 1995. *(P)*

Tagliaferro, Linda. *Galapagos Islands: Nature's Delicate Balance at Risk.* Lerner, 2000. *(I)*

Thomas, Peggy. *Reptile Rescue.* Millbrook Press, 2000. *(P; I)*

TWAIN, MARK

Aller, Susan Bivin. *Mark Twain (A & E Biography Series).* Lerner, 2001. *(I; A)*

Cox, Clinton. *Mark Twain: America's Humorist, Dreamer, Prophet: A Biography.* Scholastic, 1999. *(I; A)*

Smith, Christopher. *American Realism.* Thomson Gale, 2000. *(A)*

TYLER, JOHN

Ferry, Steven. *John Tyler: Our Tenth President.* Child's World, 2002. *(P; I)*

Ochester, Betsy. *John Tyler (Encyclopedia of Presidents, Second Series).* Scholastic, 2003. *(I; A)*

U (LETTER)

Samoyault, Tiphaine. *Alphabetical Order: How the Alphabet Began.* Viking, 1998. *(P; I)*

UGANDA

Ayodo, Awuor, and Odhiambo, Atieno. *Luo (Kenya, Uganda).* Rosen, 1995. *(I; A)*

Barlas, Robert. *Uganda.* Marshall Cavendish, 2000 (2nd ed.). *(I; A)*

Blauer, Ettagle, and Laure, Jason. *Uganda.* Scholastic, 1997. *(I; A)*

Kubuitsile, Lauri. *Uganda (Africa - Continent in the Balance Series).* Mason Crest, 2004. *(I; A)*

Wilson-Max, Ken. *Furaha Means Happy: A Book of Swahili Words.* Hyperion, 2000. *(P)*

UKRAINE

Christmas in Ukraine. World Book, 1997. *(I; A)*

Ukraine. Lerner, 1992. *(I)*

Clay, Rebecca. *Ukraine: A New Independence.* Marshall Cavendish, 1997. *(I)*

Nardo, Don. *Chernobyl.* Gale Group, 1990. *(I; A)*

UN-AMERICAN ACTIVITIES COMMITTEE, HOUSE

Alonso, Karen. *The Alger Hiss Communist Spy Trial: A Headline Court Case.* Enslow, 2001. *(I; A)*

Cohen, Daniel. *Joseph McCarthy: The Misuse of Political Power.* Millbrook Press, 1996. *(I; A)*

Finkelstein, Norman H. *With Heroic Truth: The Life of Edward R. Murrow.* Houghton Mifflin, 1997. *(I; A)*

Rappaport, Doreen. *Be the Judge, Be the Jury: The Alger Hiss Trial.* HarperCollins, 1993. *(I; A)*

Sherrow, Victoria. *Joseph McCarthy: And the Cold War.* Gale Group, 1998. *(A)*

Zeinert, Karen. *McCarthy and the Fear of Communism (In American History Series).* Enslow, 1998. *(I; A)*

UNDERGROUND MOVEMENTS

Levine, Ellen. *Darkness over Denmark: The Danish Resistance and the Rescue of the Jews.* Holiday House, 1999. *(I)*

Meltzer, Milton. *Rescue: The Story of How Gentiles Saved Jews in the Holocaust.* HarperCollins, 1999. *(I; A)*

UNDERGROUND RAILROAD

Fradin, Dennis Brindell. *Bound for the North Star: True Stories of Fugitive Slaves.* Houghton Mifflin, 2000. *(I; A)*

Gorrell, Gena Kinton; Oubrerie, Clement; and Cullen, Malcolm. *North Star to Freedom: The Story of the Underground Railroad.* Bantam Doubleday Dell, 1999. *(I)*

McKissack, Patricia C., and McKissack, Fredrick L. *Sojourner Truth: Ain't I a Woman?* Scholastic, 1994. *(I)*

Pinkney, Andrea Davis. *Let It Shine: Stories of Black Women Freedom Fighters.* Harcourt, 2000. *(I)*

Swain, Gwenyth. *President of the Underground Railroad: A Story about Levi Coffin.* Lerner, 2001. *(P; I)*

UNDERWATER ARCHAEOLOGY

Archbold, Rick. *Deep Sea Explorer: The Story of Robert Ballard, Discoverer of the Titanic.* Scholastic, 1994. *(I; A)*

Ballard, Robert D. *The Eternal Darkness: A Personal History of Deep-Sea Exploration.* Princeton University Press, 2002; *Explorations: My Quest for Adventure and Discovery Under the Sea.* Explorations: My Quest for Adventure and Discovery Under the Sea. *(A)*

Lerner Geography Department. *Sunk!: Exploring Underwater Archaeology.* Lerner, 1994. *(I; A)*

UNDERWATER EXPLORATION

Archbold, Rick. *Deep Sea Explorer: The Story of Robert Ballard, Discoverer of the Titanic.* Scholastic, 1994. *(I; A)*

Conley, Andrea. *Window on the Deep: The Adventures of Underwater Explorer Sylvia Earle.* Watts, 1991. *(P; I)*

Grupper, Jonathan. *Destination: Deep Sea.* National Geographic Society, 2000. *(P)*

Hill, Christine M. *Robert Ballard: Oceanographer Who Discovered the Titanic.* Enslow, 1998. *(I)*

Plisson, Philip, photographer. *The Sea: Exploring Life on an Ocean Planet.* Abrams, 2003. *(I; A)*

Polking, Kirk. *Oceanographers and Explorers of the Sea.* Enslow, 1999. *(I)*

Tocci, Salvatore. *Coral Reefs: Life Below the Sea; Marine Habitats: Life in the Saltwater.* Scholastic, 2005. *(P; I)*

UNICEF

Grahame, Deborah A. *UNICEF.* Gareth Stevens, 2003. *(I)*

Maddocks, Steven. *World Watch: UNICEF.* Raintree, 2004. *(I)*

UNICORNS

Giblin, James Cross. *The Truth about Unicorns.* HarperCollins, 1996. *(I; A)*

UNIDENTIFIED FLYING OBJECTS

Asimov, Isaac, and Hantula, Richard. *UFOs.* Gareth Stevens, 2005. *(P; I)*

Herbst, Judith. *UFO's (The Unexplained Series).* Lerner, 2004. *(I; A)*

UNION OF SOVIET SOCIALIST REPUBLICS

Andrews, William G. *The Land and People of the Soviet Union.* Harper, 1991. *(I; A)*

Barbour, William S., and Wekesser, Carol, eds. *The Breakup of the Soviet Union: Opposing Viewpoints.* Gale Group, 1994. *(A)*

Batalden, Stephen K., and Batalden, Sandra L. *The Newly Independent States of Eurasia: Handbook of Former Soviet Republics.* Greenwood, 1997 (2nd ed.). *(A)*

Buettner, Dan. *Sovietrek: A Journey by Bicycle across Russia.* Lerner, 1994. *(I; A)*

Conte, Francis; Kozul, Michel; Gousseff, Catherine; Sansonnens, Yves; and Sanborne, Mark, eds. *Great Dates in Russian and Soviet History.* Facts on File, 1994. *(A)*

Corona, Laurel. *The Russian Federation.* Gale Group, 2001. *(A)*

Dolphin, Laurie. *Georgia to Georgia: Making Friends in the U.S.S.R.* Tambourine, 1991. *(P; I)*

Gottfried, Ted. *Road to Communism; Stalinist Empire.* Twenty-First Century, 2002. *(A)*

Harvey, Miles. *Look What Came from Russia.* Scholastic, 1999. *(P); The Fall of the Soviet Union.* Children's Press, 1995. *(I)*

Kort, Michael G. *The Handbook of the Former Soviet Union.* Millbrook Press, 1997. *(I; A)*

Kotlyarskaya, Elena. *Women in Society.* Marshall Cavendish, 1994. *(I; A)*

Matthews, John R. *The Rise and Fall of the Soviet Union.* Lucent, 1999. *(I; A)*

Otfinoski, Steven. *Boris Yeltsin and the Rebirth of Russia.* Millbrook Press, 1995. *(I; A)*

Plotkin, Gregory, and Plotkin, Rita. *Cooking the Russian Way.* Lerner, 2003 (2nd ed.). *(I; A)*

Resnick, Abraham. *Union of Soviet Socialist Republics: A Survey from 1917 to 1991.* Scholastic, 1992 (rev. ed.). *(I; A)*

Ross, Stewart. *U. S. S. R. under Stalin.* Watts, 1991. *(I; A)*

Symynkywicz, Jeffrey B. *The Soviet Turmoil.* Silver Burdett Press, 1997. *(I; A)*

Torchinsky, Oleg. *Russia.* Marshall Cavendish, 1994 (2nd ed.). *(I; A)*

Wade, Rex A. *The Bolshevik Revolution and Russian Civil War.* Greenwood, 2000. *(A)*

UNITED ARAB EMIRATES

McCoy, Lisa. *United Arab Emirates.* Mason Crest, 2002. *(I; A)*

UNITED KINGDOM

Arnold, Caroline, and Arnold, Arthur P. *Stone Age Farmers Beside the Sea: Scotland's Prehistoric Village of*

Skara Brae. Houghton Mifflin, 1997. *(I)*

Blashfield, Jean F. *England.* Scholastic, 1997. *(I)*

Burgan, Michael. *England.* Scholastic, 1999. *(P)*

Costain, Meredith, and Collins, Paul. *Welcome to the United Kingdom.* Chelsea House, 2001. *(P; I)*

Davis, Kevin A. *Look What Came from England.* Scholastic, 1999. *(P)*

Donovan, Sandra. *The Channel Tunnel.* Lerner, 2003. *(I; A)*

Gottfried, Ted. *Northern Ireland: Peace in Our Time?* Millbrook Press, 2002. *(I; A)*

Heinrichs, Ann. *Wales.* Scholastic, 2003. *(I; A)*

Hestler, Anna. *Wales.* Marshall Cavendish, 2001. *(I; A)*

Innes, Brian. *United Kingdom.* Raintree Steck-Vaughn, 2002. *(P; I)*

Lace, William W. *Scotland.* Gale Group, 2000; *Ireland.* Gale Group, 1999; *England.* Gale Group, 1997. *(I; A)*

Lindop, Edmund. *Great Britain and the United States: Rivals and Partners.* Twenty-First Century, 1999. *(A)*

Lister, Maree; Sevier, Marti; and NgCheong-Lum, Roseline. *Welcome to England.* Gareth Stevens, 1999. *(P)*

Lyle, Garry. *England.* Chelsea House, 1999. *(I; A)*

Ross, Michael Elsohn. *Children of Northern Ireland.* Lerner, 2000. *(P)*

Stein, Richard Conrad. *Scotland.* Scholastic, 2001. *(I; A)*

UNITED NATIONS

Giesecke, Ernestine. *Governments around the World.* Heinemann, 2000. *(P; I)*

Ross, Stewart. *World Watch: United Nations.* Raintree, 2004; *The United Nations.* Heinemann, 2002. *(I; A)*

Trier, Jean. *United Nations High Commissioner for Refugees.* Silver Burdett Press, 1995. *(I; A)*

UNITED STATES

Anno, Mitsumasa. *Anno's U.S.A.* Penguin, 2002. *(I)*

Davis, Kevin A. *Look What Came from the United States.* Scholastic, 1999. *(P)*

Johnson, Linda Carlson. *Our National Symbols.* Millbrook Press, 1994. *(P)*

Leedy, Loreen. *Celebrate the 50 States!* Holiday, 1999. *(P)*

Petersen, Christine, and Petersen, David. *United States of America.* Scholastic, 2002. *(P; I)*

Quiri, Patricia Ryon. *The National Anthem.* Children's Press, 1998. *(P)*

Shearer, Benjamin F., and Shearer, Barbara S. *State Names, Seals, Flags, and Symbols: A Historical Guide.* Greenwood-Heinemann, 1994 (rev. ed.). *(I; A)*

St. Pierre, Stephanie. *Our National Anthem.* Millbrook Press, 1994. *(P)*

UNITED STATES, ARMED FORCES OF THE

Buckley, Gail Lumet. *American Patriots: A Young People's Edition: The Story of Blacks in the Military from the Revolution to Desert Storm.* Crown, 2003. *(I; A)*

Clinton, Catherine. *The Black Soldier: 1492 to the Present.* Houghton Mifflin, 2000. *(I; A)*

Harmon, Daniel E. *Your Government: The U. S. Armed Forces.* Chelsea House, 2000. *(I; A)*

UNITED STATES, ART AND ARCHITECTURE OF THE

Boulton, Alexander O. *Frank Lloyd Wright, Architect: An Illustrated Biography.* Rizzoli, 1993. *(I; A)*

UNITED STATES, CONGRESS OF THE

Aaseng, Nathan. *You Are the Senator.* Oliver, 1997. *(I; A)*

Bonner, Mike. *Your Government: How a Bill Is Passed.* Chelsea House, 2000. *(I; A)*

Jones, Veda Boyd. *Your Government: The Senate.* Chelsea House, 2000. *(I: A)*

LeVert, Suzanne. *Congress.* Benchmark, 2002. *(P; I)*

Lindop, Edmund. *Presidents Versus Congress: Conflict and Compromise.* Watts, 1994. *(I; A)*

Quiri, Patricia Ryon. *Congress.* Scholastic, 1998. *(P; I)*

Ritchie, Donald A. *The Congress of the United States: A Student Companion.* Oxford, 2001 (2nd ed.). *(A)*

Sherrow, Victoria. *Joseph McCarthy: And the Cold War.* Blackbirch Press, 1998. *(I; A)*

UNITED STATES, CONSTITUTION OF THE

Banks, Joan. *Your Government: The U. S. Constitution.* Chelsea House, 2000. *(I; A)*

Freedman, Russell. *In Defense of Liberty: The Story of America's Bill of Rights.* Holiday House, 2003. *(I; A)*; *Give Me Liberty!: The Story of the Declaration of Independence.* Holiday House, 2000. *(I)*

Fritz, Jean. *Shh! We're Writing the Constitution.* Penguin Putnam, 1998 (reissue). *(P; I)*

Graves, Kerry A. *The Constitution: The Story Behind America's Governing Document.* Chelsea Clubhouse, 2004. *(P; I)*

Quiri, Patricia Ryon. *The Constitution.* Scholastic, 1998. *(P)*

Renstrom, Peter G. *Constitutional Law for Young Adults: A Handbook on the Bill of Rights and the Fourteenth Amendment.* ABC-CLIO, 1992. *(A)*

UNITED STATES, GOVERNMENT OF THE

Fish, Bruce, and Fish, Becky D. *Your Government: The History of the Democratic Party; Your Government: The Speaker of the House of Representatives.* Chelsea House, 2000. *(I; A)*

Kronenwetter, Michael. *Political Parties of the United States.* Enslow, 1996. *(I; A)*

Nardo, Don. *The Declaration of Independence: A Model for Individual Rights.* Lucent, 1998. *(A)*

Paine, Thomas. *Common Sense.* Penguin, 2005. *(I; A)*

Parker, Nancy Winslow. *The President's Cabinet and How It Grew.* Harper, 1991. *(P; I)*

Quiri, Patricia Ryon. *The Bill of Rights; The Declaration of Independence.* Children's Press, 1998. *(P)*

UNITED STATES, HISTORY OF THE

Altman, Linda Jacobs. *Slavery and Abolition (In American History Series).* Enslow, 1999; *The California Gold*

Rush (In American History Series). Enslow, 1997. *(I; A)*

Collier, Christopher, and Collier, James L. *The Changing Face of America, 1945-2000; The Middle Road: American Politics, 1945-2000; The United States in the Cold War; The United States in World War II*. Marshall Cavendish, 2001; *A Century of Immigration, 1820-1924; Indians, Cowboys, and Farmers and the Battle for the Great Plains, 1865-1910; Progressivism, the Great Depression, and the New Deal, 1901-1941; Reconstruction and the Rise of Jim Crow, 1864-1896; Slavery and the Coming of the Civil War, 1831-1861; The Civil War, 1860-1866; The United States Enters the World Stage: From Alaska through World War I, 1867-1919*. Marshall Cavendish, 2000; *Andrew Jackson's America, 1824-1850; Building a New Nation, 1789-1801; Creating the Constitution, 1787; The Jeffersonian Republicans, 1800-1820*. Marshall Cavendish, 1998; *Clash of Cultures: Prehistory-1638; Pilgrims and Puritans, 1620-1676; The American Revolution, 1763-1783; The French and Indian War, 1660-1763; The Paradox of Jamestown, 1585-1700*. Marshall Cavendish, 1997. *(I; A)*

Feinstein, Stephen. *Decades of the 20th Century: The 1900s from Teddy Roosevelt to Flying Machines; Decades of the 20th Century: The 1910s from World War I to Ragtime Music; Decades of the 20th Century: The 1920s from Prohibition to Charles Lindbergh; Decades of the 20th Century: The 1990s from the Persian Gulf War to Y2K*. Enslow, 2001; *Decades of the 20th Century: The 1930s from the Great Depression to the Wizard of Oz; Decades of the 20th Century: The 1940s from World War II to Jackie Robinson; Decades of the 20th Century: The 1950s from the Korean War to Elvis; Decades of the 20th Century: The 1960s from the Vietnam War to Flower Power; Decades of the 20th Century: The 1980s from Ronald Reagan to MTV*. Enslow, 2000. *(I)*

Green, Carl R. *The Mission Trails (In American History Series)*. Enslow, 2001; *Blazing the Wilderness Road with Daniel Boone (In American History Series); The California Trail to Gold (In American History Series)*. Enslow, 2000. *(I; A)*

Holford, David M. *Lincoln and the Emancipation Proclamation (In American History Series)*. Enslow, 2002. *(I; A)*

Hull, Mary E. *Shays' Rebellion and the Constitution (In American History Series)*. Enslow, 2000; *The Union and the Civil War (In American History Series)*. Enslow, 2000; *The Boston Tea Party (In American History Series)*. Enslow, 1999. *(I; A)*

Landau, Elaine. *State Flowers: Including the Commonwealth of Puerto Rico*. Scholastic, 1992. *(I; A)*

Lieurance, Suzanne. *The Prohibition Era (In American History Series); The Triangle Shirtwaist Fire and Sweatshop Reform (In American History Series)*. Enslow, 2003; *The Space Shuttle Challenger Disaster (In American History Series)*. Enslow, 2001. *(I; A)*

Nash, Carol Rust. *The Mormon Trail and the Latter-Day Saints (In American History Series)*. Enslow, 1999; *The Fight for Women's Right to Vote (In American History Series)*. Enslow, 1998. *(I; A)*

Sawyer, Kem Knapp. *The Underground Railroad (In American History Series)*. Enslow, 1997. *(I; A)*

Scott, John Anthony. *The Facts on File History of the American People*. Facts on File, 1989. *(I; A)*

Spangenburg, Ray. *Political and Social Movements*. Facts on File, 1998. *(I; A)*

Sorrels, Roy. *The Alamo (In American History Series)*. Enslow, 1996. *(I; A)*

Steins, Richard. *Exploration and Settlement*. Raintree Steck-Vaughn, 2000. *(I)*

Ziff, Marsha. *Reconstruction Following the Civil War (In American History Series)*. Enslow, 1999. *(I; A)*

UNITED STATES, MUSIC OF THE

Bankston, John. *Masters of Music: The Life and Times of Duke Ellington; Masters of Music: The Life and Times of Scott Joplin*. Mitchell Lane, 2004. *(I)*

Collier, James Lincoln. *The Louis Armstrong You Never New*. Scholastic, 2004. *(P; I)*; *Jazz: An American Saga*. Henry Holt, 1997. *(I; A)*; *Duke Ellington*. Simon & Schuster, 1994. *(I)*

Krull, Kathleen. *Lives of the Musicians: Good Times, Bad Times (And What the Neighbors Thought)*. Raintree Steck-Vaughn, 1998. *(I; A)*

Wondrich, David. *Stomp and Swerve: American Music Gets Hot, 1843-1924*. Chicago Review Press, 2003. *(A)*

UNIVERSE

Asimov, Isaac, and Hantula, Richard. *The Milky Way and Other Galaxies*. Gareth Stevens, 2003. *(I)*

Clay, Rebecca. *Stars and Galaxies (Secrets of Space Series)*. Lerner, 1997. *(I)*

Couper, Heather, and Henbest, Nigel. *Big Bang: The Story of the Universe*. Dorling Kindersley, 1997. *(A)*

Datnow, Claire L. *Edwin Hubble: Discoverer of Galaxies (Great Minds of Science Series)*. Enslow, 2001. *(I)*

Gribbin, John, and Gribbin, Mary. *Time and Space*. DK, 1994. *(I; A)*

MacDonald, Fiona. *Edwin Hubble*. Heinemann, 2001. *(I)*

Redfern, Martin. *The Kingfisher Young People's Book of Space*. Houghton Mifflin, 1998. *(P; I)*

Vogt, Gregory L. *Milky Way*. Capstone Press, 2002. *(P)*; *Milky Way and Other Galaxies*. Raintree, 2000. *(I; A)*; *Deep Space Astronomy*. Millbrook Press, 1999. *(I; A)*

URANIUM

Heiserman, David L. *Exploring Chemical Elements and Their Compounds*. McGraw-Hill, 1991. *(A)*

URANUS

Asimov, Isaac, and Hantula, Richard. *Uranus: The Sideways Planet*. Gareth Stevens, 2002 (rev. ed.). *(P; I)*

Miller, Ron. *Worlds Beyond: Uranus and Neptune.* Lerner, 2003. *(I)*

Vogt, Gregory L. *Uranus.* Millbrook Press, 1993. *(P; I)*

URBAN PLANNING

Gottlieb, Robert. *Forcing the Spring: The Transformation of the American Environmental Movement.* Island Press, 2005 (2nd ed.). *(A)*

Hinds, Kathryn. *The City.* Marshall Cavendish, 2000. *(I; A)*

Lomberg, Michelle. *Healthy Cities: Improving Urban Life.* Smart Apple Media, 2004. *(I; A)*

Parker, Philip. *Global Cities.* Raintree Steck-Vaughn, 1995. *(P; I)*

URUGUAY

Jermyn, Leslie. *Uruguay.* Marshall Cavendish, 1998 (2nd ed.) *(I; A)*

Morrison, Marion. *Uruguay (Enchantment of the World, Second Series).* Scholastic, 2005. *(I; A)*

UTAH

Feeney, Kathy. *Utah: Facts and Symbols.* Capstone/Hilltop, 2000. *(P)*

Fradin, Dennis Brindell. *Utah: From Sea to Shining Sea.* Scholastic, 1996. *(P; I)*

Hirschmann, Kris. *Utah: The Beehive State.* Gareth Stevens, 2003. *(P; I)*

Kent, Deborah. *Utah.* Scholastic, 2000 (2nd ed.). *(I; A)*

Neri, P. J. *Utah.* Scholastic, 2002. *(P; I)*

Petersen, David. *Arches National Park.* Scholastic, 2000; *Bryce Canyon National Park.* Scholastic, 1996; *Dinosaur National Monument.* Scholastic, 1995; *Zion National Park.* Scholastic, 1993. *(P; I)*

Sirvaitis, Karen. *Utah.* Lerner, 2002 (2nd ed.). *(P; I)*

Stefoff, Rebecca. *Utah.* Marshall Cavendish, 2000. *(P; I)*

Tufts, Lorraine S. *Secrets in the Grand Canyon, Zion and Bryce Canyon National Parks.* National Photographic Collections, 1998. *(P; I)*

Wilkinson, Philip. *The Master Builders.* Chelsea House, 1993. *(I; A)*

V (LETTER)

Samoyault, Tiphaine. *Alphabetical Order: How the Alphabet Began.* Viking, 1998. *(P; I)*

VACCINATION AND IMMUNIZATION

Aronson, Virginia. *Influenza Pandemic of 1918-1919.* Chelsea House, 2000. *(I)*

Bankston, John. *Jonas Salk and the Polio Vaccine.* Mitchell Lane, 2001. *(I; A)*

Bredeson, Carmen. *Jonas Salk: Discoverer of the Polio Vaccine.* Enslow, 1993. *(I)*

Brynie, Faith Hickman. *101 Questions About Your Immune System You Felt Defenseless to Answer: Until Now.* Twenty-First Century, 2000. *(I; A)*

Day, Nancy. *Killer Superbugs: The Story of Drug-Resistant Diseases.* Enslow, 2001. *(I; A)*

Monroe, Judy. *Influenza and Other Viruses.* Capstone Press, 2001. *(I)*

Nardo, Don. *Vaccines.* Gale Group, 2001. *(I; A)*

Sherrow, Victoria. *Jonas Salk.* Facts on File, 1993. *(I)*

VALENTINES

Bulla, Clyde Robert. *The Story of Valentine's Day.* Harper-Collins, 1999. *(P)*

Fradin, Dennis Brindell. *Valentine's Day.* Enslow, 1990. *(P)*

Graham-Barber, Lynda. *Mushy!: The Complete Book of Valentine Words.* Bradbury, 1990. *(I)*

Landau, Elaine. *Valentine's Day: Candy, Love, and Hearts.* Enslow, 2002. *(P)*

VAN BUREN, MARTIN

Favor, Lesli J. *Martin Van Buren (Encyclopedia of Presidents, Second Series).* Scholastic, 2003. *(I; A)*

Ferry, Steven. *Martin Van Buren: Our Eighth President.* Child's World, 2002. *(P; I)*

VAN GOGH, VINCENT

Janson, H. W., and Janson, Anthony F. *History of Art for Young People.* Abrams, 1997 (rev. ed.). *(I; A)*

Lucas, Eileen. *Vincent Van Gogh.* Watts, 1991. *(I)*

Muhlberger, Richard, and Metropolitan Museum of Art. *What Makes a Van Gogh a Van Gogh?* Viking, 1993. *(I)*

VEGETABLES

Hughes, Meredith Sayles. *Green Power: Leaf and Flower Vegetables; Stinky and Stringy: Stem and Bulb Vegetables.* Lerner, 2000; *Spill the Beans and Pass the Peanuts: Legumes.* Lerner, 1999; *Buried Treasure: Roots and Tubers.* Lerner, 1998. *(P; I)*

Ridgwell, Jenny. *Fruit and Vegetables.* Heinemann, 1998. *(P; I)*

VENEZUELA

Heinrichs, Ann. *Venezuela.* Scholastic, 1997. *(P)*

Winter, Jane Kohen, and Baguley, Kitt. *Venezuela.* Marshall Cavendish, 2002 (2nd ed.). *(I; A)*

VENICE

Hinds, Kathryn. *Cultures of the Past: Venice and Its Merchant Empire.* Marshall Cavendish, 2001. *(P; I; A)*

Lusted, Marcia Amidon. *The Canals of Venice.* Lucent, 2003. *(I; A)*

Rossi, Renzo. *Great Cities Through the Ages: Venice.* Enchanted Lion Books, 2003. *(I; A)*

VENUS

Asimov, Isaac, and Hantula, Richard. *Venus: A Shrouded Mystery.* Gareth Stevens, 2002 (rev. ed.). *(P; I)*

Brimner, Larry Dane; Goodwin, Peter; and Cornwell, Linda. *Venus.* Scholastic, 1998. *(P)*

Kipp, Steve L. *Venus.* Scholastic, 1998. *(P)*

Miller, Ron. *Worlds Beyond: Venus.* Lerner, 2002. *(I)*

Schloss, Muriel. *Venus.* Watts, 1991. *(P; I)*

VERGIL

Bloom, Harold, ed. *Vergil's Aeneid (Bloom's Notes Series).* Chelsea House, 1995. *(A)*

VERMEER, JAN

Halliwell, Sarah, ed. *17th Century: Artists, Writers, and Composers.* Raintree, 1997. *(I)*

Janson, H. W., and Janson, Anthony F. *History of Art for Young People.* Abrams, 1997 (rev. ed.). *(I; A)*

VERMONT

Czech, Jan M. *Vermont.* Scholastic, 2001. *(P; I)*

Elish, Dan. *Vermont.* Marshall Cavendish, 1997. *(P; I)*

Feeney, Kathy. *Vermont Facts and Symbols.* Capstone Press, 2001. *(P)*

Flocker, Michael E., and Craven, Jean. *Vermont: The Green Mountain State.* Gareth Stevens, 2002. *(P; I)*

Fradin, Dennis Brindell. *Vermont: From Sea to Shining Sea.* Scholastic, 1996. *(P; I)*

Graff, Nancy Price. *The Strength of the Hills: A Portrait of a Family Farm.* Little, 1989. *(P; I; A)*

VERNE, JULES

Streissguth, Thomas. *Science Fiction Pioneer: A Story about Jules Verne.* Lerner, 2000. *(P; I)*

Teeters, Peggy. *Jules Verne: The Man Who Invented Tomorrow.* Walker, 1993. *(I; A)*

VESEY, DENMARK

Robertson, David. *Denmark Vesey: The Buried History of America's Largest Slave Rebellion.* Knopf, 1999. *(A)*

VETERINARIANS

Gibbons, Gail. *Say Woof! The Day of a Country Veterinarian.* Macmillan, 1992. *(P)*

Maze, Stephanie. *I Want to Be a Veterinarian.* Harcourt, 1997. *(P; I)*

VIDEO GAMES

Erlbach, Arlene. *Video Games.* Lerner, 1995. *(I)*

Pascoe, Elaine. *Virtual Reality: Beyond the Looking Glass.* Gale Group, 1997. *(P; I)*

VIDEO RECORDING

Andersen, Yvonne. *Make Your Own Animated Movies and Videotapes.* Little, 1991. *(I; A)*

Bentley, Nancy, and Guthrie, Donna. *The Young Producer's Video Book: How to Write, Shoot, and Direct Your Own Videos.* Lerner, 1995. *(P; I)*

Biel, Jackie. *Video.* Benchmark, 1996. *(P; I)*

VIENNA

Stein, R. Conrad. *Vienna.* Children's Press, 1999. *(P; I)*

VIETNAM

Vietnam . . . in Pictures. Lerner, 1998. *(I; A)*

Englar, Mary. *Le Ly Hayslip (Asian-American Biographies Series).* Raintree, 2004. *(I)*

Hoyt-Goldsmith, Diane, and Migdale, Lawrence. *Hoang Anh: A Vietnamese-American Boy.* Holiday House, 1992. *(P; I)*

Kalman, Bobbie. *Vietnam: The Culture; Vietnam: The Land; Vietnam: The People.* Crabtree, 2002 (rev. ed.). *(P; I)*

Lorbiecki, Marybeth. *Children of Vietnam.* Lerner, 1996. *(I)*

Millett, Sandra. *Hmong of Southeast Asia.* Lerner, 2001. *(I)*

O'Connor, Karen. *Vietnam.* Lerner, 1999. *(P)*

Pascoe, Elaine. *The Pacific Rim: East Asia at the Dawn of a New Century.* Millbrook Press, 1999. *(A)*

Seah, Audrey. *Vietnam.* Marshall Cavendish, 1996 (2nd ed.). *(I; A)*

Viesti, Joseph F., and Hall, Diane. *Celebrate! in Southeast Asia.* HarperCollins, 1996. *(P; I)*

Vuong, Lynette Dyer. *The Golden Carp and Other Tales of Vietnam.* HarperCollins, 1993; *The Brocaded Slipper and Other Vietnamese Tales.* HarperCollins, 1992. *(P)*

Willis, Terri. *Vietnam.* Scholastic, 2001. *(I)*

VIETNAM WAR

Denenberg, Barry. *Voices From Vietnam.* Scholastic, 1997. *(A)*

Dudley, William. *The Vietnam War.* Greenhaven Press, 1997. *(A)*

Dunn, John M. *A History of U.S. Involvement.* Gale Group, 2001. *(I)*

Galt, Margot Fortunato. *Stop This War!: American Protest of the Conflict in Vietnam.* Lerner, 2000. *(A)*

Hoobler, Dorothy, and Hoobler, Thomas. *Vietnam: Why We Fought.* Knopf, 1990. *(I; A)*

Kallen, Stuart A. *Home Front: Americans Protest the War.* Gale Group, 2001. *(I; A)*

Marrin, Albert. *America and Vietnam: The Elephant and the Tiger.* Viking, 1992. *(A)*

McCormick, Anita Louise. *The Vietnam Antiwar Movement in American History.* Enslow, 2000. *(I; A)*

Roberts, Russell. *Leaders and Generals.* Gale Group, 2001. *(I; A)*

Schomp, Virginia. *The Vietnam War.* Marshall Cavendish, 2001. *(I; A)*

Willoughby, Douglas. *The Vietnam War.* Heinemann Library, 2001. *(I; A)*

Wright, David K. *A Multicultural Portrait of the War in Vietnam.* Benchmark, 1995. *(I)*

Young, Marilyn Blatt; Grunfeld, Tom A.; and Fitzgerald, John J. *Vietnam War: A History in Documents.* Oxford University Press, 2002. *(I; A)*

Zeinert, Karen. *The Valiant Women of the Vietnam War.* Millbrook, 2000. *(I; A)*

VIKINGS

Clare, John D., ed. *The Vikings.* Gulliver, 1992. *(I; A)*

Crompton, Samuel Willard. *Hastings.* Chelsea House, 2002. *(I; A)*

Gallagher, Jim. *The Viking Explorers.* Chelsea House, 2000. *(P; I)*

Humble, Richard. *The Age of Leif Eriksson.* Watts, 1989. *(I)*

Klingel, Cynthia Fitterer, and Noyed, Robert B. *Leif Eriksson: Norwegian Explorer.* Child's World, 2002. *(P; I)*

Pitkanen, Matti A., and Harkonen, Reijo. *The Grandchildren of the Vikings.* Lerner, 1996. *(P; I)*

Simon, Charnan. *Leif Eriksson and the Vikings.* Children's Press, 1991. *(I)*

West, Delno C., and West, Jean M. *Braving the North Atlantic: The Vikings, the Cabots, and Jacques Cartier Voyage to America.* Simon & Schuster, 1996. *(I)*

VIOLENCE AND SOCIETY

Schwartz, Ted. *Kids and Guns: The History, the Present, the Dangers, and the Remedies.* Watts, 1999. *(I; A)*

Torr, James D., and Swisher, Karin L., eds. *Violence against Women.* Greenhaven, 1998. *(A)*

VIRGINIA

Barrett, Tracy. *Virginia.* Marshall Cavendish, 1997. *(P; I)*

Blashfield, Jean F. *Virginia.* Scholastic, 1999 (2nd ed.). *(I; A)*

Cocke, William. *A Historical Album of Virginia.* Millbrook Press, 1995. *(I; A)*

De Angelis, Gina. *Virginia.* Scholastic, 2001. *(P; I)*

Hossell, Karen Price. *The Thirteen Colonies: Virginia.* Gale Group, 2001. *(I)*

Pollack, Pamela, and Craven, Jean. *Virginia: The Old Dominion.* Gareth Stevens, 2002. *(P; I)*

Sirvaitis, Karen. *Virginia.* Lerner, 1991. *(I)*

VIRUSES

Aronson, Virginia. *Influenza Pandemic of 1918-1919.* Chelsea House, 2000. *(I)*

Berger, Melvin. *Germs Make Me Sick!* HarperCollins, 1995. *(P)*

Biddle, Wayne. *Field Guide to Germs.* Henry Holt, 1995. *(A)*

Day, Nancy. *Killer Superbugs: The Story of Drug-Resistant Diseases.* Enslow, 2001. *(I; A)*

Draper, Allison Stark. *Ebola.* Rosen, 2002. *(I)*

Facklam, Howard, and Facklam, Margery. *Bacteria; Parasites; Viruses.* Twenty-First Century, 1995. *(I)*

Giblin, James Cross. *When Plague Strikes: The Black Death, Smallpox, AIDS.* HarperCollins, 1997. *(I; A)*

Hyde, Margaret O., and Forsyth, Elizabeth H. *Know About AIDS.* Walker, 1997 (3rd ed.). *(I; A)*

Manning, Karen. *AIDS: Can This Epidemic Be Stopped?* Millbrook Press, 1997. *(I; A)*

Monroe, Judy. *Influenza and Other Viruses.* Capstone Press, 2001. *(I)*

Nourse, Alan Edward. *Virus Invaders.* Watts, 1992. *(A)*

Rainis, Kenneth G., and Russell, Bruce J. *Guide to Microlife.* Scholastic, 1997. *(A)*

Sherrow, Victoria. *Polio Epidemic: Crippling Virus Outbreak.* Enslow, 2001. *(I)*

VOCATIONS

Ferguson's Careers in Focus: Alternative Health Care. Facts on File, 2003. *(A)*

Preparing for a Career in the Environment. Ferguson, 1998. *(A)*

What Can I Do Now/Nursing. Ferguson, 1998. *(A)*

Apel, Melanie Ann. *Cool Careers without College for Film and Television Buffs.* Rosen, 2002. *(I; A)*

Bickerstaff, Linda. *Cool Careers without College for People Who Love to Fix Things.* Rosen, 2002. *(I; A)*

Flender, Nicole. *Cool Careers without College for People Who Love Movement.* Rosen, 2002. *(I; A)*

Frederickson, Keville. *Opportunities in Nursing Careers.* VGM, 1995. *(A)*

Fulton, Michael. *Exploring Careers in Cyberspace.* Rosen, 1998. *(I; A)*

Gard, Carolyn. *Cool Careers without College for People Who Love to Sell Things.* Rosen, 2002. *(I; A)*

Gartner, Robert. *Exploring Careers in the National Parks.* Rosen, 1999 (rev. ed.). *(A)*

Giacobello, John. *Careers in the Fashion Industry.* Rosen, 2003 (rev. ed.). *(A)*

Greenberger, Robert. *Careers without College for People Who Love to Drive.* Rosen, 2003. *(I; A)*

Hayhurst, Chris. *Cool Careers without College for Animal Lovers.* Rosen, 2002. *(I; A)*

Heaton, Barrett. *Careers in the New Economy: Careers in Teaching.* Rosen, 2005. *(I; A)*

Hinton, Kerry. *Cool Careers without College for Music Lovers; Cool Careers without College for People Who Love Food.* Rosen, 2002. *(I; A)*

Hutton, Donald B., and Mydlarz, Anna. *Guide to Homeland Security Careers.* Barron's Educational Series, 2003. *(A)*

Mannino, Stephanie. *Cool Careers without College for People Who Love Crafts.* Rosen, 2002. *(I; A)*

Maynard, Thane. *Working with Wildlife: A Guide to Careers in the Animal World.* Watts, 1999. *(I; A)*

Maze, Stephanie. *I Want to Be a Fashion Designer.* Harcourt, 2000; *I Want to Be a Chef; I Want to Be a Firefighter.* Harcourt, 1999. *(P; I)*

McAlpine, Margaret. *Working in the Fashion Industry.* Gareth Stevens, 2005. *(I; A)*

Payment, Simone. *Cool Careers without College for People Who Love to Travel.* Rosen, 2002. *(I; A)*

Reeves, Diane Lindsey. *Career Ideas for Kids Who Like Science; Career Ideas for Kids Who Like Writing.* Facts on File, 1998. *(I; A)*

Ross, Allison J. *Choosing a Career in Waste Management.* Rosen, 2001. *(I; A)*

Sayre, April Pulley. *Put on Some Antlers and Walk Like a Moose: How Scientists Find, Follow, and Study Wild Animals.* Millbrook Press, 1997. *(I)*

Seidman, David L. *Exploring Careers in Journalism.* Rosen, 2000. *(I; A)*

Strazzabosco, Jeanne M. *Choosing a Career in Cosmetology.* Rosen, 1996. *(P; I)*

Walsh, Nora, ed. *Careers in Focus: Writing.* Ferguson, 2002 (2nd ed.). *(I; A)*

Webster, Harriet. *Cool Careers without College for People Who Love to Work with Children.* Rosen, 2002. *(I; A)*

VOLCANOES

Meister, Cari. *Volcanoes.* ABDO, 1999. *(P; I)*

Rogers, Daniel. *Volcanoes.* Raintree Steck-Vaughn, 1999. *(P)*

Tilling, Robert I. *Born of Fire: Volcanoes and Igneous Rocks.* Enslow, 1991. *(I; A)*

VOLLEYBALL

Crossingham, John, and Dann, Sarah. *Volleyball in Action.* Crabtree/A Bobbie Kalman Bk., 1999. *(P; I)*

Jensen, Julie. *Beginning Volleyball.* Lerner, 1995. *(P; I); Fundamental Volleyball.* Lerner, 1995. *(I; A)*

Manley, Claudia B. *Competitive Volleyball for Girls.* Rosen, 2002. *(P; I; A)*

VOLUNTEERISM

Black, Michael A. *Volunteering to Help Kids.* Scholastic, 2000. *(I; A)*

Isler, Claudia. *Volunteering to Help in Your Neighborhood; Volunteering to Help with Animals.* Children's Press, 2000. *(I; A)*

Klee, Sheila. *Volunteering for a Political Campaign.* Children's Press, 2000. *(I; A)*

Lewis, Barbara A., and Espeland, Pamela. *The Kid's Guide to Service Projects: Over 500 Service Ideas for Young People Who Want to Make a Difference.* Free Spirit, 1995. *(P; I; A)*

Meltzer, Milton. *Who Cares? Millions Do . . . A Book about Altruism.* Walker, 1994. *(I; A)*

Murdico, Suzanne J. *Volunteering to Help the Environment.* Scholastic, 2000. *(I: A)*

Newell, Patrick. *Volunteering to Help Seniors.* Children's Press, 2000. *(I; A)*

Perry, Susan K. *Catch the Spirit: Teen Volunteers Tell How They Made a Difference.* Watts, 2000. *(I; A)*

Wandberg, Robert. *Volunteering: Giving Back.* Capstone Press, 2001. *(I; A)*

W (LETTER)

Samoyault, Tiphaine. *Alphabetical Order: How the Alphabet Began.* Viking, 1998. *(P; I)*

WALES

Wales . . . in Pictures. Lerner, 1994. *(I)*

Heinrichs, Ann. *Wales.* Scholastic, 2003. *(I; A)*

Hestler, Anna. *Wales.* Marshall Cavendish, 2001. *(I; A)*

WALLENBERG, RAOUL

Streissguth, Thomas. *Raoul Wallenberg: Swedish Diplomat and Humanitarian.* Rosen, 2000. *(I; A)*

WALRUSES

Blum, Deborah, and Hirschmann, Kris. *Creatures of the Sea: The Walrus.* Thomson Gale, 2003. *(P; I)*

Lepthien, Emilie U. *Walruses.* Scholastic, 1997. *(P)*

Rotter, Charles. *Walruses.* Child's World, 2001 (2nd ed.). *(P)*

WAR OF 1812

Bosco, Peter I. *The War of 1812.* Millbrook Press, 1991. *(I)*

Greenblatt, Miriam. *The War of 1812.* Facts on File, 1994. *(I; A)*

Santella, Andrew. *The War of 1812.* Scholastic, 2001. *(I)*

Stefoff, Rebecca. *The War of 1812.* Marshall Cavendish, 2000. *(I)*

WARSAW

Landau, Elaine. *The Warsaw Ghetto Uprising.* Simon & Schuster, 1992. *(I; A)*

WASHINGTON

Barenblat, Rachel, and Craven, Jean. *Washington: The Evergreen State.* Gareth Stevens, 2002. *(P; I)*

Blashfield, Jean F. *Washington.* Scholastic, 2001 (2nd ed.). *(I; A)*

Cocke, William. *A Historical Album of Washington.* Millbrook Press, 1995. *(I; A)*

Fradin, Dennis Brindell, and Fradin, Judith Bloom. *Washington: From Sea to Shining Sea.* Scholastic, 1995. *(P; I)*

Stefoff, Rebecca. *Washington.* Marshall Cavendish, 1998. *(P; I)*

Stein, Richard Conrad. *Washington.* Scholastic, 1996. *(I; A)*

Webster, Christine. *Washington.* Scholastic, 2003. *(P; I)*

WASHINGTON, BOOKER T.

Amper, Thomas. *Booker T. Washington.* Lerner, 2001. *(P)*

Hauser, Pierre. *Great Ambitions: From the 'Separate but Equal' Doctrine to the Birth of the NAACP.* Chelsea House, 1995. *(A)*

McKissack, Patricia C., and McKissack, Frederick L. *The Story of Booker T. Washington.* Scholastic, 1991. *(P; I)*

Schroeder, Alan. *Booker T. Washington.* Chelsea House, 1992. *(A)*

Troy, Don. *Booker T. Washington.* Child's World, 1999. *(P; I)*

Washington, Booker T. *Up from Slavery.* Airmont, n.d. *(I; A)*

WASHINGTON, D.C.

Ashabranner, Brent K. *On the Mall in Washington, D.C.: A Visit to America's Front Yard.* Twenty-First Century, 2002. *(P; I); No Better Hope: What the Lincoln Memorial Means to America.* Twenty-First Century, 2001. *(P; I); Remembering Korea: The Korean War*

Veterans Memorial. Twenty-First Century, 2001. *(I; A)*; *A Date with Destiny: The Women in Military Service for America Memorial; Badge of Valor: The National Law Enforcement Officers Memorial*. Twenty-First Century, 2000. *(I)*; *Their Names to Live: What the Vietnam Veterans Memorial Means to America*. Twenty-First Century, 1998. *(I)*; *Memorial for Mr. Lincoln*. Putnam, 1992. *(I; A)*; *Always to Remember: The Story of the Vietnam Veterans Memorial*. Scholastic, 1991. *(P; I)*; *A Grateful Nation: The Story of Arlington National Cemetery*. Putnam, 1990. *(I)*

Ashley, Susan, and Nations, Susan. *The Washington Monument*. Weekly Reader Early Learning Library, 2003. *(P)*

Doherty, Craig A., and Doherty, Katherine M. *The Washington Monument*. Gale Group, 1995. *(I)*

Elish, Dan. *Washington, D.C.* Marshall Cavendish, 1998. *(P; I)*

Feeney, Kathy. *Washington, D.C. Facts and Symbols*. Capstone/Hilltop, 2000. *(P)*

Fradin, Dennis Brindell. *Washington, D.C.: From Sea to Shining Sea*. Scholastic, 1994. *(P; I)*

Furman, Elina; Matusevich, Melissa N.; and Flynn, Margaret E. *Washington, D.C.* Scholastic, 2002. *(P; I)*

Hinman, Bonnie, and Schlesinger, Arthur Meier. *Benjamin Banneker: American Mathematician and Astronomer (Colonial Leaders Series)*. Chelsea House, 2000. *(P; I)*

Johnston, Joyce. *Washington D.C.* Lerner, 2001 (2nd ed.). *(P; I)*

Stein, Richard Conrad. *Cities of the World: Washington D.C.* Scholastic, 1999. *(P; I)*

WASHINGTON, GEORGE

D'Aulaire, Ingri, and D'Aulaire, Edgar P. *George Washington*. Doubleday, n.d. *(P)*

Feinstein, Stephen. *George Washington*. Enslow, 2002. *(I; A)*

Ferrie, Richard. *The World Turned Upside Down: George Washington and the Battle of Yorktown*. Holiday, 1999. *(I; A)*

Gaines, Ann Graham. *George Washington: Our First President*. Child's World, 2002. *(P; I)*

Giblin, James Cross. *George Washington: A Picture Book Biography*. Scholastic, 1992. *(P)*

Harness, Cheryl. *George Washington*. National Geographic, 2000. *(P; I)*

January, Brendan. *George Washington (Encyclopedia of Presidents, Second Series)*. Scholastic, 2003. *(I; A)*

Johnson, Paul. *George Washington: The Founding Father (Eminent Lives Series)*. HarperCollins, 2005. *(A)*

Jurmain, Suzanne Tripp. *George Did It*. Penguin, 2006. *(P; I)*

McNeese, Tim. *George Washington: America's Leader in War and Peace (Leaders of the American Revolution Series)*. Chelsea House, 2006. *(I)*

Old, Wendie C. *George Washington*. Enslow, 1997. *(I; A)*

WATCHES

Dash, Joan. *The Longitude Prize*. Farrar, 2000. *(I; A)*

Duffy, Trent. *The Clock*. Simon & Schuster/Atheneum, 2000. *(I; A)*

Maestro, Betsy C. *The Story of Clocks and Calendars: Marking a Millennium*. Morrow, 1999. *(P; I)*

Older, Jules. *Telling Time: How to Tell Time on Digital and Analog Clocks!* Charlesbridge, 2000. *(P)*

WATER

Berger, Melvin, and Berger, Gilda. *Water, Water Everywhere*. Chelsea House, 1998. *(P)*

Gallant, Roy A. *Water*. Marshall Cavendish, 2000. *(P; I)*

Tocci, Salvatore. *Experiments with Water*. Scholastic, 2001. *(P)*

Walker, Sally M. *Water up, Water down: The Hydrologic Cycle*. Carolrhoda, 1992. *(I)*

Williams, John. *Water Projects*. Steck-Vaughn, 1997. *(I)*

WATERGATE

Fremon, David K. *The Watergate Scandal in American History*. Enslow, 1997. *(I; A)*

Genovese, Michael A. *The Watergate Crisis*. Greenwood, 1999. *(A)*

Herda, D. J. *United States v. Nixon: Watergate and the President*. Enslow, 1996. *(I; A)*

WEATHER

Allaby, Michael. *A Chronology of Weather (Dangerous Weather Series)*. Facts on File, 2003 (2nd ed.). *(I; A)*

Bortz, Alfred B., and Shepherd, J. Marshall. *Dr. Fred's Weather Watch: Create and Run Your Own Weather Station*. Lerner, 2000. *(I; A)*

Branley, Franklyn. *Flash, Crash, Rumble, and Roll*. HarperCollins, 1999. *(P)*; *It's Raining Cats and Dogs: All Kinds of Weather and Why We Have It*. Morrow/Avon, 1993. *(P; I)*

DeWitt, Lynda, and Croll, Carolyn. *What Will the Weather Be?* HarperCollins, 1993 (reprint). *(P)*

DiSpezio, Michael. *Weather Mania: Discovering What's Up and What's Coming Down*. Sterling, 2002. *(I)*

Gardner, Robert, and Webster, David. *Science Projects about Weather*. Enslow, 1994. *(I; A)*

Gold, Susan Dudley. *Blame It on El Niño*. Raintree Steck-Vaughn, 1999. *(I; A)*

Llewellyn, Claire. *Wild, Wet and Windy: The Weather-From Hurricanes to Monsoons (SuperSmarts Series)*. Candlewick Press, 1997. *(P)*

Rodgers, Alan, and Streluk, Angella. *Cloud Cover; Forecasting the Weather; Precipitation; Temperature; Wind and Air Pressure*. Heinemann, 2002. *(P; I)*

Sayre, April Pulley. *El Niño and La Niña: Weather in the Headlines*. Millbrook Press, 2000. *(I; A)*

Silverstein, Alvin, and others. *Weather and Climate*. Twenty-First Century, 1998. *(P; I)*

Simon, Seymour. *Weather*. HarperCollins, 2006; *Hurricanes*. HarperCollins, 2003; *Tornadoes*. HarperCollins, 2001;

Lightning. HarperCollins, 1997; *Storms.* HarperCollins, 1992. *(P; I)*

Singer, Marilyn. *On the Same Day in March: A Tour of the World's Weather.* HarperCollins, 2000. *(P)*

VanCleave, Janice. *Janice VanCleave's Weather: Mind-Boggling Experiments You Can Turn into Science Fair Projects.* Wiley, 1995. *(P; I)*

Vecchione, Glen. *100 First-Prize Make-It Yourself Science Fair Projects.* Sterling, 1998. *(I; A)*

Yvart, Jacques. *The Rising of the Wind: Adventures along the Beaufort Scale.* Simon & Schuster, 1991. *(I)*

WEIGHT LIFTING

Baechle, Thomas R., and Groves, Barney R. *Weight Training: Steps to Success.* Human Kinetics Publishers, 1998 (2nd ed.). *(A)*

Lund, Bill. *Weight Lifting.* Capstone Press, 1996. *(I)*

Reef, Catherine. *Stay Fit: Build a Strong Body.* Millbrook Press, 1997. *(P; I)*

Savage, Jeff. *Fundamental Strength Training.* Lerner, 1998; *Weight Lifting.* Silver Burdett Press, 1995. *(I; A)*

WEIGHTS AND MEASURES

Bendick, Jeanne. *How Much and How Many? The Story of Weights and Measures.* Watts, 1989. *(P; I)*

WELLS, H. G.

Coren, Stanley. *Invisible Man: The Life and Liberties of H. G. Wells.* Macmillan, 1993. *(A)*

WESTERN SAMOA

Deverell, Gweneth. *Follow the Sun...to Tahiti, to Western Samoa, to Fiji, to Melanesia, to Micronesia.* Friends Press, 1982. *(P)*

WEST VIRGINIA

Fazio, Wende. *West Virginia* Scholastic, 2000 (2nd ed.). *(I; A)*

Feeney, Kathy. *West Virginia: Facts and Symbols.* Capstone/Hilltop, 2000. *(P)*

Fontes, Justine, and Fontes, Ron. *West Virginia: The Mountain State.* Gareth Stevens, 2003. *(P; I)*

Fradin, Dennis Brindell. *West Virginia: From Sea to Shining Sea.* Scholastic, 1996. *(P; I)*

Hoffman, Nancy. *West Virginia.* Marshall Cavendish, 1998. *(P; I)*

Somervill, Barbara A.; Matusevich, Melissa N.; and Doss, Georgina. *West Virginia.* Scholastic, 2003. *(P; I)*

WESTWARD MOVEMENT

Barr, Roger. *The American Frontier (World History Series).* Thomson Gale, 1995. *(I; A)*

Bentley, Judith. *Settling the West: Brides, Midwives, and Widows; Settling the West: Explorers, Trappers, and Guides; Settling the West: Farmers and Ranchers; Settling the West: Loggers and Railroad Workers; Settling the West: Miners, Merchants, and Maids; Set-tling the West: Preachers and Teachers.* Lerner, 1997. *(I; A)*

Dolan, Edward F. *Beyond the Frontier: The Story of the Trails West.* Benchmark, 1999. *(I; A)*

Duncan, Dayton. *People of the West; The West: An Illustrated History for Children.* Little, 1996. *(I; A)*

Katz, William Loren. *Black Women of the Old West.* Atheneum, 1995. *(I)*

Kozar, Richard. *Daniel Boone and the Exploration of the Frontier; Lewis and Clark: Explorers of the Louisiana Purchase.* Chelsea House, 1999. *(I)*

Marrin, Albert. *Cowboys, Indians, and Gunfighters: The Story of the Cattle Kingdom.* Simon & Schuster, 1993. *(I; A)*

Peavy, Linda, and Smith, Ursula. *Pioneer Women: The Lives of Women of the Frontier.* University of Oklahoma Press, 1998; *Women in Waiting in the Westward Movement: Life on the Home Frontier.* University of Oklahoma Press, 1994. *(I; A)*

Takaki, Ronald. *Journey to Gold Mountain: The Chinese in 19th-Century America.* Chelsea House, 1994. *(I)*

Torr, James D., ed. *Westward Expansion (Interpreting American History Through Primary Documents Series).* Thomson Gale, 2002. *(A)*

Uschan, Michael V. *Westward Expansion.* Thomson Gale, 2001. *(I; A)*

Worth, Richard. *Westward Expansion and Manifest Destiny (In American History Series).* Enslow, 2001. *(I; A)*

WETLANDS

Amsel, Sheri. *A Wetland Walk.* Millbrook, 1993. *(P; I)*

Blaustein, Daniel. *Everglades and the Gulf Coast.* Marshall Cavendish, 2000. *(I)*

Cone, Molly. *Squishy, Misty, Damp & Muddy: The In-Between World of Wetlands.* Sierra Club, 1996. *(P; I)*

Levete, Sarah. *Rivers and Lakes.* Millbrook Press, 1999. *(P; I)*

Lisowski, Marilyn, and Williams, Robert A. *Wetlands.* Scholastic, 1997. *(I; A)*

Matthews, Downs. *Wetlands.* Simon & Schuster, 1994. *(P)*

Rood, Ronald. *Wetlands.* HarperCollins, 1994. *(P)*

Sayre, April Pulley. *River and Stream; Wetland.* Millbrook Press, 1997. *(I)*

Staub, Frank. *America's Wetlands.* Carolrhoda, 1995. *(I; A)*

Taylor, Dave. *Endangered Wetland Animals.* Crabtree, 1992. *(P)*

WHALES

Berger, Melvin, and Berger, Gilda. *Do Whales Have Belly Buttons?: Questions and Answers about Whales and Dolphins.* Scholastic, 1999. *(P)*

Calambokidis, John, and Steiger, Gretchen. *Blue Whales.* Voyageur Press, 1997. *(A)*

Clapham, Phil. *Whales of the World.* Voyageur Press, 2001. *(I; A)*

Darling, Jim. *Gray Whales.* Voyageur, 1999. *(I; A)*

Gibbons, Gail. *Whales.* Holiday, 1991. *(P)*

Harman, Amanda, and Horton, Casey. *Endangered!: Whales.* Marshall Cavendish, 1996. *(P; I)*

Kelsey, Elin. *Finding Out about Whales.* Owl, 1998. *(P; I)*

Kraus, Scott, and Mallory, Kenneth. *The Search for the Right Whale: How Scientists Rediscovered the Most Endangered Whale in the Sea.* Crown, 1993. *(I)*

Lauber, Patricia. *Great Whales: The Gentle Giants.* Holt, 1991. *(P; I)*

McMillan, Bruce. *Going on a Whale Watch.* Scholastic, 1992. *(P)*

McNulty, Faith. *How Whales Walked into the Sea.* Scholastic, 1999. *(P)*

Sayre, April Pulley. *Secrets of Sound: Studying the Calls of Whales, Elephants, and Birds.* Houghton Mifflin, 2002. *(I; A)*

Thomas, Peggy. *Marine Mammal Preservation.* Millbrook Press, 2000. *(I)*

WHITE, E. B.

Gherman, Beverly. *E. B. White: Some Writer!* Simon & Schuster, 1992. *(I; A)*

LaBrie, Aimee. *E. B. White.* Chelsea House, 2005. *(I)*

WHITE HOUSE

Ashley, Susan, and Nations, Susan. *The White House.* Weekly Reader Early Learning Library, 2003. *(P)*

Quiri, Patricia Ryon. *The White House.* Watts, 1996. *(P; I)*

WHITMAN, WALT

Halliwell, Sarah, ed. *19th Century: Artists, Writers, and Composers.* Raintree, 1998. *(I)*

Loving, Jerome. *Walt Whitman: The Song of Himself.* University of California Press, 2000. *(A)*

WILDFLOWERS

Burns, Diane L. *Wildflowers, Blooms, and Blossoms.* Sagebrush Education Resources, 1998. *(P; I)*

Hood, Susan. *National Audubon Society First Field Guide: Wildflowers.* Scholastic, 1998. *(I; A)*

Ryden, Hope. *Wildflowers Around the Year.* Houghton Mifflin, 2001. *(P; I)*

WILLIAM I (THE CONQUEROR)

Crompton, Samuel Willard. *Hastings.* Chelsea House, 2002. *(I; A)*

Konstam, Angus, and Kean, Roger. *Atlas of Medieval Europe.* Facts on File, 2000. *(A)*

WILSON, WOODROW

Brunelli, Carol, and Gaines, Ann Graham. *Woodrow Wilson: Our Twenty-Eighth President.* Child's World, 2001. *(P; I)*

Feinberg, Barbara Silberdick. *Woodrow Wilson (Encyclopedia of Presidents, Second Series).* Scholastic, 2004. *(I; A)*

WINDS

Carless, Jennifer. *Renewable Energy: A Concise Guide to Green Alternatives.* Walker, 1993. *(A)*

Friend, Sandra. *Earth's Wild Winds.* Millbrook Press, 2002. *(I)*

Petersen, Christine. *Alternative Energy; Wind Power.* Scholastic, 2004. *(P)*

Rodgers, Alan, and Streluk, Angella. *Wind and Air Pressure.* Heinemann, 2002. *(P; I)*

WITCHCRAFT

Aronson, Marc. *Witch-Hunt: Mysteries of the Salem Witch Trials.* Simon & Schuster, 2003. *(A)*

Netzley, Patricia D. *Witchcraft.* Gale Group, 2002. *(A)*

WOLVES

Berger, Melvin, and Berger, Gilda. *Why Do Wolves Howl?: Questions and Answers about Wolves.* Scholastic, 2002. *(P)*

Brandenburg, Jim, and Guernsey, Joann Bren. *To the Top of the World: Adventures with Arctic Wolves.* Walker, 1995. *(P; I)*

Dudley, Karen. *Wolves.* Raintree Steck-Vaughn, 1998. *(P; I)*

Gibbons, Gail. *Wolves.* Holiday, 1994. *(P)*

Greenaway, Theresa. *Wolves, Wild Dogs and Foxes.* Raintree Steck-Vaughn, 2001. *(P; I)*

Hodge, Deborah. *Wild Dogs: Wolves, Coyotes and Foxes.* Kids Can Press, 1997. *(P)*

Martin, Patricia A. *Gray Wolves.* Scholastic, 2001. *(P)*

Milton, Joyce. *Wild, Wild Wolves.* Random House, 1992. *(P)*

Parker, Barbara Keevil. *North American Wolves.* Lerner, 1997. *(P; I)*

Simon, Seymour. *Wolves.* HarperCollins, 1995. *(P; I)*

Smith, Roland. *Journey of the Red Wolf.* Cobblehill, 1996. *(I)*

Swinburne, Stephen R. *Once a Wolf: How Wildlife Biologists Fought to Bring Back the Gray Wolf.* Houghton, 1999. *(I)*

Zeaman, John. *How the Wolf Became a Dog.* Scholastic, 1998. *(P; I)*

WOMEN'S RIGHTS MOVEMENT

Archer, Jules. *Breaking Barriers: The Feminist Movement from Susan B. Anthony to Margaret Sanger to Betty Friedan.* Viking, 1991. *(A)*

Gay, Kathlyn. *The New Power of Women in Politics.* Enslow, 1994. *(A)*

Gulotta, Charles. *Extraordinary Women in Politics.* Children's Press, 1998. *(I; A)*

Johnston, Norma. *Remember the Ladies.* Scholastic, 1995. *(I)*

Kops, Deborah. *People at the Center of: Women's Suffrage.* Blackbirch Press, 2003. *(I)*

Long, Barbara. *United States v. Virginia: Virginia Military Institute Accepts Women.* Enslow, 2000. *(I; A)*

McPherson, Stephanie Sammartino. *I Speak for the Women: A Story about Lucy Stone*. Carolrhoda, 1992. *(I)*

Weatherford, Doris. *A History of the American Suffragist Movement*. A B C-CLIO, 1998. *(A)*

Wekesser, Carol, and Polesetsky, Matthew, eds. *Women in the Military*. Greenhaven, 1991. *(I; A)*

WOOD, GRANT

Duggleby, John. *Artist in Overalls: The Life of Grant Wood*. Chronicle, 1996. *(I)*

Venezia, Mike, and Moss, Meg. *Grant Wood*. Scholastic, 1996. *(P)*

WOOD AND WOOD PRODUCTS

Cowan, Mary Morton. *Timberrr!: A History of Logging in New England*. Lerner, 2003. *(I; A)*

Jaspersohn, William. *Timber: From Trees to Wood Products, Vol. 1*. Little, Brown & Co., 1996. *(P)*

Martin, Patricia A. Fink. *Woods and Forests*. Watts, 2000. *(I; A)*

WORDSWORTH, WILLIAM

Bloom, Harold, ed. *William Wordsworth (Bloom's Major Poets Series)*. Chelsea House, 1999. *(A)*

Halliwell, Sarah, ed. *The Romantics: Artists, Writers, and Composers*. Raintree, 1998. *(I)*

WORK, POWER, AND MACHINES

Camenson, Blythe. *Real People Working in Mechanics, Installation, and Repair (On the Job Series)*. NTC, 1999. *(A)*

Hewitt, Sally. *It's Science: Machines We Use*. Scholastic, 1998. *(P)*

Lampton, Christopher. *Sailboats, Flag Poles, Cranes: Using Pulleys as Simple Machines*. Millbrook Press, 1991. *(P)*

Walker, Sally M., and Feldmann, Roseann. *Inclined Planes and Wedges; Levers; Pulleys; Wheels and Axles; Work*. Lerner, 2001. *(P)*

Woods, Michael, and Woods, Mary B. *Ancient Machines: From Wedges to Waterwheels*. Lerner, 1999. *(I)*

WORLD WAR I

Collier, Christopher, and Collier, James L. *The United States Enters the World Stage: From Alaska through World War I, 1867-1919*. Marshall Cavendish, 2000. *(I; A)*

Dolan, Edward F. *America in World War I*. Millbrook, 1996. *(I; A)*

Feinstein, Stephen. *The 1910's from World War I to Ragtime Music*. Enslow, 2001. *(I)*

Gilbert, Adrian. *Going to War in World War I*. Scholastic, 2001.

Kent, Zachary. *World War I: The War to End Wars*. Enslow, 1994. *(I; A)*

Kirchberger, Joe H. *The First World War: An Eyewitness History*. Facts on File, 1992. *(A)*

Rice, Earl, Jr. *The Battle of Belleau*. Gale Group, 1996. *(I; A)*

Stewart, Gail B. *World War I*. Lucent, 1991. *(I; A)*

WORLD WAR II

Ambrose, Stephen E. *The Good Fight: How World War II Was Won*. Simon & Schuster, 2001. *(I; A)*

Anthony, Nathan, and Gardner, Robert. *The Bombing of Pearl Harbor (In American History Series)*. Enslow, 2000. *(I; A)*

Barr, Gary. *Pearl Harbor (Witness to History Series); Pearl Harbor (Witness to History Series); World War II Home Front (Witness to History Series)*. Heinemann, 2004. *(I)*

Dunnahoo, Terry. *Pearl Harbor: America Enters the War*. Watts, 1991. *(I; A)*

Harris, Jacqueline L. *The Tuskegee Airmen: Black Heroes of World War II*. Silver Burdett Press, 1995. *(I; A)*

Inada, Lawson Fusao, ed. *Only What We Could Carry: The Japanese American Internment Experience*. Heyday, 2001. *(A)*

Knapp, Ron, and Green, Carl R. *American Generals of World War II*. Enslow, 1998. *(I)*

Krull, Kathleen. *V is for Victory: America Remembers World War II*. Random House, 2002. *(I; A)*

Morimoto, Junko. *My Hiroshima*. Viking, 1990. *(I)*

Oleksy, Walter G. *Military Leaders of World War II*. Facts on File, 1994. *(I; A)*

Perl, Lila. *Barbed Wire and Guard Towers: The Internment of Japanese Americans during World War II*. Marshall Cavendish, 2002. *(I; A)*

Pietrusza, David. *The Invasion of Normandy: Battles of World War II*. Gale Group, 1995. *(I; A)*

Rice, Earl, Jr. *Strategic Battles in the Pacific*. Gale Group, 2000; *The Battle of Britain; The Battle of Midway*. Gale Group, 1996. *(I; A)*

Tunnell, Michael O., and Chilcoat, George W. *The Children of Topaz: The Story of a Japanese American Internment Camp: Based on a Classroom Diary*. Holiday, 1996. *(I)*

Whiting, Jim. *Pearl Harbor and the Story of World War II*. Mitchell Lane, 2005. *(I)*

Zeinert, Karen. *Those Incredible Women of World War II*. Millbrook Press, 1994. *(I; A)*

WRIGHT, FRANK LLOYD

Boulton, Alexander O. *Frank Lloyd Wright, Architect: An Illustrated Biography*. Rizzoli, 1993. *(I; A)*

McDonough, Yona Z. *Frank Lloyd Wright*. Chelsea House, 1992. *(I; A)*

WRIGHT, WILBUR AND ORVILLE

Busby, Peter. *First to Fly: How Wilbur and Orville Wright Invented the Airplane*. Crown, 2003. *(I)*

Collins, Mary. *Airborne: A Photobiography of Wilbur and Orville Wright*. National Geographic Society, 2003. *(I; A)*

Freedman, Russell. *The Wright Brothers: How They Invented the Airplane*. Holiday, 1991. *(I)*

Krensky, Stephen. *Taking Flight: The Story of the Wright Brothers.* Simon & Schuster, 2000. *(P)*

MacLeod, Elizabeth. *The Wright Brothers: A Flying Start.* Kids Can Press, 2002. *(P; I)*

Old, Wendie C., and Parker, Robert Andrew. *To Fly: The Story of the Wright Brothers.* Houghton Mifflin, 2002. *(P; I)*

WRITING

Bauer, Marion Dane. *Our Stories: A Fiction Workshop for Young Authors.* Houghton Mifflin, 1996; *A Writer's Story: From Life to Fiction.* Houghton Mifflin, 1995; *What's Your Story?: A Young Person's Guide to Writing Fiction.* Houghton Mifflin, 1992. *(I; A)*

Bentley, Nancy, and Guthrie, Donna. *The Young Author's Do-It-Yourself Book: How to Write, Illustrate, and Produce Your Own Book.* Lerner, 1994. *(P; I)*

Dragisic, Patricia. *How to Write a Letter.* Scholastic, 1998. *(A)*

Fleischman, Sid. *The Abracadabra Kid: A Writer's Life.* Greenwillow, 1996. *(I; A)*

Janeczko, Paul B. *Writing Winning Reports and Essays.* Scholastic, 2003. *(I)*

Krementz, Jill. *The Writer's Desk.* Knopf, 1996. *(A)*

Lester, Helen. *Author: A True Story.* Houghton/Lorraine, 1997. *(P)*

Lindberg, Christine A. *Oxford American Writer's Thesaurus.* Oxford University Press, 2004. *(I; A)*

Nobleman, Marc Tyler. *Extraordinary E-mails, Letters, and Resumes.* Scholastic, 2006. *(I)*

Orr, Tamra. *Extraordinary Essays.* Scholastic, 2006. *(I)*

Otfinoski, Steven. *Extraordinary Short Story Writing.* Scholastic, 2006. *(I)*

Peet, Bill. *Bill Peet: An Autobiography.* Houghton, 1994. *(P; I)*

Policoff, Stephen Phillip, and Skinner, Jeffrey. *Real Toads in Imaginary Gardens: Suggestions and Starting Points for Young Creative Writers.* Chicago Review Press, 1991. *(A)*

Prelutsky, Jack. *Read a Poem, Write a Poem.* Random House, 2005. *(P)*

Ryan, Margaret. *How to Write a Poem.* Scholastic, 1996. *(A)*

Walsh, Nora, ed. *Careers in Focus: Writing.* Ferguson, 2002 (2nd ed.). *(I; A)*

Wong, Janet S. *You Have to Write.* Simon & Schuster, 2002. *(P; I)*

WYOMING

Baldwin, Ely, and Baldwin, Guy. *Wyoming.* Marshall Cavendish, 1999. *(P; I)*

Dubois, Muriel L. *Wyoming: Facts and Symbols.* Capstone/Hilltop, 2000. *(P)*

Fradin, Dennis Brindell, and Fradin, Judith Bloom. *Wyoming: From Sea to Shining Sea.* Scholastic, 1996. *(P; I)*

Frisch, Calienne A. *Wyoming.* Lerner, 1994. *(P; I)*

Kent, Deborah. *Wyoming.* Scholastic, 2000 (2nd ed.). *(I; A)*

Korman, Justine, and Fontes, Ron. *Wyoming: The Equality State.* Gareth Stevens, 2003. *(P; I)*

Petersen, David. *Yellowstone National Park.* Scholastic, 2001; *Grand Teton National Park.* Scholastic, 1992. *(P; I)*

Tufts, Lorraine S. *Secrets in Yellowstone and Grand Teton National Parks.* National Photographic Collections, 1997. *(P; I)*

X (LETTER)

Samoyault, Tiphaine. *Alphabetical Order: How the Alphabet Began.* Viking, 1998. *(P; I)*

X-RAYS

McClafferty, Carla Killough. *The Head Bone's Connected to the Neck Bone: The Weird, Wacky, and Wonderful X-Rays.* Farrar, 2001. *(I)*

Parker, Janice. *Engines, Elevators, and X-Rays (Science at Work).* Raintree Steck-Vaughn, 2000. *(I)*

Skurzynski, Gloria. *Waves: The Electro-Magnetic Universe.* National Geographic, 1996. *(P; I)*

Winkler, Kathy. *Radiology: Inventors and Inventions.* Marshall Cavendish, 1996. *(I)*

Y (LETTER)

Samoyault, Tiphaine. *Alphabetical Order: How the Alphabet Began.* Viking, 1998. *(P; I)*

YANGTZE (CHANG) RIVER

Olson, Nathan, and Hordon, Robert M. *Land and Water: The Yangtze River.* Capstone Press, 2004. *(P; I)*

Pollard, Michael. *The Yangtze.* Marshall Cavendish, 1997. *(I)*

YELTSIN, BORIS

Otfinoski, Steven. *Boris Yeltsin: And the Rebirth of Russia.* Millbrook, 1995. *(I; A)*

YEMEN

Hestler, Anna. *Yemen.* Marshall Cavendish, 1999 (2nd ed.). *(I; A)*

Marcovitz, Hal. *Yemen.* Mason Crest, 2002. *(I; A)*

Rodgers, Mary M., ed. *Yemen . . . in Pictures.* Lerner, 1993. *(I)*

YUGOSLAVIA

Andryszewski, Tricia. *Kosovo: The Splintering of Yugoslavia.* Millbrook, 2000. *(I; A)*

Dornberg, John. *Central and Eastern Europe.* Greenwood, 1995. *(A)*

YUKON TERRITORY

Levert, Suzanne. *Yukon.* Chelsea House, 1992. *(I; A)*

Z (LETTER)

Samoyault, Tiphaine. *Alphabetical Order: How the Alphabet Began.* Viking, 1998. *(P; I)*

ZAMBIA

Brown, Ernest Douglas, and Ibeanu, A.M. *Lozi (Zambia).* Rosen, 1997. *(I; A)*

Grotpeter, John J.; Siegel, Brian V.; and Pletcher, James R. *Historical Dictionary of Zambia.* Rowman & Littlefield, 1998 (2nd ed.). *(A)*

Holmes, Timothy. *Zambia.* Benchmark, 1998. *(P; I)*

Jordan, Manuel. *Chokwe (Angola, Zambia).* Rosen, 1997. *(I; A)*

Laure, Jason. *Zambia.* Scholastic, 1996 (rev. ed.). *(I)*

ZIMBABWE

Baughan, Michael Gray. *Zimbabwe (Africa - Continent in the Balance Series).* Mason Crest, 2004. *(I; A)*

Bessire, Mark H. *Great Zimbabwe.* Scholastic, 1999. *(P; I)*

Laure, Jason. *Zimbabwe.* Scholastic, 1996 (rev. ed.). *(I)*

O'Toole, Thomas E. *Zimbabwe... in Pictures.* Lerner, 1997. *(I; A)*

Rogers, Barbara Radcliffe, and Rogers, Stillman D. *Zimbabwe.* Scholastic, 2002. *(I; A)*

Van Wyk, Gary N. *Shona (Zimbabwe).* Rosen, 1997. *(I; A)*

ZINC

Heiserman, David L. *Exploring Chemical Elements and Their Compounds.* McGraw-Hill, 1991. *(A)*

ZIONISM

Chicoine, Stephen D., and Ayer, Eleanor H. *Holocaust: From the Ashes, June 1945 and After, Vol. 6.* Gale Group, 1997. *(I; A)*

Finkelstein, Norman H. *Theodor Herzl: Architect of a Nation.* Lerner, 1991 (rev. ed.). *(I; A)*

ZODIAC

Aslan, Madalyn. *What's Your Sign?: A Cosmic Guide for Young Astrologers.* Penguin Putnam, 2002. *(I; A)*

Gravalle, Karen. *Five Ways to Know about You.* Walker, 2001. *(I; A)*

ZOOS

Curtis, Patricia. *Animals and the New Zoos.* Lodestar, 1991. *(I)*

Knight, Bertram T. *Working at a Zoo.* Scholastic, 1999. *(P)*

Lauber, Patricia. *The Tiger Has a Toothache: Helping Animals at the Zoo.* National Geographic Society, 1999. *(P)*

Ricciuti, Edward R. *A Pelican Swallowed My Head and Other Zoo Stories.* Simon & Schuster, 2002. *(I)*

Smith, Roland. *Cats in the Zoo; Whales, Dolphins, and Porpoises in the Zoo.* Millbrook Press, 1994. *(P; I)*; *Inside the Zoo Nursery.* Dutton, 1992. *(I)*

Yancey, Diane. *Zoos.* Gale Group, 1994. *(I)*

ZOROASTRIANISM

Hartz, Paula R. *Zoroastrianism.* Facts on File, 1999. *(I; A)*

ZURICH

Bullen, Susan. *The Alps and Their People.* Raintree Steck-Vaughn, 1994. *(P; I)*

Harvey, Miles. *Look What Came from Switzerland.* Scholastic, 2001. *(P)*

PART II
THE STUDY GUIDE

INTRODUCTION

THE NEW BOOK OF KNOWLEDGE is a valuable source of information. Whether you are searching for the answer to a question that made a conversation with a child memorable or investigating a topic for a young student's school assignment, this encyclopedia will help you find the information you need.

THE NEW BOOK OF KNOWLEDGE can be used in a variety of settings—home, school, and library. It is written in a clear, direct style and organized so that information can be located quickly and easily. Precise and colorful photographs, illustrations, maps, charts, and diagrams assist understanding and encourage further reading and browsing. Articles are written by experts in their fields and cover topics of general interest as well as every important area of the school curriculum. Among the many categories covered are literature, language arts, history, government, geography, mathematics, social, natural, and physical sciences, technology, health and safety, art, music, and sports and physical education.

The HOME AND SCHOOL STUDY GUIDE was prepared to help teachers, librarians, and especially parents make optimal use of THE NEW BOOK OF KNOWLEDGE. The first part of the Study Guide offers suggestions about how the home-school partnership can assist the education of children. This is followed by an overview of school curriculum areas. The Study Guide then discusses the school years in three separate sections: Kindergarten through Grade 3; Grades 4 through 6; and Grades 7 through 9. Each section briefly describes what children will be learning in the classroom at those grade levels and then lists some of the articles in the set that are important to each curriculum area at those grade levels. These lists of curriculum-related articles can be used in several ways with young people. For example:

- To identify and skim through articles about a topic before it is actually covered in the classroom. This can provide important background knowledge for youngsters that will help them understand and remember information about the topic presented in class. This activity can also make the topic more interesting.
- The lists can be used to locate articles in which answers to specific questions raised in the classroom or information needed for homework assignments, research projects, or writing reports can be found. As they seek out the information they need, students will also find in the set cross-references to additional articles that will help them complete their assignments.
- Some students want to know more about subjects of particular interest to them, and they will find their interests satisfied and their learning enhanced by reading the variety of articles listed about that subject.

Learning the habit of turning to reference books for information is invaluable, as is the close association of parents and children searching for knowledge together. One of the goals of THE NEW BOOK OF

KNOWLEDGE is to help parents share in their children's learning and growing experiences.

Parents of elementary-school children will be particularly interested in the Home Activities in the STUDY GUIDE for the subject areas of Reading, Language, and Literature; Mathematics; Social Studies; and Science and Technology. These simple activities require no special materials or preparation and can be incorporated easily into a busy schedule. An estimation activity in mathematics, for example, asks the child to estimate how many puffs or flakes are in a bowl of cereal. These activities can be used to stimulate and encourage a child's interest and creativity or to help a child achieve a better understanding and increased skill in a difficult subject. There are activities for the four core subject areas in the section Kindergarten and Grades 1 through 3 and in the section Grades 4 through 6. Each set of activities for a subject area immediately follows the curriculum discussion for it. In addition, a set of twelve activities for youngsters in grades 4 through 9 is provided in the section How to Do Research for Reports and Projects. These activities may be duplicated using any copying machine. As students work through the activities, they will learn how to best use THE NEW BOOK OF KNOWLEDGE to locate and organize information and to prepare reports and projects.

Other unique features to be found in THE NEW BOOK OF KNOWLEDGE include the Wonder Questions that cover a broad range of unusual topics young people always find interesting. There are also the many activities, projects, and experiments they can do on their own, along with a complete listing of the variety of literary selections found in the set. Lists of the articles in which all of these can be found are provided in the Appendix at the end of the STUDY GUIDE. A separate listing of literary selections is organized by grade level. Each grouping is included in the lists of curriculum-related articles printed in the appropriate sections of the STUDY GUIDE: K through 3; 4 through 6; and 7 through 9.

Preschool children will also have enjoyable learning experiences with THE NEW BOOK OF KNOWLEDGE. They can wander through the set with its many illustrations and photographs of the people, places, and objects, past and present, that represent the wide range of knowledge they will acquire as they grow older. They will be delighted to listen to someone read them the nursery rhymes, poems, and stories in the set. When they ask those questions that defy immediate answers, they will observe how answers and explanations are found in its pages and thereby learn a valuable lesson and skill.

Much of the appeal of THE NEW BOOK OF KNOWLEDGE springs from the articles about subjects that may not be covered in the typical school curriculum but which will broaden a young person's overall education. Just a few of the topics that are covered include those in the cultural arts, popular entertainment, food and cooking, games, clothing and fashions, and hobbies and crafts. The Study Guide lists some of these articles in the section Hobbies and Other Leisure-Time Activities in the Appendix.

Today's educators realize that, because the world's body of knowledge is constantly and quickly changing and expanding, one of their most important missions is to teach children how to become independent discoverers, researchers, and learners. The innate curiosity of children turns them into eager questioners. In the classroom, discussions often produce dozens of questions about events, people, and places. Knowing how to find the answers to their questions is not always easy for young people. Out of the mass of resources readily available—books and textbooks, newspapers and magazines, picture files, recordings, videos, films, and electronic data bases—we often direct students to begin their search for a first answer or basic understanding in an encyclopedia.

THE NEW BOOK OF KNOWLEDGE was planned to be an early, authoritative, and efficient resource for school-age children. Many of its editors and advisers have been educators or librarians or have worked in other important ways with young people. Its contributors are experts in their fields and are able to write for young audiences. You can direct students to THE NEW BOOK OF KNOWLEDGE confident that its articles are accurate, up-to-date, and set within the contexts needed to help readers understand and use the information in them. Sometimes an article will tell students as much as they want or need to know about a particular subject. Often the encyclopedia will be only a first resource, providing an overview of basic information and stimulating the student to seek out additional resources.

Educators today are often required to fit new topics such as global studies, environmental education, multicultural studies, and substance-abuse education into their regular programs. These and similar topics have been integrated into the STUDY GUIDE'S lists of articles for traditional curriculum areas. Many educators are also concerned about helping children make connections across the curriculum. An encyclopedia is an invaluable tool for implementing such activities, and the lists of curriculum articles will be helpful in making such connections in the classroom or library, as well as in planning and helping students achieve classroom and homework assignments. As the HOME AND SCHOOL STUDY GUIDE is used with THE NEW BOOK OF KNOWLEDGE, you will discover numerous other ways in which the encyclopedia can be used to help young people become better learners.

ARTICLES OF PARTICULAR INTEREST TO PARENTS

▶ SCHOOLS, EDUCATION, AND THE FAMILY

As your children progress from infancy through childhood and adolescence into young adulthood, you will have many questions about their growth, development, and education. Questions like these:

- Is each of us born with a certain level of intelligence that will never change throughout our lives? What does an intelligence test score really mean?
- What important questions should I ask in choosing a good day-care facility? What can I do to help my children improve their learning abilities?
- Am I free to provide schooling for my children at home? Are there specific federal or state laws that regulate home schooling?.
- Does my adolescent youngster really want me to say "No" to certain requests or demands?

THE NEW BOOK OF KNOWLEDGE contains dozens of informative articles about child development, the family, schools, curriculum subjects, and various other aspects of education that will help you find answers to these questions. You will find helpful information about these topics, for example, in the articles INTELLIGENCE, DAY CARE, LEARNING, EDUCATION, and ADOLESCENCE. If you are the parent of a preschool or school-age child, you will find the following list of a few of the key articles in the set that will be of special interest to you.

FAMILY AND CHILD DEVELOPMENT

Volume	Articles
A	Adolescence
	Adoption
B	Baby
C	Child Abuse
	Child Development
D	Divorce
E	Ethnic Groups
	Etiquette
F	Family
	Foster Care
G	Genealogy
I	Intelligence
J-K	Juvenile Crime
L	Learning
P	Psychology
Q-R	Reproduction
S	Speech Disorders

EDUCATION AND SCHOOLS

Volumes	Articles
C	Children's Literature
D	Day Care
E	Education
G	Guidance Counseling
J-K	Kindergarten and Nursery Schools
L	Libraries
P	Parent-Teacher Associations
	Preparatory Schools
Q-R	Reading
	Reference Materials
	Research
S	Schools
	Storytelling
	Study, How to
T	Teachers and Teaching
	Tests and Test Taking
	Toys
U-V	Universities and Colleges

CURRICULUM SUBJECTS

Volume	Articles
A	Arithmetic
	Art
G	Geography
H	Handwriting
	Health
	History
	Home Economics
I	Industrial Arts
M	Mathematics
	Music
P	Phonics
	Physical Fitness
Q-R	Reading
S	Science

Social Studies
Spelling

W-X-Y-Z Writing An extended list of curriculum-related articles appears after each main section: Kindergarten and Grades 1 through 3, Grades 4 through 6, and Grades 7 through 9.

▶ **HOME, HEALTH, RECREATION, AND FINANCE**

Does someone among your family or friends have a health problem that you would like to know more about? Are you looking for help in decorating your home or balancing the family budget? Or are you, perhaps, searching for ideas about where to go for a vacation? THE NEW BOOK OF KNOWLEDGE contains a wealth of articles relating to the home, health, finance, recreation, and other nonacademic topics. The article INTERIOR DESIGN, for example, reveals the secret of good interior design—how to choose the style, balance and scale, color, light, pattern, and texture that will work well together in a room. In the article BUDGETS, FAMILY, you can learn how a simple six-step plan will help you get the most from your money. The article DISEASES provides information about more than 70 specific diseases, ranging from acne and bulimia to heart disease and sickle-cell anemia. THE NEW BOOK OF KNOWLEDGE is also a wonderful resource for vacation planning. There are articles filled with important and fascinating facts about each of the 50 states in the United States, every country in the world, from Afghanistan to Zimbabwe, and many of the world's major cities. There are also many special articles such as NATIONAL PARK SYSTEM, which provides listings of more than 300 of our nation's scenic, historical, and scientific treasures, including parks, monuments, historic sites, recreational areas, nature preserves, and military parks and battlefield sites. The following is just a small representative selection of the various nonacademic topics included in THE NEW BOOK OF KNOWLEDGE. As you browse through the list, you will undoubtedly find many articles of special interest to you, and those articles will lead you to many more.

THE HOME

Volume	Articles
A	Air Conditioning Antiques and Antique Collecting
B	Bread and Baking Building Construction
C	Clothing Computers Cooking
D	Decorative Arts Detergents and Soap Dry Cleaning
E	Electric Lights Electronics
F	Fashion Food Food Preservation Food Regulations and Laws Food Shopping Furniture
G	Gardens and Gardening
H	Heating Systems Homelessness Homes and Housing Homeschooling Household Pests Houseplants
I	Interior Design
P	Parties Pets Plant Pests Plumbing
Q-R	Recycling Refrigeration
T	Time Management
W-X-Y-Z	Weeds

HEALTH

Volume	Articles
A	Abortion ADHD AIDS Alcoholism Alternative Medicine Asthma Autism
D	Dentistry Disabilities, People with Diseases

Doctors
Drug Abuse
Drugs
E   Emotions
F   First Aid
H   Hepatitis
Holistic Medicine
Homosexuality
Hormones
L   Learning Disorders
M   Medicine
Mental Illness
N   Narcotics
Nutrition
O   Obesity
P   Poisons
S   Safety
Smoking
Surgery
U-V   Vaccination and Immunization
Vegetarianism

RECREATION

Volume	Articles
B	Ballet
	Books
	Botanical Gardens
D	Dance
	Drama
F	Flower Arranging
	Folk Art
	Folk Music
G	Games
H	High-Fidelity Systems
	Holidays
	Hotels and Motels
M	Magazines
	Motion Pictures

Museums
Musical Theater
N   National Forest System
National Park System
O   Opera
Operetta
P   Parks and Playgrounds
Q-R   Radio
S   Sound Recording
Space Agencies and Centers
T   Television
Theater
U-V   Video Games
Video Recording
W-X-Y-Z Zoos An extensive list of the articles about hobbies and other leisure-time activities appears in the Appendix of this STUDY GUIDE.

FINANCE

Volume	Articles
B	Banks and Banking
	Budgets, Family
	Business
C	Consumer Protection
	Credit Cards
D	Dollar
E	Economics
I	Income Tax
	Insurance
M	Money
S	Stocks and Bonds
T	Taxation
U-V	Unemployment and Unemployment Insurance
W-X-Y-Z	Wills

THE HOME-SCHOOL PARTNERSHIP

From the moment of birth, a child begins to learn. Parents or other primary caregivers are not only a child's first teachers, they may be the most important teachers a child will ever have. Children learn much in their first few years of life, and once they begin school, their home life strongly affects their school performance. A recent study found that parents make a significant difference in a child's school achievement.

Most adults feel that it is harder to be a parent today, and they consider it particularly difficult to find sufficient time to spend with their children. Nevertheless, parents want the best for their youngsters. They are concerned about preparing them for their school years, and they want to share in their day-to-day school experiences by providing support in the home for schoolwork.

▶ **THE HOME ENVIRONMENT**

When teachers across the nation were asked in a survey about what would help improve American education, their overwhelming response was that they could do their best job educating children who were sent to school in good physical condition and with positive mental attitudes toward learning.

Children need adequate food, clothing, and shelter to be physically fit to learn. It is equally important for children to develop a sense of self-worth. Children who feel good about themselves are better able to learn. Their self-esteem comes from knowing that they are valued members of the family and that they have the loving support and understanding of family members. Allowing children freedom and independence within consistent limits; providing just enough supervision and guidance for their protection; and rewarding their efforts with praise and encouragement are all ways by which children learn that they are loved and respected for who they are.

Given this kind of atmosphere in which to grow, children also need a few key learning experiences. There are at least two things par-

ents can do that will help children be successful in school—reading to them, daily if possible, and talking with them as you share time together.

Educational studies have shown that children who are read to on a regular basis come to school ready to learn to read and that they experience fewer difficulties mastering the art of reading. Fortunately, children's books are readily available. Inexpensive books for young children can be purchased at bookstore sales and in supermarket and discount stores. They can be picked up for a few coins at tag sales. Local public libraries contain shelves full of wonderful fiction and nonfiction books for children of all ages, free to anyone with a library card. School-age children are able to buy books at discounted prices at school book fairs, and teachers often encourage book sharing by providing time for youngsters to trade favorite books with their classmates. Children of any age love to be read to, and they should be encouraged to participate actively in the reading experience.

Talk with children about what they are reading. Ask them about what is taking place in the story and what they think will happen next. Have them find things in the illustrations that are named in the story. Encourage them to ask questions. Praise them when they "read" to you from a favorite book they have heard many, many times. Demonstrate to children that you enjoy reading, too. Let them see you enjoying a book, magazine, or newspaper in your leisure moments. A few minutes a day spent with children and a book can make a substantial difference to their success in school.

Talking with children is another essential learning experience. Telling stories, explaining the steps you use in preparing a meal or fixing a faucet, playing word games, posing riddles, and singing songs are just a few meaningful ways to communicate with youngsters. Encourage your children to talk to you. Show your interest in the questions they raise. Help them work out solutions to problems verbally.

Take the time to listen when they are eager to share an experience or a feeling. By learning how to use language to communicate with others, children build a speaking and listening vocabulary that will form the foundation for learning to read and write.

In addition to reading to and talking with children, parents should try to provide, as much as they are able, a wide variety of experiences for their children. Taking them for walks around the neighborhood and stopping in at local businesses, parks, playgrounds, and libraries are free activities that offer fruitful opportunities for talking and learning. Trips to museums, zoos, athletic events, and concerts have obvious benefits in broadening children's interests and knowledge.

By participating actively in your children's learning experiences, you will learn their preferences, interests, strengths, and weaknesses. You will then be better prepared to provide the successful experiences at home that will give them the confidence they need to meet the challenges of school.

▶ PARENT INVOLVEMENT IN SCHOOL

Once children are in school, they find that their learning becomes more regimented. Parents and caregivers often discover that schools today are very different from the schools they attended. They are not sure about what the school expects or what actually goes on in the classroom. Some parents come to believe that their children's education is now out of their hands and should be left to the professionals.

Research, however, documents that children do best in school when parents view themselves as being in charge of their children's education. Parental involvement has proven to be more important to children's success in school than family income or level of education. Most educators realize that well-informed parents can be strong supporters and allies in the work they do. They are reaching out more frequently to involve parents in the school and its activities.

Parents demonstrate that they think educa-tion is valuable when they continually share their children's school experiences. Getting to know your youngster's teachers is of primary importance. What do they expect of their students? Do children in their classrooms spend some of their time at their desks listening and completing teacher-directed activities? Are students expected to take responsibility for their own learning for part of the day, moving around the room, choosing from a variety of activities to work on individually or cooperatively with other children? Are students required to learn facts for tests as well as solve problems requiring critical thinking? Do their teachers evaluate the progress of students by keeping a portfolio of their work? Knowing what is required of your children will enable you to offer the most effective support.

Schools recognize the need for good home-school communication and most schools use parent-teacher conferences and written reports as a means of reporting on children's progress. Because of working hours and other responsibilities, parents or other caregivers sometimes find it difficult to keep in touch with teachers or to attend school functions. When that is the case, it is important that some other key family member make the contact or attend the meeting. When you miss teacher conferences or school functions, you are sending your children the message that school matters may not be important enough to take some of your time and concern. When the effort is made to be in regular contact with teachers and administrators, you signal your children that school and schoolwork are important and serious business for both of you. Increasingly, schools welcome parents' participation in other school activities. Many moms and dads, and grandparents, too, perform valuable services as classroom assistants and volunteer tutors or become active in parent-advisory or PTO groups.

▶ HOW IMPORTANT IS HOMEWORK?

Teachers typically assign homework to their students. But without guidance from their parents, children may find it difficult to organize their after-school time in order to complete the assignments. How important is homework? What can parents do to help children get over the homework hurdle?

Studies show that doing homework regularly and conscientiously helps raise student achievement. Teachers recognize the importance of homework in helping students become independent learners. Talk to teachers early in the school year to find out what, in general, the homework requirements will be for your children.

Work together with your children to set up ground rules that will promote good study habits. First, agree on a regular time and place for study, one that accommodates the needs of each child and the availability of a family helper, and be firm in sticking to it. Be ready to handle distractions—telephone calls, a turned-on TV set, interference from brothers and sisters. Help your children get started each day by making sure they understand what they are supposed to do for their assignments and that they have the materials they need. Do not do the homework for your children, but be ready to assist when they ask for help. Many parents, especially when younger children are involved, check completed assignments to make sure a child has not misunderstood the work. This can prevent embarrassment for youngsters and will enable you to alert the teacher to possible problems they may be having in learning the material. The articles LEARNING and STUDY, HOW TO, in THE NEW BOOK OF KNOWLEDGE include other useful homework and study tips.

Homework can help your children become better students with good study habits and keep you informed about their work in classes.

OVERVIEW OF MAJOR CURRICULUM AREAS

▶ **WHO DECIDES WHAT CHILDREN WILL LEARN?**

There is no national curriculum for American schools. In recent years, however, the federal government has supported the establishment of national education goals, including specific goals in major curriculum areas, but these goals have not yet been adopted and put into common practice. There is a body of knowledge, though, that is taught in most school systems in kindergarten through grade 12 across the entire United States. Most state departments of education develop curriculum guidelines that recommend and sometimes mandate how this knowledge should be organized and sequenced through the grades in their state. It is usually the local school district, however, that makes the final decisions about what children in their schools will learn. These decisions, to some extent, reflect the values, attitudes, concerns, and cultures of the community in which the school district is located. Although regional influences may result in differences in emphasis or in the choice of specific topics to be covered, the curriculum requirements for the major subject areas are essentially the same for almost every school district in America.

▶ **WHAT ARE CHILDREN EXPECTED TO LEARN?**

Reading, writing, and arithmetic have been the focus of education in America ever since the first public schools were established by law in Massachusetts in 1647. More time is still spent on reading, language arts, and mathematics in today's elementary, middle, and junior-high schools than on any other subjects. Four subject areas—the language arts, mathematics, science, and social studies—do make up the core curriculum for all students from kindergarten through the ninth grade. However, because most educators agree that it is essential to build a strong foundation for reading and mathematics literacy in the primary grades, other subjects are often given much less attention at the primary levels. Although children in the primary grades are exposed in

various ways to science and social studies topics, in reality, these subjects do not generally become part of the regular curriculum until the fourth grade.

Depending on budget and time constraints, the core curriculum will be rounded out with art, music, physical education, and health. Most elementary schools in the United States do not provide the opportunity for children to learn a foreign language, and the percentage of middle school and junior high school students taking a foreign language is low. In addition, students in grades 6 through 9 generally take a semester or a year of a home economics or industrial arts or technology course. Computer technology is not usually offered as a separate subject until high school, but most youngsters are exposed to computers at various grades before they reach senior high school.

▶ **READING, LANGUAGE, AND LITERATURE—THE LANGUAGE ARTS**

Reading and writing are the keystones of the school learning experience. Everything else that children learn in school depends on their success in learning to read and write. Together with listening and speaking, they are the means by which one person communicates with another, and they are essential skills for living and working in our society.

Two quite different approaches to teaching these important skills predominate in today's elementary and middle schools. The one familiar to most parents is the traditional model in which grammar and usage, reading, writing, spelling, penmanship, and oral language are treated as separate subjects, each given its own time and emphasis in the school day. A number of schools use a newer method in which listening, speaking, and the various reading, writing, and grammar and usage skills are taught together as an integrated whole. This method, usually referred to as the whole language or integrated language arts method, tends to use literature as the unifying element around which language arts activities are woven.

In the traditional reading program, teachers use a series of graded textbooks as their instructional base. The readers contain relatively short selections that may be excerpts from classic children's literature or may be selections written specifically for the textbook. Vocabulary and sentence length and structure are tightly controlled to conform to the reading level of the book. In the primary grades, the reading process is broken down into a number of decoding or phonics skills and comprehension skills that children learn in a sequenced pattern. At the end of the third grade, it is expected that the student has acquired a sizable sight vocabulary, is also able to sound out or decode new words, and can use the various subskills of reading in an integrated way to construct meaning from the text. The student should be well on the way to becoming an independent reader.

In the whole language or integrated language arts classroom, the student is more likely to learn to read from an assortment of fiction and nonfiction books, student-authored books, and other reading materials than from a traditional reader. At times the teacher may select a title for the whole class or a group within the class to read together. At other times, students make their own choices about what they will read. Reading and grammar and usage subskills are not taught in isolation or in a set sequence. Their presentation is based on the contents and the styles of the books students are reading. Listening, speaking, and writing activities also tend to be assigned to stimulate and produce student responses to what is being read. Many whole language teachers plan their instruction around theme-based units focusing on topics that touch on many of the curriculum areas.

In the middle grades, it is assumed that students have learned the basics of reading and are now ready to read to learn. They are taught more complex comprehension skills such as inferential and critical-thinking skills, and they increase their reading vocabulary. They should be ready to read content-area textbooks and reference materials for information.

Reading is not usually taught as a separate subject in grades 7 through 9, except for those students who have exhibited reading difficulties. Middle and junior high school students are, however, given opportunities to develop and apply more sophisticated and complex reading abilities in literature courses. Some curriculum specialists recommend that at these grade levels, reading instruction be incorporated into every subject, especially English, social studies, science, and mathematics.

Regardless of the type of reading program employed, students are asked to do more writing in today's classroom than in earlier times, and to spend less time practicing formal rules of English grammar and usage. Beginning in the primary grades, youngsters generally learn to write using a technique called the writing process rather than by concentrating on the mechanics of writing. They learn that there are several stages in the writing process:

- Prewriting—gathering ideas, planning, and deciding on content, purpose, audience, and style
- Drafting—focusing on content and writing style rather than on the mechanics of grammar and usage
- Revising—making changes and improvements in content and style
- Editing—making corrections in spelling, capitalization and punctuation, grammar, and usage
- Publishing—producing, either by writing down or typing, a final draft of the finished work, and sharing it with an audience

Teachers sometimes ask youngsters to spend some time every day writing in a journal on any topic they choose and often to write a longer story, report, or essay. Attempts are also made to be sure students transfer what they learn about the writing process to their assignments in each of the other curriculum areas. A goal of every school's reading, language, and literature program is to make students effective communicators so that they can read, understand, and appreciate what others have written and be able to express their own ideas and feelings effectively in writing and speaking.

MATHEMATICS

Mathematics is, more than ever before, a fundamental and basic curriculum area. As advances in different technologies cause our world to change, today's students will find it important to understand how to use mathematics to cope with these changes. The mathematics curriculum has undergone comprehensive analysis, reorganization, and modification to ensure that this instructional area reflects these changes as much as possible.

Mathematics is generally taught in a sequential and cumulative manner. Understanding certain math concepts is often necessary before one can understand higher-order, more abstract concepts. The scope of mathematics for grades K through 9 incorporates a number of strands, including:

- numbers and number patterns
- arithmetic operations involving addition, subtraction, multiplication, and division of whole numbers, fractions, and decimals
- measurement, using both standard and metric units
- geometry
- estimation and mental arithmetic
- statistics
- probability
- integers
- pre-algebra concepts and algebra

Today more emphasis than ever before is put on teaching mathematics in the context of problem solving and its applications to real-world situations. There is also less emphasis on isolated computational proficiency. Many educators believe that, while it is necessary to learn computational skills, the use of hand-held calculators should be accepted as a legitimate method of computation. Many middle school and junior high school students, therefore, are using calculators to do basic operations, allowing them more time to concentrate on the important aspects of problem solving and mathematical reasoning.

Today's mathematics classroom is not always a place where children sit at their desks quietly doing only pencil-and-paper activities. It is also frequently a place containing diverse materials that young learners can take in their hands, manipulate, and explore. Especially in the early grades, math is becoming a hands-on subject. Younger children are not yet capable of understanding abstract mathematical concepts; they learn best by playing and experimenting with concrete materials that may include pattern blocks, an abacus, Cuisenaire rods, geoboards, counting and sorting materials, and measuring tools. Computers are often available to children of all ages to help them develop data bases of statistics, create geometric displays, construct graphs, or simulate real-life situations.

Throughout the grades, students are sometimes given experiences in which problems are solved using a group approach. This process brings individuals together to work as a problem-solving team that develops strategies and achieves solutions. Students also learn in these situations that there is often more than one way to solve mathematical problems and that sometimes such problems may have more than one right answer.

The goal of mathematics instruction is to help students achieve sufficient success in mathematics to have confidence in their ability to use it both in school and in the everyday world.

SOCIAL STUDIES

The social studies program is an area of the school curriculum that focuses on people. Students in every grade, K through 9, study the diverse ways in which people work together to form societies and interact with one another in different environments and situations. In addition to history, government, civics, and geography, the social studies curriculum draws on some of the social sciences—anthropology, economics, political science, psychology, and sociology. Until junior high school, however, topics from these subject areas are not studied in any depth as separate disciplines.

Key goals for the social studies curriculum include:

- preparing young people to be informed citizens capable of fulfilling their responsibilities in a democratic society
- developing an understanding of the United States and the diversity of its political and social institutions, traditions, and values
- helping students understand and appreciate the history, diversity, and interdependence of world cultures
- involving students in identifying and analyzing local, national, and global problems and developing strategies needed to respond to them

The tremendous scope of the social studies curriculum has led to different views about how this important subject area should be taught. Some schools focus on traditional history and geography, sometimes teaching them as separate core subjects. Other schools believe that the world has become so complex and full of critical social issues that history and geography alone are not enough to provide a basis for preparing young people for their adult roles in society. In these schools, additional subjects are integrated into the social studies curriculum. State curriculum guidelines generally reflect one or the other of these views.

There is a basic or core social studies curriculum covered in most American classrooms, however. The typical framework is sometimes called the "expanding environments" or "widening horizons" organization. Children first learn about how people live together in families, neighborhoods, and communities, and in their own towns, cities, and states. At grades 5 through 9 the curriculum broadens to include separate courses on the history of the United States and on the regions and nations of the world.

Young people cannot understand the past or the present without acquiring skills that enable them to do much more than memorize names, dates, and places. Students must understand historical events and their relationship to current events and issues. In the social studies classroom students are often encouraged to go beyond their textbooks and to use a variety of print and nonprint materials as resources for information that will advance their ability to understand historical events.

To do this they are taught the research and reference skills they need to become successful gatherers of information. They are also taught how to be good critical thinkers who can analyze and evaluate information and make sound judgments about how to use it. Students are asked to read biographies and primary sources such as letters, diaries, journals, memoirs, and eyewitness accounts. They also read secondary sources ranging from encyclopedias and historical essays to novels, magazines, and newspapers that offer a variety of interpretations and points of view. Maps and globes enable students to locate places and learn about the different physical features of world regions and how such differences influence historical events. An appreciation and understanding of the world's diversity is gained also through their experiences with the literature, art, and music of different cultures, and through field trips to historical sites and museums.

Students also use various media and technology to gain insights into places and events they cannot get from print materials alone. These may include films, videotapes, videodiscs, CD-ROM's, and computer databases and simulations. Some schools also have telecommunications capabilities providing access to the Internet and other on-line systems.

Social studies homework frequently includes doing the research needed to write reports and essays, to prepare for debates, to conduct interviews or surveys, or to work on other special projects.

THE NEW BOOK OF KNOWLEDGE can be especially helpful to the social studies curriculum. It provides accurate and objective information about the people, places, and events associated with important periods in history. It provides youngsters with an excellent first source of information for each area of this curriculum they will study.

▶ SCIENCE AND TECHNOLOGY

Most children have a lively curiosity. Almost as soon as they can speak, youngsters start asking questions. The school science curriculum is committed to nurturing children's curiosity about the natural world in which they live.

In the elementary grades the science curriculum is usually broken into small units of study, each devoted to a topic from one of the scientific disciplines of life, earth, and physical science. The life science units in the early grades focus on plants, animals, human biology, and ecology. Life science expands in the middle grades to include studies of the cell, genetics, and evolution. Topics in astronomy, geology, the oceans, and weather make up the earth science units. Physical science concentrates on matter, on energy in its variety of forms (heat, light, sound, electricity, and magnetism), on physical forces and motion, on work and machines, and on chemistry. The study of technology, the science concerned with the ways in which we adapt our natural world to meet our needs, is included as it relates to specific units of study in each area.

Most students in grades 7 through 9 take separate year-long courses in life science, physical science, and earth science, although in some schools ninth graders take either a general science or a biology course.

Throughout the grades, scientific knowledge is sometimes taught within the context of major concepts and themes that help students understand connections and relationships across the different branches of science and technology. These concepts and themes may include energy and matter, scale and structure, cause and effect, patterns of change, systems and interaction, models and theories, and others.

The primary aim of the K through 9 science curriculum is to ensure that students will achieve scientific literacy. Goals often cited as important for scientific literacy include:

- knowledge of the facts, concepts, principles, laws, and theories that are used to explain the natural world
- development of a scientific habit of mind, i.e., the ability to think scientifically when answering questions, solving problems, and making decisions
- understanding the possibilities and the limitations of science and technology in explaining the natural world and in solving human problems
- understanding how science, technology, and society influence one another and having the ability to use this knowledge in everyday decision making

In addition to textbooks, many schools use an open-ended, hands-on approach to teach science that calls for the active participation of students in conducting scientific inquiries and becoming familiar with the scientific process. The classroom becomes a laboratory containing plants, small animals, and a selection of scientific equipment. Small groups of children working together use these materials to learn the steps in the scientific method through their own explorations and investigations and by thinking and acting like real scientists:

- posing a question or a problem
- developing a hypothesis or a likely explanation
- designing and conducting an experiment to test the hypothesis
- making observations
- collecting, analyzing, and organizing data
- drawing conclusions

When it is not feasible for children to carry out their own experiments, teachers often conduct demonstrations. Classroom science experiences are extended through field trips to nature centers, parks, zoos, and science museums. Some schools have their own nature trails on school grounds with interesting signs and labels to stimulate children's learning. Some states and school districts have also invested in interactive multimedia programs produced on CD-ROM and other electronic technologies to take the place of traditional textbooks.

The middle school and junior high school are transitions between the elementary program, in which concepts from each of the scientific disciplines are taught each year, and the separate subject-area departments of high school. The science teachers for grades 7 through 9 are also more likely to be science specialists or to have had training in science. At these grade levels there is instructional emphasis on laboratory and field activities.

The science highlight of the year in many schools is the annual science fair, at which individuals or teams of students plan, construct, and explain original science projects. To assist students, information and tips for preparing outstanding science fair projects can be found in the articles SCIENCE FAIRS and EXPERIMENTS AND OTHER SCIENCE ACTIVITIES in THE NEW BOOK OF KNOWLEDGE.

Students of all ages are also encouraged by their teachers to apply their interests in science to activities outside of school. Many simple experiments can be done using materials readily available in the home. Children enjoy collecting things and are often asked to make leaf, insect, shell, seed, rock, or other types of natural science collections as homework assignments. The article EXPERIMENTS AND OTHER SCIENCE ACTIVITIES describes the scientific process and gives directions for simple experiments from each of the scientific disciplines that youngsters can do at home. The many different science articles and biographies in THE NEW BOOK OF KNOWLEDGE include many other science activities and projects that can be done in or out of school. It is an excellent resource for school reports and science projects as well as for continuing one's interest in an area of science outside the classroom.

As they conduct their scientific studies throughout their school years, young people discover that reading and learning about science can be a rich and enjoyable lifelong experience.

▶ **HEALTH AND SAFETY**

Children's health and safety is an important concern of the school. Every school gives evidence of this concern by offering numerous health services, including providing a school nurse on the premises, maintaining cumulative health records for each student, and conducting screening tests to identify health and learning problems. There are also school district policies on emergency care, communicable disease control, and the administration of medication. Above all, schools attempt to provide safe and sanitary facilities for all students.

Although school personnel demonstrate their concern about students' health and safety in all these ways, not all children receive systematic, sequential instruction in health and safety as part of the standard K through 9 curriculum. Health education is usually cited as part of the curriculum in every school district. In some elementary schools, however, it may only be covered in one period a week or incidentally within the science or physical education curriculum. Many middle school and junior high school students, however, usually receive a one-semester health course that may be taught by the school nurse or by the physical education, science, or home economics teacher.

A comprehensive, up-to-date health program motivates and promotes the development of good, lifelong health habits and teaches the skills and strategies necessary to avoid risky behaviors. It encompasses physical, mental, emotional, and social health. These are usually integrated into the study of ten major health topics:

- human body systems
- prevention and control of disease
- substance use and abuse (drugs, alcohol, and tobacco)
- nutrition
- mental and emotional health
- accident prevention, safety, and first aid
- family life
- physical fitness and personal care
- consumer health
- community health, environmental health, and health care resources

In some school districts, sex education is considered part of the health program. It usually covers issues involving sexual development, as well as interpersonal relationships and gender roles. It tries to educate students about how to make responsible choices. In other school systems, special classes or one- or two-week sex education courses are offered at the middle school or junior high school level with parental permission required.

Health educators generally agree that, given today's social problems, students also need to learn and acquire decision-making and refusal skills. In many classrooms, the consequences of risky behavior are presented through role-playing, open discussion, and modeling strategies. Activities included in decision-making models, for example, help students make intelligent judgments about the course of action to take when confronted with a risky question, problem, or situation. Other models demonstrate how to resist negative peer pressure without losing good friends.

Health education is important. Good health programs produce knowledgeable students who possess the skills and motivation to become responsible individuals within families and communities.

▶ MUSIC

Music is not one of the core subjects in the school curriculum, but it is a significant element in the lives of students. All young people seem to have a natural affinity for music. Younger children sing, hum, and dance spontaneously. They enthusiastically repeat the recorded music they hear on audio systems and on radio and television. As children approach adolescence, they spend more time listening to music, often while doing some other activity, than they do watching television or reading.

Although it may not get the attention devoted to core subjects, music is, nevertheless, an integral factor in turning out well-rounded students. At the elementary level, some instruction in music is typically required for all students. In many elementary schools a music program is taught by a music specialist, who meets with each class or grade once or twice a week. The specialist strives for a balance between general musical knowledge and performance skills. If music instruction is the responsibility of the classroom teacher, it often consists primarily of listening activities.

Children in a music program in the primary grades sing, listen to different types of music, engage in rhythmic exercises and dramatic play, and play simple rhythm instruments. They begin to learn some of the basic musical elements, including tempo, pitch, melody, and rhythm.

Students in a music program in the middle grades learn musical symbols and notation and how to read music. They apply their knowledge as they perform vocally or on a simple instrument, such as a recorder, and as they improvise or compose music. By listening to live or recorded musical performances, youngsters learn to recognize different instruments and to appreciate various musical forms, styles, and periods. The history of music and the biographies of great composers and performers are often coordinated with listening experiences. There may be exposure to classical and contemporary masterworks as well as to the folk music of different cultures. Popular musical forms such as jazz, the blues, rock, and rap are often included in such courses.

Some schools offer instrumental lessons for middle grade students, who must usually be able to rent or purchase their own instrument. Instrumental lessons generally culminate in group performances.

In grades 7 through 9, students are usually offered as an elective one semester or one year of music taught by a music specialist. They also have opportunities to join a performing group, becoming active members of the school band, orchestra, or chorus or of an ensemble group for jazz, rock, or some other form of popular music. Even though rehearsals and performances occur outside regular class time, students are eager participants in these groups. They allow young people with special musical interests or talents to develop their full potential.

New technologies are appearing more frequently in general music classes. These may include computers, synthesizers, and electronic keyboards for composing and producing music.

Students who have gone through a music education program can be expected to:

- develop basic music skills that will enable them to establish a lifelong relationship to music
- understand music elements, vocabulary, and notation
- enjoy a wide variety of musical forms and styles that are part of our historical and cultural heritage
- perform and create music and respond to music through movement and dance

Youngsters who enjoy music will take pleasure in THE NEW BOOK OF KNOWLEDGE articles on musical instruments, the history and forms of classical and popular music, the biographies of famous composers and performers, and the music of other countries around the world.

▶ **ART**

Not every child has artistic talent, but most children enjoy and can benefit from art activities and experiences. Students are provided with opportunities to study art in most elementary schools, even though some states do not require that art be taught at this level. Tightened budgets and crowded school days have resulted in less frequent art instruction by specialists. When there is no art specialist available, art may be taught by the classroom teacher or may be incorporated into other subject areas. Children may illustrate stories they have listened to in reading periods or written in language arts classes, make posters with science or health themes, or construct models of historically significant structures for social studies projects.

Most schools, at the minimum, encourage youngsters to express themselves creatively, using a wide variety of art media and techniques. Children commonly have experiences in drawing, painting, printmaking, collage, sculpture, constructions, and an assortment of crafts. In well-equipped schools, students even become involved with photography, video production, and computer art.

When an art specialist is on hand, students will also learn something about the elements and principles of art and design, such as color, line, texture, and perspective. They will become familiar with all the forms art can take, ranging from architecture to painting, sculpture, and the graphic and decorative arts. A specialist may also introduce students to basics of art history and art criticism and help them begin to develop an appreciation for artworks produced by different cultures around the world.

Art fairs are popular events at many schools. Students proudly display examples of their best efforts for parents and others from the school and surrounding communities.

Art education provides a means of personal satisfaction for young people. It should also enable them to:

- perceive and understand basic elements of art and design
- use art as a means of communicating their ideas and feelings
- express themselves creatively in a variety of media
- appreciate and evaluate artworks
- enjoy art as part of our historical and cultural heritage

For students with special abilities or interests in art, THE NEW BOOK OF KNOWLEDGE offers a wealth of art information. There are biographies of famous artists; articles presenting the history of art from prehistoric to modern times; articles describing different art forms, processes, and media, many of which include special "how to" sections; and articles about the art and architecture of major countries around the world. Beautiful full-color art reproductions illustrate most of these articles.

▶ **PHYSICAL EDUCATION AND SPORTS**

Largely because of new technologies and an increase in labor-saving devices, many Americans lead sedentary lifestyles at home, in the workplace, and in their leisure activities. Consequently, many Americans are not physically fit. Although our children seem to be constantly on the move, they too have been influenced by our changing lifestyles, and numerous studies show that too many of our youngsters are out of shape and lack basic physical and athletic skills. One of the key aims of the school physical education program is to help students develop healthy patterns of activity and preferences for athletic pursuits that they will carry into their adult lives.

Only a handful of states include physical education as part of their curriculum requirements. Most elementary, middle, and junior-high schools, however, do have gym and playground facilities, even if they may not have trained physical education instructors. Much learning does take place in these facilities under the direction of the classroom teacher.

In schools with physical education specialists and regularly scheduled gym classes, the physical education program is often thorough. These schools recognize that many of their students have little opportunity for vigorous exercise and that a number of them have neither the ability nor the motivation to participate or excel in competitive team sports. The well-balanced physical education program, therefore, offers a variety of activities involving:

- physical fitness and conditioning
- movement skills, rhythmic activities, and dance
- stunts, tumbling, and gymnastics
- game skills
- individual and two-person sports
- team sports

In gym classes for younger children, the emphasis is on the coordination of large and small muscles and on the development and coordination of general motor skills through play, game, and dance experiences. Many primary-grade students also learn simple tumbling, stunt, and conditioning activities, as well as basic athletic skills they will apply in later grades to more sophisticated games and sports.

Youngsters in the middle and junior-high grades are offered activities that will help them develop agility, strength, endurance, power, flexibility, and speed. Although competitive team sports become important for many students at this level, there is equal emphasis on fitness training, individual and two-person games and sports, track and field, gymnastics, dance, and self-testing. In the middle grades, softball, basketball, soccer, and volleyball are commonly taught team sports. Football, wrestling, field hockey, racket and paddle games, and swimming, if a pool is available, are added to the program for grades 7 through 9.

Since the passage of Title IX as federal law, girls and young women must be given equal opportunity and equal treatment in all school physical education activities and programs.

In the physical education curriculum, students can experience the joy, exhilaration, and satisfaction that accompany successful physical performance. They can also develop:

- an acceptable level of fitness with a lasting desire to maintain it
- the physical and movement skills needed to participate successfully in leisure activities of their choice
- a positive self-concept
- appropriate social and emotional behaviors including sportsmanship, cooperation, self-control, and leadership
- an appreciation and understanding of specific sports

In THE NEW BOOK OF KNOWLEDGE, most team sports and games are discussed in articles written by notable athletes or other sports experts. Accurate rules, directions, and diagrams accompany these articles. In addition, enthusiasts will find information on individual sports such as skiing, golf, running, ice-skating, and many, many more.

KINDERGARTEN AND GRADES 1 THROUGH 3

▶ MEET THE EARLY SCHOOL CHILD

Even though each child grows and learns at an individual pace, nearly all children go through similar stages of development. Teachers in kindergarten and the early grades recognize these growth characteristics and take them into account when they plan a program for early childhood education.

Rapid growth and development is the primary characteristic of the child from ages 5 through 8. Most 5-year-olds are extremely active, physically and mentally. They seem to be in a state of perpetual motion and they are curious about everything. Large muscles develop more rapidly than small muscles and younger children need outdoor play with space to run, jump, and climb. Small muscle growth is aided by activities such as cutting, coloring, pasting, and drawing. Although 5-year-olds have fairly short attention spans, their eyes, ears, and other senses all come into play as they explore the world and the people around them. These youngsters are friendly, eager to please, and need interaction and secure relationships with family members, friends, and teachers. Thinking is stimulated by experiences with concrete objects and a need to relate their learning to their own personal experiences.

Kindergarten classrooms reflect the nature of the 5-year-old. Kindergarten rooms are usually large and open with movable tables and chairs and a variety of learning areas. Children select many of their own activities as they move from one corner to another. Among the activities may be building a block bridge; observing how plants grow from seeds they have planted; measuring and mixing in the cooking area; examining picture books; singing and listening to music; and fingerpainting or making clay animals. What seems like play to the casual observer is really young children's work. It is how they learn. The kindergarten teacher moves among groups and individuals, guiding, leading, facilitating their activities, and helping them develop social skills. Outdoor activity is also an important part of the typical kindergarten day.

Children from ages 6 through 8 exhibit many of the same traits as 5-year-olds, but as they grow physically and as their experiences expand, changes take place. Although they are still active, hands-on learners, primary-grade youngsters develop considerable verbal ability, are increasingly able to reason, and begin to acquire problem-solving skills. They are able to concentrate on tasks for longer periods of time. As they grow less self-centered, they become more tolerant and open-minded and they take more interest in other people. Eagerly seeking new experiences, these youngsters are constantly expanding their horizons and exploring the world beyond home, family, and school. Developing 8-year-olds become increasingly independent and they need guidance and clear limits. With many positive learning experiences behind them, as third graders they can be self-confident, enthusiastic learners.

Youngsters must make a big adjustment between kindergarten and the elementary classroom. In grades 1 through 3 learning takes place in a more serious and structured, less playful environment. Children are usually required to spend a large part of the day in quiet, small-group or whole-class activities. Teachers realize, however, that youngsters in these grade-level classrooms are still literal learners and thinkers, and they still need numerous opportunities for hands-on learning experiences.

The K through 3 years are wonderful years during which children are reaching out to a wide and exciting world. These students are still very young, however, and much is expected of them. They need support, understanding, and friendship. Above all they need to feel accepted and appreciated by family members and teachers. Enjoyable activities you and your youngsters can do together to reinforce what they are learning in the core curriculum areas—Reading, Language, and Literature; Mathematics; Social Studies; and Science—are listed after each of those sections.

The lists of articles at the very end of this

section for Kindergarten and grades 1 through 3 include many, but certainly not all, of the articles about each subject area that appear in THE NEW BOOK OF KNOWLEDGE. It is important that students look up the names of topics they want to read about in the Index or in the set itself to locate all of the information they may need or want.

▶ **READING, LANGUAGE, AND LITERATURE**

The overall objectives of the reading, language, and literature programs that begin in the primary grades are: mastering the mechanics of reading and writing; acquiring the ability to read with comprehension and to write with proficiency; and developing good, life-long reading and writing habits.

In kindergarten the focus of the reading program is on readiness skills that prepare the child for reading and writing. These include auditory and visual discrimination skills and those motor and coordination skills that will enable the young child to hold a crayon or pencil, to color and draw, and eventually to print and write. Kindergarten youngsters are also given repeated opportunities to develop and practice listening and speaking skills. They learn to follow simple rules and directions, deliver messages, ask and answer questions about their various activities, and share their ideas, feelings, and experiences with others. Inviting picture books, with and without words, are readily available to look at and use for imagining and creating stories. Their teachers tell them stories, read books and poems aloud, and lead them in word games and songs. In kindergartens using a more academic approach, youngsters will also begin to learn the relationships between alphabet letters and the sounds they represent.

In grades 1 through 3, as much as half the day may be devoted to reading instruction. Children begin to read by learning word recognition and word-attack skills. There are simple words that they may learn to recognize on sight. Children learn how to decode other words by being shown how to associate phonetic sounds with a letter or group of letters. Later, children also learn to identify words by dividing them into their structural parts. Dividing words into syllables, finding common prefixes and word endings, and breaking compound words into smaller words are all techniques for unlocking longer, more difficult words encountered for the first time. Children also learn how to identify a new word and its meaning by its context in a sentence.

By the end of the third grade, young readers will usually have acquired a literal level of comprehension. They should be able to locate details, identify main ideas, arrange events in a logical sequence, predict outcomes, and draw conclusions. In addition, many children will be able to demonstrate some appreciation of literature and a grasp of several literary elements including character, author's purpose, figurative language, and the difference between realism and fantasy.

In a traditional reading program, the class is usually divided according to reading ability into three relatively homogeneous reading groups. While the teacher works on direct instruction with one group, the rest of the class completes reading-related assignments or participates in self-directed individual or group activities. In a whole language or integrated language arts program, grouping tends to be more flexible and informal.

Primary-grade teachers are particularly alert to signs of reading difficulties, and they try to take steps to eliminate problems before they block a child's progress. Most schools also provide special reading teachers who are trained to make diagnoses and provide corrective help for children with reading problems. If you feel that your child requires special help, it is important that you approach the teacher or principal who can recommend appropriate action.

At the same time that they are learning to read what others have written, primary-grade youngsters begin to express their own ideas and feelings in written language. Kindergarten children can usually print their own names and perhaps a few other well-known names and words. In first grade, children typically learn manuscript writing because it is easier to read and write and resembles the printed words in books. Toward the end of second grade or at the beginning of third grade, children are taught how to change over to connected cursive writing.

As they are taught the steps in the writing process—drafting, composing, revising, editing, and publishing—primary-grade students also learn about proper word usage, spelling, capitalization, and punctuation, as these skills are needed. Many teachers allow youngsters to use "invented spelling" at first, writing words as they would sound when spoken, so that spelling issues do not slow down the youngsters' learning how to write down their ideas. Lessons on spelling and language mechanics are offered at a time when they will not interfere with the natural flow of ideas onto paper. By the time they enter fourth grade, students usually have developed some proficiency in writing sentences, paragraphs, and short reports, and they should enjoy expressing themselves creatively in writing.

Home Activities for Reading, Language, and Literature

- Read aloud to your children, every day if you can. Discuss the people, places, and events you read about.
- Take your children to the local library and let them share with you choosing books to bring home.
- Make up and tell stories to one another. One of you might begin a story and the other finish it. Help your children make their own books by writing and illustrating stories.
- Encourage your children to read to you from school or library books. Help them pronounce difficult words. Praise their efforts. Make this an enjoyable shared experience.
- Teach your children to observe the world around them and provide opportunities for them to talk about their experiences.
- Encourage your children to speak clearly and to listen carefully.

- Listen to your children retell favorite stories they have heard or read.
- Play simple word games. "Give a word that means the same as...." "Give a word that means the opposite of...." "Give a word that rhymes with...."
- As your children get older, urge them to do simple crossword puzzles.
- Help your children write letters, invitations, and thank-you notes to relatives and friends.
- Encourage your children to make a "New Words" dictionary, and try to add a special word to it at least once a week.
- Help your children enjoy educational television programs so that they have many opportunities to listen to how standard English is used and spoken.

▶ **MATHEMATICS**

Children in kindergarten and the primary grades work with a variety of materials to develop concepts, understandings, and skills in mathematics. Kindergarten youngsters often come to school knowing something about counting and numbers, but they must acquire math readiness skills before they will be able to work with numbers in meaningful ways.

In the kindergarten classroom, youngsters learn to sort by using simple objects such as buttons, and by comparing how objects are alike and different. They compare groups of objects to determine which group has less or more objects than another. They learn the concept of one-to-one correspondence by discovering that three oranges have the same number as three apples. They learn the concept of conservation by recognizing that three boxes are three boxes no matter how they are spread out or pulled together. Kindergarten children learn to count using cardinal (1, 2, 3) and ordinal (first, second, third) numbers. Simple geometry, measurement, money, time, and spatial relationships also have a place in the readiness curriculum. Students receive extensive practice using manipulative materials to solve math problems presented as stories that are based on real-life experiences.

Students in the primary grades are not yet abstract thinkers. They continue to use concrete objects as they learn the basic facts and techniques of computation with whole numbers. Frequent work with number lines and hands-on experiences to determine and understand place values are important activities for them. From the beginning, youngsters are also taught to estimate before making calculations as a way of judging the reasonableness of an answer. Primary students enjoy measuring length, volume, weight, time, and temperature using an assortment of measuring tools and expressing answers in both standard and metric units. They learn to identify common geometric shapes, to create and interpret simple pictorial, bar, and line graphs, and to predict outcomes and carry out simple activities involving probability. They conduct simple surveys and experiments and begin to learn how to organize and interpret statistical data. Seeing and understanding mathematical relationships and patterns is another important skill that may be introduced to them in the early grades. Helping students acquire skill in solving problems is an ongoing activity and is usually based on situations appropriate to the students' level of understanding, and experience. Students are given opportunities to try solutions using a variety of problem-solving strategies.

By the end of the third grade most youngsters will possess confidence in their ability to compute and to solve math problems in school and in their everyday lives. Many respond to the fascination of math and it becomes their favorite subject. A few will have difficulties with mathematics' abstract concepts and more complicated methods. These students may need special coaching at home as well as in school.

Home Activities for Mathematics

- Encourage your children to find and read numbers on common objects—cereal boxes, jar and can labels, calendars, newspaper ads, store signs, traffic signs.

- Ask your children to count common objects. "How many clouds are in the sky today?" "How many people are in the checkout line?"
- Ask your children to estimate quantities. "How many puffs are in your bowl of cereal?" "How much milk will this container hold?"
- Encourage your children to read the time from analog and digital clocks. Ask time questions. "How long will it take before the cookies are done?" "What time do you have to leave to get to school on time?"
- Help your children follow simple cooking recipes. Let them measure the ingredients with appropriate measuring utensils.
- Plan a party or special event with your children. Let them work out how many invitations are needed, how many favors, how much food, and how much these things will cost.
- Help your children find books in the library that contain number puzzles and math games.
- Encourage your children to look for geometric shapes such as circles, squares, rectangles, triangles, and cones in common household objects.
- Discuss with your children how you use math at home or in your job. Help them understand how math is involved in many day-to-day activities.
- Play games together that use math and probability. "How many times will the coin come up heads in 10 tries? In 15 tries? In 20 tries?"

▶ **SOCIAL STUDIES**

One of the first social studies lessons children will have is learning that they belong to a family. Youngsters also learn that belonging to a family brings with it responsibility and that the people in family groups depend upon one another. Gradually youngsters learn that each family is part of a larger group, a community, and that there are many different kinds of communities. During the kindergarten and primary school years, the social studies curriculum concentrates initially on children's families, neighborhood, and community. Youngsters learn that there are basic needs families share and that there are many different kinds of family groups in our own country and in other nations. They examine how different families live, work, and play together. They soon discover that everyone must follow rules if people are to live and work together successfully. What youngsters know about family units is then applied to the school community.

In the second and third grades, the social studies curriculum expands to include the neighborhood, local village, town, or city. Short class trips to the local post office, bank, supermarket, or police station demonstrate in a very real way how social and business institutions work in a community. Classroom visits by community workers teach youngsters about the many services needed to keep a community running smoothly. Police officers may talk about traffic rules and the reasons for them. A mail carrier may explain how letters are delivered.

Through these firsthand experiences, children also discover basic economic principles about how goods and services are produced and used and how earning money allows people to buy the things they need and want.

Classroom teachers use books, posters, films, newspapers, postcards, and photographs to help children understand that all neighborhoods and cities have many similarities but also many differences, and each has its own special needs and problems.

Primary-grade youngsters are also introduced to some key facts about our country's history and cultural heritage. Many schools focus on Native Americans, the voyages of Columbus, and the early American colonies. Facts about our history and the people who played important roles in our development as a nation are taught along with the study of national symbols, such as the American flag and the Statue of Liberty, and the celebration of national holidays.

Learning about geography grows out of the study of communities and United States history. Students begin to work with simple maps and globes. Often they make maps of their neighborhoods, pinpointing the location of their own homes and schools. Later they might also work with map puzzles and trace, draw, and color maps of the United States and of the world.

As their social studies knowledge expands and as they become more adept readers and writers, students learn and use the research skills they need to gather information and to write reports. Among the commonly taught skills for this age-group are: locating information; using library resources; using tables of contents and glossaries in books; making and interpreting diagrams and graphs; and selecting and organizing information.

Home Activities for Social Studies

- Get your children started on a stamp, coin, or postcard collection. Help them find out more about the people and places shown.
- If you can, start bank accounts for your children. Help them fill out the necessary forms.
- Give your children opportunities to earn money for work done, and help them plan how to use it.
- Talk with your children about the significance of the different holidays. Include them in activities you pursue to make and do things to celebrate each holiday.
- Read together the folklore, legends, and myths of different cultures and communities. Libraries have excellent collections of these stories.
- Watch television programs about different regions and cultures of the world. Discuss the similarities and differences between these groups and our own culture.
- When you take trips outside your community, help your children locate the destination on a map. Share with them how you have decided what direction you will take and calculate the distance. As time goes on they may be able to make such deci-

sions, too. When you arrive, discuss any special geographical features.

▶ SCIENCE AND TECHNOLOGY

The chief task of the K through 3 science program is to nurture the natural curiosity young children have about themselves, about the living and nonliving things around them, and about the forces of nature. A good primary science program provides a balanced curriculum that includes the life, earth, and physical sciences. Throughout the science program, children are introduced to basic concepts about scientific facts and principles. They begin to learn how to ask questions, make observations and predictions, plan and do simple experiments, and come to conclusions—all aspects of the scientific method.

Beginning in kindergarten, students begin to learn about the needs, habits, and relationships of living things. Youngsters might plant seeds and observe growth patterns. They might learn the special traits of mammals, birds, reptiles, amphibians, and fish and observe the life cycles of butterflies and frogs. Dinosaur studies offer a favorite way to learn about things that lived long ago. Classroom terrariums and aquariums provide an authentic means of observing the interrelationships within an aquatic, desert, or woodlands habitat. Youngsters are eager to care for the plant and animal specimens these miniature environments contain.

Young children are fascinated by space and space exploration, and they enjoy accumulating information about the sun, moon, planets, and other objects such as stars and the constellations.

Changing weather patterns are often observed and charted with youngsters measuring temperature, wind, rainfall, and humidity, describing cloud formations, and competing with the weather forecaster in making predictions about future weather.

Rock, mineral, soil, and water samples are collected to learn about the earth and its resources. The dynamics of our planet are made understandable as youngsters make mod-

els and diagrams of volcanoes and earthquakes.

By manipulating levers, inclined planes, pulleys, gears, and other simple machines that may be in their classroom, children learn about how things move and how they work. The importance of energy in their everyday lives is shown with investigations into magnetism, electricity, light, and sound.

The K through 3 years are the years when children's natural curiosity is at its peak. They are the ideal years during which to start a child on the exciting path of scientific discovery.

Home Activities for Science and Technology

- Take your children into your yard or a neighborhood park on a spring day and see how many different forms of life can be found. Include flowers, trees, grasses, large and small land animals, insects, and birds. Repeat the activity in the summer, fall, and winter.
- If you can, encourage your children to keep and care for a small pet. Ask your children to help tend houseplants or plant a garden. Let them have a special plot of their own.
- Get your children started on collections of objects from nature—small rocks, tree leaves, weeds, seeds. Borrow field guides from the library and help them identify and label the specimens.
- Help your children become sky watchers. Ask them to keep a record of the changing shape of the moon over the period of a month. Find out together what causes this phenomenon. Locate easily identifiable constellations like the Big Dipper.
- Watch science and nature programs on television together. Talk about the interesting things you learn.
- Let your children help take responsibility for household recycling of items such as paper and plastics or for plans you have made to conserve water and gas or electricity.

▶ HEALTH AND SAFETY

The early grades are a good time to help children begin to learn good health habits and attitudes that will last throughout their lives. The primary-grade curriculum introduces young children to the major body systems and organs. They also learn about some of the causes of disease and how to prevent some infections. Caring for the body so that it functions smoothly is often taught through simple units on nutrition, physical fitness, and personal care.

Like adults, children are not always happy. They, too, experience sadness, loneliness, anger, shame, jealousy, and other feelings that can be frightening. They learn that everyone has these feelings sometimes, and they begin to learn how to handle these emotions and how to get along well with others.

Primary-grade youngsters are vulnerable to many types of danger. They need to be taught safety rules that will help them avoid accidents at home, at school, and in other places. It is also important to stress that youngsters remember such safety rules when they are around strangers or in areas unfamiliar to them.

In today's society, even very young children are exposed to the dangers of drugs. A good health program teaches youngsters how to use medicines safely and encourages them to make healthy choices about alcohol, tobacco, and illegal drugs.

Young children have frequent contact with doctors, dentists, and nurses in health clinics or hospitals. The school health program helps them become familiar with the work of these people and institutions.

▶ MUSIC

Young children respond to music spontaneously. Even when music specialists are not available, kindergarten and primary-grade youngsters are offered a variety of musical activities. They sing, clap, listen to music, dance, and play simple rhythm and percussion instruments. The primary-grade teacher often knows how to play the piano or guitar and how to accompany and direct children's singing and dancing.

In a structured music program, students can learn to keep time to a beat, match pitch, identify high and low musical sounds, and sing a melody. By grades 2 and 3 they can begin to learn the basic elements of musical notation.

Youngsters are also sometimes taught how to identify different singing voices and musical instruments as they listen to recorded music. They listen and respond to marches, lullabies, American folk songs, and songs from other cultures.

The main goal of the primary music curriculum is to help and encourage youngsters to enjoy and appreciate music of all kinds and to feel comfortable expressing themselves musically.

▶ ART

The primary-grade art program provides opportunities for children to express themselves creatively with freedom and satisfaction. In the primary grades children have access to a wide variety of art materials and tools. They use poster and finger paints, sand, clay, colored paper, string, papier-mâché, and fabrics of different textures. Even common objects such as buttons, pipe cleaners, and egg cartons are used in the collages, drawings, and paintings they create. Because it is known that large muscles develop first, children are encouraged to work with large sheets of paper, large brushes, and thick crayons. By experimenting and exploring freely, youngsters discover on their own how these tools and materials work.

Teachers understand that young children are not yet ready to represent the things they see in a realistic style and that adult standards should not yet be imposed on the youngsters' creations.

Reproductions and posters of the works of great artists are sometimes examined and discussed during the art period. Students can learn something about color, line, and design as they are encouraged to talk about a master painting or sculpture.

▶ PHYSICAL EDUCATION AND SPORTS

The physical education program is designed to help children acquire physical and athletic skills, habits, and attitudes that will last beyond their school years. In many schools the regular classroom teacher is responsible for gym or physical education instruction. In others, there is a special physical education teacher.

The emphasis of the primary physical education program is often on fitness, rhythmic movement, some gymnastic activities, games, and sports.

Fitness and conditioning activities often begin with running, walking, jumping rope, or dancing. They continue with muscle stretching and strengthening exercises including bending, toe touches, crab walks, rope climbing, push-ups, and sit-ups. By the second and third grades youngsters are ready for activities that improve muscle coordination, such as the standing broad jump.

Young children enjoy discovering all the different ways in which their bodies can move. In gymnastics they run, skip, slide, hop, and gallop. They move arms and legs, manipulate objects to a rhythmic beat, and learn simple dances. Gymnastic activities sometimes include walking a balance beam and doing forward and backward rolls.

Primary-grade youngsters are taught a number of game skills basic to sports they will play when they are older. By third grade girls and boys can bounce a ball with one hand, dribble soccer balls and basketballs, strike a ball off a stationary objcct, and pass a ball in various ways to a partner. They use these skills in chasing games, relays, and team games.

In a good physical education program it is recognized that children will have varying levels of physical and athletic ability, but every child is included and involved in every activity. Every child also learns the importance of cooperation and sportsmanship in games and sports.

CURRICULUM-RELATED ARTICLES

Some of the important articles in THE NEW BOOK OF KNOWLEDGE that relate to the K through 3 school curriculum are listed here. Many other articles you or your youngsters may want to read while they are studying topics in these curriculum areas can be found by looking them up in the Index or in the set itself.

READING, LANGUAGE, AND LITERATURE

Vol.	Reading, Writing, and Language
D	Diaries and Journals
E	Encyclopedias
H	Handwriting
L	Libraries
M	Magazines
P	Phonics
R	Reading
S	Spelling
	Storytelling
U-V	Vocabulary
W-X-Y-Z	Writing

Vol.	Literature
A	Arabian Nights
C	Caldecott, Randolph
	Caldecott and Newbery Medals
	Children's Literature
F	Fables
	Fairy Tales
	Folklore
	Folklore, American
I	Illustration and Illustrators
J-K	Jokes and Riddles
N	Newbery, John
	Nonsense Rhymes
	Nursery Rhymes

Vol.	Author Biographies
A	Andersen, Hans Christian
B	Barrie, Sir James Matthew
F	Field, Eugene
	Frost, Robert
G	Grahame, Kenneth
	Greenaway, Kate
	Grimm, Jacob and Wilhelm
J-K	Kipling, Rudyard
M	Milne, A. A.
P	Potter, Beatrix
Q-R	Rowling, J. K.
S	Sandburg, Carl

	Sendak, Maurice
	Seuss, Dr.
	Stevenson, Robert Louis
T	Thurber, James
W-X-Y-Z	White, E. B.
	Wilder, Laura Ingalls
	(See also the article CHILDREN'S LITERATURE for profiles of additional authors and illustrators.)

Vol.	Selections from Literature
A	Andersen, Hans Christian—The Emperor's New Clothes
	Arabian Nights
	Aladdin and the Wonderful Lamp (excerpt)
	The Forty Thieves (excerpt)
B	Barrie, Sir James Matthew—Peter Pan (excerpt)
	Bible Stories
	Noah's Ark
	David and Goliath
	Jonah
	Daniel in the Lions' Den
	The Boy Jesus
C	Christmas Story (Gospel according to Luke)
F	Fables
	The Lion and the Mouse (Aesop)
	The Ant and the Grasshopper (Aesop)
	The Four Oxen and the Lion (Aesop)
	The Tyrant Who Became a Just Ruler (Bidpai)
	The Blind Men and the Elephant (Saxe)
	The Moth and the Star (Thurber)
	Fairy Tales
	The Enchanted Princess (German)
	The Princess on the Pea (Andersen)
	The Sleeping Beauty (Perrault)
	Little Red Riding-Hood (de la Mare)
	Field, Eugene—A Dutch Lullaby
	Silver (de la Mare)
	The Toaster (Smith, W. J.)
	Dandelions (Frost, F. M.)
	The Little Rose Tree (Field, Rachel)
	Everyone Sang (Sassoon)
	The Night Will Never Stay (Farjeon)
	Brooms (Aldis, D.)

No Shop Does the Bird Use (Coat-
sworth, E.)
Folklore—Cinderella (Korean)
Folklore, American
    Coyote Places the Stars
    Wiley and the Hairy Man
Frost, Robert
    The Last Word of a Bluebird
    The Pasture
    Stopping by Woods on a Snowy
        Evening
    The Road Not Taken

G   Grahame, Kenneth—The Wind in the
    Willows (excerpt)
Grimm, Jacob and Wilhelm
    The Shoemaker and the Elves
    Rapunzel
    Hansel and Gretel

J-K   Kipling, Rudyard—The Elephant's
    Child

M   Milne, A. A.—Missing

N   Nonsense Rhymes
    Jabberwocky (Carroll)
    Jellyfish Stew (Prelutsky)
    Habits of the Hippopotamus
        (Guiterman)
    Eletelephony (Richards)
    The Reason for the Pelican (Ciardi)
    Antigonish (Mearns)
    I Wish That My Room Had a Floor
        (Burgess)
    There Was a Young Lady of Woosester
        (Anonymous)
    There Was an Old Man with a Beard
        (Lear)
    There Was an Old Man of Peru
        (Anonymous)
Nursery Rhymes
    The Old Woman in a Shoe
    Jack and Jill
    Hey Diddle, Diddle
    Miss Muffet
    Mary's Lamb
    Humpty Dumpty

P   Potter, Beatrix—The Tale of Jemima
    Puddle-Duck

S   Sandburg, Carl
    Fog
    The Skyscraper to the Moon and How
        the Green Rat with the Rheumatism
        Ran a Thousand Miles Twice
    Stevenson, Robert Louis
    Requiem
    My Shadow
    Looking-Glass River
    The Swing

The Gardener
Bed in Summer
Kidnapped (excerpt)

W-X-Y-Z   White, E. B.—Charlotte's Web
    (excerpt)
    Wilder, Laura Ingalls—Little House on
        the Prairie (excerpt)

MATHEMATICS

Vol.	Article
A	Abacus
	Arithmetic
C	Calendar
M	Mathematics
	Money
N	Number Puzzles and Games
T	Time
W-X-Y-Z	Weights and Measures

SOCIAL STUDIES

Vol.	Family, School, and Community
A	African Americans
	Amish
C	Cities
	Colonial Life in America
D	Dentistry
	Doctors
F	Family
	Farms and Farming
	Fire Fighting and Prevention
H	Hispanic Americans
	Homes and Housing
J-K	Kindergarten and Nursery Schools
L	Learning
	Libraries
M	Money
N	Nurses and Nursing
P	Parks and Playgrounds
	Police
	Postal Service
Q-R	Restaurants
	Retail Stores
S	Schools
	Supermarkets
T	Teachers and Teaching
	Traffic Control
U-V	Veterinarians

Vol.	The United States
C	Capitol, United States Colonial Life in America Colonial Sites You Can Visit Today Columbus, Christopher
D	Democracy
E	Elections
F	Flags
I	Indians, American
L	Law and Law Enforcement Liberty, Statue of Liberty Bell
M	Mayflower Municipal Government
P	Plymouth Colony Presidency of the United States Puritans
S	State Governments Supreme Court of the United States
T	Thanksgiving Day
U-V	United Nations United States, Congress of the
W-X-Y-Z	White House

Vol.	Important People in American History
A	Adams, John Anthony, Susan B.
B	Barton, Clara Bell, Alexander Graham Blackwell, Elizabeth Boone, Daniel Bush, George Bush, George W.
C	Carson, Rachel Carver, George Washington Clinton, William
D	Douglass, Frederick
E	Edison, Thomas Alva Ericson, Leif
F	Franklin, Benjamin Friedan, Betty Fulton, Robert
G	Gates, William (Bill)
H	Henry, Patrick Hobby, Oveta Culp
J-K	Jackson, Andrew Jackson, Jesse Jefferson, Thomas Keller, Helen Kennedy, John F. King, Martin Luther, Jr.

L	Lee, Robert E. Lincoln, Abraham
M	Madison, James
P	Powhatan
Q-R	Revere, Paul Rolfe, John Roosevelt, Eleanor Roosevelt, Franklin D. Roosevelt, Theodore
S	Sequoya Stowe, Harriet Beecher Stuyvesant, Peter
T	Tecumseh Tubman, Harriet
W-X-Y-Z	Washington, George Whitney, Eli Wright, Orville and Wilbur

Vol.	Geography
A	Agriculture Atlantic Ocean
B	Biomes
C	Cities Climate Continents
D	Deserts
E	Earth Equator
F	Forests and Forestry
I	Indian Ocean Islands
L	Lakes
M	Maps and Globes
N	National Park System Natural Resources North America
O	Oceans and Seas of the World
P	Pacific Ocean and Islands
Q-R	Rivers
S	Seasons
U-V	United States
W-X-Y-Z	Weather Wetlands World THE NEW BOOK OF KNOWLEDGE contains articles on individual cities, states, countries, regions, and continents. Young readers will find information in these articles about the land, people, history, and government

of places in which they are interested.

Vol.	Holidays
C	Christmas
E	Easter
H	Hanukkah
	Holidays
I	Independence Day
N	New Year Celebrations Around the World
P	Passover
	Purim
Q-R	Ramadan
	Religious Holidays
T	Thanksgiving Day
U-V	Valentines Day

SCIENCE AND TECHNOLOGY

Vol.	Plants, Animals, and the Human Body
A	Animal Rights
	Animals
	Apes
B	Bamboo
	Bats
	Birds
	Body, Human
	Butterflies and Moths
C	Cats
D	Dinosaurs
	Dogs
	Doves and Pigeons
	Dragonflies
E	Endangered Species
F	Flowers
	Frogs and Toads
H	Hamsters
	Hibernation
	Horses
I	Insects
L	Leaves
	Life
M	Monkeys
N	Nature, Study of
P	Plants
Q-R	Rabbits and Hares
T	Trees
W-X-Y-Z	Zebras
	Zoos

Vol.	Earth and Space
A	Armstrong, Neil A.
	Astronauts
C	Climate
	Clouds
	Constellations
E	Earth-Moving Machinery
	Earthquakes
	Electricity
G	Global Warming
I	Ice
M	Magnets and Magnetism
	Milky Way
	Minerals
	Moon
P	Planets
Q-R	Rain, Snow, Sleet, and Hail
	Rainbow
	Rocks
S	Space Exploration and Travel
	Sun
T	Thunder and Lightning
	Tsunamis
W-X-Y-Z	Water
	Weather

HEALTH AND SAFETY

Vol.	Article
A	Ambulances
B	Baby
	Body Signals
D	Doctors
E	Ear
	Eye
H	Health
	Hospitals
N	Nurses and Nursing
	Nutrition
P	Physical Fitness
S	Safety
	Skeletal System
	Sleep
T	Teeth

MUSIC

Vol.	Article

B	Ballet
C	Carols
D	Drum
F	Folk Dance
	Folk Music
L	Lullabies
M	Musical Instruments
N	National Anthems and Patriotic Songs
O	Orchestra
P	Piano
Q-R	Recorder
U-V	United States, Music of the

ART

Vol.	Art and Artists
C	Cassatt, Mary
	Chagall, Marc
	Color
D	Drawing
H	Homer, Winslow
I	Illustration and Illustrators
M	Matisse, Henri
	Miró, Joan
	Moses, Grandma
	Museums
S	Sendak, Maurice

Vol.	Arts and Crafts
C	Clay Modeling
D	Decoupage
F	Finger Painting
G	Greeting Cards
O	Origami

P	Papier-mâché
	Puppets and Marionettes
Q-R	Rubbings
U-V	Valentines

PHYSICAL EDUCATION, SPORTS, AND GAMES

Vol.	Article
B	Badminton
	Ball
	Baseball
	Basketball
	Bicycling
	Bowling
C	Charades
	Croquet
F	Ferris Wheels
G	Gymnastics
J-K	Jogging and Running
	Judo
	Juggling
J-K	Karate
L	Little League Baseball
M	Martial Arts
P	Physical Education
	Physical Fitness
R	Roller Coasters
S	Skiing
	Soccer and Youth Soccer
	Softball
	Swimming
T	Table Tennis
	Track and Field

GRADES 4 THROUGH 6

▶ **THE STUDENT IN THE MIDDLE GRADES**

In grades 4 through 6, young students experience an interval of relative balance, calm, and stability compared with their earlier period of transition from home to school during the primary years, or compared with the coming years of confusion and stress that usually characterize adolescence. Physical growth continues, but the body changes in less striking ways. The mind and emotions steadily mature, and young learners are expected to have more control over their feelings and to accept more responsibility for how and what they learn.

These youngsters cherish their sense of growing independence, yet they want and accept limits. They are eager to find their place in their own age-group and to develop close relationships with friends. Peers begin to have more influence over their behavior and thinking, but family ties are still strong. This is the age of belonging—to a team, a group, a club, or a clique. It is also an age when youngsters enjoy family togetherness. They love to help plan family projects, trips, hobbies, and outings.

Middle grade students are eager to know what things are, how they work, how they were discovered, and how they are used. Children of this age have a great need to understand meanings behind facts and to see connections. Although their ability to comprehend at an abstract level is growing, these youngsters still need to learn by doing. However, attention spans are longer and interests are more intense. Children of 9 or 10 can spend hours with a favorite activity. Nevertheless, they may pass from interest to interest as they go through the grades, always ready to open doors to new experiences and understandings.

Depending on the community in which they live, students in grades 4 through 6 may attend one of three different types of school configurations. Most middle graders attend an elementary school, although it may not be the same building they attended in the primary grades. Many sixth graders and some fifth graders go to a middle school. Some sixth graders move on to a junior high school.

Those students still in elementary schools will find their learning taking place in a familiar environment. They spend most of the day in a self-contained classroom, with one teacher for all the core curriculum subjects. In some middle schools, a team-teaching approach is used. Teams of two or more teachers will share teaching responsibilities for their classes. One may teach science and math; another may teach English and social studies. In other middle schools and most junior high schools, instruction is completely departmentalized, with a different teacher for each subject.

Whatever the type of school they attend, these youngsters continue to need parental or adult guidance and support during the middle grade years. Let them know you expect them to do well. Motivate them with encouragement and praise. Help them to feel good about themselves and their abilities. Provide assistance, as needed, with homework and other school activities. Keep the communication lines with your children and your children's teachers open and active. These are important years—years in which young people must acquire the confidence, the knowledge, and the skills they will need to do well in high school and in their adult years.

Enjoyable activities you and your youngsters can do together to reinforce what they are learning in the core curriculum areas—Reading, Language, and Literature; Mathematics; Social Studies; and Science—are listed after each of those sections.

The lists of articles at the very end of this section for grades 4 through 6 include many, but certainly not all, of the articles about each subject area that appear in THE NEW BOOK OF KNOWLEDGE. It is important that students look up the names of topics they want to read about in the Index or in the set itself to locate all of the information they may need or want. For example, in the Social Studies area, articles about each of the countries of the world are not listed in this section but can easily be located by looking each one up under its own name.

▶ READING, LANGUAGE, AND LITERATURE

The foundations of reading are taught in the primary grades. Students entering the middle grades should have sound word-attack and word-recognition skills, be able to comprehend what they read at least at a literal level, and begin to understand the elements of good literature. All these skills must be applied and expanded if students are to grow in ability. The reading curriculum in grades 4 through 6 is composed of a mix of developmental reading, content-area reading, and recreational reading.

Developmental reading instruction continues at grades 4, 5, and 6 so that middle grade students learn more advanced reading skills and strategies. Emphasis is on word analysis and higher-level comprehension and critical-thinking skills. Learning prefixes, suffixes, inflected endings, and root words teaches youngsters how to decipher most words, even difficult multisyllabic words. Vocabulary and dictionary skills are taught, usually also including the study of context clues, synonyms, antonyms, and words with multiple meanings, to give students the ability to learn how to unlock the meanings of words.

Reading is primarily a process of constructing meaning from written words, and students are also taught how to apply a variety of comprehension and critical-thinking skills and strategies to do it well. These skills range from making inferences, understanding cause and effect relationships, and summarizing main ideas and key facts to understanding a writer's point of view, recognizing various persuasive devices, and being able to distinguish between fact and opinion.

In the primary grades, youngsters learned the mechanics of reading and began to read simple essays, stories, and poems. In the middle grades, students need to know how to read to learn. They must use reading to get information from many different types of books, including content-area textbooks, reference books, nonfiction books such as biographies, and many other types of resources. Reading these many different texts for information requires the use of good study skills as well as advanced reading skills, so study skills are also emphasized at these levels. Students must also know how to use the various parts of a book—the table of contents, preface, copyright page, index, glossary—to find out where the information one needs in it may be located. They also learn how to skim or scan through a book to locate information quickly; how and when to use encyclopedias, atlases, almanacs, and other reference materials; how to locate resources by referring to a library card or electronic catalog; and how to use graphic sources of information, such as tables, lists, charts, graphs, time lines, pictures, diagrams, and maps and globes. In addition, youngsters are taught to adjust their method and rate of reading depending on the type of material and their purpose in reading it. As they read their social studies, science, and math textbooks, and as they consult the variety of other print materials they need to use, students are, in effect, applying their reading knowledge as well as their thinking, comprehension, and study skills throughout the school day.

Teachers in the middle grades also recognize the importance of nurturing their students' recreational reading interests and activities, and some classroom time is provided for reading for pure pleasure. Youngsters are motivated to explore many literary genres: traditional folktales, myths, fables, and epics; realistic fiction; fantasy and science fiction; suspense and mystery; historical fiction; poetry; biographies; and books about personal experiences and adventures. Class or group discussions revolve around students' reactions to and interpretations of what they have read and include discussions of the setting, plot, characters, mood, and the author's use of language. Knowing about the elements of good literature helps children make worthwhile reading choices and enhances their reading enjoyment.

Reading growth is a complex process. Middle grade teachers remember that each child is an individual with different needs and abilities. Whether they use a traditional or whole-language approach, they try to ensure that every child's needs are met.

Children are introduced to the basics of writing in the primary grades. In grades 4 through 6 more frequent writing opportunities help students hone their skills. Introducing them to the elements of writing as a craft during these years helps them become better users of written language.

Aware that most youngsters sometimes have difficulty selecting a topic to write about, many teachers conduct prewriting brainstorming sessions. Students and teacher join in discussion of a general theme, sharing ideas and suggestions for writing topics and approaches. Once topics have been selected, students are encouraged to write a first draft quickly, concentrating on key ideas and details. Many teachers ask students to review each other's drafts, either as partners or in small groups. Youngsters learn to make thoughtful, supportive comments and recommendations during this peer review, helping each other revise and improve their writing. Once revised drafts are completed, the editing process takes over. Teachers may conduct mini-lessons at this point, focusing on an aspect of spelling, grammar, usage, or capitalization and punctuation. Other teachers hold student-teacher conferences during the revising and editing steps. When all revisions and corrections have been made, students "publish" their final versions. This may mean simply writing their pieces in their best handwriting or typing them in a computer word processing program, or turning them into booklets or books with illustrations and covers.

During the writing process, students are often encouraged to think of themselves as authors and to find a personal writing voice, incorporating humor, colorful language, or other characteristics that are natural to their own personality or use of words.

Middle grade writing assignments will usually include stories, poetry, reports, and essays. Some youngsters write articles for class or school newspapers. Direct connection to the reading curriculum is made by encouraging youngsters to use the literature they read in the classroom or at home as models for their own writing.

In schools with computers, middle graders may use simple word-processing programs. Many children find this a less cumbersome way of writing. They can edit and make changes, substitutions, and deletions quickly and easily without having to produce several handwritten copies.

English and spelling textbooks are used to provide the basic instruction children need in the conventions and mechanics of written language, and students also learn how to use a dictionary and a thesaurus. The proof of their learning, however, is their growing ability to communicate effectively in writing.

Children acquire their basic speech patterns from their parents and families, from their neighborhood friends, and from the speech of the region in which they live. Their speech patterns are largely formed by the time they start school. The school can do much, however, to improve and polish them as necessary by providing instruction in oral expression. Teachers offer many opportunities for youngsters to practice oral expression. These range from making simple announcements to taking part in group discussions. In the middle grades, students report on individual and group projects, tell about personal experiences, give and explain information and directions, tell stories, recite poetry, take part in dramatics and choral speaking, make introductions, conduct interviews, read aloud, and dramatize telephone conversations.

Students are also taught that good listening habits are important. They are shown how to be attentive and courteous while others are speaking and responsive to the thoughts and questions expressed by a speaker. Above all, students learn that listening is an important avenue for learning.

Home Activities for Reading, Language, and Literature

Continue to read aloud to your youngsters as often as possible. Listen to your youngsters read to you from books, magazines, or from stories and reports they have written themselves. Discuss authors and types of books you enjoy reading together. Find more books by the same author in your local library. Ask the librarian to recommend other authors and types of books similar to your current favorites. Help your youngsters develop the habit of looking up information in encyclopedias and other reference books. Encourage their enthusiasm and interests. Start a letter diary together. Each day, or once or twice a week, one of you write a letter to the other and ask the other person to write a response. As your youngsters come upon interesting new words in their reading or in other activities, encourage them to look up the meanings and usage of these words in a dictionary. Urge them to use these words in their own writing and conversation. Make dinner table conversation an enjoyable experience for the entire family. Tell riddles, jokes, and stories, and share with each other the day's special events and activities. This is a good age level for your youngsters to find regular pen pals. They may be friends or relatives who live some distance away. Many magazines for young people publish the names and addresses of Pen Pal Clubs or of youngsters who want to correspond with others having similar interests.

▶ **MATHEMATICS**

In grades 4 through 6, students consolidate and build on the mathematical skills they acquired in earlier grades. They are also taught how to develop their reasoning abilities further and use them to learn new, more complex and more advanced math concepts and strategies.

Middle grade youngsters apply their knowledge of addition, subtraction, multiplication, and division to larger numbers and to fractions and decimals. Their understanding of how to work with numbers is enhanced as they learn about the different properties of numbers. Concepts of prime and composite numbers, ratio, proportion, and percent are also introduced at this level. Their work is not always

done as paper-and-pencil activities. Students also learn estimation, mental arithmetic, and the use of calculators and computers.

Mathematical patterns and relationships are discovered as youngsters learn about equations, inequalities, ordered pairs, and coordinate graphs. Visual and concrete experiences help students also understand geometric concepts. Students create models and use rulers, compasses, and protractors as they explore two- and three-dimensional geometric figures, measure angles, and determine symmetry, congruency, and similarity in geometric forms.

Hands-on measuring tools, including yardsticks, meter sticks, gallon and liter containers, balance scales, and others, are often used to help students learn how to determine length and distance, weight and mass, volume and capacity, and area and perimeter. Youngsters learn to use both standard and metric units and to make conversions within both systems.

Experiences in collecting and interpreting numerical data are provided, and students present the results in the form of tables, charts, or graphs, or by calculating the mean, median, and mode of the statistical data they have collected. Experiments with coins, dice, playing cards, and other objects are often used as the basis for helping students learn the strategies they need to make probability predictions.

A key element in the middle grade mathematics curriculum is the problem-solving strand. All of the concepts and skills students learn in mathematics are applied in problem-solving situations. Students at this level learn how to use a logical sequence of steps and a variety of strategies for solving problems. Finding a pattern; using a picture, chart, or model; working backwards; making an organized list; and breaking a complex problem into two or more simple problems are among the strategies they learn to use in working out solutions to the problems they must solve.

By the time they finish the sixth grade, most students will have formed a lifelong attitude toward mathematics. Unfortunately, many youngsters lose interest in, and enjoyment of, math during the middle grade years. Many lack confidence in their ability to understand

and use math in school and in everyday life. Parents also find that it becomes more difficult to help their youngsters in math as time goes on. It is important for parents to communicate with the teacher or principal if their children start to show negative attitudes toward the subject or seem to be having difficulty doing the work. Concerned parents and teachers will want to have every opportunity to ensure that math is a positive and pleasurable experience for every child.

Home Activities for Mathematics

- Help your youngsters become aware of how large numbers are used in news articles, books, and on television programs. Ask them to read a number and talk about how big a quantity it represents. Do the same with fractions and decimals.
- If your youngsters have a special interest in a sport, encourage them to collect statistics for the sport and its players. In baseball, for example, youngsters love to rattle off batting averages, runs batted in (RBI's), home runs, base hits, stolen bases, strikeouts, and many other statistics.
- Help your youngsters use mathematics in everyday activities. Encourage them to set up budgets that include money earned, an allowance, savings, and purchases. Help them figure out best buys when shopping together.
- Ask your youngsters to estimate measurements when you are on an excursion or trip. "How high do you think that building is?" "How far is it across the lake?" "How many people will fit in the elevator?" Follow up by trying to find the answer when you can.
- Encourage your youngsters to collect interesting number facts that appear in the media or in their reading. This activity may include the sales figures for the latest recording of a favorite entertainer or the distance between the Earth and the nearest star.
- Play games involving numbers with your youngster. Card and dice games call for computation and memory skills, and many board games call for the use of play money.
- Help your youngsters interpret and use the information in everyday schedules, graphs, and tables. You can use many items to do this, including television and movie schedules, arena and theater seating diagrams, train and bus timetables, and pie and line charts and graphs you find in newspaper and magazine articles.

▶ **SOCIAL STUDIES**

Social studies in the middle grades includes history, geography, political science, economics, current affairs, and topics from the social science subjects such as anthropology, sociology, and psychology. Although the social studies curriculum varies from school to school, in general, students in grades 4 through 6 learn about their own city and state; the history and geography of the United States and other nations in the Western Hemisphere; North and South America's historical and cultural roots; and the diverse regions and nations of the world.

The study of the history of the United States usually concentrates on Native Americans, the age of the discovery and exploration of the North American continent, the colonial and revolutionary periods, and the Civil War. Major events from the late 1800's to the present may be covered, but not in depth. Emphasis on modern and contemporary history is usually given in grades 7 through 9 and in high school. Middle grade teachers try to help students understand the traditions and the political and cultural institutions of the United States and to appreciate the events and the people that most influenced our history and the development of our society.

Students learn about the geography of the United States by reading a variety of information sources and comparing and contrasting information about the different regions of the country. Physical and political maps, population tables, product maps, travel brochures, and other tools are also examined to determine how the land, the economy, the people, and the cultural traditions of one region vary from those of another. During the study of the United States, many schools include a companion study of one or more neighbors—Canada and Central and South America.

The study of world history and geography in the middle grades focuses on prehistoric, ancient, and medieval civilizations and on the cultural and social characteristics of other countries and regions. Students also learn to identify the geographic influences that affect the way people live.

Because the future of our nation and of the world depends upon intelligent and informed citizens, students also begin to study current events. Some classes subscribe to a daily local newspaper or to professionally prepared school newspapers designed for particular grade levels. Many schools use educational television or radio programs to present and stimulate interest in current events.

An important outcome of current-events studies is that youngsters become able to identify national and world issues. They enthusiastically take part in discussions and debates about such topics as the environment and conflicts between nations, as well as issues such as hunger, homelessness, and racism. Middle grade students sometimes debate serious matters that touch directly on their own lives and futures. Their increasing ability to empathize with others leads many youngsters at these age levels to begin to take seriously their rights and responsibilities as citizens in a democracy.

Teachers and school administrators commonly encourage activities that promote the development of citizenship skills. Many schools have student councils made up of elected class representatives. Parliamentary procedure is followed as students work on the council or on school committees. Youngsters also learn that there are many ways in which one person or group can be effective in bringing about change and resolving problems. They learn how to write letters and interview people. They collect and raise money for worthy causes. They campaign to save a local landmark, a stream, or an endangered species in their community and bring these issues to the attention of local, state, or federal government officials.

In the pursuit of social studies information, students also use research and problem-solving techniques. They discover that the study, research, and problem-solving skills they are acquiring in their reading, writing, and mathematics classes can be applied to their social studies projects. Working alone or in groups, youngsters use these skills when they consult an assortment of resources to locate, gather, interpret, evaluate, and organize information and then to prepare and deliver oral and written reports.

By the end of the sixth grade, youngsters will have made giant strides toward acquiring the abilities they will need to understand the complexities and the development of human societies around the world.

Home Activities for Social Studies

- Plan a trip with your youngsters. Show them how the scale and legends on a road map help you determine your route. As they develop an understanding of this kind of information, let them take charge of the road map and be responsible for directions to the driver.
- Discuss important news events at the family table. Help your youngsters distinguish between sensational gossip, unfounded rumor, and relevant facts that can be proven.
- Plan family outings or trips to include visits to museums and historical sites.
- Take your youngsters with you when you vote. Show them the ballot and voting machine. Talk about how you decide on the candidate you choose to vote for.
- Investigate and construct your family tree with your youngsters. Let them interview family members and fill in as many branches of the tree as possible. Talk about the family's origins.
- If you have a personal computer in your

home, encourage your youngsters to use educational games, data bases, and simulations with social studies themes. Let them discover how much fun this can be.

• Help your youngsters find ways of taking action on local and national matters of concern to them. They may want to write a letter to the local newspaper or to a public official, or they may want to join a special interest youth club or other organization.

• Encourage and help your youngsters locate places in the news on a map or globe.

▶ SCIENCE AND TECHNOLOGY

The middle grade science program continues the balanced approach of the primary grades in which concepts from each of the scientific disciplines—life science, earth science, and physical science—are taught each year. The scope is much broader, however. Students are introduced to a wider range of topics—from atoms to the universe, from bacteria to elephants, from light bulbs to space telescopes. They study only a limited number of concepts and principles in depth, however, as they develop an appreciation of and the habit of scientific thinking.

Youngsters in grades 4 through 6 become familiar with plant and animal life. They learn the similarities and differences in the traits of the simplest living things, such as bacteria and protozoans, and in the traits of animals with and without backbones. They trace the growth and development of flowering plants and plants with seeds or spores. As they examine the many different forms that life takes, students arrive at several key understandings: what an ecosystem is; how plants and animals make adaptations to their environments and how they change or evolve over time; how living things interact; and how the relationships among all the members of an ecosystem are intertwined.

Studies about space expand to include not only our solar system but also the other stars, galaxies, and objects that make up the universe. The wonders and riches of our own planet are presented so that students can learn about rocks, minerals, soil, water, and natural forces. They learn how weather, plate tectonics, volcanoes, and earthquakes constantly build up and wear away the surface of the planet. Students weigh the benefits of advancements in science and technology against the costs and trade-offs to human society and to the environment as they investigate air, water, land, and energy resources.

Several of the most fundamental principles and laws of physical science are first taught in grades 4 through 6. In the study of matter and its properties, students learn about the laws of the conservation of matter, and about atoms, elements, the periodic table, and how substances interact with each other physically and chemically. Isaac Newton's three laws of motion are demonstrated as students acquire knowledge about work, energy, and forces. Experiments with heat, light, sound, electricity, and magnetism lead young scientists to the understanding that although energy can be transferred from one system to another, the total amount of energy remains constant.

Middle grade students are usually ready to understand quite sophisticated scientific and technological concepts. They do this best when they are given opportunities to experiment, to draw conclusions, and to work through problem-solving activities.

Home Activities for Science and Technology

• Encourage your youngsters to find books in the library that give instructions for easy-to-do science experiments and activities. Help them do some of these activities and talk about the results.

• Youngsters at this age level have an exceptional empathy with animals. If it is possible, this is a good time to encourage them to have a pet, such as a puppy, kitten, or fish, and learn how to be responsible and care for it.

• Help your youngsters keep track of weather forecasts in the newspaper or from a radio or television newscast for a three- to four-week period. Consider together how often the forecast was correct. Was there a difference in how often short-range forecasts (one to two days) were correct compared to longer-range forecasts (four to five days)? Decide whether or not you can draw any conclusions about the accuracy of weather forecasting.

- Young people at this age are curious about how things work. Help your youngsters find instruction booklets, articles, and books written for their age level that explain how some of the electronic devices in your home work. These might include telephones, VCR's, microwave ovens, and calculators.
- Try some roadside or curbside geology investigations. Whenever you and your youngsters pass a building or park, visit a beach, or spot a fresh roadcut, examine the rocks you find. How many different samples can you find? Can you identify any? Can you find fossils in any? Examine together some books about rocks written for the age levels of your youngsters.
- Encourage your youngsters to keep a science diary or logbook. They may write about any interesting science observations or experiences they have, or they may focus their diary on one science topic such as bird-watching or stargazing.

▶ **HEALTH AND SAFETY**

The school health program for grades 4 through 6 continues to develop many of the topics begun in the primary grades, including the human body, nutrition, physical fitness, personal care, diseases, mental health, safety, and drug, alcohol, and tobacco use and abuse. Students now study these subjects in more depth.

When studying the human body, students examine its important systems in more detail. For example, as they study the structure of the circulatory system, they also learn how each of its components—heart, blood, and blood vessels—functions; how the circulatory system and the respiratory system work together; and how diet and exercise affect both systems. In addition, youngsters go beyond body systems to study simple aspects of more complex concepts such as heredity and genetics.

First aid is added to the concept of safety, and students learn the proper procedures to follow in various types of emergencies. Investigations into communicable and noncommunicable diseases expand to include heart disease, cancer, and other serious illnesses. In the area of mental health, youngsters continue to talk about effective ways of handling their feelings, and they also learn about how to improve their self-image and how to deal with stress. All children are encouraged to commit themselves to a regular exercise and fitness program and to maintain healthy attitudes toward the use of drugs, alcohol, and tobacco.

Students at this stage are ready to move beyond personal health and examine issues involved in consumer health and in community and environmental health. They learn how to use label and pricing information to make wise choices when shopping for food and health products, and they learn how to evaluate advertisements for these products. They become familiar with the various health services provided in their neighborhood: health departments, hospitals, health clinics, and emergency services.

Middle grade students often develop a keen sensitivity to environmental problems, and many youngsters become enthusiastic volunteers in environmental causes, working to reduce air, water, and garbage pollution in their homes and in their community.

Through the school health program, youngsters are provided with information and experiences that will help them maintain health-promoting attitudes and habits that are intended to last into adulthood.

▶ **MUSIC**

Music begins to become an important part of life for many children in the middle grades. At home they listen to music while working on hobbies, doing chores, or completing homework assignments. They enjoy watching music videos and often mimic popular entertainers.

Many 10- and 11-year-olds eagerly pick up popular dance steps and dance at home or at parties with their friends.

In school most youngsters participate in singing activities, frequently learning songs related to themes in the curriculum, such as songs of pioneers and cowboys and folk songs from around the world. Music teachers encourage students to read music and to experiment with part singing and harmony.

As they are asked to listen to recorded or live music, youngsters become familiar with a variety of musical styles, periods, and forms, ranging from classical and baroque to jazz and rock. In a thorough curriculum, they examine the elements a composer uses to communicate a musical message, including tempo, rhythm, melody, timbre, and harmonics. Students also learn how to pay attention to the contributions of different types of instruments and voices in a musical work.

Many children of this age learn to play a musical instrument through private lessons or at school, where they often can play in a band or orchestra. Some take voice lessons or participate in a school choral group.

Through a variety of musical activities, students can expand their appreciation and enjoyment of music.

▶ ART

Art is a very enjoyable school experience for middle grade children. They paint, draw, model in clay, design posters, construct with wood, make puppets and models, and work with paper, fabric, and many other materials and tools. They are usually allowed to base much of their creative work on personal experiences, and they are also asked to create pieces for projects in other subject areas. For example, students learning about the Middle Ages in social studies may create their own stained-glass windows using colored cellophane and black construction paper. A science unit on the ecology of a wetland may prompt the painting of a classroom mural depicting the many life-forms found in a wetland habitat.

Youngsters in grades 4 through 6 increase their knowledge of the elements of design and are encouraged to experiment with color, line, shape, space, and texture in their own works. In some programs they learn how to compare the styles of different artists and different cultures or historical periods by viewing and discussing print reproductions, slides, or videotapes of a broad range of artworks.

The school art program for the middle grades motivates youngsters to express their own ideas and feelings through art activities and to appreciate art in many of its forms.

▶ PHYSICAL EDUCATION AND SPORTS

Physical fitness, rhythmic activities, gymnastics, and game skills constitute the core of the physical education program for grades 4 through 6. A wide variety of indoor and outdoor activities including walking, running, muscle stretching and strengthening, push-ups, pull-ups, and sit-ups help youngsters gain proficiency in agility, strength, endurance, power, flexibility, and speed.

The rhythmic and gymnastic part of the program calls for folk dancing, forward- and backward-roll variations, and various skills performed on the balance beam.

There is more emphasis for this age-group on games and sports skills. Students leaving the sixth grade usually have a basic knowledge of popular games and their rules including softball, soccer, volleyball, and basketball. Most students should be able to throw, hit, and field a softball; kick, pass, and dribble a soccer ball; shoot, pass, catch, and dribble a basketball; serve and volley a volleyball; and catch, pass, and kick a football.

At this age, students are not pressured to become star performers. They are encouraged to participate in activities and games for their own well-being and enjoyment and to develop skills and abilities they can use all of their lives. The physical education program in grades 4 through 6 tries to promote a positive self-image in each child. The program helps middle school children acquire appropriate social and emotional behaviors toward others.

CURRICULUM-RELATED ARTICLES

Some of the important articles in THE NEW BOOK OF KNOWLEDGE that relate to the 4 through 6 school curriculum are listed here. Many other articles you or your youngsters may want to read while they are studying topics in these curriculum areas can be found by looking them up in the Index or in the set itself.

READING, LANGUAGE, AND LITERATURE

Vol.	Reading and Language
A	Alphabet
E	English Language
G	Grammar
L	Language Arts
P	Parts of Speech Phonics
Q-R	Reading
S	Slang Synonyms and Antonyms
W-X-Y-Z	Word Games Word Origins

Vol.	Writing
A	Abbreviations Address, Forms of
C	Compositions
D	Diaries and Journals
F	Figures of Speech
H	Handwriting Homonyms
L	Letter Writing
O	Outlines
P	Proofreading Punctuation
Q-R	Research and Reports for School
S	Spelling
U-V	Vocabulary
W-X-Y-Z	Writing

Vol.	Oral Language/Speech
D	Debates and Discussions
J-K	Jokes and Riddles
P	Plays Pronunciation Public Speaking
S	Speech Speech Disorders Storytelling
T	Tongue Twisters

Vol.	Reference, Research, and Study Skills
B	Book Reports and Reviews Books: From Author to Reader
D	Dictionaries
E	Encyclopedias
I	Indexes and Indexing
L	Libraries
M	Magazines Maps and Globes
N	Newspapers
P	Paperback Books
Q-R	Reference Materials Research
S	Study, How to
T	Tests and Test Taking Time Management

Vol.	Literature
A	Africa, Literature of American Literature Arabian Nights Arabic Literature Arthur, King
B	Ballads Biography, Autobiography, and Biographical Novel
C	Caldecott, Randolph Caldecott and Newbery Medals Canada, Literature of Children's Literature
D	Diaries and Journals Drama
E	English Literature Essays
F	Fables Fairy Tales Fiction Figures of Speech Folklore Folklore, American
G	Greek Mythology
H	Humor
I	Iliad Illustration and Illustrators

J-K	Jokes and Riddles
L	Legends
	Literature
M	Mystery and Detective Stories
	Mythology
N	Newbery, John
	Nonsense Rhymes
	Norse Mythology
O	Odyssey
P	Poetry
Q-R	Robin Hood
S	Science Fiction
	Short Stories

Vol.	Author Biographies
A	Alcott, Louisa May
	Andersen, Hans Christian
	Angelou, Maya
B	Barrie, Sir James Matthew
	Blume, Judy
	Browning, Elizabeth Barrett and Robert
	Burns, Robert
C	Carroll, Lewis
D	Dickens, Charles
	Dickinson, Emily
	Doyle, Sir Arthur Conan
	Dunbar, Paul Laurence
E	Eliot, T. S.
F	Frost, Robert
G	Grahame, Kenneth
	Grimm, Jacob and Wilhelm
H	Hawthorne, Nathaniel
	Hemingway, Ernest
	Henry, O.
	Homer
	Hughes, Langston
I	Irving, Washington
J-K	Kipling, Rudyard
L	London, Jack
	Longfellow, Henry Wadsworth
P	Poe, Edgar Allan
Q-R	Rossetti Family
	Rowling, J. K.
S	Sandburg, Carl
	Sendak, Maurice
	Shakespeare, William
	Steinbeck, John
	Stevenson, Robert Louis
	Swift, Jonathan
T	Thurber, James

	Tolkien, J. R. R.
	Twain, Mark
V	Verne, Jules
W-X-Y-Z	White, E. B.
	Whittier, John Greenleaf
	Wilde, Oscar
	Wilder, Laura Ingalls
	Williams, William Carlos
	(See also the article CHILDREN'S LITERATURE for profiles of additional authors and illustrators.)

Vol.	Selections from Literature
A	Alcott, Louisa May Little Women (excerpt)
	Andersen, Hans Christian—The Emperor's New Clothes
	Arabian Nights
	Aladdin and the Wonderful Lamp (excerpt)
	The Forty Thieves (excerpt)
B	Barrie, Sir James Matthew—Peter Pan (excerpt)
	Bible Stories
	Noah's Ark
	David and Goliath
	Jonah
	Daniel in the Lions' Den
	The Boy Jesus
	Browning, Robert—Pied Piper of Hamelin (excerpt)
	Burns, Robert—A Red, Red Rose
C	Carroll, Lewis—Alice's Adventures in Wonderland (excerpt)
	Christmas Story (Gospel according to Luke)
D	Diaries and Journals—The Diary of Anne Frank (excerpt)
	Dickinson, Emily
	A Bird Came Down the Walk
	I'll Tell You How the Sun Rose
	Doyle, Sir Arthur Conan—The Red-Headed League (excerpt)
	Dunbar, Paul Laurence
	Promise
	Fulfilment
F	Fables
	The Lion and the Mouse (Aesop)
	The Ant and the Grasshopper (Aesop)
	The Four Oxen and the Lion (Aesop)
	The Tyrant Who Became a Just Ruler (Bidpai)
	The Blind Men and the Elephant (Saxe)
	The Moth and the Star (Thurber)

Fairy Tales
The Enchanted Princess (German)
The Princess on the Pea (Andersen)
The Sleeping Beauty (Perrault)
Little Red Riding-Hood (de la Mare)
Field, Eugene—A Dutch Lullaby
Figures of Speech
Silver (de la Mare)
The Toaster (Smith, W. J.)
Dandelions (Frost, F. M.)
The Little Rose Tree (Field, Rachel)
Everyone Sang (Sassoon)
The Night Will Never Stay (Farjeon)
Brooms (Aldis, D.)
No Shop Does the Bird Use (Coatsworth, E.)
Folklore—Cinderella (Korean)
Folklore, American
Coyote Places the Stars
Wiley and the Hairy Man
Frost, Robert
The Last Word of a Bluebird
The Pasture
Stopping by Woods on a Snowy Evening
The Road Not Taken

G Gettysburg Address
Grahame, Kenneth—The Wind in the Willows (excerpt)
Grimm, Jacob and Wilhelm
The Shoemaker and the Elves
Rapunzel
Hansel and Gretel

H Hawthorne, Nathaniel—Young Goodman Brown

I Irving, Washington—Rip Van Winkle (excerpt)

L Legends
The Vanishing Hitchhiker (United States)
Roland and Oliver (France)
The Legend of Robin Hood (England)
London, Jack—The Call of the Wild (excerpt)
Longfellow, Henry Wadsworth—The Arrow and the Song

N Nonsense Rhymes
Jabberwocky (Carroll)
Jellyfish Stew (Prelutsky)
Habits of the Hippopotamus (Guiterman)
Eletelephony (Richards)
The Reason for the Pelican (Ciardi)
Antigonish (Mearns)
I Wish That My Room Had a Floor (Burgess)
There Was a Young Lady of Woosester

(Anonymous)
There Was an Old Man with a Beard (Lear)
There Was an Old Man of Peru (Anonymous)

P Poe—Eldorado

Q-R Rossetti—Who Has Seen the Wind

S Sandburg, Carl
Fog
The Skyscraper to the Moon and How the Green Rat with the Rheumatism Ran a Thousand Miles Twice (Rootabaga Stories)
Stevenson, Robert Louis—Kidnapped (excerpt)
Swift, Jonathan—Gulliver's Travels (excerpt)

T Thurber, James—The Great Quillow (excerpt)
Tolkien, J. R. R.—The Hobbit (excerpt)
Twain, Mark
The Adventures of Tom Sawyer (excerpt)
The Celebrated Jumping Frog of Calaveras County (excerpt)

W-X-Y-Z White, E. B.—Charlotte's Web (excerpt)
Wilder, Laura Ingalls—Little House on the Prairie (excerpt)
Williams, Carlos William—The Red Wheelbarrow

MATHEMATICS

Vol.	Article
A	Abacus
	Algebra
	Arithmetic
B	Budgets, Family
C	Calendar
	Computers
D	Decimal System
E	Einstein, Albert
F	Fractions and Decimals
G	Gauss, Carl Friedrich
	Geometry
	Graphs
I	Interest
M	Mathematics
	Mathematics, History of
	Money
N	Newton, Isaac

Civil War and an Expanding America

A
Abolition Movement
Addams, Jane
African Americans
Anthony, Susan B.

B
Barton, Clara
Boone, Daniel
Booth, John Wilkes
Bowie, James
Brown, John

C
Carson, Kit
Carver, George Washington
Child Labor
Civil War, United States
Clay, Henry
Compromise of 1850
Confederate States of America
Cowboys
Crockett, David (Davy)

D
Davis, Jefferson
Dix, Dorothea
Douglass, Frederick
Dred Scott Decision
Du Bois, W. E. B.

E
Emancipation Proclamation
Erie Canal
Ethnic Groups

F
Farragut, David
Frémont, John Charles
Fulton, Robert
Fur Trade in North America

G
Garrison, William Lloyd
Garvey, Marcus
Gettysburg Address
Gold Rushes
Grant, Ulysses S.

H
Hickok, James Butler ("Wild Bill")
Houston, Samuel

I
Immigration
Indians, American
Industrial Revolution

J-K
Jackson, Andrew
Jackson, Thomas Jonathan ("Stonewall")

J-K
Kansas-Nebraska Act

L
Labor Movement
Lee, Robert E.
Liberty, Statue of
Lincoln, Abraham

M
Mexican War
Monroe, James
Monroe Doctrine
Mormons

O
Oriental Exclusion Acts

P
Pioneer Life
Pony Express

Q-R
Ranch Life
Reconstruction Period

S
Scott, Winfield
Sherman, William Tecumseh
Slavery
Stowe, Harriet Beecher

T
Territorial Expansion of the United States
Tubman, Harriet

U-V
Underground Railroad

W-X-Y-Z
Washington, Booker T.
Whitney, Eli
Women's Rights Movement

W-X-Y-Z
Young, Brigham

The Modern Era

A
American Civil Liberties Union (ACLU)
American Indian Movement (AIM)
Arafat, Yasir

B
Bush, George
Bush, George W.

C
Civil Rights
Clinton, William
Cold War
Communism
Cuban Missile Crisis

D
Dawes, Charles G.
Debs, Eugene
Depression, Great
Depressions and Recessions
Dewey, George
Diana, Princess of Wales
Disarmament

F
Famine
Farrakhan, Louis
Fascism

G
Garner, John Nance

H
Hijacking
Holocaust
Hoover, J. Edgar
Human Rights

I
Iran-Contra Affair
Iraq War

J-K
Kennedy, John F.
Khomeini, Ruhollah
King, Martin Luther, Jr.
Korean War

L
League of Nations

M
Malcolm X

N	Nazism Nixon, Richard M.
O	Organized Crime Oswald, Lee Harvey
P	Panama Canal Powell, Colin
Q-R	Qaddafi, Muammar al- Qaeda, Al
Q-R	Racism Reagan, Ronald W.
S	Spanish-American War
T	Terrorism
U-V	Un-American Activities Committee, House United Nations
U-V	Vietnam War Volunteerism
W-X-Y-Z	Watergate Women's Rights Movement World War I World War II

Vol.	**The Fifty States of the United States**
A	Alabama Alaska Arizona Arkansas
C	California Colorado Connecticut
D	Delaware
F	Florida
G	Georgia
H	Hawaii
I	Idaho Illinois Indiana Iowa
J-K	Kansas Kentucky
L	Louisiana
M	Maine Maryland Massachusetts Michigan Minnesota Mississippi Missouri Montana
N	Nebraska Nevada New Hampshire

	New Jersey New Mexico New York North Carolina North Dakota
O	Ohio Oklahoma Oregon
P	Pennsylvania
Q-R	Rhode Island
S	South Carolina South Dakota
T	Tennessee Texas
U-V	Utah
U-V	Vermont Virginia
W-X-Y-Z	Washington West Virginia Wisconsin Wyoming

Vol.	**Government**
B	Bill of Rights
C	Cabinet of the United States Capitol, United States Citizenship Civil Rights
D	Declaration of Independence Democracy
E	Elections
F	First Amendment Freedoms First Ladies
G	Government, Forms of
H	Homeland Security, United States Department of
L	Law and Law Enforcement
M	Magna Carta Municipal Government
N	Naturalization
P	Presidency of the United States
S	State Governments Supreme Court of the United States
U-V	United Nations United States, Congress of United States, Constitution of the United States, Government of the
U-V	Voting
W-X-Y-Z	Washington, D.C. White House (See also names of presidents and

individual departments of the United States government.)

Vol.	Geography
A	Atlantic Ocean
B	Biomes
C	Cities
	Climate
	Continents
D	Deserts
E	Earth
	Earthquakes
	Equator
	Erosion
F	Forests and Forestry
G	Geography
	Glaciers
	Global Warming
	Greenwich Observatory
I	Indian Ocean
	International Date Line
	Islands
L	Lakes
	Latitude and Longitude
M	Maps and Globes
	Mountains
N	Natural Resources
O	Ocean
	Oceans and Seas of the World
P	Pacific Ocean and Islands
	Population
Q-R	Rain Forests
	Rivers
S	Seasons
T	Tides
	Time
	Tsunamis
U-V	Volcanoes
W-X-Y-Z	Water Supply
	Weather
	Wetlands
	World

Vol.	World Regions and Cultures

United States and Canada

A	American Literature
C	Canada
	Canada, Art and Architecture of
	Canada, Government of
	Canada, History of
	Canada, Literature of
G	Great Lakes
M	Mississippi River
	Missouri River
N	Newfoundland and Labrador
	North America
Q-R	Rocky Mountains
	Royal Canadian Mounted Police
S	Saint Lawrence River and Seaway
U-V	United States, Art and Architecture of the
	United States, Government of the
	United States, History of the
	United States, Music of the
	(See also articles on individual states and Canadian provinces, and major cities.)

Latin America and the Caribbean

A	Amazon River
	Andes
C	Caribbean Sea and Islands
	Central America
L	Latin America
	Latin America, Art and Architecture of
	Latin America, Literature of
	Latin America, Music of
P	Panama Canal
S	South America
	(See also articles on individual countries.)

Europe and the Commonwealth of Independent States

A	Alps
B	Balkans
C	Commonwealth of Independent States
	Commonwealth of Nations
E	English Art and Architecture
	English Language
	English Literature
	English Music
	Europe
	European Community
F	France, Art and Architecture of
	France, Language of
	France, Literature of
	France, Music of
G	Germany, Art and Architecture of
	Germany, Language of
	Germany, Literature of
	Germany, Music of
	Greece, Art and Architecture of
	Greece, Language of
	Greece, Literature of

I	Ireland, Literature of
	Italy, Art and Architecture of
	Italy, Language and Literature of
	Italy, Music of
M	Mediterranean Sea
Q-R	Russia
	Russia, Art and Architecture of
	Russia, Language and Literature of
	Russia, Music of
S	Scandinavia
	Scandinavian Literature
	Spain, Art and Architecture of
	Spain, Language and Literature of
	Spain, Music of
U-V	Union of Soviet Socialist Republics
	United Kingdom
	(See also articles on individual countries.)

Middle East and Africa

A	Africa
	Africa, Art and Architecture of
	Africa, Literature of
	Africa, Music of
	Amistad Rebellion
	Arabic Literature
	Arabs
C	Congo River
E	Egyptian Art and Architecture
I	Islam
J-K	Jews
	Judaism
M	Middle East
N	Nile River
P	Palestine
Q-R	Qaddafi, Muammar al-
	Qaeda, Al
S	Sahara
	Suez Canal
	(See also articles on individual countries.)

Asia

A	Asia
B	Buddha
C	China, Art and Architecture of
	China, Literature of
D	Dalai Lama
E	Everest, Mount
G	Ganges River
H	Himalayas
	Hinduism
	Ho Chi Minh
	Hu Jintao
I	India, Art and Architecture of
	India, Literature of
	India, Music of
J-K	Japanese Art and Architecture
	Japanese Literature
J-K	Khomeini, Ruhollah
S	Siberia
W-X-Y-Z	Yangtze (Chang) River
	(See also articles on individual countries.)

Southeast Asia and the Pacific

A	Aborigines, Australian
	Australia
N	New Zealand
P	Pacific Ocean and Islands
S	Southeast Asia

SCIENCE

Vol.	Astronomy
A	Armstrong, Neil A.
	Astronauts
	Astronomy
B	Black Holes
C	Comets, Meteorites, and Asteroids
	Constellations
	Copernicus, Nicolaus
E	Eclipses
G	Galaxies
	Galileo
H	Hawking, Stephen
J-K	Jupiter
J-K	Kepler, Johannes
M	Mars
	Mercury
	Milky Way
	Moon
N	Neptune
O	Observatories
P	Planetariums and Space Museums
	Planets
	Pluto
Q-R	Radio Astronomy
S	Satellites
	Satellites, Artificial
	Saturn
	Solar System

HEALTH AND SAFETY

MUSIC

Vol.	Music and Musical Instruments
B	Ballads Ballet Bands and Band Music Bells and Carillons
C	Carols Choral Music Clarinet Country Music
D	Dance Drum
G	Guitar
H	Harmonica Hymns
J-K	Jazz
J-K	Keyboard Instruments
L	Lullabies
M	Music Musical Instruments Musical Theater
N	National Anthems and Patriotic Songs
O	Opera Operetta Orchestra Orchestra Conducting
P	Percussion Instruments Piano
Q-R	Recorder Recording Industry Rock Music
S	Stringed Instruments
U-V	Violin Voice Training and Singing
W-X-Y-Z	Wind Instruments

Vol.	Music History and Biographies
A	Anderson, Marian
B	Bach, Johann Sebastian Beethoven, Ludwig Van
C	Chopin, Frederic Classical Age in Music Copland, Aaron
D	Debussy, Claude
F	Foster, Stephen
G	Gershwin, George Gilbert and Sullivan Operettas Grieg, Edvard
H	Handel, George Frederick

M	Mendelssohn, Felix Middle Ages, Music of the Mozart, Wolfgang Amadeus
O	Offenbach, Jacques
P	Prokofiev, Sergei
Q-R	Renaissance Music
S	Schubert, Franz Strauss, Johann, Jr.
T	Tchaikovsky, Peter Ilyich
U-V	Verdi, Giuseppe

Vol.	Music Around the World
A	Africa, Music of
E	English Music
F	Folk Dance Folk Music
L	Latin America, Music of
U-V	United States, Music of the

ART

Vol.	Art
A	Architecture Art
C	Cathedrals Color
D	Design Drawing
I	Illuminated Manuscripts Illustration and Illustrators
L	Louvre
M	Metropolitan Museum of Art Museums
N	National Gallery (London) National Gallery of Art (Washington, D.C.) National Gallery of Canada
O	Obelisks
P	Painting Photography Prado
S	Sculpture
U-V	Uffizi Gallery
W-X-Y-Z	Watercolor

Vol.	Art History and Biographies
B	Benton, Thomas Hart Botticelli, Sandro

	Bruegel, Pieter, the Elder
C	Cassatt, Mary
	Cézanne, Paul
	Chagall, Marc
D	Dali, Salvador
	Degas, Edgar
	Drawing, History of
	Duchamp, Marcel
	Dürer, Albrecht
E	Egyptian Art and Architecture
	Escher, M. C.
F	Folk Art
G	Gainsborough, Thomas
	Gothic Art and Architecture
	Greece, Art and Architecture of
H	Hockney, David
	Hogarth, William
	Hokusai
	Homer, Winslow
J-K	Klee, Paul
	Klimt, Gustav
L	Léger, Fernand
	Leonardo da Vinci
M	Michelangelo
	Miró, Joan
	Moses, Grandma
O	O'Keeffe, Georgia
	Orozco, José
P	Peale Family
	Picasso, Pablo
	Prehistoric Art
Q-R	Raphael
	Rembrandt
	Renaissance Art and Architecture
	Renoir, Pierre Auguste
	Reynolds, Sir Joshua
	Rockwell, Norman
	Rome, Art and Architecture of
	Romanesque Art and Architecture
U-V	Van Gogh, Vincent
	Vermeer, Jan
W-X-Y-Z	Whistler, James Abbott McNeill
	Wood, Grant
	Wyeth Family

Vol.	**Art Around the World**
A	Africa, Art and Architecture of
C	Canada, Art and Architecture of
	China, Art and Architecture of
D	Dutch and Flemish Art
E	English Art and Architecture
F	France, Art and Architecture of

G	Germany, Art and Architecture of
I	India, Art and Architecture of
	Islamic Art and Architecture
	Italy, Art and Architecture of
J-K	Japanese Art and Architecture
L	Latin America, Art and Architecture of
Q-R	Russia, Art and Architecture of
S	Spain, Art and Architecture of
U-V	United States, Art and Architecture of the

Vol.	**Decorative Arts and Crafts**
C	Ceramics
	Clay Modeling
	Collage
D	Decorative Arts
	Decoupage
F	Finger Painting
L	Linoleum-Block Printing
M	Macramé
	Mosaic
N	Needlecraft
O	Origami
P	Papier-mâché
	Posters
	Pottery
	Puppets and Marionettes
Q-R	Rubbings
S	Silk-Screen Printing
	Stained-Glass Windows
T	Tapestry
W-X-Y-Z	Weaving
	Wood Carving
	Woodcut Printing

PHYSICAL EDUCATION AND SPORTS

Vol.	**Article**
A	Archery
B	Badminton
	Ball
	Baseball
	Basketball
	Bicycling
	Bodybuilding
	Bowling
	Boxing
C	Canoeing
	Cheerleading
	Croquet

D	Darts
	Diving
F	Ferris Wheels
	Field Hockey
	Fishing
	Football
G	Gehrig, Lou
	Gibson, Althea
	Gymnastics
H	Handball
	Hiking and Backpacking
	Horseback Riding
	Horseshoe Pitching
	Hunting
I	Ice Hockey
	Ice-Skating
J-K	Jogging and Running
	Judo
	Juggling
J-K	Karate
	Karting
L	Lacrosse
	Little League Baseball
O	Olympic Games
	Owens, Jesse
P	Paddle Tennis
	Pelé
	Physical Education
	Physical Fitness
Q-R	Racing
	Racket Sports
	Robinson, Jack Roosevelt (Jackie)
	Roller Coasters
	Roller-Skating
	Rugby
	Ruth, George Herman (Babe)
S	Sailing
	Shuffleboard
	Skateboarding
	Skiing
	Skin Diving
	Soap Box Derby
	Soccer and Youth Soccer
	Softball
	Swimming
T	Table Tennis
	Tennis
	Thorpe, James Francis (Jim)
	Track and Field
U-V	Volleyball
W-X-Y-Z	Water Polo
	Waterskiing
	Wrestling

GRADES 7 THROUGH 9

▶ **THE YOUNG ADOLESCENT**

There are moments when the parents of an early teen feel that, without warning, their child has become a stranger. The son or daughter they have known since birth suddenly looks very different and behaves in unaccustomed ways. Their youngster is caring and responsible one minute and sullen and uncooperative the next. These changes are all part of the normal pattern of transition and turmoil that characterize the young adolescent.

It is a time of considerable and often abrupt physical, emotional, social, and intellectual growth and development. No longer a child but not yet an adult, the teenager may exhibit the behavior and characteristics of both. It is a stage that is often as difficult for parents and teachers as it is for the teenager.

The young adolescent's problems usually start with bodily changes. They make rapid gains in height and weight. Their arms and legs, hands and feet, seem to outgrow the rest of their body, frequently resulting in clumsy, uncoordinated actions. There are wide variations in the size and maturity of individuals of the same age or grade level, and girls often become heavier and taller and mature earlier than boys their age. Along with rapid growth may come new problems with skin conditions or body odor. Sexual development and the onset of puberty are embarrassing for some, mystifying or exciting for others.

Many youngsters accept these startling changes gracefully. Others are made anxious and worry excessively about their health and their bodies. They may translate their worries into aggressive or withdrawn behavior and may experience many mood swings. Adults can help young adolescents accept their new growth by helping them understand that what is happening to them is a perfectly natural part of growing up.

Physical and hormonal changes have an impact on the emotional and social behaviors of early teens. Strong, often conflicting, needs dominate their personalities. They are redefining their relationships with adults and are fre-

quently inconsistent in their need for independence from adult authority and their desire for guidance and regulation. They want respect and they want to be treated fairly and reasonably. They need to be able to place their trust in adult family members and teachers.

The need to conform to the code of their peers is all-important to the young adolescent. Because they are very afraid of being ridiculed, their friends' values and beliefs about right and wrong behavior, religion, drugs, sexuality, and education may conflict or seem to take precedence over the values of their family. Many inner-city youngsters face the additional pressures caused by youth gangs. Finding a place in a group takes on urgent importance at this stage, and adults should help channel this urge by helping their teenagers find appropriate clubs and other organizations to join.

Young teens are in the process of learning how to form friendships with members of their own sex and how to behave with persons of the opposite sex. At the same time they are struggling to develop a unique personal identity, and they may experiment with many roles before they find the personality that is their own. Craving success and recognition, they look to parents and teachers for guidance, understanding, and acceptance.

Along with their changing bodies, feelings, and social behaviors, early adolescents are developing intellectual sophistication. They are capable of abstract reasoning and reflective thinking. They are fascinated by concepts such as justice, democracy, friendship, and the obligations of freedom. A natural curiosity motivates their learning, and they are always ready to question and challenge the ideas and actions of others. Topics related to their own personal concerns and goals are more apt to arouse their enthusiasm and active involvement as learners.

Most students in grades 7 and 8 attend a middle school or junior high school. Ninth graders may already be in a senior high school. Most young teens will experience a more structured, departmentalized school program and will have to deal with many more teachers than they did in their earlier school years. Their school day usually consists of six periods, and each subject is given paramount importance by the instructor who teaches it.

All students study English, mathematics, social studies, and science each year in grades 7 through 9. Many begin a foreign language, usually French or Spanish. Depending on the school's facilities, physical education may be offered each year as well. In addition, students generally take at least one course in music, art, health, and home economics or industrial arts (technology education in some schools).

There is homework assigned for most subjects, and the work requires substantial time and effort on the part of the student. Tests and grades are taken very seriously and school can become yet another anxiety-producing factor in the young adolescent's life. On the other hand, many of the young person's social activities center on the school's extracurricular groups, clubs, and teams, and the school can serve as a conduit for social and emotional development as well as for intellectual growth.

For most teenagers the years of young adolescence are as scary, thrilling, and invigorating as a rollercoaster ride. Parents of young teens experience their own highs and lows, too. You can help make it a smoother ride by listening carefully to your teenagers. Pay close attention to what they tell you verbally and by their actions. Try to be patient and understanding. Let them know you are ready to take their concerns seriously, and try to help them find satisfactory solutions to their problems. They may not always admit it, but young adolescents need caring, supportive parents and adults more than ever to guide them on their quest for adulthood.

▶ SUCCESS IN SCHOOL

Young adolescents are very busy people. They spend most of their weekdays going to school, participating in after-school activities, doing homework, visiting with friends, and doing things on their own. For some teenag-

ers the only interaction with family members takes place around the table at mealtimes. Even on weekends, young teens often want to follow their own recreational agendas and can be drawn into family activities only with reluctance. Parents and teens can lose touch at this turning point in young people's lives.

Concerned parents and caregivers need to penetrate these barriers and continue to provide the support, direction, and encouragement that will help their youngsters achieve success in middle school or junior high school. The teenager who drops out of high school is often the youngster who falls behind scholastically in grades 7 through 9. It is also a fact that youngsters who do not perform to their full potential in these important years will not be sufficiently prepared to tackle the high school courses that make entry into a college or a job after graduation easier.

Parents can continue to exercise influence on their teenager's school performance in a number of direct, and sometimes subtle, ways:

- With the exception of real illness, make sure your teenagers attend classes every day. If it is absolutely necessary for them to be absent, make sure the schoolwork for all subjects is made up. If the absence has been longer than one or two days, talk to teachers yourself to get their help in making up what was missed in lectures or classroom activities.

- Young teens may lack organization skills and have difficulty setting up a homework or study plan. Refer to this STUDY GUIDE for helpful homework suggestions. Make sure each student has a quiet, private spot for study.

- Keep a regular household routine that accommodates the needs and schedules of all family members. There should be definite times set for meals, study periods, household chores, and family recreation.

- Set aside time each day for a one-on-one conversation with your teenagers. If your youngsters are reluctant to talk about school, try asking questions that require more than a simple "yes" or "no" answer.

"What's your favorite subject this semester?" "What do you like about it?" "Why do you think you did so well (or so poorly) on that last test?" "How can you do even better next time?" Talk about out-of-school interests and activities, too. Listen objectively. Try to be helpful and reassuring rather than judgmental.

- Create a home atmosphere that encourages learning. Books and newspapers should be visible—library books are fine. Try to have a good dictionary, thesaurus, and other reference books on hand—inexpensive paperbacks or second-hand books will do the job. Let young people see adults reading for pleasure as well as for information. Make a habit of watching some educational documentaries and cultural programs on television. Try to talk about current events and local issues with your teenagers.
- Include books as gifts on birthdays and holidays. Find out who the teenager's favorite authors are and what type of books are preferred. Historical? Mystery? Fantasy? Sports? Realistic? Good nonfiction books can start new interests and can support learning taking place in the classroom.
- Continue to do things as a family group. Play games together. Have a picnic. Go to athletic events, concerts, museums, plays, or art shows. In many communities there are many free cultural and sporting events. High school and local college performances and sports events can be particularly enjoyable because you will probably know some of the players or performers in them.
- Try to carry on the family reading-aloud activities that were part of your teenager's everyday life during his or her preschool and elementary school years. You probably will not get a young teen to sit still for this on a regular basis. When you have come across an especially good book, or magazine or newspaper article, however, capture a few minutes to read a particularly interesting passage and you may hook the youngster into wanting to read

it, too.
- Many middle schools and junior high schools use a tracking system in which students are assigned to classes and subjects on the basis of test scores and past performance. If any of your youngsters are in a low-track group, speak with teachers, the guidance counselor, and the principal to find ways of helping them to do well and, if it seems possible, improve enough to be moved into a higher track.
- If your teenagers have problems in school, try to pinpoint specific reasons and work with your youngsters and school personnel to create an action plan that will lead to a successful turnaround.

Above all, know your youngsters, keep informed about the expectations and requirements of their school and teachers, and provide the guidance and support they need.

The lists of articles at the very end of this section for grades 7 through 9 include many, but certainly not all, of the articles about each subject area that appear in THE NEW BOOK OF KNOWLEDGE. It is important that students look up the names of topics they want to read about in the Index or in the set itself to locate all of the information they may need or want. For example, in the Social Studies area, articles about each of the countries of the world are not listed in this section but can easily be located by looking each one up under its own name.

▶ **LANGUAGE AND LITERATURE**

The emphasis of the English curriculum for grades 7 through 9 is on reading, understanding, and appreciating literature; writing in a grammatical, well-organized, and coherent manner; and speaking effectively in a variety of situations. Unless a youngster exhibits major deficiencies in reading, most students in middle school or junior high school do not have a period in which reading skills are taught. Students will take several semesters of literature and grammar and composition courses and sometimes a course in speech or communication.

Literature courses are usually organized so that students learn the distinguishing characteristics of short stories, novels, poetry, drama, and nonfiction. Students are exposed to a broad spectrum of classic and contemporary works by well-known American authors and by writers from other countries and cultures. Students learn how to analyze literary works and to become knowledgeable about the elements writers use to communicate their ideas and feelings: plot, character, setting, theme, mood, tone, language, symbolism, and imagery. Students are asked to think, write, and talk about their reading. By learning how to communicate their interpretations and evaluations, young people also learn how to read with greater insight and deeper understanding.

In their grammar and composition course, students learn how to apply the writing process to four main types of composition: narration, description, exposition, and persuasion. They study the intricacies of grammar, mechanics, and usage and learn how to construct coherent and effective sentences, paragraphs, and themes. In their compositions students are expected to demonstrate clear and logical thinking in the support and development of a central idea. Writing assignments are often assigned for homework and may include writing a character sketch, explaining a process, writing an essay to answer a question, or writing a poem, an editorial, or an autobiography. By ninth grade most youngsters have also learned how to do a research report.

Vocabulary study is an important component of both the literature and the grammar and composition course. Youngsters encounter many new and exciting words as they read, and they are encouraged to use the dictionary and word analysis techniques to learn the meanings of words not made clear by the text. Reviewing what they know or need to learn about affixes, common roots, synonyms, antonyms, and analogies also helps them determine word meanings.

The speech course promotes self-confidence in oral communication and involves students in public speaking, group discussion, debate, and dramatic reading activities. The importance of responding courteously and appropriately to a presenter is also stressed.

▶ **MATHEMATICS**

There is variation from school to school in the types of math courses offered in grades 7 through 9. Not all students in the same grade in a particular school will take the same courses. Students with more background and ability will usually take more advanced courses than the average or weaker student. For some youngsters, middle school or junior high mathematics will consist primarily of the review, extension, and application of familiar math skills and concepts. For others, the math curriculum will consist of preparation for the more rigorous courses in algebra, geometry, and trigonometry of high school.

All students will be offered at least one course in which previously taught skills—those involving numbers, measurement, geometry, patterns and functions, statistics, probability, and logical reasoning—are strengthened and taught in greater depth. Some youngsters will take a pre-algebra class. Some will take a transition course that combines applied mathematics with pre-algebra and pre-geometry topics and concepts. Others will undertake a course made up of a combination of consumer and business applications for a variety of real-life topics and situations: earning and spending money, budgeting, banking, taxes, insurance, housing, and transportation. The more able eighth graders will be offered an algebra course.

The college-bound ninth grade student studies high school level algebra or occasionally formal geometry. Algebra is also an option for non-college-bound students, or they may study general mathematics or business math.

Some students may end their experience with school mathematics in the ninth grade. More and more states and school districts are adopting more rigorous mathematics standards, however. All students in these districts must pass high-level mathematics courses to meet graduation requirements.

American and world history and geography constitute the core of the social studies curriculum for grades 7 through 9. There are wide variations, however, in the specific courses offered at each of the grade levels by different school districts.

The study of American history may be a one-year or two-year course. It usually consists of a chronological presentation of political, cultural, social, economic, and geographic influences on the development of the United States as a nation, spanning the years from pre-colonial times to the present. More time and emphasis are assigned to the post–Civil War and contemporary eras than in earlier grades. As they survey and study important events and assess the contributions of key figures, students also learn about many of the major ideas and movements that influenced our country's past and present history. These will include abstract concepts such as democracy, freedom, responsibility, equality, and parity, as well as specific movements and processes such as the evolution of political and social institutions, slavery, immigration, the rise of industry, the impact of technology, the spread of cities and urban areas, and the role of women and diverse racial and ethnic groups.

The vast scope of world history and geography is presented in a number of different courses in different schools. These courses vary widely in their structure and emphasis. Some students study the history of Europe, Asia, Africa, and the Americas chronologically from ancient civilizations to early modern times. Other students will make in-depth investigations into selected world regions or world cultures. Still others will focus on key historical and contemporary trends, problems, and issues in a Global Studies course.

Along with their studies of America and the world, many youngsters have the opportunity to take separate courses in state history, civics, economics, or geography.

As they gather information on social studies topics, middle school and junior high school students are urged to use original primary and secondary sources; to apply critical and creative thinking to the analysis and evaluation of research data and its source; and to synthesize this information in order to make rational decisions about local, national, and international problems and issues.

▶ SCIENCE AND TECHNOLOGY

When they enter the seventh grade, most students have their first experience with science courses taught according to specific disciplines. In grades 7 through 9 science is offered in a three-year sequence by discipline: life science, physical science, and earth science, not necessarily in that order. All three courses incorporate information about technology, emphasizing its applications and its impact on society.

The life science course provides a survey of the five kingdoms into which living things are classified, according to their characteristics and relationships: the Prokaryotes (bacteria); the Protists (single-celled organisms); Fungi; Plants; and Animals. Students also conduct in-depth investigations into the structure and function of cells; genetics and the role of DNA; the evolutionary process; the structure and functions of the organ systems of humans and other animals; and the major ecosystems of the world. In many classrooms students use a microscope and do simple dissections for the first time.

In the physical science course, many topics introduced in earlier grades are extended. These include motion, forces, energy in all its forms, the properties of matter, atomic structure, and the periodic table. Students are usually ready at this age to begin new studies into the principles of chemistry. They learn about compounds, mixtures, chemical bonding, chemical interactions and reactions, and acids, bases, and salts. Demonstrations and experiments help them understand the more complex concepts of basic physics and chemistry.

Most ninth graders are offered the earth science course or a high school biology course. In earth science classes, students delve into the geology of the earth, its history, and the forces that shape it, emphasizing the role of plate tectonics. They also study the oceans of the earth, the earth's atmosphere, meteorology, and astronomy. The biology course covers the traditional life-science topics mentioned above, but with heavier concentration on the cell, microbiology, genetics, evolution, reproduction, and body chemistry.

Some ninth graders complete their science education with a general science course.

At present there is a need for people to understand the growing number of important problems in our society that require scientific and technological solutions and an equally important need for more young people to embark on science-based careers. For these reasons educators are urging students to continue their science studies through high school, and many states are mandating additional science courses as requirements for graduation. It is also important for youngsters in the middle school or junior high school to be better prepared for the more rigorous requirements of high school science.

▶ **HEALTH EDUCATION**

The study of health is especially important for the young adolescent who is experiencing physical, emotional, social, and intellectual changes. The comprehensive health program for grades 7 through 9 usually provides information about ten major health topics: human body systems; prevention and control of disease; substance use and abuse; nutrition; mental and emotional health; accident prevention, safety, and first aid; family life; physical fitness and personal care; consumer health; and community and environmental health and health care resources. It is important for students to take this opportunity to use the knowledge presented in the course they take to learn how to make healthy choices in their daily lives and to adopt positive behaviors and attitudes that will last a lifetime.

Important subtopics of particular interest to the young teen usually include: psychological well-being; fitness programs; stress management; eating disorders and weight control; alcohol and drugs; the human life cycle; human reproduction; safe and effective cosmetic and health care products; emergency care; and sexually transmitted diseases. Understanding how to cope with these concerns helps adolescent youngsters become more comfortable with the changes they are experiencing in their own lives. It also gives them confidence in their ability to deal with the day-to-day problems and situations that may affect their well-being.

▶ **FOREIGN LANGUAGE**

Most elementary schools do not provide instruction in a foreign language. Many youngsters have their first contact with another language in the seventh, eighth, or ninth grades. French and Spanish are the languages most frequently offered and students are usually given their choice between the two. Ninth graders often have more of a selection from which to choose. Depending upon the composition and interests of the local community, students may have the opportunity to learn German, Italian, Japanese, or Latin as well as French or Spanish.

Foreign language courses for grades 7 through 9 usually employ a cultural and conversational approach. Students learn to listen, speak, read, and write the language. Emphasis is on modeling the dialogue of everyday situations—visiting friends, going to school, shopping, attending sports and cultural events, or taking a bus or train ride. These dialogue situations are used as a basis for learning about the culture, geography, customs, and traditions of the country or the countries in which the language predominates.

Although students learn the basic elements of the grammar of the language, more structured grammar study is reserved for high school.

▶ **MUSIC**

In grades 7 through 9 music is usually taught by a music specialist, and students have many opportunities to participate in a variety of musical experiences and activities.

A one-semester or one-year course in music

appreciation is generally offered to all students as an elective. Youngsters are introduced to the major periods and developments in classical and popular music history and to the biographies of major composers and performers. They study musical elements such as rhythm, melody, harmony, and counterpoint and learn to recognize a variety of musical forms, including the symphony, sonata, opera, and operetta. These topics are coordinated with experiences in listening to recorded or live performances.

Some youngsters may participate in school choral or dance groups or may play an instrument in the school band or in the orchestra.

All young adolescents enjoy listening to music. Many take private voice, instrument, or dance lessons; some even begin to form their own musical groups outside of school. Certain youngsters exhibit exceptional talent in music at this age, and they should be challenged to develop it to their full potential. All students, regardless of their musical ability, should be encouraged to develop a thoughtful response to music and to continue to participate in musical activities.

▶ ART

Art instruction in grades 7 through 9 provides young teenagers with a variety of art experiences in a one-semester or one-year art course often offered as an elective.

Students experiment with an assortment of art media, tools, processes, and techniques. They may delve into poster making, lettering, painting, drawing and illustration, clay modeling, costume design, advertising design, and interior and stage decoration. They explore the use of color, perspective, proportion, dimension, line, and other elements and principles of visual composition and design.

Students become familiar with the history of art as they examine and analyze major works from different historical periods. They learn how to identify and compare stylistic differences in the works of significant artists. The role of artists in the media is also probed as students investigate the work of photographers, illustrators, costume and set designers, cartoonists, computer-graphics artists, and artists in television, video, and film production.

In some schools, students with a special ability or interest in art may be able to take additional art courses or may participate in an after-school art club.

For young adolescents, activities in art and music can provide a positive and productive avenue for releasing emotions and for expressing thoughts and ideas.

▶ PHYSICAL EDUCATION AND SPORTS

Almost all youngsters enjoy participating in sports and physical activities during their elementary school years. Enthusiasm for these activities begins to decline at about age 10. Some early teens lose all interest in keeping their bodies fit and no longer take part in games and sports on their own. The school physical education program for grades 7 through 9 plays an important role in keeping all young adolescents involved in fitness and sports activities during this crucial period of physical change and growth.

As in the earlier grades, the physical education curriculum is a combination of fitness, gymnastic activities, and games and sports. There is more emphasis on team sports at this level, although individual sports are preferred by many youngsters, and some schools add table tennis, wrestling, badminton, and paddle and racket games to their sports program. In team sports, football, basketball, baseball, and track and field are popular with boys; basketball, track and field, softball, and volleyball are generally favored by girls.

Students are usually asked to demonstrate proficiency in skills involving balance, endurance, strength, flexibility, and agility. Social attitudes and skills such as responsibility, leadership, tolerance, and a positive self-image are also stressed.

Recognizing that not all youngsters are athletes, the school physical education program is geared to helping teenagers acquire attitudes and skills that will help them maintain physical fitness in later years and remain actively involved in worthwhile recreational activities.

HOME ECONOMICS AND INDUSTRIAL ARTS

Students in middle school or junior high school usually have the opportunity to study home economics or industrial arts. In some schools, industrial arts is called technology education. These courses emphasize the learning and use of practical skills.

The home economics course focuses on the skills of day-to-day living. Topics studied usually include family life and home management; food and nutrition; clothing; home furnishings; and how to be a smart consumer. During the course, students are required to complete a number of hands-on projects, which may include planning a menu and preparing a meal, planning a room and making a three-dimensional model, or sewing a simple garment. Role playing and dramatization are used to clarify the complexities of home and community relationships and family living.

In the industrial arts or technology education course, students are introduced to hand and power tools and their applications to the basic elements of mechanical drawing or drafting. They also learn about common industrial materials such as metal, plastics, and ceramics and about the tools and processes used in electricity, electronics, printing and graphic arts, photography, and other general crafts. Students are required to complete several projects that demonstrate what they have learned about materials and processes and what level of skill they have reached with basic tools, techniques, and procedures.

CURRICULUM-RELATED ARTICLES

Some of the important articles in THE NEW BOOK OF KNOWLEDGE that relate to the 7 through 9 school curriculum are listed here. Many other articles you or your youngsters may want to read while they are studying topics in these curriculum areas can be found by looking them up in the Index or in the set itself.

LANGUAGE AND LITERATURE

Vol.	Language
A	Alphabet
E	English Language
G	Grammar
L	Language Arts
P	Parts of Speech
Q-R	Reading
S	Semantics
	Slang
	Synonyms and Antonyms
W-X-Y-Z	Word Games
	Word Origins

Vol.	Writing
A	Abbreviations
	Address, Forms of
C	Compositions
D	Diaries and Journals
E	Essays
F	Figures of Speech
H	Handwriting
	Humor
J-K	Journalism
L	Letter Writing
O	Outlines
P	Proofreading
	Punctuation
Q-R	Research Reports for School
S	Spelling
U-V	Vocabulary
W-X-Y-Z	Writing

Vol.	Oral Language/Speech
D	Debates and Discussions
J	Jokes and Riddles
O	Oratory
P	Parliamentary Procedure
	Plays
	Pronunciation
	Public Speaking
S	Speech

	Speech Disorders
	Storytelling
T	Tongue Twisters

Vol.	Reference, Research, and Study Skills
B	Book Reports and Reviews
	Books: From Author to Reader
D	Dictionaries
E	Encyclopedias
I	Indexes and Indexing
L	Libraries
M	Magazines
N	Newspapers
P	Paperback Books
Q-R	Reference Materials
	Research
S	Study, How to
T	Tests and Test Taking
	Time Management

Vol.	Literature
A	Aeneid
	Africa, Literature of
	American Literature
	Arabic Literature
	Arthur, King
B	Ballads
	Beowulf
	Biography, Autobiography, and Biographical Novel
C	Canada, Literature of
	China, Literature of
D	Diaries and Journals
	Drama
E	English Literature
	Essays
F	Faust Legends
	Fiction
	Figures of Speech
	Folklore
	Folklore, American
G	Germany, Literature of
	Greece, Literature of
H	Hebrew Language and Literature
	Humor

I	Iliad
	India, Literature of
	Ireland, Literature of
	Italy, Language and Literature of
J-K	Japanese Literature
L	Latin America, Literature of
	Latin Language and Literature
	Legends
	Literature
M	Mystery and Detective Stories
	Mythology
N	Newbery, John
	Nobel Prizes: Literature
	Nonsense Rhymes
	Norse Mythology
	Novels
O	Odes
	Odyssey
P	Poetry
	Pulitzer Prizes
Q-R	Russia, Language and Literature of
S	Scandinavian Literature
	Science Fiction
	Short Stories
	Spain, Language and Literature of

Vol.	**Author Biographies**
A	Adams, Henry
	Angelou, Maya
	Austen, Jane
B	Baldwin, James
	Balzac, Honoré de
	Bellow, Saul
	Blake, William
	Brontë Sisters
	Browning, Elizabeth Barrett and Robert
	Bryant, William Cullen
	Buck, Pearl
	Burns, Robert
	Byron, George Gordon, Lord
C	Cervantes Saavedra, Miguel de
	Chaucer, Geoffrey
	Chekov, Anton
	Conrad, Joseph
	Cooper, James Fenimore
	Crane, Stephen
D	Dante Alighieri
	Defoe, Daniel
	Dickens, Charles
	Dickinson, Emily
	Donne, John
	Dos Passos, John
	Dostoevski, Fëdor

	Doyle, Sir Arthur Conan
	Dreiser, Theodore
	Dryden, John
	Dumas, Alexandre *Père* and Alexandre *Fils*
	Dunbar, Paul Laurence
E	Eliot, George
	Eliot, T. S.
	Emerson, Ralph Waldo
F	Faulkner, William
	Fitzgerald, F. Scott
	Frost, Robert
G	Goethe, Johann Wolfgang von
	Greene, Graham
H	Hardy, Thomas
	Hawthorne, Nathaniel
	Heine, Heinrich
	Hemingway, Ernest
	Henry, O.
	Hesse, Hermann
	Homer
	Horace
	Hughes, Langston
	Hugo, Victor
I	Ibsen, Henrik
	Irving, Washington
J-K	James, Henry
	Johnson, James Weldon
	Johnson, Samuel
J-K	Keats, John
	Kipling, Rudyard
L	Lewis, Sinclair
	London, Jack
	Longfellow, Henry Wadsworth
	Lowell, Robert
M	Marlowe, Christopher
	Melville, Herman
	Milton, John
	Moliére
	Morrison, Toni
O	Osborne, John
P	Poe, Edgar Allan
	Pope, Alexander
Q-R	Racine, Jean Baptiste
	Rossetti Family
	Rowling, J. K.
S	Sandburg, Carl
	Schiller, Johann
	Scott, Sir Walter
	Shakespeare, William
	Shaw, George Bernard
	Shelley, Percy Bysshe
	Spenser, Edmund

Stein, Gertrude
Steinbeck, John
Stevens, Wallace
Stevenson, Robert Louis
Strindberg, August
Swift, Jonathan

T Tennyson, Alfred, Lord
Thackeray, William Makepeace
Thomas, Dylan
Thoreau, Henry David
Thurber, James
Tolkien, J. R. R.
Tolstoi, Leo
Twain, Mark

U-V Verne, Jules
Voltaire
Vonnegut, Kurt

W-X-Y-Z Warren, Robert Penn
Wells, H. G.
Wharton, Edith
White, E. B.
Whitman, Walt
Whittier, John Greenleaf
Wilde, Oscar
Wilder, Laura Ingalls
Williams, Tennessee
Williams, William Carlos
Wordsworth, William
Wright, Richard

W-X-Y-Z Yeats, William Butler

W-X-Y-Z Zola, Émile

Vol. **Selections from Literature**

A Africa, Literature of—African proverbs and riddles
Alcott—Little Women (excerpt)

B Bible Stories
Browning, Elizabeth Barrett—How Do I Love Thee (from Sonnets from the Portuguese)
Browning, Robert—Pied Piper of Hamelin (excerpt)
Buck, Pearl—The Good Earth (excerpt)
Burns, Robert—A Red, Red Rose
Byron, George Gordon, Lord
  Childe Harold's Pilgrimage (excerpt)
  The Prisoner of Chillon (excerpt)

C Cooper, James Fenimore—The Last of the Mohicans (excerpt)

D Defoe, Daniel—Robinson Crusoe (excerpt)
Dickinson, Emily
  A Bird Came Down the Walk
  I'll Tell You How the Sun Rose
Doyle, Sir Arthur Conan—The Red-Headed League (excerpt)

Dumas, Alexandre *Fils*—The Three Musketeers (excerpt)
Dunbar, Paul Laurence
  Promise
  Fulfilment

E Emerson, Ralph Waldo—The Concord Hymn
Essays—Essay (excerpt, Franklin)

F Frost, Robert
  The Last Word of a Bluebird
  The Pasture
  Stopping by Woods on a Snowy Evening
  The Road Not Taken

G Gettysburg Address

H Hawthorne, Nathaniel—Young Goodman Brown
Hugo, Victor—Les Misérables (excerpt)

I Irving, Washington—Rip Van Winkle (excerpt)

L Latin America, Literature of—The Heights of Machu Picchu (excerpt, Neruda)
Legends
  The Vanishing Hitchhiker (United States)
  Roland and Oliver (France)
  The Legend of Robin Hood (England)
London, Jack—The Call of the Wild (excerpt)
Longfellow, Henry Wadsworth—The Arrow and the Song

P Poe—Eldorado
Poetry
  Daffodils (excerpt, Wordsworth)
  Ode to the West Wind (excerpt, Shelley)
  Sonnet 18 (Shakespeare)
  When Lilacs Last in the Dooryard Bloom'd (excerpt, Whitman)

S Shelley, Percy Bysshe
  To Night
  Ozymandias
Short Stories
  The Tell-Tale Heart (excerpt, Poe)
  The Gift of the Magi (excerpt, Henry)
  Two Soldiers (excerpt, Faulkner)
Stevenson, Robert Louis—Kidnapped (excerpt)
Swift, Jonathan—Gulliver's Travels (excerpt)

T Tennyson, Alfred, Lord—Crossing the Bar (from The Lady of Shalott)
Thackeray, William Makepeace—Vanity

MATHEMATICS

SOCIAL STUDIES

Lewis and Clark Expedition
Lincoln, Abraham
Louisiana Purchase

M   Mann, Horace
Marion, Francis
Marshall, John
Mexican War
Missouri Compromise
Monroe, James
Monroe Doctrine
Morris, Gouverneur

N   Navigation
Northwest Passage

P   Pirates
Plymouth Colony
Pontiac
Powhatan
Public Lands

Q-R   Reconstruction Period
Revolutionary War
Rolfe, John

S   Sacagawea
Scott, Winfield
Slavery

T   Territorial Expansion of the United
States
Thirteen American Colonies
Tyler, John

U-V   Underground Railroad
United States, Constitution of the

W-X-Y-Z War of 1812
Washington, George
Webster, Daniel
Westward Movement
Women's Rights Movement

W-X-Y-Z Zenger, John Peter

Modern America Takes Shape (1865–1900)

A   Addams, Jane
African Americans
Asian Americans
Astor Family

B   Barton, Clara
Blackwell, Elizabeth
Bryan, William Jennings
Buffalo Bill (William F. Cody)

C   Carnegie, Andrew
Child Labor
Civil Rights
Civil Service
Cowboys

D   Department Stores
Dewey, George
DuBois, W. E. B.

E   Ethnic Groups
F   Field, Cyrus
G   Gallatin, Albert
Garvey, Marcus
Geronimo
Gold Rushes
Gompers, Samuel

H   Hayes, Rutherford B.
Hickok, James Butler (Wild Bill)

I   Immigration
Indian Wars of North America

L   Labor Movement
Liberty, Statue of

M   Manufacturing
Morgan, John Pierpont

O   Oriental Exclusion Acts
Outlaws

P   Petroleum and Petroleum Refining
Pioneer Life

Q-R   Ranch Life
Red Cross
Rockefeller, John D.

W-X-Y-Z Washington, Booker T.
Westinghouse, George
Women's Rights Movement

Modern America (1900–present)

A   American Civil Liberties Union (ACLU)
American Indian Movement (AIM)
American Legion
Arafat, Yasir
Automobiles

B   Bethune, Mary McLeod
Bunche, Ralph
Bush, George
Bush, George W.

C   Civil Rights
Civil Rights Movement
Clinton, William
Cold War
Commonwealth of Independent States
Coolidge, Calvin
Cuban Missile Crisis

D   Dawes, Charles G.
Depressions and Recessions
Disarmament
Douglas, William O.
Draft, or Conscription
Dust Bowl

E   Eisenhower, Dwight D.
Extinction

F   Famine
Farrakhan, Louis

I	Incas
	Islam
M	Magna Carta
	Maya
	Middle Ages
	Montezuma
P	Peloponnesian War
	Persia, Ancient
Q-R	Rome, Ancient
	(See also the list in Grades 4 Through 6—Social Studies: Early and Medieval History and Culture.)

Renaissance and Reformation (1400's and 1500's)

B	Bacon, Francis
	Bellini Family
	Botticelli, Sandro
C	Calvin, John
	Chaucer, Geoffrey
D	Dante Alighieri
	Donatello
	Dürer, Albrecht
	Dutch and Flemish Art
	Dutch and Flemish Music
E	Erasmus
	Exploration and Discovery
F	Florence
G	Galileo
	Gutenberg, Johann
H	Huguenots
	Humanism
	Hus, Jan
I	Italy, Art and Architecture of
	Italy, Language and Literature of
L	Leonardo da Vinci
	Luther, Martin
M	Medici
	Michelangelo
	More, Sir Thomas
P	Protestantism
Q-R	Raphael
	Reformation
	Renaissance
	Renaissance Art and Architecture
	Renaissance Music
S	Spanish Armada
T	Thirty Years' War
	Titian
U-V	Venice
W-X-Y-Z	Wesley, John

Absolutism, Enlightenment, and Revolution (1600's through 1800's)

B	Bach, Johann Sebastian
	Bolívar, Simón
C	Charles
	Communism
	Cromwell, Oliver
D	Darwin, Charles
	Descartes, René
E	Elizabeth I
	England, History of
	Enlightenment, Age of
F	Frederick
	French Revolution
G	Goethe, Johann Wolfgang Von
H	Habsburgs
	Handel, George Frederick
	Harvey, William
	Henry VIII
	Hume, David
I	Impressionism
	Industrial Revolution
J-K	Kepler, Johannes
L	Labor Movement
	Leeuwenhoek, Anton Van
	Locke, John
	Louis
	Louis XIV
M	Marie Antoinette
	Marx, Karl
	Mary I (Tudor)
	Mary, Queen of Scots
	Mozart, Wolfgang Amadeus
N	Napoleon I
	Newton, Isaac
P	Paris
	Peter the Great
Q-R	Rembrandt
	Revolutionary War (United States)
	Richelieu, Cardinal
	Rousseau, Jean Jacques
S	San Martín, José de
	Shakespeare, William
	Socialism
U-V	Voltaire
W-X-Y-Z	Wellington, Duke of
	Wren, Christopher

Nationalism, Imperialism, and the Modern Age (1800's through 1900's)

A	Africa
	Anarchism
	Arabs

SCIENCE AND TECHNOLOGY

HEALTH AND SAFETY

FOREIGN LANGUAGE

Vol.	Article
F	France, Language of
G	Germany, Language of Greece, Language of
H	Hebrew Language and Literature
I	Italy, Language and Literature of
L	Languages Latin Language and Literature
Q-R	Russia, Language and Literature of
S	Spain, Language and Literature of

MUSIC

Vol.	Music and Musical Instruments
B	Ballads Ballet Bands and Band Music Bells and Carillons
C	Carols Chamber Music Choral Music Clarinet Country Music
D	Dance Drum
E	Electronic Music
G	Guitar
H	Harmonica Harp Hymns
J-K	Jazz
J-K	Keyboard Instruments
L	Lincoln Center for the Performing Arts
M	Music Musical Instruments Musical Theater Music Festivals
N	National Anthems and Patriotic Songs
O	Opera Operetta Orchestra Orchestra Conducting Organ
P	Percussion Instruments Piano
Q-R	Recorder Recording Industry Rock Music

S	Stringed Instruments
U-V	Violin Voice Training and Singing
W-X-Y-Z	Wind Instruments

Vol.	Music History and Biographies
A	Anderson, Marian
B	Bach, Johann Sebastian Baroque Music Bartók, Béla Beatles, The Beethoven, Ludwig Van Berg, Alban Berlin, Irving Berlioz, Hector Brahms, Johannes
C	Chopin, Frederic Classical Age in Music Copland, Aaron
D	Debussy, Claude Donizetti, Gaetano Dvořák, Antonin
E	Elgar, Sir Edward
F	Foster, Stephen Franck, César
G	Gershwin, George Gilbert and Sullivan Operettas Gluck, Christoph Willibald Grieg, Edvard
H	Handel, George Frederick Haydn, Joseph
I	Ives, Charles
L	Liszt, Franz
M	MacDowell, Edward Mahler, Gustav Mendelssohn, Felix Middle Ages, Music of the Modern Music Mozart, Wolfgang Amadeus
O	Offenbach, Jacques
P	Palestrina Prokofiev, Sergei Puccini, Giacomo
Q-R	Renaissance Music Romanticism
S	Schoenberg, Arnold Schubert, Franz Schumann, Robert Sibelius, Jean Strauss, Johann, Jr. Strauss, Richard Stravinsky, Igor

T	Tchaikovsky, Peter Ilyich
	Toscanini, Arturo
U-V	Verdi, Giuseppe
W-X-Y-Z	Wind Instruments

Vol.	**Music Around the World**
A	Africa, Music of
	The Mbira
	The Talking Drum
D	Dutch and Flemish Music
E	English Music
F	Folk Dance
	Folk Music
	France, Music of
G	Germany, Music of
I	India, Music of
	Italy, Music of
L	Latin America, Music of
R	Russia, Music of
S	Spain, Music of
U-V	United States, Music of the

ART

Vol.	**Article**
A	Architecture
	Art
C	Cathedrals
	Color
D	Design
	Drawing
E	Engraving
	Etching
G	Graphic Arts
H	Hermitage Museum
I	Illuminated Manuscripts
	Illustration and Illustrators
L	Louvre
M	Metropolitan Museum of Art
	Museums
N	National Gallery (London)
	National Gallery of Art (Washington, D.C.)
O	Obelisks
P	Painting
	Photography
	Prado
S	Sculpture
U-V	Uffizi Gallery

W-X-Y-Z	Watercolor

Vol.	**Art History and Biographies**
A	Angelico, Fra
B	Baroque Art and Architecture
	Bellini Family
	Benton, Thomas Hart
	Bernini, Giovanni Lorenzo
	Botticelli, Sandro
	Brancusi, Constantin
	Braque, Georges
	Bruegel, Pieter, the Elder
	Byzantine Art and Architecture
C	Caravaggio, Michelangelo Merisi da
	Cassatt, Mary
	Cézanne, Paul
	Chagall, Marc
D	Dali, Salvador
	Daumier, Honoré
	Degas, Edgar
	Delacroix, Eugène
	Donatello
	Doré, Gustave
	Drawing, History of
	Duchamp, Marcel
	Dürer, Albrecht
E	Eakins, Thomas
	Egyptian Art and Architecture
	Escher, M. C.
	Expressionism
F	Folk Art
	Fragonard, Jean Honoré
	Francesca, Piero della
G	Gainsborough, Thomas
	Gauguin, Paul
	Giorgione
	Giotto di Bondone
	Gothic Art and Architecture
	Goya, Francisco
	Greco, El
	Greece, Art and Architecture of
H	Hals, Frans
	Hockney, David
	Hogarth, William
	Hokusai
	Holbein, Hans the Younger
	Homer, Winslow
J-K	Kandinsky, Wassily
	Klee, Paul
	Klimt, Gustav
L	Le Corbusier
	Léger, Fernand
	Leonardo da Vinci
M	Manet, Édouard

	Matisse, Henri
	Michelangelo
	Mies Van Der Rohe, Ludwig
	Miró, Joan
	Modern Art
	Modigliani, Amedeo
	Mondrian, Piet
	Monet, Claude
	Moses, Grandma
N	Nevelson, Louise
O	O'Keeffe, Georgia
	Orozco, José
P	Peale Family
	Pei, I. M.
	Picasso, Pablo
	Pollock, Jackson
	Prehistoric Art
Q-R	Raphael
	Rembrandt
	Renaissance Art and Architecture
	Renoir, Pierre Auguste
	Reynolds, Sir Joshua
	Rivera, Diego
	Rockwell, Norman
	Rodin, Auguste
	Romanesque Art and Architecture
	Romanticism
	Rubens, Peter Paul
S	Sargent, John Singer
	Sullivan, Louis
	Surrealism
T	Tintoretto
	Titian
	Toulouse-Lautrec, Henri de
	Turner, Joseph Mallord William
U-V	Utrillo, Maurice
U-V	Van Dyck, Anthony
	Van Gogh, Vincent
	Velázquez, Diego
	Vermeer, Jan
W-X-Y-Z	Warhol, Andy
	Whistler, James Abbott McNeill
	Wood, Grant
	Wren, Christopher
	Wright, Frank Lloyd
	Wyeth Family

Vol.	**Art Around the World**
A	Africa, Art and Architecture of
C	Canada, Art and Architecture of
	China, Art and Architecture of
D	Dutch and Flemish Art
E	English Art and Architecture
F	France, Art and Architecture of

G	Germany, Art and Architecture of
I	India, Art and Architecture of
	Islamic Art and Architecture
	Italy, Art and Architecture of
J-K	Japanese Art and Architecture
L	Latin America, Art and Architecture of
Q-R	Russia, Art and Architecture of
S	Spain, Art and Architecture of
U-V	United States, Art and Architecture of

Vol.	**Decorative Arts and Crafts**
C	Ceramics
	Collage
D	Decorative Arts
	Decoupage
E	Enameling
J-K	Jewelry
L	Linoleum-Block Printing
M	Macramé
	Mosaic
N	Needlecraft
O	Origami
P	Papier-mâché
	Posters
	Pottery
Q-R	Rubbings
S	Silk-Screen Printing
	Stained-Glass Windows
T	Tapestry
W-X-Y-Z	Weaving
	Wood Carving
	Woodcut Printing

PHYSICAL EDUCATION AND SPORTS

Vol.	**Article**
A	Ali, Muhammed
	Archery
	Automobile Racing
B	Badminton
	Ball
	Baseball
	Basketball
	Bicycling
	Billiards
	Boardsailing
	Boats and Boating
	Bobsledding
	Bodybuilding

Bowling
Boxing

C Canoeing
Cheerleading
Cricket
Croquet
Curling

D Darts
Diving

F Fencing
Ferris Wheels
Field Hockey
Fishing
Football

G Gehrig, Lou
Gibson, Althea
Golf
Gymnastics

H Handball
Hiking and Backpacking
Horseback Riding
Horse Racing
Horseshoe Pitching
Hunting

I Iceboating
Ice Hockey
Ice-Skating

J-K Jai Alai
Jogging and Running
Jones, Robert Tyre (Bobby), Jr.
Judo
Juggling

J-K Karate
Karting
Kayaking

L Lacrosse
Little League Baseball

M Martial Arts
Mountain Climbing

O Olympic Games
Owens, Jesse

P Paddle Tennis
Pelé
Physical Education
Physical Fitness
Polo

Q-R Racing
Racket Sports
Robinson, Jack Roosevelt (Jackie)
Roller Coasters
Roller-Skating
Rugby
Ruth, George Herman (Babe)

S Sailing

Shuffleboard
Skateboarding
Skiing
Skin Diving
Snowboarding
Soap Box Derby
Soccer and Youth Soccer
Softball
Special Olympics
Surfing
Swimming

T Table Tennis
Tennis
Thorpe, James Francis (Jim)
Track and Field

U-V Volleyball

W-X-Y-Z Water Polo
Waterskiing
Wrestling

HOME ECONOMICS AND INDUSTRIAL ARTS (TECHNOLOGY EDUCATION)

Vol.	Article
A	Adolescence
	Air Conditioning
B	Bread and Baking
	Budgets, Family
C	Candy and Candy Making
	Child Development
	Clothing
	Consumerism
	Cooking
	Cotton
	Crocheting
D	Dairying and Dairy Products
	Decorative Arts
	Design
	Detergents and Soap
	Dry Cleaning
	Dyes and Dyeing
F	Family
	Fashion
	Fibers
	First Aid
	Fish Farming
	Fishing Industry
	Food
	Food Preservation
	Food Regulations and Laws
	Food Shopping
	Fruitgrowing
	Furniture
G	Grains and Grain Products

H	Health
	Health Foods
	Heating Systems
	Herbs and Spices
	Home Economics
	Homes and Housing
I	Interior Design
J-K	Knitting
L	Laundry
	Leather
	Lighting
M	Macramé
	Meat and Meat Packing
N	Needlecraft
	Nutrition
	Nylon and Other Synthetic Fibers
O	Outdoor Cooking and Picnics
P	Poultry
Q-R	Recycling
	Refrigeration
	Rugs and Carpets
S	Safety
	Sewing
	Silk
T	Textiles
U-V	Vegetables
	Vitamins and Minerals

W-X-Y-Z	Weaving
	Wool
Vol.	**Industrial Arts (Technology Education)**
C	Ceramics
D	Dies and Molds
E	Electricity
	Electric Motors
	Electronics
	Electroplating
	Engraving
G	Graphic Arts
	Grinding and Polishing
I	Industrial Arts
	Industrial Design
L	Locks and Keys
M	Materials Science
	Mechanical Drawing
	Metals and Metallurgy
N	Nails, Screws, and Rivets
P	Photography
	Plastics
	Printing
T	Tools
W-X-Y-Z	Wood and Wood Products
	Woodworking

PART III
ACTIVITIES

HOW TO DO RESEARCH FOR REPORTS AND PROJECTS

▶ **INTRODUCTION**

THE NEW BOOK OF KNOWLEDGE is a valuable information resource. The twelve activities in this section are designed to help students learn how to find, organize, and use the information in the set and build good research skills in the process. The activities in Locating Information show them how to use the set's Index to find precisely the information they need. The Organizing Information activities demonstrate different ways information can be organized so that it is easy to understand and use. In Doing Research, the activities guide students through the process of researching and preparing a written or oral report and a project. Finally, in Fun with Facts, the activities show students how the set can be a useful resource in solving puzzles or playing word games. All of these activity sheets can be copied and used often.

▶ **TABLE OF CONTENTS**

ACTIVITY 1

NAME _____ DATE _____

Locating Information by Finding Key Words

You can find the answers to specific questions in THE NEW BOOK OF KNOWLEDGE. To locate the information you need, it is a good idea to write down your question first. Then decide which word or words tell what person, place, event, or object the question is about. Called **key words**, they identify the topic. Look at the questions below and underline the key word or words in each question.

1. How many stars are in the Milky Way?

2. What was Dr. Seuss's real name?

3. Which mammal can truly fly?

4. Did the first bicycles have pedals?

5. How much did the original Liberty Bell cost?

6. Why is Alaska called the Land of the Midnight Sun?

7. What famous children's book did Sir James M. Barrie write?

8. What is the largest, deepest ocean?

Next you need to locate the article where the answer to your question will be found. Look at the list of articles below. Then look back at the key words you underlined. After each article, write the number of the question it will most likely answer.

Seuss, Dr. _____   Barrie, Sir James Matthew _____

Mammals _____   Alaska _____

Milky Way _____   Liberty Bell _____

Bicycling _____   Oceans and Seas of the World _____

Now choose one of the questions above. Go to the appropriate article in THE NEW BOOK OF KNOWLEDGE and skim through it until you find the information you need. Write the answer here.

_____

_____

_____

NAME _____ DATE _____

Locating Information by Using Index Entries, Part 1

When you want to locate information in THE NEW BOOK OF KNOWLEDGE, it is best to look in the Index first. The Index is an alphabetical list of all the topics that are covered in the set. Each of volumes 1 through 20 has its own index, but Volume 21 is the Index for the entire encyclopedia. Use it for this activity. Suppose the topic you are looking up is Vikings. The following example from THE NEW BOOK OF KNOWLEDGE Index is called an **entry**. Use it to answer the questions below.

Vikings V:343

1. Is there an article about Vikings in THE NEW BOOK OF

KNOWLEDGE?_____

_____

2. In which volume will you find the article? _____

3. On what pages is the article located? _____

Here is another entry for a different topic, Rosa Parks.

Parks, Rosa (American civil rights leader) **A:**79m, 130, 143; **C:**328; **N:**28; **S:**115

4. Who was Rosa Parks? _____

5. Is there a separate article about Rosa Parks?_____

How do you know?_____

6. In which volumes can you read something about Rosa Parks?_____

_____

7. In which volume will you find information on more than one page?

_____

NAME _____ DATE _____

Locating Information by Using Index Entries, Part 2

Many topics are too big to be covered in a single article. When you look up these topics in the Index, you find a list of related topics below the main entry. These are called **subentries**. Look at this example and answer the questions below.

Whaling W:154–55

    early Massachusetts industry **M:**150

    lighting by whale oil **L:**231

    overfishing **O:**28

    protecting whales **O:**25; **W:**153

8. There is a separate article on whaling in Volume _____.

9. How many subentries are there? _____

10. If you want to know about the early whaling industry in

Massachusetts, which volume will you go to? _____

11. To prepare a report on saving the whales, which subentries would

you refer to? _____.

    Now choose a topic of your own. Find the Index entry for your topic in THE NEW BOOK OF KNOWLEDGE.

12. Is there a separate article for your topic? _____

13. If not, where can you find related information? _____

14. List two subentries that you would choose as additional references:

_____ Volume _____ Pages _____

_____ Volume _____ Pages _____

NAME _____ **DATE** _____

Locating Information by Using Cross-References, Part 1

When you look up a topic in THE NEW BOOK OF KNOWLEDGE Index, you will sometimes find the words *see also* in the entry. The *see also* listings are called **cross-references**. They refer you to another entry in the Index where you will find more information about your topic. Look at the following entry and answer the questions.

> **Bees** (insects) **B:116–21** *see also* Honey
>
> > biological classification **L:**207
> >
> > clock-compass **H:**202
> >
> > color vision **C:**428
> >
> > flower pollination **F:**285; **P:**308
> >
> > homing, example of **H:**197
> >
> > How do honeybees make honey? **H:**210
> >
> > strength of **I:**241
> >
> > vectors of disease **V:**284
> >
> > *picture(s)*
> >
> > > eggs in the hive **E:**96
> > >
> > > mouthparts **I:**238
> > >
> > > nests **B:**121

1. Where will you find the main article about bees? Volume _____

Pages _____

2. According to the *see also* cross-reference, which related topic can

you refer to in the Index? _____

3. How many of the subentries refer you to Volume H? _____

4. Where will you find a picture of the parts of the bee's mouth? _____

_____

NAME _____ DATE _____

Locating Information by Using Cross-References, Part 2

Some persons, countries, and other subjects are known by more than one name. In such cases, the Index entries are usually listed by the best-known names. If you look up the alternate name, you will find the word *see* in the entry. This is another type of cross-reference. It leads you to the Index entry where you will find information on your topic. Look at the following examples, and answer the questions below.

Bonaparte, Napoleon *see* Napoleon I

Bonney, William H. (American outlaw) *see* Billy the Kid

Mounties *see* Royal Canadian Mounted Police

Nyasaland *see* Malawi

Pyridoxine *see* Vitamin B_6

PVC *see* Polyvinylchloride

5. Do any of these cross-references include a volume number or page numbers? _____

6. Where in the Index will you look for information about Napoleon Bonaparte? _____

7. What was Billy the Kid's full name?_____

8. PVC is a shortened form of the word _____

9. Pyridoxine is another name for _____

10. Malawi is the modern name for the part of Africa formerly known as_____

11. The Royal Canadian Mounted Police are often simply called the

_____

NAME _____ DATE _____

Organizing Information by Making a Chart, Part 1

A chart is a method of organizing information. It allows you to group facts into categories and to compare what is alike or different about the items in each category. The chart below is based on information from the article BIRDS in THE NEW BOOK OF KNOWLEDGE. It is divided into three columns and nine rows. Read the headings at the top of each column. The column at the far left contains the names of different birds. The next two columns contain certain information about each bird. Use the facts in the chart to answer the questions below.

Bird	Type of Bill	Type of Food
Bald eagle	tearing	fish, frogs, birds
Blue jay	cracking	seeds, nuts
Heron	spearing	fish, frogs
Woodpecker	hammering	insects
Redpoll	cracking	seeds, nuts
Snipe	probing	small freshwater creatures
Seagull	tearing	fish, frogs, shellfish
Flamingo	filtering	small seawater creatures

1. What category is used as the heading for the middle column? _____

   _____

2. Which bird has a hammering bill? _____

3. Which bird eats small sea creatures?_____

4. Name two birds that have tearing bills. _____

5. If you were to sort birds by the type of bill they have, how many

groups would there be?_____

NAME _____ DATE _____

Organizing Information by Making a Chart, Part 2

   Practice making a chart to organize information. Choose an article of special interest to you, or use one of those listed below. Draw your chart in the space below. Decide on your headings and choose appropriate facts. You may need more columns or rows for some charts and fewer for other charts.

Butterflies and Moths	Leaves
Dinosaurs	Musical Instruments
Holidays	Planets
Indians, American	Whales

NAME _____ DATE _____

Organizing Information by Making a Web, Part 1

A web is a visual way of recording and organizing important information in an article you are reading. To make a web, start by writing the main topic of the article, or the portion of the article you are using, in the center of your paper. You will record information about the topic by working outward from the center of the web. Use boxes joined by connecting lines to jot down subtopics and specific facts that you think are important.

The sample web below is based on information from the article APES in THE NEW BOOK OF KNOWLEDGE. Use information from the web to answer these questions.

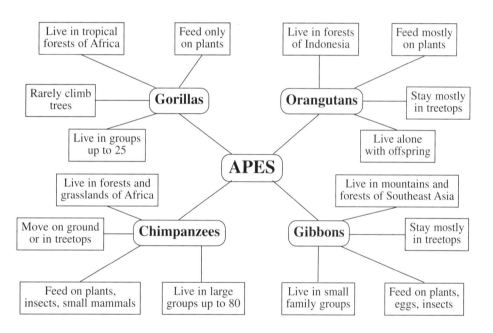

1. What are the four major groups of apes? _____

_____

2. Which groups of apes live in Africa? _____

3. Do gorillas eat other animals? _____

4. Which type of ape does not live in a group? _____

5. Which groups rarely move about on the ground? _____

NAME _____ DATE _____

Organizing Information by Making a Web, Part 2

You can make your own web organizer for any article or part of an article using the blank model on this page. Choose a topic in which you are particularly interested, or try one of these:

Africa, Music of	Eclipses
Aztecs	Folk Dance
Cats	Leaves
Colonial Life in America	Thunder and Lightning

You may not need all the boxes in this web, or you may find it necessary to add more boxes.

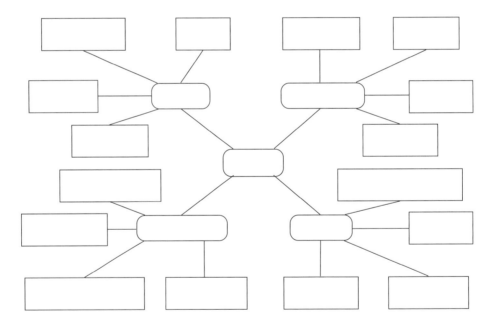

NAME _____ DATE _____

Organizing Information by Making a Time Line, Part 1

A time line is a useful way of organizing events in the order in which they happened. This time line is based on data in the article ABOLITION MOVEMENT in THE NEW BOOK OF KNOWLEDGE. The "abolition movement" is the name given to the campaign to abolish slavery in the United States. The time line is divided into 25-year periods. Key events are entered at appropriate places along the line. Use dates from the time line to answer the questions below.

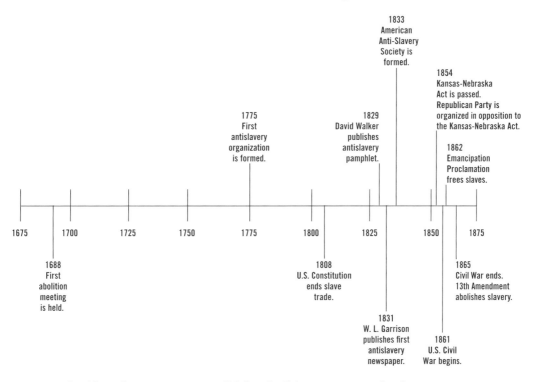

1. About how many years did the abolition movement last? _____

2. According to the time line, the United States stopped importing

African slaves in 1808. Did slavery end then? _____

3. List two events from the time line that support your answer to

question 2. _____

4. Name two writers who helped raise interest in the abolition

movement. _____

NAME _____ DATE _____

Organizing Information by Making a Time Line, Part 2

You may wish to make a time line of your own for one of the following articles, or a portion of one, from THE NEW BOOK OF KNOWLEDGE. To construct your time line, use the steps described below.

Balloons and Ballooning	Poe, Edgar Allan
Crusades	Rock Music
French and Indian Wars	United Nations
Nightingale, Florence	Women's Rights Movement

1. Draw a straight line across the middle of a sheet of blank paper. If your time line is to be put on a wall or bulletin board, you may wish to tape several sheets of paper together or use paper that comes in a roll.

2. Decide how you want to divide your time line. If you are making a time line to show important events in a person's life, you may want to divide it into 10-year periods. If you are showing key events in the history of a country, a movement, or an era, you may decide on intervals of 25 years, 50 years, or 100 years.

3. Think about the dates of the first event and last event that will be included in your time line. Then write a date on the left end of the line. It should be at an interval just before the date of the first event. Now write a date on the right end of the line. It should be at an interval just after the date of the last event.

4. Using short vertical lines, divide the time line into the intervals you have chosen. Write the appropriate date at each interval.

5. Using longer vertical lines above or below the line, record the dates of each key event at the appropriate spots along the line. Then, at each date, write out as briefly as possible what happened in each event.

6. If your time line is to be displayed, you may wish to add drawings, magazine illustrations, or photographs to the events.

NAME _____ DATE _____

Doing Research to Prepare a Biography, Part 1

A biography is a true account of a person's life. It covers the important facts about the person and describes key events and accomplishments in the individual's life. When you are doing research for a biography, THE NEW BOOK OF KNOWLEDGE is a good starting point. The Index will direct you to a biographical article, to a profile, or to other articles about the person's life or work. Read the following and answer the questions that follow it.

Sequoya was a Cherokee Indian who developed the first written Native American language. He was born in Loudon County, Tennessee, about 1770. His mother was the daughter of a chief; his father was a fur trader, a white man named either Gist or Guess.

After he suffered a crippling hunting accident, Sequoya became an expert silversmith and mechanic. He later realized the value of communication through reading and writing. Sequoya began to think his people could advance further if they had a written language of their own. He began experimenting, carving symbols on birch bark, and continued even though his family and friends ridiculed his efforts. When he tested his system on his 6-year-old daughter, he saw that children could learn the language easily.

In 1821, Sequoya completed his work. Within a few months, thousands of Cherokee learned to read and write using his system. In 1828 the *Cherokee Phoenix*, a weekly newspaper printed in English and Cherokee, first appeared. For his work Sequoya was honored by his tribe, and the Cherokee National Council rewarded him with a yearly allowance.

Sequoya died in Mexico in 1843. The giant redwood trees of California have been named sequoias in his memory.

1. What was Sequoya's major accomplishment? _____

2. Find the facts:

Date and place of birth _____

Parents _____

Main occupation _____

Honors and awards _____

Date and place of death _____

3. Why did Sequoya develop a written Cherokee language? _____

_____

4. What hardships did Sequoya have to overcome? _____

_____

ACTIVITY 7

NAME _____ DATE _____

Doing Research to Prepare a Biography, Part 2

Choose a person you would like to research for a biography. You may want to select someone from this list. Use the Biography Fact Sheet below to start your search for information for your biography.

Susan B. Anthony (American suffragist)

Simón Bolívar (South American patriot)

Elizabeth I (former queen of England)

Robert H. Goddard (American rocket scientist)

Martin Luther King, Jr. (American civil rights leader)

Wolfgang Amadeus Mozart (Austrian composer)

Jesse Owens (American track athlete)

Beatrix Potter (English writer)

Biography Fact Sheet

Name of person _____

Birthdate and birthplace _____

Parents and important family members _____

Important childhood events _____

Education _____

Main occupation _____

Key events in adult life _____

Major accomplishment _____

Honors and awards _____

Main character traits _____

Date and place of death _____

Remember, when you prepare a biography, use several different resources in addition to THE NEW BOOK OF KNOWLEDGE. These may include biographies and autobiographies, diaries, history books, magazines, newspapers, films, and videos.

ACTIVITY 8

NAME _____ DATE _____

Doing Research to Prepare a Report on a Country, Part 1

When you are preparing a report on a country, you will find much information in THE NEW BOOK OF KNOWLEDGE. Each country has its own article, and for some there are also separate articles about the country under the headings Language and Literature, Art and Architecture, and Music. The Index may have a listing of other articles related to your topic. Choose a country to report on. Then find the article about your country in the set and answer the questions below.

1. What is pictured next to the article's title? _____

2. The article is divided into sections. The headings for major sections are called **major headings**. They are printed in heavy type in capital letters. What is the first major heading? _____

3. List the other major headings in the article. _____

_____

4. **Subheadings** mark off smaller sections within major sections. Here are the subheadings under ▶ THE LAND in the article on Mexico:

The Central Plateau   **Climate**

Mountain Ranges   **Natural Resources**

Coastal Plains and Lowlands

Under which subheading would you learn

a. the name of Mexico's highest peak? _____

b. that Mexico is a leading producer of silver? _____

c. about the range of temperature in Mexico? _____

5. Find the "Facts and figures" box in your article. List the major headings in the box. _____

NAME _____ DATE _____

Doing Research to Prepare a Report on a Country, Part 2

Use the Fact Sheet below to record the data you collect for your report on a country.

Fact Sheet for a Report on a Country

Name of Country _____

The Land

    Location _____

    Major rivers, lakes, seas_____

    Major mountains and mountain ranges _____

The People

    Family life _____

    Education _____

    Language _____

    Art, music, recreation_____

    Holidays, customs, and foods _____

Industry and Agriculture

    Major industries_____

    Major agricultural products _____

    Natural resources _____

History

    Important events_____

    Type of government _____

    Major rulers or leaders_____

    Other important people _____

NAME _____ **DATE** _____

Doing Research to Prepare a Science Project

When you are preparing a project for your science class at school, for an after-school organization, or for a science fair, THE NEW BOOK OF KNOWLEDGE can be useful at each step of the process. Use the activities below to guide you as you plan your project.

A. Choosing a topic.

Because you will be spending a lot of time on your project, make sure you are really interested in the topic you select.

1. Here is a list of some of the major areas of science. Check the one that is of most interest to you.

Plants _____   Environment _____

Animals _____   Health _____

Earth _____   Computers _____

Weather _____   Chemistry _____

Astronomy _____   Physics _____

2. In the Index of THE NEW BOOK OF KNOWLEDGE, look up the area of interest you checked above. Skim through the list of subtopics under the heading. List two or three references for subjects of interest to you. Include the volume and page numbers.

_____

B. Choosing the purpose for your project.

1. Locate each of the references you listed above. As you skim through an article, think of questions that can be answered, problems that can be solved, or ideas that can be demonstrated by a science project. Write these down.

_____

2. Decide which one of these project ideas you really want to work on. Write your idea down in the form of a question, or use a sentence that states the purpose of the activity.

_____

C. Doing background research.

Before proceeding with your project, you should gather as much background information as you can. Check off in the list below the resources that you plan on using to research your topic.

Encyclopedia articles ———   Books ———

Magazines ———   Videos ———

CD-ROM or computer software ———

Interview with an expert on the topic ———

Visit to a park, museum, recycling station, or some other facility ———

You are now ready to consult your resources. Keep a record of the information you collect.

D. Planning an experiment.

Very often your science project will consist of an experiment. The article EXPERIMENTS AND OTHER SCIENCE ACTIVITIES in Volume E has many useful ideas for planning your experiment. The following passage is taken from this article. Read it and follow the steps below.

What Is an Experiment?

An experiment is one method a scientist may use to solve a **problem**. First, the problem must be recognized and clearly stated. Next, the experimenter makes an educated guess about a possible solution to the problem. This guess, based on knowledge of the subject, is called a **hypothesis**. The experimenter tests the hypothesis by following a **procedure** that can show whether the hypothesis is true or false. Certain **materials** will be needed for the procedure. During the procedure, the experimenter makes **observations** and keeps careful records of the results that are observed. Then the experimenter draws a **conclusion** about whether the hypothesis is true or false.

1. Write a hypothesis for your experiment. ————————

2. List the steps that you will use to test your hypothesis. ————

   ————————————————————————

3. List the materials you will need. ————————

4. What method will you use to record your observations and results?

   ————————————————————————

Once you have completed these steps, you are ready to collect the materials you need, set up the experiment or demonstration, conduct your test, and draw your conclusions.

NAME _____ DATE _____

Fun with Facts: A Guggenheim Game

A Guggenheim (GOOG-un-hime) is a game in which you must make up a list of words or objects that fit into particular categories, for example, cities, sports, or occupations. What makes the game challenging is the "Guggenheim word," a word that determines the beginning letters of the words in your list. You may play Guggenheim alone, against a partner, or as part of a team competition. Here is a Guggenheim for you to play. Before you start, look carefully at the Guggenheim framework and read the directions below.

	Animals	Foods	States
S			
C			
H			
O			
L			
A			
R			

1. Find the Guggenheim word that is spelled out along the left side of the framework. The word is SCHOLAR.

2. To play, you must think of words that fit into each of the three categories: animals, foods, and states. The first letter of the word must match up with one of the letters in the Guggenheim word. For example, in the first row, the names of the animal, the food, and the state you write down must all begin with the letter *s*.

3. If you get stuck and cannot come up with a name, refer to related articles in THE NEW BOOK OF KNOWLEDGE.

4. To make the game more interesting, you may wish to set a time limit for yourself. If you are playing with other people, you may use a point system as well as a time limit. Extra points can be given for less common choices. "Lemur" would probably be a less common choice than "lion," for instance, and would get extra points.

If you enjoy this game, you can make your own version of Guggenheim. Simply choose a different Guggenheim word and at least three different categories. Set up your framework and you are ready to play.

NAME _____ **DATE** _____

Fun with Facts: A Matching Game and a Wordsearch Game, Part 1

There are 16 countries of the world listed in the column on the left. Match each country to the river that flows through it. The rivers are listed in the column on the right. Use THE NEW BOOK OF KNOWLEDGE if you need help.

1. Australia _____   a. Amazon

2. Austria _____   b. Limpopo

3. Brazil _____   c. Danube

4. Myanmar (Burma) _____   d. Don

5. Canada _____   e. Ebro

6. China _____   f. Euphrates

7. India _____   g. Ganges

8. Mozambique _____   h. Huang He (Yellow)

9. Nicaragua _____   i. Irrawaddy

10. Poland _____   j. Mackenzie

11. Russia _____   k. Murray

12. Spain _____   l. Oder

13. Syria _____   m. Orinoco

14. United States _____   n. Santee

15. Venezuela _____   o. Tipitapa

16. Zimbabwe _____   p. Zambezi

NAME _____ **DATE** _____

Fun with Facts: A Matching Game and a Wordsearch Game, Part 2

Now you can go exploring. The names of the 16 rivers are hidden in this puzzle. Read forward, backward, up, down, and diagonally. Circle the name of each river as you find it.

```
O  E  U  P  H  R  A  T  E  S  X  I  E
I  A  C  E  K  N  N  I  V  Q  G  B  I
E  R  Y  P  T  O  E  P  M  T  R  H  Z
H  X  R  L  D  Z  F  I  D  O  J  W  E
G  O  F  A  G  A  V  T  A  G  M  L  B
N  R  G  B  W  M  G  A  N  G  E  S  M
A  I  Q  N  Z  A  Q  P  U  H  I  A  A
U  N  B  J  O  E  D  A  B  O  K  N  Z
H  O  D  X  L  C  I  D  E  R  D  T  O
U  C  S  M  U  R  R  A  Y  W  L  E  H
Q  O  E  I  Z  N  E  K  C  A  M  E  R
```

NAME _____ DATE _____

Fun with Facts: A Crossword Puzzle

Did you know that the first crossword puzzle was created by Arthur Wynne, a newspaperman, in 1913? Crossword puzzles are enjoyable and educational. The puzzle below is built around a theme, and most of the clues are related. If you need help with any of the answers, use THE NEW BOOK OF KNOWLEDGE. Have fun!

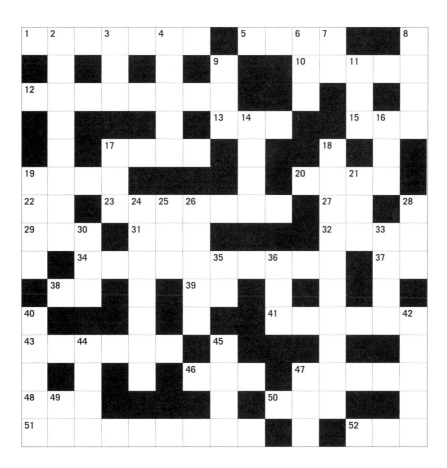

ACTIVITY 12

ACROSS

1. He invented the wireless telegraph.

5. Thomas Edison's middle name.

10. Country where paper was invented.

12. A colonial American inventor and statesman.

13. A period of history.

15. A young, furry animal.

17. He developed the Polaroid camera.

19. _ _ _ _ lite, an early plastic invented by Baekeland.

20. It was discovered by Roentgen in 1895.

22. Turn _ _ the engine.

23. The American who developed modern rockets.

27. Radio waves were aimed _ _ the target star.

29. Marie Curie won _ _ _ second Nobel Prize in 1911.

31. To be sorry for.

32. The gas that makes colored lights glow.

34. What this puzzle is mostly about.

37. Vermont, abbreviated.

38. A man's nickname.

39. One of Jupiter's moons.

41. Invention of Maiman in 1960.

43. The first space telescope.

46. A precious stone.

47. A code named for the American who invented it.

48. The short name for the Environmental Protection Agency.

50. To make a mistake.

51. It was invented by 5 across.

52. Nickname for the machine that explored the moon.

DOWN

2. It was invented by 24 down.

3. A container made of aluminum or tin.

4. The first synthetic fiber, invented by Carothers.

6. You use it to watch and record movies at home.

7. Open your mouth and say _ _.

8. James _ _ _ _, a Scottish inventor of the late 1700's.

9. The chemical in living cells used in genetic engineering.

11. It was invented by ancient Egyptians to use in writing.

14. A wheel with teeth used in automobiles and other devices with moving parts.

16. Freezing rain causes _ _ _ conditions.

17. One of four on a chair.

18. It was invented by Bardeen, Brattain, and Shockley.

19. The Danish physicist who won a Nobel Prize for his atomic theory.

21. Eat, _ _ _, eaten.

24. Wilbur Wright's brother.

25. The space flight was canceled _ _ _ to the bad weather.

26. Heavy cotton cloth used in blue jeans.

28. A powerful explosive.

30. To free from.

33. In 1785 two balloonists flew _ _ _ _ the English Channel.

35. Satellites send TV signals _ _ Earth.

36. An important liquid fuel.

40. A very early invention in transportation.

42. What 8 down used to run his engine.

44. What you can do when you complete this puzzle.

45. Inventor of the telephone.

47. Abbreviation for magnetic resonance imaging.

49. A special number used in measuring circles.

Activities Answer Key

Activity 1. Key words: 1. Milky Way; 2. Dr. Seuss; 3. mammal; 4. bicycles; 5. Liberty Bell; 6. Alaska; 7. Sir James M. Barrie; 8. ocean.

Matching:

Seuss, Dr. 2	Barrie, Sir James Matthew 7
Mammals 3	Alaska 6
Milky Way 1	Liberty Bell 5
Bicycling 4	Oceans and Seas of the World 8

Answers to questions: 1. more than 300 billion; 2. Theodor Seuss Geisel; 3. bat; 4. No, they were pushed by the feet; 5. $300; 6. For three months the sun never sets; 7. *Peter Pan*; 8. Pacific.

Activity 2. 1. Yes; 2. Volume V; 3. pages 339–43; 4. an American civil rights leader; 5. No, there is no reference for Volume P; 6. Volumes A, C, N, and S; 7. Volume A; 8. Volume W, pages 154–55; 9. five; 10. Volume M, Massachusetts; 11. overfishing; protecting whales. Answers to the last three activities will vary depending on the topic chosen by the student.

Activity 3. 1. Volume B, pages 116–21; 2. honey; 3. three; 4. Volume I, page 238; 5. No; 6. under Napoleon I; 7. William H. Bonney; 8. polyvinylchloride; 9. Vitamin B_6; 10. Nyasaland; 11. Mounties.

Activity 4. 1. Type of Bill; 2. woodpecker; 3. flamingo; 4. bald eagle, seagull; 5. six. For the final activity, students create their own chart, so answers will vary.

Activity 5. 1. gorillas, orangutans, chimpanzees, gibbons; 2. gorillas, chimpanzees; 3. No, they feed only on plants; 4. orangutans; 5. gibbons. For the final activity, students create their own web, so answers will vary.

Activity 6. 1. almost 200 years; 2. No; 3. Students may select any two of the events from 1829 on; 4. David Walker and W. L. Garrison. For the final activity, students create their own time line, so answers will vary.

Activity 7. 1. He developed the first written Native American language; 2. 1770, Loudon County, Tennessee; his mother was the daughter of a chief and his father was a white fur trader named Gist or Guess; silversmith and mechanic; tribal honors, yearly allowance from the Cherokee National Council, and the giant redwoods of California were named after him; 1843 in Mexico; 3. Because he thought it would help his people advance; 4. As a Native American he had many disadvantages. He also had to overcome a crippling disability and he was ridiculed by his own people. For Part 2's activity, students research information for a biography and record it on a fact sheet, so answers will vary.

Activity 8. 1. the country's flag; 2. The People; 3. Answers may vary but will probably include Way of Life, The Land, Major Cities, The Economy, Government, and History. 4. a. Mountain Ranges; b. Natural Resources; c. Climate; 5. Answers may vary but will probably include Official Name, Location, Area, Population, Capital and Largest City, Major Languages, Major Religious Groups, Government, Chief Products, and Monetary Unit. For Part 2's activity, students research information about a country of their choice and record it on a fact sheet, so answers will vary.

Activity 9. Answers to all activities will vary.

Activity 10. Answers to the game categories in the Guggenheim Game will vary, but all answers must begin with the letters at the beginning of the row in which they are written.

Activity 11. Answers to Matching Game: **1.** k; **2.** c; **3.** a; **4.** i; **5.** j; **6.** h; **7.** g; **8.** p; **9.** o; **10.** l; **11.** d; **12.** e; **13.** f; **14.** n; **15.** m; **16.** b.

Activity 11. Answers to Wordsearch Game.

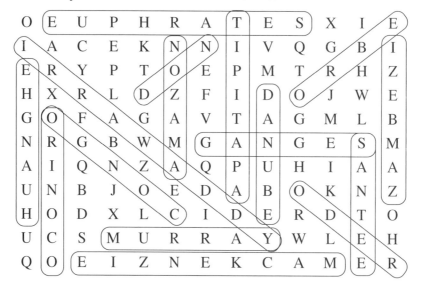

Activity 12. Answers to Crossword Puzzle.

¹M	²A	³R	⁴C	O	N	I		⁵A	⁶L	⁷V	A		⁸W
	I		A	Y		⁹D			¹⁰C	H	¹¹I	N	A
¹²F	R	A	N	K	L	I	N		R		N		T
	P			O		¹³A	¹⁴G	E			¹⁵K	¹⁶I	T
	L		¹⁷L	A	N	D	E			¹⁸T		C	
¹⁹B	A	K	E				A		²⁰X	²¹R	A	Y	
²²O	N		²³G	²⁴O	²⁵D	²⁶D	A	R	D		²⁷A	T	²⁸T
²⁹H	E	³⁰R		³¹R	U	E				³²N	E	³³O	N
R		³⁴I	N	V	E	³⁵T	I	³⁶O	N	S		³⁷V	T
	³⁸E	D		I		³⁹I	O	I		I		E	
⁴⁰W				L		M		⁴¹L	A	S	E	R	⁴²S
⁴³H	⁴⁴U	B	B	L	E		⁴⁵B			T			T
E	R		E		⁴⁶G	E	M		⁴⁷M	O	R	S	E
⁴⁸E	⁴⁹P	A				L		⁵⁰E	R	R			A
⁵¹L	I	G	H	T	B	U	L	B		I		⁵²L	E	M

ACTIVITIES • 248

Copyright © 2007 Scholastic Library Publishing, Inc.

APPENDIX

HOBBIES AND OTHER LEISURE-TIME ACTIVITIES

The favorite leisure-time activities of American families include hobbies, arts and crafts, sports, and games. Your youngsters may share their hobbies and other recreational activities with family members or with their friends, or they may choose to pursue an interest by themselves.

THE NEW BOOK OF KNOWLEDGE is an especially valuable resource for the hobbyist or the arts and crafts, sports, or games enthusiast. It contains numerous articles that describe and provide simple directions for a variety of leisure-time pursuits.

HOBBIES AND OTHER LEISURE-TIME ACTIVITIES

	Boats and Boating	**S**	Sailing
	Bobsledding		Shuffleboard
	Bowling		Skateboarding
	Boxing		Skiing
C	Camping		Skin Diving
	Canoeing		Skydiving
	Cheerleading		Snowboarding
	Croquet		Soapbox Derby
D	Diving		Soccer
F	Fencing		Softball
	Field Hockey		Spelunking
	Fishing		Surfing
	Football		Swimming
G	Golf	**T**	Tennis
	Gymnastics		Track and Field
H	Handball	**U-V**	Volleyball
	Hiking and Backpacking	**W-X-Y-Z**	Water Polo
	Horseback Riding		Waterskiing
	Horse Racing		Wrestling
	Horseshoe Pitching		
	Hostels and Hosteling	**Vol.**	**Indoor Activities and Games**
	Hunting	**B**	Backgammon
I	Iceboating		Billiards
	Ice Hockey	**C**	Card Games
	Ice-Skating		Charades
J-K	Jogging and Running		Checkers
	Judo		Chess
	Juggling (Learning the Cascade)		Crossword Puzzles
J-K	Karate	**D**	Darts
	Karting		Dominoes
	Kayaking	**F**	Folk Dance
	Kites	**J-K**	Jacks
L	Lacrosse	**M**	Magic
	Little League Baseball	**N**	Number Puzzles and Games
M	Marbles	**P**	Plays
	Martial Arts		Puzzles
	Mountain Climbing	**Q-R**	Radio, Amateur
P	Paddle Tennis	**T**	Table Tennis
	Polo	**U-V**	Ventriloquism
Q-R	Racing		Video Recording
	Racket Sports	**W-X-Y-Z**	Word Games
	Roller-Skating		
	Roping		
	Rowing		
	Rugby		

LITERATURE

As children browse through THE NEW BOOK OF KNOWLEDGE, they are often captivated by the many literary selections they come upon, sometimes returning to their favorites again and again. Parents, too, spend many pleasurable moments reading selections to youngsters not yet able to read to themselves.

The literary selections in the set include fiction, nonfiction, and poetry—classics, short stories, legends, fairy tales, fables, myths, essays, poems, and excerpts from novels and poems. Some selections accompany the biography of a famous writer. Others appear in articles that discuss a particular type of literature.

Below is a list of the literary selections contained in the encyclopedia. You will find information about selections that are particularly appropriate for your youngster's age-group in the grade-level sections of this STUDY GUIDE.

Vol.	Article	Literary Selections
A	Africa, Literature of	African proverbs and riddles
	Alcott, Louisa May	Little Women (excerpt)
	Andersen, Hans Christian	The Emperor's New Clothes
	Arabian Nights	Aladdin and the Wonderful Lamp (excerpt)
		The Forty Thieves (excerpt)
	Arthur, King	The Story of Arthur (excerpt, Malory)
B	Barrie, Sir James Matthew	Peter Pan (excerpt)
	Bible Stories	Noah's Ark
		David and Goliath
		Jonah
		Daniel in the Lions' Den
		The Boy Jesus
	Browning, Elizabeth Barrett and Robert	How Do I Love Thee (from Sonnets from the Portuguese)
		Pied Piper of Hamelin (excerpt)
	Buck, Pearl	The Good Earth (excerpt)
	Burns, Robert	A Red, Red Rose
	Byron, George Gordon, Lord	Childe Harold's Pilgrimage (excerpt)
		The Prisoner of Chillon (excerpt)
C	Carroll, Lewis	Alice's Adventures in Wonderland (excerpt)
	Christmas Story	Gospel according to Luke

Vol.	Article	Literary Selections
	Civil Rights Movement	I Have a Dream (excerpts)
	Columbus, Christopher	The Log of Christopher Columbus' First Voyage to America in the Year 1492, As Copied Out in Brief by Bartholomew Las Casas (excerpt)
	Cooper, James Fenimore	The Last of the Mohicans (excerpt)
D	Defoe, Daniel	Robinson Crusoe (excerpt)
	Dickens, Charles	David Copperfield (excerpt)
		Oliver Twist (excerpt)
	Dickinson, Emily	A Bird Came Down the Walk
		I'll Tell You How the Sun Rose
	Dogs	Famous quotes about dogs
	Donne, John	Devotions upon Emergent Occasions (excerpt)
	Doyle, Sir Arthur Conan	The Red-Headed League (excerpt)
	Dumas, Alexandre Père and Alexandre Fils	The Three Musketeers (excerpt)
	Dunbar, Paul Laurence	A Starry Night
E	Emerson, Ralph Waldo	The Concord Hymn
	Essays	Essay (excerpt, Franklin)

Vol.	Article	Literary Selections	Vol.	Article	Literary Selections
	Fables	The Lion and the Mouse (Aesop)		Grahame, Kenneth	The Wind in the Willows (excerpt)
		The Ant and the Grasshopper (Aesop)		Greece, Literature of	Parallel Lives (excerpt, Plutarch)
		The Four Oxen and the Lion (Aesop)		Grimm, Jacob and Wilhelm	Rapunzel
		The Tyrant Who Became a Just Ruler (Bidpai)			Hansel and Gretel
		The Blind Men and the Elephant (Saxe)	H	Hawthorne, Nathaniel	Young Goodman Brown
		The Moth and the Star (Thurber)		Homer	The Iliad
	Fairy Tales	The Enchanted Princess (German)		Hugo, Victor	Les Miserables (excerpt)
		The Princess on the Pea (Andersen)	I	Irving, Washington	Rip Van Winkle (excerpt)
		The Sleeping Beauty (Perrault)	J-K	Keats, John	When I Have Fears...
		Little Red Riding-Hood (de la Mare)			On the Grasshopper and the Cricket
	Field, Eugene	A Dutch Lullaby		Kipling, Rudyard	The Elephant's Child
	Figures of Speech	Silver (de la Mare)	L	Latin America, Literature of	The Heights of Machu Picchu (excerpt, Neruda)
		The Toaster (Smith, W. J.)		Legends	The Vanishing Hitchhiker (United States)
		Dandelions (Frost, F. M.)			Roland and Oliver (France)
		The Little Rose Tree (Field)			The Legend of Robin Hood (England)
		Everyone Sang (Sassoon)		Liberty, Statue of	The New Colossus (excerpt, Lazarus)
		The Night Will Never Stay (Farjeon)		Lincoln, Abraham	Excerpts from Lincoln's speeches, letters, and other writings
		Brooms (Aldis)			
		No Shop Does the Bird Use (Coatsworth)		London, Jack	The Call of the Wild (excerpt)
	Folklore	Cinderella (Korean)		Longfellow, Henry Wadsworth	The Arrow and the Song
	Folklore, American	Coyote Places the Stars	M	Melville, Herman	Moby Dick (excerpt)
		Wiley and the Hairy Man		Milne, A. A.	Missing
	Franklin, Benjamin	Quotations from Poor Richard's Almanack (attributed to Benjamin Franklin)		Milton, John	L'Allegro (excerpt)
			N	Nonsense Rhymes	Jabberwocky (Carroll)
	French Revolution	The Execution of Marie Antoinette (excerpt, Williams)			Jellyfish Stew (Prelutsky)
					Habits of the Hippopotamus (Guiterman)
	Frost, Robert	The Last Word of a Bluebird			Eletelephony (Richards)
		The Pasture			The Reason for the Pelican (Ciardi)
		Stopping by Woods on a Snowy Evening			Antigonish (Mearns)
		The Road Not Taken			I Wish That My Room Had a Floor (Burgess)
G	Gettysburg Address	Gettysburg Address			There Was a Young Lady of Woosester (Anonymous)

Vol.	Article	Literary Selections	Vol.	Article	Literary Selections
		There Was an Old Man with a Beard (Lear)		Stevenson, Robert Louis	Requiem
		There Was an Old Man of Peru (Anonymous)			My Shadow
	Nursery Rhymes	The Old Woman in a Shoe			Looking-Glass River
		Jack and Jill			The Swing
		Hey Diddle, Diddle			The Gardener
		Miss Muffet			Bed in Summer
		Mary's Lamb			Kidnapped (excerpt)
		Humpty Dumpty		Swift, Jonathan	Gulliver's Travels (excerpt)
P	Pioneer Life	Oregon Fever (excerpt from a pioneer's diary)	T	Tennyson, Alfred, Lord	Crossing the Bar (from The Lady of Shalott)
	Poe, Edgar Allan	Eldorado		Thackeray, William Makepeace	Vanity Fair (excerpt)
	Poetry	Daffodils (excerpt, Wordsworth)			
		Ode to the West Wind (excerpt, Shelley)		Thoreau, Henry David	Walden (excerpt)
		Sonnet 18 (Shakespeare)		Thurber, James	The Great Quillow (excerpt)
		When Lilacs Last in the Dooryard Bloom'd (excerpt, Whitman)		Tolkien, J. R. R.	The Hobbit (excerpt)
				Twain, Mark	The Adventures of Tom Sawyer (excerpt)
	Potter, Beatrix	The Tale of Jemima Puddle-Duck (excerpt)			The Celebrated Jumping Frog of Calaveras County (excerpt)
Q-R	Revere, Paul	Paul Revere's Ride (excerpts, Longfellow)	W-X-Y-Z	White, E. B.	Charlotte's Web (excerpt)
	Rossetti Family	Who Has Seen the Wind?		Whitman, Walt	When Lilacs Last in the Dooryard Bloom'd
S	Sandburg, Carl	Fog		Wilder, Laura Ingalls	Little House on the Prairie (excerpt)
		The Skyscraper to the Moon and How the Green Rat with the Rheumatism Ran a Thousand Miles Twice (Rootabaga Stories)		Williams, William Carlos	The Red Wheelbarrow
				Wordsworth, William	Daffodils
	Shelley, Percy Bysshe	To Night			My Heart Leaps up When I Behold
		Ozymandias		World War I	In Flanders Fields (McCrae)
	Short Stories	The Tell-Tale Heart (excerpt, Poe)		Yeats, William Butler	Under Ben Bulben (excerpt)
		The Gift of the Magi (excerpt, Henry)			The Lake Isle of Innisfree
		Two Soldiers (excerpt, Faulkner)			

PROJECTS AND EXPERIMENTS

Many articles in THE NEW BOOK OF KNOWLEDGE include useful and enjoyable projects or experiments. These excellent activities help students improve their understanding of basic concepts by giving them hands-on experiences with ideas or processes they have just read about. In addition, these activities provide many choices and ideas students can use for school projects and fairs in science, mathematics, language and literature, art, music, home economics, and personal hobbies and crafts.

Vol.	Article	Projects and Experiments	Vol.	Article	Projects and Experiments
A	Abacus	The Chinese abacus	E	Experiments and Other Science Activities	Sample report of an experiment:
	Antibiotics	How to grow a *penicillium* mold			
	Apple	How to sprout apple seeds			Controlled experiment with plant fertilizer
	Arithmetic	Using an addition table			How cold temperatures affect seed germination
		Using a multiplication table			How fast your reaction time is
		Using estimation strategies			How the length of a shadow changes with the seasons
B	Biology	How a biologist explores nature			
	Birds	Bird-watching			How to build an electric motor
	Birds as Pets	Choosing a bird			How to create layers of liquids
	Book Reports and Reviews	Choosing a book			How to identify acids and bases
		How to write a book report			How to make a pinhole camera
	Bread and Baking	Making yeast bread			How to make polymer "slime"
		How to bake a loaf of bread			How to observe the Greenhouse Effect
	Bulletin Boards	How to make a bulletin board			How to use chromatography to separate the components of a dye
C	Clowns	Suggested ways to apply clown makeup			
	Codes and Ciphers	Scytale			How your sense of smell affects your sense of taste
		Rail fence cipher	F	Falling Bodies, Laws of	Demonstration: Falling Bodies
		Pigpen cipher		Fiction	How to write fiction
		Grille		Fish	How to determine the age of a fish
	Coins and Coin Collecting	Coin collecting			
	Compositions	How to prepare a composition		Floating and Buoyancy	Demonstration: Archimedes' principle
	Constellations	Creating new constellations			How an object's buoyancy can be controlled in a fluid or in the air
	Crystals	Growing your own crystals			
D	Diaries and Journals	How to start your own journal			
	Dollhouses	How to make your own dollhouse			

Vol.	Article	Projects and Experiments	Vol.	Article	Projects and Experiments
		How shape can change an object's buoyancy		Knitting	How to make a flat kite
	Flowers	Flowers and their animal pollinators			Knitting project: squared off sweater
	Forces	Demonstrations:		Knots	How to tie knots
		How to find the sum of different forces on an object	L	Leaves	Seeing if leaves need sunlight to survive
		How the sum of three forces can be represented by vectors			Preserving leaves
				Letter Writing	How to write letters
	Fractions and Decimals	Comparing fractions		Libraries	How to use your library's reference collection
	Fungi	How to make a spore print		Light	How to produce a real image
G	Gardens and Gardening	How to grow some garden favorites			How light travels in straight lines
		How to make a backyard snack garden		Liquids	Demonstrations: Capillarity—
		How to create a container garden			The surface tension of liquids
		How to make a compost pile or bin			The effect of gravity on a drop of liquid
	Gases	Demonstrations:			The cohesive forces of water
		How air pressure can support a column of water	M	Macramé	How to do macramé
				Magnets and Magnetism	How to make an electromagnet
		How increasing the pressure on a gas reduces its volume		Maps and Globes	Be your own map maker
				Matter	Study the forms of matter
	Genealogy	Tracing your family tree		Microscopes	How to build Van Leeuwenhoek's microscope
	Genetics	How traits are inherited			
	Geometry	How to construct a polyhedron			How to care for your microscope
	Gift Wrapping	Wrapping a gift			Some things to see with your microscope
	Graphs	How to draw a bar graph	N	Number Patterns	Finding patterns in Fibonacci numbers
	Greeting Cards	How to make a pop-up greeting card			Demonstrations:
	Gyroscope	The properties of a gyroscope			Finding patterns in lattices
H	Hair and Hairstyling	How to braid hair			Finding patterns in Pascal's triangle
	Heat	Joule's experiment			Finding patterns in polygonal numbers
	Hieroglyphic Writing Systems	How to create your own hieroglyphs		Numbers and Number Systems	Recognizing numbers in everyday situations
	Houseplants	How to grow houseplants		Numerals and Numeration Systems	Can you read and write Egyptian numerals?
I	Ink	Secret messages			
	Interior Design	Decorating your room			
	Inuit	How to build a snow house	O	Osmosis	How osmosis works
				Outlines	Preparing an outline for a talk or composition
J-K	Kaleidoscope	How to build a kaleidoscope			
	Kites	How to fly your kite			

WONDER QUESTIONS

Wonder Questions have been an integral part of the encyclopedia since the original 1911 edition of THE BOOK OF KNOWLEDGE. They have always been a source of pleasure and adventure for those of us who are in constant search of interesting bits of information about everything.

Vol.	Article	Wonder Questions
A	Abolition Movement	What were the Gag Rules?
	Aerodynamics	What keeps a plane up in the air?
	Africa	What and where are the Mountains of the Moon?
	African Americans	What is Kwanzaa?
	Amish	What is Shunning?
	Apple	Who was Johnny Appleseed?
	Asia	What and where is Asia Minor?
	Astronauts	Why are astronauts weightless?
	Astronomy	How do astronomers measure distances in space?
	Atmosphere	Why is the sky blue?
B	Badminton	What makes a champion?
	Balloons and Ballooning	What makes a balloon rise?
	Bats	How do bats find their way in the dark?
	Bears	How dangerous are bears?
	Bees	Are there really "killer" bees?
	Bermuda	What is the Bermuda Triangle?
	Birds as Pets	Can people get parrot fever?
	Blindness	What is a talking book?
	Body, Human	What is the largest organ of your body?
	Books	What information is on a copyright page?
	Brain	Is it true that we use only 10 percent of our brains?
	Bridges	Why were some of the early bridges in America covered?

Vol.	Article	Wonder Questions
	Building Construction	Why is a tree or an American flag sometimes placed on the highest part of a building under construction?
		Why don't tall buildings blow down in a strong wind?
	Bullfighting	How did bullfighting begin?
	Business	What are gross income and net income?
C	Calendar	Why are the abbreviations B.C. and A.D. used with dates?
	Candles	Why do we put lighted candles on a birthday cake and then blow them out?
	Card Games	What is the origin of the suits in a deck of cards?
		Why are there three face cards in each suit?
	Cats, Wild	What is a cat's best defense?
	Cement and Concrete	How is cement made?
	Census	How is the U.S. population census taken?
	Checkers	How old is checkers?
	Circus	What was the greatest feat in the history of trapeze flying?
	Climate	How can scientists tell what climates were like a long time ago?
	Clowns	Why don't most clowns speak?
	Coins and Coin Collecting	Why are some coins grooved around the edge?
	Colonial Life in America	What did the colonists eat?

Vol.	Article	Wonder Questions	Vol.	Article	Wonder Questions
	Columbus, Christopher	Where did Columbus really land on his first voyage to the New World?		England, History of	What happened to the princes in the Tower?
				Europe	Where and what are the Low Countries?
		What were the consequences of Columbus' voyage in 1492?		Evolution	What is artificial selection?
	Communism	What are the differences between Socialism and Communism?		Exploration and Discovery	Why was the New World named "America"?
				Explosives	What is an explosive?
	Computers	Will computers ever outsmart humans?	F	Fairy Tales	Where did fairy tales come from?
	Cosmic Rays	Why are cosmic rays important?		Fallout	What was the Chernobyl accident?
D	Dairying and Dairy Products	What is a dairy farm?		Family	What is a first cousin, second cousin, and first cousin removed?
		What is Grade A milk?		Fibers	What is a fiber?
	Debates and Discussions	What is the difference between a debate and a discussion?		Fillmore, Millard	What was the Know-Nothing Party?
	Dinosaurs	What were dinosaurs?		First Aid	What is a Good Samaritan?
		What was the deadliest dinosaur that ever walked the earth?		Fish	How big do fish grow?
					What fish's "mother" is really its father?
	Disasters	Which of the following qualifies as a disaster?			Do fish sleep?
				Fission	Where does fission take place?
	Doctors	Is the Surgeon General really a surgeon?		Flowers	How big do flowers grow?
	Dogs	What are the dog days?		Fog and Smog	Why is it difficult to see through fog?
	Dollar	How can you tell if a bill is counterfeit?		Food Preservation	What makes food spoil?
	Dyes and Dyeing	What makes dyes fade?			Who was Clarence Birdseye?
E	Earth	How do earthquakes help scientists learn about the Earth's interior?		Ford, Henry	What is the Ford Foundation?
				Fossils	What is the most precious fossil in the world?
	Earth, History of	How do geologists learn about the history of the planet Earth?		Fountains	Why do people throw coins into fountains?
	Economics	What is the amazing "invisible hand"?	G	Galaxies	What are the nearest galaxies to ours?
	Ecuador	What were the enchanted islands?		Genetics	Are genetically engineered crops safe?
	Electricity	What is static electricity?		Geology	What is geomythology?
	Electric Motors	What makes electric motors run?		Geometry	What is Pi?
	Electronics	What is nanotechnology?		Geysers and Hot Springs	How did Old Faithful earn its name?
	Elements, Chemical	What is the island of stability?		Glue and Other Adhesives	What makes adhesives stick?
					What is the best adhesive?
	Elevators and Escalators	How fast can the fastest elevators climb?		Gold	What is "Fool's Gold"?

Vol.	Article	Wonder Questions
	Mountains	What is the longest mountain chain in the world?
	Muscular System	What is the levator labii superioris alaeque nasi?
	Music	What is the origin of clef signs?
		Why are so many musical terms written in Italian?
	Musical Instruments	How do musical instruments make sounds?
	Mythology	Why are similar myths found throughout the world?
N	National Cemeteries	Who can be buried in a U.S. National Cemetery?
	National Park System	What is the largest U.S. national park?
	Navigation	What is a ship's log?
		How do areas qualify to become part of the U.S. National Park System?
	Neptune	What are trans-Neptunian objects?
	Newspapers	Is the news truth?
		What is a press release?
	Noise	How does noise affect hearing?
	Numbers and Number Systems	What is infinity?
	Numerals and Numeration Systems	Who invented zero?
	Nylon and Other Synthetic Fibers	How are synthetic fibers named?
O	Ocean Liners	What caused the *Titanic* tragedy?
	Oceanography	Is there a new source of energy in the oceans?
	Onion	Why do most people "cry" when chopping onions?
	Opinion Polls	How is an opinion survey done?
P	Pacific Ocean and Islands	What is the Great Barrier Reef?
	Paper	How is paper recycled?
	Peace Movements	What is a conscientious objector?

Vol.	Article	Wonder Questions
	Pearls	What makes a pearl valuable?
		How are artificial pearls made?
	Perfumes	What are toilet water and cologne?
	Photosynthesis	How do plants get energy from sunlight?
		How can plants produce more food?
	Planets	Do planets exist beyond our solar system?
		Would you weigh the same if you lived on a planet other than earth?
	Plants	How big can a plant grow?
		Why do leaves change color in the autumn?
		Which plant has the biggest seed?
	Plays	Where did the terms "downstage" and "upstage" come from?
	Political Parties	Why are some political parties called "left" and others "right"?
	Population	Will population growth stop?
	Psychology	What is personality?
	Public Relations	What is the difference between public relations and advertising?
	Pumps	How do pumps work?
Q-R	Radiation	What is food irradiation?
	Radio	Why can you hear radio stations from farther away at night?
		What is static?
		What was "Jansky's merry-go-round"?
	Railroads	Why does the standard gauge measure 4 feet 8 ½ inches (1.4 meters)?
	Rain, Snow, Sleet, and Hail	What is the shape of a falling raindrop?
	Reconstruction Period	What were scalawags and carpetbaggers?
	Reformation	What was the Counter-Reformation?
	Renaissance	What is a Renaissance Man?

Vol.	Article	Wonder Questions	Vol.	Article	Wonder Questions
	Venus	Why are Venus and Earth so different from one another?		Waxes	Who invented wax paper?
	Viruses	Can just one virus make you sick?		Weather	What is El Niño?
	Vitamins and Minerals	Are natural vitamin or mineral supplements better than synthetic supplements?		Weights and Measures	How long is a meter?
				Westward Movement	What was the Northwest Ordinance?
W-X-Y-Z	Water	How much of Earth's water is fresh water?		Wonders of the World	What are the wonders of our world?
		How much water is in the air?		Wood and Wood Products	What is wood?
	Waterpower	Why don't we get all our electric power from water?		Wool	How is wool obtained?
				World War II	Who were the Sullivan Brothers?
					What does "D day" mean?

"DID YOU KNOW THAT . . . " Features

A younger relation of THE NEW BOOK OF KNOWLEDGE's well-known Wonder Questions, these features provide fascinating information on a wide range of topics.

Vol.	Article	Did you know that...
A	Advertising	models are not the only ones getting "made up" for advertisements?
	Animals	tiny invertebrates, called leaf-cutter ants, can carry cut-up leaves and flowers more than twice their own size?
		the bird called an oxpecker spends almost its entire life clinging to the back of a hoofed animal?
		the bee hummingbird is the smallest living bird?
		the largest structures ever built by living creatures are coral reefs?
	Antibiotics	our current antibiotics are focused on stopping only bacteria?
	Ants	ants were used as the first method of biological pest control?
	Atoms	it was not until the late 1890's that scientists began to understand the internal structure of the atom?
B	Bamboo	bamboo has a reputation for fast growth?
		bamboo is the giant of grasses?
	Bananas	Iceland grows all the bananas the country needs?
	Blood	the first successful blood transfusion was performed by the Incas of South America?

Vol.	Article	Did you know that...
	Body, Human	some 650 muscles cover the body's skeleton?
		there are more red blood cells in the body than any other kind of cell?
	Body Chemistry	not all cell types use the same amount of energy?
	Boys & Girls Clubs of America	many famous personalities are former Boys & Girls Club members?
	Brain	as many as 250,000 new brain cells are formed during a baby's development inside its mother?
C	Camping	the longest camping journey took just under two years?
	Cats, Wild	the sand cat can live without ever drinking water?
		some cats fish for their dinner?
	Citizenship	the United States Congress has granted honorary citizenship to only six people?
	Continental Congress	George Washington may not have been the first president of the United States?
D	Dairying and Dairy Products	the first cow arrived in America in Jamestown, Virginia?
	Declaration of Independence	of all the signers of the Declaration of Independence, Georgia delegate Button Gwinnett's signature is the rarest.
	Deserts	some cacti make their own anti-freeze?
	Dinosaurs	dinosaurs were watchful parents that carefully tended their young?

Vol.	Article	Did you know that...	Vol.	Article	Did you know that...
	Dollar	on average, a $1 bill lasts only 18 months before it is too worn to be circulated?	G	Gases	every time you turn on your television set you have "tuned into" a series of products that were produced with gases?
E	Emancipation Proclamation	the Emancipation Proclamation directly led to the adoption of the 13th Amendment to the U.S. Constitution?		Galaxies	the Milky Way is part of a galaxy cluster?
	Emotions	a lie detector tries to take advantage of the body's response to feelings?		Gardens and Gardening	earthworms are some of the most dedicated workers in the garden?
F	Fairies	very few fairy tales actually feature fairies?			many gardeners use quick-growing radish seeds as garden helpers and markers?
	Field Hockey	field hockey is one of the only sports whose rules are frequently examined and modified?			Thomas Jefferson was not only the third president of the United States, but also a passionate, hands-on gardener?
	Fire	the first matches were invented in China in the year 577?		Genetics	scientists have made mice glow green using DNA from jellyfish?
	Fish	Aristotle, one of the world's most influential philosophers, was the first ichthyologist?		Geysers and Hot Springs	our word "geyser" comes from one hot spring in Iceland?
		piranhas are the most ferocious freshwater fish in the world?		Global Warming	the year 1998 is the warmest year on record?
	Flowers	the first plants had no flowers?		Grapes and Berries	you can easily grow strawberries at home by using a strawberry pot?
	Folk Dance	square dancing with a caller is a uniquely American tradition?			the blueberry is known for its cancer-fighting qualities?
	Folklore	singers of epic poems can spontaneously compose works that go on for hours?		Grasses and Grasslands	many grassland plants have very deep roots?
	Founders of the United States	six men signed both the Declaration of Independence and the Constitution of the United States?			many grassland birds raise their young on the ground?
			H	Hawks	hawks can fly hundreds of miles without getting tired?
	Fungi	a fungus disease was responsible for causing a famine that resulted in the starvation and death of more than 1 million people?		Hibernation	the study of animal hibernation may lead to treatments for a number of medical problems in humans?
				Hoofed Mammals	the ability of deer to regrow antlers each year is a biological marvel?

Vol.	Article	Did you know that...
J-K	Jellyfish and Other Coelenterates	the clownfish can swim and rest among the sea anemone's deadly tentacles without getting stung?
	Jupiter	Jupiter was the first outer planet to be explored simultaneously by two spacecraft at close range?
J-K	Kingdoms of Living Things	binomial nomenclature—the naming of living things—was introduced in 1735 and is still used today?
L	Light	you see scattered light every time you look at the sky?
	Liver	the liver is one of the few parts of the body that can regenerate?
	Lobsters	an American lobster was recorded as the heaviest crustacean ever caught?
	Locomotives	steam locomotives are often classified according to their wheel arrangement?
M	Magnets and Magnetism	some living creatures can detect and use Earth's magnetic field to survive?
	Microbiology	pizza is a tasty meal because of microbes?
	Mollusks	the largest of all invertebrates (animals without a backbone) is a mollusk?
	Monkeys	the only monkeys in Europe are called apes?
	Mummies	the ancient Egyptians also mummified animals?
	Musical Instruments	many nontraditional instruments have found their way into the percussion section in the last century?
N	National Forest System	some forests actually need fire?

Vol.	Article	Did you know that...
	Newspapers	the headline to a story is almost never written by the reporter who writes the story?
	Norse Mythology	some of our modern English names for the days of the week come from Norse mythology?
	Number Patterns	it is possible to add all the counting numbers from 1 through 100 in a minute or two—without a calculator?
O	Obesity	body fat can be calculated according to the relationship between height and weight?
	Olympic Games	some sports and events at the Olympic Games have been discontinued over the years?
	Oysters, Clams, and Other Bivalves	some clams and mussels live in complete darkness?
P	Panama Canal	the lowest toll charged to pass through the Panama Canal was 36 cents?
	Percentage	there are laws regulating whether a discount or the sales tax is calculated first on a purchase?
	Photoelectricity	the photovoltaic effect was discovered in 1839 by French physicist Antoine-César Becquerel?
	Plankton	the largest animal on Earth depends on some of the smallest living things for its survival?
	Plants	a plant was responsible for causing the famous mutiny aboard the British ship H.M.S. *Bounty*?

Vol.	Article	Did you know that...	Vol.	Article	Did you know that...
		the most widely used pain reliever aspirin was named after Spiraea, a genus of flowering shrubs in the rose family?		Soils	soils act as natural filters?
		some plants can grow several inches in a matter of hours?		Space Exploration and Travel	the "space race" began on October 4, 1957, with the launch of the Soviet Union's *Sputnik 1* satellite?
	Plastics	some plastics are stronger than steel?			astronaut and geologist Harrison H. Schmitt was the first scientist to explore the moon and also the last person to set foot on the moon?
	Plays	it is all right to "cheat" when you are acting?			
	Prehistoric People	scientists discovered an important message in the bones of a Neanderthal who lived more than 30,000 years ago?			some humans have spent many months living in space?
Q-R	Railroads	railroads opened vast regions to farming, mining, lumbering, and manufacturing?			temperatures in space can be twice as high or twice as low as those in the hottest or coldest places on Earth?
	Richelieu, Cardinal	Cardinal Richelieu founded the French Academy to preserve French language and culture?		Spiders	the class Arachnida takes its name from the mythological character Arachne?
	Rivers	many of the world's great civilizations arose on the floodplains of major rivers?	**U-V**	Vegetables	many vegetables are related?
	Rocks	the oldest known rock ever found is almost 4 billion years old?		Volcanoes	volcanoes are found not only on Earth but on other planets and satellites in our solar system?
S	Science Fiction	on October 30, 1938, thousands of people across the United States were convinced that science fiction had become science fact?	**W-X-Y-Z**	Water Supply	some community-based systems date from ancient times?
					being a vegetarian can save water?
	Skeletal System	a baby has about 275 bones, while a full-grown adult has only 206 bones?		Weather	the United States experiences more severe storms and flooding than any other country in the world?

FUN WITH WONDER QUESTIONS

The following pages contain a selection of Wonder Questions from THE NEW BOOK OF KNOWLEDGE. These pages can be photocopied, and the Wonder Questions can be cut apart and handed out for use in home and classroom activities. The volume and article in which each Wonder Question and its answer appear are also given. Students can try to guess the answers to the questions and then consult the encyclopedia to find the correct answers.

A complete listing of all the Wonder Questions in the encyclopedia are in this Appendix section and can be used to create more Wonder Question activities.

WONDER QUESTION

What were the Gag Rules?

Volume A

Abolition Movement

THE NEW BOOK OF KNOWLEDGE

WONDER QUESTION

What and where are the Mountains of the Moon?

Volume A

Africa

THE NEW BOOK OF KNOWLEDGE

WONDER QUESTION

What is Kwanzaa?

Volume A

African Americans

THE NEW BOOK OF KNOWLEDGE

WONDER QUESTION

Why are astronauts weightless?

Volume A

Astronauts

THE NEW BOOK OF KNOWLEDGE

WONDER QUESTION

What makes a balloon rise?

Volume B

Balloons and Ballooning

THE NEW BOOK OF KNOWLEDGE

WONDER QUESTION

What is the Bermuda Triangle?

Volume B

Bermuda

THE NEW BOOK OF KNOWLEDGE

WONDER QUESTION

What is a talking book?

Volume B

Blindness

THE NEW BOOK OF KNOWLEDGE

WONDER QUESTION

What is the largest organ of your body?

Volume B

Body, Human

THE NEW BOOK OF KNOWLEDGE

WONDER QUESTION

Why were some of the early bridges in America covered?

Volume B

Bridges

THE NEW BOOK OF KNOWLEDGE

WONDER QUESTION

What are gross income and net income?

Volume B

Business

THE NEW BOOK OF KNOWLEDGE

WONDER QUESTION

Why are the abbreviations "B.C." and "A.D." used with dates?

Volume C

Calendar

THE NEW BOOK OF KNOWLEDGE

WONDER QUESTION

Why do we put lighted candles on a birthday cake and then blow them out?

Volume C

Candles

THE NEW BOOK OF KNOWLEDGE

WONDER QUESTION

What did the colonists eat?

Volume C

Colonial Life in America

THE NEW BOOK OF KNOWLEDGE

WONDER QUESTION

What was the deadliest dinosaur that ever walked the earth?

Volume D

Dinosaurs

THE NEW BOOK OF KNOWLEDGE

WONDER QUESTION

Where and what are the Low Countries?

Volume E

Europe

THE NEW BOOK OF KNOWLEDGE

WONDER QUESTION

Why was the New World named "America"?

Volume E

Exploration and Discovery

THE NEW BOOK OF KNOWLEDGE

WONDER QUESTION

What is a Good Samaritan?

Volume F

First Aid

THE NEW BOOK OF KNOWLEDGE

WONDER QUESTION

How big do fish grow?

Volume F

Fish

THE NEW BOOK OF KNOWLEDGE

What is the most precious fossil in the world?

Volume F

Fossils

THE NEW BOOK OF KNOWLEDGE

Why do people throw coins into fountains?

Volume F

Fountains

THE NEW BOOK OF KNOWLEDGE

What is Pi?

Volume G

Geometry

THE NEW BOOK OF KNOWLEDGE

What is "Fool's Gold"?

Volume G

Gold

THE NEW BOOK OF KNOWLEDGE

What are gargoyles?

Volume G

Gothic Art and Architecture

THE NEW BOOK OF KNOWLEDGE

Why doesn't it hurt to cut your hair?

Volume H

Hair and Hairstyling

THE NEW BOOK OF KNOWLEDGE

WONDER QUESTION

What is the Great Red Spot on Jupiter?

Volume J

Jupiter

THE NEW BOOK OF KNOWLEDGE

WONDER QUESTION

What is a yawn?

Volume L

Lungs

THE NEW BOOK OF KNOWLEDGE

WONDER QUESTION

Is there life on Mars?

Volume M

Mars

THE NEW BOOK OF KNOWLEDGE

WONDER QUESTION

What is the longest mountain chain in the world?

Volume M

Mountains

THE NEW BOOK OF KNOWLEDGE

WONDER QUESTION

Who can be buried in a U.S. national cemetery?

Volume N

National Cemeteries

THE NEW BOOK OF KNOWLEDGE

WONDER QUESTION

What is the largest U.S. national park?

Volume N

National Park System

THE NEW BOOK OF KNOWLEDGE

WONDER QUESTION

What is the outermost planet in the solar system?

Volume N

Neptune

THE NEW BOOK OF KNOWLEDGE

WONDER QUESTION

What is a press release?

Volume N

Newspapers

THE NEW BOOK OF KNOWLEDGE

WONDER QUESTION

Why do most people "cry" when chopping onions?

Volume O

Onion

THE NEW BOOK OF KNOWLEDGE

WONDER QUESTION

How is paper recycled?

Volume P

Paper

THE NEW BOOK OF KNOWLEDGE

WONDER QUESTION

Why do leaves change color in the autumn?

Volume P

Plants

THE NEW BOOK OF KNOWLEDGE

WONDER QUESTION

Who was Molly Pitcher?

Volume Q-R

Revolutionary War

THE NEW BOOK OF KNOWLEDGE

Why is it hotter in summer than it is in winter?

Volume S

Seasons

THE NEW BOOK OF KNOWLEDGE

What is the largest spider?

Volume S

Spiders

THE NEW BOOK OF KNOWLEDGE

Why do stars twinkle?

Volume S

Stars

THE NEW BOOK OF KNOWLEDGE

What makes a stomach growl?

Volume S

Stomach

THE NEW BOOK OF KNOWLEDGE

Who built Stonehenge?

Volume S

Stonehenge

THE NEW BOOK OF KNOWLEDGE

What are television ratings?

Volume T

Television

THE NEW BOOK OF KNOWLEDGE

WONDER QUESTION

How can you tell how close a thunderstorm is to you?

Volume T

Thunder and Lightning

THE NEW BOOK OF KNOWLEDGE

WONDER QUESTION

What were the fugitive slave laws?

Volume U-V

Underground Railroad

THE NEW BOOK OF KNOWLEDGE

WONDER QUESTION

What does "GI" stand for?

Volume U-V

United States, Armed Forces of the

THE NEW BOOK OF KNOWLEDGE

WONDER QUESTION

Who were the Barnburners?

Volume U-V

Van Buren, Martin

THE NEW BOOK OF KNOWLEDGE

WONDER QUESTION

Can just one virus make you sick?

Volume U-V

Viruses

THE NEW BOOK OF KNOWLEDGE

WONDER QUESTION

What was the Northwest Ordinance?

Volume W-X-Y-Z

Westward Movement

THE NEW BOOK OF KNOWLEDGE

What is the Great Red Spot on Jupiter?

Volume J

Jupiter

THE NEW BOOK OF KNOWLEDGE

What is a yawn?

Volume L

Lungs

THE NEW BOOK OF KNOWLEDGE

Is there life on Mars?

Volume M

Mars

THE NEW BOOK OF KNOWLEDGE

What is the longest mountain chain in the world?

Volume M

Mountains

THE NEW BOOK OF KNOWLEDGE

Who can be buried in a U.S. national cemetery?

Volume N

National Cemeteries

THE NEW BOOK OF KNOWLEDGE

What is the largest U.S. national park?

Volume N

National Park System

THE NEW BOOK OF KNOWLEDGE

WONDER QUESTION

What is the outermost planet in the solar system?

Volume N

Neptune

THE NEW BOOK OF KNOWLEDGE

WONDER QUESTION

What is a press release?

Volume N

Newspapers

THE NEW BOOK OF KNOWLEDGE

WONDER QUESTION

Why do most people "cry" when chopping onions?

Volume O

Onion

THE NEW BOOK OF KNOWLEDGE

WONDER QUESTION

How is paper recycled?

Volume P

Paper

THE NEW BOOK OF KNOWLEDGE

WONDER QUESTION

Why do leaves change color in the autumn?

Volume P

Plants

THE NEW BOOK OF KNOWLEDGE

WONDER QUESTION

Who was Molly Pitcher?
Volume Q-R

Revolutionary War

THE NEW BOOK OF KNOWLEDGE

Why is it hotter in summer than it is in winter?

Volume S

Seasons

THE NEW BOOK OF KNOWLEDGE

What is the largest spider?

Volume S

Spiders

THE NEW BOOK OF KNOWLEDGE

Why do stars twinkle?

Volume S

Stars

THE NEW BOOK OF KNOWLEDGE

What makes a stomach growl?

Volume S

Stomach

THE NEW BOOK OF KNOWLEDGE

Who built Stonehenge?

Volume S

Stonehenge

THE NEW BOOK OF KNOWLEDGE

What are television ratings?

Volume T

Television

THE NEW BOOK OF KNOWLEDGE

How can you tell how close a thunderstorm is to you?

Volume T

Thunder and Lightning

THE NEW BOOK OF KNOWLEDGE

What were the fugitive slave laws?

Volume U-V

Underground Railroad

THE NEW BOOK OF KNOWLEDGE

What does "GI" stand for?

Volume U-V

United States, Armed Forces of the

THE NEW BOOK OF KNOWLEDGE

Who were the Barnburners?

Volume U-V

Van Buren, Martin

THE NEW BOOK OF KNOWLEDGE

Can just one virus make you sick?

Volume U-V

Viruses

THE NEW BOOK OF KNOWLEDGE

What was the Northwest Ordinance?

Volume W-X-Y-Z

Westward Movement

THE NEW BOOK OF KNOWLEDGE